Kaua'i

8th Edition

The Most Complete Guide to Family Fun and Adventure!

Joan Conrow
Christie Stilson

Ulysses Press

Published by: Ulysses Press
P.O. Box 3440
Berkeley, CA 94703
www.ulyssespress.com

ISSN 1544-1407
ISBN 1-56975-364-4

Printed in Canada by Transcontinental Printing

10 9 8 7 6 5 4 3 2 1

Managing Editor: Claire Chun
Editor: Lily Chou
Editorial and Production: Laura Brancella, Caroline Cummins, Lisa Kester, Sarisa Nelson
Cartography: Pease Press
Cover Design: Leslie Henriques, Sarah Levin
Indexer: Sayre Van Young
Cover Photography: Robert Holmes (boy with fins)

Distributed in the United States by Publishers Group West and in Canada by Raincoast Books

Ulysses Press is a federally registered trademark of BookPack, Inc.

Write to Us!

If in your travels you discover a spot that captures the spirit of Kaua'i, or if you live in the region and have a favorite place to share, or if you just feel like expressing your views, write to us and we'll pass your note along to the author.

Ulysses Press
P.O. Box 3440
Berkeley, CA 94703
E-mail: readermail@ulyssespress.com

Table of Contents

MAPS

Introduction

Whether you're simply considering a vacation on Kaua'i—the northernmost island in the Hawaiian chain—or you've already made a decision to visit, you're definitely on the right track. Kaua'i is a special place to vacation, relax and enjoy the true aloha spirit.

The Hawaiian Islands are an archipelago of diverse natural beauty, composed of equally distinct and unique tropical ecosystems. The islands themselves are volcanoes born from the Pacific Ocean, some extinct, some dormant, some still active. They're adorned with jagged peaks, some stark and steep, others gracefully rounded or flat, and crowned with puffy clouds against a background of bright blue sky. The landscapes are arguably some of the most delightful in the world, a beautiful melding of bright blues and dark greens, accented by the white, gold, black and even green sands of the beaches, and bordered by dramatic black lava rock reefs and sheer cliffs that plunge into the sea. Nature has blessed each of the islands of Hawai'i with similar, yet different, characteristics. Although they are all somewhat alike, each has its own attributes and features, and Kaua'i arguably has a grace and charm unmatched by the other islands.

Kaua'i has long been known as The Garden Island, and it's an apt name. This island, perhaps more than the others, has the visual features and characteristics so often associated with the stereotypical "Garden of Eden." Invariably, when the subject turns to tropical islands, the word "paradise" works its way into the discussion. It's an overused term, and perhaps even unfair as an accurate description of any place. Beauty, of course, is in the eye of the beholder, and we all have our own ideas of what constitutes paradise. But it is a phrase often used by visitors and residents alike to express the splendor and *mana* (power) of Kaua'i, and in my years of residence, I've certainly been blessed with my share of Edenic experiences.

Kaua'i has many lush tropical valleys, often carved by tall cascading waterfalls that tumble into the rocky streams that feed the jungle-like vegetation that is so plentiful. The upland rainforests are dense with vegetation unique to the island, and they still host rare native birds. The island also offers scenic arid canyons of sculpted rock, narrow ridge trails with panoramic lookouts, rivers and streams winding down from remote interior valleys, and tranquil isolated beaches where only the crashing surf breaks the silence. The coastal reefs and near-shore waters, meanwhile, are host to tropical fish, endangered marine life and fragile corals.

Kaua'i is not a sedentary sort of place. Although its dramatic beauty, relaxed pace and mild climate make it a perfect place to slip into a state of blissful idleness, there's so much to do and see that it would be a shame to spend all your time lounging around a resort pool. Of course, there's nothing wrong with just "hanging loose," and everyone should devote some of the vacation to one of the favorite local pastimes. Indeed, you should plan to spend time rejuvenating yourself with a massage or other treatment that conveys the healing qualities of the island. But when the urge to explore hits, you can choose from the activities that abound. Whether you're drawn to hiking, kayaking, snorkeling, scuba diving, horseback riding, bicycling, golf or beachcombing, you'll find no shortage of places to pursue your desires and companies eager to guide you. And, of course, you'll have the pleasure of eating in the many restaurants, which range from fine dining to simple local plate lunches. The island also has a large population of talented artisans and crafters; smaller shops carry their wares, offering a chance to find items that are truly one of a kind. Hawaiian cultural opportunities are available, too, including luaus, hula performances, lei-making workshops and other interpretive and informative programs. You can even volunteer to protect some of the island's most beautiful natural areas if you're inclined. In short, the best way to truly appreciate Kaua'i is to get out and experience it, because the real Kaua'i is found in her natural places and her people.

Aloha is another word that is about as overused as paradise, but again, it is an apt description of the spirit that still dominates on Kaua'i. Our multicultural community has been able to grow together, mostly in harmony, because of our aloha, and our bonds have been strengthened by overcoming the devastation wrought by two major hurricanes within a decade. From the days of old, the people of Kaua'i have always been independent and self-sufficient—after all, it was the only island in the chain that King Kamehameha never did conquer. That spirit still prevails, and it's part of what makes the people of Kaua'i different from others you will meet in the islands.

Of course, that's a big part of Kaua'i's appeal. We have our beautiful natural environment, and we have our people. These are our greatest resources, and we hope that you will value and respect them as much as we do when you come to visit.

This is the eighth edition of this book, which was originally published in 1988. Kaua'i has changed dramatically since the first edition, but at the same time much of it remains the same. It's gotten busier, and it has many more homes, businesses, resorts and cars than it used to. But the physical features and feel of the island remain much the same. It is still predominantly rural, a place of tiny towns and extensive open space. And the genuine warmth and friendliness of Kaua'i's people is also unchanged. Those of us who live here love our home, and while we're protective of it, we're also proud and willing to share with those who also appreciate it for the true gem that it is.

As a journalist and resident of Kaua'i since 1987, I've had the opportunity to explore the island from many perspectives. I've hiked, helicoptered, boated, dove, snorkeled, kayaked, beachcombed, walked and swum all around the island, and I've spent many a happy hour enjoying the landscapes, the birds, the clouds, the marine life and, of course, the people of my adopted island home. For such a small place, there's an amazing amount to see and do and I'm not sure I'll ever cover it all. But I'll certainly have a lot of fun trying! I urge you to get out and experience the island for yourself, but don't try to see and do too much in one trip. Part of the magic of Kaua'i is simply being here, and if you're constantly dashing about, you'll miss out on the subtle way it can slow you down, rejuvenate you, and help you tune into what's really important in life. I also encourage you to take the time to read some interpretive books about the island's environment and its unique flora and fauna. The more you know about Kaua'i, the more you'll appreciate just what a treasure trove it is.

In updating the book, I've tried to add my perspective as a resident of the island, while providing information about new restaurants, activities and accommodations and updating previous entries. As I worked on this project, I was struck by just how much Kaua'i does have to offer its visitors, and how much information is packed into this volume. It has to be one of the most comprehensive on the market.

Paradise Family Guides: Kaua'i is designed to help you and your *ohana* (family) enjoy your vacation on Kaua'i to the fullest. But please consider it just the foundation for your trip, and not the final word. Too often I see visitors driving around the island with their noses stuck in a guidebook, missing all the beauty and essence of life on Kaua'i. So please use it in planning your vacation and refer to it when you get here, but most importantly, experience Kaua'i for yourself. Make your own memories, find your own favorite spots, identify your own "bests." Your trip will be far richer as a result.

To that end, you are invited to share your viewpoints and vacation experiences about Kaua'i. Send any information or inquiries to the author at: Paradise Publications, 8110 SW Wareham Circle, Portland, OR 97223, or e-mail: paradyse@worldnet.att.net.

A hui ho!
Joan Conrow

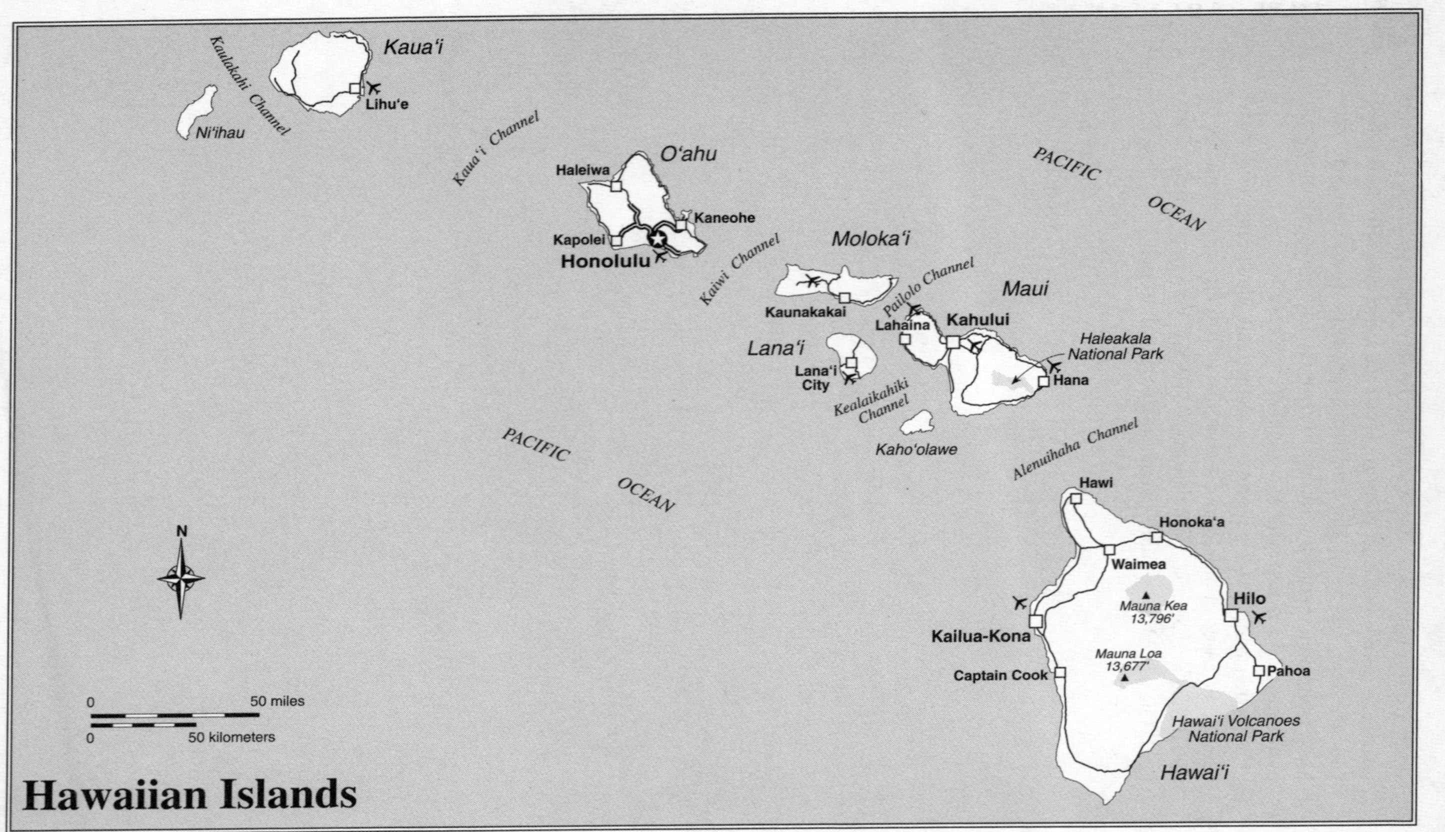
Hawaiian Islands
Kaua'i
Lihu'e
Ni'ihau
Kaulakahi Channel
Kaua'i Channel
O'ahu
Haleiwa
Kaneohe
Kapolei
Honolulu
Kaiwi Channel
Moloka'i
Kaunakakai
Pailolo Channel
Maui
Lahaina
Kahului
Haleakala National Park
Hana
Lana'i
Lana'i City
Kealaikahiki Channel
Kaho'olawe
Alenuihaha Channel
PACIFIC OCEAN
PACIFIC OCEAN
Hawi
Honoka'a
Waimea
Mauna Kea 13,796'
Hilo
Kailua-Kona
Mauna Loa 13,677'
Captain Cook
Pahoa
Hawai'i Volcanoes National Park
Hawai'i
N
0
50 miles
0
50 kilometers

CHAPTER 1

Family Paradise

Kaua'i's Best Bets

Food Splurge Friday evening seafood buffet at the Princeville Resort

Sunset and Cocktails *South Shore*: The Beach House, Po'ipu; The Point, Sheraton Kaua'i, Po'ipu. *North Shore*: The Living Room, Princeville Resort

Sunset Dining View *South Shore*: The Beach House, Po'ipu. *North Shore*: The Bali Hai Restaurant; The Hanalei Café, Princeville Resort

Beach Sunset Ke'e Beach; anywhere along the westside

Photo-Op Spot On a clear day the Kalalau Valley Lookout, Koke'e State Park. (The valley is often shrouded by misty swirling clouds covering the magnificent view, but if you're patient, it might clear.)

Photo Excursion Backcountry Tours into the mountains behind Lihu'e

Luau Value Coconut Coast Resort

Cool Treats Lappert's Ice Cream at one of their many locations. Shave ice at Halo Halo Shave Ice or Hamura Saimin in Lihu'e; anything from Beezers

Take-Home Food Products Fresh papaya salsa, Hanapepe-made taro chips, Kauai Kookies, Kilauea Bakery breadsticks, taro *mochi* from Hanalei Taro & Juice Co.

Aloha Wear Macy's, Kukui Grove

Cheap Aloha Wear Hilo Hattie's

Leis People's Market, Puhi; Blue Orchid, Koloa; Flowers Forever, Lihu'e; Pono Market, Kapa'a

Most Lavish Resort Grounds Hyatt Regency Kauai Resort and Spa

Romantic Adventure Sunset cruise on a catamaran

Excursions *Most spectacular*: Captain Andy's motor boat or kayaking trip around Napali Coast; *Most unusual*: Tour of Kamokila Hawaiian Village; *Most serene*: Grove Farm Homestead Museum; *Best adventure on foot*: Princeville Ranch hiking tours; *Most exciting cruise*: Zodiac trip along Napali Coast; *A world away*: a helicopter tour of the isolated island of Ni'ihau; *Unusual land tour*: Kipu Kai Ranch ATV rides

Chance of Getting Rained On Anywhere west of the Hanalei Bridge

Chance of Getting Sunned On Any beach along the Southshore or Westside

Kaua'i Spare-No-Expense-Get-Away-from-It-All Resort Princeville Resort; Hyatt Regency Kauai Resort and Spa

Kaua'i Bare-Bones-on-the-Cheap Adventure Lodging Koke'e Lodge at Waimea Canyon (about the only thing more economical is a tent)

Booking Agent Suite Paradise has good service and lots of rentals

Discounts Any of the activity booths around the island, but beware that you may have to sit through a timeshare presentation to receive big discounts

Flowers Sunshine Markets around the islands; People's Market, Puhi

Night Spots Lizard Lounge Bar & Grill; Rob's Good Times Grill

Unusual Gift Ideas Hawaiian motif needlepoint canvases and fabrics or an original oriental doll quilt from Kapai'a Stitchery in Lihu'e. • One of Uncle Eddie's Aloha Angels dressed in a variety of *muumuus*, hula skirts, sea shells, or *tapa* cloth (at the Hanapepe Cafe and at various hotel gift shops). • Movie buffs will enjoy *The Kaua'i Movie Book*, a full-color account of films, TV shows and documentaries shot on Kaua'i. Available at bookstores or support the nonprofit Wilcox Foundation, 808-245-1198. • The Kaua'i Products Store at Kukui Grove not only has a nice selection of locally made products, they also have homemade fudge. Made fresh daily on the premises, it comes in tropical flavors like chocolate or vanilla macadamia, Kona coffee, and piña colada. • Tropical scented lotions, soaps, and candles from Island Soap & Candle Works. Scented with island fragrances like plumeria, torch ginger, or pikake, they are all hand-made using natural ingredients

FREE GUIDED HIKES

A two-hour guided Crater Hill hike is offered daily at the Kilauea Point National Wildlife Refuge. It'll cost you $2 admission to the refuge, but the guided hikes are free. Early reservations are recommended. Call 808-828-0168 or sign up at the visitor center.

and even more fun—you can watch them being made at their factory and gift shop in the Kong Lung Center in Kilauea and Koloa Town.

Really Unusual Gift Ideas "Uncle" Bill Ford makes custom Hawaiian coconut golf clubs—a souvenir novelty gift that actually works. Contact him at P.O. Box 1403, Koloa, Kaua'i, HI 96756, call 808-742-9250 or e-mail: unclebillford@webtv.net.

T-shirts The Red Dirt shirts are a way to take a little bit of Kaua'i home with you, but Pohaku Tees in Koloa town offer good quality and original designs you won't find elsewhere.

Free Stuff

- The sunshine, fresh air and ocean breeze
- Hiking trail maps, guides, brochures from State Division of Forestry and Wildlife
- A tour of the Guava Kai Plantation in Kilauea
- The Kamalani playground for the kids at Lydgate Park
- Friday the galleries in Hanapepe host "Art Night," with at least one of them providing refreshments and an art demonstration
- Sunset torchlighting ceremony at the Hyatt Regency Kauai Resort and Spa
- Coffee tasting at the Kaua'i Coffee Company Visitor Center & Museum
- Self-guided tour of Moir Cactus Gardens and Hawaiian Gardens at the Kiahuna Plantation in Po'ipu
- The Exhibition Hall at Kukui Grove Shopping Center, a cooperative effort between the Garden Islands Arts Council and Kaua'i Society of Artists, featuring the most creative and energetic efforts of the art community
- Daily hula and Polynesian shows (5 p.m.) at the Coconut MarketPlace in Wailua
- Special events and children's activities at Borders Books at the Kukui Grove Shopping Center
- A self-guided tour of the Hawaiian artifacts at the Kaua'i Heritage Center of Hawaiian Culture & the Arts at Kaua'i Village in Waipouli. (They also offer a varied number of video presentations, lectures and workshops—many of them are free.)
- Hula show and local entertainment Friday at 6 p.m. at Kukui Grove Center
- Sunday Service in Hawaiian at the Waioli Hui Church in Hanalei or the Waimea Christian Foreign and Hawaiian Church to enjoy the exceptional choir and appreciate the great acoustics
- Lihu'e Lutheran in the Kukui Grove Center features Hawaiian music at 6 p.m.

- Admission is free at the Kaua'i Museum on the first Saturday of the month, when they offer special family activities. (For a calendar of events write to 4428 Rice Street, Lihu'e, HI 96766; 808-245-6931.)
- *E Kanikapila Kakou*, a free, 12-week Hawaiian music program that features local composers each week. Held every Monday (February through May) at 7 p.m. at St. Michael's and All Angels Parish Hall in Lihu'e. Call 808-246-3994 for schedule and more information
- The Koloa Heritage Trail, which highlights the various cultural, historical and geographical important sites of the Koloa and Po'ipu areas. Get a free trail guide/map from Po'ipu Beach Resort Association, 808-742-7444
- Free copy of *Kaua'i Update* newsletter! Send a self-addressed stamped envelope to Paradise Publications, 8110 SW Wareham, Portland, OR 97223; e-mail paradiyse@att.net, and indicate you'd like the latest copy of our Kaua'i newsletter

Best Not Quite Free, But Worth the Small Donation

- Koke'e Natural History Museum's hike with an interpretive guide along the many trails of the Koke'e area during summer months.
- Koke'e Natural History Museum, with great exhibits, interesting crafts and good information about the trails and activities in Koke'e State Park.

Gift for Friends Traveling to Kaua'i Send a self-addressed, stamped envelope for a complimentary copy of the *Kaua'i Update Newsletter* to 8110 SW Wareham, Portland, OR 97223; e-mail paradiyse@att.net. (Subscriptions also available.) Or purchase a copy of *Paradise Family Guide—Kaua'i*.

The Seven Wonders of Kaua'i

Kaua'i is a scenic tropical wonderland with varied terrain, geography and natural features. It's a lush, green Garden of Eden for the most part, little wonder its nickname is *The Garden Isle*. And there are seven special attributes that visitors shouldn't miss while there.

1. *Napali Coast*, where majestic sea cliffs rise to 4,000 feet above the uninhabited North Shore. Sea caves, lush hidden valleys, deserted white-sand beaches and some of Kaua'i's most awe-inspiring views. It's accessible by air, boat or a very strenuous 11-mile hike on the Kalalau Trail.

2. *Koke'e State Park*, a treasure trove of native plants and birds, hiking trails, scenic lookouts, and a small natural history museum.

3. *Kilauea Point National Wildlife Refuge* is one of the most visited wildlife refuges in the country. The grounds, with a historic lighthouse, sit atop a rocky peninsula on Kaua'i's northernmost point and is home to thousands of seabirds that nest on the surrounding cliffs. Whales, dolphins, seals and turtles can be seen in the ocean below.

4. *Waimea Canyon*, known as the Grand Canyon of the Pacific, is a geological wonder stretching ten miles long, 3,600 feet deep, and a mile wide. There are numerous hiking trails, picnic areas, wilderness campsites, and scenic vistas.

5. *Wailua River* can best be enjoyed by a boat or kayak trip; it's the state's only true navigable river, with two sets of memorable falls: Opaeka'a and Wailua. Upriver there's also a beautiful Fern Grotto, which is a massive lava tube adorned with lush tropical flora.

6. *Mt. Wai'ale'ale* is the second highest peak on Kaua'i at 5,208 feet, and one of the wettest places on earth, with over 400 inches of annual rainfall. This tabletop-flat mountain stands next to Kawaikini, the island's highest peak. Both can be seen and enjoyed on clear days, but neither can be reached by foot.

7. *Hanalei Valley, Bay and River* on the North Shore is rich in history and culture. It still produces the bulk of the state's taro crop, which is used to make poi.

History of Kaua'i

Although it is not the usual way to begin a historic narrative, this history of Kaua'i begins with a jump to September 11, 1992. That's the day when Hurricane Iniki's terrific winds swept across the island, leaving few structures undamaged. Although some hotels, condominiums and other island businesses were able to quickly rebuild, others took years to recover. Still other businesses closed their doors forever. But from the destruction sprang new growth and rebirth. In spite of insurance nightmares, hotels were renovated and remodeled, new restaurants opened and old ones were refurbished and improved.

Hurricane Iniki, the second storm to hit the island in a decade (Iwa struck in 1982), left a heavy footprint on the island. Besides dramatically affecting Kaua'i's economy, it changed the lives of its residents, and many left rather than face the challenge of rebuilding. Others, however, enjoyed the comraderie and opportunity to make a new start, and felt the storm slowed down the island's growth, preventing rampant overdevelopment. Overall, the island's people pulled together and Kaua'i's folks pride themselves on their self-sufficiency, strength and endurance.

THE ISLAND That said, let's go back five million years to the creation of Kaua'i. Each Hawaiian island was formed by volcanic action, and Kaua'i is the oldest of the major islands in the Hawai'i chain. The archipelago of Hawai'i spans 1,523 miles, with 132 islands, shoals and reefs that reach as far west as the Aleutian Islands of Alaska. It is the most remote inhabited land mass in the world. The Big Island is now the youngest in the chain and is continuing to grow. A new island called Lo'ihi is growing undersea southeast of the Big Island, and is expected to emerge from the oceanic depths in a few thousand years.

The State of Hawai'i is composed of eight major islands: Hawai'i, Maui, Kaho'olawe, Lana'i, Moloka'i, O'ahu, Ni'ihau and Kaua'i. The islands are organized into self-governing counties: the County of Hawai'i (often called the Big Island), the County of Maui (including Maui, Kaho'olawe, Lana'i and Moloka'i), the City and County of Honolulu (O'ahu), and the County of Kaua'i (including Kaua'i and Ni'ihau).

The major islands lie in a curving arc stretching southeast to northwest from about 18 to 23 degrees north latitude and 155 to 159 degrees west longitude in the North Pacific Ocean. Of the eight major islands, all are populated except for Kaho'olawe, which was a Navy bombing target for decades until it was returned to the State of Hawai'i for inclusion in a Hawaiian nation. Ni'ihau is only sparsely populated but is privately owned and closed to outsiders. Few are allowed to visit Ni'ihau, except on arranged hunting and fishing excursions.

The northwest Hawaiian islands are unpopulated (except for Midway Atoll) and are mostly low-lying coral atolls that are protected wildlife preserves. These islands, which stretch all the way out to near the 180th meridian International Dateline, include Nihoa, Necker, La Perouse, Gardner, Laysan, Lisianski, Pearl and Hermes, Midway, and Kure. Midway Atoll in the northwest Hawaiian islands, previously under the control of the U.S. Navy as a base, is now a part of the National Wildlife Refuge and tours of it are available, departing from Honolulu.

The northernmost islands of the eight major islands, Kaua'i and Ni'ihau, were created together, emerging from the surface of the sea at the same time. They are actually dissected domes separated by the shallow 17-mile-wide Kau'lakahi Channel. Lehua to the north and Ka'ula to the south are two tiny uninhabited islets that are also part of Ni'ihau and the County of Kaua'i.

The interpretations of the name Kaua'i prove to be varied. Harry Franck, in his 1937 publication *Roaming in Hawai'i*, noted that the translation was "to light upon" or "to dry in the sun." This derivation might possibly come from the fact that driftwood landed on the shores of Kaua'i more often than on other islands.

The island lies very much in the path of the trade winds and of ocean currents. Franck continues: "The more commonly accepted meaning of the name is 'fruitful season or time of plenty,' because in olden times Kaua'i was the only island of the group which never suffered from famine on account of drought. In very ancient times, it was known as *Kaua'i-a-mano-ka-lani-po*, which freely translated means 'The fountain-head of many waters from on high and bubbling from below.'" That is probably the most likely translation of its name.

Kaua'i is young in geological terms; its birth began about 5 million years ago and continued for about 3 million years. It lay dormant for another 1.5 million years before having the resurgence of volcanic activity that created the eastern portions of the island over the course of more than 1.5 million years. The most recent volcanic activity occurred on the southern shore more than 40,000 years ago. Compared with Maui's most recent volcanic activity, which occurred only 200 years ago, Kaua'i is the grandmother in the chain of major Hawaiian islands.

Kaua'i is much smaller today than when it was first formed. Over eons of time the crashing waves and storms eroded the North Shore, reducing the island's diameter from over 30 miles to 25—a small price to pay for the dramatic result of the erosion: the splendid and majestic Napali Coast.

Kaua'i's other phenomenon of nature, Waimea Canyon, was formed when a huge fault broke open and was further eroded by the Waimea River.

Kawaikini and Wai'ale'ale are the twin peaks of the single-shield volcano that formed the island. Mt. Wai'ale'ale is considered one of the wettest places on earth. Kaua'i today is a blend of mountains, beaches and rain forests covering 555 square miles, making it Hawai'i's fourth largest island.

Due to the years of erosion, Kaua'i has many distinct land characteristics. With a total of 136 miles of coastline, Kaua'i has more sandy beaches per square mile than any other of the major islands. Napali Coast is another of nature's wondrous creations, rising as much as 4,000 feet from the sea.

Life began in the waters surrounding the island in the form of marine creatures. Fish, mammals and microscopic animals found homes under the sea while generations of coral polyps attached themselves to the barren volcanic rock and ultimately created a coral reef. Kaua'i remains on the fringe of the coral reef system. (Many of its beaches lack a protective reef and require more caution.)

On land, life began slowly, sporadically and quite accidentally. Spores of ferns and moss, as well as tiny seeds, were carried by the winds. The few that survived altered the composition of the barren rock by breaking it down into bits of debris and fertile soil. Insects were tossed about by storms and washed ashore on floating debris.

Birds blown off course began to colonize, not only populating the island with their own species, but with larger seeds and grasses that they inadvertently carried on their feet, feathers, or in their intestinal tracts. The introduction of each species of flora or fauna was a rare event, taking thousands of years. With no predators, birds flourished, evolving into many distinct species. The only mammals to arrive without the help of man were the seal and the bat, and neither provided any threat to the birdlife of the islands. (Since the mongoose was never introduced to Kaua'i, the birds continue to fare better here than elsewhere in the state.)

According to Hawaiian legend, Kaua'i was the first home of the volcano goddess Pele, who was driven out by her sister and set up home on the Big Island, which has three active volcanoes. Kaua'i was also believed to be the first Hawaiian island populated by the Polynesians.

Although the dates vary greatly, it is thought that the first Polynesian explorers came to Kaua'i sometime between 200 A.D. and 700 A.D. from the Marquesas Islands to the far south. Findings suggest that their ancestors came from the western Pacific, perhaps as far as Madagascar. Centuries later, they were followed by the Tahitians.

POLYNESIANS The Tahitians settled on the island perhaps between the 11th and 14th centuries and began much of what we know as Hawaiian culture. The Polynesians brought their double-hulled canoes, laden with the food staples of taro and yams, as well as pigs, chickens and dogs, which supplemented their diet of fish. (Taro is the root from which poi is made, and it was used not only as a food by early Hawaiians, but also medicinally and as a dye for their *tapa* cloth.) The Polynesians also introduced a number of useful and medicinal plants, including ginger and sugar cane (to name just a few). It is estimated that by the 1700s, the Hawaiian population may have risen as high as 1 million people, spread throughout the main eight-island chain.

The Polynesians initiated a class system and the concept of *kapu*, or taboo, which was composed of rigid sanctions and religious laws. However, they also introduced the pleasures of surfing, kite flying, the beauty of the floral lei and the idea and spirit of *aloha*.

Three principal gods, Kane (the originator), Ku (the architect and builder) and Lono (director of the elements), formed the basis of the Hawaiian religion until the missionaries arrived. Rituals were an important part of their life, both in birth and death. Human sacrifices were sometimes a part of the rituals performed. (The stone foundations of *heiau*, the ancient religious temples, can still be found throughout the islands.) The governing class was called the *ali'i*, and it was they who kept order by enforcing various *kapu*. It was *kapu*, for example, for men and women to dine together. It was not until the death of King Kamehameha in about 1819 that the appointed regent of Hawai'i, Ka'ahumanu, broke the *kapu* system when she persuaded Liholiho, heir of Kamehameha, to eat with her and his mother, Keopulani, in public. Thus began the breakdown of the old *kapu* system, the old beliefs and religion. Soon after, the influence of the Western world began to spread throughout the islands with the arrival of the first missionaries from America.

On Kaua'i, the lower portion of the Wailua River was the site selected as sacred by the high chiefs and *kahuna* (priests). Here you will find remains of seven *heiau* where the early Hawaiians worshipped their gods. *Ali'i* also were born at the sacred birthing stone located here.

Although Western culture and religion have come to dominate life in the islands, Hawaiians have still maintained distinct differences from the mainland. Prayers, or *pule*, are always performed before many gatherings or activities in the islands, and blessings are required for new construction. The *kupuna*, or elders, also are still revered.

CAPTAIN COOK The islands were undisturbed by Western influence until the 1778 arrival of Captain James Cook. In search of the Northwest Passage, he first spotted and visited Kaua'i on January 19, 1778. Venerated by the local population, Cook was thought to be the returning god Lono. Cook stopped briefly at Ni'ihau and continued on to O'ahu and Maui. On a later voyage, Cook was killed in a dispute and confrontation with Hawaiians at Kealakekua Bay on the Kona Coast of the Big Island of Hawai'i.

The arrival of Europeans brought not only the near demise of the Hawaiian culture, but diseases that killed Hawaiians in huge numbers. Also introduced into the environment were many exotic plants and animals that quickly overran the island's rare and unique native ecology.

KING KAMEHAMEHA Kamehameha was born on the Big Island of Hawai'i about 1758. Kamehameha became known as a fearsome warrior with great ambition for power and control. He was the nephew of Kalaiopi, who ruled the Big Island. When Kalaiopi died, his son came to power, only to be subsequently defeated by Kamehameha in 1794. Kamehameha began his quest to conquer all the islands and unite them under one kingdom. The great chieftain, Kahekili, was Kamehameha's greatest rival. He ruled not only Maui, but Lana'i and Moloka'i, and also had kinship with the governing royalty of O'ahu and Kaua'i. King Kahekili died in 1794, leaving control of the island to his sons, Kalanikupule. A bloody battle (more like a massacre since Kamehameha used Western technology, strategy, and two English advisors) in the 'Iao Valley resulted in the defeat of Kalanikupule in 1795.

In the early 1790s, when Kamehameha was attempting to gain control of all the islands, the King of Kaua'i, Kaumuali'i, realized he had the advantage of having an island farther removed from the rest of the Hawaiian chain. He had no interest in relinquishing his power to Kamehameha. The first attempt to overtake Kaua'i was made by Kamehameha in the spring of 1796. Encountering a storm, many of his soldiers never reached the island after being forced to turn back. Others who reached the island were killed at Maha'ulepu Beach. A later attempt by Kamehameha was thwarted when typhoid struck his soldiers. In 1810, realizing the inevitable, Kaumuali'i agreed to turn over control of his island to Kamehameha. Thus, King Kamehameha the Great, as he came to be known, achieved his destiny by uniting all the islands of Hawai'i under one kingdom. However, Kaua'i still prides itself on being the only island that was never conquered.

Never returning to his home island of Kaua'i, Kaumuali'i, the last King of Kaua'i, died on May 28, 1824, on the island of O'ahu. Following the funeral services, his body was taken to Lahaina, Maui, for burial. Kapiolani, royal wife of King Kamehameha, had become close friends with Kaumuali'i. Prior to the death of Kapiolani, an arrangement had been reached that at his death Kaumuali'i would be laid to rest next to her.

RUSSIANS Kaua'i was briefly inhabited by the Russians during the reign of Kaumuali'i. The Russian traders erected several forts. (The remains of one, Fort Elizabeth, can still be found at the mouth of the Waimea River. Little remains but a few mounds of dirt at Fort Alexander, located on the bluff at Princeville. Another earthen fort in the Hanalei area called Fort Barclay, after a Russian general, has eroded completely away.) Georg Scheffer was a German who worked for the Russian American Company. This trading company sent Scheffer to recover goods from one of their vessels that had gone aground off the coast of Kaua'i.

Scheffer, a botanist and a physician, first arrived on O'ahu. After aiding the royal family when they were ill, he soon endeared himself to the King. He reached Kaua'i in the spring of 1816 and expected that he might need force to regain the merchandise that had been salvaged by Kaua'i's king. He was surprised when Kaumuali'i warmly offered to return it. For a number of reasons, Kaumuali'i was eager to be on good terms with the Russians. Gifts were exchanged and Scheffer was later given the entire valley of Hanalei. He subsequently bestowed Russian names on the Hanalei Valley, calling it Schefferthal and renaming the Hanapepe River the Don. King Kaumuali'i figured he could better protect his island from Kamehameha with the Russians as allies. Scheffer promised Kaumuali'i Russian protection. In *Kaua'i: A Separate Kingdom*, Edward Joesting writes, "The co-monarchs of Kaua'i (Kaumuali'i and Scheffer) now plotted the conquering of these islands. On July 1, 1816, they entered into a secret agreement."

When Kamehameha learned of this plan in 1817, Scheffer was ordered out of the islands. Interestingly, Georg Scheffer spent his last years in Brazil, having purchased a title for himself. He died Count von Frankenthal in 1836.

Kamehameha united all the islands and made Lahaina, Maui, the capital of his kingdom. It remained the capital until the 1840s, when Honolulu, O'ahu, became the center for government affairs.

HAWAIIAN ROYALS Liholiho, the heir to Kamehameha I (also known as Kamehameha the Great), ruled as Kamehameha II from 1819 to 1824. Liholiho was not a strong ruler and Ka'ahumanu, the widow of Kamehameha I, proclaimed herself prime minister during his reign. (While Ka'ahumanu is said to have been the most favored wife of Kamehameha I, she did not have the bloodline of the *ali'i* royalty and therefore could not be his royal wife.) Ka'ahumanu ended many of the *kapus* of the old religion, thus creating a fortuitous vacuum that the soon-to-arrive missionaries would fill.

THE MISSIONARIES The first missionaries arrived with their families from New England in 1820. On Kaua'i they were welcomed in 1821 and established mission houses around the island. The missionaries caused drastic changes to the island with their introduction of Christianity. They created a written alphabet for a language that previously had been entirely oral. It was the missionaries who set up guidelines that forbade the native women to visit the ships in the harbor. Also, horrified by the bare-breasted Hawaiian women, the missionary women quickly set about to more-thoroughly clothe the native ladies. The missionary women realized that their dresses would not be appropriate for these robust women and, using their nightwear as guidelines, fashioned garments for the Hawaiians by cutting the sleeves off and enlarging the armholes. The *muumuu* was the result (*muumuu* means "to amputate or to cut short").

SUGAR Over time, many of the missionary descendants eventually turned to business and commerce and became successful sugar planters. The island was soon blanketed with fields of green sugar cane. The first successful sugar plantation was established in Koloa in 1835 by Ladd & Company. William Hooper, a junior partner in Ladd & Company, established the plantation for that company by leasing 980 acres for $300 a year from King Kamehameha III. During the American Civil War, Louisiana's shipping of sugar had been cut off, which created a void that Hawai'i stepped into and helped fill. This was the first sugar to be exported from the islands.

While the first workers in the sugar cane industry were Hawaiians, the increasing development brought workers from the four corners of the globe. This shaped much of Kaua'i's history and cultural diversity. During the next few decades, immigrants began arriving from both Asia and Europe to work in the fields and mills. In 1838, a few Chinese laborers worked for Hooper, but it was not until 1852 that the first contract laborers from China arrived. In 1868, more than 150 Japanese laborers left their homeland to work in the islands.

The first Portuguese contract laborers were recruited in the Azores and arrived in 1877. By that year, at the height of the sugar industry on Kaua'i, eight plantations had been established. They included 'Ele'ele, Grove Farm, Hanalei, Kapa'a, Kawaihau, Kilauea, Koloa, and Lihu'e. Castle and Cooke recruited a group of 629 Norwegian men, women and children who arrived in 1880. Larger groups of Chinese and Japanese immigrants continued to arrive in the 1880s. In 1902, the first Korean laborers arrived and they were followed by laborers from the Philippines in 1906.

A variety of crops have been attempted in Kaua'i, including tobacco, tea, macadamia nuts, coffee and silk. The financial adviser to King Kamehameha I, a Spaniard named Don Francisco De Paula Marin, introduced limes, guavas, pineapples and mangos to the islands. In the 1860s, the Chinese began cultivating rice all around the islands. It became the second most important crop after sugar, and was the mainstay of Hanalei's economy until 1961, when California-grown rice killed the local rice industry.

THE PRESENT Today, tourism is Kaua'i's major industry, while sugar, coffee, guava, taro and papaya are the island's largest agricultural crops. White shrimp, raised in state-of-the-art aquaculture ponds in Kekaha, has recently become a successful export.

Kaua'i has also become well-known on the big screen. Its spectacular scenery has allowed Kaua'i to play a role in more than 50 movies and full-length television features. *Jurassic Park*, *Uncommon Valor*, *Flight of the Intruder*, *Raiders of the Lost Ark*, *Blue Hawaii*, *Outbreak*, *King Kong* and *South Pacific* are only a few. More recently, Disney's *George of the Jungle* and the sequel to *Jurassic Park*, *The Lost World*, *Jurassic Park III*, *To End All Wars*, *Dragonfly*, and *Tears of the Sun* were partially filmed on Kaua'i. (You may have noticed in the original *Jurassic Park* that when they showed an island map it was even shaped like the island.)

MENEHUNE A history of Kaua'i cannot be complete without a discussion of the *Menehune*. An early account in the logs of Captain Cook tells of a people he found in Hawai'i that were smaller in stature and lighter skin-toned than most other Hawaiians. He described them as being a servant class. The folklore says that the *Menehune* were famous for the stonework and would work at night, creating vast projects such as the *Menehune* (or Alekoko) Fishpond, and the *Menehune* ditches. Among the speculated theories, perhaps the most probable is that the *Menehune* were the island's first settlers from the

NI'IHAU

Ni'ihau, located 17 miles west of Kaua'i, is, along with Lana'i, a privately owned island. You can only visit by arranged hunting and fishing excursions via Ni'ihau Safaris, Ltd. (*See* Chapter 6, pages 335, 347). The island of Ni'ihau is slightly more than 47,000 acres, 18 miles by 6 miles. The highest elevation is 1,281 feet at Paniau. Lake Halali'i is 841 acres and although the largest inland lake in Hawai'i, it is more a salt flat that becomes a lake during heavy rains. Many native waterbirds use these wetlands.

The Western history of the island of Ni'ihau began when Mrs. Eliza McHutchenson Sinclair, a widow, relocated from New Zealand. Although she considered the purchase of a piece of beachfront property on O'ahu (now known as Waikiki) in 1863, she visited Ni'ihau following a brief rainy spell and found it quite to her liking. She purchased the parcel from King Kamehameha IV for $10,000 on January 20, 1864. It was not until later that she discovered Ni'ihau suffered from a serious shortage of water (which continues to this day). Sinclair enjoyed only three summers on her new island before purchasing land on the western side of Kaua'i in Makaweli.

At the time of Cook's visit, the population of Ni'ihau may have numbered as many as 10,000 individuals. By the time of the Sinclair purchase, the island had a population of 1,008. Dogs were raised by the Ni'ihauans for food and the Sinclairs ordered the destruction of all canines in order to safeguard the new herds of sheep and cattle. More than 700 *kanaka* (people) reportedly left the island rather than destroy their dogs.

Abrey Robinson inherited control of the family estate when Sinclair, 92, died in 1893. Born in New Zealand, he studied law at Boston University before returning to Kaua'i. Robinson implemented plans to improve Ni'ihau by undertaking reforestation, initiating irrigation systems, and introducing Arabian horses, cotton and honey to the small island while limiting outside influences. Crops proved difficult, but Ni'ihauans cultivated *kiawe* trees, from which mesquite, the pungent charcoal that is prized for cooking, is made.

The island population currently numbers in the neighborhood of 230 persons, and the Hawaiian language and culture still dominates. The island has no paved roads or telephones, and power is limited to that supplied by generators and solar cells. There are a few cars but transportation is primarily provided by donkeys and horses. The town of Pu'uwai is where the local residents live.

Today the island continues to be a working cattle and sheep ranch, but it has become most famous for its beautiful shell necklaces. Made from very small shells collected on the island's beaches, the strands come in many colors and hues. The necklaces are intricate, requiring hundreds of tiny shells and many hours to complete.

Marquesas. A census conducted in the early part of the 19th century showed that there were 65 *Menehune* living in the Wainiha Valley.

The Hawaiian Language

The Hawaiian language was first written down by American missionaries. Using the written language they created an alphabet with only 12 letters, five of which are vowels. The key to the language is to remember to pronounce each letter, except for some vowels, which run together as one. In some cases, substitute the "v" sound when "w" appears. The ' symbol you see is a glottal stop and instructs you to say each letter separately (such as *ali'i*, or ah-lee-ee). Pick up a copy of *Instant Hawaiian*; this handy guide will help you be understood.

Following are some of the more commonly used Hawaiian words that you may hear or see:

ali'i—(ah-lee-ee)—chief
aloha—(ah-loh-hah)—greetings
hale—(hah-lay)—house
hana—(HA-nah)—work
hana hou—(ha-nah HO)—to do it again, encore
heiau—(heh-ow)—temple
haole—(how-lee)—a caucasian
kai—(kye)—ocean
kahuna—(kah-HOO-nah)—teacher, priest
kama'aina—(kah-mah-ai-nuh)—native born
kane—(kah-nay)—man
kapu—(kah-poo)—keep out, forbidden
keiki—(kay-kee)—child
lanai—(lah-nah-ee)—porch or patio
lomi lomi—(loh-mee LOH-mee)—to rub or massage
luau—(loo-ow)—party with entertainment and imu-cooked food
makai—(mah-kye)—toward the ocean
malihini—(mah-lee-hee-nee)—a newcomer or visitor
mana—(mah-nah)—supernatural or divine power
mauka—(mau—*rhymes with cow*—kah)—toward the mountain
mauna—(MAU-nah)—mountain
mele—(MAY-leh)—Hawaiian song or chant
menehune—(may-nay-hoo-nee)—Hawaiian dwarf or elf
moana—(moh-ah-nah)—ocean
nani—(NAH-nee)—beautiful
ono—(oh-no)—delicious
pali—(PAH-lee)—cliff, precipice
paniolo—(pah-nee-o-low)—Hawaiian cowboy
pau—(pow)—finished

poi—(poy)—a paste made from the taro root
pua—(POO-ah)—flower
puka—(POO-ka)—a hole
pupus—(poo-poos)—appetizers
wahine—(wah-hee-nay)—woman
wiki wiki—(wee-kee wee-kee)—hurry

KAUA'I NAMES AND PLACES

Ahukini—altar (for) many (blessings)
Alaka'i—to lead
'Ele'ele—black
Ha'ena—red hot
Hanakapi'ai—bay sprinkling food
Hanalei—crescent bay
Hanapepe—crushed bay (due to landslides)
Ha'upu—recollection
Kahana—cutting
Ka Holua Manu—the sled course of Manu
Kalaheo—the proud day
Kalalau—the straying
Ka'lihi Wai—the edge, with a stream
Kaumuali'i—the royal oven
Kawaikini—multitudinous water
Kawaihau—ice water
Kekaha—the place
Kikiaola—container (acquired) by Ola
Kilauea—spewing, much spreading (volcanic eruptions)
Kilohana—lookout point
Koke'e—to bend or to wind
Lihu'e—cold chill
Mana—arid
Miloli'i—fine twist (as sennit cord)
Namolokama—the interweaving bound fast
Na'pali—the cliffs
Nawiliwili—the wiliwili trees
Niumalu—shade (of) coconut trees
Nounou—throwing
Po'ipu—completely overcast or crashing (as waves)
Polihale—house bosom
Puhi—blow
Pu'ukapele—the volcano hill
Wai'ale'ale—rippling water or overflowing water
Wailua—two waters
Waipahe'e—slippery water

For more information on Hawaiian place names consult *Place Names of Hawai'i* by Mary Kawena Pukui, Samuel H. Elbert and Esther T. Mookini.

Island Facts and Figures

Collectively, the islands are known as Hawai'i, the name coming from the largest island in the chain, known as the Big Island due to its size (larger than all the other islands combined). The name Hawai'i was given to the entire island chain after King Kamehameha the Great, of Hawai'i Island, unified the islands under one kingdom. The state has a nickname, flower, bird, mammal, tree and fish. In addition, each individual island has its own unique identity.

THE HAWAIIAN ISLANDS *Nickname*: The Aloha State; *State Flower*: Hibiscus; *State Tree*: Kukui; *State Bird*: Nene Goose; *State Fish*: Humuhumunukunukuapua'a; *State Mammal*: Humpback Whale; *State Capital*: Honolulu.

The Hawaiian State Flag was designed for King Kamehameha I in the first part of the 19th century. The British Union Jack in the corner acknowledges the early ties the islands had with England. The eight horizontal stripes of red, white and blue signify the eight major islands in the Hawaiian chain. King Kalakaua composed the state's national anthem, "Hawai'i Pono i."

KAUA'I *Nickname*: The Garden Island; *Island color*: Purple; *Flower*: Mokihana; *County Seat*: Lihu'e; *Area*: 550 square miles; *Length*: 33 miles; *Width*: 25 miles; *Coastline*: 90 miles; *Highest point*: 5,243 feet—Kawaikini; *Population*: 56,000.

NI'IHAU *Nickname*: The Forbidden Island; *Island color*: White or brown; *Flower*: Pupu shell; *Main town*: Pu'uwai; *Area*: 73 square miles; *Length*: 14 miles; *Width*: 16 miles; *Coastline*: 40 miles; Highest point: 1,281 feet—Paniau; *Population*: 250.

Island Ecology

When visiting the islands, you may never see some of the native species of birds and plant life. The more aggressive species that have been introduced over the past centuries have encroached on the native environment and many endemic (found nowhere else) species have become extinct. Several refuges and botanical gardens on Kaua'i offer the visitor the rare opportunity to see some of these species at close proximity. (*See* Chapter 6 for more information.)

INSECTS There are few dangerous land and sea creatures in Hawai'i. Mosquitos reportedly were the gift of a ship called the *Welling-*

ton, which arrived on Maui in 1826. They soon spread to the other islands and can be most irritating in the wetter, forested areas. It is worth packing a bottle of repellent. The only other creepy crawler that is to be avoided is the centipede. They spend most of their time undercover. If you see one; avoid it, the sting is extremely painful, but will gradually diminish. No treatment is needed or available.

REPTILES AND AMPHIBIANS The Bufo toad is a very friendly fellow that can be found all around the islands, but generally is more noticed after a heavy rain—or, unfortunately, flattened on the road. In 1932 this frog was brought from Puerto Rico to assist with insect control. They don't mind being held, and can be turned over and seem to love having their stomachs rubbed. However, on the bufo toad you will notice a lump behind his head that carries a poison. A handy defense, the poison awaits a sharp blow or puncture to cause it to squirt out. Dogs or cats quickly learn not to bother them because the poison can cause them to become seriously ill or die. Their body secretions can be irritating to the skin, especially eyes, and it's suggested that you just enjoy watching them instead of picking them up.

There are also a few areas on the Big Island and other islands that have recently had a couple of species of Caribbean tree frogs established. The small, but noisy, critters got into the islands by hitchhiking aboard imported plants, so the theory goes. The tiny frogs are a bit of a nuisance because they make a quite loud and very noticeable

UNWANTED SPECIES

There are no snakes in Hawai'i. However, over the past decade a few snakes have been seen, caught and destroyed. Great care is taken to ensure that snakes do not arrive in the islands unintentionally as part of ship or airplane cargo. Dogs are trained to sniff them out. The brown tree snake is among the most feared because it has virtually destroyed the wild bird population on Guam. There is an on-going program to prevent the arrival and introduction of the brown tree snake into Hawai'i.

One of the big problems is the illegal importation—smuggling—of exotic species like snakes, frogs, fish, lizards, birds and plants into the islands. Over the last several years, under the amnesty program, many species have been surrendered voluntarily. Some have been captured in the wild. Such species have included three-foot-long iguanas, a cobra snake, several types of pythons, and even several South American piranha fish. Please respect Hawai'i's native environment and do not bring in anything that is not allowed.

chirping sound, mostly at night when people are trying to sleep. It's hoped the infestation will avoid Kaua'i. But these things have a way of eventually migrating to other areas.

The other island creature that cannot go without mention is the gecko. They are finding their way into the suitcases of many an island visitor in the form of T-shirts, sunvisors and jewelry. This small lizard is a relative of the chameleon and grows to a length of three or four inches. They dine on roaches, termites, mosquitos, ants, moths and other pesky insects.

While there are nearly 800 species of geckos found in warm climates around the world, there are only five known varieties found in Hawai'i, and none are native species. They are the only lizards that can vocalize, with each species making different sounds. The house gecko is the most commonly found, with tiny rows of spines that circle its tail, while the mourning gecko has a smooth, satiny skin and along the middle of its back it sports pale stripes and pairs of dark spots. The mourning gecko species is parthenogenic, which means that there are only females that produce fertile eggs—so no need for a mate! Smaller species have a life expectancy of five to seven years; larger geckos in captivity have reached 20 years of age.

The stump-toed variety is distinguished by its thick flattened tail. The tree gecko enjoys the solitude of the forests, and the fox gecko, with a long snout and spines along its tail, prefers to hide around rocks or tree trunks. Females make sure their eggs are well hidden before leaving them forevermore. The little ones will hatch in one to three months, breaking out of their eggshell with a specially designed "egg tooth" attached to their nose.

You won't see the sly mongoose on Kaua'i. It's the only major Hawaiian island without these animals, which prey on birds and their eggs. Consequently, Kaua'i is blessed with more birdlife than other islands.

The first geckos may have reached Hawai'i with early voyagers from Polynesia, but the house gecko may have arrived as recently as the 1940s, along with military shipments to Hawai'i. Geckos are most easily spotted at night when they seem to enjoy the warm lights outside your door. They establish little territories where they live and breed so you will no doubt see them around the same area each night. They are very shy and will scurry off quickly. Sometimes you may find one living in your hotel or condo. They're friendly and beneficial animals and are said to bring good luck, so make them welcome.

BIRDS Birdlife abounds on Kaua'i, and no doubt the first you'll note are the chickens! Wild chickens? Yes! The wild chickens that you may see in the area of Koke'e and the lodge are descendants from the ones brought by the Polynesians known as *moa*. But you'll find chickens just about everywhere you turn on Kaua'i these days. Many domestic chickens escaped during the hurricanes and bred with the *moa*. The roosters can be a bit of a nuisance in rural areas where their wake-up calls are not always appreciated. Don't feed these birds, they do not need encouragement.

The songbirds of Hawai'i owe a great deal of credit to Mrs. Dora Isenberg. The *New York Herald Tribune* (September 1938 edition) carried the following historical background:

> "Thanks to the efforts of one woman, the Hawaiian islands are now the home of thousands of gaily colored songbirds from all parts of the world. Mrs. Dora Isenberg began her hobby of importing songsters forty years ago in celebration of Hawai'i's joining the United States [as a territory]. After permitting them to get acclimated in her garden on Kaua'i Island, Mrs. Isenberg gave the birds their freedom. Her first attempts were unsuccessful when fourteen larks from the Orient were released and never heard of again. But, undismayed, Mrs. Isenberg continued her efforts, and many other people took up the hobby, with the result that today the islands boast thousands of such imported birds as the Peko thrush, African ringneck dove, Mongolian thrush, Chinese thrush, Bleeding Heart dove, meadow-lark, tomtit, and cardinal."

While these birds are pretty and have a nice voice, they do carry avian malaria to native birds and also compete for food, so they are not totally benign.

MAMMALS The goats found in the Koke'e area are descendants of those brought to the islands by Captain Cook. They have done significant damage to the vegetation and hunting them is allowed. A pair of binoculars, or even a sharp lookout at one of the Waimea Canyon viewing areas and you might spot one or more. They blend in so well with the bare rocky terrain that you may almost fail to spot one even if it's standing within a few feet of you. Pigs and deer also were introduced and continue to be hunted. They also cause major environmental damage.

Traveling with Children

Traveling with children can be an exhausting experience for parents and children alike, especially when the trip is as long as the one to Kaua'i. Packing a child's goodie bag for the long flight is a must. A few new activity books or toys that can be pulled out en route can be sanity-saving. Snacks (boxes of juice are a favorite with younger children) can tide over the little ones at the airport or on the plane while awaiting your food/drink service. The squeeze-it juice drinks are portable and can be frozen in their plastic bottle, providing a cool drink when the need arises. A thermos with a drinking spout works well and is handy for use during vacations. A change of clothes and a swim suit for the little ones can be tucked into your carry-on bag. (Suitcases have been known to be lost or delayed.) Another handy addition is a small night light since unfamiliar accommodations can be somewhat confusing for little ones during the bedtime hours. Disposable diapers are a real travel convenience. And don't forget a strong sunscreen and hat.

ON THE PLANE WITH KIDS

Children may have difficulty clearing their ears when landing. Many don't realize that cabins are pressurized to approximately the 6,000-foot level during flight. To help relieve the pressure of descent, have infants nurse or drink from a bottle, and older children may benefit from chewing gum and yawning as wide as they can. If this is a concern of yours, consult with your pediatrician about the use of a decongestant prior to descent.

TRAVELING IN THE ISLANDS WITH KIDS

CAR SEATS By law, children 3 to 4 years of age must have seat belts unless they are in a federally approved car seat. Federally approved car seats are required for all children from birth up to three years in Hawai'i.

While some rental agencies do have car seats for rent, you need to request them well in advance as they have a limited number. Many rental car seats have probably seen better days, and sometimes they are not the most up-to-date design and maybe only marginal for child safety. Prices run about $5 to $15 per day. You might be better off bringing your own. Several styles are permitted by the airlines for use in flight (if you are paying for a seat for your child) or may be checked at the gate.

BABYSITTING There are no full-time childcare services on Kaua'i. Arrangements for childcare can be made through your hotel concierge or the front desk at most condominiums will be able to assist you. Service is expensive and will run you about $10 or more per hour.

CRIBS Many condominiums and most hotels will be able to provide you with a rental crib. Prices run about $5 per day, $30 per week. There are many portable cribs that can be packed into a large duffle bag. They weigh under 20 pounds and can be purchased for about the same price as a ten-day rental.

FOR EMERGENCIES *See* listing under "Medical Information" below in this chapter.

DINING A children's menu is often referred to as a "*Keiki* Menu." A few restaurants that offer menus (or child-size portions) for the young traveler include: Duke's Canoe Club, Gaylord's, Bali Hai, JR's Plantation, Oki Diner, Kountry Kitchen, Keoki's Paradise, Wailua Family Restaurant, Waipouli Deli, and Bull Shed. You can get a "Kitten's Menu" at TomKat's; feed the "Little Cowboys" at JR's Plantation; or ask for the "Menehune Menu" at any of the Camp House Grill locations. Be sure to ask for children's menus or prices wherever you dine. Look for the little girl with a hat in Chapter 4 for some of the restaurants offering children's menus.

BEACHES—POOLS

Several places offer ideal toddler and young swimmer opportunities. There is a natural kiddie wading pool at Po'ipu Beach Park that is ideal for toddlers and very young swimmers. The nearby access to bathrooms can be a plus for the traveling family as well. To the west of Po'ipu Beach is a small protected cove known as Baby Beach. Good swimming locations for the younger set also are found at Lydgate Beach Park and at Salt Pond Beach Park. Kids will love exploring a variety of sea creatures found in the tidepools here and at 'Anini Beach. Several beaches do have lifeguards on duty. Look for the shovel and pail picture for child-friendly beaches in Chapter 5.

A precaution on the beach that is often neglected is the application of a good sunscreen—always reapply after swimming! It's easy to forget that in the cool pool or ocean, you're still getting those strong rays of sun.

Unfortunately, many people underestimate the power of the ocean and drownings occur far too often on Kaua'i. If the surf is up, choose a different activity for the day, or just enjoy a picnic on the beach. Some beaches are fine for children in the summer, but are definitely *not* an option during the higher surf of winter.

The **Kamalani playground** at Lydgate Beach Park will give your lively young ones a chance to expend some of their energy. The park's volcano slide, treehouse, spider web rope ladder, tire swings, and caves were designed especially with active 6 to 10 year olds in mind. Another playground is found in the park at the entrance to the Princeville Resort on the North Shore.

A few resorts have pools with the very young traveler in mind. The Radisson Kaua'i Beach has a *keiki* pool, as does the Sheraton Kaua'i Resort and the Kaua'i Coast Resort at the Beachboy.

We recommend taking a life jacket or water wings (floaties), but do *not* count on these in the ocean. Packing a small inflatable pool for use on your lanai or courtyard may provide a cool and safe retreat for your little one. Typically resorts and hotels *do not* offer lifeguard services.

CHILDCARE PROGRAMS

Some hotels and resorts offer seasonal children and youth programs. Most are offered during summer and the Christmas–New Year holidays. A few are available year-round. Generally, only resort guests can partake of these childcare programs. However, some are open to nonhotel guests as well. In Chapter 3, look for the girl in the bathing suit. She indicates a childcare program.

Aloha Kaua'i Beach Resort has various activities in their Children's Activity Center, offered when the hotel is full. Free. 808-823-6000.

The **Hyatt Regency Kauai Resort and Spa**'s daily **Camp Hyatt** program offers the opportunity to have fun while learning about island life. The Camp's learning adventures cover such topics as archaeology, Hawaiian crafts, local history and ecological preservation. In addition to its learning adventure program, the regular Camp Hyatt schedule includes a variety of activities such as cruising down the 150-foot waterslide, face painting, tennis and Hawaiian arts and crafts like seashell sculpture, sand crafts, shell bracelet making, Hawaiian leaf stencil painting, and more. Camp Hyatt is available seven days a week to resort guests ages 3 to 12. Children under 3 may attend when accompanied by a babysitter. Camp hours are from 9 a.m. to 4 p.m. There is a ratio of one counselor for every four children, or one for every two children between the ages of 3 and 5. Night Camp is available from 4 to 10 p.m. daily, providing children 3 to 12 years with a variety of supervised activities, including games, Hawaiian crafts and computer and video games.

There are also special Holiday Activities for children during holiday seasons, including Christmas, Easter and Halloween. Easter Sunday is the only day of the year that Camp Hyatt is closed. Instead, children are invited to take part in the annual Easter Egg Parade that winds its way through the resort and ends with an Easter Egg Hunt and Festival. For Halloween, Camp Hyatt kids are assisted in making their own special costumes, then taken on a trick-or-treat excursion through the various hotel departments.

During summer, the resort hosts complimentary Family Fun Theater Nights on Wednesday in the Alii Gardens. The event offers popular movies that were filmed on Kaua'i, along with popcorn and soft drinks. Rock Club Just for Teens is held during the summer. It offers a "cool" activity room where teens can gather to socialize. Rock Club offers a variety of unsupervised teen-oriented activities such as music videos, ping-pong and darts, as well as popcorn and other munchies. The Rock Club is complimentary to teens 13 to 17 years. 808-742-1234.

The **Kiahuna Keiki Klub** at the **Kiahuna Plantation** is available for registered resort guests Monday through Friday 9 a.m. until 3 p.m. during the summer, as well as during spring and winter breaks. Kids 4 to 12 are exposed to the Hawaiian culture through activities like lei making, ukulele lessons, hula dancing, and storytelling. Other activities include beach walks, lagoon fishing and arts and crafts. Activities are based on the age level of the children participating. 808-742-5411.

Kaua'i Marriott Resort and Beach Club features a program called **Kalapaki Kids**. Provided for hotel guests only, activities include boogie boarding, hula, traditional Hawaiian games, crafts and ice cream sundae making. For example, during the hula classes, the songs that are taught are all from Kaua'i, such as "Aloha Kaua'i." Kids are exposed to the ukulele and various Hawaiian crafts like lei making and *lauhala* weaving. Reservations need to be made one day in advance. The full-day program is available Tuesday through Saturday from 9 a.m. until 3 p.m. for youth ages 5 to 12 years. The program costs $45 and includes lunch, a snack, and a Kalapaki Kids T-shirt. The program is available year-round. 808-245-5050.

Radisson Kaua'i Beach Resort's Keiki Klub is summer fun for children 5 to 12 years of age. Activities include beachcombing, ukulele lessons, movies, pool play, Hawaiian face painting, swan/duck feeding, and fishing derbies. Full- and half-day sessions. The program is available Thursday through Monday from 8:30 a.m. to 3:30 p.m. Children are exposed to Hawaiian culture through activities such as lei making, Hawaiian language games, Hawaiian legends and storytelling, hula lessons, and Hawaiian arts and crafts. Other activities include movies, fishing derbies, beachcombing, and shell collecting, as well as excursions to Smith's Tropical Paradise and Fern Grotto tours. Half-day sessions are $15 per child. Full-day program is $30 per child. Cost includes activities, excursions and refreshments. Lunch is provided only in the full-day program. 808-245-1955.

The Princeville Hotel's Keiki Aloha program is available for children ages 5 to 12 years of age and is designed with play in mind. Qualified youth counselors plan a full schedule of activities including snorkeling/beach play, sandcastle creations, Hawaiian arts and crafts, shell collecting and more. The program runs year-round, but is closed on Sunday. There is a charge of $50 per day for the first child and $40 for each additional child per family. Keiki meals are available and the lunch is charged to the parent's room based on consumption. Daytime program runs 9 a.m. to 3 p.m. and evening programs run 3 p.m. to 9 p.m. Summer program runs June 1 to August 31. For children under age 5, babysitting is available. Current babysitting rates are $10 per hour per child plus tax. For children in the same family, an additional cost of $1 per child, maximum 3 children per sitter. 808-826-9644.

Sheraton Kaua'i Resort entertains young guests with their **Keiki Aloha Children's Program**. Activities range from lei making and other Hawaiian arts and crafts to kite flying and ukulele lessons. The program is available year-round. 808-742-4016.

SHOPPING WITH AND FOR KIDS

The **Coconut MarketPlace** (808-822-3641) is one of the best all-around family malls on Kaua'i. Lots of small shops ensure that there will be something for every member of the family, and there's an equally wide array of restaurants. On the North Shore, pull off the road at Kilauea and stop in at the **Little Grass Hut** next to Mango Mama's. Unique gifts and whimsical toys along with "Baskets of Aloha" are sold to benefit the Na Kamalei School. At Princeville Center, there's the **Kaua'i Kite and Hobby Company**, and in Hanalei visit **Rainbow Ducks, Toys, and Clothing**.

MOVIE THEATERS

The twin **Coconut MarketPlace Cinemas** adjoin the shopping center and offer bargain matinees before 6 p.m. Recording: 808-822-2324. For information: 808-821-2402. **Kukui Grove Cinemas** has four screens in their theater, which is across the street from the Kukui Grove Shopping Center. Recording: 808-245-5055. **Waimea Theater** has first-run films. For showtimes and information call 808-338-0282. **Kilauea Theater** (2490 Keneke Street, Kilauea; 808-828-0438) and **Kauai Village Theater** (Kauai Village Shopping Center, 4-831 Kuhio Highway, Kapa'a; 808-823-6789) offer first-run and cult films.

OTHER ACTIVITIES WITH KIDS

The **Kaua'i Children's Discovery Museum** offers changing and permanent exhibitions, events and programs in science, culture, arts and nature. Day camps are offered during the summer and major school breaks, and drop-off child-care services for one to eight hours are available. 808-823-8222.

Storybook Theatre of Hawai'i on Kaumuali'i Highway in Hanapepe involves children in good storytelling activities and invites them to watch the filming of Cablevision's *Russell the Rooster Show*. Call for times. 808-335-0712.

Older children will enjoy a **luau**. The Kaua'i Coconut Beach has a program that offers a free luau for each child with a full-paying accompanying adult several evenings each week. Call 808-822-3455 for current schedule.

The free **hula show** at the Coconut MarketPlace (daily at 5 p.m.) often features child performers. The younger children in your traveling family might enjoy this casual, outdoor performance.

You'll find a **Fun Factory** game arcade at the Waipouli Town Center next to Foodland. They are open Monday through Thursday, 10 a.m. to 10 p.m., Friday and Saturday until midnight.

Visiting Waimea? Take time to stop at **Darri's Delites** for shave ice, pastries, popcorn—even better is their full-service crackseed. (This Asian treat is actually a form of flavored and dried fruit.) Located at 4492 Moana Road along Kaumuali'i Highway. 808-338-0113.

Paradise Fun is an air-conditioned, indoor play facility for children ages 6 months and up. Located at the Kukui Grove Shopping Center, they offer a snack bar, video arcade, big-screen TV, and soft playground. All children must be accompanied by an adult 18 or older unless you take advantage of their drop-off-while-you-shop childcare. Hours of operation: 9:30 a.m. to 6 p.m., until 9 on weekends. A great place to go on a rainy day! 808-241-7050.

Joe-Jo's Clubhouse at 9734 Kaumauli'i Highway in Waimea is a small store, but fun and festive. A good place to take the kids after the scenic wonders of Waimea Canyon. Joe-Jo's has balloons plus nachos, hot dogs, pizza pockets, *saimin*, cookies, and shave ice, with over 60 flavors. Open 10 a.m. to 6 p.m. daily. 808-338-0056.

Borders Books and Music in the Kukui Grove Shopping Center has thoughtfully created a play corner. They also have a children's section and a large Hawaiiana book section. Borders also schedules free events, from storytelling to clown visits.

Lihu'e Lanes, a completely smoke-free bowling alley, also has a snack bar with a kid-friendly menu that includes pizza, burgers and even cinnamon toast! Located in Lihu'e at the Rice Shopping Center. 808-245-5263.

EXCURSIONS AND ADVENTURES

Hiking, mountain biking, ATV tours, horseback rides, a trip to the Kilauea Lighthouse to view the seabirds, a visit to Spouting Horn or the North Shore's unusual wet and dry caves are sure to please kids—

although they'll probably be happiest enjoying the ocean or swimming pool.

Kayaking the Wailua River is a soft adventure suitable for families. Take a picnic lunch along and explore. Kayaks are available for two, so pair up with one of the kids and enjoy the scenic wonders on one of Kaua'i's navigable rivers, or take a guided tour, many of which offer a side hiking trip to a waterfall. See "Kayaking" in Chapter 6.

Especially for Seniors

More and more businesses are beginning to offer special savings to seniors. Whether it is a boating activity, an airline ticket or a condominium, be sure to ask about special senior rates.

SENIOR EVENTS Kaua'i has some interesting annual events for seniors: The Annual Seniors Extravaganza showcases talented seniors (Kaua'i War Memorial Convention Hall); a Quacker Race is a rubber duck race down the Waimea River at the Kaua'i Senior Center (Lucy Wright Park); and First Hawaiian Bank's "Prime Time Health Fair" offers displays, information and exhibits along with entertainment and bingo (Kukui Grove Shopping Center). The dates change, so check the calendar listing in *The Garden Island* newspaper when on-island.

The County of Kaua'i, Office of Elderly Affairs at 4444 Rice Street #105, Lihu'e, HI 96766; 808-241-6400 provides advocacy to elderly persons and their families.

The Lihu'e Chapter of AARP has monthly membership meetings at Lihu'e Neighborhood Center. Call the AARP office at 808-246-4500 or stop by 4212A Rice Street (look for the sign in back) to pick up brochure information or just to visit and "talk story."

KAUA'I SENIOR CENTERS There are centers in Kilauea, Kapa'a (main office), Lihu'e, Koloa, Kalaheo, Kaumakani, Kekaha, Hanapepe and Waimea. They provide programs, including dancing lessons, quilt making and health classes, weekdays 8 a.m. to noon. The main office is at 4491 Kou Street, Kapa'a, HI 96746; 808-822-9675.

Be sure to bring along your medications, and a list of what you take, along with extra prescriptions from your physician in case of emergency.

SENIOR DISCOUNTS Remember that AARP members get many travel discounts for rooms, cars and tours. And be sure to travel with identification showing your birthdate. Check the Yellow Pages when you arrive on Kaua'i for the senior discount program logo. Look for a black circle with white star in the ads.

Many restaurants and hotel dining rooms like Kukui's at the Kaua'i Marriott provide AARP discounts. Just ask about any senior discounts. Jolly Roger has lunch and Early Bird senior specials, as do Al & Don's (at the Kaua'i Sands Hotel), Kaua'i Coconut Beach in their Flying Lobster restaurant, and Aloha Kauai Resort at The Palms Restaurant in the Kuhio Dining Court. Wailua Family Restaurant offers a range of senior-priced meals all day.

Love's Bakery (4100 Rice Street) offers senior specials Tuesdays and Fridays. Gaylord's, Kaua'i Coconut Beach, and Princeville all offer senior discounts on their luaus. Just remember to ask about any applicable discount.

A number of airlines have special discounts for seniors. Some also have a wonderful feature that provides a discount for the traveling companion that is accompanying the senior. Coupon books for senior discounts are also available from a number of airline carriers.

The local Kaua'i Bus also offers discounts for senior citizens.

Travel Tips for the Physically Impaired

Make your travel plans well in advance and inform hotels and airlines when making your reservations that you are a person with a disability. Most facilities will be happy to accommodate you. Bring along your medical records in the event of an emergency. It is recommended that you bring your own wheelchair and notify the airlines in advance that you will be transporting it. Other medical equipment rental information is listed below.

Additional information can be obtained from the State Commission on Persons with Disabilities on Kaua'i at 3060 Eiwa Street, Room 207, Lihu'e, HI 96766; 808-274-3308. They can provide general information on accessibility for private and public facilities on Kaua'i. For information on accessibility features and technical assistance regarding access standards contact the Commission on Persons with Disabilities, 919 Ala Moana Blvd., #101, Honolulu, HI 96814; 808-586-8121 or interisland toll-free 800-468-4644. On Kaua'i call the toll-free local number, 800-274-3141, for a directory of individual extensions.

Contact Parents with Special Keikis c/o Easter Seal Society of Hawaii, Kaua'i Service Center, 3115 Akahi, Lihu'e, HI 96766; 808-245-7141. They provide support and education for parents of children with disabilities. Although primarily for community services for residents, another good resource is the Kaua'i Center for Independent Living. Contact them at 4340 Nawiliwili Road, Lihu'e at 808-245-4034.

ARRIVAL AND DEPARTURE On arrival at the Lihu'e airport you will find the building easily accessible for mobility impaired persons. Parking areas are located in front of the main terminal for disabled persons. Restrooms with handicapped stalls (male and female) are also found in the main terminal.

TRANSPORTATION The only public transportation is the Kaua'i Bus, which charges riders $1 per ride. Seniors, students or disabled with ID are 50 cents. A monthly pass for persons with disabilities runs $12.50. Caregivers traveling with eligible individuals will not be charged a fee. All buses are lift equipped. However, the bus does not stop at the airport and no carry-on baggage is allowed. As part of their ADA paratransit service, door-to-door pickups are available for qualified individuals. Reservations must be made 24 hours in advance; ID may be required. Each bus has a destination sign on the front and curb-side of each bus, which displays a route number. Schedules are available that show the route the bus travels and the times along that route. For additional information phone the County Transportation Office at 808-241-6410 between the hours of 7 a.m. and 5 p.m. Monday through Saturday.

ACCOMMODATIONS Each of the major island hotels offer one or more handicapped rooms, including bathroom entries of at least 29 inches to allow for wheelchairs. Due to the limited number of rooms, reservations should be made well in advance. Information on condominium accessibility is available by calling State Commission on Persons with Disability on Kaua'i at 808-274-3308. They publish the *Aloha Guide to Accessibility* available for $3 to $5 per category section. Victoria Place B&B and Po'ipu B&B Inn are two bed and breakfasts that have a handicapped accessible room.

ACTIVITIES Espirit de Corp Riding Academy has horses trained to handle physically challenged riders. 808-822-4688. Ocean Quest Watersports Co. offers diving tours and classes for the "Differently Abled." They advise you to call before you arrive as some paperwork is required for this program. Toll-free: 888-401-3483. County of Kaua'i Parks & Recreation sponsors integrated programs for youngsters with developmental disabilities. 808-241-6668. ARC of Kaua'i provides recreational programs for persons with disabilities, transportation provided. 808-245-4132. Call Easter Seals of Hawai'i on Kaua'i regarding other activities. 808-245-7141.

BEACHES Lydgate State Park, Hanalei Pavilion Beach Park and Salt Pond Beach Park are the only beach parks that currently are considered to have disabled access, but their facilities may not meet the ADA guidelines for disabled access.

MEDICAL SERVICES AND EQUIPMENT The American Cancer Society, 808-245-2942, provides equipment, including walkers and wheelchairs, on loan without charge for home use to persons with cancer. Garden Island Oxygen Supplies, 808-245-1931, rents, sells and services oxygen tanks and ancillary equipment. Home Infusion Associates, 808-245-3787, rents and sells medical equipment, including wheelchairs. Ready Rentals, 808-823-8008 or 800-599-8008, also offers wheelchair rentals. Kaua'i Hospice, 808-245-7277, has hospital beds. Gammie Home Care has an outlet in Lihu'e at 3215 Kuhio Highway, 808-632-2333; www.gammie.com and provides medical equipment rentals, from walking aides to bathroom accessories or wheelchairs, as well as oxygen services. It is again recommended that you contact any of these services well in advance of your arrival.

Accessible Vans of Hawai'i has been renting vans to travelers with disabilities visiting Hawai'i since 1979 and has units available on Kaua'i. These special vans feature lower floors, electric sliding ramps for wheelchair users plus a 4-point safety securement wheelchair tie-down system. The front passenger seat is removable to allow excellent sightseeing and viewing from the van. Accessible Vans rent by the day, week, month or long-term. Deliveries and pickups may be arranged for the Lihu'e Airport or Nawiliwili Harbor as well as hotels, island tours, or even private homes. Accessible Vans of Hawai'i works with the Kaua'i Center for Independent Living to have a local contact and delivery person for their special-needs clients. Check their website: www.accessiblevans.com. Reservations 800-303-3750 or fax 808-879-0649.

What to Pack

When traveling to Kaua'i, you won't need much. Comfortable shoes are important for sightseeing. Sandals are the norm for footwear and dress is uniformly casual. Clothes should be lightweight and easy to care for. Cotton and cotton blends are more comfortable for the tropical climate than polyesters. Shorts, T-shirts and casual dresses are the dress code here. A lightweight jacket with a hood or sweater is advisable for evenings and rain showers. It's also a good idea to throw in a pair of slacks and a sweater or sweatshirt, especially for winter trips. Tennis shoes or hiking shoes are necessary for longer hikes.

Sunscreens are a must and we recommend you toss in a bottle of insect repellent. A camera, of course, needs to be tucked in and perhaps your video camera. A hat with a brim is a good idea for protecting the head and neck from the sun while touring or just sitting on a beach. Binoculars are a good option and may be well used if you are traveling between December and May when the whales arrive for their winter vacation, or for spotting the incredible sea and land birds found on the Garden Isle.

Special needs for traveling with children are discussed above. If you leave something behind, don't worry, you can purchase it once you arrive, it'll just cost a lot more. Don't forget to leave room in those suitcases for goodies that you will want to take home!

Weddings & Honeymoons

With tropical waterfalls, lush gardens and idyllic beachfront settings, a wedding ceremony on Kaua'i can be a very pleasant experience. While the requirements are simple, here are a few tips (based on current requirements at time of publication) for making your wedding plans run more smoothly. We advise you to double check the requirements as things change.

REGULATIONS Both bride and groom must be over 18 years of age (with written consent from parents or legal guardians for those 16 or 17). Blood tests and birth certificates are not required, but you do need a photo ID, such as a driver's license or passport, to show proof of age. You do not need proof of citizenship or residence.

If either partner has been divorced, the date, county and state of finalization for each divorce must be verbally provided to the licensing agent. If a divorce was finalized within the last 30 days, then a decree must be provided to the licensing agent.

A license must be purchased in person in the state of Hawai'i. The Department of Health can give you names of the licensing agents on the island. You need to make appointments with these licensing agents. Both bride and groom must appear in person before the agent. If you are working with a wedding coordinator, she will make all the necessary arrangements. If you have questions, the local registrar on Kaua'i can be contacted at 808-241-3495; recording with information 808-241-3498. The marriage license fee is currently $50 cash, no checks. Once you have the license there is no waiting period, but the license is valid for only 30 days and only in the State of Hawai'i. For copies of current requirements and to receive necessary forms, write in advance to the State of Hawaii, Department of Health, Marriage License Section, P.O. Box 3378, Honolulu, HI 96801. 808-586-4544.

Check with the Chamber of Commerce on Kaua'i for information. For $7 ($8 on a credit card charge) they will mail you a wedding packet that includes a Kaua'i Vacation Planner, list of wedding coordinators, photographers, florists, churches and a marriage license application. Kaua'i Chamber of Commerce, 4272-B Rice Street or P.O. Box 1969, Lihu'e, HI 96766; 808-245-7363; www.kauaichamber.org.

Appointments must be made with the marriage license agents on Kaua'i. The current list, subject to change, is as follows:

- *Kawaihau District*: Lynn Kubota, 808-822-5122; Grace Apana or Walter Smith, Jr., 808-821-6887.
- *Lihu'e District*: Theresa Koki or Annabelle Pacleb, 808-274-3100.
- *Hanalei District*: Dayna Santos, 808-826-7742.
- *Koloa District*: Val Coyaso, 808-332-7076.

"**A Wedding in Paradise**" can be found at www.aweddinginparadise.com. This site offers information on wedding-related services and information on unusual and adventurous options. They also have an "estimator," which allows the viewer to calculate expenses.

The **Kaua'i Wedding Professionals Association Directory & Bridal Guide** is a great source of information. In addition to comprehensive listings and information on all their members, they offer helpful tips on wedding requirements, planning and photography. For a copy of the booklet, send $3 to KWPA, P.O. Box 761, Kapa'a, HI 96746; www.kauaiwedpro.com.

WEDDING BASICS

Island hotels and resorts frequently offer "honeymoon" or "romance" packages. Since these vary seasonally, inquire directly with the property when making your reservations.

Wedding Chapels

Aloha Church, Assembly of God, 808-241-7717.

Chapel By the Sea at Kaua'i Lagoons, Lihu'e. Beautiful site, albeit very expensive! 808-632-0505.

Koloa Church, founded in 1835, is located at 3269 Po'ipu Road. Outdoor weddings also available. Write them at P.O. Box 668, Koloa, HI 96756. 808-742-9956.

Butterflies Over Hawaii, 644 Kamalu Road, Kapa'a, HI 96746; 808-823-9408, or call 888-BUTRFLI; e-mail: butrfly@aloha.net; www.butterfly-hawaii.com. This Kaua'i-based company does the helicopter flower drop one better by releasing from 10 to 100 Hawaiian Monarch butterflies at your wedding or special event. The butterflies are raised in greenhouses with protective care and their graceful release is a humane and environmental alternative to throwing rice or releasing balloons. The butterflies' survival rate upon release is close to 100 percent. Prices range from $74.95 to $499.99 for release of 100 butterflies.

Formal Wear Rentals

A Formal Affair in Kapa'a, 808-822-0748, offers tuxedo rentals and wedding formal wear. Also for formal wear needs, try **Robert's** in Lihu'e 2976 Kress Street, Lihu'e; 808-246-4653 and 3837 Hanapepe Street, Hanapape; 808-335-5332.

Limousines

Call **Custom Limousine** 808-246-6318; **Kaua'i Limousine** 808-245-4855, 800-764-7213; **Kaua'i North Shore Limousine** 808-826-6189; **Town & Country Limousine** located throughout Hawai'i 888-563-2888.

Catering

Some caterers specialize in wedding catering and arrangements. Check below and also "Catering Services" in Chapter 4.

Heavenly Creations, custom catering and a personal chef. Special wedding and honeymoon services include a romantic dinner on the beach or a personalized treasure hunt leading to a secluded beach and a champagne picnic or buried treasure of goodies. Tel/fax 808-828-1700; 877-828-1700; www.aubergines.com/heaven.

Contemporary Flavors, 808-245-2522, in Puhi are wedding specialists preparing custom catering for all occasions, cake and ice carving, *pupus,* etc. www.gtesupersite.com/contemflavor.

Terrace Restaurant at Kaua'i Lagoons, 808-241-6010, specializes in weddings and has a variety of set menus available.

Gaylord's at Kilohana, 808-246-9333, are wedding specialists who can create all the essentials for your wedding.

Video Tape Services

Hawaiian Creative Video 808-822-5784; **I DO Video Productions** 808-823-6130; **Video Lynx** 808-245-5969.

Photographers

L. Rydell Photography 808-822-2520; **Rainbow Photography** 808-828-0555; **The Wedding Photographer** 808-245-2866; **Kilohana Studio** 808-332-9637.

Wedding Coordinators

A professional wedding coordinator can help make your wedding day a memorable event and save you much time and effort in the process. They can handle all the details. A basic wedding package costs anywhere from $250 to $750. Add a few extras and the price will increase to anywhere from $500 to $2,000 and up and up. Although each coordinator varies the package slightly, a basic package will probably include assistance in choosing a location (public or private), getting your marriage license, selecting a minister and a varying assortment of amenities such as champagne, a small cake and leis. Videotaping, witnesses or music are available for an extra charge. There are a variety of beautiful public facilities where you can be married. However, wedding companies do have a variety of private locations that may be rented for an additional fee—and this can range anywhere from $50 to $300. In addition, many hotels and resorts offer comprehensive wedding coordination services.

Aloha Kauai Fantasy Weddings, 3225 Akahi Street, Lihu'e, HI 96766; 808-245-6500; fax 808-823-8488; e-mail: mokihana@hawaiian.net; www.kauaiweddings.com. This coordinator has several different packages with various amenities available. Plumeria is $675; Lotus is $775; Orchid Deluxe is $1,900, or $2,400 with 7 nights guest house accommodations. Video packages are available: $100 to $475.

Bali Hai Weddings, P.O. Box 1723, Kapa'a, HI 96746; 808-821-2269; 800-776-4813; fax 808-822-7379; e-mail: balihai@hawaiian.net; www.kauai-wedding.com. Contact Marcia Kay Cannon. Add to the Essentials Package ($375) a variety of options, including a sunset cruise, photographer, flower archway, horse and carriage, conch shell ceremony, or limousine from $35 to $325. Assistance with travel and honeymoon accommodations.

Barefoot Kauai Weddings, P.O. Box 3185, Princeville, HI 96722; 808-826-9737; fax 808-826-1233; e-mail: bkw@verizon.net; www.barefootkauaiweddings.com. Basic wedding package $325; Aloha Barefoot $650; Deluxe Barefoot $1,160; video packages are extra.

Chapel by the Sea at Kaua'i Lagoons, 3351-A Hoolaulea Way, Lihu'e, HI 96766; 808-632-0505; 800-724-1686; fax 808-632-0303; www.gardenislandwedding.com. The use of the chapel, floral arrangements, lei or bouquet, minister and solo musician runs $1,300. Photography packages start at $350, edited video $450. Add a ride in a private white wedding carriage $400 or white limousine $250. Cake and champagne options up to $300.

Coconut Coast Weddings and Photography, P.O. Box 385, Hanalei, HI 96714; 808-826-5557; 800-585-5595; fax 808-828-0777; e-mail: cocowed@aloha.net; www.kauaiwedding.com. Complete packages with special emphasis on scenic North Shore locations and photography. Barefoot and Basic package $350; Coconut Coast package $875; Hanalei Bay Wedding $1,175; Orchid Wedding $2,075; Extra add-on amenities and services available at cost. They also offer travel services for wedding and honeymoon packages.

Gaylord's at Kilohana, 3-2087 Kaumuali'i Highway (P.O. Box 1725, Lihu'e, HI 96766); 808-245-1087; fax 808-245-7818; e-mail: gylords@aloha.net; www.gaylordskauai.com. A basic wedding package begins at $550 and includes your choice of setting, a nondenominational minister and a one-hour use of a wedding carriage. They can arrange for intimate or large receptions. You can also arrange to hold your wedding at their luau, the food and entertainment are already there and so are the "instant" family and friends.

Hanalei Colony Resort, P.O. Box 206, Hanalei, HI 96714; 808-826-6235; 800-628-3004; fax 808-826-9893; e-mail: weddings-events@hcr.com; www.wedding-in-kauai.com. Various wedding packages available at the beautiful setting on the North Shore. Simple Kauai Wedding $395; Tropical Isle Wedding $800; Wedding in Paradise $1,285; Ultimate Wedding in Paradise $1,680; various other options and amenities available.

Hyatt Regency Kauai Resort and Spa, 808-742-1234; 800-633-7313. The Hyatt's wedding department offers extensive wedding services. The wedding coordinator can provide you with a list of "10 Helpful Tips for Getting Married on Kaua'i" to help you plan your wedding before you leave home. They have various wedding and vow renewal packages available, too. Wedding packages range from $980 to $1,750. Vow renewal packages start at $730. Check with the resort for the latest details.

Island Weddings & Blessings, P.O. Box 603, Kilauea, HI 96754; 808-828-1548; 800-998-1548; fax 808-828-1569; e-mail: wedding@aloha.net; www.travel-kauai.com/islandweddings. A "Simply Special" wedding package begins at $295. Their "Island Romance Package" includes a wedding ceremony, private location, officiant, witness, tropical outdoor location, two leis, and 26 photos or a video for $695. The "Island Memories Package" adds a bouquet, boutonniere and champagne toast for $820. They offer nondenominational as well as religious ceremonies. Videos and other options available.

Kaua'i Aloha Weddings, 356 Likeke Place, Kapa'a, HI 96746; 808-822-1477, fax 808-822-7067; e-mail: haunani@aloha.net; www.kauaialohawed.com. This Hawaiian-owned and -operated company offers couples the opportunity of having their marriage performed by ordained ministers in the Hawaiian language. Each ceremony begins with the blowing of the conch shell followed by a special Hawaiian language blessing and lei exchange. Packages range from $295 to $1,395 for ceremonies that include Hawaiian songs sung to the accompaniment of a slack key guitar and hula dancer. There are basic ceremony packages, plus Fern Grotto, Historic Church, Hawaiian Wedding, and Royal Blue Hawaiian Wedding packages. Check with them for details.

Kaua'i Coconut Beach Resort, P.O. Box 830, Kapa'a, HI 96746; 808-822-6664, 800-760-8555; www.kcb.com. They offer a variety of wedding packages and have an on-site wedding coordinator.

Kaua'i Fantasy Weddings, P.O. Box 3671, Lihu'e, HI 96766; 808-245-6500. Photo packages or wedding packages available from $375 to $1,600. Hans Hellriegel has been a photographer for 30 years. He says each wedding is unique and he always falls a little in love with each bride. He has taken wedding couples to the beach, up into the mountains, to a church, with ceremonies held at sunrise, at sunset or during the day.

Kaua'i Marriott Resort & Beach Club, Kalapaki Beach, Lihu'e, HI 96766; 808-246-5091; 800-246-5620; fax 808-245-2993; e-mail: ka mika.smith@marriott.com; www.marriott.com. The Marriott has a variety of wedding packages and services plus on-site coordinators.

Mohala Wedding Services, P.O. Box 1737, Koloa, HI 96756; 808-742-8777; 800-800-8489; fax 808-823-8968; e-mail: mohala@hawaiian.net; www.mohala.com. Jona and Jim Clark work as a team to put together your wedding package. Jim is an ordained minister who performs the ceremonies, Jona and her musical partner sing the "Hawaiian Wedding Song." A Japanese garden setting, a beachside wedding, a sunset ceremony on a Kilauea estate with Makana as a backdrop or choose a garden *heiau* or gazebo with a waterfall. Packages run $275 to $1,760. Private locations run slightly more. Other options include cake, flowers, limo or carriage, musicians, tuxedo rental and video as well as a Hawaiian dove-releasing ceremony—from $50 to $365.

Princeville Hotel, P.O. Box 3069, Princeville, HI 96722-3069; 808-826-2282; 808-826-2297, 800-826-1260; fax 808-826-2288. The Wedding & Catering Service handles the various wedding services and packages.

Radisson Kaua'i Beach Resort, 4331 Kaua'i Beach Drive, Lihu'e, HI 96766; 808-246-5515; 888-245-7717; fax 808-245-3956; www.radissonkauai.com. The Radisson has an on-site wedding coordinator and a variety of packages and services available.

Rainbow Weddings & Celebrations, 6057 Lokomaikai Place, Kapa'a, HI 96746; tel/fax 808-822-0944; 888-822-0944; e-mail: vows@rainbowweddings.com; www.rainbowweddings.com. This coordination service has two wedding packages available. The standard Bali Hai Package is $325. The Paradise Package has additional amenities and services for $725.

Sheraton Kaua'i Resort, 2440 Ho'onani Road, Po'ipu Beach, Koloa, HI 96756; 808-742-4037; fax 808-742-4041; e-mail: lynn_sagucio@sheraton.com; www.sheraton-kauai.com. The on-site wedding coordinator, Lynn Sagucio, can assist with a variety of weddings services and packages. The Romance Wedding package is $1,225; Premier Wedding package is $1,650; the Nature Wedding package is $795. Extra add-ons available. Check with the coordinator for details.

Smith's Tropical Paradise Weddings, 174 Wailua Road, Kapa'a, HI 96746; 808-821-6887; 808-821-6888; fax 808-822-4520; e-mail: smthwedd@aloha.net; www.hawaiian.net/~zx/smith, offers wedding packages in the Fern Grotto and in the Smith's own gardens. Wedding times for the Grotto are 8:30 a.m., 11:30 a.m. and 4 p.m. As for ceremonies in their gardens, the hours are more flexible. They do not perform ceremonies on major holidays. Fern Grotto packages run $70 to $135 (with optional video $275 to $365). They include a private boat with entertainers, minister, photography, leis, and assorted extras. Wedding packages in the Smith's Tropical Paradise Gardens run $275 to $725. They also offer a special candle-and-torchlight wedding ceremony at 6 p.m. for $1,075.

The Vow Exchange, P.O. Box 1255, Kilauea, HI 96754; tel/fax 808-828-0336; 800-460-3434; e-mail: vowex@gte.net; www.vowexchange.com. This coordinator has various amenity packages available from $395, $1,375, $2,995 and up, including all arrangements, tropical locations or other place of your choice. Vow renewals $350. Check with them for details.

Tropical Dream Wedding, P.O. Box 422, Lawa'i, HI 96765; 808-322-5664; 888-615-5655; fax 808-332-0811; e-mail: vowex@gte.net; www.hi50.com/tdw. They specialize in custom wedding planning and also offer island concierge services, vacation activity planning, and travel arrangements. Wedding packages range from $450 to $2,845 inclusive. There are basic starter packages, and Private, Church, Specialty, and Resort packages available.

Wedding in Paradise, P.O. Box 1728, Lihu'e, HI 96766; 808-246-2779; 800-733-7431; fax 808-246-2676; e-mail: psi@hawaiian.net; www.paradiseservices.com. A basic package with a nondenominational minister and a choice of locations begins at $295. Their average packages run about $680 and include photography, leis, musician and bouquet. They provide a set of photographs with their brochure, which gives a good feeling for their location selections. Wedding sites include Terrace Garden in the Limahuli Valley, Fern Grotto Wedding (basic package $900), Japanese Garden in Kukuiolono or a private white-sand beach estate on Pakala Beach. Hosted weddings are $880 and include a wedding coordinator, table with linens, chairs, champagne, beverage and cake. Other options include photography, leis, videography, music and flowers dropped from a helicopter.

Weddings on the Beach, P.O. Box 1377, Koloa HI 96756; tel/fax 808-742-7099; 800-625-2824; e-mail: judyn@hawaiian.net; www.weddingsonthebeach.com. Packages run from $435 to $1,400 and up, depending on the location, which include Fern Grotto, an oceanfront estate, a 56-foot sailing trimaran and others. Wedding coordinator Judy Neale handles all the details: limousine service, video, food and beverages, hula dancers, musicians, flowers and photography services are available as options.

Helpful Information

FREE INFORMATION Racks located at the shopping areas can provide helpful information and lots of brochures. Some of them have coupons, which may save you a few dollars. It may save you a bit to search through these before making your purchases. We found the *Beach & Activity Guide Kaua'i* to be particularly helpful and informative, with a lot of detail and cross referencing. *This Week Kaua'i* and *Kaua'i Gold* are a couple of others worth looking through. *Menu* magazine is a great resource for restaurants that shows actual menus and enticing color photos.

Kaua'i Visitors Bureau: 4334 Rice Street, Room 101, Lihu'e, Kaua'i, HI 96766; 808-245-3971; 800-262-1400; fax 808-246-9235; www.kauaivisitorsbureau.com. The Kaua'i Visitors Bureau and the County of Kaua'i have compiled a free *Illustrated Pocket Map* that you can pick up at their Lihu'e office or order by calling their toll-free number. It is a nicely prepared island map that gives a lot of in-depth information.

Po'ipu Beach Resort Association: P.O. Box 730, Koloa, HI 96756; 808-742-7444; fax 808-742-7887; 888-744-0888; e-mail: info@poipubeach.org; www.poipu-beach.org. They provide up-to-date information on accommodations, activities, dining, shopping, transportation and service in the Po'ipu, Koloa and Kalaheo areas of Kaua'i. Contact them to request a free 36-page guide.

West Kaua'i Technology & Visitor Center: 9565 Kaumuali'i Highway, Waimea; 808-338-1332. *Hours*: Open daily except Sundays, 9 a.m. to 5 p.m. Pictorials, graphics and displays with touch-sensitive screens provide information on all of Kaua'i's activities, not just Waimea.

Communications

TELEVISION We anticipate that you'll be much too busy enjoying the island to do much television viewing. But one channel to check out is the KVIC station on either channel 3 or channel 18 (depending on your area of the island), which offers a guided tour of the island from your room. Channel listings vary depending on who is providing the service, so check the local newspaper television program listings or ask your hotel clerk.

RADIO The strongest signal on the island is KONG at 570AM/93.5FM. They play '80s and '90s adult contemporary as well as Hawaiian music and offer local news, surf and weather reports as well as what's happening on Kaua'i. KFMN-97FM also has adult contemporary, while KUAI at 720AM is a bit more eclectic—they play mostly Hawaiian music along with adult contemporary, hits from the past and young country while offering news features, local news and sports. KSRF 95.9 plays island-style music. KITH 98.9 offers island music and has information about activities and services. KKCR at 91.9FM is Kaua'i's non-profit community radio. Weekday mornings offer Hawaiian and slack key music. Other weekly programs include Vintage Hawaiian Music, Monday evening Sunset Jazz, Saturday "Rocks!" and Sunday morning classical music. Visit their website at www.kkcr.org to listen online.

PERIODICALS *The Garden Island* newspaper is published daily. They can be reached at 3137 Kuhio Highway, P.O. Box 231, Lihu'e, HI 96766; 808-245-3681; www.kauaiworld.com. Subscriptions are available by mail.

The *Honolulu Advertiser*, P.O. Box 3110, Honolulu, HI 96802; 808-525-8000; the Kaua'i Bureau contact is 808-245-3074; www.the honoluluadvertiser.com.

Honolulu Star-Bulletin, 7 Waterfront Plaza, Suite 210, 500 Ala Moana, Honolulu, HI 96813; 808-529-4700; www.starbulletin.com. The Kaua'i Bureau contact is 808-245-7575.

The Chamber of Commerce offers an extensive **Relocation Packet**, which includes the *Kaua'i Data Book* (demographics & statistics), detailed map, and information on businesses, schools, rental management companies, accommodations, auto shipping, and the local newspaper. Call 808-245-7363 to charge to your credit card ($16) or e-mail: www.kauaichamber.org.

101 Things to Do on Kaua'i is available free at stands around the island, or can be ordered by sending $5 to 101 THINGS, P.O. Box 388, Lihu'e, HI 96766. Many of the ideas are suggestions for free activities.

Kaua'i Magazine is available at bookstores or magazine stands for a cover price of $5 per copy. This quarterly, full-color magazine contains a calendar of events, local columnists, and in-depth articles on Kaua'i's people and places.

WEBSITES As the Internet continues to expand, so do various sources of information on everything Kaua'i. Website addresses are listed where possible throughout the text. E-mail addresses are also included where possible. The following are some general websites that might be of interest. These will have links to additional sources of information.

Kaua'i Vacation Planner: www.hshawaii.com/kvp is a good site with activities, feature stories, maps, calendar of events, weddings, shopping, dining and transportation information. The website is part of the larger Hawai'i State.

Vacation Planner: www.hshawaii.com. This comprehensive site on the Hawaiian islands has separate pages highlighting each island. The site is part of www.bestplaceshawaii.com. The general information about what to see around Kaua'i is well laid out. Put out by the Kaua'i Visitors Bureau, it's not a complete listing of dining, recreation and other options, but it provides quite a lot of information. While there are a few exceptions, most of the listings are folks that are members of the Kaua'i Visitors Bureau. You can get a free printed version by calling 800-262-1400.

Any individual or organization can add to the calendar website of the Hawai'i Visitor and Convention Bureau regardless of whether or not they are a Kaua'i Visitors Bureau or HVCB member. Check out the **Hawai'i Visitor and Convention Bureau** sites: www.gohawaii.com and www.visit.hawaii.org. You can also find general information at the Kaua'i Visitors Bureau site: www.kauaivisitorsbureau.com plus the County of Kaua'i site, Kaua'i: Hawaii's Island of Discovery at www.kauai-hawaii.com.

A very comprehensive and detailed site is **Hawaii.com**: www.hawaii.com or www.hawaii.net. Either of these gateways provide much information and many links on general information on living in Hawai'i, visiting Hawai'i, moving to Hawai'i and/or just dreaming about Hawai'i. The visiting Hawai'i section is very detailed. The Alternative-Hawai'i site is also a general information guide covering accommodations, restaurants, things to see and do, and much more: www.alternative-hawaii.com/index.html.

The Travel Information Network Hawai'i has the Kaua'i Travel and Vacation Guide that provides lots of additional information on visiting Kaua'i, things to do, etc. Check it at: www.travel-kauai.com.

For information on bed-and-breakfast lodgings, try: **Ohananet** at www.ohananet.com, and **Hawaii-Inns** at www.hawaii-inns.com.

Some regional destination areas on Kaua'i also have general information websites. For the South Shore and Po'ipu Resort area, try: www.poipu-beach.org.

The **Hawai'i State Vacation Planner** offers accommodation, restaurant, activity and other listings for the state, with individual sections for Kaua'i and the other Hawaiian islands: www.hshawaii.com. Discover current statistics for Kaua'i at the **Hawai'i State Data Book** at www.state.hi.us. **Hawai'i State Government** has a comprehensive website listing with all sorts of information available on the islands: www.hawaii.gov. For more specific information and data on the visitor industry or business in general, check the **Hawai'i State Department of Business, Economic Development and Tourism** site at www.hawaii.gov/dbedt.

These websites also have Hawai'i information: www.mele.com is a site for Hawaiian music. The Kaua'i Film Commission sponsors a site at www.filmkauai.com that includes Quicktime Virtual Reality 360-degree shots of some scenic spots on Kaua'i. If you're a displaced former Hawai'i resident, or someone who just needs a fix of something Hawaiian, you may find the site www.sunjose.com of interest. This electronic store has a wide product line of Hawaiiana and Hawai'i-related items. They carry everything from jewelry to hats, clothing,

Hawaiian print fabrics, books, artwork and even Hawaiian food products to give that special taste of the islands in cooking sauces, flavorings, spices, condiments, jams, jellies, macadamia nuts, and Portuguese sweet bread.

TRAVEL WEBSITES There are various websites covering Hawai'i and Kaua'i tour operators. HawaiiVisitor.com at www.hawaiivisitor.com has general information on tours, packages, activities, weddings and related information. Globus Tours/Atlas Travel Web also has general information available at: www.atlastravelweb.com.

Even if you book through a travel agent, you might be interested in checking airline flight schedules and prices on the internet. (See "Flights to the Islands" below.)

Medical Information

EMERGENCIES The main hospital in Kaua'i is found in Lihu'e. G. N. Wilcox Memorial Hospital is located at 3420 Kuhio Highway, Lihu'e; 808-245-1100.

The following clinics provide general out-patient health services to persons requiring health care:

Kauai Center for Holistic Medical and Research, in the New Pacific House building at the corner of Kukui Street and Kuhio Highway, in Kapa'a: 808-823-0994. Dr. Thomas Yarema welcomes walk-in patients, providing acute and holistic care.

Kaua'i Medical Clinic *Lihu'e (main clinic)*: 3420-B Kuhio Highway, 808-245-1500; *Koloa:* 5371 Koloa Road, 808-742-1621; *Kilauea:* Kilauea and Ola streets, 808-828-1418; *Kapa'a:* 4-1105 Kuhio Highway, 808-822-3431; *'Ele'ele:* 4392 Waialo Road, 808-335-0499

Wilcox Hospital and the above clinics are Kaiser Permanente–affiliated providers and now serve Kaiser members. Call 800-966-5955 for benefit information.

Calling 911 will put you in contact with local fire, police and ambulances.

Hazards

SUN SAFETY The sunshine is stronger in Hawai'i than on the mainland, so a few basic guidelines will ensure that you return home with a tan, not a burn. Use a good lotion (one with a high sunblock number rating) with a sunscreen, reapply after swimming and don't forget the lips. Be sure to moisturize after a day in the sun and wear a hat to protect your face. Exercise self-control and stay out a limited time the first few days, remembering that a gradual tan will last longer. It is best to avoid being out between the hours of 10 a.m. and 3 p.m. when the sun is most direct. Be cautious on overcast days when it is very easy to become burned unknowingly. Don't forget that the ocean acts as a reflector and time spent in it equals time spent on the beach.

WATER CONTAMINATION *Do not drink water from streams, waterfalls or ponds.* Drinking fresh water from streams, waterfalls or pools is not safe at any location. While there are many micro-organisms and parasites that can wreak havoc with your system, one of the most dangerous is *Leptospirosis*. This bacteria finds its way into rivers and streams in the urine and feces of rodents and feral animals and can be fatal. The symptoms are flu-like and often do not occur until 1 to 4 weeks after contamination. People who are infected may not connect their illness with the weeks-earlier contamination. *Leptospirosis* can also be contracted through the skin if there are open sores or cuts. Be sure to pack your own drinking water should you do any hiking. Or, if you do need to drink stream water, be sure to boil it thoroughly and/or treat it with water purification tablets.

SAFETY & THEFT

Do not leave valuables in your car, even in your trunk. Many rental car companies urge you to not lock your car because vandals cause extensive and expensive damage breaking the locks.

OCEAN SAFETY We cannot emphasize enough the importance of ocean safety. More folks drown off the shores of Kaua'i than any of the other islands. With the dangerous currents take heed of the signs and markers indicating beach safety, never swim alone, and please refer to the section in Chapter 5 "Beaches" for additional guidelines.

Getting There

Arrival and departure tips: During your flight to Honolulu, the airline staff will provide you with a visitor information sheet. This is used by the Hawai'i Visitors Bureau to track the number of visitors and their island destinations. This is also where you must report any animals, fruits, vegetables or plants that will need to be inspected upon arrival.

AIRLINE INFORMATION

The best prices on major air carriers can generally be arranged through a reputable travel agent who can often secure air or air-with-car packages at good prices by volume purchasing. Prices vary considerably so comparison shopping is a wise idea. Be sure to ask about senior citizen and companion-fare discounts. It is good to be an informed traveler so check on websites even if you are dealing with a travel agent or an airline. Check out www.orbitz.com or www.travelocity.com. You can register with **Travelocity** and they will send you an e-mail notice when airfares drop, whatever dollar amount you specify. **Orbitz** gives you the price for airlines departing from your home city. It's a quick way to help you begin your air travel options. Keep in mind that these websites don't necessarily post *all* airline schedules.

TRAVEL WHOLESALERS AND PACKAGES

Avalon Travel offers "theme" tours to Kaua'i that range from Culinary (with an emphasis on dining and exploring Hawaiian Regional and Pacific Rim cuisine) to Art and Garden (visit artists' homes and explore the "Garden Isle") to Wellness and Rejuvenation Retreats (created for those interested in personal growth, natural healing and spiritual enrichment). Their annual KauaiQuest is a "Festival of Spirit and Discovery" offered every October to coincide with Kaua'i's Aloha Festival Events. They promise their "insider" tours/retreats to be educational, cultural and inspirational with "programs designed for those who wish to experience the local culture and environment on a deeper and more authentic level." These "land only" tours run 7 days/6 nights and are priced from $1,899. (Price includes lodging, meal plan, presentations, professional guide, and land excursions.) Call Karol Avalon at 888-552-7375; e-mail: karol@avalontravel.com; www.avalontravel.com.

Classic Aloha Vacations P.O. Box 627, Hanalei, HI 96714; 800-200-3576 or toll-free fax 888-826-7155; e-mail: cav@aloha.net; www.classic-aloha.com. Classic Aloha offers a selection of properties on all the islands, with photos of each. Their staff of five agents on three islands are happy to answer any questions. As a Hawai'i wholesaler who sells to agencies on the mainland and Canada, the website allows them to offer excellent rates on hotels, condos, car rentals and airfare.

While you may not find the most inexpensive packages, **Creative Leisure** utilizes moderate-to-expensive, higher-end condominiums and hotels (including Whaler's Cove, Hyatt Regency Kauai Resort and Spa, Po'ipu Kai, Embassy Vacation Resort, Princeville Hotel, Kaua'i Beach Villas, The Cliffs, Pali Ke Kua, Lae Nani, Lanikai, Kiahuna Plantation, Waimea Plantation Cottages and Kaua'i Marriott). They offer the advantage of traveling any day you choose and the option of staying as long as you want. Rates are for the entire unit, not per person. Year-round discount airfares are available on United and you will receive full Mileage Plus credit for all United Airlines and Aloha Airlines travel booked through them. TravelGuard insurance is also available. You can combine and include other islands as a part of your package, or even a stopover in San Francisco. Customer service is a high priority with them, and it shows. P.O. Box 750189, Petaluma, CA 94975; 800-426-6367, 808-778-1800; www.creativeleisure.com.

Pleasant Hawaiian Holidays is one of the oldest established travel wholesalers and operators of package tours to Hawai'i. They provide a wide range of air/room packages, fly/drive/room packages, air-only packages, and land-only options. They work in conjunction with American Trans Air direct to Maui and Honolulu from Los Angeles and San Francisco. They also utilize Hawaiian Airlines, United and Delta, as well as numerous hotels and resorts, and rental car companies. Kaua'i properties include the Hyatt Regency Kauai Resort and Spa, Princeville Resort, Whaler's Cove, Aston Po'ipu Point, Kaua'i Marriott Resort, Hanalei Bay Resorts & Suites, Outrigger's Kiahuna Plantation, Aston Kaua'i Beach Villas, Radisson Kaua'i Beach Hotel, Kaua'i Coconut Beach Resort, Islander on the Beach, and Plantation Hale. A $45 fee will waive any cancellation or penalties should you have to adjust your travel plans. Their "Last Minute Desk" is for those of you trying to find space on short notice—right up to the day of departure. 800-242-9244; www.pleasantholidays.com.

★ **Suite Paradise** is a condominium rental agency that specializes in the "Best of Po'ipu." In addition to accommodations, they offer very attractive rates on car/condo packages. They can arrange ticketing on regularly scheduled airlines (United, Delta, Northwest, Continental and Hawaiian) at discounts with their air-ticketing affiliate. Call Suite Paradise at 800-367-8020 to request information on their vacation options. They have a helpful staff. Check their website at www.suite-paradise.com or e-mail them at mail@suite-paradise.com.

Sun Trips has been serving Hawai'i-bound vacationers for several years. If you are from the Midwest, you might be familiar with Sun Country, which has been flying to exotic Caribbean destinations. In 1997 they added Hawai'i. Currently they are using Oakland, California, as their gateway to the Pacific. This means that if you live in the California area you might get a great deal, but others have to make their own travel arrangements to the Oakland airport. As we go to press they have flights 6 days each week (with two on Saturday) out of Oakland. This flexibility allows you to customize the length of your vacation stay. Fly/drive, air-only, and combination packages, including rental cars, are available for O'ahu, Maui, Kaua'i and the Big Island. They offer some unique and intriguing incentives, such as free children's holidays for youngsters 2 to 18 years old. You get one free child's room accommodations if you have two full-fare adults—and you share the room (and at some places, kids can also eat free!). Travel protection insurance, in the event you have to cancel at the last minute, is available, as is travel insurance. Alamo Rent a Car handles the ground transportation (Hawai'i Rental Vehicle Surcharge of $3 per day, as well as the Fleet & Road tax of 19 cents per day, the Airport Tax of 8.10 percent and Hawaii State tax of 4.166 percent are *not* included in the price). Aloha Airlines is the carrier for the interisland flights. Single or multiple island packages are available. For airfare-only, rates are staggered based on the day of the week you depart and the time of the year. Call for a free catalog, 800-357-2400. Or request one when you visit them online: www.suntrips.com.

Remember! Be sure to check all the air carriers. Experience has taught us that a little leg work pays off. Sometimes the airlines have better deals than the agencies, so it may be worth a thorough investigation if you have the time. Always make sure you let the airline know if you are flexible on your arrival and departure days. You may be able to squeeze into some price-cut promotion window that offers an even better value on your flight dollar. Also remember that the schedules for flights to Hawai'i change greatly with the seasons. More flights are added during the summer months.

FLIGHTS TO THE ISLANDS

Most of the airlines have their own websites. These are especially handy for getting an idea of flight schedules. Only United and American Airlines offer direct flights to the Lihu'e Airport from Los Angeles and San Francisco. Otherwise, you will need to fly to Honolulu and get an interisland flight on Aloha or Hawaiian Airlines to Lihu'e. The major American carriers that fly from the mainland to Honolulu International Airport are:

Aloha Airlines—Aloha Airlines has direct flights to Lihu'e from Oakland, California. They also offer flights from Vancouver, B.C.; Las Vegas, Nevada; Orange County, California, to Honolulu. Aloha Airlines is famous for its on-time flights. Aloha also shares a mileage program with United Airlines. 800-367-5250; in Hawaii: 808-484-1111; www.alohaairlines.com.

American Airlines—American has direct flights from Chicago, St. Louis and Dallas to Honolulu. 800-433-7300; 808-833-7600 in Honolulu; in Maui: 808-244-5522; www.aa.com.

Air Canada—Air Canada flies direct to Honolulu from Vancouver, B.C. 888-247-2262; www.aircanada.com.

Continental Airlines—Continental has direct flights from Newark, Los Angeles and Houston to Honolulu. 800-525-028, 800-523-3273; www.continental.com

Delta Airlines—Delta offers direct flights from Atlanta and Dallas–Fort Worth to Honolulu. 800-221-1212; flight information 800-325-1999; www.delta.com.

Hawaiian Airlines—Hawaiian Airlines has direct flights from Los Angeles, Seattle, San Francisco, Portland, Anchorage and Las Vegas to

Honolulu. Hawaiian Airlines also has Frequent Flyer miles, and is partnered with Alaska, American, Northwest, Continental and Virgin Atlantic Airlines. 800-367-5320; in Honolulu: 808-838-1555; www.hawaiianair.com.

Northwest Airlines—Northwest flies into Honolulu from Minneapolis, Los Angeles and Seattle. 800-225-2525; 808-955-2255; www.nwa.com.

United Airlines—United has more flights to Hawai'i from more U.S. cities than any other airline. United offers a free round-trip interisland ticket on Aloha Airlines with 5,000 Mileage Plus miles. If you have miles to use, check United for information on their O'ahu flight. Reservations: 800-241-6522; flight information: 800-824-6200; www.ual.com or www.united.com.

INTERISLAND FLIGHTS

Hawai'i is unique in that its intrastate roads are actually water or sky. For your travel by sky, there are two main interisland carriers that operate between Honolulu and Lihu'e.

The flight time from O'ahu to Kaua'i is just 25 minutes. When returning to Honolulu, make sure you have plenty of time before your connecting flight to the mainland. Otherwise you might make your flight, but your baggage won't. Traveling from the main carrier to the interisland terminal is easy. Just take the *wikiwiki* shuttle, or better yet, walk and stretch your legs between flights. On both your arrival and departure flights, check your baggage all the way through to your final destination and then there's no need to pick it up and re-check it on O'ahu.

If you are traveling light and have only brought carry-on luggage with you, be advised that what is carry-on for the major airlines may ***not*** be carry-on for the interisland carriers. For example, those small suitcases with wheels and long handles that extend out to pull along behind you *must* be checked by many of the interisland carriers. Knowing this in advance, you may be able to pack those items that are more fragile in a smaller tote bag.

INTERISLAND AIR TIP

Travel agents schedule at least an hour and a half between arrival on O'ahu and departure for Lihu'e to account for any delays, baggage transfers, and the time required to reach the interisland terminal. If you arrive early, check with the interisland carrier. Sometimes you can get an earlier flight that will arrive on Kaua'i in time to get your car before returning to pick up your luggage when it arrives on your scheduled flight.

The **Lihu'e Airport** is convenient, with accessible parking, an on-site rental car area, and a restaurant that offers runway views. The Lihu'e Airport covers 804 acres and is centrally located, about one and a half miles from the town of Lihu'e. It is a blissfully simple airport, with only a handful of gates and two baggage claim areas. In addition to the chairs at the individual gates, there is a small centralized seating area surrounded by convenient pay phones and a gift shop. The airport operates three runways and offers passenger and cargo transportation. From the airport it is a 35-minute drive to the Po'ipu area, a 20-minute drive to Kapa'a and about an hour to the North Shore, depending on traffic.

INTERISLAND CARRIERS

Aloha Airlines—Aloha offers first-class service, Drive-Thru Check-In at Honolulu and nearly hourly service to Kaua'i. This airline keeps on schedule and has always had one of the lowest passenger complaint records of *all* U.S. airlines. They fly over 1,200 flights weekly, with their fleet of 17 Boeing 737s. Also weekly charter service to Midway, Johnson, Marshall Islands, Rarotonga in the Cook Islands and Christmas Island. When making reservations, you might inquire about any special promotions, AAA membership discounts, AARP discounts, or passes. United Airlines partners with Aloha and offers a round-trip ticket on Aloha for 5,000 Mileage Plus miles for connecting interisland flights from O'ahu to Kaua'i. Currently rates are $75 for one-way unrestricted tickets, $70 for a three-day advance purchase and $66 for a seven-day advance purchase. If you are an AAA member and have your membership card, you can purchase a ticket for less. Be sure to check into their Fly/Drive packages for rental cars—especially during slow season. Current flight schedule is available at www.alohaair.com/aloha-air; 800-367-5250; Honolulu 808-484-1111; Kaua'i 808-245-3681; www.alohaairlines.com.

Hawaiian Airlines—Hawaiian flies Boeing/McDonnell Douglas DC9s between Honolulu and Kaua'i. The cost is about $84 for a one-way ticket. Toll-free from the mainland and Hawaii 800-882-8811. www.hawaiianair.com.

Cruise Lines

Norwegian Cruise Lines (NCL) and parent company, Star Cruises, have enlisted the *Norwegian Star* to cruise the Hawaiian waters. The cruise line began service in the islands in 2001. The *Norwegian Star* is 971 feet in length and double occupancy can accommodate 2,240 guests along with 1,100 crew. The ship offers 10 restaurants including the Versailles Main Restaurant, Aqua Main Restaurant, Le Bistro French Restaurant, Ginza, Las Ramblas Tapas Bar & Restaurant, Endless Summer Restaurant, the SoHo Room, Market Café and Kids Café, La Trattoria, and Blue Lagoon, as well as 13 bars and lounges. Other amenities include two swimming pools, six hot tubs, a fitness center, basketball, volleyball and soccer court, Planet Kids and a themed kid's pool, video arcade, cinema and auditorium. Inside staterooms offer comfort and value, with a sitting area, two lower beds that convert to a double, TV and refrigerator. Oceanview staterooms with balconies feature two lower beds, a sitting area, a floor-to-ceiling glass door that opens onto private balcony. Also available are mini-suites and top-end suites and villas. Handicapped facilities are also available. The rack rates are listed below but there are generous discounts for early booking (20 to 40 percent off posted rack rate). All rates are based on double occupancy. The *Norwegian Star* cruises the Hawaiian islands, departing in Honolulu with stops at Nawiliwili, Kahului, Lahaina, Hilo, Kona and Fanning Island. Inside staterooms run $1,629 to $1,779. Oceanview staterooms run $1,849 to $2,179. Mini-suites are $2,279 to $2,299 and other suites and penthouses are $2,999 to $4,399. The Garden Villa with two bedrooms and private whirlpool tub with butler service runs $15,999. Extra guests (3rd and 4th) are $699, but early-book discounts bring that additional guest price down to $299.

The *Norwegian Wind* is the second of the Norwegian Cruise Line ships to operate in Hawaiian waters. This vessel is 754 feet and double occupancy can accommodate 1,748 passengers along with 700 crew. All staterooms have a TV, and bathroom with shower and hair dryer. The amenities include six restaurants: Four Seasons Main Restaurant, The Terraces Main Restaurant, Sun Terrace Italian Trattoria, Le Bistro French Restaurant, Pizzeria, and Sports Bar & Grill, along with 10 bars and lounges. Guests can enjoy Broadway-style theater, Monte Carlo casino, library and card room, Kid's Korner and video arcade, fitness center, spa and salon, two hot tubs, and two swimming pools. The rack rates are listed below but there are generous discounts for an early book (25 to 40 percent off posted rack rate). All rates are based on double occupancy. The *Norwegian Wind* currently has a fall trip that departs from Vancouver, B.C., for an 11-day cruise to the Hawaiian islands with stops at all the Hawaiian islands. Their standard fall and spring trip is a 10-day round-trip through the Hawaiian islands, with a stop at Fanning Island. In the spring they offer a 10-day trip that departs from Honolulu and travels to Vancouver, B.C. Rack rates for 10-day cruises: inside staterooms $1,779 to $1,909; oceanview staterooms $1,979 to $2,799. A penthouse runs $5,499 and owner's suite is $6,399. Third and fourth guests additional $529. Early booking reduces that to $379.

(By the way, Fanning Island is a Micronesian island to the south of Hawai'i. The reason for this later stop is that cruise ships with foreign registry must travel to a non-U.S. port. NCL is making a request to authorities to waive this requirement, so if they are successful this stop would be eliminated.)

Pre- and post-cruise packages, air add-ons, and Hawaiian shore excursions are available. For information contact your travel agent or go online to Norwegian Cruise Lines at www.ncl.com or Star Cruises at www.starcruises.com. 800-327-7030 from the U.S. and Canada.

Kaua'i's Traffic Woes

This book would be doing the visitor a disservice if it failed to mention Kaua'i's traffic woes. The fact is that Kaua'i has very few roadways—and most are just two lanes. As a result, they are very busy during daytime hours. It is a fact of life and must be understood by visitors. Some visitors arrive here thinking there will be few cars on the roads, but that's just not the case. Kaua'i is no different from any other growing community and the number of vehicles clogging the roadways continues to increase each year. There is essentially one highway that goes around the island (it doesn't quite encircle it due to the impassability of rugged Napali Coast). Smaller roads branch off from this main highway, which runs through all the towns. Be sure to use extreme caution when making left-hand turns against oncoming traffic. Better yet, avoid left-hand turns if you can. Traffic is heaviest during the morning commute and afternoon *pau hana* (after work) hours, just like elsewhere, so try to avoid driving between 7 to 8:30 a.m. and 3:30 to 5:30 p.m. The worst sections are through Kapa'a town and between Lihu'e and the turnoff to Po'ipu. It's probably not as bad as the rush-hour freeway traffic in your area, but it will be slow going nonetheless.

Being prepared for it will help you handle it. Take your time, look around, and enjoy the special beauty and appeal of Kaua'i. Resist the urge to speed or pass, both of which are considered bad form on the island, where the maximum speed limit is 50 mph. Fortunately, road rage is rare here and people drive with *aloha*. They'll wave you into traffic or let you turn; just be sure to return the favor to someone else. And when you hit those one-way bridges on the North Shore, remember to yield if you see another car waiting across the bridge. Otherwise, if there is a string of cars crossing, go with the flow and cross too. Do not go one at a time, especially at the Hanalei Bridge.

Getting Around

Here's an insider tidbit for you. If you find yourself without an essential map of Kaua'i, check out the nearest phonebook. It has some very good color maps that will get you by in a pinch. And because Kaua'i has its own peculiar idiosyncrasies, we'll pause here with a brief aside. It seems most appropriate in the category of "getting around" the island to make note of this interesting fact. The street addresses may easily confuse you as you are trying to locate a particular establishment. You may see a number such as 3-5920 next to 5924. The number in front of the dash stands for the area of the island. 0-1 is Waimea, 2 is Koloa, 3 is Lihu'e, 4 is Kapa'a and 5 is Hanalei. That seems fairly clear, but it can get a little confusing as to where the cut-off point is for each of those areas. Another problem is some people use the first number and the dash and some do not. So, all we can say is good luck, and if you're trying to find a place ask for a landmark rather than the address, which is how most locals give directions anyway.

PUBLIC TRANSPORTATION The only public transportation is **The Kaua'i Bus**, which charges riders $1 per ride. Seniors, students or disabled with ID are 50 cents. Monthly bus passes are available for $25 and provide unlimited rides. A monthly pass for senior citizens, students and persons with disabilities runs $12.50. Caregivers traveling with eligible individuals will not be charged a fee. No luggage, surfboards or bikes are allowed on board, and the bus doesn't stop at the airport. Food and drinks are prohibited. Each bus has a destination sign on the front and curb-side of bus that displays a route number. Schedules are available that show the route the bus travels and the times along that route. Call the County Transportation Office at 808-241-6410 between the hours of 7 a.m. and 5 p.m. Monday through Saturday.

LIMOUSINE SERVICES A handy way to get to your hotel with a lot of luggage is by limousine. There are several limousine services on the island. Contact: **Custom Limousine** 808-246-6318; **Kaua'i Limousine** 808-245-4855, 800-764-7213; **Kaua'i North Shore Limousine** 808-826-6189; **Town & Country Limousine** throughout Hawai'i 888-563-2888.

TAXIS A number of taxi companies service the Lihu'e airport and various communities. They include: **Ace Kaua'i Taxi** 808-639-4310; **Akiko's Taxi** 808-822-7588, 808-64-6018; **Bran's Taxi** 808-245-6533, 808-639-3609; **City Cab** 808-245-3227; **Kaua'i Taxi Company** 808-246-9554; **Kimo's Transportation Company** 808-245-4970; **North Shore Cab & Tours** 808-826-4118, 808-639-7829; **Roger Taxi** 808-652-3269; **Scotty Taxi** 808-245-7888; **South Shore Cab** 808-742-1525; **Taxi Guy** 800-829-4489; **Taxi Hanalei** 808-639-1188.

RENTAL CARS AND TRUCKS Given the state of public transportation on Kaua'i, a rental car is still, unfortunately, the best bet to get around. Rates vary, not only between high and low season, but from week to weekend and even day to day. Sample rates include: Vans and SUVs $75 to $120, Jeeps $48 to $100, Mid-size $35 to $57,

AGRICULTURAL TIPS FOR LEAVING THE ISLANDS

On your return to the mainland, you will have to take your checked as well as carry-on baggage through agricultural inspection. Where your luggage will be inspected will depend upon your travel plans. If you are checking baggage at the Lihu'e airport that will be transferred directly to your connecting flight in Honolulu, you will need to go through the agricultural inspection at the main entrance of the Lihu'e airport before proceeding to the airline ticket counter for check in. When you arrive in Honolulu and begin trekking from your interisland flight to your mainland carrier, you'll pass through an agricultural inspection center. (In case this is your first trip, they look like regular airport baggage security centers.) At this point you will need to have your carry-on baggage inspected. You'll be amazed to see the apples, oranges and other fruits stacked up on the agricultural inspection centers. Even though they may have originally come from the mainland, they will not pass inspection to get back there. Pre-inspected pineapples, papaya, orchids, tropical flowers and leis are allowed. Fruit can be purchased in inspected and sealed cartons from reputable island retailers. Generally, you will not have trouble with most flowers and/or leis. If you are unsure what is transportable, contact the U.S. Department of Agricultural at 808-877-8757 or 808-877-5261.

Compacts $25 to $45. Add to the rental price a 4 percent sales tax and a $2 per day highway road tax. Many visitors rent SUVs and jeeps, both of which cost a lot of money, eat gas and aren't needed because there are very few off-road opportunities—and rental car agreements don't allow such travel anyway. Jeeps are often very inconvenient because they provide limited rain protection. So rent the smallest vehicle you need and save money and gas. Also, if you rent a convertible, be sure you know how to put the top up before you start driving since you just might hit a passing rain shower along the way.

A trend that poses good news for travelers is that the interisland airlines, as well as many condos and hotels, are offering rental cars at discounts, greater than if you book directly. Aloha Airlines offers some very competitive rates with your interisland tickets. Some resort hotels and condominiums are offering a free rental car as a part of their package. Be sure to ask.

Rental car agencies all have the same basic policies. Most require a minimum age of 21 to 25 and a maximum age of 70. A few require a deposit or major credit card to hold your reservation. All feature unlimited mileage, with you buying the gas, which is considerably higher than on the mainland! You definitely should fill up the tank before you return your car since the rental companies charge a lot more per gallon to do it for you. In fact, all the car rental agencies will offer you a "gas deal" at rental time but decline it as it will cost you more. Please note that there are only two gas stations on the North Shore (none past Princeville) and they charge a lot more than elsewhere. Waimea is also the last stop for gas on the westside.

Insurance is an option you may wish to purchase, which can run an additional $15 to $20 a day. However, your own vehicle insurance probably will cover you, unless you're renting an SUV, in which case you must buy the additional insurance—another good reason to avoid renting those gas hogs. A few agencies require insurance for those under age 25. Most of the car rental agencies strongly encourage you to purchase the optional collision damage waiver (CDW) (Collision Damage Waiver) that provides coverage for most cars in case of loss or damage. Some credit cards now provide CDW for rental cars if you use that credit card to charge your rental fees. This doesn't include liability insurance, so you need to check to see if your own policy will cover you for liability in a rental car. *Note*: Rental companies prohibit cars on any unpaved roads, like the one to Polihale Beach in west Kaua'i. The rental agencies will provide you with a map showing restrictions. Should you travel on these roads they will hold you responsible for any damage.

Car rental discounts are few and far between. You might be able to use some airline award coupons or entertainment book coupons, but they are often very restrictive. If you are a member of AAA you can receive a discount on rental cars. Check around and compare rates. Also check car rental company websites for the latest online specials. Also check with Aloha Airlines for some great rates with their inter-island fly and drive packages. And remember that weekly rates are always a better value, even if you're only there for six days. Most of the major car rental company booths are at the Lihu'e airport, and pick-up and return areas are conveniently located behind the agency counters and across the street from the airline terminal. The rental companies offer a convenient shuttle bus to travel the short distance to their rental office.

RENTAL CAR LISTINGS The following are car rental agencies and their toll-free or local numbers: **AA Aloha Cars-R-Us** 800-655-7989; **Alamo Rent a Car** 800-327-9633; **Avis** 800-321-3712; **Bottom Dollar Cars** 800-354-2277; **Budget** 800-527-0700; **Dollar** 800-800-4000; **Hawaiian Riders Exotic Cars**—in Kapa'a: 808-822-5409—in Po'ipu: 808-742-9888; **Hertz** 800-654-3011; **National** 800-227-7368; **Pacific Island Rentals** 808-821-9090; **Rent-A-Wreck** 800-944-7501; **Thrifty** 800-367-5238; **Tropicars Classic Cruisers** 808-639-3799; **Westside U-Drive** 808-332-8644.

MOTORCYCLES, MOPEDS, BICYCLE RENTALS A number of agencies rent two-wheel vehicles.

Hawaiian Riders, 4-776 Kuhio Highway, Kapa'a, 808-822-5409; also 2320 Po'ipu Road, Po'ipu, 808-742-9888 rents mountain bikes, mopeds and Harley Davidsons.

Kaua'i Cycle and Tour, 1379 Kuhio Highway, Kapa'a, 808-821-2115; www.bikehawaii.com/kauaicycle rents Cannondale and Specialized mountain bikes. Daily and weekly rates.

Outfitters Kaua'i, 2827A Po'ipu Road, Po'ipu Beach; 808-742-9667, 888-742-9887; fax 808-742-9667; e-mail: info@outfitterskauai.com; www.outfitterskauai.com. This outfitter offers mountain bike rentals along with car racks, kid's seats, helmets, and plenty of directions. They also have a number of biking tours and biking combined with other adventures including hiking and kayaking.

Grocery Shopping

Grocery store prices may be one of the biggest surprises of your trip. If you expect things to be more expensive than at your hometown supermarket you won't be too shocked. While there are many locally grown and produced foods, nearly everything must be flown in or shipped to the islands from the mainland or elsewhere.

The various local **sunshine markets** can save you money on fresh local fruit and vegetables. Call the Office of Economic Development 808-241-6390 to check on their schedule, but currently they run: Monday—Koloa ball park at noon; Tuesday—Kalaheo Neighborhood Center at 3:30 p.m.; Wednesday—Kapa'a ball park at 3 p.m.; Thursday—Hanapepe Park at 3:30 p.m. and Kilauea Neighborhood Center at 4:30 p.m.; Friday—Vidinha Stadium parking lot in Lihu'e at Hoolako Street at 3 p.m.; Saturday—Kekaha Neighborhood Center on Elepaio Road at 9 a.m. Private **farmers' markets** are also held Saturday morning near the Kilauea post office; Tuesday at 1 p.m. at Hawaiian Farmers of Hanalei (Waipia); Monday 3 p.m. at the Kukui Grove Shopping Center; and Haupu Growers, L.L.C., daily on Koloa Bypass Road. The Hanalei Town Farmers Market operates Saturday mornings until about noon at the Hanalei Community Center, Malolo Street and Kuhio Highway, next to the soccer playing field next to Wai'oli Church.

Check the Wednesday newspaper for grocery specials. On the South Shore you can shop at **Big Save** in Koloa. On the East Side there is a **Big Save** and **Kojima's** in Kapa'a, a 24-hour **Safeway** at Kaua'i Village, and in Waipouli, the **Foodland** is open 24 hours a day and has a full-service Bank of America in the store. In Lihu'e you'll find a **Big Save** across from the state and county government buildings, and in the Kukui Grove Shopping Center there's a **Star Market**. On the West Side there is **Ishikawa's Market** and a **Big Save** in Waimea and in 'Ele'ele. On the North Shore, choose between the **Big Save** in Hanalei or **Foodland** in Princeville. All major stores accept Visa or Mastercard. Natural foods can be tracked down at **Papaya's** in Kapa'a, **Hanalei Healthfoods** in Hanalei and **Vim 'N Vigor** in Lihu'e. The best part of shopping for food in Hawai'i is discovering the interesting specialty items and local foods.

Calendar of Annual Events

There are numerous annual community social, cultural and historic events held throughout the year on Kaua'i that are of interest to residents and visitors alike. The following is not a complete list but notes some of the more popular and widely known events that have been announced. Dates and times, contact numbers and organizers change frequently, so, for the latest detailed information, specific dates, and times, it is suggested to access online events calendars or to check *The Garden Island* newspaper's calendar listing while on-island. Try: www.alternative-hawaii.com and www.gohawaii.com for more information.

January

New Year's Day Mochi Rice Pounding—Various island locations

Rainbow Arts Festival—Family fair with visual and performing arts—Hanapepe Town Park; 808-335-0712

Annual Keike Fun Run—Kilohana Plantation, Lihu'e; 808-246-9090

February

Annual Hula Ho'iki Celebration of Hawaiian Tradition—Kaua'i War Memorial Hall; 808-823-0501

Chinese New Year Celebrations—Around the island

Annual Waimea Town Celebration—Entertainment, food, crafts, games, etc., third weekend in February; 808-335-2824

Annual Captain Cook Caper Fun Run—2-5-10K Fun Runs—Waimea Town Celebration; 808-338-1475

Annual Ukulele Contest—Waimea Town Celebration; 808-335-2824

Annual Kaua'i Community College Used Book Sale; Community College in Puhi; 808-245-8239

Kilohana Long Distance Canoe Race—Kicks off Kaua'i canoe racing season; 808-335-2824

March

Garden Island Spring Fantasy Orchid Show—Hanapepe; 808-742-6600

March 26 is Prince Kuhio Day—State Holiday

Prince Kuhio Festival Celebration—Festivities take place all around the island; 808-822-5521 or 808-826-9272

Prince Kuhio Outrigger Canoe Race—Hanama'ulu to Wailua Beach; 808-822-1944

April

Slack Key Guitar Concert series—Hanalei Community Center; 808-826-1469

Annual Business Canoe Race—Hanama'ulu Beach, Kaiola Canoe Club; 808-651-8355

April through August is **Polo season**—'Anini Beach Polo Field; 808-822-3740

Annual Kaua'i Student Film Festival—Kaua'i Community College Performing Arts Center; 808-632-0272

Annual Bonsai Exhibition—Borders Bookstore, Kukui Grove, Lihu'e; 808-246-0862

May

Kaua'i Museum Lei Day Celebration—Lihu'e; 808-245-6931

May 1st, Lei Day—Celebrated around the island with various other programs and events

Kaua'i Annual Garden Fair—Kukui Grove Pavilion; 808-828-2120

Annual Royal Pa'ina—Celebration of Hawai'i's multi-ethnic heritage, food and entertainment in Lihu'e; 808-245-3373

Kaua'i Community College Orchestra Spring Concert—KCC Performing Arts Center; 808-245-8270

Annual "Visitor Industry Charity Walk"—Entertainment, food—Kukui Grove Pavilion; 808-332-5235

Kaua'i Community College Band Spring Concert—KCC Performing Arts Center; 808-245-8270

Annual Mother's Day Orchid Show—Kapa'a; 808-823-6921

Kaua'i Seniors Extravaganza—Kaua'i War Memorial Convention Hall, Lihu'e; 808-632-0122

Annual Kaua'i Chorale Concert—KCC Performing Arts Center; 808-822-5633

June

Annual Taste of Hawai'i Culinary Fair—Sponsored by Kapa'a Rotary Club—Smith's Tropical Paradise; 808-245-2903

Annual Prince Albert Music Festival—Princeville Resort musical celebration; 808-826-7546

King Kamehameha Day Celebration and Festival—Lihu'e; 808-586-0333

Annual Kaua'i Cowboy Kanikapila—Entertainment and dinner fundraiser for Waimea Boys & Girls Club; 808-338-1418

Summer O Bon Festival Season—(June–August)—Buddhist tradition of welcoming spirits of ancestors with prayers, services and bon dances plus food, games and crafts booths—Friday and Saturday nights at Buddhist temples island-wide

Kaua'i Ocean Festival—Water events, food booths, entertainment—Benefit for the Kaua'i Food Bank in Kilauea; 808-246-3809

Annual Banana Poka Festival and Forest Education Fair—Koke'e Natural History Museum; 808-335-9975

July

July 4th Concert in the Sky—Fireworks show, food, music, family fun—Vidinha Stadium, Lihu'e; 808-634-9100

Koloa Plantation Days—Week-long celebration of old Koloa Town's history and heritage; 808-822-0734

August

August 21—Admission Day—State holiday

Trout fishing season—Koke'e State Park streams and reservoir; Land and Natural Resources Dept.; 808-274-3344

Garden Island Orchid Show—Lihu'e Convention Center, Lihu'e; 808-247-3345

Aloha Festivals—Kaua'i statewide festival events kick-off; 800-852-7690

Kaua'i County Farm Bureau Fair—Vidinha Stadium, Lihu'e; 808-828-2120

September

Mokihana Festival—Annual music and dance competition, crafts, lectures, workshops; 808-822-2166

October

Annual Matsuri Kaua'i Japanese Culture Festival—Japanese cultural activities fair—Lihu'e; 808-332-8452

Aloha Festivals—Various parades, cultural and Hawaiian heritage events island-wide; 800-852-7690

Annual Eo E Emalani I Alakai Festival—Commemorates Queen Emma's journey to Koke'e and the Alakai Swamp with hula and music outdoors—Koke'e Lodge; 808-335-9975

Kaua'i Community Oktoberfest—Kaua'i Veteran's Center; 808-332-7376

Coconut Festival—Highlights importance of the coconut with food, crafts, entertainment—Kapa'a Beach Park; 808-246-0089

November

Hawai'i International Film Festival—Shows island-wide; 800-752-8193 or 808-528-FILM

PGA Grand Slam—Po'ipu Bay Resort Golf Course; 808-742-8711

Kapa'a Town Veteran's Day Parade

Hawaiian Christmas Fair—Princeville Golf Club House

Malama Pono Holiday Fundraiser—Entertainment, *pupus*, silent auction—Kaua'i Marriott; 808-822-0878

December

Kilohana Craft Fair—Kilohana, Lihu'e; 808-245-5608

Kaua'i Museum Christmas Craft Fair—Lihu'e; 808-245-6931

Kaua'i Chorale Christmas Concert—KCC Performing Arts Center; 808-245-8270—**Christmas Fantasy Faire**—Crafts, food, entertainment (call for location, it varies from Kapa'a to Lihu'e); 808-828-0014

Annual Waimea Lighted Christmas Parade and Caroling—Waimea; 808-335-2824

Santa's Village—Christmas parade, craft fairs, and holiday entertainment—Kukui Grove Shopping Center; 808-245-7784

Audubon Christmas Bird Count—Volunteers count birds—Koke'e State Park and Natural History Museum; 808-335-9975

Weather

When thinking of Hawai'i in general, and Kaua'i in particular, one visualizes bright sunny days cooled by refreshing trade winds, and this is the weather much of the time. But it can also be windy, cloudy and cool. And while some mainlanders think we have only two seasons, summer and winter, we actually have four distinct seasons. Temperatures remain quite constant year-round, although the North Shore tends to be slightly cooler and rainier. Following are the average daily highs and lows for each month.

Average Highs and Lows

January	80°F/64°F	July	86°F/70°F
February	79°F/64°F	August	87°F/71°F
March	80°F/64°F	September	87°F/70°F
April	82°F/66°F	October	86°F/69°F
May	84°F/67°F	November	83°F/68°F
June	86°F/69°F	December	80°F/66°F

Spring and winter: Mid-October through April, 70 to 80 degrees during the day, 60 to 70 degrees during the night. Tradewinds may blow strongly, but Kona winds are also more frequent, causing widespread cloudiness, rain showers, mugginess, and even an occasional thunderstorm. Eleven hours of daylight.

Summer and Fall: May through mid-October, 80-degree days, 70- to 80-degree nights. Trade winds are more consistent, keeping the temperatures tolerable. However, when the trades stop, the weather becomes hot and sticky (usually in August). Showers are also common in early morning and evening hours. Kona winds are less frequent. Thirteen hours of daylight.

Summer-type wear is suitable year-round. However, a warm sweater or lightweight jacket is a good idea for evenings and trips to the mountain areas like Koke'e. It's also wise to bring a pair of long pants. If you are interested in the types of weather you may encounter, or are confused by some of the terms you hear, read on.

Average water temperature ranges between 72 degrees in February to a warm 78 degrees by September. For additional information on weather and surf conditions on Kaua'i call the Weather Information Recording at 808-245-6001 or Marine Forecast/Hawaiian Waters for their recording at 808-245-3564.

Trade Winds Hawai'i's weather is greatly affected by the prevailing northeast trade winds, which are an almost constant wind from the northeast through the east and are caused by the Pacific anticyclone, a high pressure area. This high pressure area is well developed and remains semi-stationary in the summer, causing the trades to remain steady over 90 percent of the time. Interruptions are much more frequent in the winter when they blow only 40 to 60 percent of the time.

Kona Winds The Kona wind is a stormy, rain-bearing wind blowing from the southwest, or basically from the opposite direction of the trades. These conditions are caused by low pressure areas northwest of the islands. Kona winds strong enough to cause property damage have occurred only twice since 1970. Lighter non-damaging Kona winds are much more common, occurring 2 to 5 times every winter (November to April).

Kona Weather Windless, hot and humid weather is referred to as Kona weather. The interruption of the normal trade wind pattern brings this on. The trades are replaced by light and variable winds and, although this may occur any time of the year, it is most noticeable during summer when the temperature is generally hotter and more humid, with fewer localized breezes.

Kona Low A Kona low is a slow-moving, meandering, extensive low pressure area that forms near the islands. This causes continuous rain, with thunderstorms over an extensive area, and lasts for several days. This usually occurs from November through May.

Rain This is the stuff that keeps the Garden Island green, and Kaua'i does tend to receive more than the other islands. With the Northeast trade winds reaching the North Shore of Kaua'i first, there is a greater share of rain on this coastline. The Hanalei/Princeville area receives up to 45 inches per year. The eastside fares better, receiving only 30 inches per year. The southern and western coastlines receive between 5 and 20 inches per year. And then there is Mt. Wai'ale'ale in Kaua'i's interior, one of the wettest places on earth, with a record 665.5 inches of rain falling in 1982. The general annual average rainfall tends to be in the 450 to 475 inches range for Kaua'i's second-highest peak.

Hurricanes Hurricanes (called typhoons when they are west of 180 degrees longitude) have damaged the Hawaiian islands on several occasions. The storms that affect Hawai'i usually originate off Central America or Mexico. Most of the threatening tropical storms weaken before reaching the islands, or pass harmlessly to the west. Their effects are usually minimal, causing only high surf on the eastern and southern shores of some of the islands. At least 21 hurricanes or tropical storms have passed within 300 miles of the islands in the last several years, but most did little or no damage. Hurricane season is considered to be May through November. Hurricanes are given Hawaiian names when they pass within 1,000 miles of the islands.

In August 1950, Hurricane Hiki went to the north of Kaua'i, but still brought 70-mile-per-hour winds to the island. In 1957, Kaua'i felt the force of two hurricanes that passed nearby—both Hurricane Della in September and Hurricane Nina in December skirted a mere 100 miles from the southwestern shore of Kaua'i, bringing high winds and high surf. Hurricane Dot struck the island in August 1959, with winds nearing 100 miles per hour. Before there was much development on the island the major damage was restricted to crops. Hurricane Iwa in November 1982 passed between Ni'ihau and Kaua'i with gusts up to 100 miles per hour, causing extensive damage to crops and property.

Hurricane Iniki (which means "piercing wind") struck Kaua'i with incredible force in September 1992. It was a direct hit. By coincidence, Iniki struck Kaua'i within the same time period that Hurricane Andrew struck Florida. As Iniki crossed the Pacific, it had time to develop winds that blew at 165 miles per hour, with one gust at Napali on the Makaha Ridge that recorded a speed of 227 miles per hour. Iniki was considered a Category Four hurricane. (Category Five is the highest.) Trees were uprooted, homes were destroyed, and property damage was extensive island wide. Power and phone lines were down for weeks. Due to the remoteness of the island, help was slower to arrive to Kaua'i than to Florida. While the news media continued to focus on Florida for weeks following Hurricane Andrew, after a few days of coverage, Kaua'i was all but forgotten. The island has now fully recovered from Iniki, with only the famed Coco Palms Resort still shuttered from the storm.

Tsunami A tsunami is an ocean wave produced by an undersea earthquake, volcanic eruption, or landslide. Tsunamis are usually generated along the coasts of South America, the Aleutian Islands, the Kamchatka Peninsula, or Japan and travel through the ocean at 400 to 500 miles an hour. It takes at least four-and-a-half hours for a tsunami to reach the Hawaiian islands, unless it is caused by an earthquake on the Big Island—in which case less than 30 minutes warning is likely. A 24-hour Tsunami Warning System was established in Hawai'i in 1946. When the possibility exists of a tsunami reaching Hawaiian waters, the public is informed by the sound of the attention alert signal sirens. This particular signal is a steady one-minute siren, followed by one minute of silence, repeating as long as necessary.

What do you do when you hear the siren? Immediately turn on a TV or radio; all stations will carry CIV-Alert emergency information and instructions, including the arrival time of the first waves. Do not take chances, false alarms are not issued! Move quickly out of low-lying coastal areas that are subject to possible inundation.

The warning sirens are tested throughout the state on the first working Monday of every month at noon, so don't be alarmed when you hear the siren blare! The test lasts only a few minutes and CIV-Alert announces on all stations that the test is underway. Since 1813, there have been 112 tsunamis observed in Hawai'i, with only 16 causing significant damage.

Tsunamis may also be generated by local volcanic earthquakes. In the last 100 years there have been only six, with the last one, November 29, 1975, affecting the southeast coast of the Big Island. The Hawaiian Civil Defense has placed earthquake sensors on all the islands and, if a violent local earthquake occurs, an urgent tsunami warning will be broadcast and the tsunami sirens will sound. A locally generated tsunami will reach the other islands very quickly. Therefore, there may not be time for an attention alert signal to sound. Any violent earthquake that causes you to fall or hold onto something to prevent falling is an urgent warning, and you should immediately evacuate beaches and coastal low-lying areas.

There have been two tsunamis in recent history that struck Kaua'i, doing serious damage to property and taking human life. In 1946 and in 1957 tsunamis did the most destruction to the North Shore of Kaua'i. A tsunami alert is always taken seriously, but fortunately the most recent (1995) tsunami generated a wave of only two inches.

For additional information on warnings and procedures in the event of a hurricane, tsunami, earthquake or flash flood, read the civil defense section in the foreword of the Kaua'i phone book.

Tides The average tidal range is about two feet or less.

Sunrise and Sunset In Hawai'i, day length and the altitude of the noon sun above the horizon do not vary much throughout the year. This is because the temperate regions of the island's low latitude lie within the sub-tropics. The longest day is 13 hours 26 minutes (sunrise 5:53 a.m., sunset 7:18 p.m.) at the end of June, and the shortest day is 10 hours 50 minutes (sunrise 7:09 a.m. and sunset 6:01 p.m.) at the end of December. Daylight for outdoor activities without artificial lighting lasts about 45 minutes past sunset.

Helpful Phone Numbers

EMERGENCY: Police, Ambulance, Fire: **911**
Police non-emergency: 808-241-6711
Crime Stoppers: 808-241-6787
Weather: 808-245-6001
Poison Control: 800-362-3585
Sexual Assault Crisis (YWCA): 808-245-4144
YWCA Shelter: 808-245-6362
Consumer Protection: 808-274-3200
Kaua'i County Office of Elderly Affairs: 808-241-6400
Transportation for Elderly or Handicapped: 808-241-6400
Transportation Airports Division: 808-246-1401
Transportation Highway Division: 808-274-3111
Kaua'i Chamber of Commerce: 808-245-7363
Po'ipu Beach Resort Association: 808-742-7444
Kaua'i Visitors Bureau: 808-245-3971
The Kaua'i Bus: 808-241-6410
Time of Day: 808-245-0212
Directory assistance: Local: 1+411; interisland 1-808-555-1212
Hospitals: Both of these facilities have emergency rooms. **Wilcox Memorial** in Lihu'e: 808-245-1100; **West Kaua'i Hospital**: 808-338-9431

LAND AND NATURAL RESOURCES

Division of State Parks
Camping Permits: 808-274-3444
Main Office: 808-274-3446
Koke'e: 808-335-5871
Wailua Marina: 808-822-5065
Division of Aquatic Resources: 808-274-3344
Forestry & Wildlife: 808-274-3077

CHAPTER 2

What to See, Where to Shop

East Shore and Central Coast Area

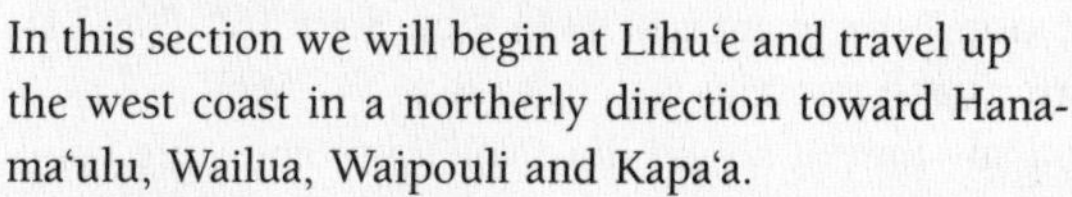

In this section we will begin at Lihu'e and travel up the west coast in a northerly direction toward Hanama'ulu, Wailua, Waipouli and Kapa'a.

Kaua'i's main airport is located in Lihu'e, so this is probably the first place you'll see. It's not exactly the garden spot of the "Garden Isle," but it is the least touristy area of the island. Lihu'e is a small town and the county seat, where all the government and many "big" business offices are located. It also has all the everyday necessities like the post office, discount shopping, banks, churches and a library, and offers the best selection of inexpensive local restaurants.

Hotels, motels and condos in Lihu'e are generally less expensive than other parts of the island and several provide convenient access to the airport. But with the exception of two resorts, accommodations are generally very basic. Even if you stay at another property for the duration of your stay, Lihu'e area lodgings are worth considering for a night if you have a late evening arrival or an early morning departure.

LIHU'E

The word *Lihu'e* means "cold chill" and according to the *Kaua'i Talking Guidebook*, the town was named in 1837 by the governor who relocated from the Big Island and named it after his own home town there. Of course, the Hawaiians had their own reasons for choosing such a name.

Because of our unusual island-state, mayors in Hawai'i govern counties that consist of one or more islands rather than areas of land. The island of Kaua'i (along with Ni'ihau) is a county of the state of Hawai'i and Lihu'e is the county seat. The historic **county building** was built in 1913 and, with its sprawling lawn and tall palm trees, it is an aesthetic focal point of Lihu'e. However, most county government agencies are located in the "round building," the county headquarters at the intersection of Rice Street and Kuhio Highway. Although government agencies are not usually high on one's list of visitor attractions, you may find the need to visit one or more while you're here on Kaua'i. The state building is next door to the historic county building.

The **Kaua'i Visitors Bureau** is always a good place to start to pick up some brochures and ask for information. It is located at 4334 Rice Street, Room #101; 808-245-3971, fax 808-246-9235. The State Parks and Recreation Department—a place you will need to go to if you plan on doing any camping or hiking—is located on the third floor of the State Building at 3060 Eiwa. This is where you will be able to pick up your permits and various maps for state trails. Phone 808-274-3444 Division of State Parks—Camping permits. The County Parks and Recreation Department is at 4444 Rice, Suite 150; 808-241-6670, or for permits and reservations phone 808-241-6660.

If you spend any time at all in Lihu'e you'll become quite familiar with Rice Street. It seems this single road can get you anywhere you want to go in town. From the Kaua'i Visitors Bureau, you can turn from Rice onto Hardy to reach the **Kaua'i War Memorial Convention Hall and the Regional Library**. The library has an excellent selection of Hawaiian titles, many of which are now out-of-print. If you are a Hawaiiana buff, you might like to include this on your itinerary! The **Kaua'i Community College**, 3-1902 Kaumuali'i Highway on the west edge of Lihu'e, also has a good Hawaiiana section in their library.

If you are hot after a day of sightseeing and shopping, take a short detour to **Halo Halo Shave Ice**. It is part of Hamura Saimin and it, too, is just off Rice Street. Just around the corner from Hamura Saimin is Ma's, a good local-style eatery; just down the street is also Barbecue Inn, a great family-style restaurant.

Farther along Rice Street is the Rice Shopping Center. It houses the island's only bowling alley, a Filipino bakery, a laundromat and a couple of local-style eateries. Beyond that, you'll find the main post office and, just across the street, the Kaua'i Museum.

The **Kaua'i Museum** is a great place to get acquainted with the island's history. It is located at 4428 Rice Street in the Wilcox Building that was originally constructed in the 1920s as the first public library. Mrs. Emma Mahelona Wilcox offered $74,000 in February of 1922 for the construction of a permanent library in memory of her husband, Albert Spencer Wilcox. The building, designed by Hart Wood, was dedicated on May 24, 1924. In 1954 work began to create a Kaua'i Museum and it officially opened on December 3, 1960. In 1969 the adjacent Albert Spencer Wilcox Library building became the central building of the Kaua'i Museum Complex. The original museum building was named after William Hyde Rice. The museum offers a combination of permanent and changing exhibits. Some tell the story of the island's volcanic creation while other displays explain the role immigrants have played in creating the multicultural community that exists here today. The ancient people and their culture, the discovery by Captain Cook, missionary occupation, royal families and agricultural history are all explored. Their 30-minute aerial film tour of Kaua'i

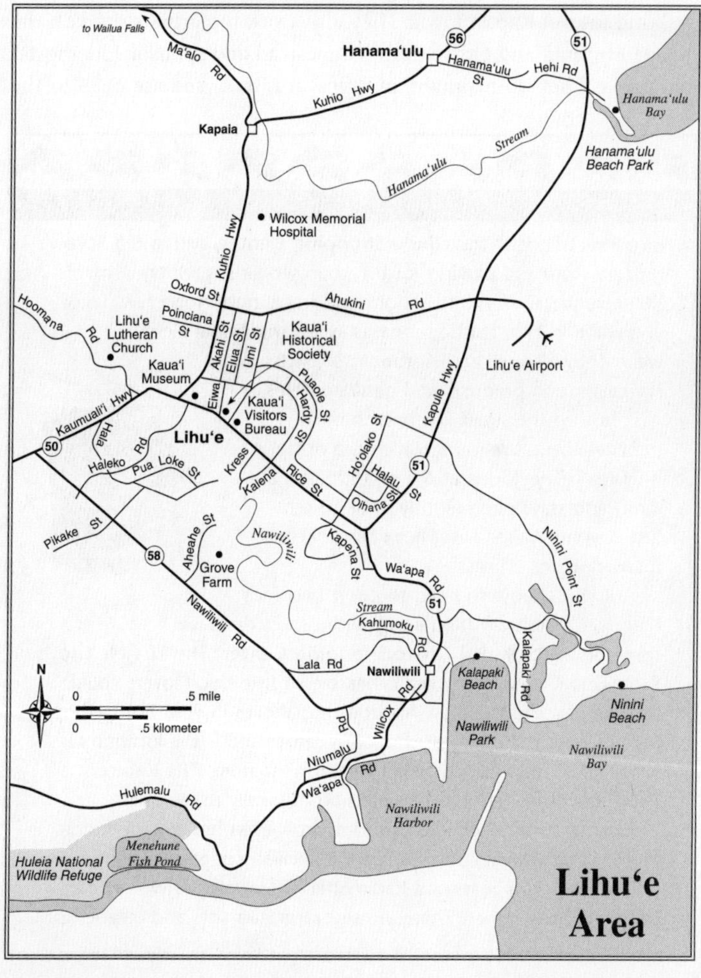

provides a great base for planning your island excursions. Art, music, dance, religion, language, farming, surfing, healing and the transition from royalty to statehood are all covered. The Kaua'i Museum gift store has quite possibly the best selection of Hawaiian titles as well as some wonderful handcrafted gift items. There is no admission charge if you wish to visit only the gift store, just advise them at the front counter. The museum is free to all on the first Saturday of each month. They have periodic special presentations and family activities. Open weekdays 9 a.m. to 4 p.m., Saturday 10 a.m. to 4 p.m., closed Sunday. 808-245-6931.

The **Kaua'i Historical Society**, located in the historic county building, 808-245-3373, is involved in various historical and educational activities on the island, including an informative historical "dune walk" that is offered in conjunction with the Hyatt Regency and a walking tour of Kapa'a town. They also work in partnership with the Kaua'i Museum and Grove Farm Homestead and sponsor Elderhostel programs. They do maintain an office in Lihu'e, and are open to the

Rice Street ends at the **Lihu'e Shopping Center**, with a Big Save grocery store and parking for the county building, where it meets Kuhio Highway. If you turn right and travel north for a few miles, you will find **Hilo Hattie**, a mainstay for traditional aloha wear. They also sell an assortment of packaged Hawaiian food products and giftware items.

Just up the street is a branch of the national chain, **Walmart**, which is a hotspot on Kaua'i. They open at 6 a.m. (Sundays at 8 a.m.) and stays open nightly until 10 p.m. Just beyond Walmart is Wilcox Hospital and many doctors' offices.

If you choose to head south, it becomes Kaumuali'i Highway (Route 50) and a short drive will take you to the **Kukui Grove Shopping Center**. The 10-hole Grove Farm Golf Course at Puakea is nearby, so those golf lovers could partake of a short game while the shopaholics in your group shop. Kukui Grove is the largest shopping center and is the location for Macy's, the island's only major department store. The **Kaua'i Products Store** has a lovely selection of locally made quilts, *muumuus*, jewelry, lotions, *keiki* clothing—even homemade fudge. **Nature's of Hawai'i** offers unusual Hawaiian curios and aloha wear, and you'll find a Sears and Radio Shack here, too, as well as many other specialty stores. There are several restaurants and eateries.

public by appointment only. Their 3,000-volume collection, however, is available to the public for research and education, Monday through Friday, by appointment only. Donations and contributions are welcomed. Family membership is $25 per year. Call for information.

Turning left (south) onto the Kaumuali'i Highway from the Kukui Grove Shopping Center and along the road a short distance, you'll find a **turnout** viewing area. This is a good location to take a glance at the magnificent Ha'upu Ridge, which rises south beyond and behind the Kukui Center. Look closely (real close!) and you will see the profile of Queen Victoria. Her head is slightly tipped back and she has a crown perched on the top of her head. A finger is pointing up as if she is reprimanding someone in the distance beyond. In fact, this natural feature is becoming more obscured with time as natural vegetation changes the distant profile line. Just beyond is **Puhi**, an old plantation town. The old town boasts a farmers market, various shops, a couple of restaurants and is home to Kaua'i Community College.

Just before you reach Puhi, you'll pass by the plantation estate of **Kilohana**. Kilohana is reminiscent of the grandeur and elegance of an earlier age when sugar was king. One of the grandest residences on Kaua'i, now known as Kilohana, was the home of Gaylord Parke Wilcox. Built in 1935, this 16,000-square-foot Tudor mansion was designed by a British architect named Mark Potter. The property was named for the large cinder cone that is located above and behind the property. The grounds are carefully landscaped and inside furniture came from exclusive Gump's in San Francisco. The Kilohana Shops and Galleries are well deserving of a bit of wandering, before or after you enjoy your meal at Gaylord's Courtyard Restaurant.

In 1865, the second sugar plantation, the Lihu'e Plantation, was established along the Wailua River. It was the first to bring immigrant workers and to use stone grinders in the processing of the cane. George Norton Wilcox, the son of island missionaries, returned to the island in 1864 following his studies at Scheffield (Yale) in engineering. He purchased 900 acres of land for $10,000. When he broached the subject of irrigation, others thought he was crazy. He proceeded to dig a ditch 11.2 miles in length to bring water from Mt. Wai'ale'ale. The ditch, dug by hand, took two years to complete. His introduction of foreign immigrants from the Philippines, Germany, Australia, Japan and elsewhere was the start of the cultural diversity that is evident in the islands today. It also launched the practice of diverting the island's many streams for agriculture, which disrupted their normal flow and forever changed stream ecosystems.

George was concerned that most of the workers would choose to return to their homelands following their contract. He approached them, inquiring what would entice them to remain. Their answer resulted in Grove Farm providing single-family, 300-square-foot homes for the workers. These camp houses were designed after those used in logging camps in Oregon and Washington and were sent to Hawai'i in ready-to-assemble units. The only differences between these cabins and those in the Pacific Northwest logging camps were the *lanais,* which were added to the front, and the use of tin for the roofs. (Because of the cane burning and risk of flying cinders, a wooden roof would have been a fire hazard.) He also introduced chemical fertilization and developed hybrid strains of cane; when the depression struck the country, George diversified. He died in 1933 at the age of 89, leaving everything to his nephew Gaylord. Gaylord built the 16,000-square-foot Kilohana home for his wife Ethel.

The **carriage ride** offers a fun, even romantic, excursion around the grounds. Carriage rides are available daily 11 a.m. to 6:30 p.m. Admission to Kilohana and its grounds is free, carriage rides are $8 adults/$4 children. Kilohana and the shops open daily at 9:30 a.m. Located just outside Lihu'e, travel east along Kaumuali'i Highway, Route 50. Kilohana is on your left just before the town of Lihu'e. If you are arriving from the north or east, travel Kuhio Highway (Route 56) south and west through Lihu'e. Bear right at the traffic light at the end of Kuhio Highway. Kilohana will be 1.4 miles down Kaumuali'i Highway on your right. Kilohana 808-245-5608.

Returning to the Kukui Grove Shopping Center, but at the opposite (Nawiliwili) end, is Big Kmart. Adjacent is **Borders Books and Music**, which is worth a stop. This is a bookstore chain, but in addition to books there is also a terrific selection of music and videos as well as the drifting scent of espresso from their in-store café. They offer special events (free!) and their children's corner is a nice touch for the traveling family. 4303 Nawiliwili Road. 808-246-0862. This is a major hangout on the island.

Also on Nawiliwili Road about a quarter mile south of the shopping center is the **Grove Farm Homestead**, which provides visitors with a fascinating look into the island's past. Kaua'i's history can be traced to the beginnings and growth of the sugar plantations. Grove Farm, one of the earliest sugar plantations, was founded in 1864 by George Wilcox, Gaylord's uncle. Today, this historic museum showcases the old sugar days and Hawai'i's politics—from the monarchy to statehood. A two-and-one-half hour tour takes visitors through the original home, which was enlarged in later years to accommodate a growing family. The property, which includes the gracious old Wilcox home and the cottage of the plantation laundress, is situated amidst tropical gardens, orchards and rolling lawns. The tours are small and intimate and the guides are knowledgeable about the island's sugar industry and its history. Minted ice tea (with homegrown mint) and

Grove Farm icebox cookies baked in an old wood stove in the farm house (Miss Mabel's favorite!) are served for refreshments.

This living legacy was left by Miss Mabel Wilcox, the last surviving niece of George Wilcox, who wanted her family home to be preserved. She lived here until her death in 1978. Most visitors miss touring the Grove Farm Homestead because reservations (required) have to be booked weeks in advance. This is quite possibly Kaua'i's best cultural experience and is well worth a phone call ahead as you plan your island itinerary. Cost is $5 per person with tours available on Monday, Wednesday and Thursday. Reservations can be made up to three months in advance. 808-245-3202. P.O. Box 1631, Lihu'e, HI 96766.

NAWILIWILI

Following Nawiliwili Road past Kukui Grove and the Grove Farm Homestead will take you toward the harbor. The route you travel is through scenic Lihu'e in the opposite direction than before. Here, Rice Street becomes Highway 51 and takes you down past the Kaua'i Marriott Resort toward the harbor.

The **Kaua'i Marriott Resort & Beach Club** is located above the Nawiliwili Harbor at Kalapaki Bay. After being closed to hurricane damage in the early '90s, the hotel sat vacant for a few years before Marriott took over the property and converted it into a combination timeshare and hotel. Major renovations converted the once European style of this lavish resort to one with a slightly more Hawaiian atmosphere. This hotel is the tallest building on Kaua'i. After its original construction in the '70s, local zoning laws changed so that no building on Kaua'i could be taller than a palm tree. Next door at Kaua'i Lagoons is the Terrace Restaurant and farther along, the Whalers Brewpub. Wedding services are available in the romantic gazebo.

In Lihu'e town, Highways 50 and 56 meet and merge with the Kaumuali'i Highway (Highway 50) heading south and west while Kuhio Highway (Highway 56) heads north through the Coconut Coast to the North Shore. You no doubt noticed passing under the old conveyor belt system of the now-closed Lihu'e Sugar Mill (very near to where Highways 50 and 56 meet). The mill closed in 2000, harvesting its last loads of cane much to the lament of many who were saddened to see the end of an era on Kaua'i. It follows the trend of the last few years all over Hawai'i where a once-thriving sugar industry has died off. Gay & Robinson operate the island's last sugar mill and plantation, on west Kaua'i.

Continuing on toward Nawiliwili Harbor, you will pass the Anchor Cove Shopping Center and the Harbor Mall, visitor-oriented shopping areas located across the street from each other on Rice Street.

Nawiliwili was named for the abundant *wiliwili* trees that once thrived in this area. Nawiliwili Harbor became Kaua'i's main deep-water harbor upon its completion in 1930. Following the completion of the harbor, Lihu'e became the island's major city. **Nawiliwili Park** has playground areas, barbecues, picnic tables and volleyball courts. If you have some recreational time consider stopping by the kayak rental at Nawiliwili's small boat harbor, which offers half-day trips up the river past the Alekoko (Menehune) Fish Pond. (*See* Chapter 7 for specifics.)

The **Menehune Fish Pond** is a spot you may easily miss. Follow Highway 51 toward Nawiliwili Harbor and look for the Wilcox Road sign. Follow it left onto Niumalu Road. Then turn right onto Hulemalu Road, where a visitors bureau sign indicates the Menehune Fish Pond. From this turn-off it is another six-tenths of a mile to the lookout, which will be on your left. The fish pond appears to be just a small pond adjacent to the Huleia River. Portions of *Raiders of the Lost Ark* were filmed along this waterway. Again, no historical background exists about the building of this pond, but legend tells that it was done by the *menehune,* who were interrupted during their nighttime work and quit, leaving the pond unfinished with *pukas* (holes) in it. Some years ago a family tried to rebuild the gates to make the fish pond a working proposition, but plans or events changed and it was never made operational. It's now being slowly destroyed by mangrove trees. The only way to see this area up close is kayak along the Huleia River. Tours up the Huleia river—which begins near the Nawiliwili boat harbor—are available from **Kaua'i by Kayak**.

The access road to the pond, and the pond itself, when reached on the river, is posted as "No Trespassing," and while that doesn't stop some people from venturing beyond, we prefer to let the property owners maintain their legal rights.

Located along the Huleia River is the **Huleia National Wildlife Refuge**, which is home to the koloa duck, coot, gallinule and stilt, all endangered Hawaiian species. In 1973, 241 acres were purchased to provide a habitat for water birds. The lands, once taro and rice fields, are now breeding and feeding grounds for a variety of waterfowl. The refuge is located in a relatively flat valley along the Huleia River, which is bordered by a steep, wooded hillside. A special permit is issued annually to a commercial kayaking business for access through an upland portion of the refuge. The refuge is not open to the public. If you continue exploring the roads beyond the Menehune Pond you'll find some nice vistas of the refuge. We also found a little fruit stand that had piles of papaya and was operated on the "honor system." The papayas were each labeled with a black marker indicating the price; we picked out the one we liked, dropped the money in the can and were on our way.

On Kuhio Highway, just past the Kaua'i Medical Center, you'll come to the intersection of Ma'alo Road (Highway 583). At the fork in the road, turn left onto Ma'alo Road, Highway 583. This is a rather narrow winding road that passes through former cane fields of Lihu'e Sugar Mill. At slightly more than three miles from the turn-off onto Ma'alo Road you will arrive at **Wailua Falls**. (You may recognize it from the opening of "Fantasy Island.") There is parking where the road dead-ends. A picturesque camera shot can be taken at this vista. There is a path which leads down to the base of the falls. However, the trail is dangerous, steep and slippery and not recommended. Many have been seriously or fatally injured and we suggest you enjoy the falls from the lookout above. Wailua, whose name means "two waters," was once actually two rivers that have merged into one. The river below is the largest navigable river in Hawai'i, and you may want to explore it during your Kaua'i stay.

The Radisson Kaua'i Beach Hotel, a few miles beyond Hanama'ulu, has several popular evening activities including a disco and a comedy club.

Retrace your route back down to Highway 56 and continue northward. At milemarker 2 you will be in **Hanama'ulu** where you'll find the Hanama'ulu Restaurant, Tea House & Sushi Bar, JR's Plantation Restaurant and a Shell gas station. Back in 1875, Hanama'ulu was a plantation camp. Cane was transported by oxen to Lihu'e until a mill was built in town. The mill continued to operate until 1918.

Harbor Mall and **Anchor Cove** are located across the street from each other on Rice Street as you head toward Nawiliwili. The Harbor Mall has several boutiques along with restaurants. At Anchor Cove you will find a Crazy Shirts outlet, a Wyland Gallery and other stores.

If you plan to be on Kaua'i for a while, especially if you are staying in a condo and plan to make some of your own meals, check out the **Holsum/Orowheat Thrift Store** at 4252 Rice Street (at the corner of Rice and Hardy) for great bargains on bread and packaged baked goods. (Visitors always ask how people can afford to live in Hawai'i when groceries are so expensive. This is one of the ways.) They are open Monday through Friday from 8 a.m. to 4 p.m., Saturday until 3 p.m., Sunday 9 a.m. to 2 p.m. Try to go on a Wednesday when their day-old products (or those nearing their expiration date) are further discounted for *mo' bettah* bread bargains. Call 808-245-6113. There is also a **Loves Bakery** at 4100 Rice Street with discounted bread items and specials for seniors on Tuesday and Friday. Open 9 a.m. to 4:30 p.m.

Just south on Highway 50 is the **Kukui Grove Shopping Center**. Located at 3-2600 Kaumuali'i Highway, it is the largest shopping center on Kaua'i, but small by mainland standards. This mall has been impacted by the economic downturn around the islands and many shop fronts are empty. You will find Macy's, Longs Drug Store, Big Kmart, convenient ATMs, a Star Market and a Borders Books along with specialty shops and restaurants. (For movie devotees, there is a nearby four-screen cinema.) Kukui Grove has a complimentary shuttle service to the shopping center with pick-up points from Po'ipu to Wailua. For shuttle service information call 808-245-7784. America Online founder Steve Case recently purchased Grove Farm, which owns the Kukui Grove Shopping Center. There likely will be some changes to the shopping center, Puakea Golf Course and the company's other holdings. It all depends on what the new owner has in mind for his new property. Stay tuned.

Kaua'i Fruit and Flower Co. is on the *makai* (ocean) side of the road as you travel north on Kuhio Highway toward Kapa'a. Stop by and visit Chucky Boy Chock (and Whitney, the dog) and sample the pineapple juice. This is the real stuff, straight from the pineapple. Or try the Dole Whip, a pineapple soft-serve ice cream. In the 1960s the building was an old wood mill where Mrs. Chock's grandfather used to work and do wood carvings. They still sell wood carvings as well as other art work and gift items, plus there is a flower shop with protea and orchids. The biggest draw of the operation is produce that you can purchase pre-packaged and pre-inspected, allowing you to take home pineapples, papayas, onions and tropical flowers. Mail orders, too. 800-943-3108 from the mainland. 808-245-1814 in Hawaii.

On Kuhio Highway you'll come to the intersection of Ma'alo Road (Highway 583). Near this intersection is a longtime shopping landmark, the **Kapai'a Stitchery**, 3-3551 Kuhio Highway. This shop will be of interest to anyone who enjoys sewing, especially quilters. They have a large selection of brightly colored fabrics, Hawaiian quilt squares and supplies, plus a variety of craft items. Needlepoint fanciers will appreciate the beautiful hand-painted canvases of local settings. The store is open 9 a.m. to 5 p.m. Monday through Saturday.

WAILUA

The Wailua area introduces what is now being called the Coconut Coast, which runs from the Wailua River to Kealia Beach. Wailua was of special religious and cultural importance to the ancient Hawaiians. Besides having many temples that are still standing, it was the area of residence for the *ali'i*.

Here, the Wailua River, the largest in Hawaii, cuts back into a verdant back country with many splendors to be shared. There are many ways to explore the river, including kayak trips or a motorized river cruise up to the **Fern Grotto**. Boat cruises run upriver daily to this natural rock cavern filled with maidenhair ferns. Boats depart every half hour from 9 a.m. to 3:30 p.m. (There is no departure at noon.) Smith's boats have musical entertainment on board. With a $15 charge for adults, $7.50 for children, it is certainly a pleasant way to spend an hour and a half, although a bit corny. The Fern Grotto gift shop was one of the few places we found that had authentic Hawaiian plant-starts packaged to pass through customs. Boat trips depart from the marina located across from Aloha Beach Resort Hotel. Call Smith's Tropical Paradise/Smith's Boats at 808-821-6895 for information.

You may wish to rent a one- or two-person kayak at the mouth of the Wailua to enjoy this lovely river at your own pace, or take a guided tour.

The 30-acre **Smith's Tropical Paradise and Botanical Gardens** is situated alongside the Wailua River and provides a wonderful opportunity to learn the names of some of the island's introduced exotic

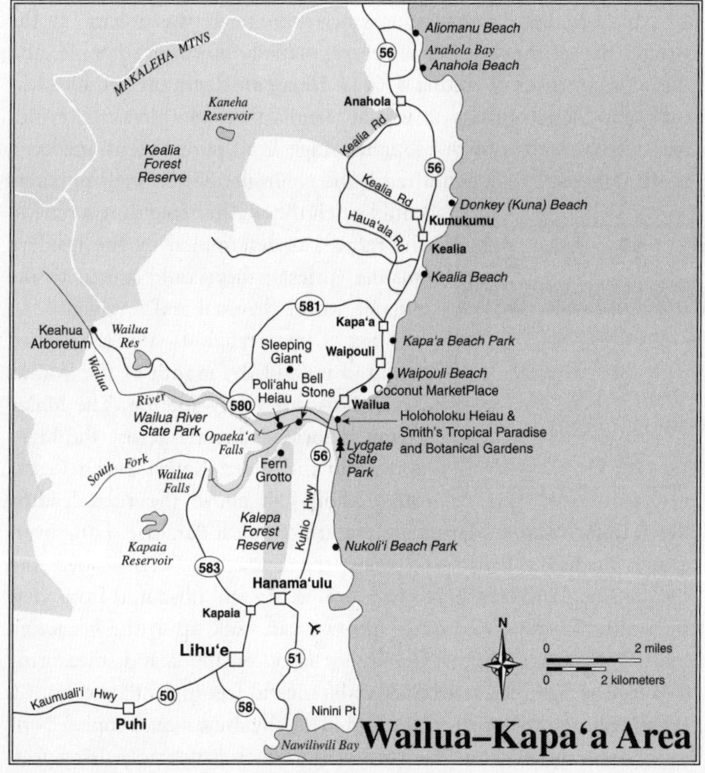

flowering trees and plants. Peacocks, ducks, colorful bantam roosters and other birds also inhabit the gardens. Bird food is available and carrying a sackful is almost certain to attract an entourage. Smith's meandering pathways will take you onto a Japanese island, through a sweet-smelling hibiscus garden, into a bamboo forest, and past a variety of fruit and nut trees. Along the way you'll see a replica of an Easter Island statue and grass huts representing several island cultures. The gardens are fairly empty in the morning; they open at 8:30 a.m. and close at 8 p.m on Monday, Wednesday and Friday. On Tuesday, Thursday and Saturday they close at 4 p.m. A luau is held on Monday, Wednesday and Friday evenings. 808-821-6895.

Turn *mauka* (toward the mountains) at the Coco Palms (still closed for renovations, with a very uncertain future) onto **Kaumo'o Road** for a short, but interesting, detour. Where the Wailua River meets the sea was, in ancient times, the place where kings were born. A series of seven *heiau* are located along the Wailua River here and you'll be winding upward toward Wai'ale'ale, the source of the mighty river. This area was an important population center in early Hawaiian times.

Located on a part of Lydgate State Park and just above the mouth of the Wailua River is the **Hauola Place of Refuge**. It's noted often as a "City of Refuge," a misnomer since there never was a "city" in the strict sense of the word. The refuge, actually more of a temple, and the adjacent ruins of **Hikina a Ka La Heiau** are distinguished by a low wall that encircles them. It was at Hauola that *kapu* breakers, criminals, or defeated warriors sought refuge from punishment and even death, provided they could reach the enclosure before their pursuers could catch them. After spending a time in the refuge, as determined by the resident *kahuna* (priest), they could return to the outside world cleansed and forgiven.

The early Hawaiians tried to preserve their royal line and one way they felt this was possible was for siblings to intermarry.

Six of these religious sites are located within a mile of the mouth of the Wailua River. Most are easily spotted. The **Malae Heiau** is located directly across the highway from the Aloha Kaua'i Beach Resort on a knoll just above the road leading down to the Wailua Marina and Smith's Tropical Paradise. Long overgrown by heavy brush and trees, the *heiau* has been cleared and restored by local Hawaiian civic groups. It's still obscured from view by a row of bushes and trees, but you can walk up to the *heiau* and marvel at its size. This is the largest *heiau* on the island, measuring 273 feet by 324 feet, with rock walls several feet high. Please respect these cultural ruins; they are sacred to the Hawaiian people. Don't enter the *heiau* or climb the rock walls, which is not only disrespectful, but could damage the structure because the stones are loose. Similarly, do not leave offerings of any kind at any *heiau* as Hawaiians take offense.

Other sites include **Holoholoku Heiau**, whose origin is in some dispute, as well as a **Royal Birthing Stone**, the spot where royalty were born. Pregnant women of the *ali'i* would give birth in huts next to the birth stone to ensure the royal status of their newborn infant. The Wailua River State Park is another 2.7 miles on the left and here you will also find the Poli'ahu Heiau. This interpretive center along the scenic bluff explains the importance of the Wailua River Valley to the Hawaiians in earlier times.

The fertile valley soil and plentiful supply of fresh water were ideal for supporting the large Hawaiian population that once inhabited this region. Adjoining the overlook is the **Poli'ahu Heiau**, reportedly built by the *menehune*. The stones were brought from the bluffs to build this religious site that was used for ceremonies until the traditional ways were abolished in 1819. This *heiau* was named after Poliahu, the goddess of snow and a sister to Pele. This is also believed to be a *luakini heiau*, which means a place of human sacrifice. An undesirable person was usually chosen: a prisoner of war, a person who had broken a *kapu* or sometimes a slave, but never a woman. A large enclosure of black lava rock was once the personal temple of Kaua'i's last king, Kaumuali'i.

You will see a dirt road just before the interpretive center. While very unimproved and rutted, the road is marked by a sign indicating the way to the **Bell Stone**. You'll find two large rocks that appear to be a gateway. By following the path to the end you will be treated to another lovely view of the Wailua Valley. At the birth of a royal child, the stone was pounded to signal the arrival of a new member of the *ali'i*, but Hawaiians prefer that you do not ring them as the stones can be damaged.

Just beyond, at 2.8 miles, is the **Opaeka'a Falls lookout** on the right side of the road and the **Wailua River lookout** on the left. Both are easily accessible and there's a paved parking lot with restrooms. The Opaeka'a Falls lookout affords a wonderful opportunity to see this 40-foot waterfall with its multiple cascades that flows year round. It's definitely worth a look. After walking the viewpoint trail you can cross the highway for a view of the Wailua River and the Kamokila Hawaiian Village.

A family-owned and -operated business, **Kamokila Hawaiian Village** is a re-creation of a Hawaiian village with huts, canoes, refurbished taro fields and demonstrations of lei making, poi making and other native arts and crafts. Located opposite Opaeka'a Falls, the Kuamo'o Road entrance is just past the Wailua Bridge. Visitors can take a narrated cultural tour, a canoeing adventure on the nearby Wailua River, or kayak to Fern Grotto to discover a secret waterfall and pool. Village Tour $5, Village and Kayak Adventure $25. Open Monday to Saturday 8 a.m. to 5 p.m. For kayak reservations or information on tour packages call 808-823-0559; e-mail: kamokila@hawaiian.net.

WAIPOULI

The inland area of the Coconut Coast—the Waipouli area of Kaua'i—offers excellent hiking opportunities. A section on hiking from *Kaua'i Hiking Trails* is included under "Hiking" in Chapter 6.

Continuing up Kuamo'o Road 4.8 miles, you will pass an Agricultural Research Station. Continue on to the Wailua Reservoir, which is one of several fresh-water fishing areas on Kaua'i. Several hiking trails have their trailheads in this area.

At 5.45 miles, you will enter the **Hawai'i State Forest Reserve**. If you plan a day of hiking, the location of the Kuilau Ridge Trail head is at 5.5 miles and just beyond is the **Keahua Arboretum**. The Arboretum offers a quiet retreat for a picnic. Several streams cross the road from here on in and, depending on the water flow and your rental car, you may choose not to proceed farther. As you retrace your path down the road, look off to the left side just beyond the Agricultural Research Station, for a small pull-out. A view of the reservoir with Nounou behind is a fine reward.

Back down to the Kuhio Highway (56), reset your odometer at zero and turn northward and continue towards Kapa'a. On your left you'll see the once-famed **Coco Palms Resort**. This area of palms was once the dream of a German plantation owner who, in the early 1800s, hoped to raise coconuts and sell copra (dried coconut meat) to the mainland. (Coconut oil can be made from the copra.) His dreams were dashed, but the tall and elegant trees remain. The Coco Palms was one of Kaua'i's first hotels. But the '92 hurricane did considerable damage to the property and it has remained closed since. Despite several proposals to rebuild the resort, none have gotten off the ground and the resort's future is in question.

Miss Sadie Thompson was filmed here, and the scene where Tatoo on "Fantasy Island" goes flying by in the jeep was also filmed in this coconut grove. Should you see the ghost of Elvis around, it is because he was also here during a portion of his filming of the movie *Blue Hawai'i*. However, you can't go into the grove since it's private property. But you can have a Blue Hawai'i wedding. Entertainer Larry Riviera (who used to perform with Elvis) still serenades wedding parties and includes an Elvis-style barge ride as part of the ceremony.

At Wailua Village in a historic sugar cane shack, you'll find **Bambulei**. They have collectibles, antique Hawaiian memorabilia, jewelry, silk and linen aloha shirts, one-of-a-kind lamps, tacky treasures and things that are both funky and elegant.

Across the street at the Kinipopo Shopping Village (356 Kuhio Highway), **The Tin Can Mailman** specializes in used and rare books, with an emphasis on Hawaiiana and South Pacific subjects. Owner Will Mauck also stocks art prints such as Matson menus and botanical prints. There are plenty of new books, too. Open 10 a.m. to 5:30 p.m.; closed Sunday.

At a brief six-tenths of a mile past the intersection of Kuamo'o Road you'll pass the largest shopping center on the east coast of Kaua'i. **The Coconut MarketPlace** has something for everyone. Located between the Wailua River and Kapa'a, it is open daily from 9 a.m. to 9 p.m.; 808-822-3641. This is one shopping center the kids may enjoy more than most—with surf and sunglasses shops, the **Magnet Factory**, the **Gecko Store** and plenty of inexpensive eateries. A selection of jewelry and art galleries as well as a two-screen movie theater are also found here.

Other unusual shops include **Bodacious**, which features petite through plus clothes, **Ye Olde Ship Store**, with scrimshaw ships in a

The lush tropical region of this area is synonymous with Kaua'i. *Nounou*, or **Sleeping Giant Mountain**, offers a majestic backdrop for this region. In her book, *Legends of Old Hawai'i*, Betty Allen retells the legend of the Sleeping Giant.

To summarize: the tale began long ago in Kapa'a where a fisherman and his wife lived. This fisherman always caught the largest of fish and one day when he pulled in his net he found the biggest fish he had ever caught. When the fish began to cry he realized it was no ordinary fish, but an *akua* (good or evil spirit) and took it home to his wife. The only thing that kept the fish from crying was when they fed him poi. His appetite was enormous, so people from all around came to feed him. The fish then transformed into a young giant who grew larger and larger as they continued to feed him poi and sweet potatoes. He grew so large that he could no longer walk and he lay down. They sent for a *kahuna* who told them that they needed to sing to the giant, but he would not reveal which song should be sung. The villagers began to sing to the giant, but to no avail. A small girl named Pua-nai was nearby looking at the rocks on the ground. Suddenly she began to sing a song she had never heard before and the giant miraculously changed to stone. They say that the giant sleeps yet today. (As long as he still sleeps, hikers can walk on his "forehead" and stand on his "face.")

bottle and ships' models. Shops do change often, so stop in and see what's new. There is often free Polynesian and Hawaiian entertainment at 5 p.m. The restaurants remain open even after the shops close. Check the restaurant section of this book for dining details.

The Kapa'a bypass is an old cane road that was converted to a narrow two-lane alternate route to alleviate the traffic congestion through Kapa'a town. The bypass road runs alongside the Kuhio Highway (56), from the Coconut MarketPlace to the Olohena Road in Kapa'a. You may want to take this if you're heading north during the afternoon rush hour traffic, unless you need to stop at the shops in Wailua and Kapa'a. Be forewarned, too, that the northbound highway drops to just one lane near the fire station, so when you see all the cars lined up on in the right lane by the MarketPlace that's why. So join the line, and don't try to cut in front of everyone or you may find yourself having to turn left into Foodland or Safeway. Just another of the many motoring quirks on the Garden Island!

At 1.3 miles past the Coco Palms begins the row of unattractive strip malls that line the highway between Wailua and Kapa'a. The first is the **Waipouli Town Center**, not to be confused with the other two Waipouli malls. A Foodland grocery store, Fun Factory (video arcade), Blockbuster, Lizard Lounge and Deli, and the popular Waipouli Restaurant are here. McDonald's and a small stream divides this center from the next.

Kaua'i Village in Kapa'a is an eight-acre shopping center featuring over 30 stores and restaurants. Tenants include Safeway, Longs Drug Store, Waldenbooks, ABC Store, Papaya's health food store, and a variety of gift and specialty shops. The Kaua'i Village Theatre, a 62-seat playhouse, shows cult, art and unusual films and occasional live productions. Be sure to check out the Hawaiian artifacts, art and handcrafted items at the **Kaua'i Heritage Center of Hawaiian Culture & the Art**. This lovely center is also a great place to sign up for lei-making and other classes.

The shopping village has a garden courtyard and two **Whaling Wall murals** by internationally known environmental artist Wyland. There is plenty of room in the open-air courtyard graced with a ten-foot waterfall and a series of landscaped ponds and streams to relax in while other members of your group are off shopping. The Village also has a **Hawaiian Garden** with indigenous and endemic plants, labeled with plaques that provide some historical information.

In the back of the center is a three-story clock tower, and under that is the **Kaua'i Children's Discovery Museum**. This little museum has permanent and changing exhibits geared toward stimulating kids' creativity and scientific interest. Kids will enjoy stopping in and playing, and the museum also offers *keiki* camps in summer and during major school holidays when parents can leave their children from one hour to the entire day. A drop-off service is also available for folks who want to give the kids something more interesting to do than hang with a babysitter. It's just $5 per hour. The museum is open from 10 a.m. to 5 p.m., Monday through Saturday. Admission is $4.25 for adults and $3 for children, a little steep, considering the facilities. But it is a nonprofit organization and the only thing of its kind on the island. 808-823-8222.

Just ahead are a string of malls and mini-malls, including **Waipouli Plaza** and **Waipouli Complex**. At the Waipouli Complex you'll find **Popo's Cookies**. The bakery makes coconut, chocolate chip, macadamia and their "granola great" cookies for all retail outlets. But you can buy them fresh and cheaper here. They also have "hard ice," thirst-quenching ice cakes in strawberry-cream, grape, orange and lemon-lime. Open Monday through Friday, 8:30 a.m. to 3 p.m., Saturday 9 a.m. to 2 p.m.; closed Sunday.

KAPA'A

Kapa'a was a center for rice cultivation until sugar cane and pineapple replaced it as the major agricultural industry. Life went along peacefully for this quiet town on Kaua'i's western shore until tourism discovered Kapa'a in the 1970s. The town is still relatively sleepy, and it hasn't been completely turned over to tourism. After all, this is the largest town on the island and the people who live here also shop and eat here, making it a good mix of residents and visitors. The town also has churches of many denominations. If you'd like to learn more about the town's past and its many historic buildings, you can take a guided walking tour offered by the **Kaua'i Historical Society**. Call for details 808-245-3373 as tour days and times change.

The southern part of town is marked by the Big Save shopping center that has a gas station with car wash, Burger King, grocery store, post office, laundromat, Fantastic Sam's and Ace Hardware. A bit further north is Pono Market, a great place to buy plate lunches and really fresh sushi and sashimi.

The best way to see downtown Kapa'a is to park and walk around. And when you need to cross the street, just venture out into the crosswalk. Unless you're assertive, you might wait a while before someone stops to let you cross when traffic is heavy. Most noticeable is the Sunnyside Market (open 8 a.m. to 7 p.m.) at Roxy Square, which sells fresh produce, tables full of papaya, bananas and more, and take-home food products. A number of nice jewelry stores can be found in this neighborhood, too, as well as **Kela's Glass Gallery**, a hemp clothing store, **Kebanu Gallery**, **South Seas Trading Company**, tropical clothing stores, a shop with hundreds of orchid plants you can ship home, a cute bead shop and **William & Zimmer**'s, which specializes in gifts and furniture made from *koa* wood. An ABC Store is right on the corner by the Kukui Street stop light, and there are two major banks within a block.

Across from ABC, check out the two-story New Pacific House "**Dragon Building**," where you'll find a natural health clinic with a practicing physician, Dr. Thomas Yarema, who has extensive emergency room experience. He will see visitors on a walk-in basis, and also offers a range of restorative therapies. The Dragon Building also houses a Bikram Yoga Studio with daily classes, and the very pleasant Day Spa provides a wide array of massage therapies and facials. There's a tattoo parlor here, too, and a sports bar, with an art gallery downstairs. Next door to the building is the Crystal Academy, with an amazing assortment of crystals for sale.

Downtown Kapa'a has a mini "restaurant row," too, as well as a liquor store and two coffee shops with internet access. Many of the restaurants are small, but you'll find a lot of good and unusual food here.

South and West Shore Areas

This section begins as we head down Highway 50 from Lihu'e through Puhi then Highway 520 (the tree tunnel) to Koloa, continuing down to Po'ipu and Lawa'i, then following back up to Highway 50 (via 530) eastward to Port Allen, Hanapepe, Waimea and Kekaha, and finally finding the way to Waimea Canyon State Park and Koke'e State Park, the west side's main attractions.

As you follow Highway 50 toward Koloa, you will turn left onto Highway 520. There's no way you can miss the stunning stand of trees that lines the road on either side. Walter Duncan McBryde was landscaping his homestead at the turn of the 20th century when he discovered he had an excess of eucalyptus trees. He donated 500 eucalyptus (also known as swamp mahogany) to the county and they were planted here. This famed eucalyptus grove known as the **Tunnel of Trees** has recovered substantially from the 1992 hurricane damage, but a little more time will be required for mother nature to rebuild the canopy effect it once had. In the days before the construction of the Kaumuali'i Highway, the tree tunnel was three times longer than its current size.

If you are staying at the Hyatt end of Po'ipu (Pe'e Road or beyond), the Koloa By-pass at Weli Weli Road now allows you to bypass Po'ipu and go straight into Koloa (and points east or north from there.

KOLOA

The last volcanic eruptions occurred on Kaua'i in the Koloa area some one million years ago. Traveling around the area you'll see cinder cones still dotting the landscape.

The word *koloa* has several meanings, but the town was mostly likely named for the prevalence of native koloa ducks in the once-vast wetlands here. The town was developed along the Waikomo Stream, which provided not only fresh water, but power for the first sugar mills. In 1835, Ladd and Company established the first successful sugar plantation in Hawai'i here. King Kamehameha III leased 980 acres to Bostonian William Hooper for $300 a year. The first mill was built in 1836 in an area known as Green Pond. The mill used large *koa* logs to grind the cane juice. The second mill was built in 1838 in the same location but used much-improved iron rollers. Ladd and Company built the third mill, powered by water and firewood that fueled the boilers, in 1841 near the confluence of the Omao and Waikomo Streams. The **chimney stack** at the park across the street from the monkey pod tree in Koloa is all that remains of this third mill, which was used until 1913. There's a **monument** there which represents the many varied ethnic groups that contributed their labors to the sugar cane industry. The "new" mill was built in 1913 and continued production for the Koloa Sugar Company until it ceased operations in 1996. McBryde—Koloa's last incarnation, once owned by Alexander & Baldwin—has shifted to coffee production as the Island Coffee Company. From its inception in 1835, and then for 21 years, this was the only sugar cane plantation in the Hawaiian islands. The quaint plantation feel of this town continues to this day.

The **Waita Reservoir**, to the east side of Koloa, is the largest reservoir in Hawaii. This manmade body of water was built on marshlands between 1903 and 1906 and covers 370 acres.

A strip of shops occupying the old wooden storefronts lines the town of Koloa. Several restaurants and various art galleries and shops carry everything from interesting old Hawaiiana prints and reprints to jewelry and souvenirs. **Island Soap and Candle Works** has an outlet here in Old Koloa Town in addition to the one up north at Kilauea.

The large **monkey pod tree** was planted in 1925 and lends its shade to the Crazy Shirts store. This building was originally built by Mr. Yamaka, who ran a hotel in the back until the mid-1920s when the Yamamoto family began their store at this site. Behind this is a small mall area with the **Koloa Museum**. This small, free museum depicts the development of the sugar industry in this area. The hours it is open seem to be sporadic.

The best deal in town is behind Sueoka's grocery. The small "**snack shop**" is reminiscent of the old Azeka's snack shop on Maui. Walk up to the window and order your grinds. Open just for lunch, it is worth the drive back from Po'ipu Beach to pick up a meal.

The **Koloa Church**, located on Po'ipu Road, was established in 1835. However, this pristine white church was not built until 1859. The design reflects a traditional New England style, typical of the missionary influence in early Hawai'i.

Another of Kaua'i's notable historic religious landmarks is found at Koloa. More than 150 years ago, in 1841, **St. Raphael Catholic Church** opened its doors on Kaua'i. The island's first Catholic church suffered severe damage in the 1992 hurricane but has been repaired. The original church had walls that were thickly built. A mortar was made by burning sand into lime and it was then mixed with pounded coral. This was used to hold together the rocks that constituted the walls. A reporting of the church's construction was published in a centennial celebration held in 1941: *The gathering of coral was a saga itself. The men and women swam out to the reef from Koloa beach and there they dived under water to break off huge slabs of coral. They would then swim with the slab back to the beach, tie it onto their shoulders and trudge the three miles across the plain to the church.* Changes to the original church over the years have included the addition of more arched windows, and a steeple was added in 1933. St. Raphael was originally a parish school and offered instruction for many years. While the main church seats only 150, you may find three times that many people in attendance on Sunday. So, in addition to the rebuilding efforts, the church also has plans for expansion. You might also visit the **Lady of Lourdes shrine**, built of lava rocks in a secluded spot at the back of the property.

Koloa Landing, about a mile-and-a-half south of town on the coast, was the state's third largest whaling port in the 1800s and was also used for exporting raw sugar and sweet potatoes. An interisland ferry cruised between the islands, bringing passengers to this port on Kaua'i. The landing as a port site was abandoned in 1928.

PO'IPU

While Po'ipu has no definitive town center, it is nonetheless a wonderful Kaua'i vacation destination. Located on the south shore, there are several excellent accommodations. Po'ipu Beach is located in front of the Kiahuna Plantation. This is one of the island's best all-around beaches for family activities, except when surf is high. The Hyatt Regency is located on Keoneloa Beach, fondly referred to as Shipwreck Beach for a long-since-gone wreck that once was beached on this stretch of coastline.

The **Po'ipu Shopping Village** is the largest and only real shopping center in this area. You will find eateries ranging from fine dining to very casual. There is also a Crazy Shirts and some other fashion shops, jewelry stores and touristy shops with fine arts and gifts. They have free Hawaiian entertainment and Tahitian dancers Monday and Thursday at 5 p.m.

Prince Kuhio Park is located on Lawa'i Beach Road. Prince Kuhio was the youngest son of Kaua'i's chief David Kahalepouli Piikoli, and the grandson of Kaumuali'i, the last King of Kaua'i. His aunt was Queen Kapiolani. Prince Kuhio was adopted by the queen and grew up in the royal household in Honolulu. The **monument** at this park marks the birth site of Prince Jonah Kuhio Kalanianaole. Prince Jonah was known as the "People's Prince" because of his achievements for his Hawaiian people. Prince Jonah was born in 1871 and elected in 1902 as a delegate to Congress, where he served until his death on January 7, 1922. You can see the foundation of Kuhio's parents' home, a royal fishpond, a shrine, Hoai Heiau where the *kahuna* meditated and lived, and a sitting bench that faced the grounds.

Located just to the east of Po'ipu Beach there is a lava rock outcropping known as **Spouting Horn**. It is named for the shooting geyser of sea water that appears during high tide. The spouting results from the surf washing into a lava tube and being sucked up through

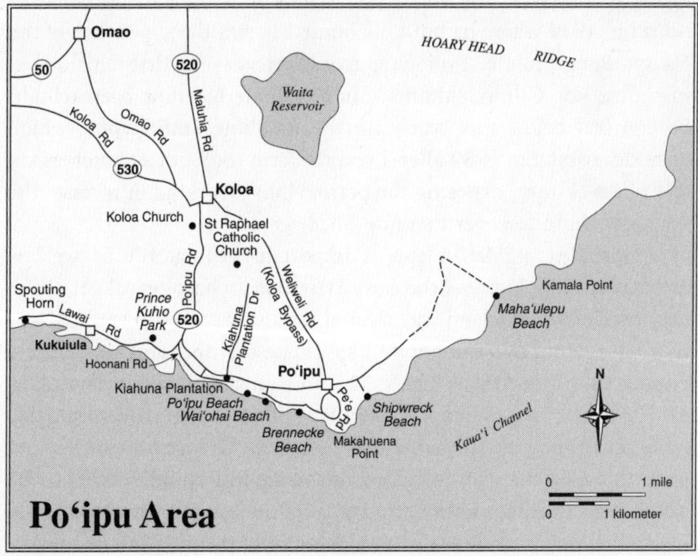

a hole in the coastal rock. The geyser reaches heights of as much as 60 feet. A popular visitor attraction, it's located at Spouting Horn County Park and is open to the public at no charge. It is easy to find: follow Highway 520 to Lawa'i Road (also known as Spouting Horn Road). Heed the posted signs that caution about the dangerous rocks. There are a number of local arts-and-crafts **vendors** with tents and booths set up next to the parking lot. Take some time to browse the fine bargains in local handmade coral jewelry, the rare and coveted Ni'ihau shell necklaces, bracelets, earrings and various artworks. You're sure to find some nice mementos of your Kaua'i visit here.

If you'd like to experience a little of the pleasures of Robinson Crusoe or Swiss Family Robinson, plan an excursion to **Maha'ulepu Beach**. This is located at the eastern end of the Po'ipu Resort area past the Hyatt Resort. It was here that King Kamehameha I made his attempt to conquer the island of Kaua'i in 1796. Unfortunately, a storm forced a retreat, but the advance forces of Kamehameha's troops arrived on the island, unaware of the order to retreat, and were quickly killed.

This is also the beach site where George C. Scott portrayed Ernest Hemingway in the movie *Islands in the Stream*. Maha'ulepu Beach is actually a collection of small beaches. Bones of ancient and now extinct flightless birds have been found in caves in this area. The beaches offer a diverse assortment of aquatic activities, including fishing, surfing, bodyboarding, body surfing, kayaking, windsurfing, snorkeling and swimming. The three areas along this beachfront are known as Gillin's Beach, Kawailoa Bay and Ha'ula Beach.

Gillin's was named for the supervisor of Grove Farm Company, Elbert Gillin, who arrived in the islands in 1912 and relocated to Kaua'i in 1925 where he built his home. He was the supervisor of the Ha'upu Range Tunnel. Following two hurricanes, all that remained of his home was Gillin's chimney, but the home has now been rebuilt. Several feet below this beach are the **Rainbow Petroglyphs**, which were discovered in 1980 after a severe storm took out as much as six feet of beachfront, exposing the petrogylphs. Working in reverse, the sea soon chose to cover them up once again.

This area of Maha'ulepu is important geologically as well as archaeologically. Many of the early Hawaiian archaeological sites were destroyed when the land was cleared for sugar cane. However, scientists have enough information to speculate that this area was heavily populated in pre-contact times. The area offered the early Hawaiians excellent fishing grounds and a fertile valley, making it a very suitable living environment. It was noted by Captain George Vancouver that from this area the glow of numerous campfires could be seen as he sailed past. Further confirmation was found by the many burial sites located in the sand dunes here. Geologically the area lies below Mt.

Ha'upu, which is now only an eroded caldera. The sand dunes have yielded other rich geological treasures, including the fossils of extinct birds. They have identified a flightless bird called a rail, several species of geese and a long-legged owl. John Clark's *Beaches of Kaua'i* notes that "several caves in the vicinity contain two extremely rare insects, one a blind wolf spider and the other a blind terrestrial amphipod."

The **Po'ipu Beach Resort Association** provides up-to-date information on accommodations, activities, dining, shopping, transportation and services in the Po'ipu, Koloa and Kalaheo areas of Kaua'i. To request a free 36-page brochure, contact: Po'ipu Beach Resort Association, P.O. Box 730, Koloa, HI 96756; 808-742-7444; fax 808-742-7887; 888-744-0888; e-mail: info@poipu-beach.org, or look up their electronic brochure at www.poipu-beach.org.

LAWA'I

Leaving Koloa and heading eastward on Highway 530, you'll travel to Lawa'i. Little is known of early Lawa'i. According to an account by David Forbes in his book, *Queen Emma and Lawa'i*, the early maps and photographs show that the valley was cultivated in taro and later in rice. Queen Emma, the wife of Kamehameha IV, probably first saw Lawa'i during her visit in 1856, but returned for a more lengthy stay during the winter and spring of 1871. On arrival she found the area rather desolate, and compared with the busy life in Honolulu, it must have seemed so. In her correspondence with her family on O'ahu she requested many items be sent, including plant slips. With these plant starts she began to develop one of the finest gardens in the islands.

Queen Emma leased the Lawa'i land to Duncan McBryde for a span of 15 years in 1876. However, she reserved her house lot and several acres of taro patch land. According to Forbes, "In 1886, after the Queen's death, Mrs. Elizabeth McBryde bought the entire Ahupua'a for $50,000. The upper lands were planted to sugar cane, and the valley was apparently leased to Chinese rice growers and taro planters."

In 1899, Alexander McBryde obtained the land and with a love of plants, continued to enlarge and cultivate the gardens that were begun by the queen. Alexander McBryde died in 1935 and the land was sold to Robert Allerton and his son John in 1938. They continued to enlarge the gardens, searching out plants from around Southeast Asia. Today Lawa'i is a horticulturist's dream, with an outstanding collection of tropical plants. The **National Tropical Botanical Garden** is a nationally chartered nonprofit organization that is actually made up of five separate gardens. Three are on Kaua'i, one is on Maui, and another is located in Florida. Each of the gardens has an individual name, but they are sometimes incorrectly referred to individually as the "National Tropical Botanical Garden."

The **Lawa'i Garden** is located on Kaua'i's southern shore in the lush Lawa'i Valley, and was the first garden site to be acquired by the National Tropical Botanical Garden. The NTBG headquarter facilities are located adjacent to the Lawa'i Garden. The headquarters complex includes a scientific laboratory, an herbarium housing nearly 30,000 specimens of tropical plants, an 8,000-volume research library, a computer records center, an educational center, and offices for staff and visiting scientists. Lawa'i Garden is a research and educational garden comprising 186 acres. The garden's extensive collections include tropical plants of the world that are of particular significance for research, conservation or culture. Special emphasis is given to rare and endangered Hawaiian species and to economic plants of the tropical world.

Of particular interest is the endangered *kanaloa kahoolawensis* (one of only four in the world). This small, woody plant is known only to exist on Kahoolawe. In 1992 two specimens of this plant were discovered there. This is the first new genus discovered in Hawai'i since 1913 and two have since been grown from seeds at the NTBG. There is also a collection of familiar household products—sugar, vanilla, cinnamon—all seen here in their natural plant state. Palm oil, sandalwood (for scent), *koa* (for wood items including canoes and furniture) and cuari (used to make sodium pentathol) can also be seen in their original form. *Three Springs* is at the interior of the Lawa'i Garden (toward the mountains). This 120-acre area was bequeathed to the Garden. As yet undeveloped, it will eventually be designed as an additional garden section, emphasizing the beautiful natural land and water features.

The nearby **Allerton Garden** is located oceanfront at Lawa'i-Kai, adjacent to the Lawa'i Garden. The entrance, located across from Spouting Horn, is a 14,000-square-foot renovated plantation home that was transplanted from West Kaua'i to become the visitor center. This was formerly a private 100-acre estate. The beautifully designed garden is managed by the National Tropical Botanical Garden pursuant to an agreement with the Allerton Estate Trust. The gardens started by Queen Emma were lovingly developed and expanded over a period of 30 years by Robert Allerton and his son John. The sculpted gardens contain numerous plants of interest, outstanding examples of garden design and water features, as well as Queen Emma's original summer cottage. The Moreton Bay fig trees here have giant buttress roots and helped create a prehistoric scene for the filming of *Jurassic Park*. While these trees appear ancient, they were actually planted in 1940. Reservations are required for tours of the Lawa'i and Allerton Gardens. Tour fee for the Allerton Garden or Lawa'i Garden is $30 adults (16 and older), $10 children (6 to 15), free for children 5 and under for each tour. For information on scheduled tours and reservations for either call 808-742-2623. P.O. Box 340, Lawa'i, HI 96765.

KALAHEO

The town of Kalaheo (meaning "proud day") was home to many immigrants at the turn of the 20th century. This was homestead land, auctioned by the government beginning in about 1910, and was originally used for growing pineapple, with Walter McBryde spearheading the pineapple industry. The population was predominantly Portuguese, Hawaiian and Japanese.

To take a short and worthwhile detour you need to turn left onto Papalina Road and head south for **Kukuiolono Park**. Many of the street names are Hawaiian words for parts of the body. For example, *papalina* means cheek, *lae* means forehead, *maka* is eye and *upu* is stomach. Glimpse off to your left as you climb the winding road and, if you are fortunate, you'll see a rainbow hanging over Po'ipu. The three huge satellite dishes on the right will warn you that your turn is just ahead. A small white sign on the right is too small and too near the turn-off to prepare you for the U-turn onto Pu'u Road. Enter Kukuiolono Park through the huge rock archway with iron gates. The park is a series of beautiful scenic gardens with sweeping Pacific and Lawa'i Valley views. Built by Walter McBryde, a founding father of the island's pineapple industry, it's a popular location for wedding ceremonies. There is also a Hawaiian garden that displays some interesting ancient stone artifacts, including huge rock bowls and a stone with a shape resembling the island called "Kaua'i iki" (Little Kaua'i). It is said by some that if you haven't seen Little Kaua'i, then you haven't seen Kaua'i. You might like to stop at the Kalaheo Coffee Co. & Café, just past the Papalina Road intersection, and pick up some of their huge sandwiches to enjoy as a picnic up at the park.

'ELE'ELE AND PORT ALLEN

Just beyond mile-marker 14 on the right is a **scenic overlook** of the Hanapepe Valley. It is a strikingly beautiful vista with the sheer canyon walls in hues of amber, ocher and red. You will first travel through 'Ele'ele and Port Allen before reaching the town of Hanapepe.

As you continue toward Waimea, you will note a series of substantial-looking electrical poles bordering the road on both sides. These were put in following the devastation caused by the 1992 hurricane. The poles are supposed to be able to withstand wind forces up to 120 miles per hour. As the road curves downhill you will reach the area of 'Ele'ele. The most notable landmark is the 'Ele'ele Shopping Center.

A Big Save and Toi's Thai Kitchen are here. Turn down toward **Port Allen** to see one of Kaua'i's two seaports. The Coast Guard has boats here and some are "drones" or target ships. They warn "Target Drone, Stay Clear" in large bold letters. Obviously these in the harbor have either not had a turn at being bombed, or they just got lucky with some misses!

You can purchase bags of Kaua'i-grown coffee and other coffee-related items at the **Kauai Coffee Company and Visitor Center,** located between Kalaheo and 'Ele'ele on a turn-off just past the old McBryde Mill. Enjoy free samples of java while you browse their store. 808-335-5497 or 800-545-8605.

You may have noticed that the dirt has become redder as you proceed around the southern coastline. That's because the soil contains a good deal of iron. A very clever entrepreneur has taken advantage of this red clay, which has a natural property for staining anything that it comes in contact with. You are sure see the "Red Dirt Shirts" at various shops around the island. If you can't wait to visit, you can order by mail. Paradise Sportswear, P.O. Box 1027, Kalaheo, HI 96741. Send for a copy of their catalog, which depicts their many varied styles.

Port Allen has reemerged as an important commercial boat harbor for visitor activities. With the banning of commercial tour boat operations at Hanalei Bay on the North Shore, most of the cruise excursions to Napali Coast now depart from this location.

HANAPEPE

Hanapepe, which means "crushed bay," was Kaua'i's largest town back in the 1920s. The area was discovered by the Chinese immigrants who began to grow rice here. Hanapepe was once again one of Kaua'i's busiest towns from World War I through the early 1950s.

During World War II this coastal village was alive with thousands of GIs and sailors who were sent from the mainland and the rest of Hawai'i to train for Pacific Theater duty, and to shore up Kaua'i's defenses. At this time Hanapepe reached its largest population and boasted restaurants, two theaters, two roller rinks, a dance hall—and a brothel! The town suffered a postwar decline and the population dwindled.

Hanapepe now boasts that it is "the biggest little town on Kaua'i." Fortunately, Hanapepe feels like a step back in time, with its plantation-era buildings and slow pace. Back when the highway was widened it was decided to bypass the town and it was probably at that time that Hanapepe began to fall into disrepair. The opening of the Kukui Grove Shopping Center in Lihu'e was another blow to shopkeepers who could not compete.

It is a quaint town that has potential for being a wonderful locale for artisans' galleries or such. You may recognize it from scenes from the TV mini-series "The Thornbirds." Many of the buildings were damaged by the 1992 hurricane and will probably not be repaired. The **Taro Ko Chips factory** is on the edge of town, and you might catch them when they are open. Mr. and Mrs. Nagamine started this business following their retirement and they cook up chips made from taro grown in fields nearby.

The Green Garden Restaurant has been hopping since the 1940s when the GIs would stop by for a meal and a piece of their wonderful pie. Yoshiura's General Store operated as Mikado until World War II and is a classic. The Hanapepe Café & Espresso is worth a visit.

By 4 p.m. most days, the town is pretty well closed up except on Friday nights! A number of art galleries have been springing up in the last several years, optimistic that perhaps this artisan community will be discovered by visitors exploring Kaua'i's western shore. These local galleries host "**Art Night**" every Friday (6 to 9 p.m.), with at least one of them providing refreshments and an art demonstration. Decorative lighting adds to the mood for visitors to enjoy a festive stroll along the old main street, watch artists painting portraits, and enjoy the hula show and local Hawaiian music. The art galleries lining Hanapepe's main street include Kauai Fine Arts, Hawaiian Kountry Art Studio, The Art Gallery, Hale Rasta, Kim Starr Gallery, Lele Aka Studio & Gallery, Hanapepe Art Center, Kamaaina Cabinets and Koa Wood Gallery, Aloha Angels Shop, Arius Hopman Studio Gallery and Dawn Traina Gallery. Hour and days open vary.

In the middle of town on the north side is a short walkway to the **Hanapepe swinging bridge** over the Hanapepe River. Take a short break and walk across the river. If you have youngsters, they will enjoy the short walk on the "swinging bridge." The bridge is a shortcut for residents living across the river to reach the town.

One of the most fascinating natural sites in Hanapepe is the salt ponds at **Salt Pond Beach Park**. The natural flats along this beach have been used by Hawaiians for generations. Today, this site continues to be used for traditional salt making. The resulting product is used for medicinal and cultural purposes. In late spring the wells, or *puna*, are cleaned and the salt-making process runs through the summer months. Mother nature has been kind enough to create a ridge of rock between the two rocky points at Salt Pond Beach, resulting in a large lagoon. The area is fairly well protected, allowing for swimming and snorkeling (except during times of high surf) and is popular for surfing and windsurfing as well. This park is well used by families and children because of its protected swimming area. This part of the island is often sunny and warmer, even when there is rain on the south and east shores. Salt Pond Beach Park can be a great day-long excursion. To reach the park, turn *mauka* off Kaumuali'i Highway on Lele Road then go past the Veterans Cemetery on Lokokai to parking area.

West Kaua'i continues to grow and evolve, somewhat reluctantly, into a visitor destination. Exploring the area, now dubbed the "West Kaua'i Sugar Heritage Corridor," begins just outside of Hanapepe. Up until a few years ago, sugar was king here and the story can be viewed along the highway and from connecting roads. It passes through Kaumakani Village, Waimea and Kekaha Town. When the sugar mill closed in Kekaha, it caused considerable economic hardship. But, as in other communities across the islands, people are retooling and not necessarily retreating. New ideas are being tried and new attempts to revitalize the community are in progress. It's a matter of time to see what works and what doesn't.

WAIMEA

Waimea is perhaps the best known, and that is a direct result of one early adventurer. Captain James Cook first landed in the Hawaiian islands in January 1778 at this site. A monument stands in his honor. In later times, rice was grown in the valleys and swamp, and sugar in the drier areas that required irrigation. The region also grew taro and raised cattle.

It is a wonderfully quaint town and, with its location on the western coastline, often has better weather conditions than other areas of the island. You can pick up a very helpful self-guided map of the Waimea area, available at the **West Kaua'i Technology & Visitor Center**. It highlights all the places to eat, picnic spots and beaches, as well as historic sites in or near Waimea, including the Russian Fort, Menehune Ditch and plantation tours of Gay & Robinson Plantation. Annual events include "Christmas in Waimea," with its annual *Lighted Christmas Parade*, the annual Falsetto Competition and Concert, and the Waimea Town Celebration.

The delightful **Plantation Lifestyles Walking Tour** provides insight into plantation life in 1900. In the future, a museum may be built near the ruins of the old Waimea Sugar Mill. The tour, led by volunteers, includes a visit to the Waimea Plantation Cottages, with a collection of relocated camp houses that now serve as visitor accommodations. Reservations are required for the Waimea Sugar Mill Camp Museum and Plantation Lifestyles Walking Tour, a one-and-a-half-hour cultural tour in an original sugar plantation village. Limited to 12 people, it's currently offered Tuesday, Thursday and Saturday at 9 a.m. Cost is $6 adults, $5 seniors 65 and older and $3 children 12 and under. Waimea Plantation Cottages, P.O. Box 1178, Waimea, HI 96796. 808-335-2824.

Hawaii's cultural history can be intimately explored through the heart of the sugar plantation. Hawaii's multicultural history is due to the need for laborers in the labor-intensive sugar fields of yesteryear. Now you have the opportunity to view field-to-factory operations at **Gay & Robinson**. The two-hour bus tour, conducted by Gay & Robinson Tours LLC, is available weekdays and includes the history of the plantation, its operation, processing, the plantation's miles of irrigation systems and views of the private lands. Harvesting operations are seasonal, with the months of April through October the best times to visit. Tour routes depend on the day-to-day operations. If you don't have time for the full tour, stop by their office and view the historic displays. The office is located in the historic Field Office (circa 1900) on Kaumakani Avenue. From Lihu'e, travel Highway 50. Just past mile-marker 19, turn left on Kaumakani Avenue, with its monkeypod trees and old-fashioned streetlights. It is open 8 a.m. to 4 p.m. Monday through Friday, with the exception of plantation holidays.

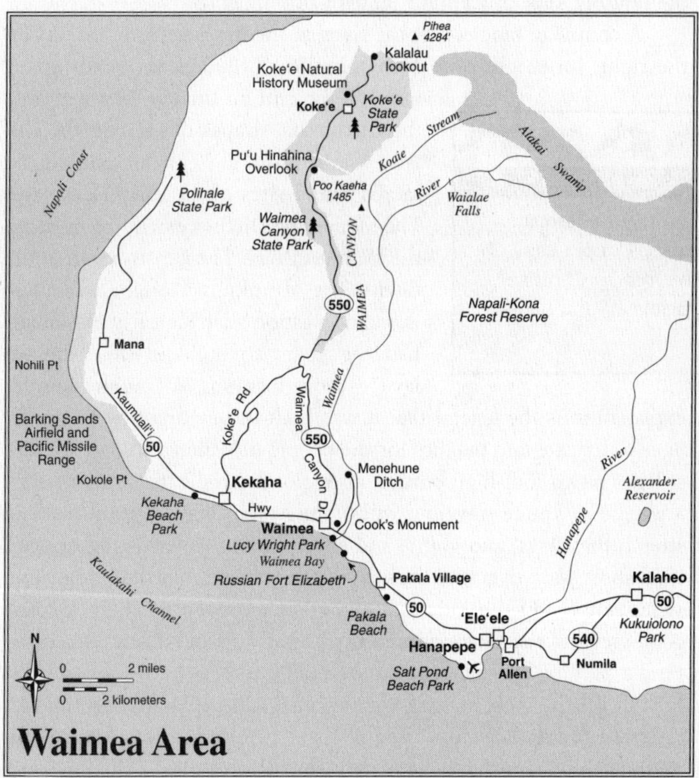

Tours are at 9 a.m. and 1 p.m. All visitors on the tour are required to wear safety equipment to enter the factory. They must also wear pants (shorts are okay) and low-heeled, closed shoes; they will be provided with safety glasses and hard hats. Cost of the tour is $30. They plan to add additional tours of their ditch systems. For tour information call 808-335-2824.

Just before you reach Waimea, before crossing the river, is **Fort Elizabeth** (also known as the Russian Fort), built on the mouth of the Waimea River in 1817 by German doctor Georg Anton Scheffer, who was employed by the Russian/American Fur Company of Alaska. When he began to fortify his fort, the native chiefs grew concerned and notified the king, who in turn ordered the Russians out of Kaua'i. (There are restroom facilities located here.)

Across the river, on the other side near the mouth, is **Lucy Wright Park**. This beach site was named for schoolteacher Lucy Kapahu Aukai Wright, who taught in Waimea for more than 35 years. She was born August 20, 1873, in Anahola. Just opposite the parking area at the beachfront is a large boulder with a bronze plaque commemorating the **landing spot of Captain James Cook** in 1778.

A couple of blocks past the river, at the Big Save Supermarket on the right, turn right onto Menehune Road. Follow the road up 1.3 miles to the cliff on the left. You will note the cactus that drapes down over the cliff face. Caverns in the cliff are said to be sacred burial sites of the early Hawaiians. The **Menehune Ditches** extend 25 miles up the Waimea River. The construction of the ditches are of unknown origin, and there is some question that the early Hawaiians had the talent to build in this "dressed lava"–stone fashion. A much simpler explanation is the legend that it was built in one night by the *menehune* to irrigate taro patches for the people in Waimea. Today, you can still see a two-foot-high portion of one of the walls that is marked by a plaque. If you're traveling with youngsters, this is a good place to stretch their legs, and yours, and walk across the "swinging bridge." It's a short walk over and back across the stream, but the bridge does swing some and the kids will enjoy the experience. There are also good views of the surrounding canyon walls up and down the stream. Find a parking space alongside the road.

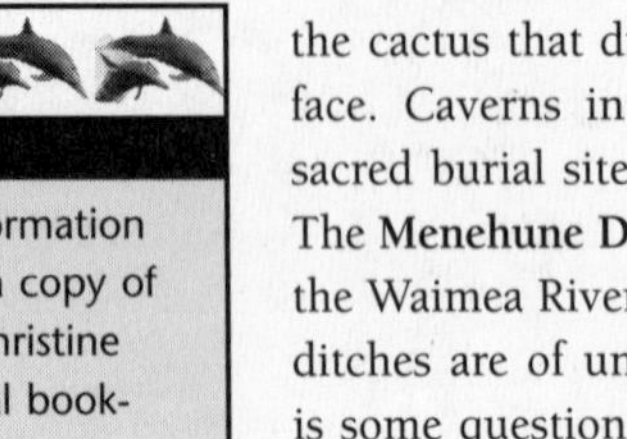

If you want more information on Waimea, pick up a copy of *Touring Waimea* by Christine Fayé, available at local bookstores.

To get the most of your Waimea visit and exploration of this historic old town, pick up a copy of the "Historic Waimea Main Street Walking Tour" brochure that details the historic sites of the town and provides a good reference and location map. Look for the brochure/map at the baggage claim area literature racks at the Lihu'e Airport upon arrival. Or, check with any businesses in Waimea to see if they have one on hand, or contact: West Kaua'i Business & Professional Association, P.O. Box 903, Waimea, HI 96796; also try West Kaua'i Main Street, 9691 Kaumuali'i Highway, Waimea, HI 96796, 808-338-9957.

The historic and restored (1999) **Waimea Theater** building is a venue for movies, live performances and conferences. This old-fashioned movie theater (it seats 250!) is located in the heart of town in a 1938 art deco building—complete with a glass ticket booth in front—and is worth a visit just to enjoy the architecture and history.

Located on Kaumuali'i Highway is the **West Kaua'i Technology & Visitor Center** (9565 Kaumuali'i Highway, Waimea; 808-338-1332). Open daily from 9 a.m. to 5 p.m., it's a good place to visit. Pictorials, graphics and displays with touch-sensitive screens provide information on all of Kaua'i's activities, not just Waimea. This high-tech, state-of-the-art, 7,500-square-foot center facility opened in 1999 with land leased from the Kikia'ola Land Co. for $1 a year for 30 years. Utilizing the theme "Enduring Engineering," visitors follow cultural and historic photographs showing the development of engineering on Kaua'i, from ancient days to modern times—from the Polynesian voyagers to NASA's most sophisticated technology. Enjoy old photographs of Waimea back in the days of grass shacks! There is even a photo of the first movie filmed on Kaua'i, *White Heat* by director Louis Weber. (The film has long since been lost or destroyed.) One unusual model is the Pathfinder, the pilotless aircraft that was flown at an altitude of 80,000 feet over Barking Sands beach. The museum blends the history of the area with information on the nearby Pacific Missile Range Facility. Not an easy task to undertake, but one that seems to work here. The center is located at the intersection of Highway 50 and 550, which is Waimea Canyon Drive.

A **monument to Captain Cook** was placed in the center of town in 1928 for the 150th anniversary of Captain Cook's first landing in the islands, which took place in Waimea. Fifty years later, the state erected a statue at Waimea's Hofgaard Park to commemorate the 200th anniversary of Cook's Landing.

The **Waimea Hawaiian Church** was built around 1865 by Reverend Rowell when he had a falling out with the Waimea Foreign Church. It was damaged by the 1992 hurricane and was totally rebuilt. You might wish to visit a Sunday morning church service, which is conducted in Hawaiian.

The **Waimea Foreign Church** was built around 1859 by Reverend George Rowell. According to John Lydgate in a speech given in the early 1900s, the church was built of sandstone blocks cut from a nearby beach. The blocks were soft when cut, but hardened when exposed to the air. They were transported by bullock-carts and secured with lime mortar. Pieces of the offshore reef were broken off by divers and a 20-foot lime kiln pit was dug. Woodwork used in the structure came from *lehua* wood that was dragged down from the mountains with teams of oxen. (By the way, "foreign" in this case means English-speaking!)

The **Gulick Rowell House** is located near the corner of Huakai and Old Missionary Row behind the West Kaua'i Technology & Visitor Center. The old home is just that. Construction of the home began in 1829 by the Reverend Peter Gulick, but was not finished until 17 years later by missionary George Rowell. It is one of the oldest surviving examples of early missionary structures in Hawaii. The 24-inch-thick walls provided natural cooling. It is privately owned and not a real visitor attraction. However, you can drive by and admire the old house and the huge spreading monkeypod tree in the yard, reputed to be the oldest such tree on Kaua'i. The grounds are nothing special, and are, in fact, overgrown with brush and weeds and generally unkempt.

At Waimea Highway 550 turns north and heads up to Koke'e and Waimea Canyon. A description of this area follows. For now, however, we will proceed northwest along the Kaumuali'i Highway (50) to Kekaha. This leads to Waimea Canyon and then you can return via Highway 550.

KEKAHA—POLIHALE

On a clear day from the coast near Kekaha, you can enjoy a clear view of **Ni'ihau**. There is also another small island farther to the north called **Lehua**, which is uninhabited. There appears to be a lower island just beyond Ni'ihau. This, however, is part of the island of Ni'ihau.

Kekaha Town was built by sugar and was a typical and thriving company town for more than 100 years. Many of the plantation-era buildings still remain in and around the mill. Kekaha Sugar celebrated its 100th anniversary in 1998 and the Kekaha Sugar Mill processed its last sugar cane harvest in 2000.

Kekaha Beach Park is a 30-acre stretch of beach with plenty of parking along the highway and restroom facilities. The weather on this side of the island is generally drier, so if you are looking for some sun visit the western coast. (Refer to the beaches chapter for more information on safety conditions for shorelines in this area.)

The nearby **Kikia'ola Harbor** has become increasingly popular because of the regulations that eliminated Hanalei Bay on the North Shore as a tour/cruise boat departure spot. The Corp of Engineers has $4.6 million set aside for renovations over the next few years.

If you continue northwest you will reach the area of the **Barking Sands Airfield** and the **Pacific Missile Range**. This is a naval base with testing facilities that runs along the Mana shore. It is said that in ancient times a Kauaian king was killed at Barking Sands and that today the sand still groans when you rub the pieces between your hands. We tried it. Maybe you will have better luck than we did! Some say that merely walking on the dry sand will cause the same effect. These days, a pass is required to enter the base and use the beaches. It requires a criminal background check, which makes the pass difficult for most visitors to obtain without prior notice.

A huge monkeypod tree in the road with a very unofficial sign will advise you that you are almost to Polihale. You may see some cars parked here. If you choose to stop, be careful your wheels don't become mired in the sand! Then proceed by foot over the dunes to a unique natural formation known as **Queen's Pond**, a lagoon protected within the reef. It can be safe for a cool dip, but only when the surf is calm.

It is another few bumpy and dusty miles along the dirt road before it ends at **Polihale State Park**. (*See* Chapter 5 for recreational opportunities afforded along the Mana coastline of West Kaua'i.) This beach is unsafe for any water activity, but while strolling along the shoreline look closely for the tiny Ni'ihau shells.

If you plan on a visit to Koke'e, it's a good idea to bring along that sweater, sweatshirt or lightweight jacket you packed in your bag. The slightly higher elevation can drop the temperature down a few pleasantly cool degrees. While the weather topside may appear overcast from below the mountain, it can also blow through quickly.

Choosing either Highway 550 from Waimea or Highway 55 from Kekaha, follow the road as it slowly winds up to Waimea Canyon. It is recommended you take an alternate route going back so that you can enjoy the dramatically different scenery each route offers. You might want to take this opportunity to check your gas gauge.

The Koke'e Road from Kekaha, Highway 55, was built in 1911, but is in fact a better road than the road from Waimea. (It is the one used by the tour bus drivers.) The Waimea Canyon Road is much steeper. After about seven miles you will reach the sign for Waimea Canyon State Park. Another .5 mile and the Koke'e Road intersects with the Waimea Canyon Road. Just before mile-marker 9 is the **Kukui Trailhead**. This is one of many trails that riddle the area and offer outstanding day-hiking opportunities. Many are reached by main roads, some are accessible by smaller dirt roads. Another 2.5 miles and the road fork will advise you of the turn-off to either Koke'e Park or Waimea Canyon.

Waimea Canyon State Park provides unsurpassed opportunities for exploration. Follow Waimea Canyon Drive as it winds its way up 12 miles into the interior of the island, hugging the rim of the canyon, for a dramatic panorama. The view of the 3,000-foot-deep canyon is staggering. Hues of orange and red are splashed against the tropical green of 1,866 acres of parkland. Mark Twain aptly described this as the "Grand Canyon of the Pacific." Contiguous with Waimea Canyon is **Koke'e State Park**.

Waimea Canyon Lookout is the first of several lookouts along the way. At an elevation of 3,120 feet, this is a stunning canyon vista. **Pu'u Ka Pele Lookout** is the next stop as you continue to climb. It offers picnic tables and another, slightly different, view of the canyon. **Pu'u Hinahina** is another vista, with a view toward Ni'ihau. Near the entrance to Waimea Canyon Park is the trailhead to the Iliau Nature Log Trail at the Kukui Trailhead. This is a good family hike that follows a short (.3 mile) trail that leads to an overview of the canyon and the waterfall on the far side of the crater. Here you'll find the iliau, a relative of the silversword plants found on Maui at Haleakala National Park and the Big Island of Hawai'i. It grows only on Kaua'i and, like the silversword, blooms with a profusion of blossoms that marks the end of its life.

KOKE'E

The **Koke'e Natural History Museum** is nestled amid one of Kaua'i's most scenic wonders. This museum, the oldest on the island, attracts more than 100,000 visitors each year and is the only museum in Hawai'i open every day of the year at no charge. The museum sponsors two annual festivals: in June it celebrates "The Banana Poka Festival" and in October the "Eo E Emalani I Alaka'i Festival." The museum also sponsors the annual December Audubon Christmas Bird Count as well as an assortment of workshops and year-round interpretive programs and exhibits. You might be interested in becoming a Hui O Laka member. Contact the Koke'e Museum at P.O. Box 100, Kekaha, HI 96752. Phone 808-335-9975, fax 808-335-6131. And check out the Koke'e Museum's Internet homepage with its hiking maps, weather report links and additional information to assist in your travel planning: www.aloha.net/~kokee. The museum store has a good selection of books about Hawai'i's wildlife, natural history and outdoors. The nearby Koke'e Lodge has a dozen housekeeping cabins available for rent to campers, hikers, etc. (*See* Chapter 4 for details.)

Adjacent to the museum is the Koke'e Lodge Café and Gift Shop that provides light breakfasts, lunch and snacks. **Koke'e State Park** offers 45 miles of named hiking trails. The main canyon stretches for 12 miles and drops 3,000 feet. The Canyon Trail leads to the east rim of Waimea Canyon and offers a breathtaking view into its depth. This is an easy trail for even the novice hiker, traversing 1.4 miles. Poomau Canyon Lookout Trail heads through a native rainforest and a series of Japanese plum trees. The 3.25-mile Awa'awapuhi Trail leads through the forest to a 2,500-foot-high vista that overlooks the Napali coast and ocean. Halemanu-Koke'e Trail offers stunning views of the Napali Coast, including Honopu Valley and the Valley of the Lost Tribe.

A short Nature Trail begins at Koke'e Museum and passes through a *koa* forest. The **Alakai Wilderness Preserve** encompasses the Alakai Swamp and is adjacent to Koke'e State Park. The swamp is ten miles long and two miles wide and spans the basin of the caldera. There are pristine nature trails and a boardwalk over the boggy terrain for viewing some of Hawai'i's rarest flora and fauna. The Alakai Swamp Trail passes through bogs and rain forests to the Kilohana Lookout above Hanalei Bay.

Besides hiking, camping and birdwatching for native Hawaiian bird species, Koke'e Park is noted for its wild plum season in late spring–early summer. The Methley plum thrives in Koke'e and when it's in season locals head to the park with bags and baskets to pick the popular fruit.

Continue up Koke'e Road another couple of miles and you will reach the **Kalalau** and **Pu'u o' Kila lookouts**. Kalalau Beach, which lies below along the coast, is that part of Napali that requires an 11-mile hike to reach. On a clear day, this is perhaps the most picturesque location on Kaua'i.

The valley falls below for 4,000 feet and is splashed by waterfalls. *Kaua'i, A Separate Kingdom*, as well as a tale by Jack London, portrays the saga of Ko'olau, his wife, and young son. During the days when leprosy patients were forced to confinement on Moloka'i without their families, Ko'olau and his family fled to this valley. (Several others fled as well, but they were eventually tracked down.) Ko'olau's son Kalei succumbed first to the disease and later Ko'olau died from the affliction. His wife, Piilani, buried him in the wilderness. Never infected with the tragic disease, Piilani returned to Waimea after the deaths of her husband and son and remarried.

North Shore Area

The picturesque beauty of the North Shore is unsurpassed in the Hawaiian Islands. Most of the attractions on this side of Kaua'i revolve around the sights provided by Mother Nature. From botanical gardens to postcard-perfect sunsets on the beach, here you can ignore the hustle and bustle and simply relax. As you take in the famed North Shore area around the small town of Hanalei, you'll see why this region was chosen as background for the many movies and TV programs filmed here over the years. It has the soaring tropical mountain peaks, jungles, beautiful beaches, plunging waterfalls and spectacular coastal panoramas typical of the Pacific islands. It's that appealing look of the mythical Paradise.

KEALIA-ANAHOLA

Following the Kuhio Highway (56) north, at mile-marker 10 you'll see a long stretch of beach that looks pleasant enough, but the water conditions are not safe. The rip currents along this beachfront are very strong. Kealia was another old plantation town and you may still see some of the old plantation buildings that remain. *Kealia* means "salt encrusted," and it was on this beach that early Hawaiians gathered the salt that had evaporated along the beachfront. From Kealia the road moves inland slightly as you continue around toward Kaua'i's North Shore.

Five miles north of Kapa'a, just prior to mile-marker 14, is what most visitors see of the town of **Anahola**—Duane's Ono Burgers. However, I think the better place to eat is across the highway at the expanded Polynesian Hide-a-way & Haw'n Bar-B-Q Chicken, a roadside stand that offers plate lunches and sandwiches, along with fresh roasted macadamia nuts.

A few steps away is Kamaka's, *the* place for shave ice and smoothies. Shave ice starts at $1.50, but splurge and get the big one for $2. (It's great shave ice—soft as cotton candy with no crunchy ice pieces!) For uninitiated mainlanders, a shave ice is a "snow cone," a popular taste treat cooler found throughout the islands. They come in a variety of flavors from strawberry to banana, mango and even more exotic local flavors! Ask for coconut or even *li hing mui* (ask the shave ice shop to explain).

Historically, the hole in the mountain (now partially collapsed) above Anahola on the seaward side carries a legend. It tells that the hole was made by the spear of an early Hawaiian giant. The giant threw it at the king of Kaua'i and missed him, piercing the mountain and leaving behind the hole. And, of course, another version says it was another chieftain who opposed the king and that Kamehameha threw the spear, which went entirely through the rock behind him.

In more recent history, late 1991, Anahola suffered the effects of a severe flood. The heavy rainfall during the night caused the stream to swell and the subsequent flooding came as a surprise to the residents. Not only property but lives were lost as well.

MOLOA'A

Continuing along the road you'll come to Moloa'a, a sleepy community that once was thriving. Prior to the turn of the 20th century, sugar cane and pineapple were booming in this region and so was the

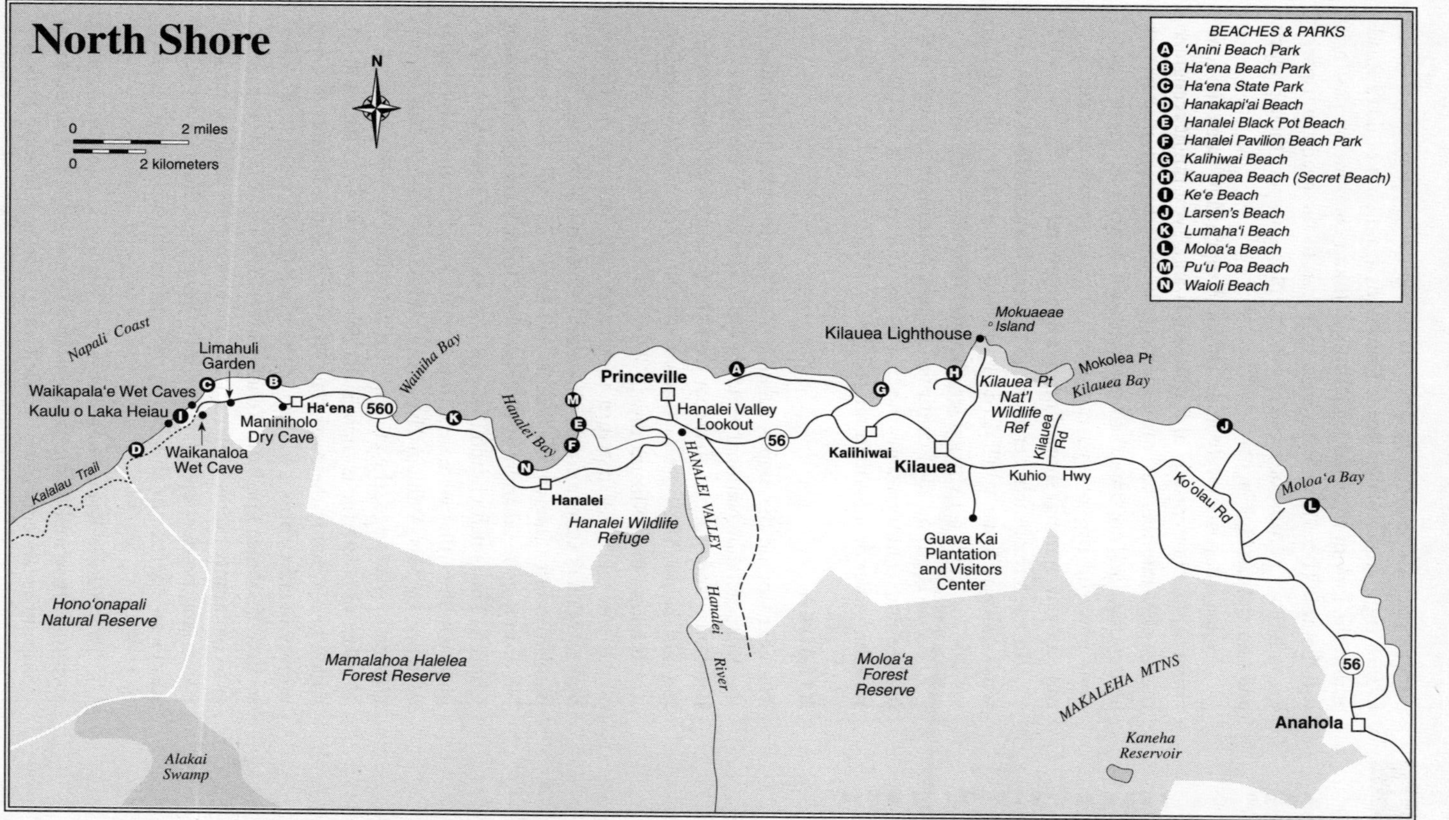
North Shore
N
0
2 miles
0
2 kilometers
BEACHES & PARKS
A 'Anini Beach Park
B Ha'ena Beach Park
C Ha'ena State Park
D Hanakapi'ai Beach
E Hanalei Black Pot Beach
F Hanalei Pavilion Beach Park
G Kalihiwai Beach
H Kauapea Beach (Secret Beach)
I Ke'e Beach
J Larsen's Beach
K Lumaha'i Beach
L Moloa'a Beach
M Pu'u Poa Beach
N Waioli Beach
Napali Coast
Limahuli Garden
Waikapala'e Wet Caves
Kaulu o Laka Heiau
Ha'ena
560
Maniniholo Dry Cave
Waikanaloa Wet Cave
Kalalau Trail
Wainiha Bay
Hanalei Bay
Hanalei
Princeville
Hanalei Valley Lookout
56
Hanalei Wildlife Refuge
HANALEI VALLEY
Hanalei River
Kalihiwai
Kilauea Lighthouse
Mokuaeae Island
Mokolea Pt
Kilauea Bay
Kilauea Pt Nat'l Wildlife Ref
Kilauea Rd
Kilauea
Kuhio Hwy
Guava Kai Plantation and Visitors Center
Ko'olau Rd
Moloa'a Bay
56
Anahola
Hono'onapali Natural Reserve
Mamalahoa Halelea Forest Reserve
Alakai Swamp
Moloa'a Forest Reserve
MAKALEHA MTNS
Kaneha Reservoir

population. Just past mile-marker 16 on Kuhio Highway you'll want to turn right onto Ko'olau Road. Then right again onto Moloa'a Road and at the fork in the road keep to the left and continue on past private homes. There is public access to a trail to the beach, but parking is limited in front of these homes, so please respect their privacy and "no trespassing" signs.

Moloa'a Bay is a lovely inlet. (If you happened to catch the lone airing of the pilot episode of "Gilligan's Island," you might recognize this bay.) While this bay can be especially dangerous during winter and spring surf, anytime there is high surf, dangerous ocean conditions powerful rip currents can occur. During periods of calm, you can enjoy swimming, snorkeling and diving here.

To reach the beaches en route to Kilauea, Ka'aka'aniu Beach (Larsen's) and Wa'iakalua, you'll need to park and take a short walk. Neither are safe for water activities. (*See* Chapter 5 for more information.)

Kuhio Highway (56) continues its trek northward through agriculture and country estates nestled along the foothills of the surrounding interior mountain ranges.

KILAUEA

The next stop on the map is Kilauea. The big attraction in Kilauea is the Kilauea Point National Wildlife Refuge, with its handsome old lighthouse and seabirds that soar over the majestic cliffs and pounding surf below. We'll get to that shortly, but there are a few things worth taking in at Kilauea town.

If you take this first turn to Kilauea onto Ho'okui, you'll find Mango Mama's Cafe, a former juice and smoothie stand that has expanded to offer sandwiches, salads and bagels as well. Take another left onto Kolo Road and you will pass the **Christ Memorial Episcopal Church**. This small church, built of lava rock, has beautiful stained-glass windows that were sent from England and a hand-carved altar designed by Mrs. William Hyde Rice. While the church had its origins many years ago, the current structure dates to 1941.

Just opposite the church is the next major street, Kilauea Road, which heads east to the coast. The **Historic Kilauea Theater & Community Event Center** is located in the Kong Lung Center at the intersection of Kilauea Road and Keneke Street. The historic theater serves as a community events center hosting movies nightly and various local events and productions. The original theater was built in 1930 and was located across the street from the current theater, which was built in 1967.

The historic **Kong Lung Center** in Kilauea is a good place for a stop to browse and shop, or for a refreshment stop. The Kong Lung Company is an emporium housed in a restored historic building.

Products include a selection of unique, "essential luxury" items. They offer Kong Lung's own T-shirts and backpack-style tote bags, swimwear, tableware and lamps. The Kong Lung Co.'s structure dates back to 1860 when it was a two-story wooden building housing the Kilauea Plantation General Store. Around 1918, the Kilauea Sugar Company's plantation manager tore down the old wooden structure. In the early 1940s the plantation rebuilt the structure, using a fieldstone construction method that is unique to Hawai'i, and the Chew "Chow" Lung store reopened as the Kong Lung Store. In the early 1970s, the Kilauea Sugar Company closed and the Kong Lung Center was purchased by local businessmen. The Kong Lung Company was restored to the authentic, plantation-style architecture and design that makes the building historically significant. In 1993, it was placed on the National Register of Historic Places. During the remodel, an old floor-safe was discovered in what is now used as a dressing room. The original butcher's freezer, dating to 1943, is now a large private dressing room. Open 10 a.m. to 10 p.m. daily. 808-828-1822, fax 808-828-1227. **Reinventions**, located up the spiral staircase, has an assortment of new and gently used clothing, with a good selection of inexpensive aloha shirts. 808-828-1125.

At the back of the center is the **Island Soap & Candle Works**, a factory and gift shop that makes and sells tropical scented lotions, soaps and candles. Scented with island fragrances like plumeria, torch ginger or pikake, they are all hand-made using natural ingredients. The "factory" looks like an old-fashioned alchemist or apothecary shop where you can watch soap and candle products being made. 888-528-SOAP; e-mail: soap@aloha.net; www.handmade-soap.com.

On Thursday afternoons and Saturday mornings, local farmers gather near the Kong Lung Store to sell their fresh produce at the **Farmer's Market**. Fresh vegetables, herbs, flowers and fruits are available, and most are organically grown. Look for signs directing you to the Farmer's Market.

Before continuing on to the lighthouse, let's begin with some history and geology about the area. **Kilauea Point** is a remnant of the former Kilauea volcanic vent that last erupted 15,000 years ago. Today, there is only a small U-shaped portion of the vent that remains, which allows for a spectacular view from the 570-foot ocean bluff. The history of the lighthouse began in 1909 when the property was purchased for a $1 token fee from the Kilauea Sugar Plantation Company. The location for the lighthouse was perfectly suited since this grass-covered bluff was surrounded by pounding surf on three sides. Winter swells of 20 feet or more were not uncommon. (We hope you have packed that pair of binoculars!) Work began on the lighthouse in 1912 and was completed in May 1913, with a light shining out to ships 21 nautical miles away. Today the lighthouse is on the National Register of Historic Places. The adjacent visitor center adjacent has displays explaining the seabirds and their sanctuaries.

Established in 1974, the **Kilauea Point National Wildlife Refuge** is recognized as Hawai'i's largest seabird sanctuary, home to more than 5,000 birds. The acquisition of land has continued, with the sanctuary presently encompassing 203 acres. The refuge is a nesting site for the red-footed booby, wedge-tailed shearwater, Laysan albatross and many other species of Hawaiian seabirds. Struck hard by the 1992 hurricane, not only was there damage to the birdlife and vegetation, but the lighthouse was also seriously affected. At Kilauea Point, they reported that about 80 percent of the native plants suffered damage. On Crater Hill at least 25 percent were lost, and an additional 50 percent damaged. Fortunately, Mokolea Point vegetation suffered little damage but Kilauea Point lost the most birds and suffered the worst damage to the habitat. The Kaua'i Natural Wildlife Refuge complex lost several buildings and had general extensive damage. But all is pretty much back to normal and it is an inspiring and peaceful place to visit.

When the lighthouse and support facilities were transferred from the U.S. Coast Guard on February 15, 1985, Kilauea Point became the 425th national wildlife refuge. Over 250,000 visitors enjoy the visitor center and wildlife-viewing areas each year. A two-hour guided Crater Hill hike is offered daily, free with the cost of admission to the refuge. Early reservations are recommended. (Call 808-828-0168, or sign up at the visitor center.) There is an on-going habitat management program that includes water development, native plant propagation, volunteer conservation group and service club, and nursery activities. Over 200 volunteers donate hours to varied refuge projects. The adjacent **Kilauea Point Humpback Whale National Marine Sanctuary** was established in 1994. P.O. Box 87, Kilauea, Kaua'i, HI 96754. Open daily from 10 a.m. to 4 p.m.; closed some federal holidays. 808-828-1413. Admission is $2, by donation.

You need to drive back to the Kuhio Highway (56) through Kilauea town in order to head north toward Princeville.

From the highway on the south edge of town, turn right onto Ho'okui into town or go a little farther and turn right on Kilauea Road at the Shell Gas Station. A short distance past Ho'okui Road on your left you will also find the entrance to **Guava Kai Plantation and Visitors Center**. There are 480 acres of guava orchards under commercial cultivation at Guava Kai Plantation, considered the "Guava Capital" of the world. Visit the plantation's visitor center and discover how guava is grown and processed into a variety of treats.

The Kilauea orchards are in the perfect spot. They receive 100 inches of rainfall each year, with temperate 65- to 80-degree weather that is very agreeable to the crop. During dry months each tree receives up to 75 gallons of water per day. The seedlings in this orchard were planted in 1977 and began producing fruit in 1979. The first commercial yield was in January 1980, with 2,000 pounds per acre harvested. Today the yield is 5,000 pounds per acre, or about 400 pounds of fruit per tree per harvest cycle. The fruit at this plantation is hand-picked and harvested year-round on a full-scale crop cycling system. Guava fruit meat can vary from white or yellow to orange or pink. The variety grown at the Guava Kai Plantation is a hybrid developed by the University of Hawai'i's College of Tropical Agriculture and has a bright pink flesh and an edible rind. The color in your glass of juice is all natural.

There is a self-guided tour of the plantation that includes a view of the orchard and of the processing plants as well as an informative eight-minute video. A manmade fish pond and an assortment of native Hawaiian plants are also here. The snack bar sells ice cream, juice, breads, bakery items and desserts that are made with guava, as well as a variety of other snacks. There are free samples of guava juice, jams, jellies and coffee. Since they are owned by Mauna Loa, they also sell Mauna Loa products at slightly lower rates than retail outlets. Guava Kai Plantation is open daily 9 a.m. to 5 p.m. 808-828-6121.

Back on the highway and continuing north toward Princeville, you'll pass **Banana Joe's**, just outside Kilauea on the *mauka* (mountain) side of the road. A landmark you will definitely want to visit if you have a thirst for a fruit smoothie! Better yet, try a "frostie"—a tropical blend of fresh fruit and nothing but fruit, pureed to the consistency of soft ice cream. Or try your papaya, banana, pineapple or mango yet another way—dried in a dehydrator by Joe's father, "Banana Tom."

At mile-marker 25 you will pass over a bridge and get a view of the Kalihiwai Valley on the *makai* side of the road, and the Kalihiwai

GOODNESS OF GUAVA

Guava has fewer calories and more vitamin C than oranges, and it is also a good source of vitamin A, potassium and phosphorus. Guava is actually not a citrus, but a berry with a fleshy seed cavity and a thick skin. The guava can survive in dry or very tropical conditions. The guava was a native of South America and introduced to the islands in 1791 by the Spaniard Don Francisco de Paula Marin, who was an advisor to Kamehameha I. The guava flourished and many now grow wild in Hawaii.

Falls on both sides of the road. Since you're passing over a narrow bridge you'll need to pull over to one side or the other to stop and get a real look at it. Definitely a great photo opportunity. During the 1957 tsunami, the original bridge was literally lifted up off the foundation and moved 50 to 100 feet upstream. Kalihiwai Falls is actually two falls, and it's on private land, accessible by hike, kayak or horseback.

You'll want to skip the first sign that says Kalihiwai Road; it dead-ends. Two miles past the Kilauea Shell Station and between mile-markers 25 and 26, take the second turn off to Kalihiwai Road down to **'Anini Beach**. A popular windsurfing location, 'Anini can be good for snorkeling during calm surf and it's one of the best beachcombing locations you'll find on the island. The kids will love sifting through the amber sand to find shell treasures! The quiet beachfront community might be an ideal location for a vacation home rental. While the real estate values in this area are sky high, there are some good vacation values available. The beach park here is nicely maintained, with covered pavilions perfect for a picnic lunch. Across the road from the beach they have polo matches each Sunday, beginning late April and running through early fall. There is another birthstone located at 'Anini Beach Park.

Back on Kuhio Highway, just before mile-marker 26, you'll pass the airport on your left and the Princeville Golf Club on your right. The breathtaking golf course vistas offered by the Princeville course may tempt even the non-golfer. Even if you aren't a golfer, you might be interested in their health club or restaurant.

PRINCEVILLE

Suddenly the entrance to Princeville appears on your right with its access to all the hotels and condominiums. The **Princeville Center** is located at this intersection as well. The **Princeville Library** is located adjacent to the Princeville Center. This beautiful facility became the 50th library in the state system. The attractive building blends with the Princeville architecture, but has a sleek, modern interior with state-of-the-art computer services and technology systems. Hours: Tuesday, Thursday, Friday and Saturday 9 to 5, Wednesday 12 to 8, closed Sunday and Monday. 808-826-1545.

The Hanalei area, ringed with gorgeous bays and beaches, has long been a place of beauty and power. In times past, the surrounding area were *kula* lands—land available to the *maka'ainana*, common person, for cultivation and fishing. History provided by the Princeville Resort tells us that "overlooking Hanalei Bay was the plateau, which is now known as Princeville—a place of spiritual power or *mana*. From the Princeville Hotel's present site to Po'oku, just beyond the highway, there is said to have been one of the largest *hala* (pandanus) groves in all Hawai'i. The grove was celebrated in many chants and stories, as *hala* was very important to the Hawaiians. The presence of the tree indicated that there were abundant water sources, and the long leaves provided weaving materials for mats and other household items. Farther up O'oku was one of Kaua'i's largest *heiau*, or temples of worship.

"The site of the hotel was known as *pu'upoa or pu'u pa'oa—pu'u* meaning mountain and *pa'oa* meaning the staff of the fire goddess, Pele, who, when searching for a new home would strike her staff in the earth to create a new crater. Directly below the hotel is a marshy area known as *kamo'omaika'i*, the site of a large fishpond. The Hawaiians were quite adept at raising fish in ponds next to the ocean. There they also built fishing shrines and altars to pay homage to the gods of the reef and the sea. This area, where ancient rockwalls are still visible, is being restored and preserved."

It was in late January of 1815 that the *Behring* went aground at Waimea Bay. The *Behring*, owned by the Russian-American Company, was headed toward Sitka with a load of seal skins when Kaua'i's King Kaumuali'i confiscated the cargo. In 1816, a German named Georg Anton Scheffer was selected by the manager of the Russian-American Company, Alexander Andreievich Baranov, to head to Kaua'i to claim their load of pelts. He arrived in Hawai'i in November of 1815, arriving on Kaua'i in May of 1816. While Scheffer and his forces were prepared to take back their cargo by force, the king returned the cargo as a show of good faith. Kaumuali'i had hopes of an alliance with the Russian Empire but Scheffer had ideas that were slightly different—his plans were to take over the entire island chain for the Russian Empire. He constructed a fort at Waimea Bay in September of that year and named it after the Russian Empress Elizabeth. He then ordered two additional forts be built—one at Hanalei and another in Princeville. His fort on top of Pu'u Poa in Princeville was named Fort Alexander, for Tsar Alexander I. After King Kamehameha learned of his plans to overthrow the government, Scheffer was ordered to depart from the islands. Scheffer made his stand at Pu'u Poa, but failed in his attempt and shortly thereafter sailed to Honolulu, then fled the islands. The grassy area just outside the porte cochere of the Princeville Hotel has the remains of the fort that was made of dirt and clay, a few rocky outcroppings. A kiosk with an interpretative center sits nearby on the plateau and offers a panorama of the Pacific Ocean.

Scottish physician Robert Crichton Wyllie came to Kaua'i in 1844 after making a fortune as a merchant in South America. He had not planned to stay in the islands but was persuaded by King Kamehameha III to accept an appointment as minister of foreign affairs, a post he held for 20 years. Wyllie desired a manor with the opulence and elegance as those found in his Scottish homeland and selected Hanalei as the site. In the early days, taro was raised here. When Wyllie purchased the property it was a coffee plantation, which he converted to a cattle ranch. Later, rice was grown in the area and now it has returned to taro cultivation. In fact, 50 percent of all of Hawai'i's poi comes from taro roots grown here.

The name Princeville was given to this area in the 1860s when Kamehameha IV and his wife Queen Emma, along with their young son, Prince Ka Haku o Hawai'i, visited Wyllie's plantation. Upon his death in 1865, Wyllie bequeathed the estate to a nephew. However, the estate was deeply in debt and the young fellow was so overwhelmed that he committed suicide. In 1867, the land was auctioned off. The area later became a cattle ranch and was then sold in 1968 for resort development. Today the Princeville Resort Community occupies 9,000 acres and is a mix of private homes, vacation rental condominiums, golf courses and the Princeville Resort Hotel.

In 1969, the first major development of the Princeville Resort area began with the state reclassifying 995 acres from agricultural to urban. There were 532 acres zoned for single and multifamily housing and hotel development, and the remaining 463 acres became the Makai Golf Club. The 27-hole golf course opened in July 1971 and by 1973, *Golf Digest* had selected it one of "America's greatest 100 courses."

In 1976, the Princeville Airstrip was completed and provided service until 1997. By 1983 the Princeville Shopping Center had expanded to 66,000 square feet and construction began that same year on the Princeville Resort Hotel. The resort opened in September 1985.

The **Princeville Resort Hotel** is worth stopping by to stroll through the lobby and public areas. With a European flare, this outstanding resort is located on a picture-perfect location. There are gorgeous views across Hanalei Bay and the North Shore area and the surrounding interior mountain peaks. Enjoy afternoon tea in the lobby lounge or plan on splurging for Sunday brunch or the Friday evening seafood buffet at Cafe Hanalei restaurant. (*See* Chapter 3 and Chapter 4 for more information.). It is a very elegant and beautiful hotel with attractive lobby and public areas.

Just past the entrance to Princeville Resort area is the **Princeville Center**. This small but busy shopping center features Chuck's Steak House, Foodland, a medical center and assorted shops that make for interesting strolling. Foodland has a very good deli with hearty sandwiches to take along on your picnic lunch. Hale O'Java serves up a great espresso along with pizza, pasta and sandwiches in their outdoor dining area. There's also a Lappert's Hawaii Ice Cream Shop next to Foodland.

Back on the highway and just past the shopping center on the left is a scenic lookout for the Hanalei Valley and Hanalei Wildlife Refuge. Be sure to pull off here to admire the beautiful panorama and take some photos of the Hanalei Valley and its checkerboard pattern of taro patches filling the valley floor.

HANALEI

The **Hanalei Wildlife Refuge** was established on 917 acres in 1972 and is located in the Hanalei Valley. Unique to many refuges, historic taro farming is allowed on a portion of the property, and another permit is granted for cattle grazing farming. These practices are compatible with the refuge's objectives, and thus are permitted to a limited degree. Administered by the U.S. Fish and Wildlife Service as a unit of the National Wildlife Refuge System, they actively manage the habitat to provide wetlands for endangered Hawaiian waterbirds, including the black-necked stilt, gallinule, coot and duck that make their homes here. Of the 49 species, 18 are introduced. There are no native mammals, reptiles or amphibians, except possibly the Hawaiian bat. The interpretive overlook on the state highway allows an excellent photo opportunity.

About one-half mile past the Wildlife Refuge lookout is another unmarked pull-off along the side of the road. It's worth a stop to get a glimpse of this beautiful valley. At the base of the hill you'll cross the rustic, circa-1912 one-lane bridge into the Hanalei Valley. (The

In 1996, Smithsonian archaeologists began surveying and excavating a wreck underwater in Hanalei Bay at the mouth of the Wai'oli Stream. *Cleopatra's Barge*, a ship that sank April 5, 1824, was once a royal vessel as well as the first ocean-going passenger ship constructed in the U.S. The Crowinshield family had the 100-foot ship built in New England in 1816 at a cost of $50,000. In 1820 the ship was sold to Liholiho (King Kamehameha II) in trade for $80,000 worth of sandalwood and was renamed *Ha'aheo o Hawai'i*, or the *Pride of Hawai'i*. Four years after the purchase, the royal yacht ran aground on a reef and sank (reportedly the captain and crew were drunk when the ship broke free from its moorings). The team was ready to terminate the search when a massive hull timber was located. Further excavation will continue. The current research is supported by the Kaua'i Historical Society and the Princeville Resort Hotel.

bridge is periodically closed for hours or even days when heavy rains cause the river to rise and partially submerge it.) You can imagine why Peter, Paul and Mary chose this magical place for their enchanted dragon, *Puff*, although they distorted the name slightly—no doubt for better lyrical flow. Look to the mountains for the many small waterfalls that glisten down the cliffs. The Hanalei River is a popular location for kayaking.

At the first stop in Hanalei town are a couple of shops that merge with the Hanalei Dolphin, one of the area's more popular restaurants. **Kai Kane** offers some interesting selections of aloha wear for gentlemen and ladies. Upstairs you'll find surf equipment for sale. The adjoining **Ola's** has glassware and other unusual gift items.

Hanalei means "crescent shaped." The **Hanalei Pier** is a scenic location, and one you'll no doubt remember it if you saw the movie *South Pacific*. The wooden pier was constructed in 1892 and then 30 years later was reinforced with concrete. It was used by local farmers for shipping their rice until it was closed in 1933. In 1979, the pier joined other landmarks in the National Register of Historic Places. To actually reach the Hanalei Pier and the parking areas along Hanalei Bay turn right on Aku Road or on Malalo Road. Both take you down to Weke Road, which runs parallel to the bay.

Continuing through the town of Hanalei you'll find an assortment of restaurants and shops to meet most of the visitors' needs. One notable shop, aptly named **On the Road to Hanalei**, offers gifts and unique items from the Pacific. Right next door is **Evolve Love Artists Gallery**, which has taken over from the Hawaiian Artists Guild. It features the multimedia work of many Kaua'i artists.

At the **Ching Young Center** you'll find a variety store, natural foods store, pizza restaurant and a Big Save Market that has a Subway inside.

Check out Paradise Adventures, operated by Byron and Dot Fears. They are former activity operators and now operate a gift shop and book island activities as well as B&Bs and vacation rentals (over 75 guest lodgings); 808-826-9999 or 888-886-4969, fax 808-826-9998, e-mail: whales@aloha.net or website www.paradise-adventures.com.

Across the street, the old **Hanalei school**, built in 1926 and listed in the National Register of Historic Places, has been converted to art and clothing shops and the Hanalei Gourmet café.

Adjoining is the Hanalei Center, where you'll find Bambo Bamboo and Neide's Salsa & Samba, a small Mexican/Brazilian eatery. Fronting the complex is the old Hanalei Coffee Company, Shave Ice Paradise and Bubba's burgers. Perhaps the most interesting shop is **Yellowfin Trading**. It is tucked in the back, a little harder to find, but worth the hunt. They have Hawaiiana collectibles and antiques along with some unusual gift items.

Following the road through town, you will pass the green **Wai'oli Church** and the **Wai'oli Mission House**. Wai'oli Mission House is open to the public Tuesday, Thursday and Saturday. Listed in the National Register of Historic Places, the home is open between 9 a.m. and 2:45 p.m. The original coral church was built in 1837 with Reverend William Alexander the first clergyman on the North Shore. In 1846, Abner and Lucy Wilcox arrived here as missionaries, and while the church was founded in 1834, the present green and white Wai'oli Church was not built until 1921. The Wilcox family established themselves on the North Shore and it was Abner and Lucy's three granddaughters who initiated the restoration of the church in 1921. The one-hour guided tour is taken on a walk-in basis with donations welcomed at the end of the visit. Sunday services performed in English and Hawaiian are fascinating. To tour the property for groups of 12 or more, please write or call in advance. Grove Farm in Lihu'e operates the tours here. Call them at 808-245-3202 for more information and reservations; Grove Farm, P.O. Box 1631, Lihu'e, HI 96766.

The **Hanalei Farmers Market** is held each Saturday morning at the Hanalei Community Center next to the soccer playing fields by the Wai'oli Church, Kuhio Highway at Malolo Street. There are various local farmers and backyard gardeners from the area selling fresh fruits, veggies and various other produce. It's a good place to pick up fresh bananas, papaya and whatever else might be in season. Free parking available.

The **Lumaha'i Valley** was once populated with Hawaiians. But it was the Japanese who farmed the first taro. Later immigrants cultivated rice. The 23-square-mile area is now used for cattle grazing.

Another landmark in Hanalei is poised along the side of the Kuhio Highway at the former Hawaiian Tel switching station. An enormous **poi pounder**, which began as a 1,500-pound boulder, now graces the frontyard of the Hanalei Poi Company. Partners Beno Fitzgerald and Hobey Beck plan to produce enough poi to saturate the Kaua'i market, processing 2,000 to 4,000 pounds of taro a week, and increasing as demand improves! Check the local grocery stores and markets for fresh Hanalei Poi.

The next few miles are dotted with one-lane bridges, but just before mile-marker 5 is the lookout to **Lumaha'i Beach**. The east end of Lumaha'i Beach, Kahalahala (which means "pandanus trees"), is where Mitzi Gaynor was filmed in her famous "wash that man right out of my hair" scene in *South Pacific*. At mile-marker 5 there is a very small pullout along the road that offers an unbeatable photo opportunity. The state acquired the land immediately behind the beach so public access and improvements may be in store but don't look for changes real soon.

Wainiha Beach is a known shark-breeding ground and not recommended for swimming or water activities. Pass the Wainiha "Last Chance" store and pick up a cold drink or sandwich. It was in this valley in the 19th century that 65 persons reported their ethnicity as "menehune."

A few miles beyond Wainiha Beach is **Powerhouse Road**: just before mile-marker 7, you'll see a road sign and road turn-off that climbs inland through the valley. The road travels through some beautiful, not-to-be-missed scenery and ends at the Powerhouse. Built in 1906, it served to provide irrigation for the McBryde Sugar Company.

HA'ENA

Ha'ena marks the last vestige of civilization. Camp Naue, a four-acre camp operated by the YMCA, is located between the 7 and 8 mile markers.

Mile-marker 8 indicates you have reached **Makua Beach**. You will probably see cars parked alongside the main road and on a short sandy side road. Makua is one of the most popular beaches on the North Shore and is commonly referred to as Tunnels Beach. You can also park down at Ha'ena Beach Park and walk down to Tunnels. While this is among the safest beaches on the North Shore and offers fair snorkeling, there can be strong rip currents even during small surf.

Throughout the North Shore area, you will notice that many of the houses are up on concrete stilts. This area was struck hard by the tsunamis of 1946 and 1957. The stilts make for a long walk up to carry groceries and anything else, but gives homeowners the added benefit of obtaining limited homeowners insurance. Whether this precaution will serve its purpose should another tsunami strike the area will hopefully never be tested.

Ha'ena Beach Park is a five-acre park maintained by the County of Kaua'i. The foreshore here is steep and therefore the dangerous shorebreak makes it inadvisable for swimming or bodysurfing. Although you may see some bodysurfing done here, it is not for novices.

Across the road from Ha'ena Beach Park is **Maniniholo Dry Cave**. This lava tube was a sea cave in earlier centuries when the sea was higher. You can travel several hundred yards and emerge at the other end. We were told that the cave was larger before it was filled in with sand by the tsunami that hit the island in 1957. Maniniholo Dry Cave, according to one legend, was created by *menehune* who had caught a great quantity of fish. There were too many fish to take them all home in one trip so they carried as many as they could to their home in the mountain, planning to return later for the rest of their catch. When they returned they discovered the remaining fish had been stolen. The *menehune* noticed a small hole in the mountain, a clue to the path that the fish thieves had taken. They proceeded to dig out the thieves and the result was this dry cave. Another legend credits the goddess Pele, who traveled along the Napali coast searching for fire in the earth. She fell in love with Lohiau, the high chief of Kaua'i, but the couple could not be together until Pele found fire beneath Kaua'i so she began to dig in search of it. She was unsuccessful and left Lohiau to go to the island of Hawai'i. The "caves" were the result of her efforts. The inner room was used as a meeting chamber by chieftains.

Limahuli Garden is one of three gardens on Kaua'i that are a part of the National Tropical Botanical Garden and is open to the public. It is located .7 of a mile from Ha'ena Park and is well marked with a sign and a Hawaii Visitors Bureau marker. This magnificent site, surrounded by towering mountains and breathtaking natural beauty, receives from 80 to more than 200 inches of rain annually. Within Limahuli Valley are two important ecosystems—the lowland rain forest and the mixed mesophytic forest. Together these two ecosystems are the natural habitat of over 70 percent of Kaua'i's (59 percent of Hawai'i's) endangered plant species. Thus, Limahuli Garden is vitally important as a botanical and horticultural resource. The Garden emphasizes rare and endangered plants of Hawai'i, as well as plants of ethno-botanical value. Limahuli Garden is also a part of an archaeologically significant site known as the Limahuli complex. The entire area has a rich history, and a series of ancient stone terraces, believed to be well over 700 years old, are visible at the garden. The oldest taro patches in Hawai'i are also located here.

Limahuli Garden encompasses 17 acres, and was gifted to the NTBG by Juliet Rice Wichman in the mid-1970s. An additional 990 acres behind the garden are set aside as a natural preserve. In 1994 the gardens were opened up to tours on a limited basis. In the future there is the possibility that they may open up a trail to the 800-foot Limahuli Falls. Guided tours are currently available only by reservation and at a fee of $15. Self-guided tours include a descriptive booklet and the cost is $10 per person. It's well worth the admission as it's a very scenic, serene park, with beautiful tropical plants that are well-managed. And the surrounding mountain scenery is inspiring. Currently open Tuesday through Friday and Sundays from 9:30 a.m. to 4 p.m. There's a gift shop that features books, posters and shirts. Parking area and restroom facilities are available. Picnic lunches are prohibited. 808-826-1053.

Just beyond Limahuli Stream are the **Waikapala'e Wet Caves**, accessible by a short hike up and behind the gravel parking area. One of the caves has a freshwater pool and is a unique phenomenon. The

Waikapala'e (the name is commonly thought to mean "water of the lace fern") Wet Cave has a cool shady cave known as the blue room. It requires a venture into the chilly waters and, depending on the water height, possibly an underwater swim through a submerged tunnel. This is one adventure we have yet to try, but we are told it is an inspiring experience. (Be cautious, however: many drownings or near-drownings have occurred here.) Apparently the reflection of the light through the tunnel causes the incredible blue effect on the cavern walls. The second wet cave, the Waikanaloa Cave, is located roadside. This cave is saltwater and not suitable for swimming.

Ke'e Beach is the end of your scenic drive (mile-marker 10). Currently there's no lifeguard service here and sometimes there are dangerous water conditions. Swimming and snorkeling are only recommended during very calm conditions and then you should use common sense. Above the beach, a walk of about 5 or 10 minutes will take you to remnants of ancient Hawaiian villages and the **Kaulu o Laka Heiau**. This sacred altar is set among the cliffs of Napali and was built for Laka, the goddess of hula. It is one of the dramatic sites on the island with views of the cliffs and ocean.

The people of Nu'alolo Kai also left remnants of their shelters. The sandstone slabs were probably used as foundations for a pole and thatch house. The people that lived in this area were agricultural. There is a low boggy area that may have grown taro. The reef fringing the area provide plenty of fish and shellfish for the inhabitants. The Bishop Museum conducted excavations in the area for five years, beginning in 1959. They determined that this area had been continuously inhabited from 1380 until 1919. The *heiau* is still used today by hula *halaus*.

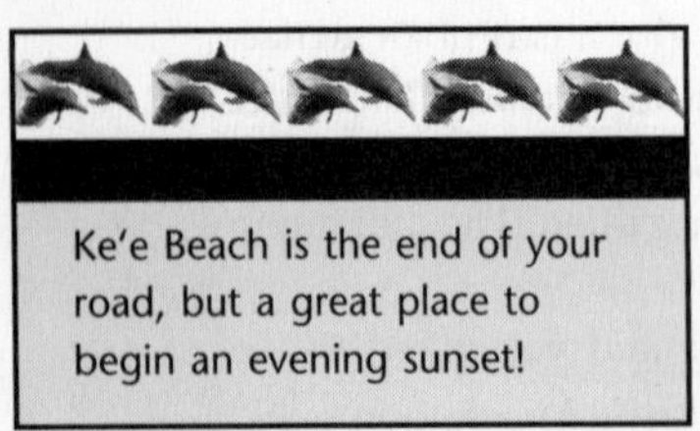

Ke'e Beach is the end of your road, but a great place to begin an evening sunset!

Beyond Ke'e is the **Napali Coast**, 11 miles of which are accessible by foot along the **Kalalau Trail**. (*Note*: I believe the correct spelling is Napali, not Na Pali, as verified by Hawaiian linguist and historian Mary Kawena Pukui.) (*See* Chapter 6 for a brief description of this scenic trail. There is a charge of $10 per person per day for use of campgrounds along the Kalalau Trail. See the camping section for details).

While some have remarked that this is the most beautiful trail in the world, be forewarned that the Sierra Club rates the 11-mile hike to the Kalalau Valley as a "ten" on their scale of difficulty. The shorter hike to Hanakapi'ai is a partial day-hike and more suited to the recreational hiker.

CHAPTER 3

Where to Stay

Kaua'i has considerable variety in lodging and accommodations in each budget category for visitors. Among your choices for lodging are self-contained, full-service, luxury resorts; hotels of all different sizes, with varying amenities and prices; bed-and-breakfast operations; time-share units; condominiums; hostels; lodges; bungalows; cottages; and dozens, if not hundreds, of vacation rentals that run the gamut from opulent beachfront homes to tiny studios located in the interior. All told, the island probably has well over 7,000 vacation units available for rent, although an exact figure is currently unknown.

The island can easily be divided into three main areas, along with some sub-areas: **East Shore and Central Coast Area**, which encompasses the region from Lihu'e to Anahola; the **South and West Shore Areas**, which comprise Po'ipu Beach, Koloa, Lawa'i, Kalaheo, 'Ele'ele, Hanapepe, Waimea, Kekaha and Koke'e; and the **North Shore Area**, which runs from Haena to Moloa'a and includes Princeville and Hanalei.

Bed and breakfasts are a booming business and an alternative that has become increasingly popular over the years. Kaua'i has a variety of economy to luxury-class B&B units around the island. The last several years have seen a rapidly expanding B&B segment in Kaua'i's hospitality industry. Whereas previously there were only a handful of such operations scattered around the island, now B&B lodgings can actually be found in just about every area. Visitors seek out B&B lodging because of the more-personalized service and experience. B&Bs often put visitors more in touch with residents who can provide unique and special insight into Kaua'i's local culture, activities, etc.—making a vacation experience that much more meaningful.

Traditionally B&B means a room in a private home, usually with a shared entrance and bath. Such rooms generally average about $55 a night. Other B&Bs, cottages, inns, condos and studios with private entrances and/or baths—more aptly called vacation rentals—range from $60 to $200 a night depending on quality, features and amenities provided. Bed & Breakfast operations are sprinkled all around the island. They are listed within each respective area as a separate group.

Also included at the conclusion of this chapter are several of the Bed & Breakfast agencies that handle many more homes than was possible to include in this volume. Related websites have been listed where available. Refer to "Rental Agents" at the conclusion of this chapter. Note that very few bed-and-breakfast facilities accept any type of charge cards. Some also do not allow young children for various reasons.

For ease in locating information, the properties are indexed alphabetically at the end of the book (*see Lodging Index*). In each of the three different geographical areas, we have divided the condominiums and listed them in order of price and then alphabetized them for quick reference.

THINGS TO KNOW ABOUT USING THIS CHAPTER

Often the management at the property takes reservations, but some do not. In some cases there are several rental agents handling units in addition to the on-site management and we have listed an assortment of these. We suggest that when you determine which condo you are interested in that you call *all* of the agents. Be aware that while one agent may have no vacancy, another will have several. The prices we have listed are generally the lowest available (although some agents may offer lower rates with the reduction of certain services, such as maid service on check-in only rather than daily maid service). You may find that one of the package options (air-condo-car) will be an all-around better value than booking each separately.

THINGS TO CONSIDER

- Remember when calling Hawai'i to adjust for the time difference. Most offices are open during business hours, Hawai'i standard time, and some only on weekdays. Bed-and-breakfast homes would no doubt appreciate calls during the afternoon or evening (Hawaiian time).
- Keep in mind that in providing directions, we may refer to the Hawaiian terms of *mauka*, which means toward the mountains, and *makai*, which means toward the ocean. On these islands it is much less cumbersome to use this form of indicating direction than the standard north, east, south and west.

Prices are listed to aid your selection, and while these were the most current available at press time, they are subject to change without notice. As island vacationers ourselves, we found it important to include this feature rather than just giving you broad categories such as budget or expensive. After all, one person's "expensive" may be "budget" to someone else.

For the sake of space, we have made use of several abbreviations. The size of the condominiums are identified as studio (S BR), one bedroom (1BR), two bedroom (2BR), and three bedroom (3BR). The number in parentheses refers to the number of people that can occupy the unit for the price listed and that there are enough beds for a maximum number of people to occupy this unit, i.e., 2BR (max. 4). The description will tell you how much it will be for additional persons over two, i.e., $10/night. Some facilities consider an infant an extra person, others allow children free up to a specified age. The abbreviations *o.f.*, *g.v.*, *o.v.* and *m.v.* refer to oceanfront, gardenview, oceanview and mountainview units. Some of the prices may be listed with a slash dividing them. The first price listed is the high-season rate, the second price is the low-season rate. More and more properties are going to a flat all-season rate. A few include the summer months as high season, and a few others have complicated matters by having a three-season fee schedule. Websites for rental agencies, hotel/resorts and individual properties have been provided where available. It is recommended that websites be checked for the latest rates as well as specials.

All listings are condominiums or vacation homes unless specified as a Hotel or Bed and Breakfast. Condos are abundant and the prices and facilities they offer can be quite varied. We have tried to indicate our own personal preferences by the use of a ★. We felt these were the best buys or were special in some way. However, it is impossible for us to view all the units within a complex, and since condominiums are privately owned, each unit varies in its furnishings and condition.

WHERE TO STAY?

As for choosing the area of the island in which to stay, we offer these suggestions:

East Shore and Central Coast Area: This region, affectionately known as the "Coconut Coast," is where you'll find the best selection of affordable and family accommodations. Centrally located, you can easily drive to either the South Shore/West Side or North Shore for the activities they offer. This is the island's major population center, as well, so you'll find lots of options available for activities, attractions, dining, shopping and lodging.

South Shore and West Shore Areas: Along the South and West shores you'll find it typically sunny and warm; the Po'ipu area generally has the best beach conditions, but the Hanapepe, Waimea and Kekaha areas are also very pleasant. In winter, the South Shore beaches are usually safer. The region has varied attractions such as Waimea—the Grand Canyon of the Pacific; Port Allen—cruise boats to the Napali Coast; Koke'e State Park; and many activity, lodging and dining choices.

North Shore Area: If you want incredible scenery and lots of lush green vegetation, then the North Shore may be for you. You can choose between luxury and moderate accommodations. The Anahola, Kilauea, Princeville and Hanalei areas have varied attractions, activities and lodging choices available. During the winter months, high surf can make the North Shore ocean conditions very dangerous, and all the greenery means rain is more abundant than elsewhere on the island.

HOW TO SAVE MONEY

Kaua'i has two price seasons: high, or "in-season," and low, or "off-season." Low season is generally considered to be April 15 to about December 15, and the rates are discounted at some places as much as 30 percent. Different resorts and condominiums may vary these dates by as much as two weeks, and a few resorts are going to a year-round rate. Ironically, some of the best weather is during the fall when temperatures are cooler than summer and there is less rain than the winter and spring months. (*See* "Weather" in Chapter 1 for year-round temperatures.)

If you are staying longer than one week, a condo unit with a kitchen can result in significant savings on your food bill. There are several large grocery stores around the island with fairly competitive prices, although most things at the store will run about 30 percent higher than on the mainland since nearly everything is shipped in. (*See* "Grocery Shopping" in Chapter 1.) Condos will also give you more space than a hotel room, but you may give up some resort amenities (shops, restaurants, maid service, etc.).

Most condominiums offer maid service only upon check-out. A few might offer it twice a week or weekly. Additional maid service may be available for an extra charge. Many vacation rental units also charge a cleaning fee. A few condos do not provide in-room phones, and a few don't have pools.

A few words of caution: Condominium units within one complex can differ greatly. If a phone or other amenity is important to you, ask. Some condos may offer free local calls while others tack on an extra fee per local call. Many have microwaves in their kitchens. Some units have washers and dryers in the rentals, while others do not. If there are no in-room laundry facilities, you will generally find that most have coin-operated laundry facilities on the premises.

Travel agents will be able to book your stay in the Kaua'i hotels and also in most condominiums. If you prefer to make your own reservation, we have listed the various contacts for each condominium and endeavored to quote the best prices available. A little phone work can be very cost effective!

We have indicated toll-free 800, 888, 877 or 866 numbers for the U.S. when available. Some toll-free numbers are not valid from Canada or for interisland calls. For additional Canadian toll-free numbers, check the rental agent list at the end of this chapter.

You might also check the classified ads in your local newspaper for owners offering units for rent, which may be an even better bargain.

Although prices can jump, most go up only 5 to 10 percent per year. You'll need to add sales tax of 4 percent plus a transient accommodations tax (currently 7.25 percent) to the prices listed. Also check the individual rental agency or hotel/condo websites for the most current room rates and discount or seasonal specials, room/car packages, senior discounts.

GENERAL POLICIES Condominium complexes require a deposit (usually equivalent to one or two nights stay) to secure your reservation and insure your room rate against price increases. Some charge higher deposits during winter or over the Christmas holiday. Generally, a 30-day notice of cancellation is needed to receive a full refund. Most require payment in full either 30 days prior to arrival or upon arrival, and some do not accept credit cards. Night owls beware! Many condos have early check-out times—often 11 a.m. (or even 10 a.m.), although some compensate by providing an earlier check-in time of 2 p.m. (instead of 3 p.m.). The usual minimum condo stay is three nights, with some requiring one week in winter.

Christmas holidays may have steeper restrictions, with minimum stays as long as two weeks, payments 90 days in advance and heavy cancellation penalties. It is not uncommon to book as much as two years in advance for the Christmas season.

All condominiums have kitchens, TVs and pools unless otherwise specified. Most condominiums have ceiling fans, but many do not have air conditioning, although you generally don't need it because of cooling breezes. After arriving from a long flight with a car full of luggage, one of the most unpleasant surprises may be to discover that you are on the third floor of a condominium complex that does *not* have an elevator. A surprising number of multilevel complexes are equipped only with stairs. That's another good reason to travel light!

Monthly and oftentimes weekly discounts are available. Room rates quoted are generally for two people. An additional person runs $10 and up per night per person, with the exception of the luxury resorts and hotels where it may be as high as $25 to $35 per person. Many complexes can arrange for crib rentals. (*See* Chapter 1.)

Variations in prices may be due to the amenities of a particular unit or the general condition of the condo. When contacting condominium complexes by mail, be sure to address your correspondence to the attention of the manager. The managers of several complexes do not handle any reservations, however, so we have indicated to whom you should address reservation requests. If two addresses are given, use the P.O. Box rather than street address for your correspondence since many communities on the island do not get home delivery.

Lodging Best Bets

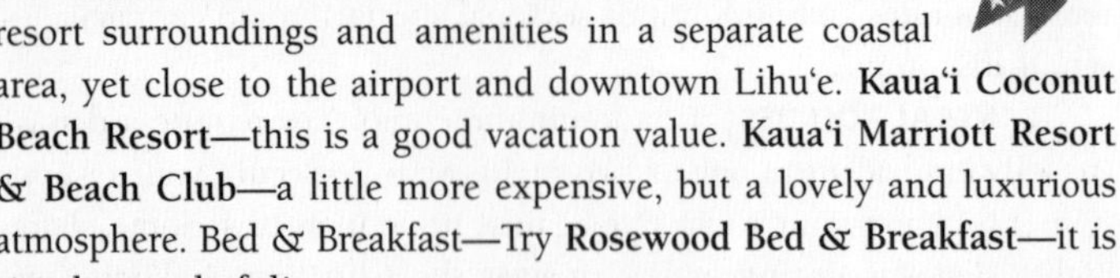

EAST SHORE AND CENTRAL COAST AREA Banyan Harbor or **Garden Island Inn**—convenient and inexpensive. **Radisson Kaua'i Beach Hotel** and **Aston Kaua'i Beach Villas**—resort surroundings and amenities in a separate coastal area, yet close to the airport and downtown Lihu'e. **Kaua'i Coconut Beach Resort**—this is a good vacation value. **Kaua'i Marriott Resort & Beach Club**—a little more expensive, but a lovely and luxurious atmosphere. Bed & Breakfast—Try **Rosewood Bed & Breakfast**—it is simply wonderful!

SOUTH AND WEST SHORE AREAS **Po'ipu Kai**—several buildings on a large property with nice condo accommodations that are value-priced. **Hyatt Regency Kaua'i**—a lovely, tropical resort. **Whalers Cove**—a more expensive but a first-class condominium in an ideal location. **Embassy Vacation Resort–Po'ipu Point**—spacious and elegant with all the amenities of a resort and a condominium combined. **Kiahuna Plantation**—well located, a beautiful upscale property with plenty of amenities. **Koloa Landing Cottages**—located near the beach in Po'ipu—very clean, comfortable and economical accommodations. Recommended B&Bs: **Po'ipu Plantation Resort**—conveniently located in heart of Po'ipu Resort area, close to beach and activities, cottage units a great value, too. Also **Marjorie's Kauai Inn**—a great value.

NORTH SHORE AREA **Princeville Resort**—elegantly wonderful, what an ideal way to enjoy Paradise! **Sealodge**—affordable with an incredible view of the Kilauea lighthouse. **Hanalei Bay Resort**—multiple amenities with views of Bali Hai and a lagoon swimming pool. **Hanalei Colony Resort**—a very pleasant resort with a fantastic location near the end of the North Shore road, great beaches, great mountain views, great peace and quiet, superb location. **North Country Farms**—a wonderful B&B/cottage set-up that's perfect for families.

East Shore and Central Coast Area

PRIVATE VACATION HOMES & COTTAGES

Anahola Beach House and Studios

4194 Anahola Road, Anahola, HI 96703, mailing address P.O. Box 609, Anahola, HI 96703. Fax 808-821-9032; e-mail: info@alohavacation rentals.com; www.alohavacationrentals.com/alohaloha.

The Anahola Beach House and Studios are located on beautiful Anahola Bay, with its miles of sandy beaches that provide one of Kaua'i's longest stretches of coastal walking beach. The bay is partially sheltered by offshore reefs, making for great swimming, snorkeling, fishing, boogie-boarding, and surfing conditions. The Beach House has superb views of the bay. Special features include surround-sound theater, hot tub, computer controlled lighting, and stereos in every room. The house is fully furnished for luxurious vacation living. There is a romantic master bedroom suite with a bathtub for two, a huge private deck, hardwood floors, two sleeper sofas in living room, spacious kitchen, hot tub, patio deck and all the amenities. The Beach House is a modified A-frame. The only thing between the house and the beach is the front lawn. The Hibiscus and Plumeria studios are self-contained units with all the amenities for a comfortable stay.

Rates: Beach House: $320 nightly for 2 people, extra person $40; $2,000 weekly, extra person $200. Studios: $75 nightly, $450 weekly and $1,400 monthly

Anahola Cottage

4488 Aliomanu Road, P.O. Box 493, Anahola, HI 96703. 808-822-4691 or 808-639-0389; fax 808-822-3591; e-mail: flo@aloha.net; www.vrbo.com/ vrbo/2425.htm.

This bright, clean, airy and spacious studio cottage, tucked under an umbrella of monkeypod trees, is a lazy 10-minute stroll down a winding, tree-lined country road to a beautiful white-sand beach. The unit is comfortably furnished with island-style decor, has a full kitchen, queen bed, ceiling fan, TV/VCR, CD player, telephone, washer-dryer and lanai with meadow view. It's just a 10-minute drive to Kapa'a town activities, shopping and dining. The host is a licensed massage therapist.

Rates: $90 nightly; $560 weekly

Anuenue Plantation Cottage

P.O. Box 226, Kapa'a, HI 96746-0226. 808-823-8335; 888-371-7716; fax 808-821-0390; e-mail: cottage@anuenue.com; www.anuenue.com/ cottage.

This is a comfortable, smoke-free one-bedroom cottage with full kitchen, living and dining areas, laundry and full bath. The bedroom opens to a lanai and has queen bed. TV/VCR, telephone available. Enjoy the panoramic tropical mountain and ocean views, waterfalls, rainbows, birds, sunsets and star-filled skies from this modern and private ridgetop cottage.

Rates: $95 nightly; discount on weekly rates

Hale Kaulana

P.O. Box 131, Lihu'e, HI 96766. 808-822-7023 or 808-634-6490; e-mail: jti@hawaiian.net; www.vrbo.com/vrbo/517.htm.

This comfortable unit is on a two-acre agricultural estate in a rural valley in the Wailua Homesteads area. It's just 7 minutes from the beach and amenities of Kapa'a town, but feels a world away. The 2-bedroom, 1-bath cottage sleeps four; full kitchen, A/C, TV/VCR, laundry; there are two kayaks available for guest use. Enjoy watching the horses and goats graze the surrounding pastures, and soak in the hot tub under the beautiful dark sky filled with stars. $100 cleaning fee.

Rates: $90 nightly (three-night minimum)

Hale O' Wailele

Mailing address 41-648 Kalanianaole Highway, Waimanalo, HI 96795. 800-775-2824; fax 808-259-6397; e-mail: kahuna@aloha.net; www.planet-hawaii.com/kahuna.

The "House of Leaping Waterfalls" is a luxurious home located on a tropical flower plantation. It's an appropriate name as the home is located at the foot of the Makaleha Mountains with unobstructed views of the waterfalls that drop off the cliffsides of these tropical mountains. This secluded three-bedroom, two-bath home offers comfortable, upscale accommodations and many amenities. Hale O' Wailele is beautifully furnished and decorated throughout with Hawaiian art, collectibles and an array of tropical flowers freshly cut from the fields of the plantation. Guest amenities include a waterfall swimming pool, two jacuzzis, gym, mountain bikes and a variety of beach and hiking gear. It's only minutes away from Kapa'a town and nearby beaches, shopping, restaurants and area activities. Suites have all amenities for relaxing vacation stay. House sleeps 6 adults.

Rates: $250 nightly for couples, honeymooners; $350 for the entire house

Kaleialoha Oceanfront Accommodations

4936 Aliomanu Road, P.O. Box 687, Anahola, HI 96703. 808-822-3000; 888-311-5252; fax 808-823-6363; e-mail: essie@hawaiian.net.

This oceanfront accommodation has varied units available and is on Kaua'i's beautiful and secluded northeast coast. There is a cozy Hawaiian bungalow ("Da Fish Shack"), a two-bedroom/two-bath upstairs unit ("Kahalekai Iluna"), a one-bedroom/one-bath upstairs unit ("Hibiscus Hale Lani") and a downstairs studio ("Hibiscus Hale Honua").

Rates: $70 to $160 nightly

Makaleha Mountain Retreat

7124A Kahuna Road, Kapa'a, HI 96746. 808-822-5131; e-mail: makaleha 007@hotmail.com; www.makaleha.com.

This is a secluded two-bedroom/one-bath cedar home at the base of the Makaleha Mountains and provides some spectacular waterfall views and sweeping landscape views. They also have a separate garden studio located in a citrus grove. It's just minutes from Kapa'a town shopping, dining, area activities and beaches. Three-night minimum stay.

Rates: Cedar Home $135 nightly; Garden Studio $60 nightly; extra person $15

Makana Crest

P.O. Box 3671, Lihu'e, HI 96766. 808-245-6500 and in Seattle, WA, at 206-242-4866; e-mail: mokihana@hawaiian.net; www.travel-kauai.com/ makanacres.

Located behind Sleeping Giant Mountain in a quiet country setting just eight minutes from beaches, town areas, etc. This cottage is 750 square feet with two furnished bedrooms and a bathroom with a shower; sleeps four. One bedroom has a queen bed, the other twins. A microwave, dishwasher, basic utensils included in the kitchen, and cable TV provided. The guest cottage is on the acreage of the owner's home. The property is landscaped with citrus and macadamia trees and a fish pond. The view features 5,000-foot Mt. Wai'ale'alae Crater. Easy access to all area activities, beaches, shopping, dining, etc. And they can even arrange a wedding.

Rates: $100 per day (three-day minimum) or $500 per week

Paradise Found

c/o Marissa Henderson, General Delivery, Anahola, HI 96703. 808-821-1567; 877-489-9197; fax 808-821-1560; e-mail: paradise@rfreedom.com; www.rfreedom.com.

This secluded honeymoon studio is located at the end of the valley road, at the beach, on Moloa'a Bay. It's in the center of a beautiful crescent bay and next to the river flowing into the bay. There's a white-sand beach around the bay and lots of marine life to spot—like whales, dolphins, turtles and an occasional monk seal. The unit has a private entry and lanai, king bed, full kitchen and bath. Quiet, except for the surf on the shoreline, and away from it all.

Rates: $150 nightly; $950 weekly

Plantation Retreat

6538 Kahuna Road, Kapa'a, HI 96746. 808-822-7832; e-mail: bananas@aloha.net; www.plantationretreat.com.

This secluded accommodation is in a lush ten-acre tropical jungle setting. The "Riverview Cottage" hangs on a cliff overlooking a rushing river. There are swimming holes, rope swings, waterfalls, caves, hiking trails and the famous 50-foot-tall tree growing out of the bathroom—the only one of its kind on the island! This environmentally friendly cottage also has a jacuzzi. Other units include the main "Polynesian Plantation House" and the secluded "Rainforest Cottage." Guests have use of mountain bikes, boogie boards, snorkels, masks and tubes.

Rates: Riverview Cottage $85 nightly, $570 weekly; Rainforest Cottage $85 nightly, $570 weekly; Plantation House $95 nightly, $640 weekly

BED AND BREAKFASTS

Alohilani Bed & Breakfast Inn

1470 Wana'ao Road, Kapa'a, HI 96746. Tel/fax 808-823-0128; 800-533-9316; e-mail: alohila@hawaiian.net; www.hawaiian.net/~alohila.

Hosts Sharon Mitchell and William Whitney offer their home, which takes its name from the Hawaiian words meaning "Bright Sky." Located upcountry from Kapa'a town, it's a five-minute drive from the beach. The "Malulani Guest Cottage" and the three guest suites offer private entrances, private baths and Alohilani home-grown breakfasts of freshly harvested tropical fruits, juices, jams and breakfast breads. Each unit features queen beds, ceiling fans, decks, lanai, kitchenettes, charcoal grills, gazebo and outdoor hot tub. The guest cottage and two suites also have sleeper sofas.

Rates: Kumulani Guest Suite $99 nightly, $650 weekly; Ko'ianiani Guest Suite $109 per night, $695 weekly; Pa'ana a ka la "Sunshine" Atrium suite $119 nightly, $750 weekly; Malulani Cottage $119 nightly, $750 weekly

A Bed of Roses Bed & Breakfast

6581B Pu'upilo Road, Kapa'a, HI 96746. 808-822-0853; e-mail: rosebedkauai@yahoo.com; www.geocities.com/rosebedkauai.

This secluded and well-hidden B&B has lots of privacy for those wanting to get away from it all, or stay in touch via a DSL line. It's just four miles from beach activities and convenient to shopping, dining and more. You can enjoy a Kaua'i sunrise from your own private lanai deck, surrounded by a peaceful garden environment. King bed, cable TV, barbecue, fridge, kitchenette, coffee maker. In season, guests can pick their own oranges, limes, bananas or macadamia nuts; coffee, juice and rolls free. Three-night minimum stay; cleaning fee.

Rates: $60 per night; $470.95 per week; $1,595.20 per month

★ *Candy's Cabin*

5940 Ohe Street, Kapa'a, HI 96746. 808-822-5451.

Located in the Wailua Homesteads. Your hostess is Candace Kepley. A studio apartment with a king-size bed, living area, private bath, lanai and refrigerator. Very roomy and adequate for a family. If you choose breakfast, you'll find some home baked goodies. Stroll around the grounds and see the family of mallard ducks that visit from the nearby stream. Located 20 minutes from the Lihu'e airport. No minimum stay.

Rates: $65 per night, for two

Hale Tutu

7230 Aino Pono Street, Kapa'a, HI 96746. 808-821-0697; 888-425-3882; fax 808-822-9091; e-mail: tutu@haletutu.com; www.haletutu.com.

This is "Grandma's House" (*Hale Tutu*), a beautiful Hawaiian-style private residence located in the cooler uplands above and overlooking the Wailua and Kapa'a areas of the Coconut Coast. There are three guest rooms and a full breakfast is offered with each. The "Nokekula (Swan) Room" has island-style furniture, large closet and private whirlpool spa, fridge, TV/VCR. The "Hawaiian Room" is furnished with Hawaiian antiques and has a large walk-in closet, fridge, TV/VCR, pool and garden views. The lower level "Nai'a Room" has a small kitchenette, TV/VCR and garden views. All rooms have queen beds, and guests have use of an outdoor spa and pool for lap swimming, plus use of fully equipped kitchen. Three-night minimum stay.

Rates: Nokekula (Swan) Room $105 nightly; Hawaiian Room $95 nightly; Nai'a Room $85 nightly

Hempey's Garden Island Bed & Breakfast

6087 Kolopua Street, Kapa'a, HI 96746. 808-822-0309; e-mail: hempey@hawaiian.net; www.hempeys.com.

This comfy B&B is nestled behind Sleeping Giant Mountain on a half-acre of beautifully landscaped tropical grounds just minutes away from Wailua Bay, shopping, dining and area activities. There are three guest rooms and a private studio with various bed arrangements (king, queen, twins), all private baths; guest rooms share a kitchenette and sitting area with full-sized refrigerator, TV/VCR, computer with internet access, phone and multiple kitchen utensils. Housekeeping, no cleaning fee. A generous Hawaiian breakfast is included. Hosts speak French, Portuguese, Italian and Spanish.

Rates: $65 to $75 nightly

House of Aleva

5509 Kuamo'o Road, Kapa'a, HI 96746. 808-822-4606.

Hosts Ernest and Anita Perry offer two upstairs rooms with a bath to share. A single room downstairs has a private bath. Breakfast tailored to your particular health needs and tastes. Located two miles inland up Highway 580 along the Wailua River and directly across from Opaeka'a waterfall.

Rates: $55 per night per couple, $40 per night single

Kakalina's B&B

6781 Kawaihau Road, Kapa'a, HI 96746. 808-822-2328; 800-662-4330; fax 808-823-6833; e-mail: klinas@aloha.net; www.kakalina.com.

Located on a three-acre working tropical flower farm in the foothills of Mt. Wai'ale'ale, your hosts are Bob and Kathy Offley. The "Hale Kolu" and "Hale Elua" units both have ocean and mountain views. Both units have a queen-size bed, ceiling fans and private bathrooms. Their newer unit is "Hale Eha," with two bedrooms, two baths, full kitchen and dining and living room. Continental breakfast included.

Rates: Full unit $175 for four people, or half unit for two people $90 per night

A mile away is their other vacation rental, the "Ginger Room." This one-bedroom home does not include the breakfast feature, but it offers a queen-size bed, living room, dining room, full kitchen and private bath.

Rates run $75 to $175, with a 10 percent discount for weekly stays

★ Kauai's Favorite Country Vacation Rentals

505 Kamalu Road, Kapa'a, HI 96746. 808-822-0166 or 808-947-6019; fax 808-822-2708, 808-946-6168; e-mail: wery@aloha.net; www.aloha.net/ ~wery/index-acb.htm.

Located on Kaua'i's east coast behind Sleeping Giant Mountain. From the outside, the main house (5,000 square feet on a two-acre estate) looks like a Spanish villa. On the inside, there are two lounge areas: a comfy Victorian sitting room with plush flower-patterned cushions and plump pillows, or the central living room remodeled with black and green marble, black leather couches, high ceilings and an enormous fireplace. Upstairs, the three private luxury suites are decorated in beautiful woods, with antique furniture, canopy beds and walk-in closets. The primary residence suite offers a king-size bed, TV, refrigerator, microwave, sitting and dining area and private bath with jacuzzi. Separate detached units in the backyard include a luxury apartment with queen bed, day bed, TV, full kitchen, sitting and dining area and large open deck. A studio apartment includes queen bed, sitting and dining area, kitchenette, private bath and TV. The two-bedroom cottage has queen beds, living room with kitchenette, dining area, one bath, TV and private front yard. Fresh flowers in all rooms and all have ceiling fans; shared laundry facilities. Nonsmokers only.

Rates: Suite I, $75, Suite II with jacuzzi $85, 2BR Presidential Suite $150 nightly. Private detached units: Apartment 1 $90, Studio Apartment $80, 2BR Cottage $120 nightly

★ K.K. Bed & Bath

4486 Kauwila Street, Kapa'a, HI 96746. 808-822-7348; 800-615-6211, code 32; e-mail: kkbedbath@aloha.net; www.kkbedbath.com.

The two guest rooms are in the old Kawamura family store warehouse next door to the building that was an old mom-and-pop store for years. Conveniently located in the center of Kapa'a town, close to area attractions and restaurants. The two guest rooms are simply furnished with queen beds, fridge, cable TV, telephone, private bath/shower; clean and nonsmoking. These are excellent budget traveler rooms. Three-night minimum stay.

Rates: $40 per person per night; $50 for two per night; $60 for three per night

Lampy's Bed & Breakfast

6078 Kolopua Street, Kapa'a, HI 96746. Phone/fax 808-822-0478 or 808-639-4779.

Located five minutes from Wailua Bay. Each of the three bedrooms is furnished with country decor and offers a private entrance and private bath; choice of king, queen or twin beds. Sitting room has TV/VCR and fully equipped breakfast bar. Breakfast is served each morning in the garden gazebo. Bright cheery accommodations in a quiet rural area. Convenient to all area beaches, shopping, dining, activities. Cash, money orders, travelers checks only.

Rates: Single $50 nightly; Double $55 nightly; Studio $65 nightly. Extra persons $10 additional. Weekly rates available

Lani Keha B&B

848 Kamalu Road, Kapa'a, HI 96746. 808-822-1605; 800-821-4898; fax 808-822-2429; e-mail: lanikeha@hawaiian.net; www.lanikeha.com.

This spacious island home is situated in the Kapa'a area of east Kaua'i nestled on three acres at the foot of Sleeping Giant Mountain. There are beautiful mountain panoramas from all the windows. Just ten minutes from area beaches, activities, attractions, shopping and dining of the Kapa'a town area. There are three guest rooms, private baths and, for guest use, a full kitchen, laundry, large lanai and TV. Two-night minimum stay.

Rates: King or twin beds, $55 to $65 per night

Mohala Ke Ola

5663 Ohelo Road, Kapa'a, HI 96746. Tel/fax 808-823-6398; 888-GO-KAUAI; e-mail: kauaibb@aloha.net; www.waterfallbnb.com.

Host Ed Stumpf invites you to "Rejuvenate in Paradise" at Mohala Ke Ola, their bed & breakfast retreat. Located above the Wailua River Valley near Opaeka'a Falls on the eastern shore of Kaua'i, there are mountain and waterfall views. Breakfast on fresh island fruit on a private terrace, enjoy the pool and relax in the jacuzzi. You can enjoy a Hawaiian *lomi lomi* massage or rejuvenate with other body treatments, including shiatsu, acupuncture and reiki. Quiet and peaceful surroundings along with a congenial and friendly atmosphere. Ed will greet you at the airport or assist if you need some shopping help. He also speaks fluent Japanese and is very knowledgeable about sightseeing and activities. They offer three guest rooms, each with a private bath and all nonsmoking. A pond and tropical landscaping are features. Three-night minimum requested.

Rates: Pool View $100 nightly; Garden and Valley View $85 nightly

Opaekaa Falls Hale Bed & Breakfast

120 Lihau Street, Kapa'a, HI 96746. 808-822-9956; 888-822-9956; fax 808-822-3911; e-mail: custland@pixi.com; www.opaekaafallskauai.ws.

This nicely maintained private home has spacious self-contained guest units with all the comforts expected. Guests enjoy over 1,000 square feet of living space, private entrance, large lanai deck overlooking the swimming pool, views of the Wailua plains and Wailua River; beautifully landscaped gardens surround the home. Featured are king and queen beds, fully equipped kitchens and dining rooms, cable TV, private bath. Conveniently near to the historic Wailua River Complex, area activities, attractions, shopping, dining and more. Hawaiian-style continental breakfast included. *Wir sprechen Deutsch.*

Rates: Royal Palm Unit (upstairs) $110 per night; Queen Emma Room (lower level) $90 per night

★ Rosewood Bed & Breakfast

872 Kamalu Road, Kapa'a, HI 96746. 808-822-5216; fax 808-822-5478; e-mail: rosewood@aloha.net; www.rosewoodkauai.com.

This home, located in Wailua Homesteads, was formerly an old macadamia nut plantation house. The area is rural, with rolling pastures and grazing cattle framed by a wide mountain range, with Mt. Wai'ale'ale in the center. After a nighttime shower, many waterfalls are visible with vivid rainbows. Since they moved to the islands 17 years ago, Rosemary and Norbert Smith have been restoring their home. A second cottage with two bedrooms, designed after the main house, is called the "Victorian Cottage." The smallest unit, designed with a Hawaiian look, is the "Thatched Roof Cottage." Additional options are their "Bunkhouse" rooms, which have proven popular with European visitors and hikers. The one-acre grounds include two ponds with small waterfalls, plus lots of fruit and flowering trees and bushes. "Thatched Roof Cottage" is a one-bedroom cottage with a king-size bed, screened lanai, kitchenette with hot plate, microwave and small refrigerator. The toilet and sink are indoors, but the hot/cold shower sits outside enclosed in the garden surrounded by native plants.

The "Victorian Cottage" offers two bedrooms and one bath, also an outdoor hot/cold shower. The master bedroom is downstairs with a queen bed, upstairs is a loft bedroom with two twin beds. A sofa opens into a sleeper bed. The full-size kitchen includes a dishwasher and a washer/dryer. The unit has a TV and phone with fax. The two "traditional" units in the main house each have a private bath. They have a king bed, which can be converted into two twins. Breakfast is left in the cottages, and, for main house guests, is served in the kitchen.

The bunkhouse has three separate rooms and a shared outside shower in a flower-bedecked gazebo. Each room has its own sink, toaster, coffee maker, small refrigerator and large lanai with gas grill. The larger room offers a microwave. One bunkhouse has twin bunk beds, while the other two have king beds. None of the bunkhouse units include breakfast or maid service. Breakfast may be provided for an additional $5 per day per person. All units are nonsmoking. Conveniently located just four miles from beaches, shopping and restaurants. Also available for rent are one- and two-bedroom oceanfront condos starting at $135 per night and beachfront cottages starting at $225 per night.

Rates: Victorian Cottage $125; Thatched Roof Cottage $105; Bunkhouses $40 to $50 per night

Waonahele at Kupono Farms

7084 Kahuna Road, Kapa'a, HI 96746. 808-822-7911; 877-822-1515; fax 808-821-0999; e-mail: kupono@aloha.net; www.planet-hawaii.com/kupono.

This is a lovely modern ranch-style home surrounded by the rainforest, thus its Hawaiian name. The home is located on a working eight-acre tropical flower and foliage farm. There are three very spacious, comfortably furnished guest rooms, each with king bed, phone, private lanai, whirlpool bath and beautiful ocean, valley and rainforest views. Includes full Hawaiian-style breakfast and daily maid service. A separate vacation home is available for honeymooners and those desiring lots of privacy (call 800-775-2824 to reserve).

Rates: m.v. $120; o.v. $140

HOTELS, CONDOS AND HOSTELS

Inexpensive Hotels, Condos and Hostels

★ Banyan Harbor Condominium Resort

3411 Wilcox Road, Lihu'e, HI 96766. 808-245-7333; 800-4-BANYAN; fax 808-246-3687. Reservations: The management company, Outrigger Lodging Services (OLS), also operates the front desk and runs the property's on-site rental program. 800-4BANYAN (422-6926) U.S. & Canada; e-mail: banyan@aloha.net; www.vacation-kauai.com. Rental agents: Maui & All Islands 800-663-6962; Prosser Realty 800-767-4707.

There are 148 units on a hilltop near Kalapaki Bay, some have a view of the Nawiliwili Harbor. The complex has a tennis court, refurbished pool and decking area, plus a separate recreation area with wet bar, shuffle board. Public volleyball courts are across the street. The rooms are crisp and clean, with television and air conditioning in all units. Washer/dryers, full kitchens (with microwave, coffee maker and dishwasher), and dining area. Townhouses have harbor views. Very convenient to the airport and an easy walk to the shops and restaurants of Anchor Cove and Harbor Mall or a short walk to the Marriott. The large front office is comfortable, with an amiable staff, and there is plenty of parking. Adjoining the property is a large orchard with the second largest banyan tree in Hawaii. Like many other facilities, they have gone to partial timeshare.

Rates: 1BR $85 to $140; 2BR $95 to $180; Room and car packages. (Mention this book and they'll give you a free upgrade from one to two bedrooms.)

★ Garden Island Inn

Located in Kalapaki Bay. 3445 Wilcox Road, Lihu'e, HI 96766. 800-648-0154; fax 808-245-7603, 808-245-7227; e-mail: info@gardenislandinn.com; www.gardenislandinn.com.

This renovated 21-room hotel, with tropical decor, has a cheery cottage feel to each of the rooms. Clean, comfortable, spacious rooms in a location convenient to activities, shopping, dining. They'll provide golf clubs and beach equipment, and you can help yourself to bananas and tangelos from the trees on the property. It's just a short walk across the road to the Kaua'i Marriott, Nawiliwili Beach Park and Kalapaki Beach. Anchor Cove Shopping Center is steps away and the Harbor Mall is just up the road with several eateries. All rooms have refrigerators, wet bars, TV, microwaves and coffee makers. One-bedroom suites are on the third floor. All units are nonsmoking and most have private balconies with ocean views and A/C. Comfortable, friendly and reasonably priced! They also have 2 two-bedroom condo units at Banyan Harbor which they rent.

Rates: $75 to $80; air-conditioned from $85 to $95; 1BR suites $95 to $125; condo units $145

Hale Lihu'e Motel

2931 Kalena Street, Lihu'e, HI 96766. 808-245-2751.

Twenty-two one-bedroom units, some with kitchenettes. No air conditioning, but rooms have table fans. Inexpensive and spartan two-story frame building located near the main business area of downtown Lihu'e. Walking distance to local restaurants, government offices, churches and banks. Rates, including tax, are the cheapest in an already inexpensive area. A little unkempt and rundown; not really what you'd envision paradise to be.

Rates: Single, double or triple occupancy $22/$25/$30; with kitchenette single $30, double $40, triple $50. Weekly discounts available

★ *Hotel Coral Reef*

1516 Kuhio Highway, Kapa'a, HI 96746. 808-822-4481; 800-843-4659; fax 808-822-7705.

This was one of the first tourist hotels on Kaua'i's Coconut Coast. This newly remodeled landmark hotel offers clean, affordable accommodations and has a prime oceanfront setting on a wide, white sandy beach in the heart of a popular vacation area. However, the highway runs right out front, so it's not exactly secluded or quiet. Ground-floor rooms are tiled, upstairs rooms are carpeted. The main building provides clean economical rooms with limited views. The oceanfront building offers spacious rooms with beach views, equipped with refrigerators and a choice of single or double beds. However, the beachfront is not suitable for swimming—but great for sunning, strolling and beachcombing. Pay telephone and TV in lobby. Daily maid service. Grocery store and restaurants nearby. Located within walking distance of a public swimming pool and many other area activities, golf, tennis. Room and car packages available.

Rates: o.f. and o.v. rooms range from $59 to $89; two-room m.v. suites $79; extra person $10; senior discounts

Kauai International Hostel

4532 Lehua Street, Kapa'a, HI 96746; 808-823-6142; www.hostels.com/kauaihostel.

This hostel is located ten miles north of Lihu'e Airport in the heart of old Kapa'a town—across from the beach park on Lehua Street that leads off from the main road, Kuhio Highway. This is *the* place on Kaua'i to meet budget travelers from around the world. Clean, friendly atmosphere, secure, safe for valuables. Oceanview dorm rooms, full kitchen and laundry facilities available plus TV, barbecue, pool table. Close to town shops, restaurants and area activities. Good starting point for adventure-seeking hikers, surfers and snorkelers, or for those who just want to explore beautiful Kaua'i beaches and its colorful culture, heritage and history.

Rates: Dorm bunk beds $20 per night; Private rooms, double bed $50

Mahina's Guest House

4433 Pahnini Place, Kapa'a; 808-823-9364; e-mail: mahinas@hawaiian.net; www.mahinas.com.

Four private rooms available. A lanai room with a twin bed, a small room with a double bed and two large rooms (one with queen and the other with a king bed). Kitchen, bath and laundry facilities all on shared basis. Clean, quiet and comfortable, plus easy access to all area activities, beaches, shopping, dining.

Rates: Twin $50 per night; double room $55 to $70; queen $55 to $80; king $75 to $90

Motel Lani

4240 Rice Street (P.O. Box 1836) Lihu'e, HI 96766. 808-245-2965; e-mail: tkn@hawaiian.net.

Located at the corner of Rice and Hardy, the center of the Lihu'e's business district, this motel has ten units, each with shower and one double or two twin beds. Some rooms have air conditioning and no TV, others have a TV and a ceiling fan. There is also a TV in the lobby for guests' use. Like Hale Lihu'e, inexpensive and very basic: "A place to sleep." Rates for one night slightly higher.

Rates: $32 to $50 per night two people, two-night minimum

Tip Top Motel

Located in downtown Lihu'e. P.O. Box 1231, Lihu'e, HI 96766. 808-245-2333; e-mail: tiptop@aloha.net.

The 34 rooms are spartan and basic, nothing fancy but clean and decent. This is a family-run operation, combining the Tip Top Motel & Café with a bakery, and has been going since 1916. They moved to their present location in the early 1960s. It's being run by the fourth generation of the Ota family. The coffee shop/café and cocktail lounge are still here, along with a Sushi Katsu Japanese Restaurant (dinner only), and a smaller version of their famous bakery. The café/bakery is noted for its oxtail soup, banana pancakes and macadamia nut cookies. If you're looking for no-frills budget accommodations with a great central location on Kaua'i, this is the place. All units are air-conditioned.

Rates: Single or double $45 (includes tax), plus $10 key deposit

Moderate Hotels, Condos and Hostels

Aloha Kauai Beach Resort

3-5920 Kuhio Highway, Kapa'a, HI 96746. 808-823-6000; 888-823-5111; fax 808-823-6666; e-mail: info@abr.com; www.abrkauai.com.

The 216-room oceanfront resort had extensive renovations and is under new management, yet again. This is an affordable full-service, activity-oriented property at the southern end of Kaua'i's Coconut Coast. This property is a good choice for couples, seniors, groups and families, especially since kids under 19 stay free—and those under 12 eat free—when accompanied by a parent. The open lobby has a nice old-Hawaiian feel and look about it. The Maile Wing and Pikake Wing feature gardenview and deluxe oceanview rooms and one-bedroom suites with various beds available. There are also 13 separate private duplex one-bedroom suite cottages. Each cottage has a master bedroom plus queen and sofa sleeper in the living area, fully equipped kitchenette. All rooms feature full amenities such as mini-fridge, coffee maker, TV, air conditioning, clocks, phones/data ports. Smoking/nonsmoking rooms available. Recreational facilities include spa, fitness room, tennis courts, shuffleboard, volleyball and two swimming pools (one geared for families). Hotel grounds feature nicely landscaped Japanese and Hawaiian gardens and a *koi* pool.

The hotel is adjacent to Kamalani Children's Playground and Lydgate State Park, which has good beach swimming and an enclosed swim/snorkel cove. Also next to the hotel grounds near the mouth of the Wailua River are the historic ruins of Hauola Place of Refuge and Hikina a Ka La Heiau. Directly across the highway is another old temple site, Malae Heiau, which has been undergoing clearing and restoration. No other hotels on Kaua'i have such important historic sites so nearby. Just below the knoll where the *heiau* sits is the famous Smith's Tropical Paradise. (*See* Chapter 2 and Chapter 6 for detailed information.) Daily maid service, laundry facilities. Restaurants and lounges include the Kahanu Snack Bar at poolside and the Kuhio Dining Court, which features a lounge, sundries shop and the Palms Restaurant. There are meeting facilities available. Inquire about special packages and kids activities when making reservations.

Rates: Gardenview $160, Oceanview $210, Junior Suite $235; 1BR Cottage Suite $435.

★ Aston Islander on the Beach

484 Kuhio Highway, Kapa'a, HI 96746. 808-822-7417; 800-847-7417; fax 808-822-1947; e-mail: www.islander-kauai.com. Rental agents: Aston Properties 800-922-7866; e-mail: res.iob@aston-hotels.com; www.aston-hotels.com. Pleasant Hawaiian Holidays 800-242-9244.

There's a total of 198 units in three-story buildings. A small understated lobby is tasteful and reminiscent of a simple, old-fashioned Hawaiian plantation. Very pleasing grounds and rooms and an excellent value for your vacation dollar. The hotel features an outdoor pool and spa, restaurant and lounge. All rooms offer king or two double beds, air conditioning, wet bar, refrigerator, microwaves in oceanfront units and suites, color TV and in-room coffee makers. Laundry facilities. Rooms are on the small side. Third and fourth persons are charged $20 per person per night. No charge for children 17 and under when sharing parents' room. Room and car packages available. Located on 6.5 oceanfront acres, next to the Jolly Roger Restaurant and across from the Coconut MarketPlace. This is one of the best beaches on the eastern shore. Check with Aston regarding any seasonal specials that might include rental car, complimentary breakfast or the fifth night free. Complimentary crib on request at time of booking.

Rates: g.v. $110; partial o.v. $120; o.v. $135; deluxe o.f. $150; Junior suite $195; extra person $20

★ Aston Kaha Lani

4460 Nehe Road and Leho Street, Lihu'e, HI 96766. 808-822-9331. Managed by Aston Resorts 800-922-7866; e-mail: res.khl@aston-hotels.com; www.aston-hotels.com. Rental agent: Maui & All Islands 800-663-6962.

Two- and three-story buildings, with a total of 74 units. More of an attractive homey apartment building than a resort. Pool, barbecue area, laundry facilities, putting green and tennis court. Full kitchens, with complimentary coffee starter kit. High ceilings, private phones, plus lanais, ceiling fans and daily maid service. One-bedroom units have two bathrooms. Located next door to the golf course on the beachfront at Lydgate Park, one of the islands better beaches. Kaha Lani is difficult to find unless you know to turn on Leho Street from the highway, but when you do, you'll be glad for the quiet seclusion. You're surrounded by a "choice" of landscaping: the soothing oceanfront, with small stretches of sandy beach; tropical gardens; or the dramatic craggy-rock-and-red-dirt road that borders the property and leads to other beach areas. The Kamalani playground at Lydgate State Park will amuse the children in your party for hours! Ask Aston reservations about special package or promotional options such as "Island Hopper Rates" if you plan on visiting other islands.

Rates: 1BR o.v. $230/$195, o.f. $270/$215; 2BR o.v. $320/$255, o.f. $350/$285

Aston Kaua'i Beach Villas

4330 Kaua'i Beach Drive, Lihu'e, HI 96766. 808-245-7711. Rental agent: Managed by Aston Properties 808-931-1400; 800-922-7866; e-mail: res.kbv@aston-hotels.com; www.aston-hotels.com. Additional rental agents: Maui & All Islands 800-663-6962; Pleasant Hawaiian Holidays 800-242-9244; Premier Resorts 800-367-7052.

Three floors (no elevator), 150 units located on 13 acres. These condominiums are part of the complex that includes the Radisson Kaua'i Beach Hotel next door. It is a short, pleasant walk along a pathway leading to the Radisson grounds and to the resort pools, restaurant, shops. The Aston pool (and whirlpool) are centralized, on an attractive raised deck reminiscent of a ship's pool deck. There are plenty of lounge chairs with barbecue grills nearby and elsewhere around the property. Rooms have a safe, washer/dryer, TV/VCR and pay movies. The beds were particularly comfortable, with velvety soft blankets and sheets. Lanais in all units. Air conditioning in bedroom suites only. Maid service. Inquire about Aston's promotional rates, special packages or "Island Hopper Discounts." The complex is on the beachfront but the beach is only suitable for strolling, exploring and sunning; swimming is not advised due to strong currents and surf.

Rates: 1BR standard $225/$190; 1BR g.v. $245/$200; 2BR g.v. $315/$250; 2BR o.v. $375/$310

★ Best Western Plantation Hale

484 Kuhio Highway, Kapa'a, HI 96746. 808-822-4941; 800-775-4253 or Best Western Worldwide 800-528-1234; fax 808-822-5599. Rental agent:

Best Western www.plantation-hale.com; e-mail: ph@aloha.net. Other agents: Maui & All Islands 800-663-6962; Pleasant Hawaiian Holidays 800-242-9244.

A total of 120 rooms in ten two-story buildings, located in the Coconut MarketPlace across the street from the beach. A good spot to stay if you don't plan on getting a rental car. The convenience of the mall provides multiple choices for restaurants and shopping. All units have one bedroom with kitchenettes and refrigerators. No dishwashers. Spas and a pool deck. Three pools, barbecue area and laundry facilities. Air conditioning and daily maid service. Nonsmoking rooms available. Second-floor units have balconies, first-floor ones have patios.

A one-block walk to the beach. The location of this property is between the road leading to the Coconut Beach Hotel and the highway. The last time we stayed there the street noise was a bit loud, but we understand they have made improvements that seem to have alleviated the problem. We'd recommend requesting one of the ocean-view rooms. There are televisions in both the living room and bedroom to help ease any program disputes!

Rates: 1BR suite w/kitchen $175 to $185; 1BR g.v. suite $185 to $195; 1BR scenic-view suite $195 to $205

Kapa'a Sands Resort

380 Papaloa Road, Kapa'a, HI 96746. 808-822-4901; 800-222-4901; fax 808-822-1556; e-mail: ksresort@gte.net; www.kapaasands.com.

The postal address is Kapa'a, but the resort is actually located in Wailua. Minimum maid service daily, with full linen change for stays of 7 nights or longer. Twenty-four individually owned studio and two-bedroom condominiums. Units all have telephone, color TV, microwaves and ceiling fans. Conveniently located behind Kinipopo Shopping Village and a short walk to additional shops and restaurants at the Coconut MarketPlace. Swimming pool, laundry facilities and attractive lanais and grounds. Located on a pleasant beachfront. If you are up early in the morning (and sometimes in the afternoon) you can watch sea turtles feeding off the reef just in front of the property.

Rates: Studio o.v. $100; studio o.f. $117 (max. 2 persons); 2BR o.v. $134 (max. 4); 2BR o.f. $152 (max. 4)

★ Kaua'i Coast Resort at the Beachboy

4484 Kuhio Highway, Kapa'a, HI 96746. 808-822-3441; fax 808-822-0843. Rental Agent: Maui & All Islands 800-663-6962.

The resort recently had an extensive renovation and reconstruction program that saw the former guest hotel units converted into 108 vacation ownership units with 69 one-bedroom, 33 two-bedroom units and a few standard hotel rooms. Rooms have air conditioning,

TV and lanais. No kitchens, but they do have a bar-size refrigerator. Daily maid service is provided. Currently guests receive a complimentary continental breakfast. There is a resort swimming pool, a children's pool and a jacuzzi, along with extensive landscaping plus an Activity and Fitness Center. Tennis courts also available and a nice restaurant, Hukilua Lanai, is on site. Located next door to the Coconut MarketPlace.

Rates: 1BR Suite g.v. $185; 1BR Suite o.v. $205; 1BR Suite o.f. $220; 2BR Suite w/kitchen g.v. $245; 2BR Suite w/kitchen o.v. $275; 2BR Suite w/kitchen o.f. $295

Kaua'i Coconut Beach Resort

P.O. Box 830, Kapa'a, HI 96746. 808-822-3455; 800-760-8555; fax 808-822-1830; e-mail: wesm@hawaiihotels.com; www.kcb.com.

This is a Hawaiian Hotels & Resorts property. The hotel is located on 10.5 acres at Waipouli Beach on the Coconut Coast and features a swimming pool/jacuzzi, three tennis courts, coin laundry and a restaurant on the property. Contemporary room decor in pastel colors and matching furnishings. Rooms provide lanai, refrigerator, coffee makers with free coffee, air conditioning. A handicapped room is also available. Summer program available for children accompanied by a parent. Offered free to guests June 1 through August 31, the activities include hula, lei making and other Hawaiian arts and crafts each morning. They also offer a "Kids Eat Free" policy for families dining on-property. Demonstrations of Hawaiian crafts are given daily year-round, as is their traditional torch-lighting ceremony each evening. Children under age 17 may stay free in rooms with their parents when using existing bedding. The proximity to nearby Kaua'i Shopping Village (with a Safeway) and just a few blocks to the Coconut MarketPlace make it ideally situated. On the down side, the parking area, while large, can be very crowded and finding a spot can be a little difficult at times. The hallways have poor lighting, making them very dark. But the hotel can be a good value, provided they continue to maintain the quality of their rooms and grounds.

A buffet breakfast is served at their Voyage Room Restaurant and is included with some of their room packages. The restaurant also serves a la carte and buffet lunches. Dinner is served at the Flying Lobster Restaurant. Nightly entertainment is at Cook's Landing Lounge. Their luau and Hawaiian revue received the Hawai'i Visitors Bureau *Kahili Award.*

Rates: Standard Room $99; o.v. $119; o.f. $159; special packages that include room plus breakfast and dinner for two, car and ohana (family) rates provide a second room free when the first room is purchased at the rack rate; check with reservations on other specials at booking time

★ *Kaua'i Sands*

420 Papaloa Road, Kapa'a, HI 96746. 808-822-4951; fax 808-822-0998. Rental agent: Sand & Seaside Hotels, 808-922-5737; 800-560-5553; e-mail: info@kauaisandshotel.com; www.kauaisandshotel.com.

This is the only Hawaiian-owned hotel chain in the world, and while it isn't fancy, it is comfortable. The rooms don't get much sun and are pretty spartan, but they are clean. Self-service laundry. The hotel sits on a beachfront, but it is better for sitting and ocean watching than for swimming and sunbathing. Rooms are air-conditioned. Al & Don's Restaurant overlooks the ocean. Located in Wailua, it is very near the Coconut MarketPlace. Discounts for AAA members and seniors. Free room upgrade for 50+ seniors, free welcome breakfast for two, daily free breakfast for AAA members.

Rates: Standard $98 to $108; Superior $100 to $110; Deluxe Poolview $125 to $135; Deluxe w/Kitchenette $135 to $145; also check on room and car packages and other specials

★ *Lae Nani*

410 Papaloa Road, Kapa'a, HI 96746. 808-822-4938; fax 808-822-1022. Located adjacent to the Coconut MarketPlace in Kapa'a. Rental agents: Outrigger Resorts 800-OUTRIGGER, toll-free fax 800-622-4852 or phone 808-921-6600, e-mail: reservations@outrigger.com, www.outrigger.com; Kaua'i Vacation Rentals 800-367-5025; Maui & All Islands 800-663-6962; Premier Resorts 800-367-7052.

They offer 84 units in three-story buildings. 1-bedroom units are 800 square feet; 2-bedroom 2-bath units are 1,072 square feet. These apartments are spacious, with nice island-style decor and furnishings; light colors with tropical accents. Amenities include an oceanfront, oversized heated swimming pool, lighted tennis courts, three barbecues. Daily maid service if booked with Outrigger. All units have ceiling fans, private lanais and full kitchens with microwaves. Laundry facilities are available on the property, but not in the units. The central office has a particularly friendly and helpful staff—meet them when you check in, stop by for your complimentary newspaper or mail (postage-free) the set of complimentary postcards that Outrigger provides for you on your arrival! This property has some outstanding oceanfront vistas. While the units are a little older and perhaps not as contemporary in style, they are very roomy and comfortable. Lae Nani is situated on five acres of lovely grounds. A small manmade rock pool along the bay has been created. The rocky promontory along the beach is a remnant of an early Hawaiian *heiau*. A free historical brochure describes a self-guided tour of Wailua and other ancient Hawaiian sites in the area.

Check with Outrigger for a variety of packages and programs, including senior discounts, first night free, room and car, and family plans.

Rates: Kauai Vacation Rental rates: 1BR o.v. $800 week; 2BR $950 week. Outrigger Resorts rates: 1BR o.v. $220; 1BR o.f. $270; 2BR g.v. $240; 2BR o.v. $280; 2BR o.f. $330

Pono Kai Resort

1250 Kuhio Highway, Kapa'a, HI 96746. 808-822-9831; 800-438-6493; www.extraholidays.com. Rental agent: Marc Resorts Hawai'i 800-535-0085, toll-free fax 800-633-5085, local 808-922-9700. Maui & All Islands 800-663-6962. Kaua'i Vacation Rentals 800-367-5025.

Amenities include pool, jacuzzi, sauna, barbecues. Units have ceiling fans, phones, lanais, full kitchens, including microwaves. Lighted tennis courts, shuffleboard, covered recreation area with kitchen facilities, tables and chairs, concierge/activity desk, video rentals. There is an attractive lagoon and bridge leading into the property from the front office and farther along, a small Hawaiian garden with pathways for a short, but pleasant stroll. Very central location on the edge of Kapa'a town. (An interesting aside is that this used to be a pineapple cannery!)

Rates: $79 to $149 nightly

★ *Radisson Kaua'i Beach Hotel*

4331 Kaua'i Beach Drive, Lihu'e, HI 96766. 808-245-1955. Radisson Hotels 888-805-3843; www.radissonkauai.com. Other rental agents: Maui & All Islands 800-663-6962; Pleasant Hawaiian Holidays 800-242-9244.

There are 347 units in a U-shaped complex of connected buildings surrounding a central courtyard and pool/activity complex on 25 landscaped oceanfront acres. All guest rooms and public areas have new furnishings and a new look from the hotel's previous incarnation. The Radisson is located three miles north of Lihu'e on Nukoli'i Beach (*nukoli'i* means the beach of the *kole* fish). There are three miles of beach for strolling, exploring and discovering, the longest stretch of beachfront of any resort on Kaua'i. While the beach is not really suitable for swimming, there are quiet coves and areas where swimming and snorkeling can be enjoyed. The resort has free scuba lessons available. But be aware that the beach can be unsafe for water activities at times.

Three swimming pools (2 adult, 1 *keiki*) and a spa amid lush tropical gardens and rockscaped waterfalls. There is also a sand-bottom pool at the front of the property closer to the actual beach and next to the Driftwood Sand Bar & Grill. Four tennis courts (two lighted), lobby shops, activity desk and fitness club round out the amenities. Wailua Golf Course is nearby. Meeting and banquet space. No laundry facilities. The rooms have daily maid service, air conditioning, refrigerator, television, direct dial phones and private lanais. Guest rooms and hallways are bright and clean; furnishings are very tasteful, with subdued tropical colors and accents.

Naupaka Terrace Steak House is open for breakfast and dinner daily. Shutters Lounge and the Driftwood Sand Bar & Grill at poolside also provide cocktails, beverages, snacks and light meals daily along with nightly Hawaiian entertainment.

A Keiki Klub summer program is available for children 5 to 12 who are guests at the resort. (*See* Chapter 1 for more information.)

Check with Radisson for special discount packages and seasonal programs including first night free, room and car, bed and breakfast and family plans. Also discounts for seniors, AARP, corporate.

Rates: Standard rooms begin at $129; Senior-Business rates $149 to $159; m.v/g.v super saver $179; m.v/g.v $209; o.v. super saver $219; lagoon $229; pool view $249; o.v. $279; 1BR suites from $309

Wailua Bay View

320 Papaloa Road, Kapa'a, HI 96746. 808-823-0960. Located overlooking Wailua Bay. Rental agent: Linda Owen 800-882-9007; www.wailuabay.com; Prosser Realty 800-767-4707; Kaua'i Vacation Rentals 800-367-5025; Maui & All Islands 800-663-6962.

As the name implies, these apartments provide a beautiful bay view. Luckily the living rooms face the ocean. Full kitchens, microwaves (in some units), dishwasher, washer/dryers. All units are air-conditioned. King or queen beds, sleeper sofa in living room. Swimming pool and barbecues. Walking distance to shops and restaurants. Daily maid service. Located on the beachfront with tennis courts across the street.

Rates: 1BR o.f. $85 to $140; Deluxe o.f. $99 and up (1 to 4, max. 4)

Expensive Hotels, Condos and Hostels

Hale Awapuhi

366 Papaloa Road, Kapa'a, HI 96746. 808-245-8841. Rental agents: Kaua'i Vacation Rentals 800-367-5025; Prosser Realty 800-767-4707; Maui & All Islands 800-663-6962.

Just nine units in this property with oceanfront pool. Convenient to shops, restaurants and the Coconut Marketplace.

Rates: Beachfront units $190 to $420; Dlx ground-floor corner unit o.v. 2BR 2BTH (1 to 4) $270/$230; 2BR w/loft (1 to 4) $330/$290; first floor 2BR 2BTH (1 to 4) nonsmoking $200/$180; 2BR 2BTH second floor nonsmoking (1 to 4) $220/$200

★ *Kaua'i Marriott Resort & Beach Club*

3610 Rice Street, Lihu'e, HI 96766. 808-245-5050. Marriott Reservations 800-220-2925; www.marriott.com. Other rental agents: Pleasant Hawaiian Holidays 800-242-9244.

Located on 51 acres overlooking Kalapaki Bay, the Kaua'i Marriott Resort & Beach Club consists of 345 hotel rooms (the Kaua'i Marriott) and a community of 232 one- and two-bedroom vacation ownership villas under the name Marriott's Kaua'i Beach Club. The villas overlook Kalapaki Beach and Nawiliwili Bay. This hotel/resort dates from the 1970s-'80s when it was at various times the Kaua'i Surf and Westin Kaua'i. A 1980s makeover left it a gaudy hotel with an overly elaborate, out-of-place design motif. In redeveloping the property in the 1990s, Marriott chose a different approach, combining time shares with a hotel property. The $30 million renovation incorporated Hawaiian history and culture into the interior design, while keeping within the existing architectural elements and scale of the buildings. The result is a much improved image for the Kaua'i Marriott—not nearly as ostentatious or garish as it once had been—more reflective of Kaua'i tropical elegance. Of course, much of the elaborate structures remain, such as the marble columns, but they have made an effort to make them less central. The elevator to the lobby is attractive and fun, kind of like "Pirates of the Caribbean" at Disneyland. The rooms are attractively furnished and spacious. Convenient in-room amenities include a mini-fridge, free HBO and hair dryers.

The villa complex features three restaurants and one lounge. Casual poolside dining is available at the Kalapaki Grill and Kukui's, as well as lunches and dinners at Duke's Canoe Club. Aupaka Terrace offers daytime refreshments or evening specialty cocktails, and an espresso and ice cream bar. The resort amenities include Hawaii's largest swimming pool and a 20,400-square-foot retail shopping center.

The resort offers the Kalapaki Kids Club, which focuses on the uniqueness of the Hawaiian Islands, Kaua'i in particular. (*See* Chapter 1 for more information.)

As for adult activities, there are plenty of those! Special activities and Hawaiian exhibits are scheduled daily, including a sunrise walk, introduction to snorkeling or windsurfing, or you can even have your portrait done! Exhibits include Hawaiian woodworking, Ni'ihau shell lei display, Hawaiian quilting or featherwork. There are eight tennis courts and nearby are the two fine Kaua'i Lagoons golf courses designed by Jack Nicklaus. The hotel offers complimentary airport shuttle service. Ask about current package options.

Rates: g.v. $309; o.v./pool view $754; o.v. $434; suites $669 to $2,800

Lanikai

390 Papaloa Road, Kapa'a, HI 96746. Rental agents: Castle Resorts 800-367-5004; Maui & All Islands 800-663-6962; Kaua'i Vacation Rentals 800-367-5025.

Two three-story buildings offer 18 units, half of these are in the rental program. These oceanfront condominiums provide large lanais, as well as full kitchens. Property amenities include pool, barbecue area. Located near Wailua State Park Beach and Kapa'a.

Rates: Castle: 1BR o.v. $250/$230; 1BR o.f. $270/$250; 2BR o.v. $295/$270; 2BR o.f. $315/$290

South and West Shore Areas

PRIVATE VACATION HOMES & COTTAGES

Anderson's Hale Nalu

8691 Kaumuali'i Highway, Kekaha, HI 96752. 808-337-9234; fax 808-337-0462; e-mail: pamshale@hawaiian.net; www.lauhala.com/halenalu.

There are two one-bedroom/one-bath homes with full kitchen, dining area and living room. Kitchens are fully equipped, living rooms have TV/premium channels/stereo, daybed and sofa sleepers. Located on the Kekaha beachside on Kaua'i's westside and away from it all. Swimming, surfing, windsurfing, snorkeling, sunbathing, fishing, whale watching are all just steps away. Public tennis courts are nearby. Some water sports and beach equipment available, plus barbecue; laundry facilities available for guests.

Rates: $85 nightly (includes tax)

Boulay Inn

4175 Omao Road, P.O. Box 522, Koloa, HI 96756. 808-742-1120; e-mail: boulayinn@hawaiian.net; www.hawaiian.net/~boulayinn.

This is a completely private upper-level one-bedroom apartment unit with wraparound lanai and expansive panoramic views of the ocean and surrounding mountains. It has island-style decor, queen bed, living room sofa bed, full kitchen, TV/VCR, ceiling fans and laundry in unit. It's just minutes away from the famed Po'ipu beach resort area, three golf courses, beaches, shopping, dining and related activities.

Rates: $65 nightly; inquire for weekly and monthly rates

Brennecke Beach Cottage

3285 Waapa Road, Lihu'e, HI 96766 (mailing address). 808-245-7575; 888-386-8786; fax 808-245-2434; e-mail: rbwhite@aloha.net; www.mmv.com/bbc.

This is a two-bedroom, two-bath plantation-style cottage located right next to Brennecke Beach in the heart of the Po'ipu beach resort area. You can walk across the street and jump in the water, stroll the beach or just watch the surf and enjoy the sun. A master bedroom has a king bed and a second bedroom sleeps two in twin beds. Cottage is complete and comfortable for island-style living and relaxation.

Rates: $1,750 weekly (one-week minimum stay)

★ Classic Vacation Cottages

2687 Onu Place, P.O. Box 901, Kalaheo, HI 96741. 808-332-9201; fax 808-332-7645; e-mail: clascot@hawaiian.net; www.classiccottages.com.

These country-style cottages are off the beaten track and away from the tourist crowds. Situated a bit upcountry from the South

Shore in the delightful Kalaheo area, and just minutes from resort activities at Po'ipu, but with easy access to the rest of Kaua'i's attractions. Choose from the Basic Studio, Garden Studio, Garden View Cottages #1 & #2, the Lake View House or the Executive House. All are fully equipped with all amenities for a relaxing vacation stay.

Rates: Basic Studio $50 to $65 nightly; Garden Studio $65 to $80 nightly; Garden Cottage #1 $80 to $95 nightly; Garden Cottage #2 $75 to $90 nightly; Lake View House, $95 nightly; Executive House $175 to $250 nightly

★ Coastline Cottages

4730 Lawa'i Beach Road, Koloa, HI 96756. 808-742-9688; fax 808-742-7620; e-mail: jds@aloha.net; www.coastlinecottages.com.

There are four separate fully equipped cottages right on the water's edge in the Po'ipu area. The studio, 1BR, 2BR and 3BR units all have private oceanfront lanais, full kitchens, living room areas, queen beds and an extra guest Murphy bed. The studio unit has mini-kitchen facilities with fridge, microwave and coffee maker. Convenient to Po'ipu Resort attractions, activities, beaches, shopping and dining.

Rates: Studio/1BR $285; 2BR $405; 3BR $650

Coco's Vacation Rental

P.O. Box 690169, Makaweli, HI 96769. 808-338-0722; e-mail: ian@hawaiian.net; www.cocoskauai.com.

This unit is a 565-square-foot guest room with private entrance in a home on a 12-acre estate located on the Robinson Family Ranch (the family owns Ni'ihau Island). The guest room has a king bed and queen sofa sleeper and accommodates 4 people. There is a full kitchen, living room and bath plus patio, barbecue and laundry. The house is surrounded by expansive ranch lands and orchards of tropical fruit trees. It's within easy walking distance of a secluded beach on Kaua'i's quiet west side, great for surfers—near some premiere breakers. Call collect for reservations.

Rates: $100 with breakfast; $90 without breakfast

Hall's Plantation Estate

3527 Papalina Road, P.O. Box 548, Kalaheo, HI 96741. 808-332-9111; fax 808-332-5408; e-mail: shelley@hallsofhawaii.com; www.hallsofhawaii.com.

This very modern and stylish country estate home sits on three-acres of well-maintained grounds overlooking the prestigious national Tropical Botanical Gardens and Lawa'i Kai Valley located behind Allerton Beach. It's also near the sunny Po'ipu resort area. The valley boasts acres of coffee orchards, plus farms growing bananas, papaya and tropical floral crops. The country home has two fully furnished guest suites, the "Kahili Mountain Suite" and the "Ficus Guest Suite." There is also the separate "Kalaheo Cottage." Each guest suite has a living room with entertainment center, fully equipped mini-kitchen, private bath and lanai, and master bedroom with king bed. The guest cottage has a living room and entertainment center, full bath, mini-kitchen and bedroom with king bed. All guests share a hot tub, barbecue and laundry facility. Ceiling fans are found throughout the units and there's tasteful contemporary Hawaiian decor. Surrounded by tropical flowers, plants and fruit trees with great ocean and mountain views.

Rates: Kahili Mountain Suite or Ficus Guest Suite $98 nightly; Kalaheo Guest Cottage $120 nightly

Jan's Kauai Kondos

Mailing address, 1565 Pe'e Road Koloa, HI 96756. 800-726-7412; e-mail: kondos@aloha.com; www.cris.com/~equities.

This 2-bedroom/2-bath condo is located in Po'ipu Sands, part of the Po'ipu Kai Resort. It has a spectacular ocean view and is just 350 yards from the beach at Keoneloa Bay. Adjacent to the Hyatt Resort and Spa plus Po'ipu Bay Golf Course. The unit has all the comforts and amenities for a pleasant vacation: laundry, full kitchen, two lanais, living room, dining room, plus nine tennis courts, large heated pool and 24-hour security. Sleeps up to 4 people.

Rates: $175 to $225 nightly

Kalaheo Plantation Vacation Rental

4579 Pu'u Wai Road, P.O. Box 872, Kalaheo, HI 96741. Tel/fax 808-332-7872; 888-332-7812; e-mail: kalaheo1@gte.net; www.kalaheo-plantation.com.

This is a finely restored and refurbished 1926-era plantation home with six available guest suites. Guest rooms have various bed arrangements—king, queen or twins—and all have kitchens or kitchenettes, private bath and entry. The home is within walking distance of five restaurants in Kalaheo and the public golf course is just around the corner. Easy access to area activities and attractions and just five miles from Po'ipu beaches. Guest rooms can be rented separately or together for larger groups.

Rates: Bamboo Room $45; Blue Ginger Room $55; Gardenia Room $65; Magnolia Suite/Hibiscus Suite $69; Orchid Suite $75; all four main-floor units $199 night/$1,399 week (max. 8); entire house, six units $350 night/$1,950 week (max. 16)

★ Kauai Condo's at Po'ipu Kai Resort

1941 Po'ipu Road, Koloa, HI 96756. 800-203-1192; fax 414-427-5325; e-mail: dickolson@hikauai.com; www.hikauai.com.

There are various nicely furnished one-bedroom condo vacation units offering full amenities, garden or ocean views, easy access to area activities, attractions, shopping, dining. Rent directly from the owner for reasonable rates.

Rates: $100 and up nightly

Kaua'i Hideaways Guest Cottages

3198A Wawae Road, P.O. Box 1082, Kalaheo, HI 96741. 808-332-6421; e-mail: ani@aloha.net; www.kauaihideaways.com.

These are unique and private modern plantation cottages. They are situated high atop a hill in a quiet neighborhood that has expansive scenery of rolling pastures and ocean views. There are four separate units with kitchen/kitchenette, laundry, TV/VCR, jacuzzi bath.

Rates: Hale Ani Studio $65 nightly; Hale Keoki Treehouse $75 nightly; Hale Guava Hillside Cabin $95 nightly; Hale Kolea Cottage $125 nightly.

Pua Hale at Po'ipu Beach

2381 Kipuka Street, Koloa, HI 96756. 808-742-1700; 800-745-7414; fax 808-742-7392; e-mail: poh@aloha.net; www.kauai-puahale.com.

A convenient South Shore location, Po'ipu and Shipwreck Beach are less than a 5-minute walk away. "Flower House" features a Japanese waterfall in a tropical garden. Eastern influence is again found in the bathroom where you can enjoy a *furo* (Japanese-style soaking tub). The home features a queen-size bed, which can be isolated by sliding *shoji* doors. The unit is within an enclosed walled tropical garden setting that allows for privacy. Four-night minimum. No smoking. No children under 8 years.

Rates: $120 per night. Weekly rate $735 with additional nights $105. Price is for double occupancy, additional persons $10 per day, maximum 4 persons. $40 cleaning fee

Sunset Kahili

1763 Pe'e Road, Koloa, HI 96756. 808-742-7434; 800-827-6478; e-mail: info@sunsetkahili.com; www.sunsetkahili.com.

There are fully equipped one- and two-bedroom condo units with great ocean views. Units are within walking distance of Po'ipu Beach. There is a pool, barbecue and nearby tennis courts. All amenities provided: laundry, full kitchen, TV/VCR, ceiling fans, etc. Easy access to resort dining, shopping, attractions and activities.

Rates: $99 to $191 nightly

BED AND BREAKFASTS

Aloha Breeze

4122 Koloa Road, Koloa, HI 96756. 808-332-9164; fax 808-332-9251; e-mail: alohabreeze@alohabreeze.com; www.alohabreeze.com.

Aloha Breeze is a delightful inn-style accommodation near the charming old sugar plantation town of Koloa and just minutes from the exclusive Po'ipu beach resort area. There are surrounding views of mountains and ocean. Guests can choose from three very nicely maintained accommodations, each with its own special tropical magic to make a stay in paradise memorable.

Rates: Garden Suite $95 nightly; Balcony House $95 nightly; Lanai Room $65 nightly

Bamboo Jungle House B&B

P.O. Box 1301, Kalaheo, HI 96741. 888-332-5115; 808-332-5515; e-mail: serene2@aloha.net; www.kauai-bedandbreakfast.com.

There are three guest suites available, each with private entrance and bath, plus full amenities. It's the only B&B with an in-ground hot tub grotto with 10-foot waterfall. Lap pool. Discounts for multiday stays.

Rates: Jungle and Safari Suites $110 nightly; Waterfall Suite $130 nightly

Coral by the Sea B&B

4538 Akekeke Road, Kekaha. P.O. Box 820, Waimea, HI 96796. 808-337-1084; 888-326-1084; fax 888-326-1084; e-mail: coralsea@hawaiian.net; www.hawaiian.net/~coralsea.

Hosts Fred and Sharon offer guests a fully equipped nonsmoking 420-square-foot studio in a residential area within one block of sandy beaches and a short drive to the Waimea Canyon/Kokee area. Queen-sized bed, sitting room, private bath with shower. A comfy couch is also a sleeper sofa. Gas grill on lanai. Stocked with fresh baked goods, coffee, fruit and juice. Bright coral on the outside, a bit dark on the inside (but it keeps it cool); ceiling fan.

Rates: Three-night minimum runs $71.50 nightly; $85 for one- or two-night stays; $357.50 weekly (tax included)

Garden Isle Oceanfront Cottages

2666 Puuholo Road, Koloa, HI 96756. 808-742-6717; 800-742-6711; fax 808-742-1933; e-mail: vacation@oceancottages.com; www.oceancottages.com.

These sea cliff cottages are located on a small ocean inlet where the Waikomo Stream meets the ocean overlooking historic Koloa Landing. Good snorkeling and scuba diving and a small sandy beach. These are oceanview units, all with private lanai. One-bedroom cottages feature queen bed in bedroom and double bed in the living room. Some have full kitchens, others kitchenettes. Washer-dryer, VCR, phone, gas barbecue. Two-night minimum stay.

Rates: $149 to $170 (depending on season), double occupancy; extra person $10

★ Gloria's Spouting Horn B&B

4464 Lawa'i Road, Koloa, HI 96756. Tel/fax 808-742-6995; e-mail: glorbb@hotmail.com; gloriasbedandbreakfast.com.

This custom-designed beachhouse features spacious oceanfront guest rooms and Hawaiian rock baths. Each of the five units includes a telephone, TV/VCR, wet bar with sink, refrigerator and microwave, along with a coffee and popcorn maker. One room offers a unique willow canopy bed, while the others offer four-poster beds of either bamboo or native *koa* wood. There are complimentary snacks and beverages, including a champagne and chocolate mac nut welcome. Beach chairs, towels, coolers and mats are provided. The buffet breakfast offers fresh fruits, cereal and a hot entree. The rooms are beautifully appointed with handmade Hawaiian quilts. This lovely property is on the high end of the price spectrum for B&B accommodations and since each room is restricted to two people, it is not for families with young children. But sleeping just 40 feet from the surf may make it worth a splurge for honeymoons, anniversaries, etc. Bob Merkle (Mr. Gloria) is a retired minister and can officiate at your wedding on the beach! No charge cards. They also offer condos and apartments at other Po'ipu locations. (www.gloriasvacationrentals.com). Three-night minimum.

Rates: based on single or double occupancy $300 ($325 during Christmas) plus tax. Weekly discount of $275 except over Christmas

Hale Hyette B&B

1663 Keleka, Koloa, HI 96756. 808-742-2877; fax 808-742-2977; e-mail: halehyette@aol.com; www.aalohakauai.com.

This unit is one spacious and nicely furnished guest room with private entrance and bath; nonsmoking facility. It features nice ocean and mountain views and the amenities of Po'ipu Kai Resort. Located near the second hole of the Po'ipu Bay Golf Course and a short walk to Po'ipu area beaches. Convenient to all resort activities, dining, shopping. No breakfast, but fruit and coffee in room.

Rates: $85 nightly

Hale Ikena Nui

Mailing address: P.O. Box 171, Kalaheo, HI 96741. Located at 3957 Ulualii Street in Kalaheo. 808-332-9005; 800-550-0778; fax 808-332-0911; e-mail: pantone@hawaiian.net; www.kauaivacationhome.com.

Hosts Dan and Patti Pantone offer a private 1,000-square-foot suite, featuring a full kitchen, queen bed, full-size sleeper couch, private phone, washer/dryer. They also have an extra B&B suite with private bath in the family residence. No charge for children 3 and under. Three-night minimum. Convenient to Po'ipu resort activities, beaches, golf, attractions, dining.

Rates: Private Suite $85 nightly, $15 per additional guests; B&B Suite $70 nightly; weekly/monthly rates available

★ Hale Kua Guests

4896-E Kua Road, P.O. Box 649, Lawa'i, HI 96765. 808-332-8570; 800-440-4353; e-mail: halekua@aloha.net; www.planet-hawaii.com/halekua.

They have a one-bedroom cottage, three one-bedroom apartments (Banana Patch, Taro Patch and condo unit), and a spacious three-bedroom unit (Coral Tree). Each unit features a queen-size bed, full bath, kitchen, queen sleeper sofa in living room. TV, VCR, telephone and washer/dryer. Views of the ocean, Lawa'i Valley and the mountains, including Mt. Kahili. Property is tucked away on the hillside of Lawa'i Valley, surrounded by lush gardens, tropical fruit and timber trees and provides a peaceful hideaway convenient to island attractions, as well as nearby restaurants, bakeries and beaches.

Rates: $90 to $125 nightly, discounts for extended stays

★ *Kalaheo Inn*

4444 Papalina Road, Kalaheo, HI 96741. 808-332-6023; 888-332-023; fax 808-332-5242; e-mail chet@aloha.net; www.kalaheoinn.com.

Units are clean and in a good location in quaint Kalaheo town. This locally owned and managed property has 15 suites of various styles and settings. The entire property is landscaped in a tropical design with banana and star fruit trees and other tropical trees and blooming flowers. Just 10 minutes drive from the sunny beaches of Po'ipu. This is an excellent lodging choice for budget-minded travellers and for those who don't need the glitz of fancy beach resorts and hotels.

Rates: $55 nightly

Kaua'i Cove Cottages

2672 Pu'uholo Road, #A, Po'ipu, HI 96756. 808-742-2562; 800-624-9945; e-mail: info@kauaicove.com; www.kauaicove.com.

This operator offers romantic and completely private cottages on Kaua'i's sunny south shore. It's located near Koloa Landing and surrounded by distant majestic mountain views and just steps from Po'ipu Beach. This is one of Kaua'i's most popular places for scuba diving, snorkeling, ocean kayaking and other activities. Stroll to nearby beaches, beachcomb, watch the turtles swim into Waikomo Stream in the evening. You're close to everything the Po'ipu resort area offers, but in a totally relaxed, stress-free environment. The cottages are non-smoking and each features vaulted ceilings, complete kitchen, private lanai and full amenities for a comfortable and memorable stay. Choose from "The Plumeria," "The Wild Orchid," or "The Hibiscus."

Rates: $95 to $125 nightly

★ *Marjorie's Kauai Inn*

3307D Hailima Road, P.O. Box 866, Lawa'i, HI 96765. 808-332-8838; 800-717-8838; e-mail: marjorie@marjorieskauaiinn.com; www.marjories kauaiinn.com.

One of the best things about staying at Marjorie's is the spectacular, panoramic view of magnificent Lawa'i Valley and the mountains. It's rural Kaua'i at its best, yet only minutes from Poipu Beach, shopping and restaurants. All the rooms have that stunning view, as well as a mini-kitchen, and on your first night you'll receive a basket with local fruits, sweet bread, juice, tea and Hawaiian coffee. Each room also has a private entrance and bath and a lanai. The premiere accommodation is the "Sunset View," with its open-beam ceilings, queen-size bed and a futon sofa/bed. It also has a private outdoor hot-tub spa in a gazebo where you can literally soak in the view. The "Valley View" and "Tradewinds" accommodations are also comfortable and well-equipped. Beach chairs, towels and a barbecue are provided and all guests can use the new 10-foot by 50-foot lap pool, which is surrounded by spacious decking for sunning—and again, you have that great view. A tropical, "grass shack" pool-side bar is in the works. There is a no-smoking policy both indoors and outdoors. And outdoors is one-and-a-half lush acres of palms, gingers, bamboo, plants and tropical fruit trees. Guests will enjoy Marjorie's personal attention; she's happy to steer you to local sights, restaurants and activities to enhance and customize your vacation. That could be why she has many repeat visitors.

Rates: Sunset View $115 nightly; Valley View $96; Tradewind $88

★ *Ole Kamaole's Beach Houses*

8663 Kaumuali'i Highway, P.O. Box 389, Kekaha, HI 96752-0389. 808-573-2865; 800-528-2465; e-mail: olehawaii@compuserve.com; www.virtualcities.com.

These units are just 80 feet from the beach and surrounded by groves of banana and papaya trees. The two units are 2-bedroom/1-bath cottages with full kitchens stocked with extensive breakfast fixings. Each cottage sleeps up to 6 people. Recreation deck has extra toilet, outdoor shower and barbecue grill. Units are on 12-foot pilings with 17-step stairs (due to heavy surf flood zone). There are miles of black-and-white-sand beaches to explore adjacent to the location on this sunny westside coast of Kaua'i. Convenient to Waimea Canyon and Kokee State Park. Just 15-minutes from Polihale Beach at the end of the road, the beach few know about or visit. The area abounds with activities and attractions. $100 cleaning fee.

Rates: $125 to $150 nightly, $15 extra person (4-night minimum stay)

★ *Po'ipu Bed & Breakfast Inn*

2720 Hoonani Road, Koloa, HI 96756. 808-742-0100; 800-808-2330; fax 808-742-6843; e-mail: info@poipu-inn.com.

This B&B includes four units located in a 1933 plantation-era home. All units have private baths, two with whirlpool tub and separate shower and two with standard tub and shower, king bed, fridge, cable TV and VCR, wicker and pine antiques. Carousel horses are used as decor in various rooms and the lobby area. Large front lanai area where an island-style breakfast is served daily. There is also a separate private condo unit on adjoining sunny Poipu property. Easy access to all Po'ipu Beach Resort area activities, shopping, dining, golf, beach.

Rates: $110 to $165

★ *Po'ipu Plantation Resort*

1792 Pee Road, Koloa, HI 96756. 808-742-6757; 800-634-0263; fax 808-742-8681; e-mail: plantation@poipubeach.com; www.poipubeach.com.

This vacation resort has two types of rental units available. There are nine cottage-style condo units, spacious one- and two-bedrooms with living/dining room, kitchens and large lanai area. Units have hardwood floors, tasteful tropical decor, queen beds, air conditioning and ceiling fans, TV/VCR and free local calls. There is a separate 1930s plantation-era bed-and-breakfast house with four rooms or suites having king or queen beds, private baths, air conditioning and ceiling fans and TV plus use of an oceanview lanai room. The Alii Ocean View Honeymoon Suite is beautiful, with turn-of-the-20th-century decor. Daily breakfast and housekeeping provided for B&B rooms. All guests have use of barbecue, hot tub and laundry facilities. Swim towels, beach mats, chairs also provided. The one-acre grounds are nicely landscaped with flowers, fruit trees and lawns. This comfortable, centrally located resort is near to beaches, tennis, golf, ocean sports, restaurants, shopping and Po'ipu resort area activities. Great swimming, snorkeling and sunning nearby at Brennecke Beach. Three-night minimum stay at cottages; two-night minimum stay in B&B rooms.

Rates: Cottage/Condo units, 1BR g.v. $105; 1BR s.v. $115; 1BR o.v. $130; 2BR s.v. $150 (max. 4); 2BR o.v. $168 (max. 4); Bed & Breakfast rooms: Queen or King Room $95; Master Room $120; Ocean View Honeymoon Suite $10; extra person $20

South Shore Vista B&B

4400 Kai Ikena Drive, Kalaheo, HI 96741. 808-332-9339 or 808-332-9201; fax 808-332-7771; e-mail: vista@aloha.net; www.planet-hawaii.com/vista.

An oceanview, fully equipped one-bedroom apartment located in the charming hillside community of Kalaheo. Just two blocks to a beautiful park and golf course, 10-minute drive to nearby beaches. Fully furnished and well-equipped, including private deck overlooking the garden. Fresh fruit, coffee, tea and cereal provided in unit, along with beach mats, towels and cooler. Three-night minimum.

Rates: $59 to $69 nightly

Strawberry Guava B&B

P.O. Box 271, Lawa'i, HI 96765. 808-332-7790; e-mail: lauria@hawaiian.net; www.hawaiian.net/~lauria.

This private home is located on the edge of the Lihu'e-Koloa Forest Reserve and at the foot of Mt. Kahili in a very quiet country setting. This is for those who appreciate nature's beauty and value solitude and privacy. B&B suites are in a separate wing, all with private entry, bath, sitting room, fridge, queen beds and marvelous country views. Close to area activities.

Rates: $65 to $75 nightly

Victoria Place

P.O. Box 930, Lawa'i, HI 96765. 808-332-9300; fax 808-332-9465; e-mail: edeev@aloha.net; www.hshawaii.com/kvp/victoria.

Three guest rooms and a studio apartment offer a choice of B&B options. Breakfast for all is served on the pool deck. The three main rooms are charming and look out onto the pool deck. The single room is a little smaller. The sitting area is pleasant, with plenty of books and lots of helpful information on touring and dining on Kaua'i. Hostess Edee Seymour is very knowledgeable and eager to share information about the island. No children under 15.

Rates: "Raindrop Room," double bed, single occupancy only $70; "Calla Lily Room" with queen bed $90; "Shell Room" with twin beds or king-size is handicapped accessible $90. "Victoria's Other Secret" is a studio apartment with private entrance, king bed, day bed, kitchen $125. Add $10 per room during holiday season (mid-December to mid-January). Additional $15 for one night only

HOTELS, CONDOS AND HOSTELS

Inexpensive Hotels, Condos and Hostels

★ Koke'e Lodge Cabins

3600 Koke'e Road, P.O. Box 819, Waimea, HI 96796. 808-335-6061.

Located at an elevation of 3,600 feet the lodge is located in 4,345-acre Koke'e State Park. A dozen housekeeping cabins furnished with refrigerators, stoves, hot showers, cooking and eating utensils, linens, towels, blankets and pillows. Wood-burning fireplaces are also available; logs can be purchased from the lodge shop. Size of units vary from one large room that sleeps three, to two-bedroom cabins that sleep seven. These cabins are *very rustic* and provide the bare essentials—no TV or phones. These are wilderness cabins in a remote forest setting, but for hikers, backpackers, outdoor enthusiasts and others of like minds, they are perfect. Maximum stay is five days; pets are not permitted.

Rates: Full payment is required for confirmation. $35 to $45 per cabin per night

★ Koloa Landing Cottages

2704-B Ho'onani Road, Koloa, HI 96756. 800-779-8773; 808-742-1470 or 808-332-6326; e-mail: info@koloa-landing.com; www.koloa-landing.com.

The cottages are located in the heart of the Po'ipu resort area and in a tropical garden setting across the street from the beachfront.

Ho'onani Road runs parallel to the beachfront. This is a quiet resort area, convenient, with easy access to area beaches, parks, golf, tennis, activities, attractions, shopping, dining in Koloa, Kalaheo, Hanapepe and neighboring towns. Right across the street from Koloa Landing, a popular spot for diving, snorkeling, fishing and canoeing. All cottages and studios include microwave, telephone, color cable TV and full kitchens. There are coin-operated laundry facilities and gas barbecue on premises. Two-bedroom cottages have large decks. Studios have a queen bed. Cottages include one queen bed and one set of twins. The studios can accommodate two persons, and the cottages sleep four people, with room for two extra persons on futon mattresses. The main house sleeps up to six people; families are welcome. These are clean, comfortable accommodations in a quiet, relaxing surrounding—a great budget-easy getaway.

Rates: Studio $85 nightly; 1BR $95; 2BR/2BTH cottage $125; 2BR/2BTH main house $140; extra person $10

Prince Kuhio

Mailing address: P.O. Box 367, Lihu'e, HI 96766. Property located at 5061 Lawa'i Road. Rental agents: Po'ipu Connection Realty 800-742-2260; R&R 800-367-8022; Grantham Resorts 800-325-5701; Prosser Realty 800-767-4707; Kaua'i Vacation Rentals 800-367-5025; Maui & All Islands 800-663-6962.

Studio, one- and two-bedroom units. All have microwave ovens, full-size refrigerators, cable TV and telephones; studios have air conditioning. Guest laundry facility on the ground floor. Barbecue, pool. Located next to Prince Kuhio Park in Lawa'i area of Po'ipu.

Rates: Studio $70 to $90; 1BR $80 to $120 nightly/$500 to $770 weekly; 2BR penthouse $135/$115

Moderate Hotels, Condos and Hostels

★ Alihi Lani

2564 Hoonani Road, Po'ipu, HI 96756. Located at Po'ipu Beach. Rental agent: Po'ipu Connection 800-742-2260, 808-742-2233.

This property has a total of six units. These condos are spacious with full kitchen plus full-size washers and dryers. Outside is a private swimming pool and sunning deck. This attractive property is located on a rocky oceanfront, but it is a short and pleasant walk down to Po'ipu Beach. With only six units in this property you won't find crowds at the pool!

Rates: $185 $250 nightly/$1,600 weekly

★ Aston at Po'ipu Kai

1941 Po'ipu Road, Koloa, HI 96756. 808-742-6464. Managed by Aston Resorts 800-922-7866; e-mail: res.ppk@aston-hotels.com; www.aston-hotels.com. Rental agents: Suite Paradise 800-367-8020; Maui & All

Islands 800-663-6962; R&R 800-367-8022; Prosser Realty 800-767-4707; Garden Island Rentals 800-247-5599; Po'ipu Connection Realty 800-742-2260; Grantham Resorts 800-325-5701; Pleasant Hawaiian Holidays 800-242-9244.

While Aston is the general property manager, other agents have several units in rental programs. Three-hundred-and-fifty condominium units. Seven resorts within a master resort, like a sprawling apartment complex made up of individual buildings—each with its own Hawaiian name. The privately owned condominiums include Po'ipu Sands, Manualoha, Makanui, Kahala and The Regency. Lanai Villas and Bayview offer private homes. The buildings and units are all different, but equal in stature and category of accommodations. Two-story townhouses are stylish and modern with a two bedrooms and two bathrooms on the lower (entry-level) floor. Roomy bathrooms with luxury shower and tub. Living room, full kitchen and half-bath upstairs. High ceilings, ceiling fans, wet bar, good assortment of small appliances and kitchen utensils. Washer/dryer with handy starter supply of detergent; complimentary HBO, private phone. Interior decoration varies with each owner, but island-style furniture is generally very attractive and comfortable. Po'ipu Kai shares Shipwreck Beach with the Hyatt and fronts Po'ipu Beach Park at the other end of the property. A great location for beach aficionados! Shop around, prices vary greatly depending on rental agent (as can quality of the unit). Prices may reflect location in resort or amenities such as maid service.

Rates: Studio g.v. $195/$150; 1BR g.v. $270/$205; 1BR o.v. $350/$285; 2BR g.v. $350/$285; 2BR o.v. $435/$355; 3BR/4BR g.v. $465/$305. Inquire with Aston about special packages, promotionals, senior or "Island Hopper" discounts

Garden Island Sunset Vacation Rentals

Rental agent: Kaua'i Vacation Rentals 800-367-5025.

This oceanfront 4-plex offers wonderful sunsets and views of Ni'ihau. A short walk to Waimea Town. All units are 2BR, 1BTH and sleep 4.

Rates: $650 weekly

Hale Hoku

4534 Lawa'i Road, Koloa, HI 96756. Tel/fax 808-742-1509; e-mail: halekoku@hawaiian.net; www.hshawaii.com/kvp/hoku.

This two-bedroom, two-bathroom unit provides a full kitchen, washer/dryer, cable TV. Outdoor pool, outdoor shower and barbecue. Ten-night minimum during high season. Four-person occupancy; additional $15 for fifth guest.

Rates: 2BR deluxe o.f. $225/$200

Kuhio Shores

5050 Lawa'i Beach Road, Koloa, HI 96756. Located near Prince Kuhio Park. Rental agents: Po'ipu Connection 800-742-2260; R&R 800-367-8022; Prosser Realty 800-767-4707; Garden Island Rentals 800-247-5599.

These are one-bedroom and two bedroom oceanfront condominiums.

Rates: 1BR and 2BR o.f. $110 to $125 nightly/$900 weekly, plus cleaning fee

Lawa'i Beach Resort

5017 Lawa'i Road, Koloa, HI 96756. 808-742-9581; fax 808-742-7981. Rental agents: Grantham 800-325-5701; Maui & All Islands 800-663-6962; Suite Paradise 800-367-8020.

This property has turned into timeshare, but a few units are still in the vacation rental program. Cable TV with HBO, private phone, washer/dryer. Pool, jacuzzi, barbecue grill, limited maid service; coin-op laundry; telephones.

Rates: 1BR/2BR o.f. $189 to $310

★ Makahuena

Located in Po'ipu. Mailing address: 1661 Pe'e Road, Koloa, HI 96756. 808-742-2482. Rental agents: Castle Resorts 800-367-5004; Grantham Resorts 800-325-5701; R&R 800-367-8022; Maui & All Islands 800-663-6962; Po'ipu Connection Realty 800-742-2260.

Seventy-nine condominiums. Resort includes pool, tennis court, jacuzzi and barbecue area. We stayed in a deluxe 2BR 2BTH operated by Po'ipu Connection. It was really oceanfront, with a blowhole right outside our lanai! It was a pleasure to open the double doors into the entranceway and be greeted by such a spacious, luxurious unit. The size was enhanced by wall mirrors and high cathedral ceilings and it seemed "huge," but once we settled in, found it to be comfortable and intimate. The furniture was attractive, with warm shades made tropical with lots of cane and bamboo. The bedrooms had *shoji* doors, there were ceiling fans throughout, programmed lighting and air conditioning controls, wet bar, dishwasher, washer/dryer, microwave and plenty of dishes and utensils. The unit was clean and fresh and a nice soft carpet. All units have ceiling fans, full kitchens and washer/dryer.

Po'ipu Connection rates: 2BR 2BTH deluxe o.f. $1,600 weekly. Grantham rates: 2BR o.f. $205/$185; 2BR premium o.f. $300; 3BR o.v. $195/175. Castle Resorts rates: 1BR g.v. $180/$160; 1BR o.v. $195/$175; 1BR o.f. $235/$200; 2BR g.v. $185/$165; 2BR o.v. $220/$190; 2BR o.f. $250/$225; 2BR deluxe o.f. $365/$340; 3BR g.v. $295/$275; 3BR o.v. $335/$310

Nihi Kai Villas

1870 Ho'one Road, Koloa, HI 96756, located up the hill from Brennecke Beach. Grantham Resorts 808-742-2000; 800-325-5701; fax 808-742-9093; e-mail: info@grantham-resorts.com; www.grantham-resorts.com. Rental agents: Prosser Realty 800-767-4707; Maui & All Islands 800-663-6962; R&R 800-367-8022; Suite Paradise 800-367-8020; Po'ipu Connection Realty 800-742-2260; Garden Island Rentals 800-247-5599.

Seventy units with 1, 2 and 3 bedrooms. Phones, TV, microwave, kitchens, washer/dryer. Many oceanview. Oceanfront swimming pool and tennis courts. Nearby beach is popular for body surfing.

Garden Island Rates: 1BR $125/2BR 2BTH $135 plus cleaning fees. Suite Paradise Rates: For minimum 7-day stay, 2BR 2BTH unit $250 to $305. Grantham: 1BR deluxe g.v. $159/$139; 2BR deluxe o.v. $179/$159; 2BR deluxe o. f. $420/$240; 3BR luxury o.f. $285/$260

Po'ipu Crater

2330 Ho'ohu Road. 808-742-7260. Rental agents: R&R 800-367-8022; Po'ipu Connection Realty 800-742-2260; Maui & All Islands 800-663-6962; Suite Paradise 800-367-8020; Grantham Resorts 800-325-5701.

Thirty condominiums in a garden setting. Each two-bedroom, two-bath bungalow is furnished with phone, cable TV, VCR, microwave, washer/dryer, plus full kitchen. Located near Brennecke Beach. Resort features tennis, swimming pool, sauna, barbecue.

Grantham rates: 2BR 2BTH garden $139/$119; Po'ipu Connection rates: 2BR 2BTH $750-$850 weekly; Suite Paradise rates: 2BR 2BTH garden $195 with 7-day minimum stay

★ Po'ipu Kapili

2221 Kapili Road, Koloa, HI 96756. 808-742-6449; fax 808-742-9162. On-site rental agent: Po'ipu Ocean View Resorts (same address) 800-443-7714; e-mail: aloha@poipukapili.com; www.poipukapili.com.

Sixty one- and two-bedroom condominiums in seven low-rise oceanfront buildings. The property features traditional Hawaiian plantation architecture located in the Po'ipu Beach resort community. Kitchens fully equipped, including microwave ovens. One-bedroom units are 1200 square feet, two-bedroom units are 1,800 square feet. These are very spacious units with lots of room to move around and relax in, which is what you want on a vacation. Units are well-appointed, very nice, clean furnishings and equipped with all the conveniences needed for a great stay. Laundry facilities are available on the property, but two-bedroom units have their own washer and dryer. Oceanview pool and complimentary tennis courts lighted for night play. The property is very private and the attractive and well-cared-for grounds add to the appeal. As nice as some other units costing much more. Room and car packages are available. (Christmas holiday rates are higher than the high season rates that follow.)

Rates: 1BR o.v. $260/$200; 1BR o.v. dlx $300/$225; 2BR o.v. $350/$260; 2BR o.v. dlx $400/$300; 2BR superior $425/$325; Penthouse $550/$450

Po'ipu Makai

1677 Pe'e Road, Po'ipu, HI 96756. Rental agents: Prosser Realty 800-767-4707; Grantham Resorts 800-325-5701; Maui & All Islands 800-663-6962; Kaua'i Vacation Rentals 800-367-5025; Po'ipu Connection Realty 800-742-2260.

Each of 15 units fronts the ocean. Depending on the rental agent and unit, prices vary greatly! Small swimming pool.

Po'ipu Connection Rates: 2BR 2BTH $120-$165, 3BR 2BTH $1,250 weekly; Kaua'i Vacation Rental Rates: 2BR ocean $170/$150; 3BR ocean $205/$180

Po'ipu Palms

1697 Pe'e Road at Po'ipu Beach. 808-245-4711. Rental agents: R&R 800-367-8022; Prosser Realty 800-767-4707; Po'ipu Connection 800-742-2260; Maui & All Islands 800-663-6962.

There are 12 oceanfront units in this complex. Attractive, homey apartments with two small bedrooms and two baths. There's also a pool.

Rates: $1,050 to $1,250 weekly

Sunset Kahili

1763 Pe'e Road, Koloa, HI 96756. 800-82-POIPU; 808-742-7434. Rental agent: Maui & All Islands 800-663-6962.

There are 36 condominiums in a five-story building. Pool. Full kitchens, television, telephones, ceiling fans, washer/dryer, lanais and swimming pool. One block to Brennecke Beach.

Rates: 1BR $120 to $125/$110 to $130; 2BR $135 to $150/$150 to $160

Waikomo Stream Villas

Located in Po'ipu. Rental agents: Grantham Resorts 800-325-5701; Maui & All Islands 800-663-6962; Prosser Realty 800-767-4707.

Sixty one- and two-bedroom units in tropical setting. Units have private lanais and are equipped with kitchen, telephone, cable TV, VCR, microwave, washer and dryer. Free tennis, barbecue area and an adult and children's swimming pool are amenities.

Rates: 1BR 1BTH g.v. $115/$85 (1-4); 2BR 2BTH g.v. $149/$119 (1-6)

★ *Waimea Plantation Cottages*

P.O. Box 367, Waimea, HI 96796. 808-338-1625; 800-9-WAIMEA. Rental agents: Managed by Aston Properties 800-922-7866; e-mail: res.wpc@aston-hotels.com; www.aston-hotels.com; Maui & All Islands 800-663-6962.

Each of the cottages, originally built between 1880 and 1950 to house plantation employees, has been fully restored and updated. Located in a lovely grove of palms, these individual houses are just what you'd expect a Hawaiian home to be. There are 47 cottages spread among 27 acres. The property information sheet includes the following history: "In 1884, Hans Peter Fayé, a Norwegian engineer and farmer, secured a lease from Kalakaua, King of Hawai'i, for about 200 acres of Mana swamp land, where he successfully grew sugar cane. He and nearby planters combined their lands to form the Kekaha Sugar Company in 1898, one of Hawai'i's most profitable cane producers. By 1910, W.P. Fayé, Limited, had privately purchased the neighboring Waimea Sugar Mill Company. Today, Fayé's descendants manage Waimea Sugar Mill lands as Kiki'aola Land Company, Ltd."

The Alan E. Fayé Manager's Estate is a two-story house circa 1900. This five-bedroom home is 4,000 square feet. H.P. Fayé's first home, originally in Mana 20 miles away, was relocated to the entryway where it now serves as the front desk. The property is divided into several areas: Seaside, Historic Mill Camp, Hanawai Courtyard and Coconut Grove. (They also have a 1916 two-story beachhouse and cottage located on the shore of Hanalei Bay available for rent.) They have a Waimea Sugar Mill Camp Museum and Plantation Lifestyles Walking Tour. (*See* Chapter 2 for more information.) Weekly maid service, color cable TV, phones, laundry facilities, complimentary tennis, swimming pool. A recreation room has a large-screen TV, lounge area, video games and a gift shop, which includes a small museum.

These units are full of history—looking at the tiny doors, old-fashioned dressers and end tables and rattan furniture, you can actually imagine what it would have been like to be a plantation worker coming in the back door and putting your lunch tin on the oil cloth on top of the tiny table in the quaint kitchen. But the plumbing has been modernized and though the bathrooms are a bit small, they have a great walk-in tiled shower with plenty of room. The lighting fixtures are new, but have an old look. Air conditioning, ceiling fans, TV, stereo, coffee maker. The pool area, overlooking the ocean, is spacious and completely open. (It can be noisy what with the gravel driveways, crowing roosters and squeaky floorboards, but it just adds to the ambiance!) Visa and Mastercard accepted.

Rates: Studio w/kitchenette $150/$140; 1BR/1BTH Grove View $220/$185; 1BR/1BTH Superior Grove View $225/$195; 1BR/1BTH Superior Oceanfront $250/$225; 2BR/1BTH Grove View $260/$220; 2BR/2BTH Superior Grove View $270/$230; 2BR/1BTH Superior Oceanfront $270/$310; 3BR/2BTH Superior Grove View $300/$255; 3BR Superior Oceanfront $335/$295; 4BR/3BTH Oceanfront $400/$370

Expensive Hotels, Condos and Hostels

★ *Embassy Vacation Resort–Po'ipu Point*

1613 Pe'e Road, Koloa, HI 96756. 808-742-1888. Managed by Marc Resorts. Reservations: Marc Resorts Hawai'i 800-535-0085, toll-free fax 800-633-5085, local 808-922-9700. Other rental agents: Maui & All Islands 800-663-6962; Pleasant Hawaiian Holidays 800-242-9244.

They have 218 units, some are timeshares. This is another very pleasant luxury property with an architectural style similar to the Moana Hotel on O'ahu. The decor is reminiscent of an English country estate, with dark greens accented by antique floral patterns. The bathrooms are spacious, with big showers and deep tubs. The units have a full kitchen with washer/dryer, microwave and dishwasher. Rooms have stereos, TVs, VCRs and there is enough game software to keep the kids happy! Nightly two-hour manager's cocktail party includes beverages and *pupus*. Coffee in rooms with complimentary breakfast in the Club Room by the pool. Breakfast includes assorted juices, fresh fruit and breads, but be prepared for the activity talk! The landscaped pool area and whirlpool are surrounded by sand (that is similar to aquarium gravel), with lawn chairs around the border. One-bedroom suites have a king bed and sleeper sofa. The two-bedroom suites have a king bed and two twin beds plus a sleeper sofa in the living room. The Health Club features workout equipment, steam and sauna baths. Toddler pool and a nice touch are the many sand toys available for the use of those little guests. Check out the volcanic lava flow out on the beachfront and see the family of green turtles that frolic in the surf. Great amenities that are sure to enhance your vacation! Also, Pleasant Holidays and Maui & All Islands offer special package rates and free-night discounts.

Rates: (Marc Resort year-round rates): 1BR g.v. (max. 4) $309; 1BR partial o.v. $360; 1BR o.v. $395; 1BR o.f. $460; 2BR g.v. (max. 6) $360; 2BR partial o.v. $435; 2BR o.v. $500; 2BR o.f. $575; Presidential 3BR 3.5 BTH w/ kitchen $1,100

★ *Hyatt Regency Kaua'i Resort & Spa*

1571 Po'ipu Road, Koloa, HI 96756. 808-742-1234; fax 808-742-1557. Reservations 800-633-7313; www.kauai-hyatt.com. Other rental agents: Pleasant Hawaiian Holidays 800-242-9244.

This Hyatt, while not on as grand a scale as some other Hawai'i Hyatt properties, still has a grand feeling, and it's arguably the nicest resort on the island. This property is located on 50 oceanfront acres in the Po'ipu Beach district. The classic traditional Hawaiian architecture is reminiscent of the 1920s and 1930s. It is very open and elegant, with a regal Hawaiian look. Even during high occupancy, this resort doesn't feel crowded. A pleasant surprise are the pools, which are heated. With two swimming pools, three jacuzzis and another "action" pool, with waterfalls, slides, water volleyball, a children's area and five acres of meandering saltwater swimming lagoons featuring islands, each with its own landscaping. Kids will love these pools, and even if you aren't staying here, you can buy a daily pool pass. There are also four tennis courts with pro shop and tennis professional on the property as well. The Dock offers poolside coffee,

HAWAIIAN CULTURE VISITED

The Hyatt Regency Kaua'i has developed an innovative Hawaiian program, free to the general public. Activities conducted by the Kaua'i Historical Society include the "Archaeology and Dune Walk" along the 500-yard white-sand beach fronting the resort and "Talk Story" sessions that focus on the lore and legends of Kaua'i. Leilani Bond, the Hyatt's *kumu* (respected teacher) oversees the Hawaiiana program. She and the 250 students of her hula *halau* share their knowledge of Hawaiian culture. Traditional arts and crafts are offered Monday through Friday and include *poi*-pounding demonstrations, modern hula instruction, quilting demonstrations, flower lei making and even ukulele lessons.

Traditional Hawaiian music is featured each evening in the Seaview Terrace from 6 to 8 p.m. A torch lighting ceremony (accompanied by chanting and traditional hula) is a part of the evening guest entertainment four nights a week. A weekly schedule of the resort's Hawaiian program activities is available at the concierge desk.

beverages, snacks and light meals. The Seaview Terrace has a comfortable living room feel, very open and airy, with a beautiful view.

The Stevenson's Library is a cruise ship–type bar area—a combination gaming room (complete with pool, backgammon, chess and more), library and bar—although very unbar-like. The Ilima Terrace embraces the true Hawaiiana feeling and serves breakfast, lunch, Sunday brunch and dinner in an open-air arrangement with plenty of foliage and *koi*-filled lagoons. Tidepools restaurant is housed under a thatched roof surrounded by a lagoon island. Dondero's is the fine-dining Italian restaurant. The Po'ipu Bay Bar & Grill is also part of the Hyatt.

While the beachfront is pleasant, the winds and surf can come up and make it unsafe for swimming. The Hyatt does post ocean safety flags. The guest rooms are light and bright with plantation-style furnishings. As with many Hyatt properties, they offer the Regency Club—special floors offering guest amenities such as complimentary breakfast, beverage service and late-afternoon hors d'oeuvres. The resort also features the ANARA Spa. Salon facilities, exercise room, aerobics and yoga classes, as well as an array of wonderful facial and body treatments can certainly be a memorable part of your Kaua'i vacation. Their spa services are highly recommended by this author. (*See* "Spas & Fitness Centers" in Chapter 6 for more information.)

Rooms have recently had a facelift, freshening up this lovely hotel. Rates are single/double occupancy. No charge for children 18 and under when sharing their parents' room using existing bed space. For additional persons 19 and older, $30 charge per night; $50 per night for the Regency Club. Maximum four adults or two adults and two children per room.

Rates: Garden $320; Mountain $395; Lagoon $440; Partial Ocean $490; Deluxe Ocean $580; Regency Club $650; Hyatt Suites: Ocean $795; Regency Club Ocean $905; Deluxe $1,270; Regency Club Deluxe $1,370; Presidential $3,000

★ ***Kiahuna Plantation***

Located in Po'ipu. Mailing address: 2253 Po'ipu Road, Koloa, HI 96756. 808-742-6411; fax 808-742-1698. Rental agent: Outrigger Hotels & Resorts manages part of the property and Castle Resorts the other part, which makes it all a bit confusing. And there are other property manager agents who handle bookings as well. The reservation number for Outrigger is 800-OUTRIGGER, 808-921-6600, toll-free fax 800-622-4852; e-mail: reservations@outrigger.com; www.outrigger.com. Castle Resorts 800-367-5004; e-mail: reservations@castleresorts.com; www.castleresorts.com. Other rental agents: Grantham Resorts 800-325-5701; Maui & All Islands 800-663-6962; Suite Paradise 800-367-8020; Pleasant Hawaiian Holidays 800-242-9244.

Kiahuna is the largest resort condominium on Kaua'i, with 333 units in two- and three-story buildings situated on 35 acres of lush gardens and expansive lawns that were once part of Hawai'i's first sugar cane plantation. The historic manor house was originally the home of the plantation manager and now is home to the Plantation Gardens Restaurant.

This is what might be called "Classy Hawaiian." The rooms are very attractively decorated and have the feel of a comfortable beach home. They have high ceilings and are nicely furnished with wicker and wood, with the bedroom set off in a cozy nook of its own. The kitchens have coffee makings and a microwave with complimentary microwave popcorn. The property has plenty of amenities as well: the Kiahuna Keiki Club; crafts and Hawaiian activities; and free tours of the grounds. The comforts of a condo and the amenities and convenience of a hotel earn this property a star. One- and two-bedroom units have various gardenview, oceanview and oceanfront categories. All units include living and dining rooms, private lanai, fully equipped kitchen, color TV, video tape player and ceiling fans. Daily maid service, laundry facilities, complimentary beach chairs and towels, gas barbecues. Pool and ten tennis courts. Free tours available of the incredible cactus in the Moir and Hawaiian gardens, located on this resort property. Excellent location on Po'ipu Beach and even more family-friendly with their Keiki Klub Summer Program! (*See* Chapter 1 for more information.)

Castle Resorts rates: 1BR: g.v. $215/$180, o.v. $313/$225, o.f. $440; 2BR: g.v. $395/$330, o.v. $495/$405, o.f. $660. Grantham rates: 1BR o.f. $265/$205. Outrigger rates: 1BR: suite g.v. $199, royal g.v. $215, partial o.v. $240, o.v. $315, o.f. $425 (1, max. 4); 2BR: suite g.v. $340, royal g.v. $370, partial o.v. $400, o.v. $480 (1, max. 6). Suite Paradise rates: 1BR 1BTH $265

Po'ipu Shores

1775 Pe'e Road, Koloa, HI 96756. 808-742-7700. Managed by Castle Resorts. Rental agents: Castle Resorts 808-524-0900; fax 808-596-0158; 800-367-5004; www.castleresorts.com; Suite Paradise 800-367-8020; Maui & All Islands 800-663-6962.

Thirty-three oceanfront condominiums, one, two and three bedrooms. All suites feature fully equipped kitchens, color TV, washer/dryer and private lanai. Both the living room and bedroom have oceanviews. The units are more appealing inside than out, with light furniture and walls and attractive lighting. Wood and marble kitchens are fully equipped with microwaves and plenty of counter space. Many of the privately owned units are equipped with VCRs, paperbacks and even CDs. There is a raised deck area surrounding the pool and a club room complete with kitchen, plus magazines and games. The older elevators tended to make a bit of noise, but happily, it was drowned out by the crashing of the waves. While most of the accessible parking area fills up quickly, it is a nice enough property, centrally located and a good value in this price range.

Rates: Castle Resorts rates: 1BR o.f. $250/$215; 2BR o.f. or dlx o.f. $290/$225, $310/$275; 3BR o.f. $340/$305; Penthouse 2BR o.f. $400/$375 Suite Paradise rates: 2BR 2BTH $335

★ *Sheraton Kaua'i Resort*

2440 Ho'onani Road, Koloa, HI 96756. 808-742-1661; fax 808-742-4041. Sheraton Reservations: 800-782-9488; www.sheraton-hawaii.com.

The resort is situated on 20 acres of oceanfront gardens adjacent to Kaua'i's popular Po'ipu Beach. The resort comprises 413 air-conditioned rooms (including 14 suites). Three wings, each no higher than four stories, provide guests with ocean vistas and tropical gardens with *koi*-filled ponds. The Garden Wing is located across the street. The resort's artwork and interiors showcase the traditions of Hawaiian culture and diversity of the island. Guest rooms are decorated in natural earth tones and the rooms' furnishings and fabrics use Hawaiian *tapa* (bark cloth), lei and floral motifs. The property features guest services and facilities include massage and fitness center, tennis courts, beach activities booth with rental equipment and instruction and the Keiki Aloha Club children's center. Two swimming pools are available for guest use—the nicest one is oceanside, offering a slide, two children's pools and a whirlpool. The oceanfront pool and surrounding area feature tropical landscaping and they have done a particularly nice job restoring the surroundings to their natural, simple state of ocean and sand rather than trying to improve on nature with a lot of complicated manmade landscaping. The *koi* ponds, tropical gardens and waterfalls enhance the natural landscape. In-room amenities include coffee and coffee maker, mini-refrigerator, complimentary safe, hair dryer, cable color TV, in-room movies, Sony PlayStation and video checkout. They have a daily menu of activities and a full-service salon and fitness center. Check it all out at the Beach Activities Center at the oceanfront pool. Try out scuba with a free lesson offered twice daily. Hawaiian arts classes can be attended in the Garden Lobby (reservations required) and include lei making or hula lessons. The Hawaiian Cultural Court features displays and demonstrations daily in the Garden Lobby.

The Sheraton Kaua'i Resort entertains young guests with their Keiki Aloha Children's Program. (*See* Chapter 1 for more information.)

Guests can enjoy Shells, the resort's signature dining room, which hugs Po'ipu Beach, and serves breakfast, lunch and dinner. Lighter fare and a panoramic ocean vista (with live local entertainment evenings) are offered at The Point, which has both indoor and outdoor seating. A dramatic tile mural of a canoe paddler carving a path across a cresting wave welcomes guests to this casual dining spot. (Great for sunsets and one of the happening nightlife locations.) Overlooking tropical gardens and carp-filled pools is Naniwa, a Japanese dinner restaurant designed to resemble a traditional Japanese inn. The Oasis Bar & Grill and The Garden Terrace, both poolside, serve sandwiches and salads. You'll often find live Hawaiian music as a backdrop here.

Sheraton has followed the lead of other resorts and charges a hotel fee. While this one includes some nice amenities, it is unclear why the extra charge is made. Since everyone is required to pay them, why don't they just raise the rates $10? The $10 automatic hotel charge includes free local phone calls, continental breakfast, tennis, fitness center, internet and more.

Check with Pleasant Hawaiian and other package retailers regarding air/room packages that include a stay at this lovely resort.

Rates: Garden $260; Lagoon $310; Deluxe Ocean Front $370; Ocean Luxury $440; Garden Suite $490; Ocean Front Suite $670

★ *Whalers Cove*

Located in Po'ipu. Mailing address: Koloa Landing at Po'ipu, 2640 Puuholo Road, Koloa, HI 96756. 808-742-7571; 800-225-2683; fax 808-742-1185. Premier Resorts 800-367-7052. Rental agents: Suite Paradise 800-367-8020; Maui & All Islands 800-663-6962; Pleasant Hawaiian Holidays 800-242-9244.

Thirty-eight very luxurious and roomy units. Oceanside pool and barbecue. Located on a promontory overlooking the ocean. Years ago whaling ships anchored at this cove to unload passengers and cargo. A swimming beach is one mile away. The cove fronting the property offers very good snorkeling. The units are comfortable, with very nice furnishings, artworks, fully equipped kitchens, dining area and large patio/lanais. Third-floor units have jacuzzi tubs overlooking the ocean. Discounts for longer stays. Great location, convenient to Po'ipu resort attractions, activities, shopping, dining, golf, tennis. Two-night minimum stay.

Premier Resorts rates: 1BR o.v. $310 to $445 (max. 2); 2BR $380 to $545 o.v. (max. 4); Suite Paradise: 2BR 2BTH $455

North Shore Area

PRIVATE VACATION HOMES & COTTAGES

The North Shore has a plethora of homes to meet most any need or group size and there are almost as many rental agents to assist you. Following are a few homes and cottages that proved of special interest.

Aloha Condos

78-261 Manukai Street, #203, Kailua-Kona, HI 96740. 360-385-9291; 877-782-5642; fax 928-438-8272; e-mail: jim@alohacondos.com; www.alohacondos.com.

This condo booking service has fully equipped deluxe condos at Hanalei Bay Resort on the North Shore; available at reduced rates directly from the owners.

Rates: $145 to $325 nightly

★ An Angel Abode

4064 Ka'ahumanu Place, P.O. Box 3597, Princeville, HI 96722. Tel/fax 360-456-4040; e-mail: gail@travelkauai.com; www.travelkauai.com.

This is a private, custom-designed modern vacation rental home with three large bedrooms, each with private bath. Rooms have large picture windows and french doors opening onto a lanai providing distant ocean and mountain views. Located in the prestigious activity-oriented Princeville Resort, convenient to golf, tennis, ocean activities, hiking and exploring the North Shore area.

Rates: $95 to $150 per night; $325 per night for whole house

Anchorage Point

Rental agent: Na Pali Properties 800-715-7273.

Located in Ha'ena, this 2BR 2BTH home is elevated, with a spacious living/kitchen/dining room offering a panoramic ocean view. It resembles a large cabin with simple furnishings. One of the bedrooms has an adjoining shower large enough to hold a small party. The location of this is a plus and the ocean view couldn't get much better. There is some need for a bit of updating, but the price is a plus.

Rates: $1,050 to $1,250 per week for two, $300 deposit, $85 cleaning fee

Anini Beach Cottages

P.O. Box 837, Hanalei, HI 96714. 808-828-0068; 800-323-4450; fax 808-828-2067; e-mail: cottage@aloha.net; www.aloha.net/~cottage.

This accommodation offers four separate guest cottages: Plumeria is fully equipped and sleeps 6; Orchid Guest Cottage sleeps 3; the Lily Pad and Mango cottages each sleep 2. All amenities provide for a relaxing vacation; located on Kaua'i's famed North Shore. Four-night minimum stay.

Rates: $125 to $175 nightly; inquire about weekly or monthly rates

Anini Beach Hale

P.O. Box 419, Kilauea, HI 96754. 808-828-6808; 877-262-6688; e-mail: aloha@yourbeach.com; www.yourbeach.com.

This is a modern, well-equipped 2-bedroom/2-bath vacation home located just 100 paces from 'Anini Beach. A nonsmoking home set amid the exclusive enclave of vacation homes. It sleeps four in two king beds. Fully and comfortably furnished, with kitchen, living room, laundry, dishwasher and all the amenities. Enjoy one of Kaua'i's best beaches, with its calm lagoon waters ideal for swimming, snorkeling, kayaking, fishing or just lounging on the sandy shore.

Rates: $1,400 weekly (one-week minimum stay)

Anne's Condos & Studios at Princeville Resort

4890 Ka Haku Road, Princeville, HI 96722. 760-753-2763; 800-481-4991; e-mail: annkauai@gte.net; www.choice1.com/princeville_golf_condo.htm.

These nicely furnished condo units and studios are conveniently located on the Princeville Resort Golf Course. Golf nuts will enjoy the easy access to the links. It's also close to beaches, scenic lookouts, waterfalls, botanical gardens, hiking trails, adventure activities, area dining and shopping.

Rates: Studio $60 and up nightly, $400 and up weekly; Condo unit $85 and up nightly, $550 and up weekly

Devaki's Vacation Rental

P.O. Box 622, Hanalei, HI 96714. 808-826-6735; e-mail: kevdev@poi.net; www.devaki-kauai.com/hanalei-vacation-rental.

This is a spacious one-bedroom beach house located directly across from Hanalei Bay, with a backdrop of mountains and waterfalls. The unit has a large two-person outdoor shower plus a large indoor bathroom with a two-person shower. There's a fully equipped kitchen. Amenities include king bed, comfortable sofa and loveseat, laundry,

TV/VCR, private lanai and barbecue. There is also a separate studio that offers privacy for one or two people. Lots of natural lighting and air circulation. The carpeted room has sliding glass doors that open to a small private lanai. There is a fold-out futon, small fridge, microwave and bathroom with shower. The host is a personal fitness trainer who can provide healing massage and traditional Hawaiian *lomi lomi* massage.

Rates: Beach House $750 weekly; Studio $60 nightly

★ Glo Manor House

P.O. Box 221, Kilauea, HI 96754. 808-828-6684; e-mail: glomanor@hawaiian.net; www.hawaiian.net/~glomanor.

This is a private seaside 8,000-square-foot manor house located at the end of 'Anini Beach on Kaua'i's picturesque North Shore. The beach and lagoon, with a resemblance to those found in Tahiti, is protected by a large outer reef that makes it safe for swimming, snorkeling and great beachcombing. There are two separate guest studios and an 1,800-square-foot 2-bedroom apartment, fully furnished and equipped. The King's Place is a 2-bedroom/2-bath apartment unit. The Garden Studio has a king bed, kitchen and bath. The Crow's Nest studio has a queen bed and private bath.

Rates: King's Place $115 nightly; Garden Studio $75 nightly; Crow's Nest $65 nightly

Hale Honu Townhouses

4800 Hanalei Plantation Road, P.O. Box 223414, Princeville, HI 96722. 808-826-1084; 888-686-1084; fax 603-754-7027; e-mail: coral-c@aloha.net; www.aloha.net/~coral-c.

There are two well-kept and attractive 3-bedroom, 2-bath vacation condo units in the Princeville Resort on the Makai Golf Course. Great location for golfers or anyone wanting a convenient North Shore location. It's a short walk to the beach from these fully equipped units, complete with kitchens, dining rooms, lanai, laundry facilities. The two townhouses can accommodate a group of up to 15 people. Great for families.

Rates: $92 nightly (max. 4), $650 weekly; ask about large group rates

Hanalei Properties

P.O. Box 748, Hanalei, HI 96714. 808-826-6111; e-mail: hanaleibay@aol.com.

This agency has three distinctive vacation rental homes available in historic Hanalei town. The Plantation Guest House is an upscale oceanview home. The Bed, Breakfast & Beach Home is a moderately priced home just 125 yards from beautiful Hanalei Beach. Tutu's (Grandma's) Cottage is a private two-bedroom, one-bath home that sleeps four people.

Rates: Plantation Guest House $130 per night; Bed, Breakfast & Beach House $80 to $135 per night; Tutu's Cottage $950 per week for two people, $1,050 for three and $1,150 for four

Hardy's Happy Hula Hut

4515 Emmalani Drive, Princeville, HI 96722. 808-826-7168; 510-444-2913; e-mail: hardy@aloha.net or hardyic@aol.com; www.hardyshappyhulahut.com.

This is a comfortable one-bedroom condo unit with a fantastic cliffside ocean view. It's located in the resort community of Sealodge at Princeville. Next to the complex pool there is a path down to a secluded beach. The unit is fully equipped with kitchen, laundry, TV/VCR, king bed, etc. Easy access to all area activities: golf, tennis, hiking, shopping and dining.

Rates: $100 nightly, weekly rates available (three-night minimum stay)

★ ***Jungle Cabana, Jungle Bungalow and Jungle Paradise House***

Wainiha. 808-826-5141; 888-886-4969; e-mail: info@junglebungalow.com; www.junglebungalow.com; www.junglecabana.com; www.kauai-jungle-paradise.com.

The Jungle Bungalow, Jungle Cabana and Jungle Paradise Home are privately situated on 2.25 acres of lushly landscaped jungle alongside a rushing mountain stream with Wainiha Valley as a backdrop. Rent one for a romantic getaway or all three for a fun family reunion. Located a few minutes' drive to beaches, ten minutes to Hanalei or the Napali Coast.

The **Jungle Bungalow** is a secluded modern structure with a different charm. If you seek tropical style, like to kick back in a hammock, listen the sound of a rushing river and birds singing and think that relaxing in an outside clawfoot tub set in a beautiful garden is bliss, then this is *the* place for you. This two-story accommodation sleeps up to five guests. There is a complete kitchen with quality cookware. The bungalow provides total privacy for those needing a bit of quiet romance. Mountain views and private gardens complement the tropical atmosphere. Four-night minimum stay.

Rates: $135 per night dbl, $900 per week; extra nights $125; extra guests $10 each/$50 week; $90 clean-out fee

Jungle Cabana is a cozy first-class-studio-style lodging with about 350 square feet of interior space that is paneled primarily in woven bamboo and trimmed with bamboo accents. It opens up to soothing views of the rushing mountain stream and spectacular Wainiha Pali. The tropical Zen-type decor is enhanced with a bamboo sofa and furniture. There is a complete kitchen that overlooks the rushing jungle stream. The main living space is the "nature that surrounds." Bathing is in a private riverside garden setting with clawfoot tub and shower.

Here you can surely transcend reality and enjoy a private and romantic setting! Four-night minimum stay.

Rates: $110 per night; $730 per week; extra nights $100; $60 clean-out fee

Jungle Paradise House is situated along the edge of the Wainiha River. You'll find 3 bedrooms, 2 bathrooms, living room, dining room, river room, family room and a well-supplied kitchen all done with the decorative feel of Old Hawaii. The furniture and beds are new, as are the bamboo flooring, Berber carpets and ceiling fans. There is even a computer hook up if you can't tear yourself away from your laptop. Soak in the jacuzzi tub or enjoy the outdoor shower under the avocado and palm trees. If you are looking for privacy and seclusion this is the spot for you. This is the Hawaii many seek but seldom find. Four-night minimum stay.

Rates: $195 per night for up to 4 people; $1,300 per week; extra guests $15 each/$75 week (up to 4 additional guests); clean-out fee $120; refundable damage deposit $300

★ *Kai Mana Cottage*

Rental office (California): 415-388-7195; e-mail: gina@shaktigawain.com.

Kai Mana is a private 1BR 1BTH cottage located near the end of a quiet cul-de-sac in rural Kilauea. Just west of the Kilauea Lighthouse, the wildlife refuge and above Secret Beach, this unique, circular-designed cottage has a full kitchen, living room, deck, hot tub, TV/VCR. The hammock on the lanai offers a peaceful retreat. The cottage overlooks a secluded beach with a private trail leading down to it. Great for private sunning, beachcombing or super sunsets. A very secluded retreat replete with tasteful Hawaiian decor.

Rates: $185 per night or $1,200 for a 7-night weekly rental

Kauikeolani Estate and Hanalei Plantation Cottages

P.O. Box 81, Hanalei, HI 96714. 808-826-1454; 888-900-1454; fax 808-826-6363; e-mail: info@hanaleiland.com; www.hanaleiland.com.

Kauikeolani, the historic beachside plantation home of Albert Spencer Wilcox, has stood for over 100 years. Wilcox was a successful sugar planter and the fourth son of missionaries Abner and Lucy Wilcox. The estate is bounded by the Hanalei River and guests can look out upon an expansive lawn to the beautiful wide beach fronting Hanalei Bay. Mountains of the surrounding Hanalei Valley provide additional panoramic views. The estate has been restored with great attention to detail of the historic 1890s era when it was built. Kauikeolani means "vision that come in the early morning mist" and the home was named after Albert's wife, Emma Kauikeolani Napoleon Mahelona. The estate includes the main Kauikeolani seven-bedroom home, plus four other 2BR and 3BR cottages: Palaka, Umetsu, Paniolo and Nalu. These cottages were the housing provided for the plantation worker families in the early days of the estate. The main home and cottages are strictly nonsmoking. Special day rates are available for banquets, incentive groups and weddings. Three-night minimum for all cottages, plus cleaning charges apply on all rentals. This is a very special and historic place.

Rates: Kauikeolani Main Home 7 BR (max. 12), $10,000 week, $30,000 month (one-week minimum stay); Umetsu Cottage 2BR (max. 4), $300 night, $2,000 week, $7,000 month; Palaka Cottage 2BR (max. 5), $250 night, $1,500 week, $5,000 month; Paniolo Cottage 3BR (max. 6), $450 night, $3,000 week, $10,000 month; Nalu Cottage 3BR (max. 6), $450, $3,000 week, $10,000 month

Love Nest Cottage

P.O. Box 167, Anahola, HI 96703. 877-828-1700; e-mail: info@heavenly creations.org; www.heavenlycreations.org/lovenest.htm.

These secluded hideaway units appeal to the romantically inclined. The Love Nest Cottage is spacious and roomy, with beautiful interior decor, fully equipped kitchen, hammock for two. There is a king-sized canopy bed and extra sleeper sofa. Private jungle area for casual exploration. The Romantic Bamboo Bungalow is also secluded, comfortable and spacious, with king bed, large bathroom with tub and shower, full kitchen, indoor hammock (Tantra swing available). The Romantic Suite has a spacious deck, limited kitchen facilities and lovely decor. There is a VCR (no TV reception), fresh flowers in the rooms, dining either indoor or outdoors, beach gear. Any meal can be served upon request for an extra charge ($20 for breakfast for two), including romantic beachside dinners. Located on a tropical fruit-and-flower farm within minutes of sparkling northeast coast beaches. A quiet and peaceful location south of Kilauea for those intimate privacy-needed times.

Rates: Love Nest $115 nightly, $693 weekly; Romantic Bamboo Bungalow $693 weekly; Romantic Suite $445 weekly (nightly rates available)

Om Orchard Retreat

4420 Kahili Makai, P.O. Box 1190, Kilauea, HI 96754. 808-828-0111; fax 808-828-6758; e-mail: om@aloha.net; www.omorchard.com.

This is a comfortable and well-kept cottage featuring large glass windows with a nice nature view. The bedroom loft is a roomy 560 square feet and the cottage is furnished in comfortable island-style decor and furniture. There is a large bathroom and a unique private outdoor lava-rock shower surrounded by banana trees. Take your shower *au naturel*! There is also a fully furnished kitchenette with all amenities.

Rates: $135 nightly (September through May); $150 nightly (June through August); three-night minimum stay

River Estate

5-6691 Kuhio Highway, P.O. Box 169, Hanalei, HI 96714. 800-484-6030, security code 2468; 808-826-5118; e-mail: info@riverestate.com; www.riverestate.com.

River Estate is a two-acre riverfront botanical garden one block from a secluded beach. This property specializes in private group retreats, honeymoons, weddings, family vacations, private gatherings, etc. The Guest House has two bedrooms, two baths; The Treehouse has three bedrooms, two baths. Units come with full furnishings and are fully equipped for guest comfort and enjoyment.

Rates: $175 and up nightly

BED AND BREAKFASTS

The following are some of the bed & breakfast options offered on the North Shore. See the end of this chapter under "Rental Agents" for companies that offer a wide range of B&B units around the island.

Aloha Aina Bed & Breakfast

P.O. Box 1232, Hanalei, HI 96714. 808-828-1155; e-mail: iam@aloha.net.

This B&B is located on a secluded 3-acre estate in beautiful Kilauea, with open mountain and ocean views. There are tropical fruit and flower gardens, a tranquil valley for walking, full kitchen, king-size bed, jacuzzi, stone lanai and all the expected comforts.

Rates: $80 nightly

★ Aloha Plantation

4481 Malulani Street, Kilauea, HI 96754, mailing address: P.O. Box 683, Hanalei, HI 96714. 808-828-1693; 877-658-6977; e-mail: alohaplantation@hawaiian.net; www.garden-isle.com/aloha.

This is a vintage 1920-era plantation manager's home on the North Shore. There are two guest rooms. One room has a double bed and shared shower. The second room has two double beds and a private bath. The home is decorated with Hawaiian antiques, including comfortable wrought-iron beds with whispering ceiling fans overhead. There is a screened porch overlooking a tropical courtyard.

Rates: $50 nightly, room with shared shower; $60 nightly, room with private bath

★ Hale 'Aha

3375 Kamehameha, P.O. Box 3370, Princeville, HI 96722. 808-826-6733; 800-826-6733; fax 808-826-9052; e-mail: kauai@pixi.com; www.haleaha.com.

This is the only B&B overlooking the Prince Golf Course, located along 480 feet of fairway. There is a nearby trail leading to a secluded beach. The upstairs house is reserved for guests; the living room is pretty and pastel, with a cozy fireplace and dining area set up for breakfast. Rooms are cushy and comfy. Everything is very homey, especially the hospitality of your innkeepers, Billie and Gary Sparks. They put the coffee on at 7 for early risers who might want it with a muffin or cereal on the run. But if you wait, you'll be treated to a full spread that includes hot homemade bread (with guava butter), muffins, fresh fruit, granola or cereal, a tropical smoothie, fresh fruit, steamed brown rice with brown sugar, crushed almonds, raisins and fruit plus a baked apple with whipped cream. Rooms have TVs, mini-refrigerators, bathroom amenities and extra towels and pillow. Guests are entitled to substantial golf discounts at the course. They take Visa and MC, but they don't allow children, making this a better choice for those vacations when you leave the kids at home. The penthouse suite is the top floor of the property, with 1,000 square feet of room, separate living area, large whirlpool tub and washer and dryer. Three-night minimum stay.

Rates: $115 to $275 per night

★ *Hale Ho'o Maha*

2883 Kalihiwai Road, P.O. Box 422, Kilauea, HI 96754. 808-828-1341; 800-851-0291; fax 808-828-2046; e-mail: hoomaha@aloha.net; www.aloha.net/~hoomaha.

This B&B is located in a country farm-like setting (in fact a bull lives just down the road), surrounded by ponds and streams with the ocean and bay just a bit farther away. The decor is whimsical and eclectic, with lots of wood and wood artifacts and an aquarium in the living room. Each room has a personality of its own: the Pineapple Room has a round bed with pineapple bedspread, rugs and knick-knacks; the romantic Guava Room has a canopy bed with sheer, wispy draping. Breakfast includes Anahola Granola (made just a few miles away), muffins and a plate of fresh fruit that not only offers papaya, pineapple, bananas and grapes, but tropical rambutans in season, too. Located on 5 acres, this home is within walking distance of two beaches. Visa or Mastercard accepted. Your hosts are Toby and Kirby.

Rates: Four varied accommodations from $60 to $85 per night, double or single occupancy; $20 per night charged for additional person. A 50 percent deposit is required to confirm your reservation for each room

★ *Hale Manu Bed & Breakfast*

Kokea Farm, Kilauea, mailing address P.O. Box 3500, Princeville, HI 96722. 808-828-6641; 888-828-6641; www.bnbweb.com/halemanu.html.

Hale Manu is on Kaua'i's spectacular North Shore in the middle of a three-acre tropical gardener's paradise. All types of tropical plants, orchids, flowers, palms and more make Hale Manu a botanical garden and working flower farm. Lots of birds inhabit the area as well. There is a spacious one-bedroom guest apartment, nicely furnished with all the expected amenities and comforts.

Rates: $95 nightly

★ *The Historic Bed & Breakfast*

P.O. Box 1662, Hanalei, HI 96714. 808-826-4622; e-mail historicbnb@hotmail.com; www.historicbnb.com.

Built in 1901, this home is included in the National and State Historic Registry as the oldest Buddhist mission on Kaua'i. Following years of neglect, the building was scheduled for demolition but in 1985 a few local businesspeople banded together and the building was moved across the island and converted into a residence. Over 95 percent of the original building was saved. Rooms are furnished with antique bedding and *shoji* Japanese screen sliding doors that open onto a long hallway of polished wood. The B&B is located next to Postcards Café and within walking distance of the beach. Owner Kelly Sato offers a full breakfast.

Rates: Shared bath $85, private bath $105. Two-night minimum stay

North Country Farms

P.O. Box 723, Kilauea, HI 96754. 808-828-1513; fax 808-828-0805; e-mail: ncfarms@aloha.net; www.northcountryfarms.com.

North Country Farms is a four-acre organic vegetable, fruit and flower farm. The 1BR redwood guest cottage includes a full-service kitchenette for snacks and meals. The two one-bedroom guest cottages (the Garden Cottage and Orchard Cottage) include full-service kitchenettes for snacks and meals. Cottages have covered lanais, queen bedroom, extra sleeping accommodations in living room, stereo CD, lots of books, magazines, games, puzzles, etc. Your hostess, Lee Roversi, adds that her family of four (three teenagers) love to open the farm to other families. It's a great place, with lots of aloha. The cottages and farm are completely child-friendly. Guests are invited to pick their own fruit and veggies; aloha breakfast basket provided upon arrival. As the guest houses are separate accommodations, they lend themselves very well to a traveling family. This is a lovely area, quiet and close to many North Shore attractions—and a good deal for the price.

Rates: $110 per night

Pavilions at Seacliff

Contact: Estate Manager, P.O. Box 3500-302, Princeville, HI 96722. 808-828-1185; fax 808-828-1208. Rental agents: 'Anini Beach Vacation Rentals 800-448-6333 or 808-826-4000; Homes & Villas in Paradise 800-282-2736, 808-262-4663; Prosser Realty 800-767-4707.

The property is bordered by the Kilauea Point Wildlife Bird Refuge and Kilauea Lighthouse. The house offers three oceanview master suites and 3.5 baths. A lap pool with jacuzzi. Washer/dryer, fax machine, plus a complete workout room. Three-night minimum stay. Rates are for up to 6 guests. 10 percent monthly discount. $1,000 deposit required.

Rates: $700/600 nightly

HOTELS, CONDOS AND HOSTELS

Inexpensive Hotels, Condos and Hostels

★ *Hale Moi Cottages*

5300 Ka Haku Road, P.O. Box 899, Princeville, HI 96714. 808-826-9602. Rental agents: Marc Resorts 800-535-0085; Na Pali Properties 800-715-7273.

Forty units in two-story buildings. Hotel rooms, studio suites with kitchens, 1.5-bedroom suites with kitchens. Mountain and garden views. Full kitchens and washer/dryer, except in hotel units. All have remodeled kitchens and bathrooms. The studios are spacious—one very large room with a nice, full kitchen. The hotel units are actually mini-suites, with a small bedroom and living area. A tiny alcove provides some basic kitchen-type amenities: mini-fridge, coffee maker, microwave, eating utensils, glasses, cups and dishes. The units are an interesting cross between a hotel room, condo unit, private cottage and small apartment! They are just big enough, with a charming cottage look, both inside and out. Located next door to Winds of Beamreach Restaurant. Check in at Pali Ke Kua office across the street.

Marc Resort year-round rates: Hotel Room m.v. $129 (2); Studio Suite m.v. w/kitchen $159; 1.5 BR, 2BTH Suite m.v. $179

★ *Hanalei Inn*

5468 Kuhio Highway, P.O. Box 1373, Hanalei, HI 96714. 808-826-9333 or 808-826-1506. Owners are Michelle and Parnell Kaiser.

Full kitchen, queen beds (third person or child okay on futon). Small, rustic apartments, clean and well-kept. Outdoor phone for free local calls. This place is strictly for the backpackers, nature freaks, adventurers, kayakers, hikers, surfers, etc., who only require a bare-bones roof over their heads, a sack and a shower. Not for the fussy.

Rates: $65 per night; unit without full kitchen $55

Paniolo

Located in Princeville. Rental agent: Hanalei Vacations 800-487-9833.

There are two-bedroom, two-bath cottages as well as studios and one-bedroom, two-bath condo units. Swimming pool. It's a short walk to shopping and the beach.

Rates: 2BR/2BTH cottages, Studio and 1BR condo units $80 to $120 nightly

Sandpiper Village

Located in Princeville. Rental agents: Hanalei Vacations 800-487-9833; Oceanfront Realty 800-222-5541.

This property offers hotel rooms, one-, two- or three-bedroom units. Pool and hot tub. Some two-bedrooms have lofts and some units have washers/dryers. Not all rooms have phones.

Rates: g.v. studio units $85 nightly/$535 weekly; 2BR plus loft $150 nightly plus clean-out fee charged.

★ *Sealodge*

Located in Princeville. Rental agents: Carol Goodwin rents her J-7 unit with a fabulous view of the Kilauea Lighthouse (plus other units at Sealodge). Write: 3615 Kingridge Drive, San Mateo, CA 94403 or call 650-573-0636. Oceanfront Realty 800-222-5541; Maui & All Islands 800-663-6962; Hanalei Vacations 800-487-9833; Prosser Realty 800-767-4707.

These are oceanview units located along the bluff at Princeville. The exterior is cedar shake, which is reminiscent of accommodations on the Oregon beachfront. While each unit has a different view, those on the far eastern end have a spectacular view of Kilauea Lighthouse and the Pacific coastline. Watch the waves come in over the extensive reef, enjoy the seabirds frolicking in the air currents, or during the winter, enjoy this outstanding whale-watching lookout. Just make sure you pack your binoculars! The trail down to the beach is marked by a "use at your own risk" sign and is steep and very slippery when muddy—recommended only for the hale and hearty. The trail ends on a rocky shore and you will need to clamber over the rocks to your left to reach the crescent-shaped stretch of white-sand beach that is the length of a football field. Because of the enormous 'Anini reef, this piece of coastline is fairly well protected year-round from high ocean swell and surf. With all the comforts of home, an outstanding vista, and value priced, you could hardly do better on the North Shore. (Cleaning fee charged for stays of less than five nights.)

Rates: 1BR 1BTH $109 nightly/$723 weekly; 2BR 2BTH $135 nightly

Moderate Hotels, Condos and Hostels

Alii Kai I

3830 Edward Road, Princeville, HI 96722. Rental agents: Kaua'i Paradise Vacations 800-826-7782; Hanalei Vacations 800-487-9833; Hanalei North Shore Properties 800-488-3336; Oceanfront Realty 800-222-5541.

Two-bedroom, two-bath units, some ocean front. Depending on the owners, units furnished with two double beds, one queen or one king. Most units have sleeper sofas. Some units have full-size washer/dryer. Pool.

Rates: 2BR 2BTH Deluxe $130 to $145 nightly/$850 to $955 weekly

Alii Kai II

3830 Edward Road, Princeville, HI 96722. On-property management 800-648-9988. Rental agent: Kaua'i Paradise Vacations 800-826-7782; Hanalei Vacations 800-487-9833; Hanalei North Shore Properties 800-488-3336; Oceanfront Realty 800-222-5541.

Some units with view of the ocean, others offer mountain vistas. Most units are 1,100 square feet. and have been recently redecorated. Most include microwave, TV and washer/dryer. Pool and hot tub.

Rates: 1BR studio $95 nightly/$605 weekly; 2BR 2BTH $135/$120

(The) Cliffs at Princeville

3811 Edward Road, Princeville. Managed by Premier Resorts. Rental agents: Premier Resorts 800-367-7052; Kaua'i Paradise Vacations 800-826-7782; Maui & All Islands 800-663-6962; Hanalei Vacations 800-487-9833; Hanalei North Shore Properties 800-488-3336; Kaua'i Vacation Rentals 800-367-5025; Oceanfront Realty 800-222-5541; Prosser Realty 800-767-4707.

There are 202 vacation studios, 1-bedroom 2-bath, 2-bedroom 2-bath and even 4-bedroom, 4-bath units available through some rental agents. There is an on-site activity director offering a variety of classes, hula-aerobics and even a weekly local farmers market. Attend a free movie night or try out your talents at karaoke! Amenities include pool, 4 tennis courts, two jacuzzis, sauna, barbecue area and a recreation pavilion. Units have ceiling fans, lanais, full kitchens. Daily maid service. Beach nearby.

Rates: Prosser Rates: Oceanfront 4BR/4BTH $175; Premier Resorts Rates: start at $165 for a one-bedroom g.v. with two-night minimum required; Oceanfront Realty Rates: 1BR $130 nightly/$840 weekly; 2BR $160 nightly/$1,550 weekly; 2BR deluxe $175 nightly/$1,225 weekly

Emmalani Court

Located in Princeville. Rental agent: Pacific Paradise Properties 800-800-3637; Kaua'i Vacation Rentals 800-367-5025.

Two-bedroom, two-bath unit with ocean and golf course views.

Rates: Nightly $175, weekly rate $1,050/$1,200; cleaning fee $75 per stay

Hanalei Bay Villas

5300 Ka Haku Road, Princeville, HI 96714. Rental agents: Oceanfront Realty 800-222-5541; 808-826-6585; fax 808-826-6478; e-mail: kauai@oceanfrontrealty.com; www.oceanfrontrealty.com. Marc Resorts 800-535-0085; Na Pali Properties 800-715-7273.

These condominium units are actually single structures with views of the golf course, mountains and Hanalei Bay in the distance. The condos are 2BR 2BTH with the upper level providing living area, kitchen, dining room and half bath. On the downstairs level are two bedrooms and two bathrooms. Beautifully furnished in pastel hues, lots of extras, including lanais off both the top and lower levels. Located across from Pali Ke Kua Condo and Winds of Beamreach Restaurant.

Oceanfront Realty Rates: 2BR $130 to $205; 3BR $130 to $260; Marc Resort Rates: 2BR Dlx 2.5BTH suite w/kitchen m.v. $199, or bay view $231, maximum 6.

★ *Hanalei Colony Resort*

5-7130 Kuhio Highway, mailing address P.O. Box 206, Hanalei, HI 96714. 808-826-6235; 800-628-3004 U.S. & Canada; fax 808-826-9893; e-mail: aloha@hcr.net; www.hcr.com. Rental agent: Prosser Realty 800-767-4707.

Hanalei Colony Resort, located on 4.5 acres of beach front, is a village of condominiums (13 two-story buildings, each with four condominiums) that offers very comfortable two-bedroom accommodations (most with two baths). Situated just prior to the end of the road at Haena, near the beginning of the famed Napali Coast, it's the last vestige of civilization on the North Shore. The rooms are decorated island-style and they are open and airy, with fabulous large picture-window coastal and mountain views—and the beach is in your front yard. Other condos and resorts are more luxurious perhaps and have more upscale furnishings and amenities, but you'll get the feel of the South Pacific here, with its remoteness and sense of being close to nature. It's reminiscent somewhat of places like Moorea and Bora Bora in French Polynesia, with the beautiful beaches, jagged mountain peaks and lush green environment. This is truly a place to get away from it all because they don't have TVs, stereos or phones (although there is a telephone by the pool where guests can make complimentary local phone calls). Units closer to the beach have nicer views (i.e., #G3). It's a short walk from any unit to the parking lot. They do offer a weekly complimentary poolside breakfast with tea, coffee and juice and a selection of fresh fruits and freshly baked pastries, as well as a weekly afternoon mai tai party. These are both held at the new oceanfront Makana Room, which is used for banquets, weddings and other events, with full catering service available. Each morning between 8 and 10 a.m., it's open to guests as a lounge area, and has internet access. The Napali Coffee House & Art Gallery, in the front of the Makana building, sells morning coffee, espresso and pastries, as well as lunch-time deli sandwiches, salads and fresh smoothies. Hand-crafted island art and jewelry are displayed and sold. Other guest amenities also include pool and jacuzzi. Twice weekly maid service. Car and condo packages available. Weekly discounts. And if you are planning a wedding on Kaua'i, they also have a wedding coordination service and special wedding packages available. If you're looking for the one place on all of Kaua'i to really get away from it all, look no further. This is it. Online booking through their website.

Rates: 2BR g.v. $195/$180; o.v. 1BTH $225/$205; o.v. 2BTH $230/$215; o.f. 2BTH $280/$255; premium o.f. $335/$300

Kamahana

Located in Princeville. Rental agents: Oceanfront Realty 800-222-5541; Prosser Realty 800-767-4707; Pacific Paradise Properties 800-800-3637.

One- and two-story condominiums overlooking the golf course. Rooms have high, slanted ceilings that offer lots of sun during the day, though stay cooler at night. Ceiling fans. Spacious, airy, modern kitchens are well-equipped with all the necessities. The picture windows and sliding glass doors are all around and offer plenty of vistas. Room extras include things such as a closet full of books and cards, beach chairs, golf balls and even a boogie board. Since each unit is privately owned amenities will vary between units. Small, uncrowded pool area with "rec room" for gatherings. Located next to Sealodge.

Rates: 2BR 2BTH o.v. $109 nightly/$723 weekly; Deluxe $145 to $160 nightly/$995 to $1,100 weekly

Pali Ke Kua

5300 Ka Haku Road, P.O. Box 899, Princeville, HI 96714. 808-826-9066. Rental agents: Marc Resorts Hawai'i 800-535-0085, toll-free fax 800-633-5085, local 808-922-9700. Hanalei Vacations 800-487-9833; Kaua'i Paradise Vacations 800-826-7782; Kaua'i Vacation Rentals 800-367-5025; Pacific Paradise Properties 800-800-3637; Oceanfront Realty 800-222-5541; Maui & All Islands 800-663-6962; Hanalei North Shore Properties 800-488-3336.

Located on the cliffs at Princeville, adjacent to the Princeville golf courses. Ninety-eight units in two-story wooden buildings with Hawaiian-style roofing. 1BR units are 763 square feet, 2BR are 1,135 square feet. Each unit is like a small, private apartment with a well-equipped kitchen and washer/dryer (with a starter box of detergent). The furniture is light bamboo with fabrics in rich colors and patterns. The units are fresh and particularly clean and well maintained. There are a number of nice appointments, such as eyelet-edge lace on the sheets and large counter space in both the kitchen and bathroom. Outdoor amenities include pool and jacuzzi. A short walk to a small beach. Winds of Beamreach Restaurant located on property.

Rates: Marc Resorts year-round rates: 1BR dlx m.v. or g.v. $167; o.v. $183; o.f. $207; 2BR dlx m.v. or g.v. $207; o.v. $223; o.f. $263

Pali Uli

Ka Haku Road, Princeville Resort, HI 96714. Rental agents: Hanalei Vacations 800-487-9833; Oceanfront Realty 800-222-5541; Prosser Realty 800-767-4707.

This is a very private, small complex of individual cottage-style units but very well-appointed and fully equipped for vacation comfort. Kitchen, dining area, living room. Each 2BR/2bath unit has a unique soaking tub on a very private lanai. Great ocean views, privacy, quiet and all of Princeville Resort's amenities nearby.

Rates: 2BR/2BTH $75 to $95 nightly, $525 to $750 weekly

Puamana

Located on golf course in Princeville. 808-826-9768. Rental agents: Oceanfront Realty 800-222-5541; Prosser Realty 800-767-4707.

Two-bedroom, two-bath units, many with ocean views. Swimming pool.

Rates: 1BR 2BTH $85 to $99 nightly/$595 to $693 weekly; Deluxe $120 to $150 nightly/$840 to $1,050 weekly; Premium $175 nightly/ $1,225 weekly

Expensive Hotels, Condos and Hostels

★ Hanalei Bay Resort

5380 Honoiki Road, Princeville, HI 96722. Aston Hotels & Resorts 800-922-7866; e-mail: info@aston-hotels.com; www.aston-hotels.com. Rental agents: Quintus Resorts 800-827-4427; Maui & All Islands 800-663-6962; Pleasant Hawaiian Holidays 800-242-9244; Hanalei Vacations 800-487-9833; Oceanfront Realty 800-222-5541; Kaua'i Paradise Vacations 800-826-7782.

The Hanalei Bay Resort offers three floors with 153 rooms in one building plus another 75 one- , two-, and three-bedroom suites in separate complexes. No elevators. Suites are equipped with a complete kitchen, offering a full-size refrigerator, stove/oven, microwave, dishwasher and coffee maker. Units are spacious and nicely furnished; the suites have both a homey and a luxuriant feel. The high-beamed ceilings have tropical fans. Telephones in both living room and bedroom. The upholstered chaise longue is romantic, elegant and comfortable. One-bedroom suites are 1,091 square feet with two TVs. Two-bedroom suites are 1,622 square feet with two bathrooms and three televisions. Three-bedroom suites are 2,085 square feet with three bathrooms, four TVs and service for eight guests. Pay-per-view TV on command is available for all. The suites are a bit of a walk from the lobby and some walkways are steep climbs, especially if you have luggage.

There are a lot of free activities for guests: slide presentations, scuba lessons and a tennis clinic. The on-site Bali Hai restaurant has a spectacular view. Sunday afternoon there is jazz in the Happy Talk Lounge. The pool and jacuzzi are built in a natural lagoon setting surrounded by waterfalls, with an island in the middle. It almost looks like it was there before and the hotel was built around it. The bathrooms are unusually decorated with a Victorian look: green tile and floral decor make it more homey and a lot less sterile than most hotel bathrooms. Resort amenities include the over-sized lagoon swimming pool and eight complimentary tennis courts (some lighted for night play). Rooms feature balconies, air conditioning, telephones and daily maid service. Nonsmoking rooms available on request. Hotel rooms are 521 square feet and studios are 570 square feet. The Princeville Makai and Prince Golf Courses are adjacent to the property (a total of 45 holes), with golf shuttle service. Conference facilities available.

Rates: Hotel m.v. $190; Studio m.v. $205; Hotel g.v. $210; Studio g.v. $225; Hotel o.v. $270; Studio o.v. $285; 1BR m.v. $345; 1BR o.v. $385; 2BR m.v. $430; 2BR o.v. $50; 3BR o.v. $735. Inquire with Aston on special promotional packages, senior discounts or "Island Hopper" specials.

★ *Princeville Resort*

5520 Ka Haku Rd., P.O. Box 223069, Princeville, HI 96722. 800-826-4400 from the U.S. & Canada, locally 808-826-9644; 800-325-3535; fax 808-826-1166; e-mail: info@princeville.com; www.princeville.com. Booking also through Pleasant Hawaiian Holidays 800-242-9244.

The handsome 252-room Princeville Resort opened in 1985. The resort has won wide acclaim in the media over the years, being ranked as one of the world's top resorts by readers of prestigious magazines like *Conde Nast Traveler* and *Golf Magazine*. It is a stunning property set gracefully on 23 acres on Pu'u Poa Ridge above Hanalei Bay, with Bali Hai mountain forming a majestic backdrop. From the moment you enter the spacious lobby you will feel worlds away. While not traditionally Hawaiian, this hotel has classic elegance, with a European flare. The use of water throughout the lobby, above the restaurant and in the foyer creates reflecting pools that glimmer and glisten. With a lobby so enormous and opulent, it is surprisingly simple to find a quiet corner. Off to one side is the library lounge, a popular spot for taking afternoon tea, reading a good book or watching the sun slowly sink from either the veranda or a cozy sofa indoors.

The resort comprises three separate buildings that terrace down Pu'u Poa Ridge, reaching from the top plateau of Princeville to the beach of Hanalei Bay. The lobby and entrance are located on the ninth floor, the pool and beach are on the first floor. A total of six rooms are available for the physically impaired. There is a freshwater swimming pool and three whirlpool spas plus an exercise room and an in-house cinema showing movies daily. A thoughtful addition in the guest rooms is a "Do Not Disturb" light that you can switch on from next to the bed that glows out in the hallway. The bathrooms are divine, filled with oversized bathtubs, marble double vanities, tele-

Text continued on page 176.

PRIVATE VACATION HOME RENTAL AGENTS

'Anini Beach Vacation Rentals

P.O. Box 1220, Hanalei Bay, HI 96714. 800-448-6333; 808-826-4000; fax 808-826-9636; e-mail: anini@aloha.net; www.anini.com.

They offer a variety of two-, three- and four-bedroom rental cottages, beachfront and executive homes on the North Shore. Rates: cottages $100 and up nightly; beachfront homes $200 and up nightly; executive homes $600 and up nightly.

Bali Hai Realty, Inc.

5-5088 Kuhio Highway, Hanalei Bay, HI 96714. 808-826-7244; 800-404-5200; e-mail: info@balihai.com; www.balihai.com.

This realty management company has a large inventory of beachfront vacation homes and condo rental units, specializing in the North Shore area and Princeville.

Grantham Resorts

3176 Po'ipu Road, Suite 1, Koloa, HI 96756. 808-742-7200; 800-325-5701 and 800-742-1412; fax 808-742-9093; e-mail: info@grantham-resorts.com; www.grantham-resorts.com.

Grantham Resorts offers 100 Po'ipu Beach rental properties at ten different beach resorts in Po'ipu ranging from bungalows to oceanfront condominiums.

Hanalei North Shore Properties

P.O. Box 607, Hanalei, HI 96714. 808-826-9622; 800-488-3336; e-mail: hnsp@aloha.net; www.planet-hawaii.com/visit-kauai.

Condominium rentals, plus many outstanding cottages and celebrity homes. Charo's own beachfront villa is available for vacation rental. It is situated on three oceanfront acres, complete with 4 master suites and 6 baths. Located on Tunnels Beach. Or how about "Club Nash," the premier beachfront estate of Graham and Susan Nash. 4 bedrooms, 3.5 baths on Hanalei Bay. This Old Hawaiian–style home was completed in 1992 and runs between $4,200 to $5,000 per week. Other homes from $750 to $5,600 per week. Condos from $500 per week.

Harrington's Paradise Properties

P.O. Box 1345, 5-5408 Kuhio Highway, Hanalei, HI 96714. 808-826-9655; 888-826-9655; fax 808-826-7330; e-mail: hpprop@aloha.net; www.oceanfrontkauai.com.

A varied selection of homes and cottages in many price ranges, primarily on the North Shore. Five-night minimum stay most of the year, with the exception of summer (one-week minimum) and Christmas (two-week minimum).

Incredible Journey

Mailing address, P.O. Box 563, Applegate, CA 95703. 530-878-4988; 888-729-6899; fax 530-878-8515; e-mail: jc@incrediblejourney.net; www.incrediblejourney.net.

This booking service offers several unique B&Bs, condos, cottages and private homes around Kaua'i. Accommodations range from moderate to deluxe. Rates from $55 and up nightly.

★ Maui & All Islands Condominiums & Cars

P.O. Box 947, Lynden, Washington 98264. 800-663-6962; toll-free fax 888-654-MAUI; www.mauiallislands.com.

Rental homes on the North Shore and around Kaua'i, as well as a large selection of condominiums.

★ Na Pali Properties

P.O. Box 475, Hanalei, HI 96714. 808-826-7272; 800-715-7273; fax 808-826-7665; e-mail: kauai-1@aloha.net; www.napaliprop.com.

Specializes in rental homes on the North Shore. They earn a star for having a wide range of selection and prices. They offer quaint cottages, five-bedroom homes and even an outstanding historic three-bedroom home on Hanalei Bay built in 1904. Prices begin at $450 per week and go up to $2,000.

Princeville Real Estate

3651 Albert Road, Princeville, HI 96722. 808-826-4492; fax 808-826-7475; e-mail: info@kauaigolfproperties; www.kauaigolfproperties.com.

This realtor carries a large inventory of vacation rental homes and condominiums at all price ranges in the Princeville Resort and North Shore areas. They specialize in golf vacation home/condo rentals for the Princeville Resort golf courses.

★ Prosser Realty

4379 Rice Street, P.O. Box 367, Lihu'e, HI 96766. 808-245-4711; 800-767-4707; fax 808-245-8115; e-mail: realty@aloha.net; www.prosserrealty.net.

Prosser Realty gets special mention for having a very interesting selection of rental homes, they also rent condominiums from a wide inventory of properties around Kaua'i. They promise to find you the best possible vacation accommodations for the lowest possible price.

Summers Realty

1310 Inia Street, Kapa'a, HI 96746. 808-822-5876; fax 808-822-6933; e-mail: summerre@gte.net; www.summers-realty-kauai.com.

This realtor has a number of vacation rental homes and condos available island-wide, all price ranges.

Tropical Properties

4489 Aku Road, P.O. Box 826, Hanalei, HI 96714. 808-826-1616; 888-826-3211; fax 808-826-1089; e-mail: kody@aloha.net; www.kauaitropicalproperties.com.

This realty company has a number of vacation rentals, homes, cottages, condos available on the North Shore. All price ranges available, check for the latest rates.

phones and music speakers. In each bathroom there is a "magic" window that electronically changes to allow for view or opaqueness. Tasteful additions such as the fresh orchids in the vase in the bathroom, add to that pampered feeling. The view is one of the primary amenities here and from every possible angle of the hotel, they've incorporated its picture-perfect setting. The resort is beautiful during the day, but perhaps even more spectacular at night. The Living Room Lounge has a very comfortable and homey feel and you can enjoy afternoon tea while appreciating the view. Inquire about the Princeville Golf Club passes that offer multiple rounds for multiple days at discounts. Resort packages are also available including the Prince Package (which offers golf discounts and breakfast), Luxury Romance Package, Luxury Taste Package, Luxury Holiday Package.

Cafe Hanalei is much more spectacular than its name seems to indicate. In fact, it doesn't have much at all in common with a café. The Hanalei Bay below and the cliffs best known as Bali Hai create a lovely and romantic dining ambiance for breakfast, lunch, dinner or Sunday brunch. (*See* Chapter 4 for reviews of the restaurants.) The resort also has available a very nice selection of meeting and banquet facilities.

Activities include their Hawaiian Cultural program of Hula and Hawaiian implement demonstrations, Hawaiian storytelling and *lau hala* weaving. Should you feel the need for extra pampering, the Prince Health Club and Spa is located at the Prince Golf and Country Club. Short-term membership rates are $12 per person per day, weekly fee $45, two-week fee $65, monthly fee $95. All users must be at least 16 years of age. (*See* "Spas & Fitness Centers" in Chapter 6 for more information.)

The Princeville Hotel's Keiki Aloha program is available for children 5 to 12 years of age and designed with play in mind. Qualified youth counselors plan a full schedule of activities including Hawaiian crafts, sandcastle building, beach and pool games, evening movies. (*See* Chapter 1 for more information.)

Even if you are not fortunate enough to have the opportunity to stay at this resort, be sure to stop and visit and you are sure to make plans for a stay during another vacation to Kaua'i.

Rates: Mountain/Garden $390; partial o.v. $450; o.v. $555; Prince Junior Suites $650, Executive Suites $1,150; Presidential Suites $2,900; and Royal Suite $3,700. Third adult an additional $60 per night

Pu'u Po'a

5300 Ka Haku Road, P.O. Box 899, Princeville, HI 96714. 808-826-9602. Rental agents: Marc Resorts Hawai'i 800-535-0085, toll-free fax 800-633-5085, local 808-922-9700; Hanalei Vacations 800-487-9833; Kaua'i Vacation Rentals 800-367-5025; Kaua'i Paradise Vacations 800-826-7782;

Oceanfront Realty 800-222-5541; Maui & All Islands 800-663-6962; Hanalei North Shore Properties 800-488-3336; Pacific Paradise Properties 800-800-3637.

Fifty-six units in four-story buildings with ultra-modern exterior. Pool and tennis court. Units have washer/dryer, ceiling fans, full kitchens and daily maid service. Two-night minimum stay.

Rates: 2BR dlx o.v. $223; 2BR luxury o.v. $263; 2BR o.f. $195 to $214/$1,365 to $1,500 weekly (max. 6)

Retreats/Large Groups/Reunions

Island Enchantment

P.O. Box 821, Anahola, HI 96703. 808-823-0705; 888-281-8292; e-mail: enchant@aloha.net; www.aloha.net/~enchant/kauainaturesites.html.

Humberto and Tatiana Blanco provide accommodations, in addition to offering art, yoga and poetry classes. This riverside retreat is five minutes from a lovely cove beach and close to the Anahola mountains. Your stay may be combined with a 6- to 8-day tour. Their outdoor adventures offer an opportunity to learn and practice the elements of yoga, body/mind techniques, meditation and massage, plus swimming beneath secluded waterfalls. Nicely furnished rooms with private bath facilities.

Rates: Single/double w/private bath $90 nightly, $575 weekly

Kahili Mountain Park

4035 Kaumuali'i Highway, P.O. Box 298, Koloa, HI 96756. 808-742-9921; fax 808-245-3100; e-mail: aua@hawaiian.net; www.sdamall.com/kahilipark.

Owned and operated by the Seventh Day Adventist Church, this camp is 20 minutes from Lihu'e airport and 7 miles from Po'ipu Beach. There are 43 cabins located on 197 acres of beautiful garden park in an area of natural beauty—a rustic getaway in the rolling foothills of Kahili Mountain. Cabins and cabinettes accommodate up to 6 people. Cabinettes offer 5 twin beds, 2 that can be made into kings, a kitchenette with a two-burner stove; shared bathrooms and showers. Cabins have two twin beds and one double and sleep up to 4 people. (Two cabins sleep up to 6.) Each has a half-bath inside and an outdoor private shower. The kitchen includes a two-burner stove and small refrigerator. The newer cabins have two twin beds and one queen bed, a kitchen with two-burner stove. Full indoor bath and shower and screened porch. Laundry on premises. They provide linens (including bedding and towels), dishes, dish soap, cookware.

Rates: Cabinettes $40; Cabins $60; extra person $6

★ *Kauikeolani Estate and Hanalei Plantation Cottages*

P.O. Box 81, Hanalei, HI 96714. 808-826-1454; 888-900-1454; fax 808-826-6363; e-mail: halelea@aloha.net; www.hanaleiland.com.

(See above listing under the North Shore area's "Private Vacation Homes & Cottages" for detailed information.) Available for banquets, incentive groups and weddings. three-night minimum for all cottages.

Keapana Center

5620 Keapana Road, Kapa'a, HI 96746. 808-822-7968; 808-822-7968; e-mail: keapana@aloha.net; www.planet-hawaii.com/keapana.

Located on six acres, the emphasis here is on a nurturing, healthful environment. A jacuzzi, steam bath and massage are available. Five minutes to Kapa'a town and the beach. Continental breakfast included (island fruits and fresh-baked bread). Rooms share bath facilities.

Rates: Single $40-55; Double $55-70

YMCA Camp Naue

c/o YMCA, P.O. Box 1786, Lihu'e, HI 96766, Office 808-246-9090; fax 808-246-4411, Camp: 808-826-6419. Camp Naue is located on four beachfront acres between the 7 and 8 mile markers on the State Highway, past Ha'ena on the North Shore.

They offer two co-ed bunk houses that sleep up to 50 people and a bathhouse with hot/cold showers and restroom facilities. The kitchen seats 60 people. They also have a two-bedroom/one-bath beach cabin that sleeps up to 6 people. The beach cabin may be rented as part of a group reservation or for individual use. The beach cabin must be rented in order to receive exclusive use of Camp Naue. Because of the capacity of the camp, they only accept reservations for groups of 15 or more, except for the cabin, which requires no minimum, but a maximum of 6 people.

Camp Naue Rates: Bunk Houses—Kaua'i resident $11 per person/ non-resident $12 per person. Tent use—one person with tent $10. Each additional person in the same tent $7 per person. Cabin (renter furnishes bedding) with group $40 per day, individual rental $50 per day. Kitchen use: $25 per day and is non-refundable

YWCA Camp Sloggett

YWCA of Kaua'i, 3094 Elua Street, Lihu'e, HI 96766. 808-245-5959; fax 808-245-5961, camp phone 808-335-6060; e-mail: kauaiyw@pixi.net; www.pixi.com/~kauaiyw.

The YWCA hostel and campground Camp Sloggett is located in the heart of Koke'e State Park on the island's west side, above the Waimea Canyon. The grounds offer 2 acres of open field space, covered fire pit for camp fires, barbecue area, volleyball and badminton nets. Sports and recreation equipment are available. Henry and Etta Sloggett built the lodge in 1925 as a mountain retreat for their friends and family. Following Henry's death, the Sloggett children generously donated the house and grounds to the Kaua'i YWCA and in 1938 YWCA Camp Sloggett was established. They offer accommodations in Sloggett Lodge, which sleeps 10 in 2 bedrooms (3 people in each) and 4 in the main room. The kitchen facilities offer commercial double ovens and 6-burner stove, 2 refrigerators, cookware and table settings for 58 people. A covered lanai space of 800 square feet is suitable for dining, meetings or recreational use. The Weinberg Bunkhouse sleeps 40 people with mixed single and bunk-style beds. Two staff rooms sleep 4 each and two common rooms offer space for 16 each. Baths/ kitchens available.

Camp rates are $15 per person per night for Kaua'i residents; $18 per person per night for Hawai'i residents; non-residents are charged $20 per person per night. Children age 5 and under are free. A minimum of 5 people weekdays and 8 people weekends. They require a ten-person minimum on weekends during peak season—May through September. Tent camping is available to Kaua'i residents for $5 per person per night; Hawai'i residents $7 per person per night; non-residents $10 per person per night. A two-night minimum on weekends and three-night minimum over holidays is required. Kitchenette facilities available. Hostel accommodations are in the Weinberg Bunkhouse and tent sites only and include use of bath and recreational facilities. Barbecue, microwave and refrigerator are available on the lanai. No reservations. Individuals accommodated on a space-available basis.

Rental Agents

BED & BREAKFAST AGENCIES

Affordable Paradise Bed & Breakfast, Hawaii

332 Kuukama Street, Kailua, HI 96734; 808-261-1693; fax 808-261-7315; e-mail: barbara@affordable-paradise.com; www.affordable-paradise.com.

All Islands Bed & Breakfast

463 Iliwahi Loop, Kailua, HI 96734; 808-263-2342; 800-542-0344; fax 808-263-0308; e-mail: cac@hawaii.rr.com; www.home.hawaii.rr.com/allislands.

Bed & Breakfast Hawai'i

P.O. Box 449, Kapa'a, HI 96746; 808-822-7771; 800-733-1632; fax 808-822-2723; e-mail: reservations@bandb-hawaii.com; www.bandb-hawaii.com.

Bed & Breakfast Honolulu (Statewide)

3242 Kaohinani Drive, Honolulu, HI 96817; 808-595-7533; 800-288-4666; fax 808-595-2030; e-mail: rainbow@hawaiibnb.com; www.hawaiibnb.com.

Bed & Breakfast Kaua'i

4170 Kalani Place, Princeville, HI 96722 (Liz Hey); 808-822-1177; 800-822-1176; fax 808-826-9292; e-mail: heyliz@bnbkauai.com; www.bnb kauai.com.

Go Native

4408 Deer Valley Road, Rescue, CA 95672; e-mail: sales@go-native.com; www.go-native.com/hawaii/hi.shtml.

Hawaiian Islands B&B

572 Kailua Road, Suite 201, Kailua, HI 96734; 808-261-7895; 800-258-7895; fax 808-262-2181; e-mail: hi4rent@aloha.net; www.lanikaibb.com.

Hawai'i's Best Bed & Breakfasts

P.O. Box 563, Kamuela, HI 96743; 808-885-4550; 800-262-9912; fax 808-885-0559; e-mail: bestbnb@aloha.net; www.bestbnb.com.

CONDOMINIUM AND HOME RENTAL AGENCIES

Aston Hotels & Resorts

2155 Kalakaua #500, Honolulu, HI 96815; 800-922-7866; from Hawaii 800-321-2558; 808-931-1400; fax 808-922-8785; e-mail: info@aston-hotels.com; www.aston-hotels.com.

Captain Cook Resorts

1024 Kapahulu Avenue, Honolulu, HI 96816; 808-738-5507; 800-854-8843; fax 808-737-8733; e-mail: info@captaincookresorts.com; www.captaincookresorts.com.

Castle Resorts & Hotels

1150 South King Street, Honolulu, HI 96813; 808-591-2235; 800-367-5004 U.S. & Canada; toll-free fax 800-477-2329; e-mail: info@castleresorts.com; www.castleresorts.com.

Garden Island Rentals

P.O. Box 57, Koloa, HI 96756; 808-742-9537; 800-247-5599; fax 808-742-9540; e-mail: gir@kauairentals.com; www.kauairentals.com.

Grantham Resorts

3176 Po'ipu Road, Suite 1, Koloa, HI 96756; 808-742-7200; 800-325-5701; fax 808-742-9093; e-mail: info@grantham-resorts.com; www.grantham-resorts.com.

Hanalei North Shore Properties

P.O. Box 607, Hanalei, HI 96714; 808-826-9622; 800-488-3336; fax 808-826-1188; e-mail: hnsp@aloha.net; www.kauai-vacation-rentals.com.

Hanalei Vacations

P.O. Box 1109, Hanalei, HI 96714; 808-826-7288; 800-487-9833; e-mail: rentals@aloha.net; www.hanalei-vacations.com.

Harrington's Paradise

5-5408 Kuhio Highway, P.O. Box 1345, Hanalei, HI 96714; 808-826-9655; 888-826-9655; fax 808-826-7330; e-mail: hpprop@aloha.net; www.oceanfrontkauai.com.

Kauai Paradise Vacations

5161 Kuhio Highway #205; P.O. Box 1708, Hanalei, HI 96714; 808-826-7444; 800-826-7782; fax 808-826-7673; e-mail: kpv1@aloha.net; www.planet-hawaii.com/paradise.

Kaua'i Vacation Rentals

3-3311 Kuhio Highway, Lihu'e, HI 96746; 808-245-8841; 800-367-5025; e-mail: aloha@kvrre.com; www.kauaivacationrentals.com.

Marc Resorts Hawai'i

2155 Kalakaua Avenue, 7th floor, Honolulu, HI 96815; Hawai'i 808-922-9700; 800-535-0085 U.S. & Canada; toll-free fax 800-663-5085; e-mail: marc@aloha.net; www.marcresorts.com.

Maui & All Islands Condominiums & Cars

U.S. Mail only: P.O. Box 947, Lynden, WA 98264; Canadian Mail only: P.O. Box 1089, Aldergrove, BC V4W 2V1; 800-663-6962 U.S. & Canada; toll-free fax 888-654-MAUI; local fax 604-856-4187; e-mail: paul@mauiallislands.com; www.mauiallislands.com.

Na Pali Properties

P.O. Box 475, Hanalei, HI 96714; 808-826-7272; 800-715-7273; fax 808-826-7665; e-mail: nal@aloha.net; napaliprop.com.

Oceanfront Realty

P.O. Box 3570, Princeville, HI 96722; 800-222-5541; Princeville office 808-826-6585; fax 808-826-6478; e-mail: kauai@oceanfrontrealty.com; www.oceanfrontrealty.com.

Outrigger Hotels & Resorts

2375 Kuhio Avenue, Honolulu, HI 96815; 800-688-7444 U.S. & Canada; toll-free fax 800-622-4852; 808-921-6600; e-mail: reservations@outrigger.com; www.outrigger.com.

Pleasant Hawaiian Holidays

2404 Townsgate Road, Westlake Village, CA 91361; 818-991-3390; 800-2-HAWAII (429244); fax: 805-495-4972; www.pleasantholidays.com.

Po'ipu Connection

P.O. Box 1022, Koloa, HI 96756; 808-742-2233; fax 808-742-7382; Reservations 800-742-2260; e-mail: poipu@hawaiian.net; www.poipuconnection.com.

Premier Resorts

P.O. Box 4800, Park City, UT 84060; 800-367-7052; e-mail: stay@premier-resorts.com; www.premier-resorts.com.

Prosser Realty

4379 Rice Street or P.O. Box 367, Lihu'e, HI 96766; 808-245-4711; 800-767-4707; fax 808-245-8115; e-mail: realty@aloha.net; www.prosserrealty.net.

RE/MAX Kaua'i Vacation Rentals

P.O. Box 223609, Princeville, HI 96722-3609; 808-826-9675; 877-838-8149; fax 808-826-1229; e-mail: info@remaxkauai.com; www.remaxkauai.com.

R&R Realty and Rentals

1661 Pe'e Road, Po'ipu, HI 96756; 808-742-7555; 800-367-8022; fax 808-742-1559; e-mail: randr@aloha.net; www.rnr-realty-rental.com.

Suite Paradise

1941 Po'ipu Road, Po'ipu, HI 96756; 808-742-7400; 800-367-8020; fax 808-742-9121; e-mail: mail@suite-paradise.com; www.suite-paradise.com.

CHAPTER 4

Where to Dine

The cultural diversity of the Hawaiian islands provides many benefits to visitors and residents alike. Over the past 150 years or so, immigrants arrived from various places, many to labor on the once vast sugar and pineapple plantations which were the backbone of Hawaii's agri-based economy for so long. These immigrants, from such diverse places as Japan, China, Korea, the Philippines, Puerto Rico and Portugal, brought with them the many varied foods, culinary traditions, flavorings and cookery styles from their native lands. As the story goes, the plantation workers shared their meals, thus introducing each other to the flavors and tastes of their respective homelands. This gave rise to modern Hawaii's diverse mix of culinary influences, which has resulted in a happy blend of exotic food and flavors. There is probably no other state in the USA that can claim the diversity and range of ethnic cuisines than Hawaii has. The blending of Hawaii's ethnic foods has given rise to Hawaiian Regional Cuisine, recognized as a special culinary approach that utilizes the distinct cookery methods, foods, local produce, flavorings and innovative fusion of Asia/Pacific tastes.

Although Kaua'i previously had a reputation as being dullsville for diners, that has happily changed. Visitors will now find dining out to be an exciting adventure, with the chance to sample many different ethnic cuisines, as well as the distinctive local style of cooking. A number of restaurants also feature local ingredients, including organic salad greens, corn, tropical fruits, pork, fish, goat cheese and other items from right here on-island, ensuring its freshness and quality. Whether you want to splurge on fine dining at one of the island's many quality restaurants or dive into a simple plate lunch from a local lunch counter or drive-in, you'll find what you're looking for. In addition, diners can savor an authentic Hawaiian luau, complete with traditional *imu* (underground oven) roast pig, *laulau*, poi and a variety of other authentic Hawaiian foods, with the bonus of a Polynesian music and hula show. The range of cuisine and dining options is actually quite extraordinary for a small island like Kaua'i. So get out and explore the many food and dining discoveries awaiting you. *Bon appetit*!

Kaua'i is indeed fortunate to have a wide range of restaurants, cafes, coffee shops, upscale dining rooms and island-style eateries. There's something for just about everyone, but like most things in life, not everyone agrees on what and where is the best. There are friendly disagreements and differences of opinion about dining out on Kaua'i, just as there are everywhere else. When it comes to eating, everybody has his/her own personal favorites.

In addition to the dining experiences of this book's author, a great effort has been made to gather opinions and experiences about dining out on Kaua'i from many people, readers included. And while it's doubtful that anyone can attest to having dined in every restaurant on "The Garden Island," it is hoped that this section will provide insight into the variety of restaurants and cuisines that are available.

You may also be pleased, or disappointed, depending on your habits, to discover that all eating establishments are now designated non-smoking due to a recently enacted ordinance on Kaua'i.

The restaurants in this section are divided into the same three sections of the island as the "Where to Stay" chapter. Hopefully this will simplify locating that special place for breakfast, lunch or dinner depending on wherever you find yourself when hunger strikes. The restaurant listings are also indexed alphabetically as well as by cuisine. The restaurant descriptions/listings below are divided by geographical area, separated by price range and listed alphabetically in those price ranges. These ranges are: *inexpensive dining*—under $10 per person; *moderate-priced dining*—$10 to $25 per person; and *expensive dining*—$25 and up per person. The price ranges were decided by comparing an average dinner meal, exclusive of tax, alcoholic beverages and desserts. Due to changes in menus, management, supplies or other factors, restaurant prices are obviously subject to change at any time. If you are a senior citizen, be sure to ask about a Senior Citizen Discount as more restaurants are extending such a courtesy.

For simplicity, the restaurant listings in this section do not include fast-food outlets like McDonalds, Burger King, Kentucky Fried Chicken, Pizza Hut, 7-Eleven Food Stores and other convenience stores, which are, unfortunately, located all around the Garden Island. Most folks are aware of the type of food to be had in such operations and they don't merit a separate listing in this book. Suffice it to say that if you hanker for that sort of comfort food, you'll have no trouble finding it on Kaua'i, although it's primarily located in Lihu'e and Kapa'a.

This book uses a one-star rating system in recommending restaurants instead of multiple-star designations. It seemed a simple solution to the problem of trying to compare restaurants of different stature and caliber that happen to have equally good food, service, decor, etc.—sort of like comparing apples and oranges. It's like comparing the excellent Korean BBQ in Wailua with the superb A Pacific Café just down the road. Each was wonderful for what it was, but did Korean BBQ deserve only one or two stars just because it has a very different ambiance? Likewise, did A Pacific Café deserve four or five stars because it is a fine dining room, has great service, tasteful decor and equally tasty creative Hawaiian Regional Cuisine? The answer lies in the fact that both types of places are great places to eat for different people at different times and for different reasons. Thus they deserve to be treated equally. They both get a star!

We've also noted our favored restaurants or eateries based on their quality, individuality and value. So as you read through the restaurant chapter, we've highlighted these special restaurants with our mark of excellence—a single ★. Those restaurants marked with a ★ indicate an exceptional value in quality of food and service, decor and ambiance, or unique and unusual cuisine. A real effort has been made to ensure that those restaurants so marked have in fact earned the accolade. This has been done through personal visits and evaluations of a meal, or by close and careful consultation with reliable patrons, reader reviews and others. In spite of this, restaurants, like everything else, can and do change over time. What may have been an enjoyable dining experience last week or last month may well be a complete disaster the next time around. The consistency factor of good food and service for the level of dining carries much weight in the evaluation and consideration. Those restaurants marked as an exceptional value have proven themselves consistent on these last points noted.

Readers are encouraged to check ahead with restaurants and call them for specific hours and days of service. One thing for which the restaurant business is well-known for is the frequent change of days and hours open, plus meal service provided. Several restaurants seem to change their hours seasonally. So check with a given restaurant before traveling any distance to be sure they are open when you expect them to be to avoid disappointment. The same thing applies to menu selections and prices. It is reasonable to expect that menus and prices at even the best restaurants will fluctuate from time to time, seasonally and/or with a change in chefs, owners, etc. This book cannot guarantee that changes will not occur in restaurants, menus or service. The only thing guaranteed is that changes probably will occur.

The restaurants have been divided into **East Shore and Central Coast Area**, which will offer dining options for Lihu'e, Kapa'a, Nawiliwili and Wailua. **The South and West Shore Areas** includes Po'ipu, Koloa, Lawa'i, Port Allen, Hanapepe, Waimea, Kekaha and Koke'e. Finally, the section on dining on the **North Shore Area** features restaurants in the towns of Anahola, Princeville and Hanalei.

Finally, as you travel around the Garden Island, you may come across a restaurant or dining place not listed in this book. The reason is either that the specific restaurant opened after this book went to press or, for whatever reason, the author deemed the establishment unworthy to be included.

Ethnic Foods

A little background on some ethnic foods may tempt you to try a few new foods as a part of your dining adventure on Kaua'i. You're sure to find many of these foods on the various restaurant menus you come across. So, let your imagination flow and sensibilities go—embark on a new culinary and taste adventure. Grab all the gusto you can! And if you have questions about the menu, just ask.

CHINESE FOODS

Bean threads: thin, clear noodles made from mung beans
Char siu: roasted pork with spices
Chow mein: thin noodles prepared with veggies and meat in various combinations, also cake-noodles style
Egg/Spring/Summer roll: deep-fried or fresh pastry roll with various veggie, meat or shrimp fillings
Kung pao chicken: deep-fried or sauteed spicy chicken pieces
Long rice: clear noodles cooked with chicken and vegetables
Mongolian beef: thinly sliced charbroiled beefsteak
Peking duck: charbroiled duck with *char siu* flavoring
Pot stickers: semisoft pan-fried filled dumplings
Sweet-and-sour sauce: sugar-and-vinegar-based sauce with tomato sauce, salt and garlic flavorings
Szechuan sauce: hot chili–flavored sauce used extensively in beef, chicken, pork, seafood dishes
Won ton: crispy deep-fried dumpling with meat or veggie fillings; also soft style cooked in soups or noodle dishes

FILIPINO FOODS

Adobo: chicken or pork cooked with vinegar and spices
Cascaron: a donut made with rice flour and rolled in sugar

Chicken papaya: chicken soup with green papaya and seasonings
Dinadaraan: blend of prepared pork blood and meats
Halo halo: a tropical fruit sundae that is a blend of milk, sugar, fruits and ice
Lumpia: fried pastry filled with vegetables and meats
Pancit: noodles with vegetables or meat
Pinacbet: stir-fry of bitter melon, okra, pork and various seasonings
Pork and peas: traditional entree of pork, peas, flavorings in a tomato paste base
Sari sari: soup entree of pork, veggies and flavorings

HAWAIIAN FOODS

Haupia: a sweet custard made of coconut milk
Kalua pig: roast pig cooked in an underground *imu* oven, very flavorful
Kulolo: a steamed pudding using coconut milk and grated taro root
Laulau: pieces of pork or chicken, flavored with butterfish, topped with luau (taro) leaves, wrapped in ti leaves, then steamed
Lomilomi salmon: diced and salted raw salmon with tomatoes and green onions
Opihi: these saltwater limpets are eaten raw and considered a delicacy
Poi: pureed taro corms, best eaten fresh
Poke: raw fish that has been spiced. A variety of fish are used and are often mixed with seaweed; for example, *ahi poke* is raw tuna or *tako poke* is marinated octopus

JAPANESE FOODS

Chicken katsu: deep-fried, breaded chicken pieces served with *katsu* sauce
Donburi: chicken, pork or fish entree with veggies and special soy sauce served over steaming rice and topped with egg
Kamaboko: fish cake of white fish and starch steamed together
Miso soup: soup of fermented soy beans
Sashimi: very fresh firm raw fish, usually yellowfin tuna (*ahi*), sliced thin and dipped in *wasabi-shoyu* sauce;
Shabu shabu: thinly sliced beef with veggies, noodles and *ponzu* sauce
Soba/saimin: thin noodles served with/without broth; cold soba served as salad with vegetables
Sukiyaki: thinly sliced beef with veggies, noodles and tofu in a broth
Sushi: white rice rolls or cakes with various seafood, seaweed and veggie fillings
Tempura: deep-fried shrimp, fish, seafood and veggies dipped in a light flour batter
Teriyaki: flavorful, savory soy sauce and ginger marinade for beef, chicken, pork and seafood

Tonkatsu: pork cutlet grilled golden brown, served with *tonkatsu* sauce

Udon: noodles served with soup broth, green onions, fish cake slices, optional meat

Wasabi: very spicy green horseradish root used to dip sushi into

KOREAN FOODS

Kalbi ribs: flavored similarly to teriyaki, but with chili pepper, sesame oil and green onions

Kim chee: spicy pickled cabbage flavored with ginger and garlic

Mandoo: fried dumplings with meat and vegetable fillings

Mandoo kook, Bi bim kook, yook kae jang: soups served with *mandoo* dumplings, noodles, vegetables, variety of meats

Meat or fish jun: fried or broiled beef or fish with teriyaki-type sauce

Spicy barbecue beef, chicken or pork: broiled soy sauce–flavored beef, chicken or pork laced with spicy hot chili

LOCAL FAVORITES

Bento: a box lunch might include tempura shrimp, veggies, scoop of noodles, sushi roll or rice

Loco moco: a combination of hamburger patty atop a bowl of rice with fried egg and gravy

Plate lunches: a traditional favorite might include teriyaki beef or chicken, hamburger with gravy, roast pork, fried fish or any of several other entrees, always served with rice and often a scoop of macaroni salad

Saimin: noodles served in broth with fish cake, veggies

Shave ice: ground ice—mainlanders know it as snowcones, except the ice is more finely shaved—topped with a variety of flavored syrups such as strawberry, pineapple, guava, vanilla, mango, root beer, *lilikoi*.

THAI/VIETNAMESE FOOD

Fried noodles/fried rice: crispy/soft fried noodles with meat entree and soft rice with meat and vegetables

Green curry: choice of meat entree with peas, string beans, coconut milk and sweet basil

Mein noodles: egg noodle soup with shrimp, seafood or other entree

Musaman curry: curry with onion, peanuts, carrots and potatoes in coconut milk

Pad Thai: Thai-style pan-fried noodles with choice of meat entree or veggies garnished with sprouts

Pho noodle soup: noodle soup with beefsteak, meatball, chicken or combination with veggies

Red curry: choice of meat entree with bamboo shoots in coconut milk and sweet basil

Rice noodle soup: rice stick noodles with shrimp, pork, fish cake, squid or other seafood

Satay sticks: broiled chicken, pork or beef on skewer sticks, served as a side dish

Vermicelli cold noodles: thin, clear noodles combined with meat or seafood entree and veggies

Yellow curry: chicken with coconut milk and potatoes

A FEW WORDS ABOUT ISLAND FISH

Whether cooking fish at your condominium or eating out, the names of the island fish can be confusing. While local shore fishermen catch shallow-water fish such as *aholehole* or *papio* for their dinner table, commercial fishermen angle for two types. The steakfish are caught by trolling in deep waters and include *ahi*, *ono* and mahimahi. The more delicate bottom fish include *opakapaka* and *onaga*, which are caught with lines dropped as deep as 1,500 feet to shelves off the island coastlines. Here is some background on what you might find on your dinner plate.

Ahi: yellowfin (Allison tuna) is caught in deep waters off Kaua'i and weighs 60 to 280 pounds; pinkish red meat is firm yet flaky and popular for sashimi.

Aku: a blue-fin tuna, and has a stronger taste than *ahi*.

Albacore: a smaller version of the *ahi* averages 40 to 50 pounds and is lighter in both texture and color; also called *koshibi*.

Au: the broadbill swordfish, or marlin; a dense and sometimes dry fish.

Ehu: orange snapper.

Hapu: Hawaiian sea bass.

Lehi: a silver-mouth member of the snapper family, with a stronger flavor than *onaga* or *opakapaka* and a texture resembling mahimahi.

Mahimahi: called the dolphin fish, but has no relation to Flipper or his friends; caught while trolling and weighs between 10 to 65 pounds; excellent white meat that is moist and light and is very good sauteed; a seasonal fish that causes it to command a high price when fresh. **Beware**: while excellent fresh, mahimahi is often served in restaurants having arrived from the Philippines frozen, making it far less pleasing. A clue as to whether fresh or frozen may be the price tag. If it runs less than $10 to $15 it is probably the frozen variety. Fresh mahimahi will run more.

Onaga: caught in holes that are 1,000 feet or deeper, this red snapper has an attractive hot-pink exterior with tender, juicy, white meat inside.

Ono: also known as *wahoo*; a member of the barracuda family, its white meat is firm and more steaklike. *Ono* means "delicious" in Hawaiian.

'Opae: shrimp

Opakapaka: pink snapper; meat is very light and flaky with a delicate flavor.

Papio: a baby *ulua* caught in shallow waters.

Uku: grey snapper, light, firm and white meat with a texture that varies with size.

Ulua: also known as pompano, this fish is firm and flaky with steak-like, textured white meat.

Dining Best Bets

It's difficult to identify the best places to eat that please everyone. And that's because everyone has different likes and dislikes and tastes. Without a doubt, there will be disagreements. Understandably so. This section attempts to identify what this writer has found to be pleasant, exceptional, enjoyable or otherwise good places to eat. It is hoped that readers will concur with these suggestions.

Asian Cuisine Hanama'ulu Restaurant has good local-style Chinese and Japanese food, Restaurant Kiibo in Lihu'e and Tokyo Lobby. Ba̧ Le has wonderful Vietnamese cuisine. Sukhotai, King & I, and Pattaya Asian Café for Thai food.

Bakery Kilauea Bakery.

Breakfast Kountry Kitchen, Kalaheo Coffee Co. & Café, Ono Family Restaurant, Olympic Café and the Po'ipu Bay Grill & Bar.

Breakfast Buffet Ilima Terrace at the Hyatt Regency Kaua'i.

Breakfast Value Ma's in Lihu'e.

Dining Value Garden Island BBQ.

Dinner Buffet Hanalei Café at the Princeville Resort, the Ilima Terrace at the Hyatt, Japanese cuisine buffet at Hanama'ulu Restaurant on Sunday nights.

Family Dining Olympic Café.

Fine Dining Dondero's at the Hyatt.

Fine Dining in a Casual Atmosphere Beach House Restaurant and A Pacific Café.

French Toast Hanalei Wake-up Café.

Good and Cheap Hamura Saimin, Wong's, Korean BBQ, Waipouli Deli & Restaurant.

Hamburgers Ono Family Restaurant—try the buffalo burgers and Po'ipu Tropical Burgers.

Hawaiian/Local-style Food Aloha Diner has true Hawaiian food, or try Ma's or Okazu Hale in Lihu'e.

Island-style Ambiance Keoki's Paradise or Kauai Hula Girl Bar & Grill.

Italian Pomodoro: be sure to try the spumoni ice cream cake.

Mexican Maria's and La Playita Azul.

Most Outrageous Desserts Roy's chocolate souffle, Keoki's Hula Pie and Toasted Hawaiian at A Pacific Café.

Pizza Brick Oven Pizza—a long time favorite. Pau Hana Pizza gets points for its variety of unusual toppings, and pesto pizza at Pizza Hanalei is *ono*.

Plate Lunches Hanalei Mixed Plate, Kalena Fish Market, Polynesian Hide-a-way.

Pupus Keoki's or Duke's (try the calamari) and "The Kiss" at Casa di Amici Po'ipu.

Salad Bar There are very few, but Duke's could hold its own—even with a lot of competition!

Salads Warm *ahi* salad at A Pacific Café; the Oriental chicken salad at Princeville Restaurant & Bar; Cobb salad at Olympic Café, mixed greens at Blossoming Lotus.

Sandwiches The lean turkey Reuben at Joe's (either one), the chicken salad sandwich at Lizard Lounge & Deli, fresh and colorful veggie sandwich at Mango Mamas, taro hummus on taro roll at Hanalei Taro & Juice Co.

Seafood Beach House Restaurant, Coconuts Island-Style Bar & Grill, A Pacific Café.

Shave Ice Halo Halo Shave Ice in Lihu'e or Kamaka's small roadside stand in Anahola.

Smoothies Mango Mamas in Kilauea, fantastic poi and fresh fruit smoothies at Hanalei Taro & Juice Co.

Sushi Tokyo Lobby, Princeville Restaurant & Bar (Monday night only, but truly authentic), great variety at Wasabi's, Koloa Fish Market.

Vegetarian Blossoming Lotus in Kapa'a has fantastic vegan fare, Hanapepe Cafe & Espresso is excellent, and Zababaz One World Café and Papaya's Natural Foods have good casual fare.

View Al & Don's has a wonderful ocean view, try it for breakfast. Fabulous sunset and ocean views at the Beach House Restaurant. If you can afford it, Café Hanalei at the Princeville Resort wins hands down. (*Tip*: Go for lunch.)

East Shore and Central Coast Area

Inexpensive-priced Dining

Al & Don's (American cuisine)

420 Papaloa Road, Kaua'i Sands Hotel, Kapa'a; 808-822-4221.

Hours: Breakfast 7 to 9:15 a.m. Dinner 6 to 8 p.m. No lunch. *Sampling:* Large selection of hotcakes (with a variety of tropical fruit toppings and special coconut syrup), waffles or waffle sandwich, French toast, omelets and egg dishes ($4 to $6). Dinners include French bread, choice of pasta or whipped potatoes and vegetable. There is spaghetti, roast turkey (or hot turkey sandwich), leg of lamb, chicken stir-fry, mahimahi, lasagna, pineapple baked ham or ham and turkey combination dinner ($7 to $10). Senior specials nightly. Chocolate dream cake, strawberry shortcake, cream pies, cheesecake, hula pie or sundae. *Comments:* They serve old-fashioned food at old-fashioned prices. Children's menu at half price. Breakfasts are the best bet, but anytime before sunset buys you a great beachfront view. Karaoke on weekends.

★ *Aloha Diner (Local cuisine)*

971-F Kuhio Highway, Kapa'a, in the Waipouli Complex; 808-822-3851.

Hours: Lunch Monday through Saturday 10:30 a.m. to 2:30 p.m. Dinner Tuesday through Saturday 5:30 to 9 p.m. Closed Sunday; lunch only on Monday. *Sampling:* Local plates for lunch and a few more expensive ones for dinner: *Kalua* pig or *laulau* with *lomi* salmon and rice or poi; with chicken luau, *haupia or kulolo* and tea or coffee for dinner ($6 to $9). Other lunches include tripe or beef stew and various combinations ($6 to $8). Dinner with additional items as above and in combination ($9 to $11). All specials items available a la carte, along with won ton and saimin. *Comments:* This is the only place on Kaua'i devoted solely to true Hawaiian food.

Ara's Sakana Ya Fish House (Japanese/local cuisine)

4301 Kuhio Highway, Hanama'ulu; 808-245-1707.

Hours: 8 a.m. to 7 p.m. Sunday until 5 p.m. *Sampling:* Sushi, *poke*, boiled peanuts or soy beans, *kim chee*, shrimp and scallop salad. Plate lunches include rice, potato salad and *kim chee* ($5 to $7). *Comments:* Eat in or take out.

★ *Ba Le (Vietnamese cuisine/sandwiches)*

4-831 Kuhio Highway, Kapa'a (Kauai Village Shopping Center); 808-823-6060.

Hours: 10 a.m. to 9 p.m. daily. *Sampling: Pho*, a fragrant beef-broth noodle soup, is the specialty here, offered with chicken, shrimp, vegetables and tofu, steak prepared rare or well-done or beef brisket

($6.50 to $8.95). Vermicelli (long rice noodle) bowls with grilled pork, shrimp, sirloin, sauteed lemongrass steak or chicken and egg roll ($6.50 to $7.95). Rice plates, with steamed veggies and choice of grilled chicken, pork loin, chicken *katsu*, mahi *katsu*, tofu eggplant, garlic shrimp and lemongrass chicken, tofu and several kinds of beef ($5.95 to $8.50). Even the sandwiches are unique, with lemongrass chicken, tofu, ham and steamed pork, steak or tuna, served with pickled carrot and daikon. Also, fresh-fruit smoothies ($3.75) and both hot and iced Vietnamese condensed milk coffee ($2.95). *Comments:* This is the kind of place that we wish had opened long ago. It's got incredible food, great prices and it's easy to find. You can eat in the small and busy dining room or take out. The only problem is that it was immediately popular, so they are often busy. Still, it's well worth the occasional small wait to eat at this restaurant, where the flavors are complex and delectable and the variety is quite amazing. They bake their own bread daily for the sandwiches, and the tapioca pudding (try the one

CATERING SERVICES

If you have guests coming, have a group to feed, or are simply planning a party or celebration and don't want to do all the prep work involved, call one of the many island catering services that can prepare, serve and clean up afterward, leaving you to simply enjoy the event. You'll find that most hotels and resorts have a catering service, as do many local restaurants. There are several private catering companies on Kaua'i offering custom catering and a personal chef for all occasions. Just give your favorite hotel or restaurant a call. Or you can try one of the following catering services:

Contemporary Flavors, 1610 Haleukana Street, Lihu'e, HI 96766; 808-245-2522; fax 808-245-2744; e-mail: conflvr@gte.net; gtesupersite.com/contemflavor.

Gaylord's at Kilohana, 3-2087 Kaumuali'i Highway, Lihu'e, HI 96766; 808-245-9333; www.gaylordskauai.com.

Green Garden Restaurant, Highway 50, Hanapepe, HI 96716; 808-335-5422, 808-335-5528.

Heavenly Creations, P.O. Box 167, Anahola, HI 96703; 808-828-1700; 877-828-1700.

Koloa Fish Market, 5482 Koloa Road, Koloa, HI 96756; 808-742-6199.

Lemm's Luau & Catering Service, Anahola; 808-822-4854

Puhi Fish and Catering, 4495 Puhi Road, Lihu'e, HI 96766; 808-246-6925.

Terrace Restaurant at Kaua'i Lagoons, 3351 Hoolaulea, Lihu'e, HI 96766; 808-241-6010.

with taro) is a cheap ($1.50) and a yummy conclusion to any meal. We have not had one unhappy experience at this place, and judging from the testimonials pasted to their walls and take-out menu, visitors and locals alike have had the same good time.

Beezers (Family dining)

1378 Kuhio Highway, Kapa'a; 808-822-4411.

Hours: 9 a.m. to 11 p.m. daily. *Sampling:* Breakfast served all day: scrambled eggs, omelets, "Scramble" (eggs, mushrooms, onions, peppers, potato with cheese and picante sauce), and *loco moco* ($4 to $8); or order from a serious selection of burgers ("Cheezer," Boca veggie, chili, egg, char-grilled chicken breast or fresh fish, patty melt), plus turkey club, BLT, cold pastrami, grilled veggie, "Stacker" (ham, roast beef or fresh-roasted turkey breast), tuna melt, fried egg, grilled ham and cheese, hot dog, peanut butter with jelly, banana or bacon and homemade Sloppy Joe or meatloaf sandwiches ($5 to $9). Homemade soup and chili; salads like the Beezers'Ceezer (with grilled chicken or fish), chef's, turkey or tuna with homemade dressings. Quench your thirst with a flavored Coke, ice cream soda, egg cream or black cow, then get into the thick of it with a malt shake or smoothie. And there are all sorts of ice cream desserts, pies, fudge brownies, cakes, cookies, etc. *Comments:* A Beezer is somebody who loves ice cream and this old-fashioned ice cream parlor is the kind of the place that only a Beezer can love. The decor is malt-shop chic, from the booths in the back to the soda fountain in front. Order at the shiny counter and enjoy the photos from the '50s and the collection of labels and logos—and linoleum—from long ago.

Big Kahuna (Sandwiches/salads)

939B Kuhio Highway, Kapa'a; 808-822-7553.

Hours: 11 a.m. to 8 p.m. *Sampling:* Philly cheese steak subs, gyros, teriyaki chicken subs, Greek, chicken-grilled steak and chef salads, deli subs of turkey, roast beef, etc. ($4.50 to $8.70). Eat in or take out. They'll also pack you a lunch for hiking or kayaking. *Comments:* Small, clean café with good, simple food served in portions ranging from small to large, to meet your appetite, as well as kids' sizes.

Borders Café Espresso (Coffee/espresso, sandwiches and snacks)

Inside Borders Books at 4303 Nawiliwili Road, Lihu'e; 808-246-0862.

Hours: Monday to Thursday 7:30 a.m. to 9:30 p.m. Friday and Saturday until 10:30 p.m. Sunday 8 a.m. to 7:30 p.m. *Sampling:* Sandwiches, soups, salads (and combinations), vegetarian chili, eggrolls ($4 to $6). Flavored slushies and smoothies. Italian sodas, coffee and tea drinks. Chocolate crumb cake, baklava, brownies, cookies. *Comments:* Small café with separate entrance or through Borders. Coffee bar or tables and chairs. Light meals and/or beverages served with plenty of reading material, including out-of-town newspapers. Very popular.

Bubba's (Burgers)

1421 Kuhio Highway, Kapa'a; 808-823-0069; e-mail: obubba@aloha.net; www.bubbaburger.com.

Hours: 10:30 a.m. to 6 p.m. *Sampling:* Bubbas, double bubbas, hubba bubbas plus hot dogs, corn dogs and Budweiser beer chili. "Alternative" burgers include fish, chicken, *tempeh* and Italian sausage or fresh-fish sandwich with pineapple lemongrass salsa ($2 to $6). Side orders of Caesar salad, French fries, onion rings, frings (fries and rings), or chili fries ($2 to $4). *Comments:* With a name like Bubba's you were expecting maybe escargot? Old-fashioned counter and stools, murals and memorabilia on the walls and ocean-view seating on the veranda. They've got another hamburger joint in Hanalei; both locations have take-out and T-shirts. Buy a hat or shirt and if you wear it when you order your burger, you'll get a free drink.

Coconut MarketPlace

484 Kuhio Highway, Kapa'a.

Lappert's ice cream, Tradewinds Bar and several small restaurants (inexpensive for the most part) make this shopping center into a kind of extended food court. Some of the larger restaurants and/or those having something particular to recommend are listed individually and alphabetically.

- ***Aloha Kaua'i Pizza***; 808-822-4511. *Hours:* 11 a.m to 8 p.m. *Sampling:* Variety of pizzas ($5 to $23). Their signature pizza is "Artichoke Eddie" with fresh garlic butter and marinated artichoke hearts, sweet red onions, tangy green olives, *fume bueno* cheese and tomatoes ($7 to $23); calzone ($5 to $7), lasagna ($7), Italian sandwiches ($6), salads ($4 to $7). Fresh ingredients, turkey meatballs, sausage and sauces from a 120-year-old family recipe have made this an Entertainment Book winner several years running.
- ***Eggbert's Family Specialty Restaurant***; 808-822-3787. See listing below.
- ***Fish Hut***; 808-821-0033. Open daily 11 a.m. to 9 p.m. Sunday to 7 p.m. *Sampling:* Fish-n-chips plus *ahi*, *ono*, mahimahi, charbroiled fish, fried seafood (shrimp, scallops, oysters) in combinations with French fries and homemade cole slaw. Also sandwiches, fish burgers, fish wraps, fish tacos and fish salads ($5.95 to $11.95).
- ***Harley's Ribs-n-Chicken***; 808-822-2505. *Hours:* 11 a.m to 8 p.m. *Sampling:* No surprise, they serve ribs and barbecue chicken!

- ***Kauai Hula Girl Bar & Grill***; 808-822-4422. See Moderate-priced listing below.
- ***Palm Tree Terrace***; 808-823-1040. *Hours:* Lunch 11 a.m. to 2 p.m. Dinner 5 to 9 p.m. *Sampling:* Sandwiches include grilled garlic chicken, pastrami, crab, mahimahi; appetizers range from calamari rings, mozzarella sticks, jalapeño poppers to *lumpia*; salads include grilled chicken salad, tuna and crab; dinner entrees include choices like beef or chicken kabobs, pork chops or New York steak; there are several pastas such as chicken alfredo, chicken sienna and seafood linguini; seafood choices include mahimahi, fish-and-chips and shrimp ($5 to $17).
- ***TC's Island Grill***; 808-823-9181. *Hours:* 11 a.m. to 9 p.m. *Sampling:* Local-style breakfasts plus hot dogs, burgers, salads, sandwiches, chili and teriyaki beef or fried chicken platters.

★ Dani's (Local cuisine)

4201 Rice Street, Lihu'e; 808-245-4991.

Hours: Breakfast 5 to 11 a.m. Lunch 11 a.m. to 1:30 p.m. Closed Sunday. *Sampling:* Breakfast meats, eggs and omelets including *kalua* pig and Dani's special with fish cake, green onion and tomato ($5 to $7). Pineapple, banana, papaya hotcakes and sweet bread French toast ($4 to $6). Breakfast and lunch specials include combinations of *laulau*, *kalua* pig, beef or tripe stew, and lunch entrees offer hamburger steak, pork chops, roast pork, veal, beef or chicken cutlet, fried shrimp, oysters or scallops, plus burgers and sandwiches ($5 to $9). *Comments:* This is a very popular local coffee-shop eatery. It has a large open dining room with numerous tables. The standard here is good local-style food and pleasant, friendly service in a clean, neat atmosphere.

Deli & Bread Connection (Deli/sandwiches)

Kukui Grove Shopping Center, 3171 Kuhio Highway, Lihu'e; 808-245-7115.

Hours: 9:30 a.m. (from 10 a.m. on Sunday) to 7 p.m. (until 9 p.m. on Friday and 6 p.m. Sunday). *Sampling:* Sandwiches on freshly baked bread or rolls include roast beef, pastrami, corned beef, smoked ham, liverwurst, chicken salad and crab meat ($4 to $6). French dip, tuna or chicken with avocado, Reuben, BLT, meatloaf or club, sub or poor boy with choice of ingredients ($5 to $8). Vegetarian sandwiches and daily homemade soups ($3 to $6). *Comments:* Good food and big portions, but very busy at lunch time. Bakery breads include rye, wheat, sour dough, French and their signature Oriental sweet bread, plus giant muffins and cookies, cinnamon rolls, *manju*, brownies and pies. Indoor and outdoor seating.

Driftwood Sand Bar & Grill (Coffee/espresso, sandwiches & snacks)

Radisson Kaua'i Beach Resort, 4331 Kaua'i Beach Drive, Lihu'e; 808-245-1955.

Hours: Lunch and snacks continuously from 10 a.m. to 6 p.m. daily. This resort poolside bar and grill features beverages, cocktails, snacks and light meals, burgers, sandwiches, salads and general light fare.

Eggbert's Family Specialty Restaurant (American cuisine)
Coconut MarketPlace—by the water wheel; 808-822-3787.

Hours: Breakfast 7 a. m. to 3 p.m. Lunch 11 a.m. to 3 p.m. Dinner 5 to 9 p.m. *Sampling:* Eggs Benedict in five styles (combos of veggie, ham or turkey) and two sizes or create your own with additional ingredients, all with Eggbert's own Hollandaise made fresh with tangy lemon ($8 to $11). Omelet varieties include ham, Portuguese sausage, mushrooms, sour cream and chives, tomato and cheese and Denver—or you can choose your own fillings ($4 to $10). Egg plates, pigs-in-a-blanket, French toast (with cinnamon and vanilla), and banana hotcakes round out the breakfast menu ($4 to $8). Lunch specialties include turkey or ham club sandwiches, fried rice crowned with a crepe-thin omelet, pork and cabbage, and the definitive brunch dish: Eggbert's Big "O" omelet sandwich with choice of ingredients ($5 to $8). Dinner entrees include New York steak, fresh catch, stir-frys (fish, chicken, beef or pork), meatloaf, roast pork and barbecue chicken ($9 to $16). Senior and children's portions available. *Comments:* Eggs Benedict, along with *keiki* favorites like banana pancakes and pigs-in-a-blanket, are among their specialties. Their water wheel–corner of the Coconut MarketPlace is open and airy, with comfortable space between the tables and a veranda that's perfect for people watching.

Endless Summer (Snacks/farmers market)
3366 Wa'apa Road (adjacent to Anchor Cove), Lihu'e; 808-246-8854.

Hours: 9 a.m. to 9 p.m. (Monday 9 a.m. to 5 p.m.). *Sampling:* Hot dogs, chili and rice, smoothies, shakes, Lappert's ice cream ($3 to $6). *Comments:* Fresh fruit stand and mini-farmers market in front. Try an Endless Summer smoothie with papaya, banana, pineapple, *lilikoi* and coconut juice.

Fish Express (Seafood)
3343 Kuhio Highway, Lihu'e (by Wal-Mart); 808-245-9918.

Hours: 10 a.m. to 7 p.m. Monday through Saturday. Sunday until 5 p.m. *Sampling:* Plate lunches, *kalua* or *laulau* plate, seafood lunch ($6 to $8). Prepared fish with a variety of sauces: Provençal, passion-orange and tarragon, ginger-curry, blackened with guava-basil. Also variety of *poke* and sashimi. *Comments:* Seafood deli with limited seating.

★ Garden Island BBQ and Chinese Restaurant (Chinese/local cuisine)
4252 Rice Street, Lihu'e; 808-245-8868.

Hours: Monday through Saturday 10 a.m. to 9 p.m. Closed Sunday. *Sampling:* Chicken, beef, pork and shrimp dishes, plus chow mein, barbecue, soups and combination plates like lemon chicken, beef curry, pork with bitter melon, shrimp with eggplant, *loco moco*, barbecue short ribs, sweet-and-sour spare pork, scallop soup, rainbow tofu soup and House "Chop Suey Chow Mein" ($4 to $8); burgers and sandwiches ($2 to $3). *Comments:* Good selection, good food, good portions. It's always busy and popular with locals.

★ *Hamura Saimin & Halo Halo Shave Ice (Local cuisine)*

2956 Kress, Lihu'e, just off Rice Street; 808-245-3271.

Hours: Monday to Thursday 10 a.m. to 11 p.m. Friday and Saturday until 1 a.m. Sunday until 9:30 p.m. *Sampling:* No surprise, they serve saimin—in small, medium, large and extra-large portions. Also barbecue, *udon*, fried noodles and won ton soup. The most expensive item on the menu is the shrimp or the special (with lots of meat, veggies and hard-boiled egg)—saimin at $5. Fresh *lilikoi* pie is a specialty dessert. *Comments:* This is another of Kaua'i's original hole-in-the-wall diners. It's a somewhat rundown-looking and tacky sort of place with U-shaped formica-covered counters and a variety of unmatched stools. This is a very popular place with the locals or anyone who likes slurping noodles. The menu is on the wall and is limited, so ordering and receiving your food is quite speedy. A good thing, too, because during peak meal hours you may have to wait for a vacant stool. Don't overlook the chicken and beef sticks. The meat is a good-size portion, moist and very flavorful. Order at least one to accompany your noodles. Hamura Saimin is not only popular during regular meal hours—it's a busy late-night hang out. Oh yes, and heed the warning posted, no sticking gum under the counter. You may see locals picking up boxes of raw saimin noodles to send home with visiting family and friends. Hamura Saimin has something of a cult following throughout the islands. Among noodle connoisseurs it's a bit overrated. Still, it's an experience. You may have to hunt for parking on the nearby narrow and crowded streets.

Higashi (Local cuisine)

1415 Kuhio Highway, Kapa'a; 808-822-5982.

Hours: Monday through Friday 6 a.m. to 2 p.m. Saturday 6 a.m. to 1 p.m. Closed Sunday. *Sampling:* Two eggs, breakfast meat, rice and toast or omelets. Sandwiches: hamburger (teriyaki or barbecue), egg, tuna, ham, bacon and egg; saimin, oxtail soup, *loco moco*, chicken *moco*; beef or curry stew, *shoyu* chicken, roast pork, mahimahi, beef or pork cutlet ($3 to $8). *Comments:* This is another hole-in-the-wall, local-style eatery.

Hiroko's Okazuya (Local cuisine)

3630 Lalo Road, across from the school; turn up the hill just past Nawiliwili Harbor; 808-245-3450.

Hours: Breakfast and lunch 7 a.m. to 2 p.m. *Sampling:* Breakfast ($5 to $6); daily plate-lunch specials: chicken *hekka*, pork peas and pimento, fried rice and hot dog, mayo baked chicken, roast beef or pork, sweet-and-sour meatballs or mixed plate with two pieces of chicken, two pieces of cooked meat, noodles, luncheon meat, corned beef hash, two scoops rice and one scoop macaroni salad ($5 to $7). *Comments:* Sodas and juices. Benches outside with soda machine for after hours.

Hong Kong Café (Chinese food)

Wailua Shopping Center, 4-361 Kuhio Highway, Kapa'a; 808-822-3288.

Hours: Open daily except Tuesday: 10:30 a.m. to 2:30 p.m. and 4:30 to 9:30 p.m. *Sampling:* Lunch and dinner plates and combos include rice, macaroni salad and sweet-and-sour cabbage. House specialties include kung pao stir-fry chicken, pork or beef, hot and spicy eggplant with meat, stir-fry cashew nut or almond with meat, spicy sauteed shrimp and sweet-and-sour pork ($7 to $10). Other menu items include chicken *katsu*, roast duck, fried shrimp, lemon chicken, barbecue beef stick, fish cutlet, *char siu*, sweet-and-sour chicken and fried stuffed eggplant ($5 to $8). Sizzling platters offer seafood, fish or pepper steak ($8 to $10). Vegan specials include stir-fry mushroom with snow peas, stir-fry eggplant with tofu, kung pao tofu and Mongolian broccoli ($6 to $8). A la carte dishes range from the traditional to the unusual. You can order your *mu shu* pork with beef, chicken or vegetables instead—either way, the portions are generous with tasty filling and just enough pancakes and *hoisin* sauce to make everything come out even. Deep-fried crab and cream cheese won tons are just one of the ways to start, but the Chinese chicken salad with shredded walnut and crispy noodle is not to be missed. Roast duck is a specialty, as is their spicy eggplant with chicken, minced pork, beef or shrimp—both are excellent choices ($5 to $20). Chow mein, lo mein, saimin and several vegetarian dishes round out the menu. *Comments:* The ambiance is clean and comfortable, and there's a colorful aquarium as a focal point. They use fresh Kaua'i products—fresh fish and vegetables—and serve purified, filtered water. The food is quite good, with friendly, efficient service to match.

Kahanu Snack Bar (Coffee/espresso, sandwiches and snacks)

Aloha Kauai Beach Resort, Wailua; 808-823-6000.

Hours: 11 a.m. to 6 p.m. *Sampling:* Mahimahi or chicken sandwich, cheeseburger, hot dog on Hawaiian sweet bread bun, garden or fruit salad ($4 to $8) plus fries, onion rings, corn dogs, ice cream and shakes. Traditional tropical drinks like Blue Hawaii, Tropical Itch, Piña Colada or Chi Chi, and Holiday Punch. *Comments:* This poolside restaurant also offers an ocean view.

Kalapaki Beach Hut (Coffee/espresso, sandwiches and snacks)

Overlooking Kalapaki Bay, 3474 Rice Street, next to Anchor Cove Shopping Center; 808-246-6330.

Hours: Daily 7 a.m. to 7 p.m. Breakfast until 10:30 a.m. *Sampling:* Breakfast egg or pancake sandwich, *loco moco*, omelets, mahimahi and eggs, buffalo and eggs (really!), Branola French toast ($3 to $7). Lunches feature their flame-broiled beef or buffalo burgers with a variety of toppings. Caesar salad; fish-and-chips; mahimahi, chicken, tuna or vegetarian sandwiches ($4 to $6). *Keiki* menu available. *Comments:* Not that cheap, but tasty, eats in a casual outdoor setting—or buy your burger or plate lunch to go. Seating available upstairs for a view of the park and bay area or dine at the counter on the lower level.

Kalapaki Grill (Snacks/light meals)

Located poolside Kaua'i Marriott; 808-245-5050.

Hours: 11 a.m. to 4:30 p.m. *Sampling:* Grilled burgers, jumbo hot dog, sandwiches (turkey, grilled chicken, tuna), garden, chicken Caesar or rotelle pasta salad, shrimp cocktail, jalapeño poppers ($5 to $10). *Comments:* Appetizers served in *dim sum* baskets. Shave ice in eight flavors, from coconut to lemon-lime. *Keiki* menu available. Beer, wine and tropical drinks.

★ Kalena Fish Market (Local/Korean food)

2985A Kalena Street (next to Lihu'e Fishing Supply), Lihu'e; 808-246-6629.

Hours: Monday to Friday 10 a.m. to 7 p.m. Saturday until 5 p.m. Closed Sunday. *Sampling: Kalua*, *laulau* or special Hawaiian plate; Korean plates (barbecue beef, chicken or short ribs; meat *jun*, *bi bim bap*, fried *mandoo*, *kim chee* soup) with two scoops of rice and choice of vegetable ($5 to $8). *Comments:* Fish or *tako poke*, *opihi*, *lomilomi* salmon, scallop salad, smoked or dried fish and other *pupus* from the deli. Always fresh and tasty and good variety.

Kaua'i Chop Suey (Chinese food)

In Harbor Mall, 3501 Rice Street, Nawiliwili; 808-245-8790.

Hours: Lunch Tuesday to Saturday 11 a.m. to 2 p.m. Dinner Tuesday to Sunday 4:30 to 9 p.m. Closed Monday. *Sampling:* House specials include Kaua'i chop suey with mushrooms ($8) or *hon too mein* for 4 to 6 persons ($28). Also chicken, duck, shrimp, scallop, beef, pork, vegetarian, sweet and sour, egg and noodle dishes ($6 to $10). Chow mein and noodle soups as well as rice dishes, including special fried rice with chicken, pork, mushrooms, beans, shrimp and more ($4 to $9). Their sizzling-rice platters like beef, chicken, scallop or shrimp with lobster sauce (with 10 pieces of jumbo shrimp) are a specialty ($7 to $9). *Comments:* Big Chinese banquet room divided into three areas with round archways and red and gold decor. They don't have a liquor license, so bring your own if you so choose. The food is nicely seasoned and the sizzling platters (which arrive crackling and steaming) are always fun!

Kaua'i Community College/Queen Victoria Room (Continental cuisine)

Inside the Campus Center, 3-1901 Kaumuali'i Highway #50, Lihu'e; 808-245-8243.

Hours: When classes are in session during spring and fall semesters on Wednesday and Friday 11:30 a.m. to 1 p.m. *Sampling:* Three-course Continental and Pacific Rim lunches ($9 to $13) are the fine-dining options for spring; fall is more like a coffee shop, with diner/coffee shop–style cooking and a casual atmosphere. Salads, sandwiches and homecooked entrees ($3 to $8), with paper plates, paper napkins, etc. For the fine dining and tableside-cooked lunches, they bring out the good china, silver and linen napkins. *Comments:* Separate dining room offers lunch while school is in session as part of the Culinary Arts training program. Students learn all aspects of the restaurant business: they shop, serve, clean and wait on the tables. The program is only offered during the school year, so be sure and call to check on availability and schedule a reservation. Good food at a good price and a fun concept.

Kaua'i Kitchens (Local cuisine)

Rice Shopping Center, 4303 Rice Street, Lihu'e; 808-245-4513.

Hours: 7 a.m. to 2:30 p.m. Saturday 7:30 a.m. to 1:30 p.m. Closed Sunday. *Sampling:* Sandwiches, plate lunches, *bentos*, sushi (*maki* cone) and daily specials ($2 and up): chicken cutlet, fresh corned beef, breaded crab croquette, baked pork chops, roast turkey with stuffing, lemon chicken, seafood curry, fish filet, pork adobo plus Hawaiian, Filipino and Oriental plates ($5 to $7). They also sell Kaua'i Kookies, baked foods and T-shirts retail from the Kaua'i Kookie Kompany. *Comments:* "Quick Tasty Island Style" that you can eat in or take out. They have another location in Koloa and one in Waimea, in the Big Save grocery store.

Kaua'i Mix Plate & Deli (Hawaiian/Local-style cuisine)

3204 Kuhio Highway, Lihu'e; 808-246-8898.

Hours: 7:30 a.m. to 9:30 p.m. *Sampling:* This local-style fast-food counter serves up a variety of inexpensive fare. Breakfast items include omelets ($5 to $6), steak and eggs ($7), *loco moco* and eggs ($6), and pancakes ($3 to $4). For lunch/dinner, choose from burgers ($1 to $3), stew/chili/curry ($3), Oriental chicken salad ($5), different varieties of stir-fry noodles ($5 to $7), plate lunches like lemon chicken, teriyaki beef, mahimahi, barbecue chicken, *katsu* curry, pork *katsu*, shrimp, *loco moco*, beef stew and more ($5 to $7) with mini-plates ($4 to $5). *Comments:* Beach packs and party pans for take-out also available. Eat in or take out.

★ Kawayan (Local/Filipino/Thai/vegetarian cuisines)
Puhi Industrial Park, 1543 Haleukana Street, Puhi; 808-245-8823.

Hours: Monday to Friday 10 a.m. to 6 p.m. Closed weekends. *Sampling:* Pork adobo, *pancit guisado*, *pinkabet* and Thai chicken served daily ($6 to $7) along with *lumpia* and spring rolls. Plate lunches have 1, 2 or 3 choices of entrees and are featured as daily specials ($6 to $8), like curry chicken, pork and peas, chicken papaya, beef *senigang*, fish or vegetable curry, chow fun, chicken adobo, Thai fried rice with shrimp and pork, pork *tocino*, Thai curry, mongo beans, beef *tocino*, fried rice. Vegetarian selections. *Comments:* Nice outdoor dining area and tasty fresh food. They also have *halo-halo*, shave ice and frozen appetizers (*lumpia*, spring rolls) by the dozen. Popular with the lunch crowd.

K.C.L. Barbecue & Chinese Restaurant (Local and Chinese food)
3100 Kuhio Highway, Lihu'e, 808-246-3829; and in the Waipouli Complex, 4-971 Kuhio Highway, Kapa'a, 808-823-8168.

Hours: Daily 9 a.m. (9:30 a.m. in Lihue) to 10 p.m. *Sampling:* Eggs, omelets, *loco moco*, French toast or pancakes for breakfast ($4 to $6). Burgers, barbecue chicken, shrimp, mahimahi or teriyaki beef sandwiches and hot dogs ($2 to $4). The menu is an extensive list of 138 items including chicken (lemon, *katsu*, cutlet, barbecue, ginger), roast duck, *char siu*, mahimahi, pork chop, *loco moco*, teriyaki steak, sweet-and-sour spare ribs, shrimp curry, and combinations (mixed or barbecue mixed plate, *bento* box, New York steak and garlic shrimp, seafood or chicken combo, and fried chicken) with macaroni salad and rice ($4 to $8). Chinese dishes include chop suey, pot roast, chicken with cashew nuts and vegetables, shrimp with straw mushrooms, beef broccoli, pork with bitter melon, chicken with eggplant, shrimp with black bean sauce and squid with ginger and onion ($6 to $8). *Comments:* It's hard to find a hamburger for $1.25—or for that matter, mahimahi, fried shrimp and scallops for under $7—but you can here. Of course, you also get what you pay for. This is sort of a greasy-spoon place, but the portions and prices make it popular.

Kim Chee #9 Restaurant (Korean food)
3-2600 Kaumuali'i Highway, Lihu'e; 808-246-0106.

Hours: Sunday to Thursday 10:30 a.m. to 8 p.m. Friday to Saturday 10:30 a.m. to 9 p.m. *Sampling:* This small restaurant features a Korean menu. Choose from entrees like barbecue chicken or beef ($7), *kalbi* ribs ($15), barbecue pork ($7), meat *jun* ($7), chicken *katsu* ($8), shrimp tempura ($10), squid tempura ($9), chicken tofu

($7), steamed *mandoo* ($6), mahi *katsu* ($8), and chop *chae* long rice ($8) plus many other selections. *Comments:* This is probably one of the most unusually named restaurants on Kaua'i. Located next to Longs Drugs on the outside corner near the parking lot in Kukui Grove.

★ *Korean BBQ (Korean food)*

In the Kinipopo Shopping Center, 356 Kuhio Highway, Wailua; 808-823-6744.

Hours: Wednesday to Monday 10 a.m. to 9 p.m. Tuesday 4:30 p.m. to 9 p.m. *Sampling:* Korean entrees like *bi bim bob*, *kalbi* ribs, teriyaki beef, meat or fish *jun*, fried or rolled *mandoo*. Combination plates served with four vegetables, potato salad and two scoops of rice featuring barbecue chicken, stir-fry squid or long rice (tofu, chicken or beef), chicken cutlet or *katsu*, hamburger steak ($6 to $8); also *kim chee*, miso and *kooksoo* soup. *Comments:* This is one of our favorites. It's always good, the prices are right (two can eat heartily for under $15) and it has a wide variety to choose from. And it serves a lot more vegetables than any other local-style eatery.

Kountry Kitchen (American cuisine)

1485 Kuhio Highway, Kapa'a; 808-822-3511.

Hours: Breakfast 6 a.m. to 2 p.m. Lunch 11 a.m to 2 p.m. *Sampling:* Pancakes and waffles (plain, strawberry or banana), French toast, pork chop and eggs, corned beef hash, *loco moco*, omelets (Polynesian, Denver, ham and cheese, fresh mushroom, hamburger, tuna, chili or build your own) with cornbread, and vegetable, turkey or traditional eggs Benedict ($4 to $10). Lunch fare includes patty melt, BLT, grilled ham and cheese and tuna sandwiches or create your own burger with your choice of a variety of toppings ($5 to $7). Lunch plates of hamburger steak, grilled pork chop, mahimahi, sirloin steak or fried chicken served with vegetable, rice or fries and cornbread ($7 to $9). Ice cream and blueberry or apple crisp. *Comments:* Looks like an old-fashioned coffee shop of the '50s, but with wood, brick and copper accents. Family-style restaurant, but they do have beer and wine. *Keiki* menu available. Good breakfasts!

Kukui Grove Shopping Center

3-2600 Kaumuali'i Highway, Lihu'e.

The draw of most of these small restaurants is their location in the Kukui Grove Shopping Center. We've listed them with a capsule review. Most are inexpensive. Some of the larger restaurants, or those having something particular to recommend, are also listed individually.

- ***Deli & Bread Connection***; 808-245-7115. See listing above.
- ***Ho's Chinese Kitchen***; 808-245-5255. Open Monday to Thursday and Saturday 9:30 a.m. to 6 p.m. Friday 9:30 a.m. to 9 p.m.

Sunday 9:30 a.m. to 5 p.m. *Sampling:* Chinese dishes such as lemon chicken, cold ginger chicken, roast duck on rice, beef broccoli chow mein, beef chow fun, pork with Chinese peas, beef tomato, shrimp Canton, mahimahi black bean, various soup, chop suey, noodle, rice and egg specialties ($5 to $7).

- ***Joni Hana***; 808-245-5213. *Hours:* 10 a.m. to 8 p.m. *Sampling:* Menu changes daily and features things like chow mein, teriyaki chicken or beef, lemon *shoyu* chicken, chow fun, beef stew, sweet-and-sour spare ribs, chicken broccoli, shrimp tempura, *nishime*; plate lunches; *bentos*; local-style grinds at good prices ($4 to $8).
- ***Kaua'i Bakery***; 808-246-4765. *Hours:* 7 a.m. to 7 p.m. *Sampling:* Donuts, turnovers, cinnamon buns and local pastries (*manju*, *malasadas*), plus *haupia*, *lilikoi* and guava cakes.
- ***Kim Chee #9 Restaurant***; 808-246-0106. See listing above.
- ***Myron's***; 808-245-5178. *Hours:* 9:30 a.m. to 7 p.m. *Sampling:* Filipino and local food, plate lunches; menu items such as pork or chicken adobo, tripe stew, chicken papaya, pork and peas, barbecue spare ribs, chicken long rice, *lumpia* ($5 to $7).
- ***Zack's Famous Frozen Yogurt & Café***; 808-246-2415. See listing below.

Lihu'e Bakery & Coffee Shop (Filipino cuisine)

Rice Shopping Center, 4303 Rice Street, Lihu'e; 808-245-7520.

Hours: Monday to Friday 5 a.m. to 6 p.m. Saturday 5 a.m. to 4 p.m. Sunday 5 a.m. to 10 a.m. *Sampling:* Unusual Filipino baked goods, also donuts and muffins. Hot Filipino entrees served cafeteria style from 5 a.m. through lunch ($4 to $6). *Comments:* Macaroons, turnovers and lots of baked goods.

Lihu'e Café (Local cuisine)

2978 Umi Street, Lihu'e; 808-245-6471.

Hours: Lunch only. Tuesday to Friday 10:30 a.m to 1:30 p.m. *Sampling:* Menu changes daily and may include such local-style favorites as chicken *hekka*, roast pork, *nishime*, pork tofu, chicken curry, beef stew, roast turkey, chili dogs, along with specials like chow fun, sweet-and-sour spare ribs or fried chicken with rice, *kim chee* and salad ($5 to $7). Teriyaki or chop steak plate; saimin, won ton mein, *bento* ($3 to $6). *Comments:* Most popular at night as a bar and lounge, but they serve lunch from a small buffet table.

Lizard Lounge & Deli (Sandwiches/pizza)

Waipouli Town Center, 771 Kuhio Highway, Waipouli; 808-821-2205.

Hours: 10 a.m. to 2 a.m. *Sampling:* Pizza by the slice ($2 to $3) and a selection of ham, salami, turkey, veggie, tuna, chicken salad or roast beef sandwiches named after the seven major Hawaiian islands

($5). They're served on a large French roll (fresh and soft) with dill pickles on the side. Chef salad, buffalo wings or chicken breast sandwich ($7). Smoothies, coffee drinks and good homemade cole slaw and potato salad. Imported beers and microbrews, modern martinis and tropical drinks like the Po'ipu Passion, Kapa'a Cooler and a piña colada that they'll put up against any on the island. *Comments:* This bar has plenty of seating at tables and chairs or the bar/counter. Live entertainment, billiard tables, electric and steel-tip dart boards—even playing cards—make this a popular hang-out. It's one of the few places on Kauai open until 2 a.m.

L&L Drive Inn (Local cuisine)

733 Kuhio Highway, Kapa'a; 808-821-8880.

Hours: 10 a.m. to 10 p.m. *Sampling:* At L&L you can get plate lunches including seafood, chicken, pork, beef and vegetarian Asian dishes, plus burgers, hot dogs, saimin, chili, curry and stew ($4 to $6). Combination plates ($4 to $7) include up to three entree items, plus prime rib plates ($6 to $8). Varied daily entrees from the buffet steam table range from beef with broccoli, orange chicken, vegetable chop suey, black-pepper chicken strips, or sweet-and-sour pork, and much more ($5 to $7). *Comments:* This is the L&L chain's Kaua'i outlet and they feature local-style plate lunches and favorites at reasonable prices.

★ Ma's (Local/homestyle cuisine)

4277 Halenani Street, Lihu'e; 808-245-3142.

Hours: Monday to Friday 5 a.m. to 1:30 p.m., Saturday and Sunday to 11:30 a.m. *Sampling:* Eggs, Irish omelet, Doctor's omelet (egg whites only), bacon, Portuguese sausage, *pipi kaula* and waffles or pancakes that come plain or with pineapple, papaya or banana ($5). Lunch entrees vary daily but may include things like meatloaf, veal/pork cutlets, fresh *ahi* or *akule* fish, Ma's fried noodles with teriyaki meat, beef or tripe stew, curry beef ($4 to $7). Hawaiian specials include *kalua* pork and eggs, *pipi kaula* and eggs, *laulau* and eggs, *lomilomi* salmon and eggs, corned beef hash and eggs ($5). Specialty sandwiches such as roast beef and pork plus hamburgers are available ($2 to $4). *Comments:* Ma's opened in the mid-1960s and its big portions and low prices make it a local favorite. The breakfasts are a real bargain. Try a local variety of Spam and eggs, or omelets, pancakes, or French toast made with Portuguese sweet bread. This is definitely a hole-in-the-wall, greasy-spoon restaurant, but that's what makes it so much fun. The service is genuinely warm and sincere, a reflection of Kaua'i itself. Ma herself, a very gracious and grandmotherly lady, may be the one to greet you with a smile and plunk down a big thermos of coffee so you can serve yourself. (The coffee is free with meals.) Turn off Rice Street onto Kress Street and make another left onto Halenani. It's just around the corner from Hamura Saimin and Barbecue Inn. Limited street parking in front and on nearby narrow streets and lanes.

Mark's Place (Local cuisine)
In the Puhi Industrial Park, 1610 Haleukana Street, Kapa'a; 808-245-2722.

Hours: 10 a.m. to 7 p.m. *Sampling:* Plate lunches with hamburger steak, beef curry or stew, teriyaki or Korean chicken, *loco moco*, chicken cutlet or *katsu* in regular or mini sizes ($4 to $6). Mixed plate with chicken *katsu*, teriyaki beef and beef stew ($6). Burgers and hot teriyaki chicken or beef sandwiches ($2 to $4). Daily specials might include garlic and herb *ahi*, a half-roasted chicken with mashed potatoes and corn on the cob, or miso pork with eggplant ($6 to $7). Fresh salads change daily; mini or large *bento*. Homemade desserts like strawberry Bavarian parfait ($2) or blueberry streusel, *haupia* bread pudding and banana nut bread. *Comments:* This is a real dining discovery, an out-of-the-way place worth searching for. Located just off Puhi Road and Hanalima Street. It's local food upgraded. They also offer take-out and catering as Contemporary Flavors, Inc.

Mele Lounge (Sandwiches/pupus)
Lobby of Radisson Kaua'i Beach, Lihue; 808-245-1955.

Hours: Sandwiches 12 p.m. to 8 p.m. *Pupus* served until 10 p.m. *Sampling:* Cheeseburger; hot dog; turkey, ham-and-bacon club; smoked ham-and-Swiss sandwiches ($7 to $9). Crab or pork won tons; spicy chicken wings; potato skins; jumbo onion rings; nachos; and grilled Portuguese sausage on sauteed Kaua'i onions ($5 to $9). Teas, espressos and coffee drinks. Smoothies with or without rum. *Comments:* Cocktail lounge with nightly Hawaiian entertainment.

★ Mermaid's Café (International cuisine)
1384 Kuhio Highway, Kapa'a; 808-821-2026.

Hours: Monday to Saturday 9 a.m. to 9 p.m. Closed Sunday. *Sampling:* Tofu or chicken satay plate; tofu or chicken coconut curry plate; stir-fry noodle plate; *ahi nori* wrap; chicken satay wrap; *ahi* cilantro wrap; organic salad; black-bean burrito; foccacia sandwich with *ahi* tuna or chicken; also breakfast bagels, scones, French toast, eggs and more; beverages include international teas, coffees, etc. All meals for under $10; sidewalk seating and tables. *Comments:* This is a tiny eatery, but the food is made fresh and uses quality ingredients and the menu has flair. Definitely worth a stop.

Naupaka Terrace and Sushi Bar (Breakfast/pupus and sushi bar)
Poolside at the Kaua'i Marriott, Lihue; 808-245-5050.

Hours: Continental breakfast 6 to 10:30 a.m.; appetizers and sushi bar 5 to 10 p.m. *Sampling:* Pastries, bagels, fruit, yogurt, Anahola granola. In the evening, try the Hawaiian nachos, cheese quesadillas, fish fingers, volcano wings, shrimp cocktail, jalapeño poppers, burgers, teriyaki chicken sandwiches, or Caesar salads ($6 to $10). The sushi bar offers a variety of sushi and sashimi and *maki* sushi rolls ($5 to $16). *Comments:* An attractive restaurant resembling a large gazebo in a park. Choose from a dozen liqueur coffee drinks and specialty martinis. Cigars and board games available upon request.

Nawiliwili Tavern (Italian food)

At Kalapaki Bay near the Anchor Cove Shopping Center, 3488 Paena Loop, Lihue; 808-245-7079; www.nawiliwili.com.

Hours: Dinner 4 to 8 p.m., bar open until 2 a.m. *Sampling:* Spaghetti with marinara sauce, meat sauce, spinach and mushroom, white clam, meatballs and combination sauces, or chicken parmesan served with green salad and fresh-baked sourdough bread ($6 to $8). Burgers, too. Dessert specialty is creamy amaretto tiramisu. *Comments:* Pool tables, darts and video games, satellite live sports, plus free e-mail; karaoke every Tuesday. Pub-style atmosphere, located in the historic Hotel Kuboyama.

Okazu Hale (Japanese/local cuisine)

4100 Rice Street, Lihu'e; 808-245-6554.

Hours: Monday to Saturday 11 a.m. to 2 p.m., 5 to 9 p.m. *Sampling:* Spicy chicken and eggplant, shrimp and vegetable tempura, teriyaki beef or chicken, pork chops and chicken cutlet served with rice and tossed salad ($6 to $9). *Donburi* with chicken, beef, stir-fry or tempura ($6 to $8). Saimin and good sushi as well. *Comments:* Daily specials include *ahi* and stuffed cabbage, oxtail soup, stuffed chicken, pot roast and meatloaf ($6 to $8); Saturday-night sushi and tempura dinner ($16). Sushi is fresh and a good value here. Tiny dining room, but fast service; also take out.

Oki Diner and Bakery (Local cuisine/bakery)

3125 Kuhio Highway, Lihu'e; 808-245-5899.

Hours: 5 a.m. to 2 a.m. *Sampling:* For breakfast they have omelets, egg dishes, pancake sandwich, fried rice with meat and blueberry or banana hotcakes ($4 to $8). The rest of the menu covers everything else: burgers, sandwiches, *dim sum*, saimin or *won ton min*, fried noodles and noodle salad ($3 to $7) and local favorites like *laulau*, *kalua* pig, pork adobo, *loco moco*, spaghetti, *kalbi* ribs, beef stew, fried chicken, pork chops, tempura, ginger chicken and oxtail soup—all served with rice and salad ($6 to $10). Create your own stir-fry from a selection of meats and vegetables. *Keiki* menu available. Pies from their own bakery, with fresh cream topping: *lilikoi* chiffon, banana or chocolate cream, custard and lime. *Comments:* It's like a fast-and-friendly bus station for food: there's a large dining room and a full bakery filled with coconut or apple turnovers, large cookies, butter *mochi*, *manju*, brownies, oversized cream puffs with custard filling, apple squares and their yummy specialty—pumpkin crunch. Very casual atmosphere and furnishings. The food isn't anything special, but they have lots of choices, the prices are low and they're open 21 hours.

★ Ono Family Restaurant (Local cuisine/family dining)
1292 Kuhio Highway, Kapa'a; 808-822-1710.

Hours: Breakfast 7 a.m. to noon. Lunch 11 a.m. to 2 p.m. *Sampling:* The breakfast menu offers a variety of egg dishes and omelets, including meat, cheese and vegetable combinations (like tomatillo and avocado, fried rice with *kim chee* and homemade chorizo). Ono burritos, Ono-style Portuguese pork and eggs, as well as pancakes (including banana or tropical), French toast and other standard breakfast fare round out the breakfast menu ($4 to $7). The lunch menu offers sandwiches like cod, veggie, tuna melt, turkey, a 24-special (half turkey-and-egg-salad sandwich with macaroni salad and soup) and a farmer's sandwich (turkey, ham, jack cheese with fries and soup) ($4 to $7.50). There is also a diverse burger menu, including teriyaki, mushroom, bacon, *paniolo* barbecue, chili, patty melt and several specialty burgers made from mahimahi, bacon and avocado, buffalo and charbroiled chicken ($6 to $7). Lunch specials range from fresh island fish, chicken or beef stir-fry, meatloaf and charbroiled beef to fish-and-chips, saimin and fried noodles ($6 to $8). For dessert, try a piece of their *onolicious* homemade pies; these are genuinely tasty, and the coconut, macadamia-nut custard, coconut vanilla and macadamia-nut vanilla cream are sure to please. *Keiki* menu available. They also sell Auntie Ono's homemade pineapple-papaya jam, jelly, coconut syrups and Kona coffee blends. *Comments:* This is a funky old place, in a historic building in downtown Kapa'a. It has an antique island–style decor, with woven coconut hats on the wall, some artwork and miscellaneous odds and ends for decorative accents around the booths and tables. Their service has always been outstanding: friendly, attentive, sincere small town–style. It's a local institution with local style–comfort food in a wholesome family atmosphere.

Papaya's Natural Foods (Vegetarian cuisine)
Kaua'i Village, 4-831 Kuhio Highway, Kapa'a; 808-823-0190.

Hours: 9 a.m. to 7 p.m. Closed Sunday. *Sampling:* Rosemary potatoes, steamed eggs and brie, multigrain pancakes, tofu scramble, granola, *tofutos rancheros*, or frittata to start you off ($3 to $7), then a variety of sandwiches and entrees for lunch or dinner: *tempeh* or tofu burgers, falafel, hummus or Mediterranean salad plate, Thai vegetable stir-fry, baked tofu, fresh fish tacos, veggie pizza and spinach and herb lasagna ($5 to $8). Good selection of muffins, scones, breads, cookies and brownies and serious desserts. *Comments:* Teas, coffee drinks and smoothies, plus a variety of fat-free, sugar-free, wheat-free and vegan items. This is Kaua'i's biggest health food store, so the menu reflects high quality and organic ingredients. Order at the counter, then bring your selections to the tables outside where you can enjoy great people watching. It's a good value for your dining dollar, but it can get busy and then service slows.

Po's Kitchen (Local cuisine)

4100 Rice Street, Lihu'e; 808-246-8617.

Hours: Monday to Saturday 6 a.m. to 2 p.m. *Sampling: Bento* and box lunches in three sizes: small/regular/deluxe ($5 to $7). Box lunches include fried chicken, teriyaki meat, egg roll, rice ball, potato salad, luncheon meat, hot dog, side dish and pickled cabbage. Also teriyaki chicken, meat, or short ribs plate lunch and hot entree that changes daily ($5 to $8). *Comments:* Simple and very inexpensive menu. The fried chicken was a wingette, the luncheon meat is a piece of Spam. All the portions in the small *bento* were appetizer-sized. A good place to sample some unusual local dishes with a lot of small sides and snack items, but it's a bit of a greasy-spoon.

Puakea Bar & Grill (American and local cuisines)

Puakea Golf Course, across from Kukui Grove Shopping Center to the south, 4315 Kalepa Street; 808-245-8756.

Hours: Saturday to Tuesday 9 a.m. to 6:30 p.m. Wednesday to Friday until 7:30 p.m. *Sampling:* Burgers, hot dogs, sandwiches (turkey, egg or white-meat chicken salad, grilled ham-and-cheese, roast beef, BLT, club, albacore tuna), fish-and-chips, chicken Caesar and chicken or beef taco salad ($4 to $6). Chili and rice, onion rings, Spam and cabbage, chicken wings with fries, diced hot dog and onions ($3 to $4). Beer and wine, sodas, raspberry tea, pink lemonade, snacks. *Comments:* Small café across from the pro shop with counter and table seating.

★ Restaurant Kiibo (Japanese cuisine)

Just off Rice Street, 2991 Umi Street, Lihu'e; 808-245-2650.

Hours: Lunch 11:30 a.m. to 1:30 p.m. Dinner 5:30 to 9 p.m. *Sampling:* Lunch special with entree, rice, miso soup and salad ($5 to $7). Teriyaki chicken, beef or pork, plus light-and-fluffy tempura, fresh sushi, sukiyaki, sashimi, *nabe*, butterfish *nitsuke*, saba *shioyaki*, fried salmon or chicken, ramen, chicken or pork tofu, noodles, fresh fish and special house *bentos* ($7 to $18). *Comments:* The decor and food are authentic and very traditional. It's one of the better places to get Japanese food on Kaua'i. Usually busy, especially at lunch.

Rob's Good Times Grill (American cuisine)

4303 Rice Street, Lihu'e; 808-246-0311.

Hours: 11 a.m. to 9 p.m. *Sampling:* Lots of appetizers/*pupus* like sauteed mushrooms, chicken sticks, won tons, egg rolls, fresh veggies, fried chicken or zucchini, *kalua* pork and cabbage, boiled peanuts, chips and homemade salsa ($3 to $6). Sashimi, grilled steak, seared *poke*, or mixed *pupu* basket. Tuna or Oriental chicken salad ($5 to $6). Pastrami and Swiss, mahimahi, egg salad, tuna, grilled chicken or turkey, BLT and turkey club sandwiches ($5 to $7). Burgers include mushroom, bacon or chili ($5 to $7). *Comments:* Pub mirrors and beer signs on the walls with satellite TV and a dart board. Music, entertainment and karaoke. During football season, they open at 7 a.m. for breakfast with *loco moco*, omelets, or sweet bread French toast. Later at night, this is more of a bar scene, often with live entertainment and dancing.

Sampaguita's/Big Wheel Donut Shop (Local cuisine)

Old Hanamaulu Trading Post; 808-245-5322.

Hours: Donuts from 4 a.m. to 11:30 a.m. Breakfast 5 a.m. to "whenevah." *Sampling:* Plate lunches ($4 to $6); breakfast: eggs, bacon and hotcakes ($4). *Comments:* These are two different places, but in such a small building that it's almost impossible not to list them together. Big Wheel also serves coffee, makes their donuts fresh and frequently has a "Sorry out of donuts" sign in front. Not surprising, since they start serving them at 4 in the morning! The donuts are the best choice here.

The Shack (Burgers/sandwiches)

4-139 Kuhio Highway, Kapa'a; 808-823-0200.

Hours: 11 a.m. to midnight, or 2 a.m. (if there's a crowd). *Sampling:* Buffalo wings, onion rings, chili and rice, potato skins, chicken strips, zucchini strips ($3.25 to $6.25), plate lunches like chicken *katsu*, teriyaki beef, hamburger steaks, fresh fish, chili dog and combo plates, all served with two scoops rice and macaroni salad ($5.50 to $7.25). Thirteen kinds of burgers, including topped with bacon and bleu cheese, guacamole, chili, Swiss cheese and mushrooms, patty melt, Reuben burger, Ortega chili burger and the double shack cheeseburger—a half-pounder topped with Portuguese sausage. ($4.75 to $6.50). Eight kinds of chicken sandwiches, such as Hawaiian style, spicy, guacamole, Ortega ($5.50 to $6.50). Also a host of other sandwiches, such as Philly cheesesteak, pastrami Reuben, turkey club, grilled honey-mustard ham, tuna melt and fresh fish ($5.72 to $6.25). Fries or salad can be added to any order for $1.95. Fish-and-chips, New York steak and shrimp-and-chips ($6.50 to $8.95). Dinner, chef, Caesar and Oriental chicken salads round out the menu. *Comments:* This restaurant chain is new to Kaua'i, taking over the Kapa'a Fish & Chowder House, but it's been serving burgers in Southern California, O'ahu and

Colorado for over 30 years. Prices are reasonable, portions are large and there's plenty of room in the spacious dining area, as well as some outside tables. It bills itself as a family restaurant and sports bar, with big-screen TV, large bar, games and other activities. Live entertainment some evenings. They'll stay open until 2 a.m. if there's a crowd, making it one of the few places you can eat late at night. Small kids' menu.

Sri's Snack Shop (Local cuisine)

Rice Shopping Center, 4303 Rice Street, Lihu'e; 808-246-3910.

Hours: Breakfast 6 to 9 a.m. Lunch 11 a.m. to 3 p.m. Closed Sunday. *Sampling:* Oxtail soup, pork tofu, chicken or beef stew ($4 to $7). Weekly specials may features roast beef, roast chicken, roast pork, roast duck and roast turkey (Friday). *Comments:* This tiny local café also has *guri guri*, a local-style creamy sherbet.

Surf and Turf Café (Steak/seafood)

Kinipopo Shopping Village, 356 Kuhio Highway, Wailua; 808-822-0560.

Hours: 11 a.m. to 8:30 p.m. Closed Sunday. *Sampling:* Hot and cold sandwiches of turkey, roast beef, grilled and fried fish, hamburgers and taro burgers ($5.95 to $6.95). Also fish-and-chips, steak, shrimp, *kalua* pork, seafood platters, grilled chicken and meatloaf ($6.95 to $7.95). Caesar, chef and green salads ($4.95 to $5.95). Same menu served all day. *Comments:* The name isn't inspiring, but the food is good and the portions are generous, especially for the low prices that make it a good value. Oceanview mural, relaxed, low-key setting. A nice stop for a quick, casual meal.

Terrace Restaurant at Kaua'i Lagoons Resort (Continental/international cuisines)

Kaua'i Lagoons Golf Course, 3351 Ho'olaule'a Way, Lihu'e; 808-241-6080.

Hours: Breakfast 8 to 11 a.m. Lunch 11 a.m. to 1:30 p.m. *Sampling:* Fruit, cereal, egg dishes, Spanish or *kim chee* omelet, Hawaiian sweet bread French toast, banana-nut hotcakes, crab cake Benedict, steak and eggs ($3 to $10). Burgers, sandwiches (curried tuna croissant, barbecue teriyaki sirloin, fresh fish or turkey, ham-and-cheese); grilled *ahi*, shrimp, fruit, or chicken Caesar salad ($7 to $10); Oriental stir-fry (veggie, chicken or shrimp), *donburi* teriyaki beef or chicken and double garlic linguine ($9 to $10). Luncheon buffet with soup, salads, hot entrees, sandwich bar and desserts. *Comments:* Attractive setting overlooking a gazebo garden. Not bad if you're golfing or staying at the Marriott, but not worth a special trip.

Tip Top Café (Local cuisine)

3173 Akahi, Lihu'e; 808-245-2333.

Hours: Breakfast daily 6:30 to 11:30 a.m. Lunch Tuesday to Sunday 11 a.m. to 2 p.m. *Sampling:* Macadamia or banana pancakes, sweet bread French toast, *loco moco*, omelets, *bento* ($3 to $6). Burgers, grilled ham-and-cheese, BLT and tuna sandwiches plus beef stew, saimin and oxtail soup, a popular specialty ($3 to $5). Daily specials: meatloaf, corned beef and cabbage, pork tofu, spaghetti and chili ($5 to $7). *Comments:* Move over Hard Rock Café, the Tip Top souvenir shop has T-shirts and hats. The bakery continues to make yummy macadamia-nut cookies, cream puffs and eclairs. This is a typical local-style spot and it's busy at breakfast and lunch. The macadamia pancakes are light and fluffy and the French toast is very good. They're known for their oxtail soup. Prices are a little high for what you get, but it's filling, casual and family style. The café is part of the Tip Top Motel. Their sushi bar and Japanese restaurant, Sushi Katsu, is part of the café. (See individual listing in Moderate-priced section below.)

★ Waipouli Deli & Restaurant (American/local/Asian cuisines)

771 Kuhio Highway, Kapa'a; 808-822-9311.

Hours: Breakfast and lunch 7 a.m. to 2 p.m. Dinner Monday to Saturday 5 to 9 p.m. *Sampling:* Eggs with breakfast meats, pancakes, French toast and homemade corned beef hash ($3 to $6). Lunch entrees of shrimp tempura, roast pork, chop suey, chow mein, pork tofu, beef broccoli, fried chicken, pork or chicken cutlet, liver with bacon and onions, beef or chicken *hekka*, mixed plate ($6 to $8). Burgers and burger platters, sandwiches and saimin ($2 to $6). Dinners include fries or rice, salad and iced tea or coffee. Beef stew, egg foo yung, barbecue teriyaki steak, beef tomato and most of the lunch entrees ($9 to $15). *Comments:* Small local restaurant in the Foodland Shopping Center next to Blockbuster. Children's half-order portions available on lunch and dinner entrees. When a restaurant is always packed, you know they must be doing something right. The service is very friendly, the food is decent, the prices are reasonable—overall, a good dining value.

Zack's Famous Frozen Yogurt & Café (Coffee/espresso, sandwiches and salads)

Kukui Grove Shopping Center, Lihu'e; 808-246-2415.

Hours: Monday to Thursday and Saturday 11 a.m. to 5:30 p.m. Friday until 9 p.m. Sunday until 5 p.m. *Sampling:* This dessert-and-snack shop offers a menu of hot dogs, hamburgers, vegetarian specials, soups, salads (Caesar, chicken sesame, or chicken papaya) plus ham, French dip, roast beef and chicken sandwiches and beef, ham or veggie wraps, pizza ($3 to $7). There are also dishes like chili or stuffed baked potatoes, including bleu cheese, chili, hot dog, broccoli, cheese and bacon bits for toppings ($3 to $6). Chicken and ham plates come with pineapple-papaya sauce and a fresh papaya slice ($5 to $6). Rounding out the menu are dessert goodies such as ice cream, yogurt, frosted brownies, macadamia-nut cheesecake bars, *lilikoi* pie and more. *Comments:* Lots of homemade touches like soups (Portuguese bean, green papaya chicken), cole slaw and potato salad and fresh salads with homemade bleu cheese and other dressings—even homemade croutons!

Moderate-priced Dining

Aussie Tims (Barbecue)

Kuhio Highway, Wailua; 808-822-0300; www.kauaimenu.com.

Hours: Lunch 11 a.m. to 2 p.m. Dinner 4 to 8 p.m. *Sampling:* Offering Kaua'i's only authentic Texas barbecue, with pork ribs, St. Louis ribs, Texas brisket, smoked links, pulled pork, mixed grill, smoked turkey and chicken, smoked Cajun shrimp ($7.95 to $16.95). All plates feature meat smothered in a tasty and spicy barbecue sauce, beans and a choice of corn or slaw and bread. Also sandwiches of pulled pork, smoked chicken, smoked turkey, beef brisket or hot links, all served with potato-mac salad or slaw ($6.96 to $7.95). Side dishes of cornbread, baked bean, corn on the cob, rice. *Comments:* True barbecue is virtually nonexistent on Kaua'i, so if you're hankering for some this is the place to go. Located in a small shopping center across from Kinipopo Shopping Center.

★ *Barbecue Inn (American/Japanese cuisine)*

2982 Kress Street, Lihu'e; 808-245-2921.

Hours: Breakfast 7 a.m. to 1:30 p.m. weekdays. Dinner 5 to 8:30 p.m., Monday to Saturday. Closed Sunday. *Sampling:* Breakfast meats and eggs dishes, pancakes and Asian breakfast of miso soup, teriyaki fish, scrambled egg with green onion, rice and hot tea ($5 to $8). Lunch and dinner menus change daily. The lunch menu may feature specials like grilled fresh-island fish—*ono*, *ahi* or mahimahi, fresh fish *laulau*, lamb shank, shrimp scampi, pork with squash, beef stew, *char siu* duck, roast beef, chicken Caesar salad, grilled liver and onions, pork tofu and veggies, chow mein with chicken or ribs and more ($8 to $13). The dinner menu may include items like sauteed pork tenderloin medallions, macadamia nut–crusted fresh *ono*, T-bone or New York steak, sauteed breast of chicken and shrimp pasta, *kalua* pork and cabbage, chicken cutlet and more ($9 to $19). Both lunch and dinner feature daily chef's specials, house sandwiches and Japanese specials like teriyaki, tempura, *yakitori*. *Comments:* Lunch specials include soup or fruit, drink and dessert. Their homemade cream pies are a delight. Dinner also comes with salad. All sandwiches come on their freshly baked bread. The Sasaki family has owned and operated the restaurant in the same location since 1940, and although there are now a few token barbecue items on the menu, the barbecue in the name referred to a hibachi, which back then was just the common way of cooking. They have added a few more gourmet-style entrees and now serve champagne or wine, but basically, this is still a nice family-style restaurant (*keiki* menu for both lunch and dinner) with booths and curtains. Generous portions, good value and friendly, attentive, efficient service. Good food, good prices, good service—a real Kaua'i kind of place. You may have to hunt around for parking on the narrow streets nearby since this is a popular local spot, but it's worth the effort.

★ Blossoming Lotus (Vegan cuisine)

1384 Kuhio Highway, Kapa'a; 808-822-7678.

Hours: 11 a.m. to 10 p.m. *Sampling:* Bountiful salads featuring vegan substitutes for eggs and tuna, live-food pates, curried *seitan* (a wheat-based meat substitute), grilled tofu with choice of chutneys or sauces, spinach spanikopita and excellent *nori* (seaweed) wraps filled with such goodies as sun-dried tomato pesto, veggies and other ingredients ($7.99 to $11.99). The cornbread ($4.50) is almost a meal in itself. Some 16 types of cuisine are represented in this restaurant, which bills itself, aptly, as a fusion-style eatery. An extensive tea menu and wholesome baked goods and desserts round out the menu. *Comments:* The excellent food, creative menu, warm, friendly service and relaxed, clean atmosphere will make happy diners of even the most die-hard carnivores. It's vegan—meaning no animal products—but you won't miss them. Local and organic ingredients, lots of vegetables and grains, cooked in interesting and extremely delicious and innovative ways. Very good value for low prices. Outdoor tables right on the main street are grand for checking out the local scene, and the indoor dining is soothing and attractive. Discounts for local residents and pregnant *wahines*. This is one of our favorite places on Kaua'i. How can you not love a place where they prepare your food with consciousness, love and blessings? Take-out also available, and they don't use styrofoam boxes.

Bull Shed (Steak/seafood)

796 Kuhio Highway, Waipouli; 808-822-3791/822-1655.

Hours: Cocktails from 4:30 p.m., dinner 5:30 to 10 p.m. *Sampling:* Their trademark prime rib is $21. Other meaty offerings include garlic tenderloin, beef kabob, teriyaki chicken or top-sirloin, Australian lamb rack, garlic chicken and pork baby back ribs ($14 to $22). Shrimp, scallops, crab, lobster and fresh island fish ($16 to market price); and in combination with steak or chicken ($17 to market price). Salad bar (included) offers basic ingredients, but a few unusual items like peas, fresh pineapple and garlic bread. Mud pie for dessert; *keiki* menu of teriyaki chicken or fresh fish. *Comments:* This is a true local favorite, with a surprisingly good ocean view. If you're expecting a dark and dingy steakhouse, you're in for a surprise. It's light, bright and very open, with picture windows. The food is consistently good and with rice, bread and salad bar included in the meal you get a lot for your money.

Café Portofino (Italian cuisine)

Harbor Mall, 3501 Rice Street, Nawiliwili; 808-245-2121.

Hours: Dinner 5 to 10 p.m. *Sampling:* Roasted bell peppers, steamed clams, calamari, mozzarella (fried or with tomato), *ahi* carpaccio and prosciutto are offered as antipasti ($8 to $10). Gazpacho, minestrone or soup of day ($4). Featured pastas are penne with broccoli and spinach, fettuccine with shrimp and mushroom or alfredo, linguine carbonara, pesto, or with clams, ravioli, canneloni and lasagna ($14 to $20). Choose veal or chicken parmigiana, marsala, or Portofino-style (with shrimp and scallops in lemon sage sauce) or veal piccata or chicken in wild mushroom sauce, sauteed with artichoke hearts or cacciatore ($15 to $21). Specialties include osso buco, Provençale or lemon wine scampi and eggplant parmigiana ($16 to $26). Profiteroles, caramel custard and tiramisu are some of the homemade desserts. *Comments:* The restaurant is located in the Harbor Mall, which has undergone extensive renovation. Located on the complex's upstairs level, the dining room features paned windows, beamed ceilings and a patio where you can dine al fresco overlooking the Kalapaki Beach area. Nice bar and lounge areas with live music (usually jazz) on weekends. The cuisine is authentic Italian with ingredients imported from Italy. Breads, ice creams and desserts made on the premises. Good Italian food in comfortable surroundings.

Caffe Coco (Vegetarian cuisine)

Wailua Village, 4-369 Kuhio Highway; 808-822-7990.

Hours: Breakfast 9 a.m. to noon. Sunday until 2 p.m. Continuous menu until 9 p.m. Closed Monday. *Sampling:* Fruit bowl, homemade granola, scrambled egg croissant or egg or tofu burrito, roast veggie omelet for breakfast ($3 to $8). Light meals include potstickers, Greek or tofu salad, sandwiches on foccacia bread (barbecue or roast turkey, seared *ahi*, roast eggplant and cheese) and wraps: tofu and roast veggie, Greek salad or fish ($6 to $9). Platters with rice and salad offer spiced tofu, seared fresh fish, macadamia sesame-encrusted *ahi*, pasta *del giorno* ($11 to $15). Moroccan-spiced seared fish or tofu, fish burrito, *ahi nori* wrap, gumbo and rice, homestyle pot pie, sweet potato cakes, spanikopita, pizza and Thai pumpkin coconut might be some of the blackboard specials. Pumpkin spice cake, *haupia* pudding with tropical fruit sauce, banana fruit tart, Mexican chocolate tofu pie (vegan), or black mocha ice cream roll are some of the homemade desserts. Coffee drinks and espresso. *Comments:* Café and art gallery surrounded by abandoned cane fields in a restored plantation home. Eclectic collection of tables and chairs in various corners and cozy nooks inside; garden seating amid hanging foliage, orchid ferns and *lilikoi* shade trees are very pleasant on nice days. The display case offers savory items like curried vegetable *samosa* plus homemade pastries and desserts. The food is good and well made, but the service can be very slow, so be prepared to wait. Take the time before or after dinner to browse the Bambulei furniture and gift shop next door. Live music some nights.

Camp House Grill & Bar (American cuisine)
4-831 Kuhio Highway, Kapa'a 808-822-2442.

Hours: 6 a.m. to 9:30 p.m. *Sampling:* Breakfast quesadilla, pancakes, omelets, waffles, French toast, biscuits and gravy, eggs Benedict, omelets and a variety of breakfast sandwiches—Monte Cristo with hash browns, or BLT (and egg), pancake or French toast with bacon and eggs ($4 to $9). They have early-bird specials before 8 a.m., but as they say on the menu: "After 8:01, No Way!" Lunch features a variety of burgers, salads, Camp House *huli* barbecue chickens, barbecue pork ribs, varied chicken breasts, sirloin steak Polynesian and fresh catch served with soup or salad and choice of side ($6 to $16). Dinner entrees include pork chops, prime rib, steak of the day, scampi, snow crab legs, or fresh island fish ($12 to $20). They're known for their homemade pies, so save room for dessert. Or, you can buy a whole pie to take with you. Pies include pineapple cream cheese macadamia pie, chewy chocolate chip macadamia nut and coconut, banana, or chocolate cream, plus Paradise Pie made with macadamia nut, pineapple and coconut. *Comments:* Camp House is known for its home-style cooking and homemade pies. *Menehune* (children's) menu available for lunch and dinner. This restaurant features the same family-style atmosphere and home-style cooking that have been traditions at the original Camp House Grill for more than a decade, although portions are a bit skimpy and the food is rather uninspired.

★ Coconuts Island-Style Bar & Grill (Pacific Rim cuisine/seafood)
919 Kuhio Highway, Kapa'a; 808-823-8777.

Hours: 4 to 10 p.m. Closed Sunday. *Sampling:* Grilled filet mignon, tempura-dipped *ono*, roasted veggies with pasta, wok-seared *pad Thai*, teriyaki-dipped grilled salmon, boneless pork chops, burgers, seafood paella ($11.95 to $22.95); spinach, Caesar and organic local green salads ($6.50 to $8.50); appetizers like Asian chicken tacos, fried calamari, lobster ravioli ($7.75 to $9.95); and satisfying desserts like creme brulee and baked banana bread pudding. *Comments:* Although this place has a Southern California sort of feel, the food and cheerful ambiance quickly made it popular with residents and visitors alike. Like the colorful and eclectic art on the walls, the food has variety and zip, with bold flavors. The fish is never over-cooked and the portions are good-sized. There's something for everyone on the menu. It's a fun, interesting and tasty place to eat.

Duke's Canoe Club (Steak/seafood)

Kalapaki Beach, Kaua'i Marriott; 808-246-9599.

Hours: Lunch and Barefoot Bar menu 11:30 a.m. to 11:30 p.m. Dinner 5 to 10 p.m. *Sampling:* Pizza, burgers and sandwiches, salads, *pupus* and Hawaiian local plates for lunch ($4 to $12). Stir-fry chicken cashew, pork ribs, fish tacos, roast beef and cheddar sandwich and grilled mahi Caesar are just a few of the options; fresh fish, seafood, steaks and prime rib are among the most popular dinner offerings ($14 to $22). All include a very serious salad bar that has a fresh Caesar salad station, fresh greens and variety of veggies, as well as prepared salads like macaroni, cole slaw, pasta and potato, plus warm breads, macadamia lemon muffins and carrot muffins. The menu includes innovative dishes like Thai seafood coconut curry; linguine with basil and sun-dried tomatoes, Thai chicken pizza (with a delicious sweet chile sauce and light, homemade pizza crust); and appetizers of macadamia nut and crab won ton, *poke* rolls (with Maui onion), and thick sticks of perfectly prepared calamari ($7 to $20). For desserts, the hula pie is the best, but the Kona coffee cheesecake can hold its own. *Comments:* Named in honor of legendary surfer Duke Kahanamoku, the restaurant features an extensive collection of Duke memorabilia, including photos, an impressive 40-foot outrigger canoe and three of his surfboards. The 30-foot lava rock waterfall is quite dramatic, creating a unique centerpiece as it splashes into a *koi* pond. There is a spacious and attractive area upstairs and a separate area with a salad bar and wide plantation-like veranda that overlook the ocean. (Part of the beachfront lanai is portioned off for private parties, a great place to celebrate a special occasion—anniversary or birthday—in your own little corner of the world!) Strolling musicians in the dining room; live music and entertainment in the Barefoot Bar on weekends.

Fishbowls (Steak/seafood)

733 Kuhio Highway, Wailua; 808-822-7833.

Hours: 5 to 10 p.m. daily. *Sampling:* Appetizers range from oyster shooters and shrimp cocktail to escargot and crab cakes ($8.95 to $9.95). Portuguese bean soup, *ahi poke*, Maui onion soup and clam chowder, Caesar and green salads ($7.95 to $9.95). Cioppino ($19.95), clam, spinach or shrimp linguine ($12.95 to $16.95), scallops, scampi, lobster, crab legs and fresh-fish specials ($17.95 to $34.95) and baby back ribs, pork or lamb chops, steaks, prime rib and combo plates ($14.95 to $29.95). *Comments:* The menu is typical surf-and-turf, with an interesting Euro-Pacific Rim accent. There's also a nice bar known as the Hana Pa'a lounge that often has entertainment in the evenings. It's a nice enough place, but the location is nothing special and the food seems a little pricey for the quality. For the money, you could probably do better.

Flying Lobster (Seafood)

Kaua'i Coconut Beach Resort, Kapa'a; 808-822-3455.

Hours: 5:30 to 9:30 p.m. *Sampling:* Signature lobster dinners plus steak, scampi, herb-roasted or honey-macadamia chicken, barbecue ribs and fresh catch; crab legs ($13 to $25). All-you-can-eat pasta (with mix-and-match pastas and sauces) includes a small salad ($9). Combination dinners from chicken-and-ribs to steak-and-lobster ($15 to $27). Limited menu of burgers and sandwiches plus Caesar salad with shrimp and appetizers of calamari rings, crab legs, shrimp, hot crab dip with garlic toast or Clams Casino ($4 to $8). Dinners include soup or salad bar, starch and vegetable. Desserts include cakes, pies, ice cream and Kaua'i Coconut Beach Sand Pie. *Comments:* Early-bird specials nightly, 5:30 to 6:30 p.m.; Friday and Saturday prime rib and seafood buffet. The food isn't outstanding, but it's pleasant and they have Hawaiian-style entertainment in the evenings. This is called The Voyage Room at breakfast and lunch; see separate listing below.

★ Hanama'ulu Restaurant, Tea House & Sushi Bar (Chinese/ Japanese cuisine)

Just north of Lihu'e Airport, 3-4291 Kuhio Highway #56, Hanama'ulu; 808-245-2511.

Hours: Lunch Tuesday to Friday 10 a.m. to 1 p.m. Dinner Tuesday to Sunday 4:30 to 9 p.m. Closed Monday. *Sampling:* Chinese dishes with noodles, pork, beef, chicken and seafood plus baked mussels and lobster ($5 to $10). Japanese salads, soups, beef, chicken, pork, seafood and vegetarian specials ($7 to $11). Also soups and appetizers from potstickers to *robatayaki*. Complete dinners such as the 9-course Chinese or Japanese dinner for 2 or more are available ($16 per person). Special tempura or seafood platters ($14 to $16). Chinese, Japanese or teriyaki plate lunches and also available at dinner ($6 to $9). Sunday-night Asian buffet from 5:30 to 8:30 p.m. features sushi, sashimi, salads, fish, chicken, crab, teriyaki beef and dessert ($22). *Comments:* The front room is used for lunch and is decorated in a pleasant Asian style, but the Japanese Dining Room (where you sit on the floor Japanese-style) toward the back is nicer, overlooking a beautiful garden with *koi* ponds. Restaurant offers *robatayaki* cooking grilled in front of you, as well as a full sushi bar. The food is reliably good and has been for over 75 years, making it popular for local parties and family gatherings. Hanama'ulu is often overlooked by folks passing through in their haste to head north toward Kapa'a and the North Shore. But this is one of the best Asian restaurants and most-reasonably priced on Kaua'i. A good option for a family meal.

Hawaiian Classic Desserts (Bakery/café)

4479 Rice Street, Lihu'e; 808-245-6967.

Hours: Monday to Saturday 7 a.m. to 3 p.m. Closed Sunday. *Sampling:* French toast or pancakes (with apple smoked chicken sausage), omelets, *loco moco*, eggs with *lup cheong* and green onion fried rice and homemade corned beef hash ($6 to $9). Plate lunches; ham hoagie, turkey, Hawaiian-style Philly steak sandwiches (with teriyaki beef), and burgers ($8 to $9); salads with seared *poke*, broiled lemon-pepper salmon, grilled eggplant, or chicken Oriental ($9). *Comments:* Open kitchens in both the restaurant and behind the dessert bar where you can watch owner and pastry chef Fenton Lee create your "just desserts!" As you'd expect, the sandwiches are all on freshly baked bread and buns.

Kauai Hula Girl Bar & Grill (Steak/seafood)

Coconut MarketPlace, 4-484 Kuhio Highway, Kapa'a; 808-822-4422.

Hours: 11 a.m. to 10 p.m. *Sampling:* Sandwiches, plate lunches, grilled fresh fish and burgers ($6.95 to $10.95) for lunch. Dinner offers steak and lobster ($30.95), *char shui* ribs, *hulihuli* chicken, filet mignon and New York steaks ($13.95 to $20.95), fresh fish prepared a variety of ways ($17.95 to $23.95), two types of pasta, Caesar and green salads, soups. *Comments:* Surf-and-turf, with an island twist. They advertise "surfer-sized" portions, which are large. Also children's menu and senior discounts. Family-style, casual and friendly, and often there's live Hawaiian-style music.

JJ's Broiler (Steak/seafood)

Anchor Cove Shopping Center, Kalapaki Bay, 3416 Rice Street, Lihu'e; 808-246-4422.

Hours: Lunch 11 a.m. to 5 p.m. Dinner 5 to 10 p.m. Cocktails 5 to 11 p.m. *Sampling:* Cheeseburgers come with avocado, bacon, mushrooms, pineapple or chili ($7 to $9). Salads include Asian grilled chicken, Cobb, Caesar, seafood and spinach, and there's ocean chowder, French onion, or beef-and-vegetable soup ($5 to $10). Sandwiches of pastrami and Swiss, turkey club, mahimahi, fried egg and avocado, teriyaki chicken or beef, steak, French dip, Monte Cristo and Reuben are available ($9 to $13), as are a number of vegetarian offerings, Kaua'i garden or marinated tofu sandwich and vegetable pizza on a flour tortilla. Before dinner, there are oysters, mussels, escargot, scampi, crab cakes, or Peking chicken tacos ($8 to $11). Seafood entrees include sauteed scallops, baked lobster tail, coconut shrimp, tempura platter and fresh island fish; charbroiled meats include New York steak, filet mignon, roasted macadamia lamb rack, prime rib, barbecue pork ribs, Cornish hen and JJ's signature Slavonic steak ($17 to $25). Other specialties include black-bean shrimp with Asian polenta, spicy wasabi ribeye steak, *ahi* and crab Napoleon, beef medallions with lobster saute, sugar cane shrimp, chicken fettuccine, seafood linguini, tortellini primavera and baby lamb chops with penne pasta ($16 to $28). Entrees include table salad bar and choice of starch. Key lime pie, JJ's sea of chocolate and double-decker ice cream pie are some of the after-dinner treats. *Comments:* Nice outdoor patio and deck for lunch; dinner is served upstairs with a big picture window overlooking the beach. If the food was as good as the view, this place would be worth recommending.

JR's Plantation Restaurant (Steak/seafood)

3-4221 Kuhio Highway 56, Hanama'ulu; 808-245-1606.

Hours: Dinner 5 to 9:30 p.m. *Sampling:* Appetizers include their special Asian ginger shrimp, escargot and Cajun stuffed mushrooms ($6 to $8); a la carte items offer seafood pasta, jumbo burger, roast beef, Hawaiian luau platter, or salad bar. Entrees include salad bar, rice or potato and homemade garlic bread: New York steak, prime rib, scampi, lamb chops, fresh catch, Hawaiian luau platter, lobster combo, Cajun teriyaki or garlic chicken breast, fried shrimp or their signature Cajun fish and shrimp with ginger scallion sauce ($13 to $20). "Little Cowboy" dinners include a trip to the salad bar ($6 to $8). Homemade desserts are hula pie; strawberry or blueberry cream cheese pie or try JR's strawberry *haupia*! *Comments:* Tropical drinks served with or without alcohol.

Jolly Roger (American cuisine)

Just behind Coconut MarketPlace next to The Islander, 484 Kuhio Highway, Kapa'a; 808-822-3451.

Hours: Breakfast and Sunday breakfast buffet 6:30 a.m. to noon. Lunch 11 a.m. to 4:30 p.m. Dinner 3 to 10 p.m. *Sampling:* Omelets, eggs Benedict, French toast, steak-and-eggs, plus apple pancakes or waffle with cinnamon apples and macadamia nuts ($4 to $8). Sunday breakfast buffet has eggs, bacon, sausage, corned beef hash, French toast pancakes, waffles and fresh fruits ($5 to $8). Burgers, salads and sandwiches, including a chicken or tuna avocado melt, French dip, turkey and mahimahi ($4 to $8). Specialties include teriyaki steak or chicken, fettuccine alfredo with mushrooms or chicken, spaghetti and stir-fry for lunch ($8 to $10), for dinner ($10 to $15). Other dinners include fresh or fried fish, seafood platters, chicken Polynesian, fried calamari, scallops, smothered chicken and create-your-own combinations ($13 to $16). Then there are sundaes, hot fudge cake, or Mauna Kea crunch—a chocolate chip cookie with sundae toppings. *Comments:* Familiar chain with a traditional menu, though there are a few creative surprises. Specials like steak and all-you-can-eat shrimp and a senior menu with a choice of teriyaki steak or chicken, ground beef, mahimahi, *ono*, sirloin steak, spaghetti, or hibachi chicken, including vegetable, potato or rice, soup or salad and coffee or tea. Food is nothing exotic, but affordably priced with a broad menu offering something for every family member. The breakfast specials are a good value. Karaoke on weekends.

★ King & I Thai Cuisine (Thai food)

Waipouli Plaza, 4-901 Kuhio Highway, Kapa'a; 808-822-1642.

Hours: Lunch Monday to Friday 11 a.m. to 1:30 p.m. Dinner 4:30 to 9:30 p.m. *Sampling:* Start with the spring rolls with fresh mint and cucumber, ready to wrap in lettuce and dip, then try the lemongrass or coconut soup, green papaya salad, or King & I noodles with shrimp, pork or chicken, or satay meat skewers and fried calamari ($7 to $11). You can choose from red, green or yellow curry ($8 to $10) and smell the aroma of jasmine rice and enjoy the Siam fresh basil, spicy eggplant, ginger fish, garlic shrimp and other Thai dishes, with choice of beef, pork, chicken, shrimp, calamari, tofu or fish ($8 to $10). Thai iced tea or coffee are a must and for dessert be sure to try the delectable coconut milk and black rice, the natural color of the herbal rice from Thailand. If you don't want to make a decision, they offer set menus for 2, 3 or 4 persons that include five items with rice, tea and dessert ($28 to $50). *Comments:* The owners/chefs grow their own herbs and spices so when the dish says fresh basil or fresh mint, it really is. The curries are wonderful, perfectly seasoned and an ideal accompaniment with fresh fish. Many vegetarian selections. Lovely dining room, with Thai furnishings and lots of blooming orchids.

La Bamba Mexican Restaurant (Mexican food)

Kukui Grove Center, Lihu'e; 808-245-5972.

Hours: Monday to Saturday 11 a.m. to 10 p.m. Sunday 4 to 9 p.m. *Sampling:* Seafood salad on a tortilla, taco salad in a shell, plus the usual selection of tacos, burritos, enchiladas and quesadillas ($2 to $9). The *carnitas* or *carne asada* burritos are the house specialties ($7 to $11). *Chile verde*, tamales or *chiles rellenos*; fajitas with chicken, steak or seafood for one or two people ($11 to $24). *Comments:* Big portions, booths or tables. Take-out available, but no liquor license so you are welcome to BYOB.

★ *La Playita Azul (Mexican food)*

Kaua'i Shopping Village, 831 Kuhio Highway, Kapa'a; 808-821-2323.

Hours: Lunch 11 a.m. to 2:30 p.m. Dinner 4:30 to 9:30 p.m. No lunch Sunday. *Sampling:* Enjoy some authentic and creative Mexican cuisine. This small eatery serves up a big menu of creative and traditional Mexican fare. Chicken *mole* enchiladas ($8), enchiladas *verdes* ($8), quesadillas ($8), taquitos ($8); try the nachos ($9), chimichangas ($9), Monico's veggie burritos ($9), burrito *con carne asada* ($9), burrito *con pollo* or burrito *al pastor* ($9). Other specials include *costilla en chile verde tradicion* ($10), taco *de pescado* ($11), burrito *de pescado* fresco ($11), *mole poblano de pollo* ($12), seafood burrito ($13), *camarones al mojo de ajo*—garlic shrimp ($15), and *camarones a la diabla*—shrimp in chipotle sauce ($15). *Comments:* This is one of the best Mexican restaurants on Kaua'i and very good value for the money. Eat in or take out. Located just around the corner from Safeway. It gets busy and then things slow down, so be patient.

Lemongrass Grill & Seafood (Pacific Rim/Asian cuisine)

4-885 Kuhio Highway, Kapa'a; 808-821-2888.

Hours: 5 to 10 p.m. *Sampling:* Enjoy such appetizers as fried *ahi* sushi roll, *furikake* seared *ahi*, crispy fried *ahi lumpias*, Kilauea prawns or *ahi poke* in Thai rice paper ($6 to $9). Salads include Caesar, spinach salad, shrimp and Moloaa papaya and Kapahi ginger chicken ($6 to $7); soups include papaya bisque and clam chowder ($5). Dinner entrees include specialties like stuffed calamari with chili garlic sauce, braised short rib Walker Hill, Chinese-style steamed fish, braised spicy short rib Jardinere, grilled salmon ginger lemongrass aioli, lemongrass seafood stew, braised lamb shank, hoisin barbecue chicken breast, pork loin with tropical mango pineapple relish and other tempting items ($15 to $20). *Comments:* This eatery is located in a small house facing the highway, with both inside and outside dining; they also have a sushi bar. Interior decor carries splashy Thai batik accents; dishes are bright, colorful and attractively presented. The Lemongrass Gallery (808-822-1221), which features "Pacific Fine Collectibles," is in a separate building behind the restaurant. Browse through the unique selection of antiques, sculptures, gifts, art and accessories before or after dinner.

Maria's (Mexican food)

3-3142 Kuhio Highway, Lihu'e; 808-246-9122.

Hours: Monday to Friday 11 a.m. to 8 p.m. Saturday 5 to 8 p.m. Closed Sunday. *Sampling:* A la carte nachos, quesadillas, burritos, tostadas, enchiladas and tacos ($2 to $5). Combination plates with tacos, enchiladas, *chiles rellenos*, taquitos and veggie or pork *sopes* ($6 to $9). Beer, wine or homemade sangria available. Dinners to-go serve

2 to 6 people ($17 to $42). *Comments:* Yes, there really is a Maria and she learned to cook traditional family recipes from her grandmother in Jalisco, Mexico. Located next to 7/11 and across from the Lihu'e McDonald's, this small, friendly restaurant doesn't take credit cards—but not to worry, they're also located next to an ATM. If you want authentic, quality Mexican food, this is a good choice.

Naupaka Terrace Steak House (Steak/seafood)

Radisson Kaua'i Beach, 4331 Kauai Beach Drive, Lihu'e; 808-245-1955.

Hours: Breakfast 6:30 to 11 a.m. Dinner 6 to 10 p.m. *Sampling:* Standard breakfast fare includes omelets, pancakes, Belgian waffles, sweet bread French toast, tropical fruit platter, plus continental breakfast ($7 to $10). The dinner menu features appetizers such as fried calamari, stuffed mushrooms, Hanamaulu chicken fritters, Naupaka quesadillas and prawn cocktail canoe ($9 to $10). Salads range from Caesar chicken, Naupaka peppered *ahi* salad to a standard salad bar ($11 to $16). Entrees include filet mignon, New York strip steak, top sirloin, ribeye, prime rib, filet mignon and lobster, Wailua chicken, Kauailoa seafood grill, fresh island fish, chilled prawns, pasta Kauai Beach and vegetarian divine ($14 to $33). *Comments:* The arrangement of terraced private alcoves with tables and booths with pleasing tropical color combinations, accents and furnishings create a pleasant dining atmosphere. The dining room provides courtyard and pool views. Pleasant setting for quiet intimate dinners or family meals.

Norberto's Café (Mexican food)

4-1373 Kuhio Highway, Kapa'a; 808-822-3362.

Hours: Monday to Saturday 5:30 to 9 p.m. Closed Sunday. *Sampling:* Taquitos, tacos, burritos, quesadillas, nachos and chimichangas are just some of the items offered a la carte ($3 to $8). Dinner specialties include *rellenos tampico*, burritos *rancheros*, burrito *el café*, fajitas made with Kaua'i steak or chicken, fish specials, enchiladas *grande*, with beef or chicken and a special homegrown Hawaiian taro-leaf enchilada in veggie style or with beef, chicken or fish ($13 to $16). All entrees come with soup, vegetables, rice and beans, corn chips and salsa. Their homemade desserts, if you can find room, are chocolate cream pie, hula pie and rum cake. *Comments:* They serve Mexican beer and a variety of good margaritas with unusual flavors (Midori, passion fruit and raspberry) available by the glass or by the pitcher. Their unique *taro* enchilada and fish specials are the best choices. Kitschy (but not too) cantina atmosphere. It's a fun place that makes for good family dining—and they have a kid's menu to prove it.

★ *Olympic Café (American/Mexican/Italian cuisines)*
1387 Kuhio Highway, Kapa'a; 822-5825.

Hours: Breakfast 6 a.m. to 3 p.m. *Sampling:* Breakfast burrito or quesadillas, a variety of omelets and scrambles, coconut pineapple or blueberry pancakes and guava jelly-stuffed toast. Several burger options plus sandwiches including barbecue or blackened chicken, mozzarella and pesto, tuna, BLT and chicken avocado club. Very good salads: Caesar, Greek, Cobb, tuna, taco or grilled chicken, all made with fresh local greens, plus several Mexican entrees and lunch specials. *Comments:* This airy room opens onto the sidewalk along the main street of Kapa'a. The yellow color scheme, with colorful *tapa* print chairs, blends with the colorful books in the used-book library—available for both browsers and buyers. And those go very well with the selection of teas, juices, coffee drinks, fresh muffins and pastries available from the espresso bar. The food is very good, reasonably priced, and the atmosphere is casual and great for families. The service is friendly, too.

(The) Palms Restaurant (Hawaiian Regional/Pacific Rim cuisine)
Holiday Inn Sun Spree Resort, Wailua; 808-823-6000.

Hours: Breakfast buffet 6:30 to 10:30 a.m. Dinner 5:30 to 9 p.m. *Sampling:* Breakfast buffet offers fresh fruits, breads and pastries, cereals, plus hot selections of eggs, potatoes, pancakes and breakfast meats ($12). Dinners begin with shrimp cocktail, sashimi, calamari rings, steamer clams, chicken Caesar salad, Wailua mesclun salad, spinach and papaya salad, seafood chowder or soup du jour ($3 to $12). Entrees include Togarashi-crusted *ahi* $19, salmon Kekaha $22, shiitake-crusted chicken $18, *pulehu* strip steak $22, Thai crab and shrimp cakes $19, mango *li hing mui* chicken $17, plus various pastas $15 to $17. Lighter fare includes sandwiches, burgers, fried fish, quesadillas and more ($7 to $13). Assorted sweets and ice cream for dessert options. There is live Hawaiian entertainment in the evenings. *Comments:* This is a large restaurant in the hotel's Kuhio Dining Court, which includes a small sundries shop and cocktail lounge. The dining room is made more intimate with the addition of tall wood columns and smaller table groupings. The wood-and-green accent colors give it a rich, cozy look and feel. The food is average, but we note it for the value: kids under 12 eat free per each adult that orders from the main menu.

Panda Garden (Chinese food)
Kaua'i Village Shopping Center, 4-831 Kuhio Highway, Kapa'a; 808-822-0922.

Hours: 4:30 to 10 p.m. *Sampling:* Over 100 offerings of both Cantonese and Szechuan dishes. Appetizers, soups, chicken and duck, beef and pork, seafood, eggs, sizzling platters, vegetarian, chow mein and rice ($6 to $12). Scallops with peppery salt, lobster with black-bean sauce or ginger and onions, steamed island fish, pot roast chicken, beef with sesame sauce, pork hash, shrimp with chile garlic sauce and tenderloin steak with black pepper are just a few of the diverse selections ($7 to $20). Plate-lunch specials offer a choice of eight entrees with soup, won ton and rice ($6), and set dinners for 2 to 10 people are available ($25 and up). *Comments:* They offer both the unusual and the traditional, but seafood is a particular specialty. Their hot, spicy dishes are marked with a star. Beer and wine; take-out available. Food is fair to good and service is efficient.

Paradise Seafood & Grill (Steak/seafood)

1850 Kaumuali'i, Puhi; 808-246-4884.

Hours: Lunch 11 a.m. to 3 p.m. Dinner 5 to 9 p.m. *Sampling:* A variety of burgers including fish and chicken plus smoked turkey, chicken salad and club sandwiches ($6 to $8). Caesar salad, fried chicken, lasagna, fish-and-chips and seafood: on a platter, in a salad or linguine ($6 to $8). Dinner starts with steamed clams, fried mushrooms, crab cakes, oysters, mussels or calamari ($6 to $10). Entrees include fresh fish, scampi, baby back pork ribs, crab legs, steak, prime rib and mushroom or teriyaki chicken ($15 to $25). Chocolate cappuccino brownie, mud pie, or cheesecake for dessert. Wine, beer and espresso. *Keiki* menu available. *Comments:* Take-out or seating outside on the lanai or back patio.

Poor Boy's Pizza (Pizza/sandwiches)

1384 Kuhio Highway, #104, Kapa'a; 808-822-7985.

Hours: Monday to Saturday 10 a.m. to 10 p.m. Sunday from noon. *Sampling:* Pizza in 12-, 16- and 29-inch sizes, plus individual 7-inch pizzas ($12 to $30). Calzones, stromboli and Italian or ham-and-cheese sandwiches on fresh-baked bread ($7 to $10), plus breaded zucchini, hot wings, or seasoned fries ($3 to $6). Strawberry or tropical fruit smoothies, too. *Comments:* Take-out or delivery available, or just sit in front and people-watch in the heart of old Kapa'a town.

Restaurant Kintaro (Japanese cuisine)

370 Kuhio Highway, Kapa'a; 808-822-3341.

Hours: 5:30 to 9:30 p.m. Closed Sunday. *Sampling:* Tempura, sukiyaki and *yakitori* dinners, *yosenabe*, *nabeyaki* noodles, broiled steaks and fish combinations, plus complete *teppanyaki* dinners, with appetizer: oysters, chicken or New York steak teriyaki, filet mignon, hibachi shrimp, fish with scallops or lobster tail and tenderloin steak ($13 to $30). *Comments:* Fish and steaks; also hand-rolled sushi and soft-shell crab. Stylized, attractive Japanese ambiance with a sushi bar and aquarium. There are two serving sections: the less expensive general seating area and a moderately expensive area with *teppanyaki* tables, where you can enjoy your meal cooked before your eyes. While it is a bit more expensive, the *teppanyaki* room is worth it for the show. The service is excellent on both sides. This restaurant is consistently popular with locals and visitors, but it's certainly not the best place on the island for either sushi or Japanese food.

Sukhotai (Thai/Chinese cuisines)

Kapa'a Shopping Center, 1105 Kuhio Highway, Kapa'a; 808-821-1224.

Hours: 10:30 a.m. to whenever. *Sampling:* Soups (ocean golden, lemongrass shrimp or chicken, long rice, spicy fish, coconut chicken); salads like seafood, papaya or calamari ($8 to $14). Appetizers of spring roll, chicken crepe, chicken sticks, *satay*, papaya salad and fried tofu ($7 to $12). Thai entrees include cashew chicken, *pad* eggplant, coconut chicken or seafood, garlic mixed vegetable, *pad ben-ja-lung* (shrimp and vegetables), and fish *prig prow dand* red, green, yellow, Pa Nang, pineapple and *musaman* curries ($8 to $16). Chinese dishes include chop suey, egg foo yung, lemon chicken, *lo mein*, garlic calamari, seafood broccoli, pepper steak, Asian fish, stir-fried long rice, or sweet and sour ($8 to $15). House specials offer seafood with chile paste, whole snapper with garlic, crispy duck with vegetables, spicy chicken angel and shrimp stuffed with minced chicken in peanut sauce ($14 to $18). For dessert there is fried ice cream, tapioca pudding with coconut sauce, or rambutan stuffed with pineapple. *Comments:* They also have Vietnamese and vegetarian dishes. Anything on the menu can also be ordered vegetarian style. Order your meal mild, medium or spicy Thai hot to suit your taste. Same menu served all day. They run the Asian gift shop next door that has a variety of Asian gifts, souvenirs and artworks.

Sushi Katsu (Japanese cuisine)

3173 Akahi Street, Lihu'e; 808-246-0176.

Hours: Lunch (sushi only) Tuesday to Sunday 11 a.m. to 2 p.m. Dinner 5:30 to 9:30 p.m. Closed Monday. *Sampling:* Lunch: *chirashi* sushi, maki mono roll, *tekka ju*, regular or big California roll and sushi combinations ($4 to $14). Special rolls such as soft-shell crab, spicy *ahi*, fresh salmon, or *inari* sushi. Sushi combination and sushi and sashimi deluxe assortment; *udon* and *soba* noodles ($3 to $22). Dinners (including soup and rice) feature shrimp tempura, teriyaki beef or chicken, chicken *katsu*, tempura and sushi, *oyako donburi*, or catch of the day ($10 to $14). Green tea ice cream for dessert. *Comments:* This Japanese restaurant and sushi bar is part of the legendary Tip Top Café.

★ Tokyo Lobby (Japanese/sushi bar)

Harbor Mall, 3501 Rice Street, Nawiliwili; 808-245-8989.

Hours: Lunch Monday to Friday 11 a.m. to 2 p.m. Dinner 4:30 to 9:30 p.m. *Sampling:* Unusual and creative sushi offerings like *nigiri* sushi assortment, *futomaki* roll, *makimono nori* roll, *inari* sushi with soybean, *chirashi* sushi ($9 to $14). Appetizers include teriyaki chicken on skewer, *tori karaage* ginger chicken, *shu-mai* pork dumplings, soft-shell crab and others ($4 to $8). Lunch entrees include tempura, *katsu*, chicken teriyaki and *yaki sakana* grilled mackerel ($8 to $10); *donburi, udon* noodles ($6 to $12). Japanese dinners include *nabemono* soups like seafood *yosenabe*, sukiyaki and *nabeyaki udon*, plus beef or chicken teriyaki, shrimp or veggie tempura, *katsu*, curry chicken, lemon herb chicken, calamari steak, *una-jyu* broiled eel, barbecue salmon and a special Tokyo Lobby *donburi* ($10 to $16). The specialty is the "Tokyo Lobby Love Boat," a choice of three combination dinners ($22 per person) brought to the table in a head-turning artistic Japanese wooden boat. Top off your meal with refreshing ice creams in green tea, coconut pineapple, Kona coffee, or Japanese-made red bean. *Comments:* The tempura was light, crispy and fresh, not mushy or greasy. The sushi was attractively presented in tasty and unusual combinations. They have expanded and added on a garden room—a very bright and open conservatory-like room surrounded by windows on all sides. Jack Ho is the owner. His mom Lin Ho is the manager, a sweet, friendly and gracious hostess. "Mom" talks and visits with everyone who comes in and even if the sushi weren't as good as it is, she'd be worth the designation of a star.

Voyage Room (American food/Sunday brunch)

Kaua'i Coconut Beach Resort, Wailua; 808-822-3455.

Hours: Breakfast 6:30 to 10 a.m. Until 9 a.m. on Sunday (brunch 10 a.m. to 1:30 p.m.). Lunch 11 a.m. to 1:30 p.m. *Sampling:* Breakfast buffet with fruit, pastries, breads, cereals, eggs, breakfast meats and potatoes ($12). Also a la carte omelets, pancakes, Belgian waffle, or roast beef hash Benedict ($7 to $10). For lunch, there are sandwiches of turkey, ham, tuna or chicken salad, fresh catch and burgers plus saimin or ravioli and fruit, Cobb, chef, Greek and chicken or shrimp Caesar salads ($6 to $10). Island-style iced tea is available with cane sugar and pineapple and there are a variety of cakes, pies and ice creams for dessert. *Comments:* Some of the hotel packages include the breakfast buffet with your room, which is a real bonus. The Sunday brunch is a good value, offering a carving station of roast meats plus sushi, salads, Belgian waffles, omelet station, hot entrees, selection of pies and cakes and an ice cream sundae bar. The restaurant stays the same, but the name changes at dinner—it then becomes the Flying Lobster (see separate listing above).

Wailua Family Restaurant (Local/American cuisines)

Wailua Shopping Plaza, 4361 Kuhio Highway, Wailua; 808-822-3325.

Hours: Breakfast 6:30 to 11 a.m. Lunch 11 a.m. to 4 p.m. Dinner weekdays 4 to 9:30 p.m. Friday and Saturday 4 to 10 p.m. *Sampling:* Breakfast: eggs, pancakes, French toast, ham and turkey Benedict, *loco moco,* omelets ($3 to $9). Burgers and sandwiches (corned beef, fish, club, patty melt, French dip, BLT and salads ($6 to $8); stir-fry or combination platters of steak, fish, chicken or shrimp ($7 to $8). Dinners offer similar combinations plus dozens more with seafood, ribs, pork and a variety of steaks (ribeye, New York, sirloin, T-bone) or prime rib, plus seafood choices like lobster platter, giant fried shrimp, fried oysters, fried scallops, grilled *ahi*, mahimahi or *ono* and combo plates ($10 to $23). All-you-can-eat salad buffet ($4 to $9) has more than just salads: there's soup, a seafood bar, taco bar, plus puddings and cookies. *Comments:* Senior dinners and children's menu served all day from 10 a.m.

★ *Wailua Marina Restaurant (American cuisine)*

Wailua River State Park, Building B (near Smith's Tropical Plantation), 5971 Kuhio Highway, Kapa'a; 808-822-4311.

Hours: Lunch 10:30 a.m. to 2 p.m. Dinner 5 to 9 p.m. Closed Monday. *Sampling:* Chinese chicken, pineapple boat and chef's salads and BLT, tuna, egg, turkey, French dip, ham, pastrami, mahimahi, club, burger, steak, barbecue or teriyaki chicken, Reuben and Monte Cristo sandwiches ($7 to $10). Many dinner entrees available for lunch ($7 to $10). Baked stuffed pork chop or chicken (with plum sauce), Chinese-style steamed mullet, charbroiled calamari, prawns or *ahi* stuffed with crab meat, prime rib, sauteed seafood, teriyaki steak, scampi, filet mignon, spaghetti or spare ribs ($10 to $18). Oxtail soup; shrimp, steak and chicken mixed plate ($9 to $12). Hot lobster salad is a specialty ($20). Desserts include homestyle cream pie (coconut, macadamia nut or chocolate), ice cream pies (mud, fudge, brownie or spumoni) or *lilikoi* chiffon pie (like Key lime, only better!). *Comments:* This is a classic restaurant, popular with locals and offering a lovely view of the Wailua River in a relaxed setting. The stuffed pork chops are big and thick, but you can cut them without a knife! The fish is always fresh and priced at least a couple of dollars less than it would be elsewhere. With more than three dozen entrees on the dinner menu, you are sure to find something for everyone. There are extra-long tables for families or groups, with a separate banquet room and cocktail lounge. Seating on the lanai can be more pleasant, however. Wall murals may amuse the younger kids in your family, one across the back wall has 3-D sea turtles, shells and fish.

★ *Wasabi's (Japanese/sushi bar)*

1394 Kuhio Highway, Kapa'a; 808-822-2700.

Hours: 11 a.m. to 9 p.m. *Sampling:* They specialize in a wide variety of sushi. For dinner choose chicken *yakitori*, shrimp or fish tempura or fresh fish of the day ($13 to $15). A la carte items include *yakitori* chicken, grilled veggies, tofu tempura, soft-shell crab tempura or grilled squid ($6 to $13). House-favorite sushi include lava roll (smoked salmon or island fish; $13), black dragon roll (seared *maguro;* $11), lollipop roll (*hamachi*, *maguro* and salmon; $12), *pokepine* rolls (*maguro* with *ponzu* sauce; $12), or *wasabi* balls (mushrooms stuffed with seafood mix; $12). Special sushi rolls include choices like Rainbow Roll—five types of fish with crab, avocado and cucumber ($9); Sunrise Roll—*hamachi*, *maguro*, *tobiko*, papaya and cucumber ($8); Kauai Roll—*unagi*, papaya, avocado and macadamia nuts ($8); Full Moon Roll—shrimp, scallops, crab and veggies ($9); Green Dream Roll—*anago*, crab, avocado and asparagus ($8). They also have an assortment of *nigiri* and *maki* rolls and fresh sashimi. *Comments:* This is a very small restaurant with a cheerful decor and friendly staff. Best of all, the prices are right and the food is fresh, good and unique. BYOB from the liquor across the street; located right on Kuhio Highway in the heart of Kapa'a town.

Whaler's Brewpub (American cuisine)

Beyond the Marriott at Fashion Landing Shopping Center, Kaua'i Lagoons, 3132 Ninini Point, Lihu'e; 808-245-2000.

Hours: Lunch 11:30 a.m. to 2:30 p.m. Dinner 5 to 10 p.m. Sunday brunch 10 a.m. to 3 p.m. *Sampling*: For lunch, try the blackened chicken pasta, amber ale–batter fish-and-chips, teriyaki chicken, pork ribs or saimin, along with a variety of sandwiches: turkey club, Philly chicken, roast beef, salmon bagel or specialty spiced mahimahi ($8 to $12). Fresh fish or garlic stir-fry with tofu, shrimp or chicken ($13 to $16). Dinner entrees also include fiery shrimp harpoons, lamb chops, New York steak and Hawaiian mixed grill ($17 to $25). Their signature "whale of a burger" is a specialty for both lunch and dinner. Also soups, salads and *pupus* that include egg rolls, calamari rings, teriyaki-chicken skewers, chicken quesadillas and nachos ($5 to $10). *Comments:* This open-air microbrewery is located at the back of Kaua'i Lagoons and offers a spectacular view of the ocean with the lighthouse in the background. Casual lanai seating outside; attractive wood booths inside. Their trademarked Pacific Rim Beer Cuisine incorporates the flavors of nine (brewed-on-the-premises) ales in a lot of their menu items—especially *pupus* like the beer-batter fish, coconut shrimp bites and flowering onion. Other seasonings range from Asian to Cajun, and when they say they have "One Whale of a Burger" they mean it! This isn't a hamburger, it's a buffet on a bun. The 20 ounces of ground beef is served on a huge, homebaked bun and served on a platter filled with a ton of fries, an assortment of onions, tomato, lettuce and other good, fresh toppings, plus a variety of condiments. And the best part is that it feeds two or more. They also have a Beer and Brunch Buffet every Sunday that includes all nine microbrews plus salads, carved prime rib, omelets and a variety of hot entrees and desserts. There's a 4,000-gallon marine aquarium, a pool room upstairs and live music on the weekends.

Expensive-priced Dining

★ A Pacific Café (Pacific Rim/Hawaiian Regional cuisine)

Kaua'i Village Shopping Center, Kuhio Highway, Kapa'a; 808-822-0013.

Hours: Dinner 5:30 to 10 p.m. *Sampling:* The menu changes daily, but your first taste might begin with an appetizer like poached scallop ravioli with *tobiko* pearls (scallop flavor, but with a different texture) and lime-ginger sauce, deep-fried curried oysters with scallion sauce, firecracker salmon with sweet Thai chile sauce or their signature tiger eye *ahi* sushi tempura ($8 to $11). Soup might be Thai coconut curry with island fish and shrimp or you might opt for a salad of spicy *ahi*, grilled Indonesian shrimp with mango vinaigrette or the tasty Japanese eggplant with goat cheese fritter ($8 to $10). Entrees from the wood-burning grill might include fire-roasted *ono* with shrimp risotto and Thai coconut green curry sauce (smokey, but lively and flavored with flair), Moroccan marinated veal chop with couscous, New York steak with gorgonzola cabernet sauce, smoked chicken breast with mushrooms, spinach, fontina cheese and white truffle mashed potatoes with black truffle *jus* or lacquered *ahi* with mushroom compote and orange-soy-caramel sauce. Specialties might feature their signature wok-charred mahimahi in garlic-sesame crust with lime-ginger sauce; penne pasta with shrimp, tomatoes, capers with black olive butter; mushroom-spinach-stuffed chicken breast on garlic mashed potatoes; Pacific salmon with griddle rice cake and miso-ginger vinaigrette; Chinese roast duck with braised baby bok choy, scallion flat bread and caramelized pineapple glaze; or grilled beef tenderloin with feta-herb crust, crispy shrimp and roasted potato terrine and cabernet Stilton sauce ($23 to $28). They offer a prix-fixe "tasting menu" where you can select a combination of one of the evening's appetizer, entree and dessert selections, with suggested wines for a set price. Distinctive desserts include hot macadamia-nut tart, banana *lumpia*, chocolate *bombe* (with macadamia mousse filling), a *haupia* coconut cake or creme brulee. *Comments:* Celebrity owner/chef Jean-Marie Josselin is one of the 12 acknowledged Hawaiian Regional cuisine chefs in the islands (he's written several cookbooks) and has garnered more than his share of accolades and awards over the years. The restaurant grows its own salad greens, vegetables and fresh herbs on its organic farm. Everything on the menu is good. The only drawback is the noise level, which detracts a bit from the meal.

★ *Gaylord's Restaurant (American cuisine)*

Kilohana Plantation 3-2087 Kaumuali'i Highway, Lihu'e; 808-245-9503; www.gaylordskauai.com.

Hours: Lunch Monday to Saturday 11 a.m. to 3 p.m. Sunday brunch 9:30 a.m. to 3 p.m. Dinner from 5 p.m. *Sampling:* Menus change daily. Innovative lunch salads might include papaya stuffed with shrimp, Oriental chicken, Greek-style roasted vegetable, Caesar with red peppers and mild goat cheese coated with macadamia nuts, or *salpicon* local greens with bell pepper, onion, tomato, *ahi*, cactus, avocado and feta cheese ($9 to $11). Sandwiches come with soup or salad and fries or rice: San Francisco Reuben (on sourdough), turkey and avocado, a variety of burgers, Monte Cristo and a tasty ground *ahi* burger, with pickled ginger and a special sauce ($8 to $11). Signature lunch dishes range from baby back ribs to sweet-and-sour chicken, or try the Farmer's Pie (vegetables under a crust of whipped potatoes), grilled Alaskan salmon, honey-dipped chicken, or capellini pomodoro ($9 to $13). Dinners might feature appetizers of coconut shrimp, spicy crab cakes, pan-seared sashimi, hot crab and artichoke-heart dip and honey-baked or garlic brie ($9 to $11); entrees of steak, fresh fish, baby back ribs, rack of lamb, seafood rhapsody, prime rib (regular or blackened), and chicken served Florentine, Greek or Kaua'i-style with papaya, pineapple and macadamia-nut wine sauce ($18 to $30). Sauteed venison is a specialty and the prime rib and lobster duet remains one the most popular double entrees ($30 to $38). The dessert list is extensive, starting with linzer torte, Kilohana mud pie, passion fruit parfait and double chocolate mousse. Their chocolate truffles are deep fried with coconut on the outside and melting chocolate inside and the homemade banana cream pie tastes of real banana. A good selection of premium wines are offered by the glass. For Sunday brunch, entrees are accompanied by a plate of fresh fruit and home-baked cinnamon roll and feature eggs Benedict, spinach quiche, strawberry French toast, tropical Belgian waffle, crepes, banana macadamia pancakes, a variety of pastas and their signature sweet potato hash with chunks of purple sweet potatoes and chicken breast topped with two poached eggs and *maltaise* sauce ($12 to $16). *Comments:* The atmosphere and ambience make this a special place to dine. Unfortunately, the dining area is along the courtyard and during cool or rainy periods, they drop down canvas walls with plastic windows. While this helps keep the elements out, it does detract from the setting. (Sort of gourmet dining in a tent!) The food is usually quite good, however, and dining here is certainly worthy of a recommendation, but preferably on a warm and sunny afternoon or early evening to enjoy the full experience of its unique ambiance. Reservations recommended. They also offer a twice-weekly luau; see the "Luaus" section at the end of this chapter for more information.

★ *Hukilau Lanai (Hawaiian Regional cuisine)*

Kauai Coconut Coast Resort, Coconut MarketPlace, Kapa'a; 808-822-0600.

Hours: Tuesday to Sunday 5 p.m. until about 9 or 10 p.m. *Sampling:* Appetizers include shrimp bisque, Mongolian lamb baby back ribs, sweet potato ravioli, seafood cakes with Thai spices, seared *ahi*, spinach and luau-leaf dip and ginger-miso littleneck clams ($5.95 to $10.95). Salads are grilled *ahi*, Kilauea greens with goat cheese, Caesar and mixed greens, in full and half portions ($2.95 to $14.95). Entrees run the gamut from ribeye steak to shiitake mushroom meatloaf, sugar cane shrimp and mango chicken grilled on a skewer, pork tenderloin, chicken, ribs. Then there's the pasta, such as one made with shrimp and Portuguese sausage and a rizo with vegetables ($13.95 to $22.95). They also serve several types of island fish each day, like *opah*, *ahi* and *wahoo*, or whatever is good and fresh, as well as a mixed-fish plate for those times when you can't make up your mind ($18.95 to $23.95). Desserts are excellent and original and include a goat cheese creme brulee, praline-and-coconut macadamia cheesecake, a fabulous cake made from Big Island chocolate and served warm, the frozen lava souffle with tropical fruit flavors and Lappert's ice cream ($2.95 to $8.95). *Comments:* A casual, airy setting, much like sitting out on a friend's pleasant lanai, make this restaurant very relaxing and enjoyable. The ambiance and the service are both island-style, meaning it's laidback and moves at a slow pace, but that's a good thing, not a detraction. This is a place where you can just hang out and have a leisurely meal and the food is original and well-prepared. It's run by the same folks who manage Gaylord's, so they know what they're doing. It's also a nice place to have a drink and some *pupus*, as the torch-lit lanai overlooks the ocean.

Kukui's Restaurant & Bar (Pacific Rim cuisine/buffets)

Kaua'i Marriott Resort, Lihu'e; 808-245-5050).

Hours: Breakfast 6:30 to 11 a.m. Lunch 11 a.m. to 2 p.m. Dinner 5:30 to 10 p.m. Pizza Café noon to 8:30 p.m. Sunday brunch 8 a.m.

to 2 p.m. *Sampling:* Unusual breakfast offerings should wake up your taste buds: shrimp-and-crab Benedict, vegetable frittata, breakfast burrito (with scrambled eggs, Portuguese sausage and island salsa), macadamia-nut pancakes and Hawaiian sweet bread French toast with sun-dried fruits ($5 to $14). Continental and full-breakfast buffet ($14 to $17). Lunch begins with sausage nachos, crab and shrimp quesadillas, vegetable rice paper roll, Maui onion soup plus a variety of salads including ceviche, Oriental chicken *soba*, or seafood Caesar ($6 to $10). Entree selections feature Jawaiian chicken, eggplant or swordfish sandwich, fish tacos, shrimp and crab cakes, mushroom ravioli, burgers, seafood melt and tempura-batter fish-and-chips ($7 to $16). Roasted garlic chicken, brie and asparagus, smoked salmon and eggplant, artichoke and goat cheese are some of the pizzas ($8 to $16). Dinners include seafood-crusted mahimahi, roasted *char siu* pork, *paniolo* steak, lemon rosemary chicken and pasta with seared tiger prawns or garlicky scallops ($16 to $29). Chocolate mousse, passion fruit cream tart, chocolate macadamia-nut pie, coconut rice pudding and Kahlua cheesecake are the desserts. Weekly prix-fixe specials, with soup or salad, bread with seafood mousse, cheesecake and coffee. Specialty dinner buffets are featured on the weekend from 5:30 to 9:30 p.m.: Friday is prime rib and King crab with Hawaiian music ($30), Saturday is Pacific Rim with a *keiki* hula show ($30). Their excellent Sunday brunch ($28) offers salads, fresh fruit, cheese, fish and sushi platters, breakfast dishes, hot entrees, an omelet station, Anahola granola and other cereals, with a selection of nuts and sweet toppings including an unusual treat of dried tropical fruits. Choose pancakes, French toast or potato pancakes at the griddle station, rotisserie spiced mahimahi at the Southwest wrap-and-roll station, prime rib at the carving station, or try some of the innovative creations at the sushi bar—like tempura sushi with lightly fried edges and soft sushi middles! *Comments:* This open-air pavilion-style restaurant is located at the edge of the resort's 26,000-square-foot pool, the largest in the Hawaiian islands.

South and West Shore Areas

Inexpensive-priced Dining

Da Imu Hut Café (American/local cuisines)

3771 Hanapepe Road, Hanapepe; 808-335-0200.

Hours: Breakfast 8 to 10:30 a.m. Lunch 10:30 a.m. to 2 p.m. Dinner 5 to 8:45 p.m. (Friday until 9:45 p.m.) Closed Saturday and Sunday. *Sampling:* French toast, omelets, meat, egg and rice plates ($4 to $6). Local plates: Hamburger steak, teriyaki beef or chicken, saimin (fried or bowl), *kalua* or *laulau* ($4 to $7). "Burgas," egg or tuna sandwich ($2 to $4).

Da'li Deli & Café Cara (Italian deli/American cuisine)
Old Koloa Town; 808-742-8824.

Hours: Deli Monday to Saturday 8 a.m. to 3 p.m. Café Cara Tuesday to Saturday 5:30 p.m. to whenever. *Sampling:* Deli menu-board features items like German pancakes, French toast, frittata, lox platter, bagelwich, granola, fruit plate, or egg breakfast ($5 to $9). Create your own sandwich from a choice of deli meats, cheeses, toppings and condiments on a variety of freshly baked breads ($4 to $7). Specialty sandwiches include marinated eggplant on foccacia, turkey with cranberry relish, Italian sub, or spinach and smoked turkey wrap, plus quiche and Greek, chef's or curry-chicken salad ($4 to $7). Breads, flavored bagels, pies, tortes, cookies and other baked goodies from the bakery, plus coffee drinks and smoothies. Café Cara is a recent expansion of the deli and offers a full dinner menu of authentic Italian specials. Choose from appetizers like *arincini*, bruschetta, polenta or antipasto misto ($5 to $10), soups and pastas like *ribolitta* ($5), risotto asparagus ($9), risotta *di mara* ($9), fusilli *alla pappone* ($9), and salads like *rucola* ($6), caprisce ($7). Main courses are bright and innovative such as *fettuccine alla Toscana* ($11), cannelloni vegetarian style ($12), salmon *ai Capperi* ($13), *Agnello alla Diavola* ($15). Varied desserts and beverages round out the menu. *Comments:* Everything is baked fresh on the premises. Sandwiches are all served on home-baked bread using organic vegetables and fresh deli meats. They even roast their own turkey and make their own traditional boiled-in-water bagels! The dinner menu features excellent creative Italian cuisine—the menu changes every two months—and the service is very friendly. It's a small dining room—no fancy decor—but some colorful local tropical-style artwork on the walls create a generally pleasant ambiance. No liquor available but BYOB. Minimal glassware charge applies on BYOB.

The Dock (Coffee/espresso/sandwiches/snacks)
Hyatt Regency, 1571 Po'ipu Road, Po'ipu; 808-742-1234.

Hours: 10:30 a.m. to 5 p.m. *Sampling:* Deli sandwiches, hamburgers, salads (Caesar, grilled or Oriental chicken, pasta, chef's, tuna and a signature smoked seafood salad with *lilikoi* vinaigrette), plus grilled specialty sandwiches like barbecue chicken, garden burger, fresh fish, spiced beef on foccacia and a Reuben wrapper ($4 to $9). Ice cream, frozen yogurt, cookies, fresh fruit ($2 to $4). *Comments:* Located poolside. *Keiki* meals available.

★ Grinds Espresso (Coffee/espresso/sandwiches/snacks)

'Ele'ele Shopping Center, Kaumuali'i Highway; 808-335-6027.

Hours: 5:30 a.m. to 9 p.m. *Sampling:* Skillet breakfasts with potatoes, green pepper and potatoes or rice with a choice of meat (sausage, salami, pepperoni) plus omelets, French toast and burger-steak, or mahimahi breakfast and a Not-So-*Locomoco* ($4 to $7). Sandwiches ($5 to $7) on homemade bread are served hot (chicken club, bacon and pineapple, mahimahi, pesto cream cheese and salami, chili burger) or cold (Italian, smoked turkey and jack cheese, veggie, ham and cheddar). Salads include regular house green salad, an organic Caesar, chicken and walnut, and chef's ($4 to $8). Local plate lunches include mahimahi, barbecue, Cajun or *shoyu* chicken, and *shoyu* beef patty or chili rice ($5 to $7). Pizzas come in 15" and 18" sizes ($12 to $23). Espresso and coffee drinks, smoothies, Italian sodas ($2 to $4). *Comments:* There is patio seating with lattice work and flowers if you don't want to dine inside. Good variety and well-made food make this a great choice for dining.

★ Kalaheo Coffee Co. & Café (Coffee/espresso/sandwiches/snacks)

At the light in Kalaheo, 2-2436 Kaumuali'i Highway; 808-332-5858; e-mail: java@kalaheo.com; www.kalaheo.com.

Hours: Monday to Friday 6 a.m. to 3 p.m. Saturday 6:30 a.m. to 3 p.m. Sunday 6:30 a.m. to 2 p.m. *Sampling:* Breakfast ($3 to $7) is served until noon and the menu offers Anahola granola, scrambled egg or veggie sandwich, pancakes, Belgian waffles, breakfast burritos. Special breakfasts like "Up-Country," "Paniolo" or "Kahili," and "Bagel Bennys," are offered, or you can build your own omelets until closing. Lunch is served from 10:30 to closing and includes Kaua'i-grown salads (with bulgar wheat, herb chicken, or Oriental veggie), homemade soups and deli or grilled sandwiches such as hot pastrami, tuna melt, Cajun tofu and eggplant, chicken and bulgar salsa wrap, grilled Reuben, turkey burger, or fresh vegetable on focaccia ($5 to $7). Ice cream shakes and pastries, including muffins, scones, delicious big cinnamon rolls, cheesecake, apple pie, carrot cake and chocolate raspberry cake. And, of course, they have plenty of espressos, coffees and teas. *Comments:* The fresh salads are excellent and the sandwiches are piled high. This is a great place to stop on the way to, or from, Waimea Canyon, or to pick up some lunch to eat up at Kukuiolono Park.

Kaua'i Kitchens (Local cuisine)

Near Big Save, 5516 Koloa Road, Koloa; 808-742-1712.

Hours: 7 a.m. to 2:30 p.m. *Sampling:* Sandwiches, plate lunches, *bentos*, sushi-*maki* cone ($1 to $2 and up); plus daily specials like chicken cutlet, fresh corned beef, breaded crab croquette, baked pork chops, roast turkey with stuffing, lemon chicken, seafood curry, fish filet, pork adobo, plus Hawaiian, Filipino and Asian plates ($5 to $7). They also sell Kaua'i Kookies, baked foods and T-shirts from the Kaua'i Kookie Kompany. *Comments:* "Quick Tasty Island Style" that you can eat in or take out. (Also located at Rice Shopping Center in Lihu'e and inside the Big Save grocery store in Waimea.)

Koke'e Lodge (American cuisine)

3600 Koke'e Road, Waimea; 808-335-6061.

Hours: 9 a.m. to 3:30 p.m. *Sampling:* Continental and light breakfasts, quiche, cornbread, muffins ($2 to $6). Varied lunch sandwiches are served on 12-grain bread ($6 to $7). Pear, Greek or Moroccan salads ($7). And the Koke'e Lodge offers specialties like chili, Portuguese bean soup and cornbread; desserts include carrot cake and *lilikoi* or coconut pie ($3 to $5). Wine and Kaua'i beer. *Comments:* Rustic atmosphere—and the only place to eat "up the mountain." Considering you're in what seems to be the middle of wilderness, the food is remarkably good. Nothing like a bowl of bean soup with a side of cornbread to warm you up after a cool afternoon adventure in the mountains.

Koloa Country Store & Internet Café (Coffee/espresso/sandwiches/snacks)

The Courtyard, 5356 Koloa Road, Bldg. 9, Old Koloa Town; 808-742-1255.

Hours: Monday to Saturday 8 a.m. to 8.p.m. Sunday 9 a.m. to 5 p.m. This small cafe is located in a shopping complex opposite the main intersection of Maluhia and Koloa roads. It's a combination country store and internet cafe. The menu features snacks, baked goodies and pastries, desserts, espresso and varied coffees, tea and soft drinks ($2 to $5). Lounge area and local arts-and-crafts display; they provide access to e-mail and the internet for a fee.

★ Koloa Fish Market (Fresh fish/plate lunches)

5482 Koloa Road, Koloa; 808-742-6199.

Hours: Monday to Friday 10 a.m. to 6 p.m. Saturday until 5. Closed Sunday. *Sampling:* Smoked fish, seared *ahi*, *poke*, *lomilomi* salmon, scallop salad and other deli items. Lunch specials change daily and might include fresh island fish, *laulau*, *kalua* pork, beef stew, chili and rice, teriyaki chicken, chicken *katsu* ($5 to $7). Sides of macaroni and rice; sushi and sashimi trays ($3 to $4). *Comments:* Tiny market at the Koloa Town Center; mostly take-out, but a few tables and chairs outside. Real local-style food, variety of flavors, great eating adventure. Sushi and *poke* always fresh.

Kupono Café at the ANARA Spa (Vegetarian food)

Hyatt Regency, 1571 Po'ipu Road, Po'ipu; 808-742-1234.

Hours: 6 a.m. to 2 p.m. *Sampling:* Fresh fruits, cereals and tropical muffins, along with fresh fruit juices and smoothies ($3 to $7).

Low-fat lunches include red lentil chili with yogurt and baked corn chips, garden burger and island-grown salads ($5 to $8). *Comments:* Located right at the spa so you can enjoy a healthy breakfast or lunch after indulging in a facial or massage, working out in their fitness room, or swimming laps in their 25-yard lap pool. (Although it sounds like an appropriately ethereal and Asian name, ANARA is actually an acronym for A New Age Restorative Approach.)

Linda's Restaurant (Local cuisine)

3840 Hanapepe Road, Hanapepe; 808-335-5152.

Hours: Monday to Friday 10:30 a.m. to 1:30 p.m. Tuesday to Friday 5:30 to 8:30 p.m. *Sampling:* Continuous menu features a variety of burgers (mushroom with Swiss, teriyaki beef or chicken) plus tuna, egg or grilled cheese sandwiches ($2 to $3) as well as miso soup, saimin and won ton *min* ($3 to $5). Plate specials served with rice, macaroni salad and hot vegetable: teriyaki chicken or beef, *loco moco*, mahimahi, pork chop, veal cutlet, beef stew and honey-dip chicken ($5 to $7). There are also entrees such as chicken cutlet, chicken *katsu* and breaded teriyaki beef or chicken ($6 to $7). Daily specials might include roast beef, *shoyu* chicken, meatloaf, chicken *hekka* and baked mahimahi ($6 to $7). *Comments:* Small coffee shop that's been serving up good local-style meals for over 30 years.

Mi Casita (Mexican food)

By the post office, 5470 Koloa Road, Old Koloa Town; 808-742-2323.

Hours: Monday to Saturday 11 a.m. to 9:30 p.m. Sunday 4 to 9 p.m. *Sampling:* Pork, beef or chicken burritos, beef or chicken chimichanga ($9 to $10). Fajitas for 1 or 2 ($13 to $23), with chicken, steak, seafood, or a "Fiesta" combination. Specialties include enchiladas *rancheras*, *chile verde*, *carnitas*, *chiles rellenos*, enchiladas, tacos, taquitos and tostadas ($8 to $12). Taco salad or seafood salad in a shell, plus a variety of nachos, quesadillas, potato skins and buffalo wings appetizers ($6 to $9). *Comments:* This sister-restaurant of La Bamba in Lihu'e doesn't have a liquor license, but invites you to BYOB.

Oasis Bar & Grill (Coffee/espresso/sandwiches/snacks)

Sheraton Kaua'i Resort, 2440 Ho'onani Road, Po'ipu; 808-742-1661.

Hours: 11:30 a.m. to 6 p.m. *Sampling:* Sandwiches, salads, fresh fruit and ice cream ($2 to $7). Hot items include fried chicken, jalapeño poppers, nachos, burgers, pizza, hot dogs (or turkey dogs), fish burgers, chicken fingers, buffalo wings and chicken teriyaki sandwiches ($5 to $10). *Comments:* This is the hotel's casual poolside restaurant and is close to the beach. (The Garden Terrace—open only during high season—also offers snacks and light meals.)

(The) Point (Lounge/appetizer/dessert menu)

Sheraton Kaua'i Resort, 2440 Ho'onani Road, Po'ipu; 808-742-1661.

Hours: 3 p.m. to 1 a.m. Grill 4 to 10 p.m. *Sampling:* Hot and cold appetizers (suitable for grazing!) include crusted seared *ahi*, cheese plate, prawns and sashimi, plus nachos, won tons, chicken wings, burgers, fish or chicken sandwich and tempura ($5 to $10). Their drink menu offers some creative choices in liqueur coffee drinks, alcoholic (and non) tropical drinks and martinis plus beer and wine, ports, cognacs and cigars. Try the "Banana Paradise" with macadamia-nut liqueur, banana cream, vodka and Bailey's or the "Menehune Magic" with mango cream, cranberry juice and Stoli Razberi. *Comments:* So what is The Point? It's an airy, poolside lounge that offers appetizers (enough for a light meal) and an extensive drinks menu in an upscale Hawaiian atmosphere with live music—jazz, Hawaiian—and other entertainment. A special cigar room with pool table is located next door. Tall, glass windows surround both The Point and the adjacent Shells restaurant, offering the dramatic ocean waves as a panoramic backdrop.

Poolside Grill and Bar (Snacks/light meals)

Embassy Vacation Resort, Po'ipu Point; 808-742-1888.

Hours: 10:30 a.m. to 8 p.m. *Sampling:* Homestyle burgers (including *ahi* and chicken), sandwiches (turkey, tuna, peanut butter and jelly), salads (turkey Caesar, penne pasta, fresh fruit), honey-dipped chicken, fish-and-chips, nachos, saimin ($4 to $9) and a variety of pizzas ($9 to $13). Ice cream treats from sundaes to Melona melon bars—a creamy melon popsicle ($2 to $6). *Comments:* A good place to enjoy a light lunch or warm-day snacks and cooler treats after a spell in the pool or at the beach.

Pualini's Farmer's Market (Hawaiian/local-style cuisine)

On the south side of the highway on the west edge of town, just before the turn onto Waimea Canyon Road, 9652 Kaumuali'i Highway, Waimea; 808-338-9722.

Hours: 9 a.m. to 6 p.m. This is a combination small-farmers produce stand and snack shop. In addition to seasonal fruits and veggies, they have a limited menu of sandwiches like roast turkey, roast pork or beef Alabama style, tuna salad, honey-baked ham, egg salad and veggie ($5 to $6). Salads include tuna and Nelle's Hawaiian curried chicken salad ($5 to $6). Smoothies range from mango mambo to Patrick's pride, Pualani's best and several others ($3 to $4). Frosties—frozen fruits eaten with a spoon—include banana and strawberry, pineapple and strawberry, banana and mango, mango and strawberry, pineapple and papaya and more ($4), plus there are a variety of other homemade snacks, plate-lunch specials, bagels and other goodies.

There are a few sidewalk/patio tables or you can take your lunch or snacks away. Don't forget to check the fruit and veggie tables for bargains on bananas, papaya, pineapples, fresh island coffee, tomatoes and other fresh island produce.

Shipwreck Subs & Ice Cream (Sandwiches/ice cream)

Po'ipu Shopping Village, 2360 Kiahuna Plantation Drive, Po'ipu; 808-742-7467.

Hours: 11 a.m. to 6 p.m. *Sampling:* Create your own 6" or 13" subs on fresh white or wheat bread with turkey, roast beef, ham, pastrami, salami, tuna or egg plus choice of Swiss, provolone, cheddar, jack or pepper jack cheese, plus condiments. With one meat ($5 to $6), two meats ($6 to $7) or three meats ($6 to $8). Potato and pasta salad sides ($1 to $2). Lots of ice cream treats. *Comments:* They have a kid's special for ages 12 and under, a peanut butter-and-jelly sandwich with chips and a small soda ($3). We have had good reports from readers who have been particularly pleased with their fresh breads, meats sliced to order, friendly service and reasonable prices.

Sueoko's Snack Shop (Local cuisine)

Next to Sueoka's Grocery Store, Koloa; 808-742-1112.

Hours: Monday to Friday 9:30 a.m. to 3 p.m. Saturday 9:30 a.m. to 3 p.m. Sunday 11 a.m. to 3 p.m. *Sampling:* Plate lunches, sandwiches and burgers, local foods. *Comments:* This is Kaua'i's original hole-in-the-wall eatery because that's almost what it is. It's an unobtrusive little structure attached to the side of Sueoka's grocery store. But they have some incredible bargains on some good sandwiches and great local-style plate lunches. This is a chance to sample some local dishes—and they serve a variety of plate lunches with specials that change daily. The specials are listed on papers stuck on the window and as they sell out of a particular item, they pull the paper off. You'll see plenty of local folks picking up their lunch during their break. Hamburgers, grilled cheese sandwich, fish burger or saimin ($2 or less). The teriyaki sandwich seemed like a splurge at $2.50. It was not a huge sandwich, but very tender and flavorful and at this price you could order two! Plate lunches like fried chicken, tripe stew, chili dog, teriyaki beef, hamburger steak, chopped steak, mahimahi and roast pork ($3 to $5 or less). No place to sit and eat, so we recommend you take your order over to the beach and enjoy a bargain oceanfront meal.

★ ***Taqueria Nortenos (Mexican food)***

Po'ipu Plaza, 2827 Po'ipu Road, Po'ipu; 808-742-7222.

Hours: 11 a.m. to 10 p.m. daily except Wednesday. *Sampling:* Mexican fare, still nothing much over $6 (with add-ons); most items priced $2 to $4. *Comments:* Burritos and the works. The usual enchiladas, tacos, tostadas, plus *chalupas* (crispy corn cups filled with beans and cheese), and *bunuelos* (dessert chips sprinkled with cinnamon sugar). This is the epitome of a Mexican hole-in-the-wall restaurant. The few tables in a small room behind the walk-up counter resemble a large closet full of jumbled misfits. But don't be misled. This place has really great food. The prices appear average, but wait until you see the portions. You can fill up and then some for $6 or less. Since the ambiance isn't much, grab some food to go and head to one of Kaua'i's beautiful parks or beaches.

Waimea Bakery & Deli (Sandwiches/bakery)
9875 Waimea Road, Waimea; 808-338-1950.

Hours: 6 a.m. to 3 p.m. *Sampling:* Breakfast burritos, eggs and meat, ham, egg, cheese and pineapple melts, deli sandwiches (chicken, roast beef, ham), a good and unusual taro-teriyaki burger, fish plates and other specials ($4 to $8). *Comments:* This is a tasty little place for breakfast or lunch and the macadamia-nut cinnamon rolls, fresh pastries, Hawaiian sweet bread and tropical fruit turnovers are well worth a stop alone. Also, fruit smoothies, milk shakes and ice cream floats. Eat in or take out.

★ *Waimea Canyon Snack Shop (Coffee/espresso/sandwiches/snacks)*
Waimea Canyon Plaza at the foot of Koke'e Road, Highway 552, Kekeha; 808-337-9227.

Hours: 9 a.m. to 5 p.m. *Sampling:* This small food counter offers a short menu of sandwiches like tuna and chicken salad, burgers, hot dogs and various other snacks, plus assorted cold beverages, coffee. It is also a Lappert's Ice Cream Shop so you can indulge in some Kaua'i-made ice cream. *Comments:* Good place to stop for a refreshing drink or snack on the way to Waimea Canyon and Koke'e Park or on the way back.

Moderate-priced Dining

Brennecke's (Steak/Seafood)
Across from Poi'pu Beach Park, 2100 Ho'one Road, Po'ipu; 808-742-7588; www.brenneckes.com.

Hours: Lunch 10 a.m. to 4 p.m. Dinner 4 to 10 p.m. Early-bird Dinner 4 to 6 p.m. Happy hour 2 to 5 p.m. *Sampling:* Burgers, sandwiches, soups and salad bar served all day until 10 p.m. ($5 to $12). *Pupus* all day, too: ceviche, sashimi, nachos, black-and-blue *ahi*, teriyaki chicken sticks, Asian or local-style samplers ($8 to $14). Early-bird and regular dinner choices include scampi, pasta with vegetables or clams with pasta, prime rib, New York steak, shrimp skewers, Oriental chicken stir-fry, Hawaiian spiny lobster, barbecue pork ribs and fresh island fish ($14 to $30). *Comments:* Excellent children's menu includes cheese or pepperoni pizza, beach burger, fish sandwich, teriyaki chicken sticks and more ($4 to $9). Salad bar has some interesting items, like whole red skinned potato salad, baby corn, pasta salad and a good choice of dressings. Things are a bit pricey, especially in light of the average quality of the food, but all meals come with a salad bar and the great across-the-road view of the beach park. Brennecke's also has T-shirts and a beach activity center and beach deli downstairs.

★ Brick Oven Pizza (Italian food)

2555 Kaumuali'i Highway, Kalaheo; 808-332-8561.

Hours: Tuesday to Saturday 11 a.m. to 10 p.m. Sunday 3 to 10 p.m. Closed Monday. *Sampling:* Whole-wheat or white crust with the usual pizza toppings, plus homemade Italian sausage, lean beef and green onions, imported anchovies, smoked ham and pineapple, salami, bay shrimp; varied sizes ($10 to $29). Pizza breads and hot sandwiches with sausage, seafood, meats and vegetables, or "*pupu*" pizza: pizza dough with garlic and cheese and a side of pizza sauce or dressing for dipping ($4 to $7); green veggie or chef's salads ($2 to $7). Desserts include aloha pie or ice cream sundae cups; beer and wine. *Comments:* Hearth-baked pizzas at this family-owned operation that has been pleasing residents and visitors alike since it opened in 1977. Good homemade sausage and excellent pizza crust, soft and doughy, but beautifully browned—like a soft pretzel. The garlic butter on the crust is an added flavor treat. Widely viewed as the best pizza on the island.

Camp House Grill (American cuisine)

Kaumuali'i Highway, Kalaheo; 808-332-9755.

Hours: Breakfast 6:30 to 10:30 a.m. (to 11 weekends and holidays). Lunch and Dinner 10:30 a.m. to 9 p.m. *Sampling:* Breakfast quesadillas, pancakes, omelets, waffles, French toast, biscuits and gravy, eggs Benedict, omelets and a variety of breakfast sandwiches—Monte Cristo with hash browns, or BLT (& egg), pancake or French toast with bacon and eggs ($4 to $9). They have early-bird specials ($2 to $3) before 8 a.m., but as they say on the menu: "After 8:01, No Way!" Grilled fish, veggie, BLT or turkey BLT sandwiches; chili ($4 to $8). Lunch and dinner offerings include a variety of burgers, salads, several grilled chicken entrees, barbecue pork ribs, Camp House *huli huli* chicken, sirloin steak Polynesian, pork chops, snow crab legs, shrimp scampi and fresh catch served with soup or salad and choice of side ($4 to $19). *Comments:* They're known for their homemade pies, so if you don't save room for dessert, you'll just have to buy a whole one from the glass case on your way out. Pineapple cream cheese macadamia or chewy chocolate chip macadamia-nut sound good enough to eat (and they are!) and so do the cream pies of coconut, banana and chocolate or the Paradise Pie made with macadamia-nut, coconut and pineapple. The burgers are good, but the ribs are better. This looks like a funky neighborhood diner, which it is, but it's comfortable and casual. It's home cooking all the way and home baking as far as the pies are concerned. The children's menu is available for lunch and dinner. (There's another Camp House Grill in Kapa'a.)

★ *Green Garden (Family dining)*

Kaumuali'i Highway, Hanapepe Town; 808-335-5422/335-5528.

Hours: Breakfast Monday to Friday 8:30 to 10:30 a.m. (from 8 a.m. on Saturday, 7:30 a.m. Sunday). Lunch 10:30 a.m. to 2 p.m. Dinner 5 to 9 p.m. Closed Tuesday. *Sampling:* Breakfast of eggs, breakfast meats, waffles, hotcakes and French toast ($4 to $5). For $5.20 you can have dessert for breakfast: a waffle with ice cream, whipped cream, coconut and strawberry topping. Lunch sandwiches include salad, fries and beverage and offer roast pork, mahi-melt, burgers and a variety of clubs ($6 to $7). Entrees also include vegetables and feature chicken chow mein, shrimp tempura, sweet-and-sour spare ribs, barbecue *ahi*, barbecue chicken, shrimp Louie salad and more ($7 to $9) and specials like seafood curry, breaded liver, or chicken tofu. Dinners are complete with homemade soup, salad, rice or potatoes, vegetables, rolls and beverage. Appetizers include a choice of escargot-stuffed mushrooms, shrimp cocktail, mussels, sashimi or *pupu* platter ($4 to $7). They offer some of the same lunch entrees at only slightly higher prices, as well as kiawe-broiled pork chops, steaks, kabobs or chicken peppercorn, as well as Chinese, Japanese or Hawaiian plates, *ahi a la Arashiro*, rack of lamb and teriyaki chicken. Daily specials might include roast turkey or pork, prime rib, crab legs, fresh fish, chicken cutlet, or their house special—baked seafood salads—($9 to $21).They're known for their "mile-high" pies like coconut, macadamia-nut, or chocolate cream and especially the *lilikoi* chiffon ($3). *Comments:* This family-owned restaurant has been here since 1948, serving an eclectic mix of local, homestyle and gourmet meals in large portions for small prices. Wine and tropical drinks; their house special is a *lilikoi* (passion fruit) daiquiri. Good selection of children's choices. Very casual and informal with the spacious garden look of a greenhouse. Long family-style tables, generally pleasant atmosphere and courteous small town–style service. Many folks stop just to try the homemade pies. This is a true Kaua'i institution.

★ *Hanapepe Café & Espresso (Gourmet vegetarian food)*

Located in the old Igawa Drugstore, 3830 Hanapepe Road, Hanapepe Town; 808-335-5011/335-8544.

Hours: Breakfast Tuesday to Saturday 9 to 11 a.m. Lunch 11 a.m. to 2 p.m. Dinner Friday only 6 to 9 p.m. *Sampling:* Breakfast naturally begins with espresso and other coffee drinks and there are multigrain waffles and pancakes, homemade oatmeal, home fries and baked frittatas ($4 to $9). Lunch includes soups and salads, healthnut or grilled vegetable sandwich, pasta and garden burgers with various combinations of pesto, sun-dried tomatoes, sauteed mushrooms and artichoke hearts ($5 to $8). Dinners change monthly and might include an appetizer of stuffed tomatoes, ricotta dumplings, roasted garlic bread and macadamia-nut pesto, roasted goat cheese cakes, or seared polenta salad ($7 to $12). Entrees may include dishes like vegetable and potato Charlotte, Southwest-style lasagna, garbanzo-bean flour cakes with eggplant and tomatillo relish, four-cheese lasagna, primavera and linguine crepes, quesadillas with pesto and portobello mushrooms, purple sweet potato quiche with raisins, cheese and sauteed mushrooms, puree of onion with fresh spinach and a daily fresh pasta ($13 to $19). Desserts include macadamia-nut creme brulee, passion fruit bread pudding with raspberry sauce and vanilla ice cream, tiramisu and chocolate cake with *lilikoi* glaze ($6 to $6.50). *Comments:* This funky little eatery offers quality homemade-style food and gourmet vegetarian dinners that even meat-eaters like. They're made with an Italian flair and with such fresh, flavorful vegetables that most don't know anything's "missing." (In fact, 90 percent of their customers aren't vegetarian!) The dishes are creative and colorful, mixing and matching ingredients for bursts of flavor that are both familiar and exciting. BYO wine. Live music on dinner nights with regular or Hawaiian slack-key guitar. Reservations are recommended for dinner.

Joe's on the Green (Coffee/espresso/sandwiches/snacks)

Located at the Kiahuna Golf Course, Po'ipu; 808-742-9696.

Hours: Breakfast 7:30 to 11:30 a.m. Lunch 11:30 a.m. to 2:30 p.m. Dinner Wednesday and Thursday only 5:30 to 8:30 p.m. Cocktails and *pupus* until 6 on weekends. *Sampling:* Breakfast specials include Joe's special scramble made with ground beef, eggs and taro leaf; biscuits-and-gravy; eggs Benedict, *huevos rancheros* and a variety of tropical fruit pancakes ($5 to $9). For lunch, try the *kalua* pork sandwich, beer-battered fish-and-chips, Joe Mama burger, tuna melt or a Caesar salad ($7 to $9). Dinner (and great sunsets!) are offered on Thursday night. The lively and inventive menu features some surprising combinations that really work: prawns wrapped in phyllo with banana-curry sauce; *kalua* pork and *lomi* salmon ravioli; and fresh mahimahi in coffee lime beurre blanc sauce are just a few of the nighttime specials ($15 to $23). *Comments:* No longer just a snack bar, the wide, open-air bar and pleasant seating area is now enhanced by a real restaurant. The country club setting overlooks the golf course and offers a great panoramic view. Live Hawaiian music on Thursday nights.

Lawa'i Restaurant (Local/Asian cuisine)

2-3687 Kaumuali'i Highway, Lawa'i; 808-332-9550.

Hours: Monday to Friday 10 a.m. to 9 p.m. Saturday to Sunday from 9. *Sampling:* Extensive menu (about 300 items) of local and Asian dishes: soup, pork, beef, poultry, seafood, chop suey, eggs, vegetarian, saimin, cake noodles, salad, sushi roll, Filipino dishes, curries, Japanese dishes plus sandwiches, steaks and seafood. Chinese sausage, crispy duck with plum sauce, ham and egg foo yung, seafood spaghetti, duck noodles with vegetables, chicken papaya, *sukiyaki don*, shrimp tempura, fish teriyaki, barbecue meatballs ($5 to $12). Full seafood, Chinese, or steak combo dinners ($10 to $16). *Comments:* This small eatery is very popular with local residents. Despite the rather dingy atmosphere, the food is good and the choices are amazing. There are three pages full of dishes on the printed menu, with even more on a blackboard.

Pacific Pizza & Deli (Pizza/deli)

Part of and adjacent to Wrangler's Steak House across from Big Save, 9652 Kaumuali'i Highway, Waimea; 808-338-1020.

Hours: 11 a.m. to 9 p.m. *Sampling:* A variety of "international" pizzas in small, medium and large ($9 to $20) sizes and calzones such as Pacific seafood, Japanese, Portuguese, Mexican, Veggie, Thai, *Hapa haole* (pesto with sun-dried tomatoes, mushrooms, zucchini, Canadian bacon and Hawaiian pineapple), *lomilomi* salmon and Filipino with homemade *langanizsa* sausage ($4 to $6). Deli sandwiches (on choice of bread) or cold wraps rolled in a tomato-basil tortilla come in turkey, ham pastrami, roast beef, seafood and tuna ($5 to $6). House salad ($4) plus special deli salads sold by the pound. *Comments:* Eat in or take out. Good pizza and sandwiches.

★ Pattaya Asian Café (Thai/Chinese food)

Po'ipu Shopping Village, 2360 Kiahuna Plantation Drive, Po'ipu; 808-742-8818.

Hours: Lunch Monday to Saturday 11:30 a.m. to 2:30 p.m. Dinner nightly 5 to 9:30 p.m. *Sampling:* Spring or summer rolls, fish cakes, *sateh*, calamari, *mee krob* appetizers ($7 to $11). Lemongrass or Thai ginger coconut soup with chicken or seafood ($8 to $15); fresh papaya, shrimp or beef salad ($6 to $11). Lemon chicken, stir-fried eggplant, broccoli with oyster sauce, *pad Thai* noodles, Evil Jungle Prince, garlic with coconut, pineapple with curry sauce, stir-fried bell pepper and a variety of curries are the entrees ($8 to $17). *Comments:* The emphasis at this shopping center–sidewalk restaurant is on authentic and traditional Thai cuisine, combining the unique and exotic flavors with Southeast Asian cookery style.

Pizzeta (Italian food)

5408 Koloa Road, Koloa Town; 808-742-8881.

Hours: 11 a.m. to 10 p.m. Happy Hour 3 to 6 p.m. *Sampling:* Appetizers include mozzarella sticks, garlic bread sticks, stuffed mushrooms and bruschetta ($6 to $8). Varied salads include blackened-chicken Caesar, veggie chop salad and Greek salad, and there is a soup of the day ($3 to $10). A wide selection of pastas range from spaghetti marinara, to spaghetti and meatballs, fettuccini with clams, fettuccini Lucia and penne *siciliano* ($8 to $12). Specialties include cheese ravioli, lasagne, chicken parmesan, eggplant parmesan, chicken cacciatore, chicken marsala and a fresh island fish of the day ($12 to $15). The menu also features a number of pizza pies in medium and large sizes such as barbecue chicken, sun-dried tomatoes, Florentine, Puttanesca, Margarita, shrimp pesto, pizza bianca, meat lovers and more ($13 to $24). Calzones include veggie, Hawaiian, Italian sausage, spinach and ricotta, pesto and mushrooms, pepperoni and others ($9); and there are Italian grilled specialty sandwiches like *vento* blackened chicken, calabrese salami, roma herbal cream cheese, hot meatball sub and chicken parmigiana ($6 to $8). Delightful desserts like cheesecake, ice cream, chocolate decadence and a perfectly textured tiramisu complete the menu ($4 to $6). *Comments:* Full beverage selection with Italian sodas, tropical iced tea, juices, espressos and coffee drinks as well as wine and beer. They feature good family-style Italian cooking and use many homemade ingredients in their recipes.

Po'ipu Bay Grill & Bar (American cuisine)

Just past the Hyatt Regency on the golf course at Po'ipu Bay, 2250 Ainako, Po'ipu; 808-742-1515.

Hours: Breakfast 6:30 to 10:30 a.m. Lunch 10:30 a.m. to 3 p.m. (Sandwiches and *pupus* Thursday to Friday 3 to 7 p.m., until 11 on Saturday). *Sampling:* Variety of breakfast meats and egg dishes plus *loco moco*, eggs Benedict, omelets, corned beef or crab hash with poached eggs, Belgian waffle, cinnamon rolls and a great selection of tropical and fruit pancakes: banana, macadamia, mango, berry and raisin ($6 to $9). Japanese breakfasts ($13 to $15). Lunch options include salads (Caesar, grilled salmon or eggplant), sandwiches (grilled *ahi*, Korean barbecue steak, hot dog, club, crab melt), and burgers ($5 to $10). Korean and Hawaiian plate lunches ($9 to $10). Buffalo wings, chili, calamari, nachos (regular or criss-cut potato), *ahi* sashimi and spicy onion rings are some of the *pupus* ($5 to $9). For dessert there's mud pie, apple pie and ice cream ($3 to $5). *Comments:* Windows all around, with views of the golf course. Looks like an old-fashioned hotel or country club dining room. Good reviews on the breakfast for quality and price (especially the eggs Benedict and home fries, and we liked the Asian-style cole slaw and garlicky criss-cut French fries served with their sandwiches). This dining room is operated by the Hyatt Regency and for guests' enjoyment they have pool tables, a dart board, video games and plenty of sports-filled televisions, as well as live entertainment from 8 to 11 p.m. on Saturday.

Po'ipu Tropical Burgers (American cuisine)

Po'ipu Shopping Village, 230 Kiahuna Plantation Drive; 808-742-1808.

Hours: 6:30 a.m. to 9:30 p.m. *Sampling:* Fresh fruit, omelet creations, pancakes and French toast, egg specials ($4.95 to $7.95) for breakfast (omelets served until 3 p.m.). Lunch includes soups, salads (Caesar, Cobb, Oriental chicken) and a wide range of deli types sandwiches served with French fries and "gourmet" burgers prepared with Kaua'i beef, including specialties like a rum-guava barbecue burger, a surfer burger and a beefless burger ($5.95 to $8.95). The same menu is offered for dinner, along with specials, such as fresh fish, steak, chicken and pasta, with salads, ($11.95 to $19.95). Wine, beer, espresso and desserts. *Comments:* This casual, open-air restaurant is great for families because it has a wide choice of inexpensively priced items, even at dinner, so everyone can find something they like. They even have kids' specials. The portions are ample; the staff is friendly. A good addition to the southside.

★ Pomodoro (Italian food)

Rainbow Plaza, 2-2428 Kaumuali'i Highway, Kalaheo; 808-332-5945.

Hours: Dinner 5:30 to 10 p.m. *Sampling:* Antipasti of calamari *fritti*, mozzarella marinara, or prosciutto and melon ($6 to $10), a variety of pastas—spaghetti, ravioli, cannelloni, manicotti, baked penne and lasagna, the house special ($12 to $17) and Pomodoro specialties like veal parmigiana, *pizzaiola*, piccata or scallopini; eggplant or calamari parmigiana, scampi, chicken cacciatore and chicken saltimbocca—an unusual change from veal ($16 to $20). Italian desserts like zabaliogne, tiramisu and spumoni are featured. Entrees are served with pasta, vegetable and homemade garlic focaccia bread. *Comments:* Surprisingly attractive tables and settings for its relatively hidden location on the second level of a shopping complex. They have a separate cocktail lounge. The food is fresh and flavorful—everything is made to order. The lasagna deserved its designation as house special: it was made with both beef and sausage and just the right amount (lots!) of cheeses. The spaghetti and meat balls were excellent—and a very generous portion. The calamari was perfect in texture and preparation and the spumoni ice cream cake easily became one of our Best Bets! The service was excellent (both personable and efficient) and we appreciated the attention to the little things—like napkins under our water glasses. Generally moderate prices on most menu items and there are things for the children to enjoy as well.

Toi's Thai Kitchen (Thai food)
'Ele'ele Shopping Center, 'Ele'ele; 808-335-3111.

Hours: Lunch 10:30 a.m. to 2:30 p.m. Dinner 5:30 to 9 p.m. Closed for lunch on Sunday. *Sampling:* Soups (such as *tom yum*, long rice, tofu and saimin) are served with rice, papaya salad and dessert ($6 to $15). Appetizers include spring rolls, *mee krob* and deep-fried tofu, plus salads with beef, pork or chicken; shrimp, mahimahi or calamari and beef, chicken or pork *laab* ($8 to $10). *Pad Thai*, Thai fried rice, *lad na and* fried noodle with broccoli are offered with pork, beef, chicken, shrimp, mahimahi, calamari, tofu or vegetables ($9 to $12). Dinner entrees include green papaya salad and choice of jasmine, brown or sticky rice: *jub chai*, buttered garlic *nua*, satay, ginger sauce *nua, nua krob*, cashew chicken, or shrimp, *panang* chicken and red, green, yellow or Matsaman curry ($11 to $16). "Toi's Temptation" (choice of meat simmered in coconut milk and chile paste with lots of lemongrass) is a specialty, as is "Pinky in the Blanket"—deep-fried shrimp marinated in white wine and wrapped in rice paper with satay peanut sauce ($11 to $16). American plates (chicken, pork, mahimahi or shrimp with fries, salad and dessert) are available for the non-adventurous types ($9 to $11). Lunch menu features the same items as dinner, most at $1 to $3 less. *Comments:* Attractive contemporary Asian decor accents; bright flower pots on each table and individual lace curtains on the windows. The bar is on one side with an open dining area on the other. This is true homestyle Thai cooking, very different from what you'll find at most other Thai restaurants and well worth a stop if you're in 'Ele'ele (near Hanapepe). Karaoke at 9:30 p.m. with late-night *pupus* (including saimin, pork won ton, calamari, or onion rings, wing dings, poppers, fried mushrooms—$5, sashimi—$8) until 1 a.m. Friday and Saturday.

TomKats Grille and Bar (American cuisine)
5402 Koloa Road, Old Koloa Town Center; 808-752-8887.

Hours: 11 a.m. to 10 p.m. Happy Hour 4 to 6 p.m. *Sampling:* Nibblers like fried onion rings, mushrooms, mozzarella sticks, or zucchini plus chicken fingers, calamari rings, jalapeño poppers and buffalo wings ($5 to $8). Chef, chicken and seafood salads ($6 to $9). Good choice of burgers and sandwich traditions like a patty melt, Really Reuben, French dip, New York steak, mahimahi, turkey "Klub" or veggie burger ($7 to $9). Hawaiian, Italian, *paniolo* or teriyaki chicken sandwiches ($6 to $7). Homemade chili

($3 to $4). Also seafood or steak kabobs and rotisserie chicken, plus nightly dinner specials (from 5 p.m.) like barbecue pork ribs, chicken marinara, or seafood linguine or kabobs, fresh "Katch" or prime rib ($9 to $17). Wash it all down with a white tiger, banana cow, or a mai tai made with passion fruit and guava juice. *Comments:* The name of the restaurant was derived from the first names of owners, Tom and Kathy Podlashes and Katnip is behind the bar. Casual outdoor seating on wooden decks in a rustic garden setting. Very good desserts and Tom makes the carrot cake himself. Menu for Kittens 12 and under.

Waimea Brewing Co. (Continental cuisine)
Waimea Plantation Cottages, 9400 Kaumuali'i Highway; 808-338-9733.

Hours: 11 a.m. to 9 p.m. Bar and brewery until 11. *Sampling:* A restaurant and brew pub combination. Start with such innovative appetizers as Caribbean jerk-seared *ahi* sashimi with fire-roasted corn salsa, *kalua* duck *lumpia* with black-bean *hoison* sauce, taro leaf goat cheese dip, fiery chicken wings with bleu cheese papaya dipping sauce, *gado gado* chicken skewers with peanut sauce, or the "twisted" Caesar salad, with grilled lettuce and their own non-traditional dressing ($5 to $7). Burgers topped with everything from bleu cheese to fried egg, plus grilled fish, chicken or portobello mushroom sandwiches ($7 to $9). "Big Plates" of baby back ribs, fresh catch, *kalua* pork, or Mediterranean roasted chicken ($13 to $16), and *keikis* can order a peanut butter and jelly sandwich, grilled cheese, hot dog, or popcorn chicken off the Short Pants Club menu ($3 to $4). Nightly dinner specials might offer appetizers of lemongrass-crusted *ahi* satay or smoked marlin lasagna ($9 to $11) and entrees like "quill" pasta with Kekaha shrimp (served with tomato, lime and Hawaiian chile pepper sauce and cilantro macadamia-nut pesto), herbed mahimahi with spicy passion fruit sauce, or grilled *ono* with green curry–lime leaf *beurre blanc* ($16 to $21). Roasted banana cheesecake, *lilikoi* poundcake and "Chocolate is my Master" are the desserts ($3 to $5). *Comments:* This restaurant has a nice plantation-style ambiance that is attractive, but not too upscale and food that has just the right balance of familiarity and creative innovation. There are petroglyph designs throughout and the bar is made from red dirt (cemented and polished). A view of the gleaming brew tanks. The patio deck has old-fashioned park-bench chairs. Try their "Damn Good Fries," with hand-harvested Hawaiian salt, bok choy cabbage or Java slaw and "beginners" (not too hot) *kim chee.* You can wash it down with a tart, fresh *lilikoi* margarita, but you'll probably opt for one of the handcrafted brews from their brew pub: Pakala Porter, Alakai Stout, West Side Wheat or Napali Pale Ale. They also have brew label T-shirts and mugs with their petroglyph logo designs.

★ *Wong's Restaurant & Omoide Bakery (Chinese food)*

1-3543 Kaumuali'i Highway, Hanapepe; 808-335-5066.

Hours: Deli open 8 a.m. to 9 p.m. Wong's dinner service 5 to 9 p.m. Closed Monday. *Sampling:* In the deli: breakfasts of eggs, pancakes and omelets ($3 to $7), appetizers of spring roll, won ton, *gau chee*, *loco moco*, fried shrimp ($3 to $7), sandwiches, burgers, Spam ($3 to $4), saimin ($7), lunch and dinner plates like spare ribs, oyster chicken, or beef broccoli ($5 to $7) and dinner specials like roast pork and New York chop, or pepper steak ($8 to $13). *Char siu* pork or roast duck from $7.25 a pound. Wong's has an extensive Chinese dinner menu complete with chicken, duck, beef, pork, egg, seafood, vegetarian and noodle dishes that are quite good. You can choose your own meal from a steam table set-up. Crispy skin chicken, "duck-in-the-nest," Mongolian beef, pork with eggplant, shrimp foo yung, steamed sea bass with ginger and onions, Szechwan tofu and roast pork saimin are just a few examples ($6 to $9). "Gringo" steak and shrimp entrees ($10 to $24). The bakery has pies (*lilikoi* or chocolate chiffon, macadamia-nut cream custard, pumpkin) cakes (*haupia*, guava, chantilly, "chocolate dream"), plus cheesecake (raspberry, fudge, "turtle pecan") and almond float. *Comments:* The restaurant is a banquet room that also does a lot of parties and catering. They're famous for their *lilikoi* chiffon pie. Good food; good value.

Wrangler's Steakhouse (Steak/seafood)

Across from Big Save, 9852 Kaumuali'i Highway, Waimea; 808-338-1218.

Hours: Lunch Monday to Friday 11 a.m. to 4 p.m. Dinner Monday to Friday 4 to 9 p.m. Saturday 5 to 9 p.m. Closed Sunday. *Sampling:* Burgers, sandwiches, fresh fish ($7 to $11) or the "Kau Kau Tin" lunch: Oriental shrimp tempura, teriyaki chicken and Japanese pickled vegetables served in a plantation worker's tin ($8). Shrimp Louie and chicken Caesar salads, too. Dinners include tempura, pork chops, barbecue ribs and fresh-fish specials ($15 to $20) as well as a wide variety of steaks that are served broiled, pan-fried, sizzling (their house specialty) or with seafood combinations ($16 to $20). *Keiki* menu ($5 to $7). *Comments:* This steak house serves meals in a large open-beam-ceiling room and is attached to their next-door operation, Pacific Pizza & Deli.

Expensive-priced Dining

★ *Beach House Restaurant (Pacific Rim cuisine)*

On the way to Spouting Horn, 5022 Lawa'i Beach Road, Po'ipu; 808-742-1424.

Hours: Dinner 5:30 to 10 p.m. *Sampling:* The Beach House has a well-deserved reputation for creative and innovative dishes in a beautiful setting. The dining room looks out at the ocean, making for dreamy sunset dining. The menu offers exotic appetizers such as sea scallops on green papaya salad with white truffle vinaigrette and cranberry essence, grilled artichoke, shrimp *pulehu*, crab cakes and a "taster" of *ahi* prepared as sushi, in a taco and in a hash spring roll. Seafood minestrone or Kaua'i asparagus salads are other starters ($6 to $12). Entrees range from Asian duck breast to crispy sesame chicken, lemongrass-crusted sea scallops, local paella with shrimp, scallops, seared crusted macadamia-nut mahimahi with citrus miso sauce and seared pork chops with *lehua* honey and whole-grain mustard glaze. Or try *kiawe*-grilled coriander-marinated lamb chops, grilled *ahi* with black-bean chili sauce, fire-roasted eggplant cannelloni, New York steak with truffles, grilled *ono* with caper pesto or Kaua'i shrimp with spinach and mushrooms ($18 to $30). Dessert options ($6 to $8) might be *Kahlua* poi cheesecake, a fabulous molten chocolate desire, warm chocolate tart with white chocolate gelato, coconut butter *mochi* sundae, fruit quiche, *sorbetto martini* or apple banana Foster. *Comments:* The Beach House consistently scores high marks for both its food and romantic setting from various travel magazines and surveys and we can echo the praise. Between the wonderful and consistently high-quality food, attentive service and gorgeous setting, it easily rates as one of the island's top restaurants. If you're looking for a special evening out or simply want to enjoy a drink and *pupus* while watching the ocean, this is the place to go. Reservations recommended.

Casa di Amici Po'ipu (Italian-Mediterranean cuisine)

2301 Nalo Road, Po'ipu; 808-742-1555.

Hours: Dinner 6 to 9:30 p.m. *Sampling:* Appetizers include such tempting exotics as *bandolini* filled with prosciutto, asiago and sage in pancetta, tomato and sage sauce, shrimp and *ahi* Thai sticks with wasabi aioli or risotto with *kalua* pork and cabbage or enjoy "The Kiss," a garlicky brie wrapped in filo dough, baked and topped with marinara sauce—a meal in itself ($8 to $10). Salads include a Caesar, *insalata di Pomodoro*, *mista*, Greek *salade mesclun* or Asian *salade mesclun* ($6 to $8). Entree specials might include rosemary-garlic-olive oil lamb loin with cassis-mint sauce, sauteed duck breast with Jamaican-spiced sauce, fennel-crusted lamb with orange-*hoison*-ginger sauce, salmon and shrimp in Thai coconut lobster sauce, black tiger prawns with ravioli of lobster thermidor in paella sauce, porcini-crusted chicken breast in cherry port wine, *tournedos rossini* in Madeira-shallot sauce with Asian spice pate or Japanese mahogany-glazed salmon with jalapeño tequila aioli and black-bean *chinitos* ($18 to $28). There's also a full page of pastas and sauces to mix and match ($19 to $23; light portions from $14) plus lasagna, fettuccine putanesca and linguine primavera ($20 to $23). Chicken or veal prepared marsala, piccata or gorgonzola–styles ($18 to $23). Creative desserts include bananas Foster, frozen mango mousse and delicate tiramisu ($6 to $8). *Comments:* This restaurant is tucked away in a quiet neighborhood in the Poipu resort area and is surrounded by homes and condos. Turn left above the curve just past Po'ipu Beach Park (as you're heading east). The cuisine, a blend of Italian-Mediterranean, makes Casa di Amici a unique Kauai dining experience, while the alfresco dining and grand piano music makes for a romantic dining experience. Unfortunately, they've never quite gotten their service down pat, making for some rather maddening waits for your food. But if you're not in a hurry, it's fine. Reservations recommended.

★ *Dondero's (Italian food)*

Hyatt Regency Kaua'i, 1571 Poi'pu Road, Po'ipu; 808-742-6260.

Hours: 6 to 10 p.m. *Sampling:* Antipasti consists of porcini mushroom crepes; beef carpaccio; bruschetta; fresh triangle pasta with shrimp, asparagus and mushrooms; minestrone soup; artichoke with crab fondue and several salads including portobello mushroom and goat cheese ($6 to $13). Pastas include ricotta cannelloni with walnuts; veal rigatoni; seafood spaghettini; fettuccine with roasted chicken, porcini mushroom, prosciutto and parmesan cream sauce and risotto with grilled vegetables ($17 to $27). Savory entrees include veal scallopini with lobster; bucco; chicken stuffed with spinach, mushroom and fontina cheese; filet medallions with marsala sauce; risotto-crusted fresh fish with lobster and shrimp cannelloni; and cioppino ($24 to $29). Desserts ($5 to $6) include a delicate tiramisu, gelato, flourless chocolate cake, fresh-fruit torte, amaretto cheesecake souffle or *Zuppa Inglaise*, the Italian version of an English trifle. *Comments:* Extensive wine list. The dining room is beautifully decorated with marble flooring, patterned tile accents and colorful Franciscan murals that lend the feel of an Italian bistro and make for an intimate dinner setting. The food is classical Italian, with a unique difference that should appeal to purists, as well as the more adventurous Italian food lover. The dining room is elegantly casual and they do request men wear shirts with collars. The outside terrace is especially delightful on a warm evening. The service is impeccable, easily the best on the Garden Island, an area where most of the island's fine-dining establishments fall a bit flat.

With its superior service and outstanding food, this is probably the best fine-dining on Kaua'i. It's expensive, but worth it. (Not exactly the place for dining kids-in-tow.) Reservations suggested.

Ilima Terrace (Continental cuisine/buffets/brunch)

Hyatt Regency Kaua'i, Po'ipu; 808-742-6260.

Hours: Breakfast 6 to 11 a.m. (buffet until 10), Sunday brunch 10:30 a.m. to 2 p.m. Lunch 11 a.m. to 2:30 p.m. Dinner 6 to 9 p.m. *Sampling:* Assorted cereals, fruits, pancakes, Belgian waffles, banana French toast, smoked salmon plate, omelets ($4 to $13) and a daily breakfast buffet ($17). Sunday champagne brunch ($30). Lunch starts with a sashimi sampler, smoked chicken quesadillas with sweet chile cream, buffalo wings, Thai summer rolls or a variety of salads: Cobb, pasta, fruit, Caesar or sesame-shrimp and seafood ($6 to $16). Burgers, pizza, pasta or entree specialties like Korean chicken, seared *ahi* loin steak, prawn noodles or red-hot chicken spaghetti, along with healthy offerings such as red lentil chili, grilled salmon salad or whole-wheat tortilla chicken sandwich ($6 to $17). Limited dinner menu with pizza, sandwiches and salads ($6 to $12) or a nightly theme buffet ($30) that includes salad bar, breads, fruits and cheeses, pastries and varied buffet food depending on the night. Call to confirm the evening's selection from among Italian Night, Hawaiian Seafood Night, Prime Rib Night or Surf-and-Turf Night—the buffet themes change nightly. *Comments:* The Ilima Terrace features lush tropical gardens and lagoons filled with *koi* surrounding the open-air dining area. Warm air and sunshine make this a very relaxing dining spot and while the food isn't outstanding, it's a great place to people-watch while soaking up the ambiance of this fine resort. Reservations suggested.

Kalaheo Steak House (Steak/seafood)

4444 Papalina Road, Kalaheo; 808-332-9780.

Hours: Dinner 6 to 10 p.m. *Sampling:* Clams by the pound, artichokes, sauteed parmesan mushrooms, shrimp cocktail or teriyaki steak stix will start you off ($5 to $10). The dinner menu features choice Midwestern steaks like top sirloin, New York cut, filet mignon and prime rib, plus pork tenderloin, baby back ribs or chicken breast and Cornish game hen, in addition to seafood specials like Kalaheo shrimp, teriyaki shrimp, Alaska king crab legs or fresh island fish ($15 to $25). There are also various combination platters ($18 to $22). Meals come with all-you-can-eat salad, fresh rolls, plus baked potato or rice. For dessert, there's rum cake, ice cream or a daily special cheesecake ($2 to $4). *Comments:* Cozy wood decor with hanging plants. Located on a quiet street just off the main highway. The portions are ample and a good value; their Portuguese soup with a house salad makes a satisfying light supper.

★ *Keoki's Paradise (Steak/seafood)*

Po'ipu Shopping Village, 2360 Kiahuna Plantation Drive, Po'ipu; 808-742-7534.

Hours: Lunch 11 a.m. to 2 p.m. Dinner 5:30 to 10 p.m. Café menu for lunch; also seafood and taco bar 11 a.m. to 11:30 p.m. *Sampling:* Sashimi, fisherman's chowder and Thai shrimp sticks with guava cocktail sauce to start ($4 to $9) and entrees of fresh fish (with several preparations), pesto shrimp macadamia, Pacific Rim rigatoni (with seafood), steaks, Koloa pork ribs, Balinese chicken (in garlic and lemongrass) and vegetarian lasagna ($12 to $21). Ice cream, triple chocolate cake and "The Original Hula Pie" ($3 to $5). The cafe menu has burgers and sandwiches (chicken, steak, roast beef, Reuben); fish tacos, nachos, chicken quesadillas and a selection of *pupus* from the dinner menu, as well as their superb calamari strips ($4 to $10); also Hawaiian plates—pork, fish and chicken ($10). *Comments:* This is one of the popular TS restaurant chain that also owns Duke's Canoe Club on Kaua'i and in Waikiki, as well as Kimo's and Hula Grill on Mau'i. The predictable food is a good value, but is not fine-dining cuisine—it's much more casual. Dinners come with salad, a basket of hot rolls, carrot muffins and herbed rice. Appetizers are worth the extra few dollars, especially the calamari—the thick strips are about perfect in taste and texture. The atmosphere at Keoki's is creative, with plenty of family appeal. The lagoons, with *koi*, waterfalls and plenty of lush greenery in this open-air, multilevel restaurant, create a jungle setting that adds to the overall appeal. The kids will love eating in the tropics. Get there before 6 p.m. for early-bird specials. This place is usually hopping, so reservations are a good idea.

Naniwa (Japanese food)

Sheraton Kaua'i Resort, 2440 Ho'onani Road, Po'ipu; 808-742-1661.

Hours: Dinner 5:30 to 9:30 p.m. *Sampling:* Start with *ahi* carpaccio, sliced beef with citrus *ponzu* sauce, smoked salmon with fresh fruit/prosciutto ham with asparagus, chilled tofu, tempura, seafood *laulau* and a variety of sushi including Hawaiian roll *poke* style ($7 to $10). Assorted sashimi or sushi ($19 to $23). Glass noodle, seafood or Manoa leaf and papaya salads ($7 to $9). Dinner entrees of beef striploin steak, broiled chicken, butter fish, assorted tempura or sushi, buckwheat noodles with tempura, plus fresh fish or lobster and crab ($17 to $23). Complete dinners with salad, miso soup, rice and pickled vegetables ($23 to $30). East–West desserts range from *ujikintoki* (ice cream, shaved ice and red azuki beans) to cappuccino *grasse* (coffee gelatin with ice cream and Kahlua); *mitsumame* (fruit, gelatin, ice cream and azuki beans) to *haupia* with fresh fruit ($4 to $6). Beer, wine and sake. The Saturday-night Japanese buffet features sushi, sashimi, salads, entrees, cold seafood, tempura station and desserts ($32). *Comments:* Naniwa blends Hawaiian ambiance into a Japanese inn setting surrounded by *koi* ponds and lagoon gardens. The food reflects the same blend of Japanese with Hawaiian (and European) touches. Like the other restaurants at the resort, the ambiance is upscale, but not intimidating.

★ Plantation Gardens Restaurant (Pacific Mediterranean cuisine)
Kiahuna Plantation, 2253 Po'ipu Road, Po'ipu; 808-742-2216.

Hours: Dinner 5:30 to 9:30 p.m.; *pupus* and drinks from 4:30 p.m. at the bar. Formerly Piatti, the restaurant has changed its name back to the original Plantation Gardens Restaurant. But that's about the only thing that's changed. The cuisine is still Pacific-inspired with Mediterranean accents. This lovely, airy dining room is set in the historic 1930s-era Moir House, an old plantation home. The room has an elegant yet homey atmosphere, with rich Brazilian cherrywood floors, *koa* wood trim, rattan seating and a large verandah for alfresco dining that overlooks the well-kept manicured botanical gardens. The dining room has earned numerous awards and wide acclaim over the years, including top-honors in the *Zagat Restaurant Survey* and a much-deserved star-rating by this book. *Pupus* include daily plantation homemade soup, fresh-island *ahi* sashimi, Hawaiian baked oysters, Kekaha shrimp and fish won tons, Koloa asparagus and pancetta, wok-seared scallops, pork ribs, crab-stuffed shiitake mushrooms and a Pacific platter ($6 to $11). Salads range from plantation Caesar (optional fresh fish, lava spiced grilled or sesame seed crusted), to Big Island palm salad, tempura soft-shell crab, grilled chicken, plus pears and caramelized onions ($7 to $21). The younger set may enjoy fresh pizzas from the wood-burning ovens, including sausage and peppers, Hawaiian *imu* chicken, veggie and Puna goat cheese and pesto ($14 to $21). Entrees include: fresh island fish of the day, veal and chanterelle stew, Hawaiian bouillabaisse, Parker Ranch Black Angus New York steak, macadamia-nut lamb chops, seafood *laulau*, rotisserie chicken, center-cut pork chop, grilled veggies and tofu. Pasta and risotto choices consist of island-style paella risotto, fresh fish-and-green curry risotto, jumbo scallops, Kekaha prawns and black coral fettuccini and shrimp wasabi ravioli ($18 to $29). Scrumptious tropical desserts round out the menu. Attentive, courteous service; reservations suggested.

Roy's Po'ipu Bar & Grill (Hawaiian Regional/Pacific Rim cuisine)
Po'ipu Shopping Village, 2360 Kiahuna Plantation Drive, Po'ipu; 808-742-5000.

Hours: Dinner 5:30 to 9:30 p.m. *Sampling:* The menu changes nightly and includes both a choice of chef's specials and old standbys from Roy's chain. There's also a special Japanese menu served with different samples of sake. Appetizers might include potstickers, crispy coconut shrimp sticks, crab cakes, escargot cassoulet and spring rolls with curry mango sauce ($6 to $9). Lemongrass grilled chicken, green apple and bleu cheese, and grilled portobello mushroom and roasted eggplant are a few of the salads ($5 to $7). *Kiawe* wood oven–baked pizzas may include Mongolian short rib, Cajun shrimp, eggplant and tomato, pesto summer squash ($6 to $8). Entrees might feature Chinese duck with *lilikoi* mango sauce, parmesan-crusted lamb shank, *imu*-roasted pork pot roast, garlic mustard grilled short ribs and lemongrass-crusted shrimp with Thai peanut curry sauce ($17 to $20). Other special entrees may include wood roasted rack of lamb with five-spice Kona coffee sauce, sesame-crusted *ono* with *wakame* miso shrimp sauce and soba noodles and *kiawe*-grilled filet mignon with black-bean chile sauce ($20 to $25). Their nightly "mixed plates" offer a chance to try two entrees as one ($26 to $30). Roy's signature dessert is the dark chocolate souffle, literally swimming in rich chocolate with raspberry sauce. Or there's apple-and-macadamia-nut strudel, blueberry cheesecake, *lilikoi* custard tart, Key lime brulee or chocolate mousse toffee bars ($6 to $7). *Comments:* Roy's Po'ipu location is one of over a dozen restaurants owned by chef Roy Yamaguchi, one of the founders of Hawaiian Regional cuisine. He has enclosed the kitchen behind huge glass windows, so you can watch the chefs as they prepare your meal. The setting isn't special, with a rust and green theme carried throughout and weather permitting, the side panels are opened up to make it a bit more open air. No view—you're looking out on a shopping center. Although Roy's is popular and busy, we've found the food to be a bit overpriced and overrated. We also found the service to be cloying, without being especially efficient. In short, if you've eaten at Roy's and love it, stop in. Otherwise, there are better places to spend your money on the southside.

Shells (International cuisine)

Sheraton Kaua'i Resort, 2440 Ho'onani Road, Po'ipu; 808-742-1661.

Hours: Breakfast 6:30 to 11 a.m. Sunday brunch 10 a.m. to 2 p.m. Dinner 5:30 to 9:30 p.m. *Sampling:* A la carte breakfast omelets, egg dishes, corned beef hash, French toast, pancakes, Belgian waffles, fresh fruit, cereals and heart-healthy selections ($4 to $14); Continental breakfast ($11); full buffet ($16). Dinners begin with appetizers like crab-and-prawn cake, *ahi* carpaccio, oysters Rockefeller, tropical fruit cocktail, shrimp with *poha* sauce and gazpacho or Maui onion soups ($3 to $8). Salad bar ($10) or with a la carte entree ($5). Choice of complete dinners with salad, dessert and beverage ($15 to $28) or a la carte ($24 to $33). Dinner entrees feature prime rib, grilled lamb chops, roasted pork loin (with *hoisin* citrus sauce), filet mignon, macadamia-crusted chicken breast or fresh fish plus pasta primavera, cannelloni, seafood fettuccine, prawn scampi or Oriental pasta with tofu. They also offer a Friday-night seafood buffet (5:30 to 9:30 p.m.) with sushi, salads and cold seafood, plus hot fish and seafood entrees, a shrimp tempura station, beverages and desserts—including hot chocolate souffle with a variety of sauces and toppings ($35). *Keiki* menu ($3 to $8). *Comments:* The Sheraton Kaua'i Resort is a luxury facility that really is suited for families: the restaurants are attractive, but not upscale and intimidating. The focal point of both Shells and The Point lounge is not the interior decoration, but the tall, glass windows that offer the ocean as a full-wall natural mural. You can dress up, but you can also bring the family.

Tidepools (Steak/seafood)

Hyatt Regency Kaua'i, 1571 Po'ipu Road, Po'ipu; 808-742-6260.

Hours: Dinner 6 to 10 p.m. *Sampling:* The menu changes frequently, but you might start with almond shrimp cakes, fried oysters, *ahi* sashimi, grilled sweet chile shrimp and *ahi*, "Kauaian" ribs or mussels and clams ($7 to $10). Follow up with Kaua'i onion soup or clam chowder and Caesar (with crisp onions and Puna goat cheese); Kaua'i onion and tomato, fresh fruit or green salad ($5 to $8). Then enjoy a wide selection of entrees: there's pan-fried *somen* noodles with grilled tofu and vegetables or a "cupboard" of potato, vegetable and noodle dishes for the vegetarian ($18 to $20) and filet mignon, prime rib, pork chops or roast chicken from the grill ($23 to $28). Specialties of the house include charred *ahi* sashimi, shrimp and crab strudel, skewered shrimp scampi, seafood mixed grill, Tidepools' signature macadamia-nut–crusted *ahi*, ($25 to $29), and live Maine lobster (market price). Fresh Hawaiian fish is prepared several ways and a variety of meat-and-seafood combination plates are available. Desserts range from skillet-baked apple pie to mud pie, ginger creme brulee and white chocolate cheesecake ($5 to $7). *Comments:* Tidepools offer contemporary Hawaiian cuisine featuring Kaua'i-grown products like onions and sweet corn, plus vegetables and herbs from an Omao farm, Chinese noodles from Kaua'i Noodle Factory, island-grown fruit and Hawaiian fish. The choice of entree combinations is a great way to taste and sample—a diverse selection of menu items can really make dining an experience here. Try some of the more unusual fish offerings like *hebi*, *ehu* or *monchong*. Selected entrees are available for the kids in your family at half price, making this rather expensive dining choice a more affordable one. The restaurant is built like a series of open-air *pili* grass-thatched Polynesian *hales* over a tranquil lagoon—it definitely puts you in the mood for seafood and is fun. The children in your party will enjoy the Robinson Crusoe atmosphere, while the adults will appreciate fine dining in a romantic setting. Reservations recommended; appropriate resort attire suggested.

North Shore Area

Inexpensive-priced Dining

Amelia's (Coffee/espresso/sandwiches/snacks)

Princeville Airport, 3541 Kuhio Highway; 808-826-9561.

Hours: noon to 8 p.m. Music and dancing Friday to Sunday until 2 a.m. *Sampling:* Turkey, ham, tuna, barbecue beef, roast beef or French dip sandwich ($6 to $7), hot dogs, chili, nachos ($4 to $5). *Comments:* Like a neighborhood roadhouse, with more character than most bars, enhanced by interesting Amelia Earhart–decor and a great mountain view. Television with satellite sports.

Bubba's (Coffee/espresso/sandwiches/snacks)

Hanalei Center, Kuhio Highway, Hanalei Town; 808-826-7839; e-mail: obubba@aloha.net; www.bubbaburger.com.

Hours: 10:30 a.m. to 6 p.m., until 8 p.m. in the summer. *Sampling:* It's mostly burgers here—Bubbas, double bubbas, hubba bubbas, plus hot dogs, corn dogs and Budweiser beer chili. "Alternative" burgers include fish, chicken, tempeh and Italian sausage ($2 to $6)—or fresh-fish sandwich with pineapple lemongrass salsa ($2 to $6). Side orders of Caesar salad, French fries, onion rings, frings (fries and rings) or chili fries ($2 to $4). *Comments:* With a name like Bubba's, you were expecting maybe shrimp? Located in a small building just off the street and in front of the Hanalei Center complex, they have a counter to place and pick up your order and a large wall menu. Seating is a couple of benches and stools at the verandah counters. A good place to have a burger and people-watch at the same time, if you can find a seat. They do have take-out—and T-shirts. Buy a hat or shirt and if you wear it when you order your burger, you'll get a free drink. If you're hungry for a burger, this is as good a place as any.

Duane's Ono Burgers (Coffee/espresso/sandwiches/snacks)

On the highway in Anahola; 808-822-9181.

Hours: Monday to Saturday 10 a.m. to 6 p.m.; from 11 a.m. on Sunday. *Sampling:* The teriyaki burger is the biggest seller here, but there are lots of other burgers to choose from: barbecue, bleu cheese, avocado, mushroom and combos like "Duane's Special," with 1,000 island dressing, grilled onions, pickles, sprouts, cheddar and Swiss, or the "Local Girl," which comes with teriyaki, Swiss cheese and pineapple ($4 to $6). There are other sandwiches, too, such as fish, chicken, patty melt, tuna, grilled cheese and a veggie burger ($3 to $7). Side orders of fries, onion rings or salad ($2 to $3). They have *keiki* burgers and sandwiches, beverages ($3). *Comments:* The burgers are piled high with lots of "stuff," like a Dagwood burger. Try the fries with the special seasoning they have on the counter—*ono* (delicious)! The few outdoor tables have a mountain view, but please, don't feed the wild chickens. They're enough of a nuisance already. This place has long been a popular burger stand, but it's lost some of its appeal and charm since Duane sold out—recent visits found it a bit greasy. Still, the visitors line up.

★ Hanalei Mixed Plate (Hawaiian/local-style food)

Ching Young Village, Kuhio Highway, Hanalei; 808-826-7888.

Hours: Monday to Saturday 10:30 a.m. to 8:30 p.m. Closed Sunday. *Sampling:* Standard mixed-plate entree choices are *kalua* pork and cabbage, *shoyu* ginger chicken and vegetable stir-fry or chow mein (all with white or brown rice) ($5 for one choice; $6 for two, $8 for three). Other dishes include vegetarian Thai coconut curry; *ahi* ginger stir-fry; grilled Cajun *ahi*; or grilled sesame chicken; mahimahi enchilada; roasted red bell pepper pesto and creamy garlic basil mahimahi ($7). Sauteed mahimahi, *kalua* pork, grilled *ahi* and teriyaki or *shoyu* chicken sandwiches ($7 to $11); chicken or mahimahi Caesar and garden salads ($4 to $10). Corn dog, chili dog or hot dog; cheeseburger, tempeh, garden or buffalo burger ($5 to $7). Baskets with fish, chicken, shrimp or spring rolls, with chips ($4 to $9 or any two combo for $11.) *Comments:* Mostly take-out, with a small patio area and open-air tables for eating here. This is one of a very few places left that has "Bison-on-a-bun." It's a little coarser and gamier, but not at all tough or chewy. Mixed-plates are a good value; the vegetables are fresh and colorful—it's hard to decide when they all look so appetizing. Good local-style food for reasonable prices. Definitely worth a stop. Parking in Ching Young Village shopping center parking lot next door.

★ Hanalei Taro & Juice Co. (Smoothies/sandwiches)

East edge of Hanalei Town, next to Kayak Kaua'i, Kuhio Highway; 808-826-1059.

Hours: 10 a.m. to 4 p.m. *Sampling:* These smoothies offer a special ingredient: poi. It's blended with fresh fruit for a hearty and delicious taste ($3.50)—and you can have protein powder and spirulina added. No one makes smoothies like this and the poi is home-milled from taro grown just up the road. The sandwiches (turkey and taro hummus) are served on delicious homemade taro rolls ($5.50). For dessert, the taro *mochi,* a pudding-like confection that quickly becomes addictive, is outstanding (the container serves several people—if they're willing to share!) ($4.50). There's also a trailer selling fresh local produce and fruit. Folks will help you pick out items that are ripe and give information on how to prepare some of the more unusual offerings. They often have fresh coconuts, too. *Comments:* This little stand is a hidden gem, with quality food that is unique.

Hanalei Wake-up Café (American/Mexican food)

Aku Road, Hanalei; 808-826-5551.

Hours: Breakfast 6 to 11:30 a.m. Lunch Monday to Saturday 11:30 a.m. to 2:30 p.m. *Sampling:* For breakfast there's homemade granola, pancakes, French toast, veggie tofu, a scrambled egg quesadilla and build-your-own omelets ($4 to $7). Or try the custard French toast made with Portuguese sweet bread and topped with pineapple, coconut and whipped cream ($5). For lunch, there is veggie, tofu, chicken or *ahi* stir-fry ($6 to $8), or plate lunches with chile pepper *ahi* or chicken, hamburger steak, teriyaki chicken, chicken cutlets or charbroiled *ahi* ($6 to $8). Chinese chicken, Caesar and garden salads or sandwich choices of BLT, ham-and-cheese, tuna melt, beef or veggie burgers and *ahi* ($5 to $7). Mexican entrees include taco or enchilada plates with choice of chicken or *ahi* ($7 to $8). *Comments:* Small coffee shop–type restaurant, family-owned and -operated. The custard French toast called "Over The Falls" is to die for and while it appears to be a small portion, it is plenty filling—more custard than toast. The breakfast quesadillas are good-sized portions that should appease those hearty morning appetites. The Mexican meals are flavorful, not too heavily spiced and served in ample-sized portions. The motif here is "surf," from the photos and trophies to the video playing on the television. The atmosphere is strictly casual and most folks that come in look like they just came from the beach, which is probably about right. This is Hanalei, after all, and not downtown Honolulu.

Kilauea Farmers Market (Sandwiches/salads)

Next to Kong Lung Center in the Kilauea Theatre Building, Keneke Street, Kilauea; 808-828-1512.

Hours: Lunch counter 10 a.m. to 3 p.m. Store and take-out deli 8:30 a.m. to 8:30 p.m. *Sampling:* Sandwiches served on freshly baked Kilauea Bakery bread: turkey, roast beef, ham-and-cheese, fresh fish, pastrami, peanut butter, chicken salad or subs. Hummus, tabbouli, pasta, pesto, three-bean, tofu and garden salads. Homemade soups with garlic toast (fish, minestrone, chicken noodle and chowder with corn fresh off the cob). Menu prices range from $3 to $7. *Comments:* This small lunch counter and kitchen is located inside a gourmet grocery store that offers everything from organic coffees and Thai cooking ingredients, to microbrew beers, organic wines and local organic produce.

Mango Mamas Café (American food)

Just off Kuhio Highway, 4460 Ho'okui #56, Kilauea; 808-828-1020.

Hours: 7:30 a.m. to 6 p.m. *Sampling:* Fresh fruit and vegetable juices and smoothies (just juice and fruit—no additives) in tropical combinations of mango, banana, pineapple, coconut, guava and passion fruit. ($3 to $6). They also have sandwiches like avocado, hummus, rice or soy cheese, peanut butter and jelly, ham, turkey, tuna, wraps, vegetarian tamales, veggie or tempeh burgers ($3 to $5), plus fresh fruit, salads and soup. Sprouted wheat and spelt bagels, with various toppings, organic granola, Suzi's pastries ($4 or less); for beverages, choose from flavored coffees, coffee drinks, tea and chai extra spicy with ginger ($4 or less). *Comments:* This former smoothie-and-juice stop is now a café with a friendly, enthusiastic, young staff. If we had a category for "prettiest sandwich" they offer it—light green avocado, with orange carrot shreds, red tomato and dark green lettuce piled up on "basic beige" bread in a bright yellow wrapper. Fresh, colorful, filling—and delicious!

Old Hanalei Coffee Company (Coffee/espresso/sandwiches/snacks)

Hanalei Center, 5183 Kuhio Highway, Hanalei; 808-826-6717.

Hours: 7 a.m. to 6 p.m. (summer until 8). *Sampling:* In addition to flavored coffees, they offer espresso, lattes, cappuccinos, frosted or hot mochas, teas ($2 to $4), with free refills on most of the "basic" beverages, smoothies ($3 to $4), waffles ($5 and up) and bagels, plus muffins, macadamia-nut brownies, cookies, pies and cakes—all baked fresh daily. Lemon bars and aloha bars—macadamia-nut crust with chocolate chips and toasted coconut—are popular, quick snacks. *Comments:* Waffles served 7:30 to 11:30 a.m. Start with a plain waffle and add toppings like papaya, banana, kiwi, mango, raspberries, blueberries, strawberries, coconut, macadamia nuts, chocolate chips and whipped cream, or try a Kaua'i waffle with papaya, banana, mac nuts and whipped cream. The menu offerings are limited, but what they have is good. Casual and pleasant atmosphere—homey with curtains and a small selection of gifts. They also offer mail-order coffees from their Island Java Roasting Co.; 888-452-8244.

Polynesian Hide-a-way & Haw'n Bar-B-Q & Kamaka's Shave Ice (Hawaiian/American food)

4404 Kuhio Highway, Anahola; 808-821-8033.

Hours: Sunday to Monday 11 a.m. to 4 p.m. Tuesday to Saturday 10 a.m. to 5 p.m. *Sampling: Huli-huli* chicken, teriyaki beef, barbecue pork, fish and grilled cheese sandwiches ($4 to $5), burgers ($5 to

$7), and island favorites, including pork or chicken *laulau*, *kalua* pig, *loco moco*, smoked meat and hamburger steak ($6 to $7). *Comments:* Dine in or take out at this roadside stand. The food is plentiful and the owners are friendly. Try the fresh roasted macadamia nuts. They're flown in daily from the Big Island and roasted fresh on the premises. Price per bag: $4 (¼ lb.), $7 (½ lb.), $12 (1 lb.).

Tropical Taco (Mexican food)

5088 Kuhio Highway #56, Hanalei; 808-827-8226.

Hours: Monday to Saturday 11 a.m. to 8 p.m. Closed Sunday. *Sampling:* Tacos, tostadas and burritos made fresh daily. The menu is rather limited but they offer some good Mexican food. Choose from a tropical taco with beans, meat, lettuce, salsa, cheese and sour cream; the tropical fish taco consists of fresh fish deep-fried in beer batter; the regular taco comes with the works; the tostada is a flat taco with the works; Fat Jack has cheese, meat, beans and is deep fried and topped with the works; the chili burrito has beans, meat and the works; the veggie burrito has everything but the meat; the fresh-fish burrito has fish and the works; and the baby burrito has cheese and beans only ($4 to $8); ice-cold lemonade to quench that thirst. *Comments:* This North Shore eatery used to operate out of a dark green mobile taco van, which now has been retired. Located in the new Halele'a Building at the east edge of Hanalei town right on the highway. Tables to eat here or take out.

Village Snack & Bake Shop (Deli/bakery/coffee shop)

Ching Young Village, Kuhio Highway, Hanalei; 808-826-6841.

Hours: Breakfast 6 to 11 a.m. Lunch 11 a.m. to 4 p.m. (Sunday until 3 p.m.) *Sampling:* Breakfast sandwiches, eggs, pancakes, rice, Spam. *loco moco* ($3 to $6). Tuna melt, teriyaki beef or chicken, BLT, sandwich; burgers, hot dogs ($2 to $5). Side orders ($1 and up); plate meals (fried or chile pepper chicken, hamburger steak, teriyaki beef) or fish-and-chips ($5 to $7). Beach or picnic lunch to go includes sandwich, soda, fruit or salad ($5 to $7). *Comments:* This a definitely a greasy-spoon kind of place, but the desserts are excellent, especially the chocolate cake and coconut cream pie. Worth stopping in for those and other baked goodies.

Zababaz One World Café (Vegetarian food)

Ching Young Village, Kuhio Highway, Hanalei; 808-826-1999.

Hours: 9 a.m. to 7 p.m. *Sampling:* Organic vegetarian dishes like lasagna, enchiladas, quiche, veggie burgers, potato or green salad, hummus wrap and several Thai items. Fresh bakery goodies include their popular brownies and oatmeal chocolate chip cookies. The cornbread and banana walnut bread are made with maple syrup instead of sugar. They also have Lappert's ice cream as well as smoothies, juices and espresso drinks. Prices average $3 to $6. *Comments:* Small vegetarian café and juice bar located in the original Ching Young Store. Limited seating at picnic tables with benches. Good food and pleasant service.

Moderate-priced Dining

Bamboo Bamboo (Hawaiian Regional/Pacific Rim cuisine/Italian)

Hanalei Center, 5-511 Kuhio Highway, Hanalei; 808-826-1177.

Hours: Lunch 11:30 a.m. to 3 p.m. Dinner 5:30 to 9:30 p.m. Reservations suggested. *Sampling:* The menu is a somewhat eclectic collection of Italian dishes like pasta and pizza ($9 to $20) plus Hawaiian Regional and Pacific Rim entrees like fresh island fish, potato-crusted mahimahi, bamboo salad with fresh *ahi*, Creole Haena, filet mignon and herb roasted chicken on garlic mashed potatoes ($17 to $24). Appetizers include crispy *ahi* spring rolls, veggie summer rolls, *ahi* sashimi, fresh clams, won ton and smoked salmon bruschetta, plus soup of the day and house salad ($5 to $10). *Comments:* The pleasant open-air dining room is located in one of Hanalei's busy shopping/dining complexes. The main room has a contemporary feel—with lots of warm woodwork accents. There's an adjoining patio area for alfresco dining. However, that's shared with the restaurant next door (Neide's Salsa & Samba), bringing additional traffic and noise from their side. But it can be a good vantage point for people-watching.

(The) Beach (Coffee/espresso/sandwiches/snacks)

Princeville Resort; 808-826-2763.

Hours: 11 a.m. to 5:30 p.m. *Sampling:* Turkey club, New York steak, fresh fish, tuna in pita, wrapped Caesar chicken sandwich, or Black Angus burger ($13 to $15). Cobb, Caesar, grilled chicken (with avocado, papaya and fresh berries) or taco salad ($12 to $17). Spring rolls, buffalo wings, nachos, crabmeat quesadillas or *ahi* trio plate ($10 to $17). Desserts ($4 to $6). *Comments:* Wine and beer and a good selection of tropical drinks. *Keiki* menu ($4 to $8). Prices are high, but it *is* Princeville.

Hanalei Dolphin (Steak/seafood)

Kuhio Highway, Hanalei Town; 808-826-6113.

Hours: Lunch 11 a.m. to 3:30 p.m. Dinner 5:30 to 10 p.m. *Pupus* 11 a.m. to 10 p.m. *Sampling:* Lunch sandwiches such as teriyaki chicken, chilled fish salad, fresh fish, calamari or tempeh veggie burger on sesame seed roll or Dolphin squaw bread ($7 to $8). Dolphin salads include two kinds of lettuce, Chinese cabbage, bean sprouts and tomatoes and are topped with calamari, chicken, grilled fish or fish salad ($6 to $9). Appetizers include ceviche, seafood chowder, artichoke, sashimi, artichoke and stuffed mushrooms ($5 to $7 or market price). Seafood entrees of fresh island fish, calamari, scallops, shrimp and Alaska king crab plus *Haole* or Hawaiian chicken, filet mignon steak, New York steak and steak and seafood combinations ($12 to $28). Homemade dessert selections change daily, but they always have Dolphin ice cream pie ($5) with banana, macadamia nut and coconut ice cream in an Oreo cookie crust. *Comments:* Quite a few of the entrees are under $20 and all come with salad, steak fries, penne pasta or rice and hot homemade bread. They also offer *menehune* (kid) portions ($12) or light dinners: broccoli casserole, seafood chowder or salad and bread ($9 to $16). This is just good, simple basic food. They don't take reservations and unless you arrive early, you will probably have a wait. Put in your name and spend your time browsing through the adjoining gift and clothing stores. The food is hearty, some of the sauces are a bit on the heavy side, but the salads are a very pleasant surprise. Served family-style in a bowl, the mixed greens are accompanied by homemade garlic croutons and an assortment of dressings you can add yourself. They have a fish market, too, open from 11 a.m. to 8 p.m.

Hanalei Gourmet (Continental cuisine)

Old School Building, Hanalei Center, 5161 Kuhio Highway, Hanalei; 808-826-2524.

Hours: Breakfast 8 to 11 a.m. Lunch 10:30 a.m. to 4:30 p.m. *Pupus* and grilled sandwiches until 5:30. Dinner 5:30 to 9:30 p.m. *Sampling: Pupus* include Asian crab cakes, *ahi* nachos, crab-stuffed mushrooms, sauteed mussels, deep-fried artichoke and artichoke toast—broiled with their unusual and flavorful artichoke dip and lots of gooey cheese ($6 to $10); boiled shrimp ($9 for a quarter-pound, $24 for a pound). Salads include chicken in papaya or avocado boat, Hanalei Waldorf with mango vinaigrette, Oriental *ahi* pasta, Waioli salad veggies with Sonoma goat cheese vinaigrette, roasted garlic Caesar and good ol' green salad ($6 to $9). Pastas include eggplant or seafood marinara, Greek, or gorgonzola chicken. Basic sandwiches like grilled chicken breast, charbroiled island fish, turkey, roast beef, corned beef, chicken salad and tuna ($5 to $9) on fresh baked bread with "the works." More gourmet varieties ($7 to $8) include Oregon bay shrimp (open-faced with melted jack cheese and remoulade sauce), *ahi* with dill mayo, ginger chicken and roasted eggplant and red pepper with provolone cheese, a sour-cream-lime-cilantro sauce and sweet red onions. Gourmet burgers with gorgonzola or avocado with bacon ($7 to $9). Dinner entrees include specialty pastas like pasta du jour, Greek pasta with New Zealand mussels, shrimp scampi linguini, gorgonzola chicken and gourmet stir-fry with veggies and *udon* noodles

($11 to $20). Other entrees include fresh island fish, sauteed scallops *meuniere*, pan-fried crab cakes, macadamia-nut fried chicken and charbroiled pork chops ($16 to $20 or market price). Breakfast offerings include *huevos* Santa Cruz, muesli, bacon-and-egg sandwich ($5 to $8) or fruit, bagels and pastries ($2 or less). *Comments:* The place is generally busy and it's not bad—but nothing to write home about.

★ *Kilauea Bakery & Pau Hana Pizza (Bakery/pizzeria)*

On the way to the Lighthouse Kong Lung Center, Kilauea Road at Keneke Street, Kilauea; 808-828-2020.

Hours: 6:30 a.m. to 9 p.m. Pizza served from 11 a.m. to 9 p.m. *Sampling:* Croissants, cinnamon buns, scones and other freshly baked pastries, plus unusual breads like *limu* sourdough with sea algae, sun-dried tomato and fresh basil, poi bread, feta cheese and sweet red bell pepper, Hawaiian sourdough (fermented from a guava starter), and Na Pali brown bread, made with fennel, caraway, orange rind and cocoa. Pizzas are just as innovative with a lot of unusual toppings and combinations: the "Barbecued Chicken" has barbecue chicken, roasted onions and red peppers, mushroom and mozzarella cheese; the "Classic Scampi" has tiger prawns, tomato, roasted garlic, capers, asiago and mozzarella cheeses; and the "Billie Holiday" has smoked *ono*, swiss chard, roasted onions, gorgonzola rosemary, sauce and mozzarella cheese ($11/17/24). Regular pizzas are priced by size and toppings ($7 to $28); or try their Abrezone, an open-faced vegetable calzone. They have a tasty selection of cream cheese spreads, with everything from mango-pineapple to red pepper and garlic to tapenade or hummus to put on your bagel. They also have coffee drinks and espressos ($1 to $4). Pizza/salad lunch specials ($6). *Comments:* Pastries and breads baked daily. Pizza crust is extra crispy. And the staff are extra nice. Owners Tom and Katie Pickett started the bakery in their home, expanded, then added pizza. If you don't have a big appetite or a family, you can order pizza by the slice. Or, try their flavored breadsticks in chile pepper, garlic butter, or sesame and *alae* (red) salt. (They make a great made-on-Kaua'i gift to take home!) Their signature bakery items include the sourdough and Na Pali brown breads and tropical fruit layer cakes with whipped cream icing. In addition to the bakery operation, they have a full-service espresso bar with limited cafe seating inside and a courtyard with a few umbrella tables outdoors. This is a very popular stop for lunch, pizza or a quick snack.

Lighthouse Bistro (Continental cuisine)

On the way to the Lighthouse, Kong Lung Center, Kilauea Road at Keneke Street, Kilauea; 808-828-0480.

Hours: Lunch 11 a.m. to 2 p.m. Dinner 5:30 to 9:30 p.m. *Sampling:* Soups, salads, hamburgers, sandwiches and tacos for lunch. For dinner, there are appetizers, soups and salads, pastas, seafood and varied entrees. Lunch offerings include fish tacos, falafel taco, hummus wrap, chicken Caesar wrap and pasta marinara ($7 to $9); sandwiches include fresh-fish burger, cheeseburger, teriyaki chicken, garden burger, Italian sausage and French dip ($7 to $9). For dinner, start with appetizers like tossed antipasto (served on wild greens), Jawaiian seared scallops, artichoke piccata, or chicken *satay* with peanut sauce ($10 to $12). There are salads like Caesar (with fish or chicken), mesclun, or garden Romaine lettuce salad ($6 to $9). Soups include seafood bisque and soup of the day ($6). Feast on pastas like fettuccini alfredo, tri-colored tortellini (with sun-dried tomato pesto) or pasta marinara ($11 to $13). Varied entrees (served with soup or salad) include stuffed shrimp in phyllo, filet *au poivre*, mango cherry chicken breast, seafood linguini, rib-eye steak, chicken pesto, veal piccata, cannelloni *quatro formaggio* or Cajun-barbecue shrimp ($17 to $25). Seafood selections include fresh island fish offered in four styles: broiled (and served with tropical salsa), blackened, sauteed or pan-seared with mango sesame sauce ($24 or market price). *Comments:* The dining room is clean, bright and airy with an old plantation-style feel. They feature premium bar drinks and an extensive wine list, featuring a different selection each night. Live entertainment Thursday to Saturday.

Neide's Salsa & Samba (Mexican/Brazilian food)

Hanalei Center, 5161 Kuhio Highway, Hanalei; 808-826-1851.

Hours: 11 a.m. to 9 p.m. *Sampling:* Quesadillas, burritos, enchiladas, tostadas and chimichangas, plus *huevos rancheros*, *carne asada*, steak *ranchero* and fish tacos ($7 to $12). Brazilian dishes ($7 to $14) include vegetarian (pumpkin stuffing) or chicken *panqueca* (crepe), *muqueca* (fresh catch with coconut sauce, shrimp and cilantro), *ensopado* (baked chicken and vegetables, *bife acebolado* (steak and onions) or *bife a cavalo* (steak with an egg on top). *Comments:* The courtyard dining area is shared with Bamboo Bamboo Restaurant so it does get a bit busy with some people traffic and noise. But the food is good and authentic and the Brazilian influence sets it apart from other places.

Paradise Bar & Grill (American food)

Princeville Shopping Center, 4280 Kuhio Highway, Princeville; 808-826-1775.

Hours: 11 a.m. to 11 p.m. *Sampling:* Start with peel-and-eat shrimp, spring rolls, teriyaki chicken skewers, jalapeño poppers, potato skins, soup or salad ($4 to $8). Fish or shrimp and chips, chicken strips or crab cake "nuggets," plus steak, fish, teriyaki chicken sandwiches and burgers ($6 to $9). Dinner entrees (served from 5 p.m.) include rice and baked potato and two steamed veg-

etables: Fresh fish, rib-eye steak, teriyaki chicken, garlic shrimp, sauteed beef tips, crab legs, vegetable platter ($13 to $16) or combine any two ($18). *Comments:* Beer and wine, fruit smoothies and the basic tropicals, plus a featured microbrew draft of the month. There's also a *keiki* menu ($3 to $4).

Pizza Hanalei (Pizza)

Ching Young Village, Kuhio Highway, Hanalei; 808-826-9494.

Hours: 11 a.m. to 9 p.m. *Sampling:* The name says it all. This place is all about pizza. Choose your toppings or combine them from pepperoni, homemade sausage, Canadian bacon, pineapple, bell pepper, meatless sausage, onion, mushroom, jalapeño, fresh garlic, zucchini and more. Small ($10 to $14), medium ($13 to $15) or large ($20 to $28). They also feature special pizzas like veggie, pesto and barbecue chicken special. Slices (served all day—only cheese at night) or side of garlic bread ($3 or less). Spinach lasagna, pizzarito (pizza ingredients rolled up in a pizza shell like a burrito), Caesar or garden salad ($4 to $7). *Comments:* Pizza Hanalei has been around for a long time and has sustained its popularity. The pizzas are all handmade to order. Sauce is homemade as are the crusts: whole wheat with sesame seeds or white. The pesto pizza is especially good.

Princeville Restaurant & Bar (American/Asian food)

Just before Princeville, Princeville Golf Club, 3900 Kuhio Highway; 808-826-5050.

Hours: Breakfast 8 to 11 a.m. Lunch 11 a.m. to 3 p.m. *Sampling:* Breakfast sandwich, *loco moco*, omelets, Belgian waffle, French toast or banana pancakes topped with macadamia nuts or blueberries ($5 to $8). For lunch they have burgers, sandwiches (French dip, Reuben, teriyaki chicken or grilled *ahi*), local-style plates and variety of chef's specials ($5 to $10). Salads are excellent: The Oriental chicken is fresh and crisp, so big it covers the entire plate and the *wasabi*-sesame dressing is fantastic. The seared *ahi* is served on fresh greens and goes great with their papaya-seed dressing. All the portions are really big. They also have a number of heart-healthy selections for spa-goers (yogurt, granola, veggie burgers) along with mineral and oxygen-enhanced water. On Monday night they offer a special menu of authentic Japanese cuisine and sushi—from 5:30 to 8:30 p.m. (dinners $15 to $18). On "Pau Hana Fridays" there is a limited *pupu* and sushi menu with draft beers and karaoke from 6 p.m. The "Sunday Sports Brunch Buffet" (9:30 a.m. to 2 p.m.) offers eggs Benedict, breakfast meats, an omelet station, green salad, chicken and beef entrees, sushi, cheese blintzes, potatoes, rice, fruit, cereal, assorted Danishes and desserts with beverage/beer included ($19, children $9). *Comments:* The restaurant is downstairs in a cool atrium with palm trees, ceiling fans and garden furniture in pink and green, yet the elegant building looks like a mini version of the Princeville Resort with a gorgeous view of the golf course. It's like fun food in a fine atmosphere. You may wonder, what's a casual restaurant doing in a marble-and-glass palace like this? And that's a good question, but then, everything about Princeville is a bit overstated. It's definitely worth checking out on Monday night for the Japanese food.

Tahiti Nui (Continental/International cuisine)

Kuhio Highway, Hanalei; 808-826-6277.

Hours: Breakfast 7 to 11 a.m. Lunch 11 a.m. to 2 p.m. Dinner 5:30 to 10 p.m. *Luau* on Wednesday at 6 p.m. (separate entrance and admission). This nondescript eatery is located in an older wood-frame building right alongside the Kuhio Highway #56 and close to the east edge of town. It still has the '50s-style Polynesian Bar with South Seas bamboo walls and ceiling fans. The lanai out front faces the highway and is still a great place to people watch. While Tahiti Nui has been in place for over 35 years now, the menu has gone through various reincarnations, trying to find its place among the mix of restaurants now found in Hanalei. At present, the menu is a general combination of Continental and mixed international cuisine. Appetizers include stuffed mushrooms, won ton and chicken wings. Dinner entree selections include New York steak, calamari Provencale, chicken teriyaki, pasta primavera, fresh island fish and varied daily specials ($15 to $20). For information on their luau, see section on "Luaus" at the end of this chapter.

Winds of Beamreach (American food)

Pali Ke Kua Resort, 5300 Ka Haku Road, Princeville; 808-826-6143.

Hours: Dinner 5:30 to 9:30 p.m. *Sampling:* Appetizers include sashimi, *poke*, steamed clams, gulf shrimp cocktail and chicken teriyaki ($8 to market price). Entrees are served with soup or salad and fresh baked rolls: smoked Hawaiian pork tenderloin, macadamia-nut or garlic-herb chicken, pasta marinara, pineapple shrimp, beef or chicken stir-fry, fresh island fish, seafood medley, New York steak, filet mignon ($16 to $24). For dessert, there's Tahitian lime pie, macadamia-nut custard pie, chocolate or rum caramel sundae, hula pie and lava flow ($3 to $7). Early-bird specials (5:30 to 6:30 p.m.) offer fresh-fish kabob, chicken teriyaki, beef or chicken stir-fry, hamburger steak or linguini alfredo ($11 and up). *Comments:* Fresh fish steamed Hawaiian style with fresh ginger, garlic and green onion is a specialty. The teriyaki steak is also popular. The desserts, salad dressings and soups are all homemade in this family-owned and -operated eatery. No ocean view here, but they do overlook the pool, so at least there's water, as well as a nice view of the mountains.

Expensive-priced Dining

Bali Hai Restaurant (Hawaiian Regional/Pacific Rim cuisine)

Hanalei Bay Resort, 5380 Honoiki Road, Hanalei; 808-826-6522.

Hours: Breakfast 7 to 11 a.m. Lunch 11:30 a.m. to 2 p.m. Dinner 5:30 to 9:30 p.m. *Sampling:* Unusual island-style items for breakfast like sliced bananas with coconut cream, macadamia-nut waffles or the Taro Patch Breakfast—with two eggs, Portuguese sausage, poi pancakes and taro hash browns ($4 to $13). Lunch offers Kaua'i onion soup, smoked tofu salad, quiche, island *papillotte* (fresh fish steamed in a banana leaf), chicken Hanalei (breaded with peanuts and *panko*), and a good selection of sandwiches: Reuben, seafood salad, turkey club and burgers ($4 to $13). Save your decision-making energy for later and start your dinner with a *pupu* platter of pork ribs, chicken skewers and prawns *katsu* or shrimp cocktail, diced *ahi* "fiesta," blackened seared *ahi*, Bali Hai crab cakes or fresh island sashimi ($12 to $14). Follow with a Caesar or vegetable salad with chicken or shrimp ($7 to $11), or go straight to one of the special fresh-fish preparations: Bali Hai Sunset, pan seared over a crispy crab cake with sweet potatoes; Tropical Breeze, sauteed with papaya and pineapple salsa; Rock Jumping Fisherman, broiled with coconut milk, sweet chile and peanut sauce; Black Pot *Pulehu*, broiled and glazed with sweet lime Oriental sauce; or Kauai Rich Forest, pan seared and served over veggie medley with shiitake mushroom sauce ($25). Other menu entrees include steak Olowalu home-style lamb chops, breast of chicken linguini, pan-seared shrimp and scallops, chicken stir-fry or beef steak Makawao ($16 to $32). Children-sized portions on selected items. If you want to end with a dessert, banana *lumpia*, passion-fruit mousse cake, coconut macadamia tartlette, fresh berries and Grand Marnier cheesecake, tropical fruits in a pastry shell or creme brulee are the choices ($6 to $10). *Comments:* Whatever you order, it comes with a stunning, panoramic view of the Bay and Makana (Bali Hai), which is one of the best things about this restaurant. Reservations suggested.

★ Café Hanalei (Pacific Rim/Japanese food)

Princeville Resort; 808-826-2760.

Hours: Breakfast 6:30 to 11 a.m. Lunch 11 a.m. to 2:30 p.m. Dinner 5:30 to 9:30 p.m. Breakfast buffet until 10:30 a.m. (9:30 Sunday). Sunday brunch 10 a.m. to 2 p.m. (Sushi bar menu: Tuesday to Wednesday and Saturday to Sunday 5 to 9:30 p.m.) *Sampling:* Order an a la carte breakfast ($5 to $13) or sample their buffet featuring crepes, pastries, fruits, omelets, pancakes and breakfast meats ($20.95). For lunch there are salads like stir-fry chicken, Cobb, *soba* and *somen* noodle and fresh tropical fruit, burgers and sandwiches such as a club with avocado, grilled chicken on focaccia, fresh albacore or vegetarian wrap ($12 to $17); Japanese entrees ($15 to $19). Dinner appetizers include Thai curry-and-coconut soup, crab cakes, spinach salad wrap, salmon tartar, *ahi* trio plate, coconut prawns and California rolls ($6 to $16). Entrees feature seafood curry, steak and prawns, *hoison* barbecue lamb chops, Hawaiian bouillabaisse, grilled chicken breast, fresh fish or Japanese *unaiu*: freshwater eel with miso soup, pickled vegetable and green salad ($20 to $34). They also offer a set three-course dinner with your choice of appetizer, entree, dessert and beverage ($45). For dessert try a duo of Kona coffee and ginger creme brulees, chocolate torte, Thai tapioca with jellied berries or *lilikoi* cheesecake ($5 to $8). Sunday brunch offers an elegant buffet for $31.95; $38.50 with champagne. There are salads, fresh seafood, sushi, pastas, hot entrees, carved roast beef, an omelet bar, fruit crepe bar, waffle bar and plenty of desserts. *Keiki* menu available ($3 to $6). *Comments:* Nestled below the opulent lobby at the foot of two elegant staircases, this restaurant has *the* perfect view of Hanalei Bay—with a full-length picture window to gaze and glory in the view unencumbered. The Friday-night seafood buffet (5:30 to 9:30 p.m.) is pricey, but worth the splurge ($45). An entire buffet of hot seafood dishes—from shrimp lasagna to crab and lobster sausage, seafood paella and bouillabaisse, to salmon *en croute* to escargot with curry butter. There are at least a dozen choices before moving to the cold seafood display filled with sushi, sashimi, fresh Dungeness crab, shrimp and mussels and seafood salad selections—from spicy calamari to bay shrimp with cilantro and avocado. Save room for the barbecue, where a chef will cook your fresh fish to order. We had a selection of fresh *ono* or salmon or a skewer of scallops and prawns. Did we mention the heavily laden dessert table? Go for lunch so you can make the most of the incredible view.

CJ's (Steak/seafood)

Princeville Shopping Center, 4280 Kuhio Highway, Princeville; 808-826-6211.

Hours: Lunch Monday to Friday 11:30 a.m. to 2:30 p.m. Dinner nightly 6 to 10 p.m. *Sampling:* Lunch offers a good selection of burgers and salads (including shrimp and/or crab Louie) plus several hot and cold sandwiches (turkey Swiss, teriyaki beef or chicken, barbecue prime rib, tuna melt or shrimp, crab and bacon) plus fries, skins or rings ($4 to $13). Start your dinner with mushrooms sautee, steamed artichoke or shrimp cocktail ($5 to $9).

Dinners include salad bar, bread and rice. Entrees include fresh island fish, shrimp Hanalei, Alaska king crab and Hawaiian spiney lobster, plus prime rib, top sirloin, New York cut or Kansas City–cut Black Angus sirloin, barbecued pork ribs, New Zealand rack of lamb and several steak and seafood combinations ($18 to $29); crab or lobster at market price. There's always mud pie for dessert ($4) or a choice of daily specials. *Comments:* This used to be Chuck's Steak House and while it has a new name and new owners, the menu and kitchen staff have remained essentially the same. They feature choice Midwest corn-fed Black Angus beef and fresh Kaua'i-caught seafood and Kaua'i-grown produce. In addition, there is a children's and seniors' menu with slightly smaller portions of teriyaki chicken, barbecue ribs, hamburger or shrimp Hanalei, including salad bar ($9 to $14). Casual, rustic look with a lot of woodwork trim.

La Cascata (Italian food)

Princeville Resort, 5520 Ka Haku Road, Princeville; 808-826-2761.

Hours: 6 to 10 p.m. *Sampling:* Antipasto beginnings include kabocha squash soup with pistachios, beef carpaccio, crispy calamari, seared *ahi* Nicoise salad, potato-crusted crab cakes, arugula salad with pear, gorgonzola cheese and walnut vinaigrette, espresso-lacquered lamb chop or tomato and eggplant Napoleon ($7 to $14). Seafood linguini, smoked chicken ravioli, rack of lamb, stuffed chicken breast, veal piccata, grilled *ahi* with mushroom risotto, swordfish with couscous and snapper with spinach gnocchi are the entrees prepared with an Italian accent ($23 to $33). The desserts are varied: mango cheesecake, cappuccino creme brulee, Tia Maria parfait, tiramisu, chocolate cake with *lilikoi* puree or macadamia-nut pie ($6 to $8). *Comments:* Dinners begin with focaccia bread squares and olive oil or tomato and garlic sauce to dip them in. A complete three-course dinner is available with your choice of appetizer, main entree, dessert and coffee beverage ($45). They have an extensive selection of wines by the glass and by the bottle. *Keiki* menu available ($3 to $6). The food is good, but you'll pay the price—slightly more forgivable with its extraordinary panoramic view of Hanalei Bay.

(The) Living Room (Afternoon tea/hors d'oeuvres/desserts)

Princeville Resort, 5520 Ka Haku Road, Princeville; 808-826-2760.

Hours: Afternoon Tea 3 to 5 p.m. Hors d'oeuvres 5 to 9:30 p.m. Sushi bar Tuesday to Wednesday and Saturday to Sunday 5 to 9:30 p.m. Desserts 5 to 10:30 p.m. *Sampling:* An exquisite afternoon tea offers tea sandwiches, scones with Devonshire cream and strawberry preserves, English tea bread, miniature pastries, fresh-fruit tarts and, of course, a lovely hot "cuppa" ($18). Prawn cocktail, California rolls, crab cakes, vegetable crudités, *ahi* trio plate, spring rolls, Caesar salad, cheese plate or even a cheeseburger or grilled sirloin are offered as hors d'oeuvres or a light supper ($9 to $20). *Maki* and *nigiri* sushi ($4 to $10), sashimi ($9 to $13). Desserts are from the hotel's Hanalei Café: a duo of Kona coffee and ginger creme brulees, chocolate torte, Thai tapioca with jellied berries, *lilikoi* cheesecake ($6 to $8). *Comments:* Wine and beer, tropical cocktails, brandies and cognacs and a selection of cigars are also available to enjoy with nightly entertainment from 7 to 11 p.m. This is a charming and elegant room where you can take delight in the view across Hanalei Bay to the mountains beyond from the comfortable, intimate groupings of couches and chairs. It does look and feel like a living room, but one belonging to someone a whole lot richer than anyone we know. Some folks partake in the afternoon tea just for the experience.

Postcards (Seafood/gourmet vegetarian)

5075A Kuhio Highway, Hanalei; 808-826-1191.

Hours: 6 to 9 p.m. *Sampling:* Dinners begin with taro fritters, grilled prawns with teriyaki plum sauce, seared *ahi*, Thai summer rolls or "rocket-shaped" salmon strips with sweet chili, ($9 to $11). Caesar (with eggless dressing) or Kaua'i-grown salads ($5 to $8) can be ordered with crostinis or prawns. Entrees feature Thai coconut curry, primavera Postcards, seafood Sorrento and Taj Triangles—peas, carrots and potatoes with Indian spices in phyllo pastry ($15 to $22)—and fresh island fish ($ market price). Desserts include ginger-spice cheesecake, pineapple-upsidedown cake, chocolate raspberry torte, *lilikoi* mousse and macadamia-nut pie ($6), as well as some delectable non-dairy offerings. *Comments:* This is a charming restaurant in a restored plantation-style house, with a warm and cozy feel. The food is primarily vegetarian, along with fish dishes, and they are often creative in their preparation and presentation. However, both the food and the service are inconsistent, which would be a bit more forgivable in a less-pricey place. But perhaps it will be good when you visit and it is one of the better choices in Hanalei—where outstanding food is in short supply.

Sushi Blues & Grill (Hawaiian Regional/Pacific Rim cuisine)

Ching Young Village, Kuhio Highway, Hanalei; 808-826-9701; www.sushiandblues.com.

Hours: Dinner 6 to 9:30 p.m. Closed Monday. *Sampling:* Naturally, appetizers include sashimi ($ market price); sushi rolls ($8 to $13) such as tempura shrimp roll, asparagus roll and tuna roll, rainbow roll, veggie roll, caterpillar roll with avocado and eel, grasshopper roll with eel, shrimp and macadamia nuts. *Pupus* include crab cakes, shrimp and vegetable tempura and garlic sake–sauteed mushrooms, sesame *shoyu poke*, seared *ahi* Caesar, gingered crab *tiki* salad ($5 to $18). Oriental, Caesar, spicy tuna, salmon skin and tempura shrimp salads ($5 to $12). Entrees come with miso soup, sauteed veggies, three-piece California roll, *wasabi* mashed potatoes or rice. Entrees include sizzling seafood stir-fry, coconut shrimp with Thai chili plum sauce, kiwi-teriyaki chicken, linguini and scallops, hibachi shrimp scampi, sweet-and-sour pork ribs and rib-eye steak with shiitake mushroom *au jus* ($19 to $22, fish at market price). Fresh fish is served in several styles: grilled with garlic sake cream; wok-charred with mango barbecue glaze; or sesame-crusted with coconut passion fruit *beurre blanc*. Desserts include green tea or mango ice cream, chocolate mousse cake or mud pie ($4 to $5). *Comments:* This upstairs eatery is one of the latest popular sushi-plus restaurants. You can have your sushi and eat dinner, too. There's a full page of sake (rice wine), with samplers available, several specialty martinis, international beers, plus wines and tropicals. Live music several nights a week—ranging from blues to jazz to Hawaiian and swing band dance music—may be the best reason to dine here since the food isn't particularly outstanding.

Zelo's Beach House (Continental/International cuisine)

Ching Young Village Shopping Center, 5156 Kuhio Highway, Hanalei; 808-826-9700; www.zelosbeachhouse.com.

Hours: Lunch 11 a.m. to 3:30 p.m. Happy Hour 3:30 to 5:30 p.m., with limited lunch and *pupu* menu. Dinner 5:30 to 10 p.m. *Sampling:* Stuffed baked potato, lunch omelet, fish-and-chips, fish tacos or all-you-can-eat spaghetti ($8 to $12); entree-sized chicken or fish Caesar, Mediterranean or Chinese chicken salads ($9 to $17). Philly steak, turkey club or French dip sandwiches; tuna, hummus, Cajun chicken or seafood quesadillas wraps ($7 to $10), plus an extensive variety of beef, chicken or fish burgers ($6 to $9). Dinner entrees feature crab-stuffed fresh fish, Hawaiian chicken, coconut shrimp, prime rib, slow-cooked baby back pork ribs, fresh island fish, seafood fajitas, fish tacos, beer-battered fish-and-chips and mushroom-smothered chicken ($14 to $30, fish is market price). There are a variety of pastas: smoked salmon linguini, sun-dried tomato rigatoni, fettuccini alfredo (or with Cajun chicken, fresh fish or seafood artichoke piccata), cheese ravioli, chicken pesto tortellini, linguini with clams and toasted pine nuts or all-you-can-eat spaghetti ($10 to $22). The fresh fish is prepared several ways: charbroiled with pineapple-papaya salsa, Cajun pan-blackened with garlic aioli sauce, sauteed in lemon piccata sauce or prepared with a Thai satay peanut sauce over crisp rice noodles. If you still have room for dessert, order carrot cake, macadamia-nut cream pie, chocolate suicide cake, or grasshopper pie ($4 to $5). *Comments:* Their logo is the Greek symbol for exuberance—and it shows. The portions are huge and the menu is wide and eclectic so most anyone in your party should find something to eat. The verandah dining area is also popular at this funky beachhouse-style eatery.

Luaus

Gaylord's at Kilohana Plantation ("Reflections of Paradise")

Kilohana Plantation, 2087 Kaumuali'i Highway, Lihu'e; 808-245-9593; e-mail: info@gaylordskauai.com; www.gaylordskauai.com.

Luau guests gather outside on the Kilohana Estate grounds and pick up their mai tais as they enter the historic Carriage House for the luau dinner and show. After dinner, a cloud of mist draws your attention to the stage as your M.C. Mikela introduces the opening number—a medley of 1940s *hapa haole* songs accompanied by hula dancers in colorful cellophane skirts. A group of talented musicians guides you through a travelogue of Polynesian, Hawaiian, Tahitian and Maori dances culminating in a Samoan Fire Knife Dance. The best and most unusual numbers in the show center around fire—literally! In one intriguing bit of choreography, bowls of fire were featured intimately as dancing partners. Then in the poi-ball number (an already mesmerizing display of talent and skill), the excitement was enhanced with twirling poi balls on fire! The costumes were attractive and well-designed, especially the skirts made from a provocative collection of leaves and bark, with color and texture that certainly made for a unique fashion statement. The buffet consisted of *kalua* pig, mahimahi, teriyaki beef, pineapple chicken, fried rice, *imu*-baked sweet potato, fresh vegetables, poi rolls, sweet bread and a variety of salads and fresh fruit. The macaroni-potato salad was quite good, with chunky bits of potato and a well-textured dressing and the strawberry papaya was particularly sweet and tasty. The fried rice was spicy and tasted like it might have had Portuguese sausage in it. The teriyaki beef was good and tender, but the chicken was presented in big bone-in pieces and messy to eat. The pig was good, with poi in tiny little white cups and the taro rolls were a nice touch. Tropical fruit-filled cakes and a potentially interesting *imu*-baked rice pudding were the desserts. After the show, the dancers and

Chief Manu, the fire dancer, greet the guests and pose for photos. The luau is offered Tuesday and Thursday at 6:30 p.m. Rates: adults $50; 55 and over $45. Children 6 to 14 $20; children 5 and under free. They also perform group and wedding luaus as well as special luaus with turkey for holidays.

Hyatt Regency Kaua'i ("Drums of Paradise")

1571 Po'ipu Road, Po'ipu; 808-742-1234; www.hyatt.com.

The luau program includes Hawaiian crafts and displays and a cocktail social, along with a Hawaiian buffet and Polynesian show of music and dance. The buffet begins with fresh sliced tropical fruits; Garden Isle greens with cucumber, tomatoes and carrots topped with croutons, grated cheese and papaya-seed dressing; *lomilomi* salmon; spinach, *pipikaula* and macadamia-nut salad; and poi. Entrees of *hulu huli* chicken; fresh island fish with macadamia-nut butter; *kalua* pig and teriyaki steaks are offered with stir-fry vegetables; Hawaiian sweet potatoes; steamed island rice; rolls and butter. Pineapple cake, bread pudding and *haupia* are the desserts. The luau is held outside in the Grand Gardens every Sunday and Thursday at 6 p.m. Adults $60, juniors (13 to 20 years) $40, children (6 to 12 years) $30 and children under 5 free.

Kaua'i Coconut Beach Resort Luau

Coconut Plantation, Kapa'a; 808-822-3455 ext. 651; www.kcb.com.

This has received the "Kahili" Award from the Hawai'i Visitors Bureau for its "Keep it Hawai'i" program. It features the dances, legends and lore of Kaua'i and includes a show of *kahiko* hula, the traditional ancient style of Hawaiian dance. The show is choreographed by *Kumu hula* Kawaikapuokalani Hewett. The dancers are beautifully dressed and make some very speedy costume changes. They put the pig in the *imu* at 10:45 in the morning, so if it works out with your schedule, stop by the Luau Halau Pavilion and see how it is done. The luau begins at 6 p.m. with the blowing of the conch shell, torchlighting ceremony and a shell lei greeting. Seating is family style, however, and it does get a bit crowded around the tables. *Haupia* and fresh pineapple are on the table when you arrive. The buffet is a pleasant mix, with fried rice, mahimahi, *kalua* pork, baked taro, teriyaki beef and tropical chicken, combined with fresh fruits and assorted salads. The *kalua* pork was wonderful and the teriyaki beef was surprisingly moist and flavorful. Dessert options were coconut cake, *haupia* and a pasty, flavorless rice pudding. Arrive early and wait in line for the better seats. Open bar throughout the evening. They do have smoking and non-smoking sections. *Luau* rates: $55 adults, $50 seniors (55 years), $33 teens 12 to 17 and $23 children 3 to 11. Family Night (currently offered every Monday, Tuesday, Friday and Saturday) allows one child to be admitted free when accompanied by an adult paying full price. Additional children charged at the regular children's rate. *Luau* held nightly; advance reservations required.

Princeville Resort Beachside Luau ("Pa'ina 'O Hanalei")

5520 Ka Haku Road, Princeville; 808-826-9644; www.princeville.com.

Held poolside under a pavilion (and partial tent) with Hanalei Bay as a backdrop, this luau begins with the blowing of the conch shell and participation in a traditional luau ceremony. The food is better than most, with a buffet of *kalua* pig, chicken *laulau*, grilled marinated chicken with macadamia-nut sauce (tender strips of chicken breast in a tasty sauce), mahimahi with lemon seaweed sauce, *soba* noodles with vegetables and ginger and lemongrass marinated beef. There was also rice and Hawaiian (purple) sweet potatoes. Two excellent salads were featured: cold roasted vegetables and a salmon combination that was part grilled and part *lomilomi* style—a delicious blend of textures, flavors and colors! Other Hawaiian-style salads included *tako* with *kim chee*, cucumber and seaweed, bean sprout and watercress, as well as Garden Isle salad greens and fruits. The dessert table featured pineapple upsidedown cake, *haupia*, *imu*-baked rice pudding, large cookies and slices of banana bread attractively dusted with powdered sugar. Beer, wine and mai tais. The entertainment features Ho'ike Nani 'O Ke Kai (A Show of Splendor by the Sea) in a program that offers *kahiko* hula along with a *paniolo* number, The Hawaiian War Chant and ultimately two fire knife dancers, one of whom creates (with slight-of-hand dexterity) a sudden "line of fire" at his feet—very impressive! The luau is priced at $60 for adults, $30 for children 6 to 12 and $48 for seniors (65 years). Held Monday, Wednesday and Thursday at 6 p.m.

Radisson Kaua'i Beach Resort

4331 Kaua'i Beach Drive, Lihu'e; 808-245-1955, 808-246-0111.

The Radisson hosts its "Old Style Island Luau" every Monday evening beginning at 5:30 p.m. Guests are greeted with a shell lei upon entering the luau site next to the pool and receive a complimentary mai tai cocktail. Watch the torchlighting ceremony, followed by the presentation of the traditional roast pig. Guests then indulge in an all-you-can-eat feast of traditional luau fare,

NIGHTLIFE

Bar and lounge hours and live entertainment and music offerings noted in the following section are subject to change at any time without notice.

Hap's Hideaway on Rice Street in Lihu'e is a sports bar.

The bar at **Keoki's Paradise** seems to be a popular hang-out for locals and visitors. Live contemporary Hawaiian music Thursday to Saturday.

Jazz in the **Happy Talk Lounge** at Hanalei Bay Resort is a Sunday-afternoon tradition from 3 to 7 p.m.; another tradition is the Aloha Friday "happy hour" from 4 to 6:30 p.m. with special *pupus* and drinks. Also live entertainment Monday to Saturday from 6:30 to 9:30 p.m.

Hanalei Gourmet has entertainment most nights.

Karaoke at **Rob's Good Times Grill** in Lihu'e; **JR's** in Hanama'ulu; **Tahiti Nui** in Hanalei; and **Jolly Roger** in Kapa'a.

Stevenson's Library at the Hyatt is a quiet retreat with a large aquarium, chess tables and bookcases. Read, browse or just relax and soak up the atmosphere. The library is open from 6 p.m. to 1 a.m., with jazz nightly from 8 to 11 p.m.

Live entertainment, electric and steel-tip dart boards and other games at the **Lizard Lounge and Deli** at Waipouli Town Center and **The Shack** in Kapa'a.

Enjoy Hawaiian music and other nightly entertainment in the **Living Room Lounge** of the North Shore's Princeville Hotel.

Sushi Blues in Hanalei has entertainment several evenings a week—usually jazz on Wednesday, blues on Friday and Saturday and Hawaiian swing music on Sunday.

including roast pig, *huli-huli* chicken, beef stir-fry, grilled mahimahi and a long list of salads, vegetables and exotic desserts. Then sit back, relax and enjoy a full Polynesian Revue by Na Punua O Kaua'i featuring *keiki* hula (children), Tahitian and Hawaiian dance numbers, plus a thrilling Samoan fire knife dance. Adults $55, seniors $52, children ages 6 to 13 $28, age 5 and under free. For show only, adults and seniors $25, children $15.

Smith's Tropical Paradise

174 Wailua Road, Kapa'a; 808 821-6895.

Smith's luau grounds are located on their 30-acre botanical and cultural garden. The luau begins with a traditional *imu* ceremony at 6 p.m., but the gates open an hour early for touring of the grounds, either on your own or with an optional guided tram tour. They have an open bar with live music that opens at 6:15 and closes at 7:30,

Live Hawaiian music at **Joe's on the Green** during their dinners from 5:30 to 8:30.

Jazz at **Hale O'Java** Wednesday nights 6:30 to 9 p.m. (Flamenco guitar Tuesday and Thursday, 4 to 6 p.m.)

Po'ipu Bay Bar & Grill is open Thursday to Saturday evenings with live music (and a *pupu* menu) from 8 p.m.

Live entertainment Thursday to Saturday at the **Lighthouse Bistro** in Kilauea.

Duke's Canoe Club hosts Tropical Friday every week from 4 to 6 p.m. with live music and tropical drink and food specials. Live music in the bar Thursday to Sunday night from 9 to 11:30.

Amelia's at the Princeville Airport has TV with satellite sports, plus music and dancing Friday to Sunday until 2 a.m.

JJ's Broiler has live music Thursday to Sunday at their Anchor Cove location.

Lihu'e Cafe Lounge has dancing on Friday and Saturday, karaoke on Tuesday and Thursday and free pool on Monday and Wednesday.

Local-style music nightly at the **Kaua'i Coconut Beach Resort** and **Kauai Hula Girl** in Coconut MarketPlace.

Whalers Brewpub offers a variety of live music: reggae, rock and more from both local and mainland bands.

serving beer, wine and mai tais. Dinner is served at 6:30—an all-you-can-eat buffet of Garden Isle greens, poi, jello, three-bean, *nimasu* and macaroni salads, Asian fried-rice, *lomilomi* salmon, fresh fruits, *kalua* pig, teriyaki beef, adobo chicken, sweet and sour mahimahi, hot vegetables, snowflake and sweet potatoes, hot vegetables and *haupia*, coconut cake and rice pudding for dessert. At 8 p.m. Madame Pele introduces the luau show with a fiery welcome in the garden's covered lagoon amphitheater. The "Golden People of Hawaii" is an international pageant depicting dances and songs from the South Pacific. Featured are Tahiti, China, Japan, the Philippines, New Zealand and Samoa, in addition to, of course, Hawaii. The luau is held Monday, Wednesday and Friday at a cost of $54 for adults, $29 for ages 3 to 12 years and $20 for children 3 to 6 years. The luau show alone is $16 adult/$9 child. Reservations are required.

Tahiti Nui Luau

Kuhio Highway, Hanalei; 808-826-6277

This North Shore luau is offered twice a week on Wednesday and Sunday at 6 p.m. Held indoors in the back of the Tahiti Nui restaurant, it is a narrow room with long tables and a stage at the end. This is a family-style luau and there are always lots of kids. The food is authentic—no glitz or glamour—casually displayed in serving trays and Tupperware-like dishes; it's as if you went to someone's home for a luau dinner and the guests took turns getting up to perform. This is a small luau room (as luaus go), with the advantage that you have a good view of the stage from most any table and they are not so squeezed together that it is difficult to get in and out of your seat. (Important when you want to hit that buffet line!) A more intimate and local luau with a friendly atmosphere. They cook the pig in an *imu* out in back, not a very attractive pit, but then it is authentic *imu* cooking. The menu is an all-you-can-eat Tahitian and Hawaiian buffet with mai tais. Buffet items feature *kalua* pig, fresh fish, teriyaki chicken, *poisson cru*, chicken with coconut milk, fish or chicken *laulau*, sweet potatoes, *poi*, *lomilomi* salmon, green salad, potato/macaroni salad, fresh fruit slices, garlic bread, *haupia* and chocolate cake. *Luau* rates include free mai tai cocktails: $54 adults; $32 teens (12 to 17), $22 children (3 to 11), with one child admitted free when accompanied by a full paying adult.

CHAPTER 5

Beaches

Kaua'i, being the oldest of the major Hawaiian islands, has beaches that have been worn with time. Because of this, you will not find exotic dark-sand beaches, but rather those of golden sand that has been gently polished over millions of years. If you are the active beachgoer who likes to snorkel or swim, or the type that prefers to find a quiet shady beachfront spot, Kaua'i offers a diverse selection.

Not every beach on Kaua'i has a full description, but this section focuses on those that are especially noteworthy or have amenities. Wherever possible, the Hawaiian names for the beaches have been used, while including the local names as an aside. For more information on Kaua'i's beaches, the ultimate book is *Beaches of Kaua'i and Ni'ihau* by John R.K. Clark, published by University of Hawai'i Press. This reference will provide you with everything you want to know, and perhaps a little bit more.

"It has been calculated that 44 percent of its coastline is fringed by fine white-sand beaches, double the percentage of any other Hawaiian Island" (*Ten Years, 250 Islands* by Ron Hall). With ratings of average, outstanding and world-class, Ron Hall has rated Kaua'i as world-class in sandy beaches, coastal spectacle and island scenery. Most beaches are accessible by foot, three are accessible by water only, and six are by water or by trail. Kaua'i has more linear miles of sandy shoreline than any of the other major islands—approximately 113 miles.

The beaches of Kaua'i offer many opportunities to view rare marine life and large sea birds. You may even be lucky enough to see a critically endangered Hawaiian monk seal basking on the beach. This is normal behavior so don't try to chase them back in the water or wet them down. They are shy creatures, so be quiet and keep a good distance. They can also bite and are very protective of their pups, so show a little respect and never do anything dumb, like try to perch your child atop one for a picture. (Yes, people have tried!) Like turtles, dolphins and whales, seals are protected by federal law and it is illegal to approach any of these marine animals or do *anything* that causes them to change their behavior. So don't get too close and please, resist the urge to swim with the dolphins and touch the turtles. These animals are in near-shore waters because they are resting and feeding, and interactions with humans disrupt that behavior, no matter how much you might think they might want to hang out with you! Similarly, feeding the fish is also not advised. Remember, these are all wild creatures, so leave them in peace.

Besides having a good population of marine life, Kaua'i's beaches are an essential source of recreation and food for local families. Locals often use the beaches in a manner that is different than a visitor, and you can avoid conflict and ill feelings by showing respect. So here are some dos and don'ts—if you see someone fishing, don't enter the water in that area and never walk between the ocean and a fisherman preparing to cast a throw net; remember to keep a space bubble if you can—in other words, don't throw down your towel next to someone if there's plenty of space elsewhere, as there generally is.

As with all of the Hawaiian islands, the beaches of Kaua'i are publicly owned and most have right-of-way access; however, the access is sometimes tricky to find and parking may be a problem. Please note: public access to some Kaua'i beaches is on or through private property and the state of Hawai'i exempts landowners from liability. In other words, you may use their land, but they are *not* responsible—*you* are! Parking areas are provided at most developed beaches, but they are often small.

In any parking lot (but even to a greater degree in the undeveloped areas where you will have to wedge your vehicle along the roadside), it is vital that you leave nothing of importance in your car as the occurrence of theft, especially at some of the more remote locations, is very high.

For recreation, especially for families, Kaua'i has many wonderful beaches. Foremost among them is Po'ipu Beach on the South Shore, which was named as the top beach in Hawai'i for kids by readers of *Hawaii Magazine*, and best family beach by the Travel Channel in 2002. It also ranked number one in the entire U.S. for 2001 by the Dr. Beach National Beach Ratings, conducted by Dr. Stephen Leatherman of Florida International University. There is a natural kiddie wading pool at Po'ipu Beach Park that is ideal for toddlers and very young swimmers. The handy nearby access to bathrooms can be a plus for the traveling family, too!

To the west of Po'ipu Beach is a small protected cove known as Baby Beach. This can be accessed from Spouting Horn Road to Ho'ome Road. Good swimming locations for the younger set also are found at Lydgate Beach Park and at Salt Pond Beach Park. At both locations you'll find an ocean pool made from boulders. Kids will love discovering a variety of sea creatures found in the tidepools here and at 'Anini Beach.

At the larger, developed beaches, a variety of facilities are provided. Many have convenient rinse-off showers, drinking water, restrooms and picnic areas. A few have children's play or swim areas. Some have lifeguards on duty. The beaches near the major resorts often have rental equipment available for snorkeling, sailing and boogie boarding and some even rent underwater cameras. These beaches are generally clean and well maintained. (See "Camping" for more information about beach facilities.)

In the winter, Kaua'i's most gentle beaches are found on the southern coastline, while in summer the North Shore waters are often lakelike. However, wind and storms can affect the condition of beaches all around the island at any time of year. Seasonally, there is also a great change in the island's beaches. While any beach you visit may be calm and idyllic in the summer, there may be high and treacherous surf during the winter months. Unlike Maui, whose southern and western beaches form part of a protected area sheltered by the islands of Kahoolawe and Lana'i, Kaua'i has beaches that are more exposed.

The North Shore of Kaua'i often has higher surf during the months of September through May. On the east coast, high surf from the east and north is also more frequent during the same months. The South Shore receives high surf during the summer months. Lydgate and Salt Pond beaches have two sea pools that are protected from the surf and ideal for young children. You'll find lifeguards on duty at Lydgate Beach, Po'ipu Beach, Salt Pond Park, Ke'e, Kekaha, Hanalei Pavilion, Kealia and Wailua.

Seasonal conditions can also affect the beach itself. Sand is eroded away from some beaches during winter to be re-deposited during the spring and summer.

Beach Precautions

WATER SAFETY

Here are some basic water safety tips and terms. Most of the north and west shore beaches of Kaua'i do not have the coral reefs or other barriers that are found on the south and eastern shores. These wide expansive beaches pose greater risks for swimmers, with their strong currents and dangerous shorebreaks. You may see swimmers or surfers at some of the beaches where we recommend that you enjoy the view and stay out of the water. Keep in mind that just because there is someone else in the water, it doesn't mean it's safe. Some of these surfers are experts in Hawaiian surf, and we advise that you do not take undue risks. Others might be visitors just like you, but not as well informed.

A **shorebreak** is when the waves break directly on the beach. Small shorebreaks may not be a problem, but waves that are more than a foot or two high may create undertows and hazardous conditions. Most drownings on Kaua'i happen with a shorebreak. Conditions are generally worse in the winter months. Even venturing too close to a shorebreak could be hazardous, as standing on the beachfront you may encounter a stronger, higher wave that could catch you off guard and sweep you into the water.

A **rip current** can often be seen from the shore. They are fast-moving river-like currents that sometimes can be seen carrying sand or sediment. A rip current can pull an unsuspecting swimmer quickly out to sea, and swimming against a strong rip current may be impossible. Unfortunately, these currents are another leading cause of drownings in Kaua'i. They are common in reef areas that have open channels to the sea.

Undertows happen when a rip current runs into incoming surf. This accounts for the feeling that you are being pulled down. They are more common on beaches that have steep slopes.

We don't want to be alarmists, but we'd prefer to report the beaches conservatively. Always, always use good judgment.

Kona winds generated by southern-hemisphere storms cause southerly swells that affect Po'ipu and the southern coastline, while creating offshore conditions that make for glassy seas on the north and east sides.

Northerly swells caused by winter storms northeast of the island are fairly common, but can cause large surf, particularly on the northern and eastern beaches in winter.

Using the historical drowning rates as a measure, the five most dangerous beaches on Kaua'i are Hanakapiai, Lumahai, Wailua, Hanalei and Waipouli. Other beaches with high incidents of drownings are Polihale, Anini, Kalalau, Larsen's and Kealia. These beaches share such cautionary features as a lack of a protective reef, a large channel in a reef where a strong current forms during high surf, and a river emptying into the sea. Most of them are also fairly remote and response times are prolonged.

Please, treat Kaua'i's wild beaches with respect. Since many have no restroom facilities, try to use the bathroom somewhere else before you stop. If you must relieve yourself, go well away from the waterline and bury your deposit and any tissue you used. Also, pack out your trash and bring out a little bit that someone else left, too.

TIPS

Here are some additional beach safety and etiquette tips:

- "Never turn your back to the sea" is an old Hawaiian saying. Don't be caught off-guard; waves come in sets, with spells of calm in between.
- Use the buddy system, never swim or snorkel alone.
- If you are unsure of your abilities, use flotation devices attached to your body, such as a life vest or inflatable vest. Never rely on an air mattress or similar device from which you may become separated.
- Study the ocean before you enter; look for rocks, shorebreak and rip currents.
- Duck or dive beneath breaking waves before they reach you.
- Never swim against a strong current, swim across it.
- Know your limits.
- Small children should be allowed to play near or in the surf *only* with close supervision and should wear flotation devices. And even then, only under extremely calm conditions. The protected pools at Lydgate and Salt Pond are safe alternatives.
- When exploring tidepools or reefs, always wear protective footwear and keep an eye on the ocean. Also, protect your hands.
- When swimming around coral, be careful where you put your hands and feet. Urchin stings can be painful and coral cuts can be dangerous. You can also damage or injure the coral. Yes! Coral is living and it grows very slowly so don't knock into it or stand on it while snorkeling.
- Respect the yellow and red flag warnings when placed on the developed beaches. They are there to advise you of unsafe conditions.
- Avoid swimming in the mouths of rivers or streams or in any areas of murky water.
- Always use fins when boogie boarding.
- Don't feed the fish.
- Keep your distance from pole and net fishermen.
- Remember, it's illegal to do *anything* that causes a dolphin, monk seal, turtle or whale to change its behavior, so stay away from them.

Surface **water temperature** varies little with a mean temperature of 73 degrees Fahrenheit in January and 80.2 degrees in August. Minimum and maximum range from 68 to 84 degrees. This is an

OCEAN MENACES

Kaua'i's ocean playgrounds are among the most benign in the world. There are, however, a few ocean creatures that you should be aware of. We will attempt to include some basic first-aid tips should you encounter one of these. Since some people might have a resulting allergic reaction, we suggest you contact a local physician or medical center should you have an unplanned encounter with one of them.

Portuguese Man-of-War are sea animals seen only rarely but caution is in order. It's one of those ocean critters to be avoided. These very small creatures are related to the jellyfish and are adrift in the ocean via the currents and the wind. These unique sea creatures are sometimes blown on shore by unusual winds and can cover the beach with their glistening crystal orbs filled with deep blue filament. If they are on the beach, treat them as if they were still in the water—stay away. On rare occasions they will be seen drifting in the ocean during a snorkeling cruise or sea excursion and the cruiseboat staff may change snorkeling destinations if this is the case. The animal has long filaments that can cause painful stings. If you are stung, rinse the affected area with sea water or fresh water to remove any tentacles. If you need to pick out the tentacles, do not use your bare fingers; use gloves, a towel or whatever is available to protect yourself. Vinegar, isopropyl alcohol and human urine, once considered effective remedies, are no longer recommended treatments.

In the water, avoid touching **sea urchins**: the pricking by one of the spines can be painful. And if you do encounter one, be sure the entire spine has been removed. Soaking the wound in vinegar helps to dissolve the spine; for pain, soak the puncture in hot water for 30 to 90 minutes.

Coral is made up of many tiny living organisms. Coral cuts require thorough disinfecting and can take a long time to heal. If an inflamed wound's redness begins to spread, it suggests an infection and requires medical attention. So stay off the coral—and don't touch it!

almost ideal temperature (refreshing, but not cold) for swimming and you'll find most resort pools cooler than the ocean. Of course, if it's windy, it may feel chilly when you get out of the water.

Note: Ulysses Press, Paradise Publications and the authors of this guide have endeavored to provide current and accurate information

Cone shells look harmless enough, are conical and come in colors of brown or black. The snails that inhabit these shells have a defense mechanism that they use to protect themselves—and to kill their prey. Their stinger does have venom so it is suggested that you just enjoy looking at them. Cleaning the wound and soaking it in hot water for 30 to 90 minutes will provide relief if you're stung.

Eels live among the coral and are generally not aggressive. You may have heard of divers who have "trained" an eel to come out, greet them and then take some food from their hands. We don't recommend you try to make an eel your pal. While usually non-aggressive, their jaws are extremely powerful and their teeth are sharp. And as divers know, sea animals could mistake any approach or movement as an aggressive or provoking act. Just keep a comfortable distance—for you and the eel. Also, should you poke around with your hands in the coral, they might inadvertently think your finger is food. This is another reason you shouldn't handle the coral. Eels are generally not out of their homes during the day, but a close examination of the coral might reveal a head of one of these fellows sticking out and watching you! At night during low tide at beaches with a protective reef, you might try taking a flashlight and scanning the water. A chance look at one of these enormous creatures out searching for its dinner is most impressive.

Sharks? Yes, there are many varied types of sharks. However, there are more shark attacks off the Oregon coastline than in Hawai'i. In the many years of snorkeling and diving, we have only seen one small reef shark, and it was happy to get out of our way. If you should see one, don't move quickly, but rather swim slowly away while you keep an eye on it. Avoid swimming in murky waters near river mouths after it rains. Also, stay out of the water if you have open cuts and remember, urine has blood that might attract sharks, so don't pee in the water in that area. *Kaua'i Guide to Beaches* is an excellent resource for beach exploration. It's published by Magic Fishes Press and can be ordered direct: P.O. Box 3243, Lihu'e, HI 96766.

on Kaua'i's beautiful beaches. However, remember that nature is unpredictable and weather, beach and current conditions can change. Enjoy your day at the beach, but utilize good judgment. Ulysses Press, Paradise Publications and the authors of this guide cannot be held responsible for accidents or injuries incurred.

Best Bets

The following are some of Kaua'i's best beaches. But beach-goers should keep in mind that daily and seasonal climate, weather and ocean conditions affect the quality of the beach conditions and the water. Also, it may be useful to keep in mind that in general, the South Shore has better beach conditions in the winter and the North Shore has better conditions in the summer. That said, here's our list:

Snorkeling *Beginners*: Po'ipu Beach; Lydgate Beach; *intermediate*: Makua Beach (Tunnels)

Windsurfing *Beginners*: 'Anini Beach Park; *intermediate*: Maha'u-lepu Beach

Best for Children Lydgate Beach; Kapa'a Beach Park; Salt Pond Park; Po'ipu Beach

Swimming Po'ipu Beach; Hanalei Bay (summer only); Salt Pond Park

Sunsets Ke'e Beach; Kekaha Beach; Salt Pond Park

Sunrises Lydgate Beach; Maha'ulepu Beach

Tidepools Kapa'a Beach Park

Beachcombing Nukole (Nukoli'i) Beach; Maha'ulepu Beach; Kapa'a Beach Park

Using This Chapter

The following listings refer to a variety of beaches and beach parks. However, some are not true beaches. For example, Spouting Horn is a beautiful beach location, but only for viewing and not good for aquatic activities.

The **pail and shovel** icon indicates beaches that are recommended for family activities. They are more protected and most likely have lifeguards on duty.

East Shore and Central Coast Area

Kalapaki Beach

This site is of historic significance in surfing history as the location where ancient Hawaiians practiced the skill of bodysurfing. The wave conditions continue to attract surfers and bodysurfers, and the gentle off-shore slope makes it a good option for swimmers during calm seas. During periods of high surf, surfers come out in droves. However, we advise that you leave the high surf to the experienced surfers.

William Harrison Rice and Mary Sophia Rice arrived on Kaua'i as missionaries in 1841. Their son, William Hyde Rice, purchased the land around this beach from Princess Ruth Ke'elikolani and built his home here. Several lodging facilities have been established on this wonderful beachfront. At one time the Westin Kaua'i Resort, boasting an elaborate architectural style that most islanders found garish, was built. In 1992, Hurricane Iniki performed a great favor by virtually destroying the resort, which sat empty for several years. Despite the proximity of Lihu'e and the Marriott Resort, this beach is not usually crowded. Better protected than some, except during east swells, you should heed caution at all times.

Recommended for: Swimming, windsurfing and bodyboarding during low surf conditions.

Facilities: Barbecue grills, restrooms, rinse-off showers.

Access: Beach access is at the left side of the bay or through the Nawiliwili Park public access on the right.

Parking: Public parking area at the west end next to the stream that enters this bay.

Ninini Beach

There are two beaches located here. Both can be affected by high surf and Kona storms. Snorkeling at the larger sandy stretch can be good when the ocean is calm. During high surf enjoy watching the bodysurfers. Sometimes it is referred to as Running Waters Beach because of the irrigation runoff that once occurred here. Nearby you'll see the Nawiliwili Light Station located at the point. This area is popular with shore fishermen catching reef fish.

Recommended for: Snorkeling on rare calm days (only for the very experienced).

Facilities: None.

Access: Turn at Ahukini Road and follow the dirt road 2.6 miles to Ninini Point.

Parking: No official parking.

Hanama'ulu Beach Park

A lovely location for a picnic in this 6.5-acre park, however, the bay waters are murky. The *Beaches of Kaua'i* by John Clark noted that "Hanama'ulu Stream crosses the southern end of the beach, discharging its silt-laden waters into the bay." He also added that "mullet and sharks, particularly juvenile hammerheads, are also found in the bay."

Recommended for: Picnics.

Facilities: Tables, toilets, pavilion, barbecue and showers.

Access: Located .5 mile from Hanama'ulu town.

Parking: Plenty available.

Camping: With county permit.

Text continued on page 290.

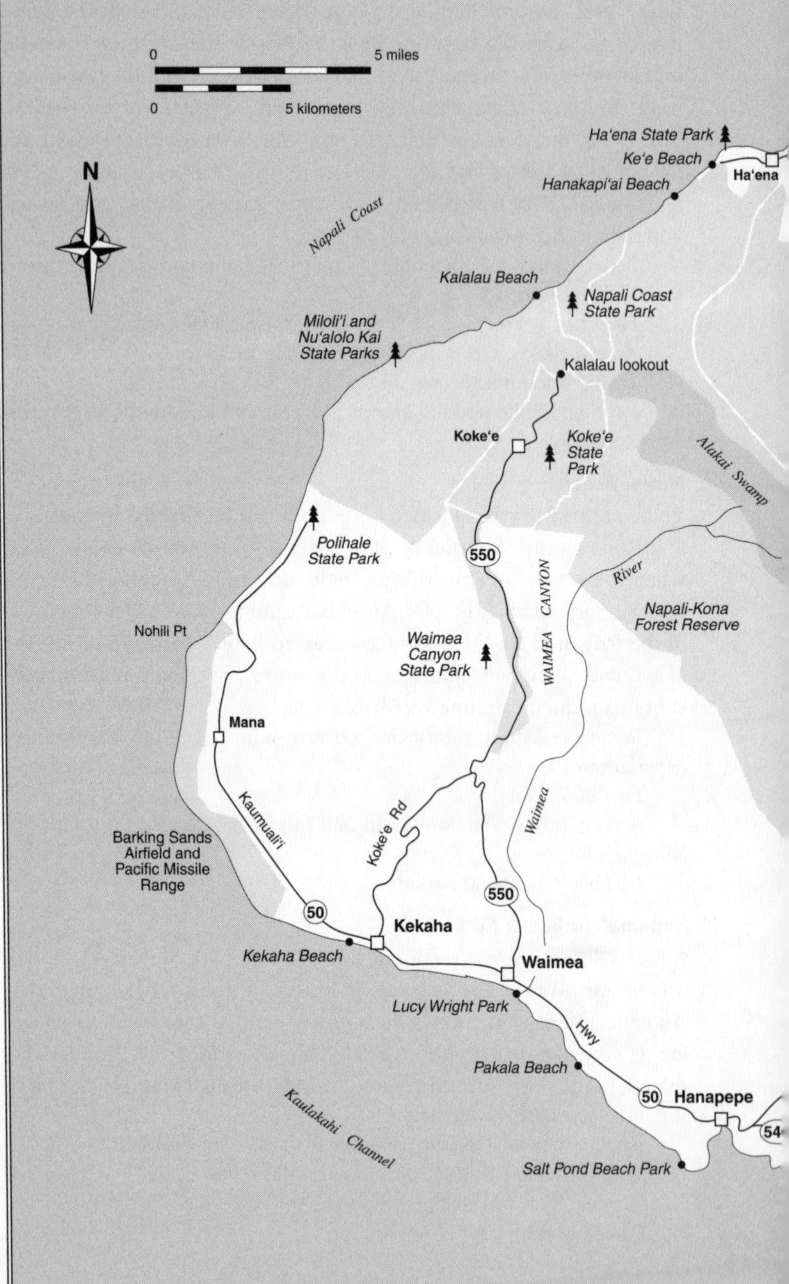
Kaua'i Beaches
0
5 miles
0
5 kilometers
N
Ha'ena State Park
Ke'e Beach
Ha'ena
Hanakapi'ai Beach
Napali Coast
Kalalau Beach
Napali Coast State Park
Miloli'i and Nu'alolo Kai State Parks
Kalalau lookout
Koke'e
Koke'e State Park
Alakai Swamp
Polihale State Park
550
River
WAIMEA CANYON
Napali-Kona Forest Reserve
Nohili Pt
Waimea Canyon State Park
Mana
Kaumuali'i
Koke'e Rd
Waimea
Barking Sands Airfield and Pacific Missile Range
550
50
Kekaha
Kekaha Beach
Waimea
Lucy Wright Park
Hwy
Pakala Beach
50
Hanapepe
Kaulakahi Channel
Salt Pond Beach Park

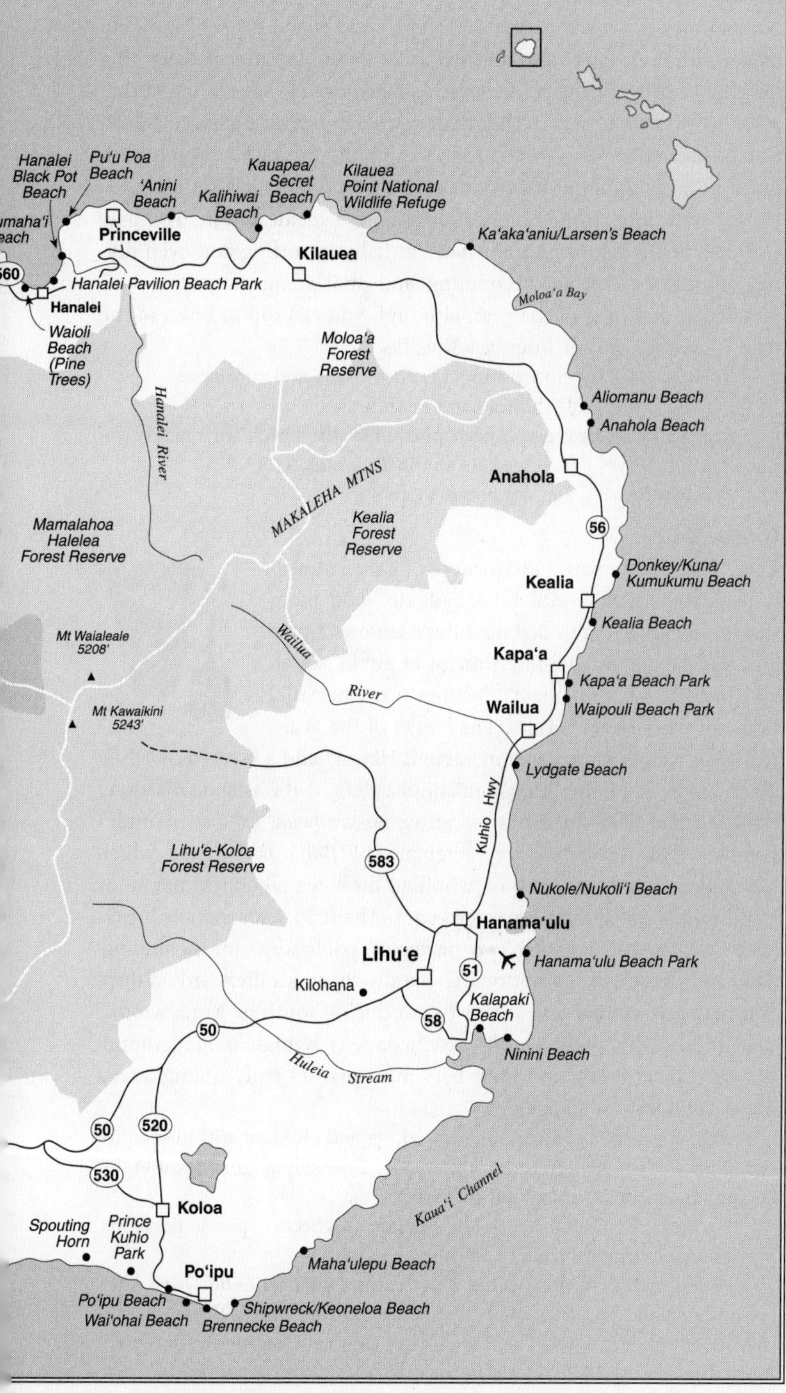
Hanalei Black Pot Beach
Pu'u Poa Beach
'Anini Beach
Kalihiwai Beach
Kauapea/ Secret Beach
Kilauea Point National Wildlife Refuge
Princeville
Kilauea
Ka'aka'aniu/Larsen's Beach
560
Hanalei Pavilion Beach Park
Hanalei
Waioli Beach (Pine Trees)
Moloa'a Bay
Moloa'a Forest Reserve
Hanalei River
Aliomanu Beach
Anahola Beach
Anahola
MAKALEHA MTNS
Kealia Forest Reserve
56
Mamalahoa Halelea Forest Reserve
Donkey/Kuna/ Kumukumu Beach
Kealia
Kealia Beach
Mt Waialeale 5208'
Wailua River
Kapa'a
Kapa'a Beach Park
Wailua
Waipouli Beach Park
Mt Kawaikini 5243'
Lydgate Beach
Kuhio Hwy
Lihu'e-Koloa Forest Reserve
583
Nukole/Nukoli'i Beach
Hanama'ulu
Lihu'e
Hanama'ulu Beach Park
51
Kilohana
Kalapaki Beach
58
50
Ninini Beach
Huleia Stream
50
520
530
Koloa
Kaua'i Channel
Spouting Horn
Prince Kuhio Park
Maha'ulepu Beach
Po'ipu
Po'ipu Beach
Shipwreck/Keoneloa Beach
Wai'ohai Beach
Brennecke Beach

Nukole/Nukoli'i Beach

Nukole means "beach of the kole fish," and is the proper Hawaiian name, although it is now referred to as Nukoli'i, after a dairy that once had cattle grazing in the area. Archaeological events suggest that prior to that there was a Hawaiian settlement. The Radisson Kaua'i Beach, located on this beachfront, maintains the public beach park pavilion and adjoining bathrooms. This beach stretches for approximately two miles from Hanama'ulu Bay to Lydgate Beach. You may see local residents trying their hand at fishing, surfing and even diving on this beachfront. Swimming and snorkeling are not recommended at any time of the year, although you can dip in holes in the reef. It's wonderful for long beach walks.

Recommended for: Sunbathing, beachcombing and sunrises.

Facilities: Rinse-off showers and restrooms.

Access: To reach the southern portion of the beach turn *mauka* on Kaua'i Beach Drive, which leads to the Radisson Hotel.

Parking: Parking area for about 15 cars.

Lydgate Beach

This 40-acre state park (administered by the county) is dedicated to Reverend John Lydgate, who more than a century ago founded the Lihu'e Union Church and was a force in the establishment of public parks and historic sites on Kaua'i. Wailua was once the home of the island's royalty. The banks of the Wailua River were a sacred area in ancient Hawai'i and a favored dwelling place reserved for the kings and high chiefs of the island. All along the river and near the mouth is an extensive *heiau* (ancient temple) complex. At Lydgate Park are the remains of *Hikina'akala Heiau*, which was a place of refuge for those who had broken a taboo. Do not sit or stand on the walls; these are sacred sites. About 25 years ago the breakwater was added, creating two protected pools ideal for swimming. The pools have a sandy bottom. Generally there is a lifeguard on duty. You may see windsurfers at this beach during south or Kona winds.

Another highlight of this beach park is **Kamalani Playground**, designed by children and built by volunteers. It's truly unique and a joy for children of all ages.

Recommended for: Swimming for adults and children within the protected pools. Not advised beyond the pools. Snorkeling: good location for beginning snorkelers to try out their skills.

Facilities: Restrooms, rinse-off showers, barbecues, picnic pavilions, playground. Lifeguard usually on duty.

Access: South of the Wailua River turn *mauka* on Leho Drive, then continue *mauka* on Nalu Road. If you are heading north, the turn-off is easy to spot; it is just past the Wailua Golf Course. Heading south there is no marked entrance; if you get to the golf course, you've missed it.

Parking: Large parking area.

Camping: Permits available from the county.

Wailua Beach

This is a nice half-mile crescent stretch of beach on the north side of Wailua River. At the north end of the beach are several condos and hotels. *The Beaches of Kaua'i* by John R.K. Clark noted that the surfers' shorebreak here is Horners, named after Albert Horner, a pineapple industry pioneer. His mansion was built on this beachfront in 1929 and was later moved to an inland location in Wailua. Dangerous currents much of the year make this beach advisable only for walking and sunning. There are numerous resorts located along here, and Al & Don's Restaurant in the Kaua'i Sands has a nice oceanview location. There is one small protected pool at Alakukui Point, which during calm surf is safe for wading. Also at Alakukui Point are some remnants of an old *heiau*.

Recommended for: Beachcombing, walking, sunning.

Facilities: Phones, lifeguard.

Access: Off Kuhio Highway north of the Wailua River to Kapa'a.

Parking: Parking area near Wailua Bridge and limited parking on Papaloa Road.

Waipouli Beach Park

This narrow strip of beach runs from the Coconut Plantation Resort to the Waika'ea Canal in Kapa'a. The Kaua'i Coconut Beach Resort is located on this beachfront. While the pedestrian trail among the ironwood trees above the shoreline is popular for joggers or walkers, the beachfront is covered by beach rock, and very strong offshore currents make it unsafe for swimming year-round. Some marginal swimming might be pursued at the southern end of the beach, but even then, only under very calm surf conditions. A popular fishing location.

Recommended for: Swimming is marginal in the summer months.

Facilities: Only for hotel guests.

Access: Off the pedestrian path behind the Coconut MarketPlace.

Parking: Coconut MarketPlace—some designated beach parking stalls near the Sheraton Coconut Beach.

Kapa'a Beach Park

With its location nearer to civilization, and the adjoining canal used as a boat launch, you are likely to find this beach more populated than some. It also has a protected swimming area known as Baby Beach great for very small children. Kapa'a Beach Park has encountered severe shoreline erosion over the last 30 years. You'll note that some human measures have been made to stop the erosion, such as jetties at the mouth of the canal. In the evening you might want to stroll down the beach (on a moonlit night) and perhaps you'll be lucky enough to see fishermen practicing *lamalama* (torch fishing).

Recommended for: A few areas of the beach offer adequate swimming when the surf is calm, but not especially recommended. Shore fishing is popular here. Great sunrises!

Facilities: Restrooms, rinse-off showers, public swimming pool.

Access: Turn toward the ocean off Kuhio Highway at Niu Street, near the Kapa'a ballpark.

Parking: Parking area.

Kealia Beach

Once the town of Kealia was a thriving plantation town, complete with a train depot, and at the nearby landing an interisland steamer would stop for passengers. Little is left today except a post office, store and, of course, a big and beautiful beach. The word *kealia* means "salt encrusted." (Interesting to note that almost every island in Hawai'i has a beach named Kealia.) Although you'll see many surfers and boogie boarders in the water, strong currents make it generally unsafe for water activities; it's particularly dangerous during high surf.

Recommended for: Walking, sunbathing, swimming in calm times.

Facilities: Lifeguard.

Access: Highway 56 at mile-marker 10.

Parking: Parking in designated lots along the roadside.

Kuna Beach (Donkey Beach or Kumukumu Beach)

Apparently before the advent of machinery, mules were used to haul cane seed to the fields. Some say that there were only mules and no donkeys, but whatever the case, the name Donkey Beach stuck. Located 1.5 miles from Kealia Beach, Donkey Beach has a very pastoral setting, although the ongoing development of the exclusive Kealia Kai subdivision on the bluffs above may change all that. It takes about 15 minutes to walk to the beach from the highway, and nearly half an hour to reach it along the shoreline trail from Kealia. Its inaccessibility has made this beach a popular site for nude sunbathing (which is illegal in Hawai'i), so if you don't want to see that, don't go here.

Recommended for: Sunbathing.

Facilities: None.

Access: Follow the trail from the parking lot off Kuhio Highway.

Parking: A lot off the highway at mile-marker 11, north of Kealia Kai.

Anahola Beach and Aliomanu Beach

This is a popular park for local residents. There is an outside fringing reef and pockets of sand that create pools that are pleasant for swimming and even safe enough for kids. The Anahola River is found at the south end of the beach, while Aliomanu Beach is at the north side of Anahola beach. Both are located on Anahola Bay. It is widely used by fishermen and is a nice walking beach.

Recommended for: Fishing, picnics, swimming (watch for currents).

Facilities: Picnic tables, restrooms, rinse-off showers, camping.

Access: Highway 56, look for Anahola Road.

Parking: Parking lot.

Camping: With county permit.

South and West Shore Areas

Maha'ulepu Beach

This is a beautiful and rugged coastline and beach that still has a wilderness feel. It was here that King Kamehameha I made his attempt to conquer the island of Kaua'i in 1796. Unfortunately, a storm forced a retreat, but the advance forces of Kamehameha's troops arrived on the island, unaware of the order to retreat, and were quickly killed. This is also the beach site where George C. Scott portrayed Ernest Hemingway in the movie *Islands in the Stream*. Maha'ulepu Beach is actually a collection of smaller beaches that offer an assortment of aquatic activities, including fishing, surfing, bodyboarding, bodysurfing, kayaking, windsurfing, snorkeling and swimming.

The three areas along this beachfront are *Gillin's Beach*, *Kawailoa Bay* and *Ha'ula Beach*. Gillin's was named for the supervisor of Grove Farm Company, Elbert Gillin, who arrived in the islands in 1912. He relocated to Kaua'i in 1925 and built his home at this beach. He was the supervisor of the Ha'upu Range Tunnel. Following two hurricanes, all that remained was Gillin's chimney, but the house has since been rebuilt. Several feet below this beach are the **Rainbow Petroglyphs**. Discovered in 1980 when a severe storm took out as much as six feet of beachfront, the petrogylphs were suddenly exposed. Working in reverse, the sea soon chose to cover them up once again. Gillin's may be good for the experienced snorkeler during calm surf. Maha'ulepu is the south shore's most dangerous beach, and currents at Kawailoa Bay make it unsafe for swimming or snorkeling.

Recommended for: Walking, sunbathing, observing marine life.

Facilities: None. Be sure to bring your own water.

Access: Access to these beaches is over private land owned by the Grove Farm Company and is open during daylight hours only—7 a.m. to 6 p.m. The gate is locked at night. Since access could be denied at any time, it is requested that you take all your litter with you and be respectful of the right to use these gorgeous beaches of Kaua'i. Take the dirt road at the end of Po'ipu Road and turn right onto the cane road. To reach Kawailoa Bay take the dirt road at the end of Po'ipu Road and turn right onto the cane road: Gillins and Kawailoa Bay can both be reached from this road. To reach Ha'ula Beach you may park on the east side of Pa'o'o Point and walk to the shore by trail.

Parking: On the side of the dirt road.

Camping: None.

Keoneloa Beach (Shipwreck Beach)

This sandy shore fronts the Hyatt Regency. Keoneloa and Maha'ulepu are a part of the same beach. It is commonly referred to as Shipwreck Beach for the long-gone ship that ran aground years ago. Most of the ship has long since washed away, but the motor may still be occasionally visible. A good spot to watch surfers and windsurfers, but swimming, even during calm seas, may not be advised. The Hyatt does erect flags to indicate the condition of the surf, but still use your own good judgment.

Recommended for: Sunning, watching windsurfers and surfers.

Access: Take the unpaved haul cane road that picks up where Po'ipu Road ends. Follow the narrow dirt road that heads toward the ocean.

Facilities: Public restrooms, shower facilities for Hyatt guests.

Parking: Parking area at bottom of the dirt road.

Po'ipu Beach

Po'ipu area's main attraction is, of course, Po'ipu Beach. The beach is fronted by the popular Po'ipu Beach Park and a few resorts. The beach is actually is series of small golden-sand crescents strung together. Here beachgoers will find snorkeling, swimming, sunning, wading, strolling, surfing and windsurfing. Palm trees are scattered along the coastline here and the park has expansive grassy lawns. The surf spots are just offshore, where a reef creates perfect wave-breaks for beginner, intermediate and advanced surfers. Closer in to shore, swimmers can enjoy the relatively calm waters and snorkel around some interesting rocky points where fish and marine life congregate. There is also a natural and safe kiddie wading pool at Po'ipu Beach Park, perfect for toddlers and young swimmers.

The younger set also will enjoy the playground, with its segmented play areas for younger and older children. The playground is also fully ADA-accessible.

In 2002, Po'ipu Beach was named the "top beach for kids" in Hawai'i by readers of *Hawaii Magazine*, and "best family beach" by the Travel Channel. In 2001, it was ranked number one in the U.S. by the "Dr. Beach National Ratings," conducted by Stephen Leatherman of Florida International University.

Po'ipu Beach Park is a four-acre stretch of land fronting the eastern section of Po'ipu Beach as well as Brennecke Beach. This park has been the centerpiece of the Po'ipu Beach resort area for decades. It is popular with families of young children and novice swimmers, and the kiddie wading pool gets good use. The offshore reef provides substantial protection for the shoreline. There is a lifeguard on duty seven days a week year-round. Snorkeling around the right side of Nukumoi Point is very good. The beach is protected by Nukumoi Point and a shorebreak on the east. Bodyboarders are attracted to the waves offshore. High surf can occur April through September.

Here you will find another one of Hawai'i's eight *tombolos*. Without knowing it was something special, you probably wouldn't have noticed it at all. This is a strip of sand that connects one island to another or to the mainland. There are only eight *tombolos* in Hawai'i. On the rocky volcanic shore to the east be on the lookout for green sea turtles frolicking in the waves. This is a great area for swimming and snorkeling during calm seas.

The area is divided into three separate beaches. They are:

Po'ipu Beach—The sand is fine and great for sunning, sitting, strolling and watching others. The beach has good snorkeling as a result of the offshore reef. Boogie boarding is popular here and you might see surfers riding the waves farther out. Windsurfers enjoy this site as well. Dangerous water conditions during high surf, however. Snorkeling and swimming is good during calm seas but stay inside the reef area. Located at the east end of Ho'onani Road.

Brennecke Beach—At this beach on Ho'one Road, the shorebreak on the rocks with a small beachfront can be hazardous to the boogie boarder. At one time this beach had what many considered the best body surfing on Kaua'i and is still very good. However, things changed a bit when Hurricane Iniki stripped away most of the sand. Since then, a great deal of sand has been dumped on the beach to help give Mother Nature a hand in its restoration. Brennecke Beach Center across the street rents beach equipment.

Wai'ohai Beach—This is actually a part of Po'ipu Beach, but is known as Wai'ohai Beach. It was the original site of the old Knudsen home before resort development began in this area in the early 1960s. Vlademar Knudsen was the son of the premier of Norway, who first went to California and made a fortune in the Gold Rush before relocating to Kaua'i and making a second fortune as founder of Kekaha Sugar Company. Anne Sinclair was the daughter of Elizabeth Sinclair, the lady who purchased the island of Ni'ihau in 1864. Anne Sinclair and Vlademar Knudsen married in later years and it was Wai'ohai that Anne Knudsen chose for the location of her beach house. This sandy beach is good for surfing, swimming and snorkeling during calm seas. High surf generates dangerous conditions. Wai'ohai can be reached from the adjoining beach on Ho'one Road. There is parking available in the gravel/dirt parking lot next to Brennecke.

Recommended for: Po'ipu Beach is popular with surfers, swimmers and snorkelers.

Facilities: The beach park has lifeguard, pavilions, comfort stations, picnic tables, sidewalks and showers, plus a convenience store and restaurant right across the road.

Access: From Po'ipu Road, turn south onto Ho'owili Road and drive one block straight south to Ho'one Road and the beach park.

Parking: There are designated parking areas nearby.

Koloa Landing

In the height of the early plantation days, Koloa Landing was the departure and arrival port for passenger and cargo vessels, as well as whaling ships. Today this old boat launch, a remnant of history, is used as a departure for beach scuba dives.

Recommended for: Beach dives.

Facilities: None.

Access: At the western end of Hoonani Road.

Parking: Paved and unpaved parking off the *makai* side of the landing.

Prince Kuhio Park

This beach park is dedicated to Prince Jonah Kuhio Kalaniana'ole. He was born in 1871, and in 1902 was elected to be a delegate to Congress, where he served until his death on January 7, 1922. He was known as the "People's Prince" because of the achievements he made for the Hawaiian people. Prince Kuhio was the youngest son of Kaua'i's chief David Kahalepouli Piikoli, and the grandson of Kaumuali'i, the last king of Kaua'i. Prince Kuhio was adopted by Queen Kapiolani, his aunt, and grew up in the royal household in Honolulu.

You can see the foundation of Kuhio's parent's home, the royal fishpond, and *Hoai Heiau,* where the *kahuna* (priests) meditated and lived, as well as a sitting bench that faced the grounds. The monument at this park marks Kuhio's birth site.

Recommended for: Swimming, snorkeling and sunning during low tide and calm seas. During high tide, it becomes just a park, with no beach. Great sunsets.

Facilities: Public restrooms.

Access: Located on Lawa'i Beach Road.

Parking: Paved parking area.

Beach House Park

Located alongside the road, this narrow beach is primarily usable only during low tide. Swimming and snorkeling can be good during low surf. The reef makes snorkeling good for even a beginner. This is a very, very small beachfront located right off the road, tucked between hotels and the restaurant, with plenty of traffic going past. Not a very scenic or picturesque beach location. It's known as "Acid Drop" among surfers.

Recommended for: Swimming, snorkeling during calm surf, sunsets.

Facilities: Restrooms, showers.

Access: Enter from Highway 520, the road forks into Po'ipu Road on one side and Lawa'i Road on the other (also known as Spouting Horn Road). It is not as far down as Spouting Horn, and is located across from the Lawa'i Beach Resort.

Parking: Paved parking area across the road from the beach.

Spouting Horn

There are a number of places around the Hawaiian islands that have the perfect conditions to form a blowhole. The best displays at Spouting Horn are during high surf, when the water and air rushing together make a fine display. The geyser can reach heights of 60 feet. As you'll note by the many cars, tour buses and vendors booths, this is a popular visitor destination. There is no access to the ocean. "Do Not Enter" signs post the danger of being on the rocks should you attempt to descend down. The obvious danger is that you could be hit by a wave and pulled down.

Recommended for: Enjoying one of nature's wonders, a blowhole!

Facilities: Restrooms, vendors selling their wares.

Access: Enter from Highway 520, the road forks into Po'ipu Road on one side, Lawa'i Road on the other. From Lawa'i Road (also known as Spouting Horn Road) it is two miles to the blowhole, which is located along the roadside.

Parking: Large paved parking area.

Port Allen

Port Allen is the second largest port on Kaua'i. Port Allen has little to offer in the way of a beach or beach activities, but many boat tour companies depart from here.

Recommended for: Tour boat departures only.

Facilities: Restroom, boat launch.

Access: In 'Ele'ele turn *mauka* off Kaumuali'i Highway on Waialo Road, follow it to the parking area at the boat launch.

Parking: Free large paved parking lot at the harbor.

Hanapepe Beach Park

This dusty and well-used park is near the Hanapepe River mouth, but is not recommended for ocean activities.

Recommended for: Picnicking and non-water beach activities.

Facilities: Picnic area, restrooms, showers, pavilions.

Access: Take Lele Road from Kaumuali'i Highway; beach park is at west end of the bay.

Parking: Parking available.

Salt Pond Beach Park

The natural flats along this beach have been used by Hawaiians for generations. Today, this site continues to be used for traditional salt-making. In late spring the wells, or *puna,* are cleaned and the salt-making process runs through the summer months. Mother Nature has been kind enough to create a ridge of rock between the two rocky points at Salt Pond Park, resulting in a large lagoon area that is fairly well protected, except during times of high surf. Popular for surfing and windsurfing as well. And, because of its protected swimming area, this is an ideal spot for families and children. A lifeguard is generally on duty.

Recommended for: Swimming and snorkeling most of the year, except during high surf. Popular for surfing and windsurfing as well.

Facilities: Picnic areas, barbecues, restrooms, rinse-off showers, lifeguard.

Access: From the highway turn onto Lele Road, past the cemetery, turn right onto Lokokai Street. From the highway Lele Road is marked Highway 543.

Parking: Paved parking area.

Camping: With county permit.

Pakala Beach

Great offshore waves make this a popular summer surfing spot, but it otherwise has little to redeem it as a family beach destination.

Recommended for: Surfing.

Facilities: None.

Access: Along a dirt path off Kaumuali'i Highway, 1.4 miles east of Waimea River.

Parking: Roadside.

Lucy Wright Park

Lucy Kapahu Aukai Wright was born August 20, 1873, in Anahola. She was a well-loved school teacher in Waimea for 35 years until her death in 1931. This beach is dedicated to her memory. An earlier, very notable visitor arrived at this beach site: Captain James Cook. Cook landed here on his arrival to the Sandwich Islands in January 1778.

Because of the location of this beach on the west side near the mouth of the Waimea River, the beach collects assorted debris, and the water is murky. It's not popular for sunbathers or swimmers, but you might see surfers offshore.

Recommended for: Fishing.

Facilities: Restrooms, showers, parking area, picnic tables at Waimea Pier.

Access: On the Waimea side of the bridge over Waimea River, turn *mauka* on Lawa'i Road off Kaumuali'i Highway and follow to the park.

Parking: Paved parking lot.

Camping: By county permit on grassy area.

Kekaha Beach

This is a 15-mile stretch of coastline reaching from Kekaha to Polihale, located on the western end of the town of Kekaha and along the Kaumuali'i Highway. Along the roadside the beach park is attractive and includes facilities nearby. Several decades ago, this shoreline had severe erosion problems. In 1980, a seawall was constructed along the roadway. Strong rip currents are generated here during high surf that are particularly dangerous during winter and spring months. Surfers occasionally enjoy the surf at a couple of locations along this beachfront. If the wind is blowing up at Polihale, chances are you might find you can enjoy your picnic lunch with less sand in your sandwich at Kekaha. Shorebreak and rip currents year-round make this a dangerous beach for water activities. However, it is an excellent beach for sunsets, walking or a picnic lunch.

Recommended for: Picnics, beach play and sunsets.

Facilities: Picnic pavilions, showers, restrooms.

Access: Follow the Kaumuali'i Highway past Kekaha.

Parking: Along Kaumuali'i Highway.

Polihale State Park and Barking Sands Beach

The Polihale State Park marks the southern end of Napali Coast. Dangerous surf conditions preclude swimming and ocean sports. And be sure to bring shade with you because you won't find much here! Still, it's a gorgeous beach for walking and sunning.

The Polihale State Park extends for five miles along the eastern shore and encompasses 140 acres. Large dunes are formed along the back of the beach that can reach up to 100 feet high. You'll know you have arrived at Barking Sands when you see the military installation, and then you have to keep going to reach the state park.

More than 100 years ago, the sand from this area was studied by the California Academy of Sciences and it was discovered that it had small holes or "blind cavities." The resulting vibration when the sand is rubbed between the hands causes a sound similar to barking or singing. Hence the name for this beach area.

Does the sand really bark? Well, you'll have to try it yourself and see. Some seem to think so. Others are unconvinced. A similar anomaly occurs on one beach on O'ahu and another on Ni'ihau. A few other places in the world have sand with this remarkable property.

While you may see locals driving along the beach, this is not advisable. Not only will the rental car companies not be pleased should you become stuck, but there is also a plant unique to this area that is threatened by beach driving. The *ohai* is an endangered beach plant found only in Hawai'i. On Kaua'i, the only place these 30-foot shrubs grow is at Polihale and officials fear that the damage caused by beach traffic is further endangering the survival of this species.

The *Polihale Heiau* is a four-terraced temple found on the slopes above the beach, almost indistinguishable after centuries of erosion. This *heiau* was sacred to Miru, the God of Po. It was said that this was a jumping-off place for the dead. (You can see the sculpted cliffs at the end of the beach.)

In the early days, the Hawaiians living on this side of the island constructed small houses made of grass. There was one large living room and two doors on opposite sides. Eric Knudsen, an early pioneer on Kaua'i, recalled that his father was curious as to why all the houses were built with their gable-ends east and west and doors facing toward the mountains and the sea. The obvious reason might be for tradewinds to create cool breezes through the home, or perhaps for those wonderful ocean and mountain vistas. However, when he questioned a fellow he was told, "Why, you know that Po, the abode of the dead, lies under the ocean just outside Polihale, where the cliffs and the ocean meet and the spirits of the dead must go there. As the spirits wander along on their way to Po, they will go around the gable-end of a house but if the house stood facing the other way, the spirits would walk straight through and it would be very disagreeable to have a spirit walk past you as you were eating your meal. In fact we can always tell when a battle has been fought by the number of spirits passing at the same time."

Recommended for: An opportunity to experience the sand dunes, take a very long beach walk, picnics, a glimpse of the south end of Napali, camping.

Facilities: Picnic pavilions, showers, restrooms.

Access: The access road is a miserable five-mile-long, badly rutted and pot-holed old cane haul road, now more of an offroad four-wheel-drive vehicle trail. Your rental car agency frowns on taking cars on this road and your rental agreement probably stipulates that it's a violation. So, you're on your own if you choose to go there! Follow the Kaumuali'i Highway at Mana to the end and then follow signs along the cane roads approximately five miles. There are no state signs posted, but some smaller, difficult-to-read signs might be noted along the way. It's a well-rutted, well-used road, as you'll see.

Parking: In a large beachfront lot or near the pavilions.

Camping: Allowed, but permits from the state are required.

North Shore Area

Moloa'a Bay

This is as pristine a bay as you may find on Kaua'i, although the development of homes and vacation rentals has spoiled a lot of its charm, and made it nearly impossible to park. James Garner fans might note that Moloa'a was the film location for *Castaway Cowboys*. While this bay can be especially dangerous during winter and spring surf, anytime there is high surf dangerous ocean conditions and powerful rip currents can occur. During periods of calm, you can enjoy swimming, snorkeling and diving here.

Recommended for: Snorkeling and swimming only during periods of calm.

Facilities: None.

Access: Just past mile-marker 16 on Kuhio Highway as you head toward Princeville. Turn right on Ko'olau Road, then turn right again onto Moloa'a Road. At the fork in the road, keep to the left, following the road in front of private residences to the public access trail.

Parking: Parking is wherever you can squeeze in between the "No Parking" signs.

Ka'aka'aniu Beach (Larsen's Beach)

Named for the site where L. David Larsen, a Swedish-born plant pathologist, built his home. Larsen arrived in Hawai'i in 1908 and later managed the Kilauea Sugar Plantation. Dangerous rip currents and a shallow rocky shore make this unappealing for swimmers, and many snorkelers have drowned here. The offshore reef is a popular location for the harvesting of *limu kohu*, a type of seaweed. During times of low tide you may see the harvesters at work, or net-throwers catching fish. (Never walk between the net-throwers and the water as you'll scare the fish.) The county access, purchased in 1979, was sold with the condition that the access not continue all the way to the beach. This was done in hopes of making the beach less attractive and therefore less populated, so it will take a little bit of effort to reach this sandy crescent. Once you reach the head of the path, it will take about 10 minutes to walk down to the beachfront.

Recommended for: Beachcombing, fishing.

Facilities: None.

Access: There is public access 1.2 miles from the north intersection of Ko'olau Road and Kuhio Highway. It's a 10-minute hike to reach the shoreline.

Parking: Very limited, along the access road.

Waiakalua Iki Beach

Dangerous rip currents at Waiakalua Iki make it inadvisable for water activities, but it's a popular fishing location. The twin beach, Waiakalua Nui is just slightly east and is covered with beach rock.

Recommended for: Fishing.

Facilities: None.

Access: Near the end of North Waiakalua Road is a public access to the shoreline. Take the steep trail down—a 15-minute walk.

Parking: Very limited parking.

Kilauea Point National Wildlife Refuge

Although you cannot reach a beach from here, it is a beautiful spot to enjoy the scenic North Shore coastline and observe whales and seabirds. (*See* Chapter Two for more information.) Open 10 a.m. to 4 p.m., closed some federal holidays. Admission to the refuge is $2 and it's well-worth the price.

Recommended for: Bird watching and whale watching.

Facilities: Bookstore, restrooms, visitor center.

Access: Turn off Kuhio Highway at Kilauea and follow Kolo Road to Kilauea Lighthouse Road; take it to the end.

Parking: Large paved parking area inside the refuge.

Kauapea Beach (Secret Beach)

This 3,000-foot-long beach lies between Kalihiwai Bay and Kilauea Point. It's a little tricky getting there given that you can't see the beach from the highway, and the access is not clearly marked. The path to the beach is also steep and rough, and very slippery after rains. The "beautiful people" of the 1960s referred to it as Secret Beach, and unfortunately it is still called this today. A strong shorebreak and dangerous currents make this a poor choice for water activities year-round, especially during the winter. You can sometimes see whales and dolphins in the summer. This is another place where you'll likely encounter nude sunbathing. From this beach you can see Moku'ae'ae, a small rocky outcropping that's a bird sanctuary and part of the Kilauea Refuge.

Recommended for: Beachcombing, fishing, sunbathing.

Facilities: None.

Access: One-half mile west of Kilauea from the Kuhio Highway, turn onto Kalihiwai Road, which dog-legs to the left. Off to the right is a dirt road with an embankment on either side. Travel down the road and there is a parking lot. Then take the trail leading to the beach. The trail down requires a 15-minute hike (longer on the way up).

Parking: Parking area at end of access road. *Note:* The parking area is notorious for rip-offs so don't leave anything of value in your car.

Kalihiwai Beach

This crescent of white sand is fringed with ironwood trees. You'll see boardsurfing in the winter, although it's only for experts as it's a very dangerous break. The shorebreak is daunting in winter, so stay out of the water then and avoid the river mouth, where strong currents form. It can be quite pleasant and calm for swimming in the summer. You can kayak up the river except during heavy rains or flooding.

Recommended for: Swimming only on calm summer days.

Facilities: Picnic tables, porta-potties.

Access: Take Kalihiwai Road (eastern exit) to the end.

Parking: At the beach under the ironwood trees.

'Anini Beach Park

This beach was named "Wanini," but sometime over the years the name was abbreviated. With a two-mile offshore reef, this beach is popular for various types of fishing (pole, spear, throw-net) and seaweed harvesting. It's also a nice camping beach, and has a boat launch area. Snorkeling, windsurfing, beachcombing and boating are also to be found here. Water conditions are very dangerous during high surf, which causes strong rip currents. This beachfront was the location for several scenes in *Honeymoon in Vegas*.

Recommended for: Windsurfing; snorkeling and swimming only during very calm summer surf. Stay away from the west end of the beach where there is a channel, and stay inside the reef when snorkeling.

Facilities: Picnic facilities, showers, restrooms.

Access: Follow Kuhio Highway to the western Kalihiwai Road and take Anini Road to the beach.

Parking: Long stretch of grass for parking, with an open area next to it for boats and trailers.

Camping: With county permit.

Princeville Beaches

Princeville is a 2,000-acre tract of land lying between Hanalei Bay and 'Anini Beach Park. The resort development began in 1968 and is composed of condominiums, private homes and several hotels. Most of the development sits along the bluffs, with only three small beaches in the area—Pu'u Poa Beach, Kaweonui Beach, Kenomene Beach. Access and parking are very limited, especially in light of the overall size of the community. Just six easements provide public access to this shoreline. None of these beaches are safe for winter-time water activities.

The Princeville Hotel Resort is located on the Pu'u Poa hill. Below is the Pu'u Poa Beach, which stretches about 1,200 feet between the resort and the mouth of the Hanalei River. Only during calm summer seas will you find an opportunity to snorkel amid the reef here. Pu'u Poa is the best of the three Princeville beaches. Kayaks to explore Hanalei River can be rented at the Beach Activities Center at the Princeville Hotel Resort.

Pu'u Poa Beach is just below the Princeville Hotel—a long, narrow sandy beach fronting reefy waters that are often murky because the Hanalei River enters the sea here.

Recommended for: Sunbathing, picnics, fishing; advanced surfers only in winter months; snorkeling and swimming during summer months only.

Facilities: Toilets and showers. Princeville Hotel offers food and beach gear rental.

Access: Below the Princeville Hotel: follow access signs on the left (east) side of lobby area.

Parking: Some parking for beach guests at a tiny lot before the Princeville Hotel guard shack on Ka Huku Road. Or use the hotel's valet parking.

Kaweonui Beach

This pocket beach is below the Sealodge condominiums and is a mix of rocky reef and sand with large *hala* and *kamane* trees offering some shade. It is known as Little Glass Shacks surf break.

Recommended for: Fishing.

Facilities: None.

Access: The trail starts at the west end of the Sealodge condominiums' parking lot. A hike of 15 minutes down a very steep goat-like trail is required to reach the shoreline. Please be aware that this trail is very dangerous and slippery, and it remains muddy even when it's not raining. Use it strictly at your own risk.

Parking: In the Sealodge parking lot off Keoniana Road.

Kenomene Beach

This bit of shoreline offers a narrow sandy beach and is known as Hideaways for its surf break.

Recommended for: Swimming and snorkeling during calm summer days. Advanced surfing only.

Facilities: None.

Access: Near the Pali Ke Kua condominiums, just before the gate at the Princeville Hotel there is a path down to the beach. It will take a 10-minute walk down the stairs and trail to reach this beach. Guests of Pali Ke Kua have a private trail to another (separate) part of Kenomene Beach.

Parking: In the tiny public lot before the guard shack at Princeville Hotel, or in the Princeville Hotel lot.

Hanalei Bay

The Hanalei Bay begins its two-mile sandy stretch at Pu'u Poa marsh, where the river empties into the bay, and ends at the Makahoa Point toward the west. The entire coastline is accessible through several beach parks that line this area. See below for information on Black Pot Beach, Hanalei Beach Park (Pavilions), Waikoko Beach and Wai'oli Beach Park (Pine Trees). There are three parking areas. The historic pier at Black Pot has been restored.

Hanalei Black Pot Beach

One of the few Kaua'i beaches with no true Hawaiian name, this site was dubbed "Black Pot" for the huge cooking pot that was shared here by fishermen. Black Pot Beach Park is located where the Hanalei River meets the ocean on the eastern end of the bay. This is a popular site for local residents to gather for swimming and other water sports. During periods of big surf, it is very crowded. The Hanalei Pier is a scenic location, and one you'll no doubt remember if you saw the movie *South Pacific*. The wooden pier was constructed in 1892 and then 30 years later was reinforced with concrete. It was used by the local farmers for shipping their rice crops to market until it was closed in 1933. In 1979 the pier joined other landmarks on the National Register of Historic Places. Swimming is good for kids near the pier (they also like to jump off during the summer months).

Recommended for: Bodyboarding, surfing, windsurfing; swimming and kayaking during calm summer surf.

Facilities: Restrooms, showers, lifeguard.

Access: From the parking lot at the end of Weke Road, through Black Pot Park.

Parking: Parking lot on Weke Road.

Camping: With county permits.

Hanalei Pavilion Beach Park

Hanalei means "crescent shaped." The beach at this park can be calm and serene during low summer surf, but extremely treacherous during winter and spring high surf. A lifeguard is often on duty here.

Recommended for: Picnics anytime, summertime swimming.

Facilities: Picnic tables and restrooms, lifeguard.

Access: Turn right on Aku Road, and a second right onto Weke Road.

Parking: Designated lot.

Waioli Beach (Pine Trees)

This is the third major recreational area for Hanalei Bay. Swimming isn't the best here, even in summer, but it's a popular winter surf spot known as "Pine Trees."

Recommended for: Picnics anytime, boogie boarding, surfing.

Facilities: Picnic tables and restrooms, wash-off showers.

Access: Turn right on Aku Road, and a second left onto Weke Road

Parking: Large lot.

Waikoko Bay

Waikoko, which means "blood waters," is the last of the beaches along Hanalei Bay. It offers an offshore reef, making this narrow beach a good place for children to swim. The offshore water is very shallow, in fact, too shallow for most adults.

Recommended for: Swimming for children in the shallow, reef protected ocean during calm seas only.

Facilities: None.

Access: Located along Highway 56, a half-mile past mile-marker 4.

Parking: Alongside the road.

Lumaha'i Beach

In 2001, the state acquired several acres of land behind the beach area from the Wilcox Family Estate. That land is mostly a *lauhala* (pandanus) tree forest—the plant widely used for woven mats, baskets and other utility items. It is unknown whether the state will provide more public access and facilities at this popular beach in the future. The beach is tucked beneath some lush cliffs and became famous for a well-known scene in the 1957 film *South Pacific*. Actually, it was the eastern end of this beach, which has a separate name, *Kahalahala* (which means pandanus trees), where Mitzi Gaynor filmed her famous "Wash that man right out of my hair" scene. A more scenic stretch of beach is hard to imagine. Unfortunately, this is one particularly dangerous stretch of coastline. The width of Lumaha'i Beach is said to vary as much as 360 feet with the seasonal movement of the sand from one end to the other. With the steep shore comes the danger of high surf, dangerous shorebreak and strong currents. There is no protective reef so the ocean drops off very quickly. The nearby Lumaha'i River may rise dramatically as a result of flash floods. This, in combination with the danger of rough waves, most common during high surf, makes even wading along the shore unadvisable. You may see body or boardsurfers enjoying this beach, but when the surf becomes even slightly rough, you'll see that even experts stay out of the water.

You may have heard of *o'opu*, a unique freshwater fish that spends its first few months in the sea before returning to the freshwater stream. They have adapted well to their surroundings by using their lower front fins as suction cups to hold onto rocks, even those extremely steep rock walls that form waterfalls. Using their tails to propel themselves, *o'opu* travel slowly upstream. The adults come down the rivers in late summer and fall, spawn, and then the young head for the ocean. The young (larvae) mature into juveniles called *hinana* and return to their freshwater origins and migrate upstream. These interesting creatures are found only in Hawai'i and are highly valued as a table fish.

Recommended for: Enjoying the view—an outstanding photo opportunity at the 5-mile marker post or at several other small pullouts along the road. Swimming is safe at Kahalahala only on the *very* calmest of summer days.

Facilities: None.

Access: Along the highway at mile-marker 4 before the bridge and parking along mile-marker 6 nearer the river.

Parking: Very limited along the roadside.

Wainiha Beach

Wainiha means "unfriendly waters." This beach has no reef, so it is completely unprotected from the open ocean. High surf, therefore, creates very dangerous conditions—resulting in rip currents and shorebreaks. It is not recommended for any water activities, but beachcombing on the dry sandy shore can be good.

Recommended for: Beachcombing.

Facilities: None.

Access: Through the trees, off Kuhio Highway near mile-marker 7.

Parking: Off-road parking only, near mile-marker 7.

Makua Beach (Tunnels Beach)

You are not likely to find anybody referring to this stretch of beach by its Hawaiian name *Makua*, but you can show you know a little something by using it yourself. This popular—bordering on overused—beach is better known as "Tunnels," named for the underwater lava tubes and caves here. Located on Ha'ena Point, it's one of the more frequented beach sites on the northern shore of Kaua'i. While the shoreline has a lot of beach rock, making it less attractive to swimmers, the offshore reef offers good snorkeling and excellent diving during calm seas.

During the spring and winter, high surf creates very strong currents, and even during low surf, the current offshore can be treacherous. During high surf this beach is a popular surfing spot, but only for the expert. You may also see fishermen using spears or nets along the reef. You may recognize this beach as one of the main locations for the television mini-series "The Thorn Birds."

Recommended for: Swimming and snorkeling and scuba diving during periods of low and calm sea, and beachcombing during high seas. Surfing and windsurfing also. Very dangerous during winter months.

Facilities: None.

Access: Two public accesses, one at the east side of Ha'ena Point, the other to the west. You'll find the first .3 mile past mile-marker 8 on Highway 560 and the second .5 mile past the same marker.

Parking: Very limited parking off Kuhio Highway, or park at Ha'ena beach park and walk east.

Ha'ena State Park

This is a five-acre park maintained by the County of Kaua'i. In the past, this beach, then called *Maniniholo* (traveling manini fish), was a *hukilau* site, where fishermen would come and throw their nets out into the sea and pull their catch onto shore. This is different from net fishing, which you might see done by a single fisherman. Today the *hukilau*-style of fishing is rarely done. The mountains are stunning behind this beach, making it one of the most scenic on the island, and in calm seas, the water is a gorgeous aqua due to the white sands beneath.

The foreshore here is steep. The resulting shorebreak is dangerous and makes it unsafe for swimming or bodysurfing in rough seas. Although you may see some bodysurfing done here, it is *not* for the novice.

Across the road from Ha'ena Beach Park is **Maniniholo Dry Cave**. (*See* Chapter 2 for more information.)

Following another .2 of a mile past Ha'ena State Park and just beyond Limahuli Stream are the Waikapala'e Wet Caves, accessible by a short hike up and behind the gravel parking area. (*See* Chapter 2 for information.)

Recommended for: Swimming and snorkeling in the summer with calm seas, particularly dangerous during winter months.

Facilities: Restrooms, showers, picnic pavilions.

Access: Located on the Wainiha side of Ha'ena.

Camping: Permits available from the county.

Parking: Parking in designated lot along the roadside.

Ha'ena State Park and Ke'e Beach

Highway 56 ends at this beach. This is the beginning of Napali Coast and Napali Coast State Park, which is only accessible by boat or by hiking trail. Swimming here is only advisable during calm conditions. The 230 acres of Ha'ena State Park include a number of ancient archaeological sites. Remnants of ancient Hawaiian villages and the *Kaulu o Laka Heiau* can be found here. This sacred altar is set along a series of tiers on the cliffs of Napali and was built for Laka, the goddess of hula. It is still used today by hula *halau*; do not leave any offerings or climb on the walls.

This area was also the site of the famous Taylor Camp, which was populated by over 100 flower children during the 1960s and 1970s. Howard Taylor, Elizabeth Taylor's brother, offered this hippie community refuge at his seven-acre property when its members were evicted from a public beach park and threatened with jail time. The hippies, however, were not welcomed by the locals in the area who objected to their nudity and trash. Howard Taylor eventually left, turning the land deed over to the state in 1974. The state took over the park in 1977, evicting the hippies and burning their camp and its treehouses.

If you're over 40, you may remember the *puka*-shell fad. It reportedly began when hippies from the Taylor Camp gathered the distinctive white shells with holes in the center (*puka* means hole) and strung them to make necklaces. Elizabeth Taylor, donning one of these necklaces (a gift from her brother), apparently created the craze. Great story, eh?

At the very end of the beach park, and road, is lovely Ke'e Beach. Like Makua Beach, it is another of those beautiful spots that is sadly overused. You'll find good swimming and snorkeling, but again (are you tired of hearing this?) only if the sea conditions are calm. Stay inside the lagoon as the area beyond the reef can have strong currents.

Ke'e may look familiar to you because it is where the final scene of *Body Heat* was filmed starring Kathleen Turner.

Recommended for: Good swimming and snorkeling at Ke'e in the summer with very calm surf, great sunsets.

Facilities: Lifeguard, picnic area, restrooms, showers.

Access: Located at the trailhead to Napali Coast State Park.

Parking: Parking areas near the end of Kuhio Highway. If the lot at Ke'e is full, there is more parking beyond the restrooms.

Napali Coast State Park

This 6,500-acre state park is composed of dramatic cliffs, dense rainforests and lush coastal valleys. There are 15 miles of shoreline between Ke'e Beach and Polihale Beach on Kaua'i's eastern shore and five major beaches within the state park: Hanakapi'ai, Kalalau, Honopu, Nu'alolo

Kai and Miloli'i. By the way, "Napali" means "the cliffs." (You'll often see it written as "Na Pali" but *Hawaiian Place Names*, written by historian Mary Kawena Kukui, spells it as one.)

Hanakapi'ai Beach can be reached in a day's hike. It is a distance of two miles from Ke'e and may take an hour or two to reach. Remember, it has no facilities, so pack plenty of drinking water, include sunscreen lotion and a hat, and wear comfortable shoes. It might be recommended to also include a small first-aid kit with an ace support bandage. In the valley behind the beach, you may see remnants of a fishing village and a farming community that once resided here. Please treat historic sites with respect.

Due to the remoteness of this coastline, beach lovers need to use extra caution. As mentioned before, this is a wilderness area and help would be a long time in reaching you should you become ill or injured. The surf and currents are extremely hazardous, especially in the winter.

The trail to this beach can be quite muddy after rainfall. Another rough and tumble trail that travels two miles inland from the beach will take you to **Hanakapi'ai waterfall**. The falls flow down for about 300 feet to the pool below. Avoid swimming beneath the falls, and resist the urge to drink the water as it may contain harmful *leptospirosis* bacteria.

From this beach, the trail continues another nine miles to **Kalalau Beach**. Due to the rugged terrain and steep elevations, it takes an entire day to reach the beach.

Again, the summer months are most advisable for visiting Napali Coast, although the whales and winter surf are beautiful to see. The area was inhabited by Hawaiians until 1919. In the late 1960s and early 1970s the area was repopulated, this time by hippies. With serious sanitation problems the state implemented a program that limited access to the area by restricting the number of camping permits. Boat and helicopter landings also came under restrictions. Camping is allowed only in designated areas and water must be treated. With no fronting reef and strong currents, it is dangerous to swim here any time of the year.

The remaining three of Napali's beaches are only accessible by boat. Permits are required for camping and day hikes past Hanakapi'ai.

Hanakapi'ai Beach

We recommend you simply stay out of the ocean here. This North Shore beach is particularly dangerous, and the #1 beach for drownings between 1970 and 1988. This, combined with the remoteness of the shoreline, means that beach lovers need to be careful.

The Hanakapi'ai River flows into the ocean at this sandy beachfront, creating dangerous currents any time of year, and especially during winter months. Even the Department of Land and Natural Resources recommends you avoid the ocean. There are some pools along the stream for a quick dip, but keep an eye out above the valley as rain in the uplands can result in flash flooding. A reminder, as with any fresh water on the island, it needs to be boiled or otherwise treated before drinking. (*See* Chapter 6 for more information on this beach area.)

Recommended for: Indescribable scenic beauty.

Facilities: Composting toilets.

Access: A two-mile trek from the trailhead at Ke'e Beach, at the northwest end of Kuhio Highway.

Parking: It is not recommended that you park and leave your car overnight. Several companies can arrange to drop you off and pick you up.

Camping: By permit with the state.

Kalalau Beach

The trail from the Hanakapi'ai Valley to the Kalalau Valley is a difficult one and should not be attempted as a day trip. An 11-mile hike from the trailhead at Ke'e Beach, it traverses along scenic ocean cliffs and winds through narrow hanging valleys, with significant elevation changes (meaning a lot of ups and downs!). The beach is long and narrow during the summer, but with close shorebreak, it is unsafe at all times of the year. During the winter, the beach often disappears. No water activities can be recommended at this location. This is one of Kaua'i's five most dangerous beaches, based on incidents of drowning. As with other valley beaches, the Kalalau River mouth area is subject to rip currents that are very hazardous. Also, be alert to the possibility of flash floods during rainfall in the upper region. This is the last beach accessible by foot along the Napali Coast. The remaining beaches are accessible only by boat. (*See* Chapter 6 for more information on this beach area.)

Recommended for: Scenic beauty only, camping.

Facilities: Toilets.

Access: Eleven strenuous miles on foot along the Napali Coastline from the trailhead at Ke'e Beach at the northwest end of Kuhio Highway.

Parking: It is not recommended that you park and leave your car overnight. Several companies can arrange to drop you off and pick you up.

Camping: By permit with the state.

Honopu Beach and Nu'alolo Kai and Miloli'i State Parks

Accessible only by boat, Honopu has no facilities and camping is not allowed. Nu'alolo is a popular summer destination for the charter/cruise boats. Several companies have state permission to land at this beach, others must anchor offshore. Snorkelers need to stay clear of the shallow reefs due to the danger of surges. Miloli'i is popular with locals for fishing during the summer.

Recommended for: Snorkeling at Nualolo Kai during calm summer months.

Facilities: Composting toilets.

Access: Charter/cruise boats.

Na Naia Hulahula: The Dancing Dolphins

Ne'e papa like lkou,
me ta maita'i.
Na Nai'a hulahula
i lila i H'ena
Nã pua 'o ta moana tai,
'oia nã ãnela ki'ai,
Na Nai'a hulahula
i lila i K'?
Ha'aheo e Npali,
i ta holo tit,
Na Nai'a hulahula,
i lila i Hanakp'ai
He mele te a nou
na Nai'a hulahula,
Ha'aheo e Npali,
na pua 'o ta moana tai

Their graceful moves,
all in unison.
The dancing Dolphins,
there at Ha'ena
Flowers of the sea,
the guardian angels.
The dancing Dolphins,
there at Ke'e
Pride of Napali,
swiftly moving.
The dancing Dolphins,
there at Hanakapi'ai.
Tell the story,
the dancing Dolphins.
Pride of Napali,
flowers of the sea.

Used with permission of Chucky Boy Chock

CHAPTER 6

Recreation and Tours

Kaua'i, The Garden Isle, has much to interest the outdoor-oriented visitor. Whether it is the land, the air or the ocean that beckons, there are a variety of activities to tempt even the die-hard lounge-chair athlete. This chapter lists activities in alphabetical order.

There are a number of activity booking agencies on Kaua'i that can assist you with booking the recreational activity of your choice. Pick up a free copy of the *Beach & Activity Guide Kaua'i*. They list companies that give 5 percent, 10 percent or 15 percent discounts if you book directly.

It is highly advisable that prior to your arrival on Kaua'i you check out the online websites and addresses of related tour operators, vendors and activity booking agencies listed in this chapter to inquire about current discount rates—special internet rates, direct-booking rates, etc.—that may be available. You can often save a considerable amount on related tours and activities by booking online or directly with the operators and/or vendors. Also, keep in mind that prices for various tours and activities do change without notice. Prices quoted in this book were the most current prior to publication, but may well have changed by the time you read this.

(*Author's note*: "Napali," as in Napali Coast, means "the cliffs." You will often see it written as "Na Pali" in some travel literature and advertising of cruise boat and helicopter tour companies. But *Hawaiian Place Names*, written by authoritative historian Mary Kawena Pukui, spells it as one word, thus her spelling is followed in this book.)

Best Bets

For great snorkeling try Lydgate or Po'ipu Beach on the South Shore or Makua Beach (also known as Tunnels) on the North Shore.

The golf aficionado will delight in the Prince Course at Princeville. Rated as the number-one course by *Golf Digest*, it is well deserved. Excellent play and outstanding scenery! The same can be said for the Po'ipu Bay Golf Course, a spectacular layout along the Po'ipu Coast, challenging and beautiful. Home of the annual PGA Grand Slam event.

If the whales are in residence during the winter months, you can take advantage of a whale-watching excursion to view these beautiful mammals a bit more closely.

For an underwater thrill, consider an introductory scuba adventure, no experience necessary.

For an eye-popping, spectacular aquatic adventure, take a snorkel cruise of Napali Coast.

For hikers, try any of the trail systems in Koke'e Park/Waimea Canyon. The moderately difficult Awa'awapuhi Trail to the North Shore is one of the better ones; the Waipo'o Falls trek is also a great, moderately challenging adventure hike.

Take a guided tour up the Wailua River to the Fern Grotto and hike to a secluded waterfall.

Hike the Kalalau Trail, an 11-mile trek along rugged Napali coastline. Not for the novice hiker.

The Grove Farm Homestead tour is one of Kaua'i's best cultural and historical experiences. Reserve your space long before your arrival, as they take very small groups.

Enjoy a hiking excursion in the summer months with an interpretative guide from the Koke'e Natural History Museum.

Spend a day, or part of one, at the ANARA Health Spa at the Hyatt Regency Kaua'i.

Take a bottle of something bubbly and watch a romantic sunset at Ke'e or Kekaha Beach.

Take advantage of an incredible golfing value on the picturesque 9-hole Kukuiolono Golf Course. Start your play around 3 p.m., miss the crowds, and if you don't finish you won't feel bad: green fees are a bargain at only $7!

The horticulturist or amateur gardener will not want to miss visiting one or all of the island's lovely botanical gardens.

The following is a list of just some of the activities that might be enjoyed on the island, along with the price per person you might expect to pay for a typical excursion or rental period. Remember to always check the local brochures for coupons, and don't be afraid to ask if they're running a special offer. Also check outfitter/vendor websites, where available, for specials and discounts available only by booking online.

Adventure hike-bike trek (½ day)—from $85
Deep-sea fishing (½ day trip)—from $95
Downhill Waimea Canyon bike ride—from $72
Fresh-water fishing (½ day trip)—from $105
Golf (9 holes, private course)—from $50 to $65
Golf (18 holes, private course)—from $75 to $170
Golf (9 holes, public course)—from $7
Golf (18 holes, public course)—from $32 to $44
Hawaiian luau—from $50
Helicopter tour (55 to 60 minutes)—from $150
Horseback riding (3 hours)—from $90
Land tours (island guided bus tours)—from $65
Moped day-rental—from $50
Motorcycle day-rental—from $185
Napali Coast ocean excursion—from $75
River kayak (½ day guided)—from $60
River kayak self-guided rental—from $26
Scuba diving (2-tank, with equipment)—from $100
Sunset sail along Napali Coast—from $85

Activity Booking Services

There are several activity booking services on Kaua'i that provide tour and activity reservations with many of the leading air, water and land tour operators, vendors and outfitters. And they often do it at discounted rates because they are tour wholesalers. For whatever tour, excursion or activity you have in mind, it might be good to check and compare with any of these booking services to inquire about the current special rates and discounts that are being offered. Depending on season and demand, it might be better to book with one of these services rather than with the tour operator directly. But be sure to always compare and inquire about special rates or discounts being offered, including senior rates.

Activity Connection—9561 Kaumuali'i Highway, Waimea; 808-338-1038

Activity Hut—2253 Po'ipu Road, Koloa; 808-742-9522

Activity Warehouse—4-788 Kuhio Highway, Kapa'a; Kapa'a 808-245-4600, Po'ipu 808-742-2300, Princeville 808-826-4100

Activity Wholesalers—5077 Kuhio Highway, Hanalei, 808-826-9983; in Anchor Cove Shopping Center, 3416 Rice Street, Nawiliwili, Lihu'e, 808-245-3926; www.livekauai.com

Activity World—800-235-7771; Lihu'e/Kapa'a 808-245-3300; Po'ipu/South Shore 808-742-9800; Princeville/North Shore 808-826-6500

Activities of Kaua'i—3-3222 Kuhio Highway, Lihu'e; 808-245-1664

Activities Unlimited Kaua'i—6281C Hauaala Road, Kapa'a; 808-821-1313

Cheap Tours—888-822-5935; 808-246-0009, 808-742-7000; www.cheaptourshawaii.com

Adventures and Tours

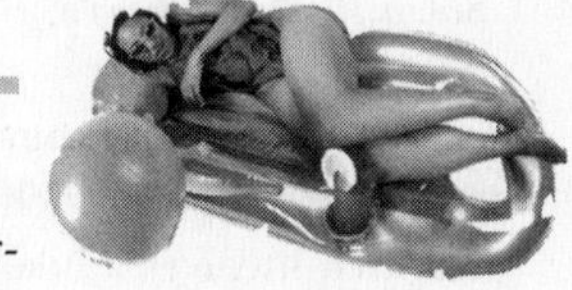

ALL-TERRAIN VEHICLES

Kaua'i ATV This outfitter offers two different outdoor all-terrain adventures in Kaua'i's lush, tropical landscape, exploring backcountry areas, old cane plantation roads into the fields, valleys and mountain areas. Beautiful views of mountains, coastline and forest areas. Learn from guides about the social, cultural and natural history of the region, wildlife, plants, etc. The Koloa Tour is three hours; Waterfall Tour is four hours. They even have dune buggies suitable for six passengers (including young kids) and a two-passenger mud bug for rent. ATV riders must be over 16. The tours are offered three times daily, and range from $99 to $145 per person. The dune buggy rents from $79 to $145. Mud clothes can be rented. Located in old Koloa Town on Weliweli Road. *P.O. Box 800, Kalaheo, HI 96741; 808-742-2734, 808-742-9654; e-mail: kauaitv@gte.net; www.kauaiatv.com.*

Kipu Ranch Adventures Take a leisurely ATV ride or ride in the mule if you are under 16 or not inclined to drive your own ATV. Ride through mountain trails, tropical forests, river valleys and rolling pastures on this working cattle ranch and see areas where many movies were filmed. You can even hang from the same rope swing used by Indiana Jones in *Raiders of the Lost Ark*. Beautiful panoramic scenes of forest and mountains, wildlife and tropical plants. Standard tour is three hours. Call for directions, current tour times and rates. *Kipu Road, Lihu'e, HI 96766; 808-246-9288, 808-634-5478; www.kiputours.com.*

BICYCLING/MOTOR BIKING

Chris the Fun Lady This rental equipment operator has all sorts of recreational equipment available and can book tours, cruises, excursions. They rent mountain bikes, too. *4-746 Kuhio Highway, Kapa'a, HI 96746; 808-822-7759.*

Gary's Motorcycles of Kaua'i They rent a full line of Harley Davidson motorcycles, many models. Daily rates: Road King $185, Sportster $185, Wide Glide $185, Heritage Softail $185, Harley Buell Blast $150, moped $50. They also have a special custom-built Trike with a Chevy 350 engine, seats 5 people, hardtop, CD/stereo for $225 day. *4558 Kukui, Kapa'a, HI 96746; 808-822-4644; e-mail: customhogs@hotmail.com; realkauai.com/garysmotorcycles.*

Hawaiian Riders They rent mountain bikes ($10 to $16 day, $7 to $10 half day). They also rent mopeds ($50 day, hourly rates available), Harley Davidsons (begin at $69 day) or exotic automobiles ($119 to $399 day). Located in Kapa'a across from McDonald's. *4-776 Kuhio Highway, Kapa'a, HI 96746, 808-822-5409; also 2320 Po'ipu Road, Po'ipu, 808-742-9888.*

★ ***Kaua'i Adventure Trek*** This outfitter offers a basic half-day adventure trek that includes biking, hiking and optional swimming. The trek involves a bike ride through the Grove Farm lands, once a leading sugar cane plantation. The trek follows meandering back-country cane roads through the scenic grazing lands and mountains of Haiku country between Lihu'e and Koloa. Bikers pass through the long dark tunnel of the old cane road separating the east side of the island from the south side. The ride continues gradually downhill through rolling hills and fields to the abandoned Koloa Sugar Mill for a stop. The trek continues through fields of coffee, corn and papaya groves to the beach on the Po'ipu coast. A picnic lunch stop on the beach allows time to relax and savor the beautiful beach of the South Shore. You can swim or explore the beach before heading on the last leg of the journey, a short hike over the hilly coastline of Maha'ulepu to a lovely secluded beach and cove. Informative guided narration details the history, culture and heritage of this region of Kaua'i. This is an excellent family adventure for young and old alike. Safe mountain bikes included; tandem bikes available. Includes picnic lunch and drinks. Two treks daily, leaving from Kilohana Plantation. Rates: $85 per person. *3-2087 Kaumuali'i Highway, Lihu'e, HI 96766; 808-245-3440; cell 808-635-8735; e-mail: info@alohakauaitours.com; kauaiadventuretrek.com.*

Kaua'i Coasters This outfitter offers 12 miles of scenic downhill biking from Waimea Canyon to the coast at Kekaha. Includes bikes, gear, guides and breakfast at the crater rim. Their motto: "We've been going downhill since we started!" This is a very pleasant, safe ride; narration on culture, natural history, ecology, heritage and a short walk on the canyon nature trail. Half-day adventure ride excursion.

Rates: $70 per person. *P.O. Box 3038, Lihu'e, HI 96766; 808-639-2412; e-mail: coast@aloha.net; www.aloha.net/~coast.*

Kaua'i Cycle and Tour They rent Cannondale and specialized mountain bikes. Rates: $15 to $35 day; $40 to $85 for three days; $75 to $150 for one week. Open Monday through Friday 9 a.m. to 6 p.m. Saturday 9 a.m. to 4 p.m. Closed Sunday. *1379 Kuhio Highway, Kapa'a, HI 96746; 808-821-2115; www.bikehawaii.com/kauaicycle.*

Outfitters Kaua'i This outfitter offers mountain bike rentals for your own exploration, along with car racks, kid's seats, helmets and plenty of directions. They have a number of biking tours and biking combined with other adventures, including hiking and kayaking. Their Bicycle Downhill Canyon to Coast is a guided trip at sunrise or sunset; includes a light breakfast, snacks, beverages. Downhill Bike Ride rates: Adults $72, children 10 to 14 years old $60. *2827-A Po'ipu Road, P.O. Box 1149, Po'ipu Beach, HI 96756; 808-742-9667, 888-742-9887; fax 808-742-9667; e-mail: info@outfitterskauai.com; www.outfitterskauai.com.*

BILLIARDS

Garden Island Billiards This is an air-conditioned, smoke-free billiard parlor that offers ten full-size tables. Open daily 6 p.m. until midnight. They have liquor and offer ice-cold beer. A smoking room is also available. *Next to Anchor Cove Shopping Center, 3366 Wa'apa Road; 808-245-8900.*

Other places to play pool include the **Stevenson Lounge** at the Hyatt Regency, the **Nawiliwili Tavern** and **Sheraton Lounge** (The Point).

BOAT TRIPS (*See* Sea Excursions; Snorkeling)

BOWLING

Lihu'e Bowling Center A smoke-free environment is offered at Lihu'e Bowling Center, where there are 28 lanes open everyday. Saturday nights they offer teen disco-bowling, with popular music and a light show. The snack bar features kid-friendly foods, including burgers, pizza, clam chowder and cinnamon toast; pro shop, video games, billiards, lounge. Open 9 a.m. to midnight Monday to Saturday, Sunday noon to midnight. *In the Rice Shopping Center, 4303 Rice Street; 808-245-5263.*

BRIDGE

Everyone has a passion. You know, that hobby or recreational activity that, in your estimation, exceeds all others. Well, if the game of bridge is yours, then you are in luck on Kaua'i! Visitors are invited to stop by any of three bridge clubs around the island. Locations and playing times vary. Contact Mable Haas at 808-822-5373 or Colleen Lawshe at 808-332-9738.

CAMPING

When planning your camping vacation on Kaua'i, remember that space is very limited at the most popular campsites so make arrangements well in advance. Only tent camping is allowed at County of Kaua'i parks. Hawai'i State Parks allow tent camping, while cabins are available only at Koke'e State Park through concessionaire Koke'e Lodge.

County Parks that allow camping include Anahola County Park, 'Anini Beach Park, Ha'ena Beach Park, Hanama'ulu Beach Park and Lucy Wright Park. Camping permits are required. Contact: Parks Permit Section, Division of Parks and Recreation, County of Kaua'i, 4444 Rice Street, Moikeha Bldg., Suite 150, Lihu'e, HI 96766; 808-241-6660 during regular business hours Monday through Friday, 8 a.m. to 4 p.m., closed weekends and state holidays. There is a non-resident permit fee for tent and vehicle camping, $3 per adult per night. Permits are available at the campgrounds from park rangers at $5 per night for each adult. Youths under age 18 are free. Hawai'i State residents are exempt from camping fees. Campsites are on a first-come, first-served basis. Permits may be purchased by mail, but require 30 working days in advance to process. Contact the above office for information. See individual listings under County Parks for information.

State Parks that allow tent camping or offer cabins include Polihale State Park, Napali State Park and Koke'e State Park. Camping permits are required for state parks and are available by contacting: Hawai'i State Parks, Kaua'i District Office, Department of Land & Natural Resources, 3060 Eiwa Street, Room 306, Lihu'e, HI 96766-1875; 808-274-3444 during regular business hours; permits are issued only Monday through Friday 8 a.m. to 4 p.m., closed weekends and state holidays. Camping permits cost $5 per campsite per night for all state campgrounds except for Napali Coast State Park, which is $10 per person per night for camping at the beach parks on Napali Coast. All campgrounds, except the parks along Napali Coast, are equipped with restrooms, cold showers, drinking water, fireplaces and picnic tables. There are restrictions as to the number of nights you are allowed to camp. Permits for the Kalalau Trail/Napali Coast are in high demand and you should apply months in advance. Permits may be obtained through correspondence; however, you will be required to submit photocopies of identification (passport, driver's license) for each adult (age 18 or older) and the names and ages of minors in your group. See individual listings under "State Parks" below for information.

State Forest Reserves have some limited wilderness campsites available for tent camping only. These are hike-in campsites only. Expect hunters and dogs in these areas. No-fee permits are required. For information, contact: Hawaii State Forestry & Wildlife Division, Kaua'i District Office, Department of Land & Natural Resources, 3060 Eiwa Street, Room 306, Lihu'e, HI 96766; 808-274-3433 during regular business hours Monday through Friday, 8 a.m. to 4 p.m., closed weekends and state holidays. See the individual listings below under "State Forest Reserve Campsites" for information on each site.

Camping Equipment There are a few outfitters that provide camping equipment. They include **Pedal and Paddle** 808-826-9069; fax 808-826-7869; www.pedalnpaddle.com and **Kayak Kaua'i** 808-826-9844, both in Hanalei on the North Shore. Backpacking, camping and survival gear are available, as well as kayak, canoe, mountain bike and beach equipment rentals.

CULTURAL TOURS (*See* Museums)

DANCING

There are two dance groups that are active on the island: **USABDA**, which is a national organization, and the **Hawaiian Ballroom Dance Association**. For information on events contact Janine at her e-mail address: jb@aloha.net.

There are also dance opportunities, in limited degrees, at **The Point** at the Sheraton in Po'ipu, 808-742-1661.

FISHING

Freshwater Fishing

Kaua'i offers some diverse fishing options. Area reservoirs are home to several varieties of bass, including the peacock bass, which is also only found in Columbia and Venezuela. Since there is no restocking program, your outfitter will release all fish that are caught. Several areas are stocked with rainbow trout, although trout season is limited to the first 18 days of August, and then only on weekends and holidays through September. And did you know that the largest body of fresh water in Hawai'i is found on Kaua'i? The 422-acre manmade reservoir is Lake Waita. Check with the Department of Land and Natural Resources, Division of Aquatic Resources at 808-274-3344 regarding licensing for freshwater fishing. Ask about seasonal (usually August through September) trout fishing at Koke'e.

Cast & Catch Fresh Water Bass Guides They offer guided freshwater bass trips aboard their 17-and-a-half-foot boat to catch large-mouth bass, peacock bass and small-mouth bass. Beverages and tackle supplied. Hotel and airport pick-up available. A four-hour trip is $115 for the first person, $190 for two, $260 for three or more. Eight-hour trips also available. *P.O. Box 1371, Koloa, HI 96756; 808-332-9707.*

JJ's Big Bass Tour Sample bass fishing at one of the various reservoirs of Kaua'i. They supply tackle and refreshments along with hotel pick-up. The 17-foot *Monarch* bass boat accommodates up to three people. A half-day trip for one person is $110, full-day $190; for two persons it's $190 half-day, $300 full-day. *4550 Puuwai Road, Kalaheo, HI 96741; 808-332-9219; pager 808-654-4153.*

Ocean Fishing

It may come as a surprise to you, but sport-fishing charter boats in Hawai'i generally retain the rights to any fish caught, not the usual practice in other parts of the country. However, the captain will often cut enough of the catch for you and your family to enjoy for dinner, if you wish. You might wish to check with your boat crew before the trip to determine their policy. Half-day shared fishing trips run $75 to $150 per person; half-day private charters can run $450 and up. Full-day private charters can be as much as $600—and up. Cold beverages and water are usually provided, but guests are expected to bring their own lunch and snacks.

'Anini Fishing Charters This is a 33-foot twin diesel fishing boat specializing in sport and bottom fishing charters as well as Napali Coast tours. Rates are per person, shared boat: 4 hour $90; 6 hour $110; 8 hour $140. Call for latest private charter rates. Bob Kutkowski is the owner/operator of *Sea Breeze V. P.O. Box 818, Kilauea, HI 96754; 808-828-1285; e-mail: kauaifishing@hawaiian.net; www.kauaifishing.com.*

Captain Don's Sport Fishing and Ocean Adventures This water adventure operator has a custom 22-foot power catamaran for exploring Kaua'i's coastal areas for fishing, snorkeling, dolphin and whale watching, etc. Short-term 2-, 3- and 4-hour charters are available. Call for current rates. *Nawiliwili Harbor, Lihu'e, HI 96766; 808-826-6264, 808-639-3012.*

Capt. Harry's Sportfishing The *Happy Hunter* is a 35-foot Bertram Sportfisher that fishes the south and east coasts of Kaua'i for all Hawaiian game fish—marlin, mahimahi, yellowfin tuna, *ono*, *ulua*, *aku*, etc. Call for rates. *Nawiliwili Harbor, Lihu'e; 808-246-0399, 808-639-4351.*

Hana Pa'a Charters Captain Tim and Julie Hale invite you aboard their 38-foot Bertram, the *Maka Hou*. Exclusive and shared charters, night *ahi* fishing, trolling and bottom fishing, private sightseeing and whale watching. Call for rates. *Nawiliwili Small Boat Harbor, Lihu'e; 808-823-6031.*

Kai Bear Sportfishing Charters Located at Nawiliwili Harbor, the *Kai Bear* is a 38-foot Bertram Convertible Sportsfisher. It offers two staterooms with a galley at your disposal and adjacent salon with sofas, chairs, dining table, stereo, VCR and TV, plus it's air-conditioned. On their 8-hour charter only, fish are guaranteed! You'll receive your choice of a 3- to 5-pound portion of the catch, or a $20 gift certificate for a fish dinner at one of Kaua'i's fine restaurants. This is a professional outfit, with the crew in uniform. Maximum is six passengers. Rates: 4 hours, $550; 6 hours, $750; 8 hours, $950 for private. Ask about their special of $149 each for four passengers for four hours. They also have a 42-foot Bertram Luxury that departs from Port Allen. *P.O. Box 3544, Princeville, HI 96722; 808-639-4556; fax 808-826-4556; www.kaibearsportfishing.com.*

Kekaha Fishing Co. The *Susan Lee* is a 34-foot fiberglass fisher that departs from Kekaha's Kikiaola Harbor in west Kaua'i. Charter fishing tours along west Kaua'i and Napali Coast trips are offered. Seasonal whale watching, too. Call for rates. *P.O. Box 1289, Kekaha, HI 96752-1289; 808-337-2700; e-mail: gofish@hawaiian.net.*

Lahela Ocean Adventures This 34-foot Sportfisher operator offers light tackle, sport- or bottom-fishing excursions, half- or full-day, private or shared charters. Fish for marlin, tuna, mahimahi, *ono*, *ulua* and more. Snorkeling and whale watching, too. Rates: Shared charter fishing, half-day economy $99; deluxe $135 to $170; private charter fishing half-day, $475; 3/4-day, $575; full-day, $775. *Slip 109, Nawiliwili Harbor, Lihu'e; 808-635-4020; e-mail: lahela-adventures@aloha.net; www.lahela-adventures.com.*

McReynolds Fishing Charters Shared and exclusive charters on their 30-foot Napali-style Wilson fishing boat, the *Ho'omaika'i*, which means to make good or thanksgiving. Half- and full-day trips on the North Shore for marlin, *ahi*, mahimahi, *aku*, *ono*, *ulua*, *kahala*, *kamanu*, out of 'Anini Beach. *P.O. Box 1002, Kilauea, HI 96754; 808-828-1379.*

Napali Sportfishing This fully equipped Bertram Sportfisher, the *Kai Runner II* does 4-, 6- and 8-hour fishing tours; fishing for blue marlin, yellowfin tuna, mahimahi, *ono* and *aku*. They take extended trips to Ni'ihau and other known fishing hotspots around Kaua'i. Call for rates. *P.O. Box 569, Waimea, HI 96796; 808-635-9424, 808-335-9909.*

Open Sea Charter Fishing This is a luxurious 36-foot Hatteras, the *Carol Ann*. Fishing the south and west shores of Kaua'i for marlin, *ono*, yellowfin tuna, *aku*, mahimahi and shark out of Port Allen Harbor. 4-, 6- and 8-hour fishing tours available. Call for rates. *P.O. Box 634, Waimea, HI 96796; 808-332-8213.*

Sport Fishing Kaua'i This outfitter operates a fully equipped Bertram Sportfisher boat. Rates: Private charters for boat, half-day,

$475; 3/4-day, $675; full-day, $875; Ni'ihau tour, $1,075; shared boat rates per person: half-day, $95; 3/4-day, $135; special rates for children, too. *P.O. Box 1195, Po'ipu, HI 96756; 808-639-0013; e-mail: info@fishing-kauai-hawaii.com; www.fishing-kauai-hawaii.com.*

True Blue Charters & Ocean Sports This is a 55-foot Delta vessel *Konane Star* equipped with microwave, TV, VCR, hydrophone (whale listening device), hot and cold freshwater showers, restrooms. Rates: half-day share trips (4 hours) $95 to $175; 3/4-day (6 hours) $125 to $225. (The price reflects the number of anglers.) Exclusive charters $650 to $800. Spectators on share trips half price. They also operate Island Adventures, kayak trips and Rainbow Runner Sailing aboard a 42-foot trimaran. *P.O. Box 1722, Lihu'e, HI 96766; departs Nawiliwili Small Boat Harbor Slip #112; 888-245-1707, 808-246-6333; fax 808-246-9661; e-mail: funkauai@hawaiian.net; www.kauaifun.com.*

Wild Bill's Fishing Charters This is a 28-foot Radon Sportfisher; fish the south and east coasts of Kaua'i for marlin, *ahi*, *ono*, mahimahi, *aku* and more. 4-, 6- and 8-hour fishing trips available. Call for rates. *P.O. Box 413, Kapa'a, HI 96746, Nawiliwili Harbor, Lihu'e; 808-822-5963.*

Fishing Supplies **Lihu'e Fishing Supply**—If the "big one" gets away, you can always go next door to the Kalena Fish Market. *2985 Kalena Street; 808-245-4930.* **Rainbow Paint & Fishing Supply Inc.**—All you need to catch and land a trophy. *Waialo Road, Hanapepe; 808-335-6412.*

GARDEN TOURS (*See* Museums)

GOLF

Kaua'i offers seven 18-hole golf courses at five different locations, plus one 9-hole course and one 10-hole course. Each course takes advantage of mountain and ocean views and utilizes the natural elements of the island to add character to each course.

Grove Farm Golf Course at Puakea This golf course is built on more than 200 acres of historic property that was once a sugar cane field. It is unusual with its massive ravines, lakes and volcanic cliffs. Definitely more to the course than you might expect for central Kaua'i! Course rating is 76.2, with slope rating of 135. There are four tee boxes. Designed by architect Robin Nelson, the course is adjacent to the lot on which *Jurassic Park: The Lost World* was filmed. Reservations for the 10-hole course (yes, that is *ten*) can be made 30 days in advance. Lessons available. Rate: $65 for 20 holes; $50 after 2 p.m.; $45 for 10 holes. *4315 Kalepa Street, Lihu'e, HI 96766; 808-245-8756; www.golfgrovefarm.com.*

Kaua'i Lagoons Golf Club Facilities include a driving range, pro shop, putting green, restaurant and bar. Tee times can be made 29 days in advance. Both the Kiele Course and the Mokihana Course make up this facility. Rental clubs and shoes available. *3351 Ho'olaulea Way, Lihu'e, HI 96766; 808-241-6000, 800-634-6400.*

★ **Kiele Course**—Designed by Jack Nicklaus, this 18-hole, par-72 course is 7,070 yards. The course features deep ravines, ocean cliffs and a wedding chapel. Each hole is named for an animal and a white marble statue of the animal adorns each tee. *Golf Digest* rated this course #3 in Hawai'i and #88 in the United States. With the nearby Kaua'i Lagoons Chapel by the Sea, perhaps this is the perfect course for the groom-to-be (or bride-to-be) to combine a few holes of golf before or after the ceremony! General public $170, Kaua'i Marriott guests $120, other guests staying in Kaua'i hotels are $130.

★ **Mokihana Course**—Also designed by Jack Nicklaus, this 18-hole course (par-72) has 6,942 yards of play. This course was named in honor of the *mokihana*, the official flower of Kaua'i. This course is less demanding than neighboring Kiele, but the Scottish links–style course is popular with the recreational golfer. It has a forgiving layout, with wide fairways and four tees for all skill levels. Green fees general public $85; Kaua'i Marriott guests $75; after 11 a.m. $65 and $55.

Kiahuna Golf Club Robert Trent Jones, Jr., designed this 18-hole, par-70 course located in Po'ipu. Kiahuna features ocean and mountain views, as well as some surprises. Lava rock walls, a huge lava tube, a Blind Eye Spider cave and other Hawaiian archaeological sites add to the personality of this course as it winds around remnants of an ancient Hawaiian village. Championship 6,353 yards. Facilities include driving range, pro shop, putting green, snack shop and bar. Green fees, including cart: $75 morning; after 2:30 p.m. $45. *2545 Kiahuna Plantation Drive, Koloa, HI 96756; 808-742-9595.*

★ ***Kukuiolono Golf Course*** This public course is situated on top of Kukuiolono Park and the fourth and fifth holes have spectacular views. It features ample fairways, a Japanese garden and ancient

STAND-BY GOLF

This is a great option for golfers interested in some serious savings. They feature discounted rates at public and private courses. They sell unsold tee times beginning about 6 p.m. until 9 p.m. for the next day of play and after 7 a.m. for the same day. They book your game at a guaranteed price and time. Discounts range from 10 percent on the lowest-priced courses up to 33 percent and more. Prices always include the cart. Definitely worth a phone call. They don't book municipal courses, however. Bookings are handled by telephone and you pay with a credit card. 888-645-2665.

Hawaiian rock structures. Play is on a first-come basis, no reservations. The 9 holes are a par-36, with 2,981 yards of play. Facilities include a driving range, pro shop, putting green and snack shop. Golf club rentals available. At $7 for all-day play, it is hard to go wrong. This course is usually very crowded. We suggest you tee off about 3 p.m.—you get through a fair part of the course (and see that spectacular view at the fourth and fifth hole)—and for the price it doesn't matter if you don't finish. Open 6:30 a.m. to 6:30 p.m.; no tee-offs after 4:50 p.m. Carts are optional at $6. *Papalina Road, Kalaheo; 808-332-9151.*

★ ***Po'ipu Bay Resort Golf Course*** Po'ipu Bay Resort Golf Course is an 18-hole championship course situated on 210 oceanfront acres adjacent to the Hyatt Regency Kaua'i Resort and Spa. The course is a Scottish links–style course with a par-72 designed by Robert Trent Jones, Jr. It boasts some outstanding ocean vistas and seven holes with water hazards. Set between lush mountains and rugged ocean bluffs, the course includes over 35 acres of landscaped tropical plants and flowers. An archaeological site has been incorporated into the course. During winter, golfers can even catch glimpses of the whales as they pass offshore. And don't be surprised if you see some *nene* (Hawaiian geese) wandering about. It's an absolutely beautiful course to play but can be subject to strong winds from mid-morning on. Over the years Po'ipu Bay has won numerous awards and has consistently been rated among the top golf courses in the U.S. and Hawai'i. It has been rated the #1 golf course in Hawai'i on the Gold List as chosen by the readers of *Conde Nast Traveler*. The course has played host to the annual PGA Grand Slam of Golf, hosting golf luminaries like Tiger Woods and company. Greens fees: Hyatt Hotel guest before noon $120, $105 after; others $170 before noon, $115 after; after 3 p.m. $65. They also feature a half-off Junior Golf Special Rate for kids 17 years and under when accompanied by a paying adult. Inquire about any special hotel guest or other discounted rates; also check their daily clinics and lessons. Facilities include a driving range, pro shop, clubhouse (with restaurant, lounge and snack bar), putting green and practice sand bunkers. Golfers can also reserve tee times online through EZLinks Golf, Inc. at www.ezlinksgolf.com. *2250 Ainako Street, Koloa, HI 96756; 808-742-8711; www.kauai-hyatt.com.*

Princeville Golf Club The Princeville Resort offers stellar golfing opportunities.

Makai Course—Designed by Robert Trent Jones, Jr., this is actually three courses rolled into 27 holes: The Lakes, The Ocean and The Woods are each nine holes, par-36, with the clubhouse at the hub. With waterfalls, beaches, mountains and spectacular Makana (Bali Hai) as backdrops, it's a gorgeous setting. Facilities include driving range, pro shop, putting green and snack bar. The Prince Course has been listed in *Golf Digest* Top Resort Courses and in America's 100 Greatest Golf Courses for the last 16 years. The Makai Course has hosted the LPGA Women's Kemper Open more than once. $120 regular rate, $105 for Princeville area guests, $100 for Princeville Hotel guests. Twilight rate (after 1:30 p.m.) is $80. Sunset rate (after 4 p.m.) is $45. An additional round is $35. Club rental $35, shoe rental $15, riders fee $25. *4080 Leiopapa Road, Princeville; 808-826-3580.*

★ **Prince Course**—This 18-hole layout is a par-72, with 7,309 yards of play. Scenic vistas include the rugged cliffsides and the famous Makana and other beautiful mountains. You may also see albatrosses nesting here in winter. The course fits snugly along the cliffsides of Kaua'i's North Shore, with hole #13 featuring a waterfall backdrop. With a USGA course rating of 75.3, this course is ranked as the most challenging in the state. However, multiple tees on each hole accommodate the casual golfer as well. Driving range, pro shop, putting greens, restaurant and bar are available. *Golf Digest* ranks this course #1 in the state of Hawai'i and in the top 50 in the United States. It's one of 11 courses in the U.S. to have a five-star rating. The Prince Course charges $175 standard rate, $145 for Princeville area guests and $125 for Princeville Hotel guests. Rates after noon are $115 standard rate for all; $55 replay rate. *5-3900 Kuhio Highway, Princeville, 808-826-5000.*

★ ***Wailua Municipal Golf Course*** On the eastern shore between Lihu'e and Kapa'a, the course features an 18-hole, 6,981-yard, par-72 layout. It's considered by some to be the best municipal course in the state, with shaded ponds, Pacific Ocean views and fairly low green fees. This is a great option for the budget traveler who really wants to golf but can't afford the much higher fees at the resort courses. The only cheaper course is Kukuiolono at Kalaheo. Facilities include a driving range, pro shop, putting green, restaurant and bar. Rates: $32 weekday, $44 on weekends and holidays. Ask about their afternoon specials. Club rental $15. Charge is $20 per cart (cart is optional). This is a very busy course with many local folks golfing here. *3-5351 Kuhio Highway, Lihu'e, HI 96766; 808-241-6666.*

HANG GLIDING

Birds in Paradise Here is an opportunity to experience hang glider ultralight flying. Tandem instructional tours are offered in these powered ultralights and a wing-mounted video of your flight is available. Rates: Mini-Intro Lesson (25 to 30 minutes), $100; Full Intro Lesson (50 to 60 minutes), $175; Advanced Lesson (80 to 90 minutes), $255; Round-the-Island Lesson (110 to 120 minutes), $330. Microlight

Pilot Certification is typically 10 to 12 hours. *Port Allen Airport, 543 Lele Road, Hanapepe, HI 96716; 808-822-5309, fax 808-822-5309; e-mail: birdip@birdsinparadise.com; www.birdsinparadise.com.*

HELICOPTERS

A helicopter tour will set you back some bucks, but some visitors feel it is a worthwhile experience. Many residents, however, have some strong feelings about such tours, as they severely disrupt the peace and quiet of our island, and they're especially intrusive in wilderness areas like Waimea Canyon and Kalalau. You may want to think twice about whether you want to support such an activity. If you decide to do it anyway, choose a clear, sunny day or else you won't see much—helicopters still fly in cloudy weather, even though your experience is greatly diminished. Helicopters fly around Kaua'i in a clockwise direction, so seating on the right side of the craft offers the best viewing. However, the seat assignment is based on weight and yes, they sometimes have you step on a scale to make sure you're honest. Some helicopter companies are owner-operated and brochures often talk about the owner's flying experience. In some cases, this may not be the person piloting your helicopter tour. In other cases, you'll find that it's indeed the owner that operates each and every tour. Most flights depart from Lihu'e Airport or Princeville Airport. Those departing from Port Allen Airport on the westside are listed, but not recommended, since residents have complained about the expansion of helicopter flights out of the main airports and the controversy over the use of this airfield for such flights. Tours offered by Jack Harter and Will Squyres are most highly recommended because they have been the most responsive to efforts to control helicopter flights and select routes that are the least intrusive to residents and hikers. They are also the oldest firms on the island.

There have been some revisions in regulations regarding kids. Children 1 to 35 pounds must have an infant life preserver. Children 36 to 90 pounds must have a child life preserver. Children over 90 pounds are considered an adult and must have an adult life preserver. Children under two are permitted to sit on a parent's lap. For a single-engine flight over water *everyone* must wear a vest. For a twin-engine flight over water, a vest is not required, but must be easily accessible. On Kaua'i, most tours include a scenic pass along Napali Coast. Due to weather conditions, and just the view vantage point, the flights must be able to fly out over the water. The only company on Kaua'i currently operating a dual rotor helicopter is Hawai'i Helicopters.

While most young children don't go on helicopter trips, we were told that there are lots of infants that go as lap riders. So inquire if you are traveling with a babe in arms, or want to take a youngster up.

★ ***Air Kaua'i Helicopter Tours*** Chuck DiPiazza and staff fly air-conditioned A-Stars with a two-way intercom and custom bubble windows providing exceptional visibility. They are also equipped with a compact disc player and a special noise-canceling system. They offer one concise tour, a one-hour deluxe air experience that includes Waimea Canyon, Napali and Wai'ale'ale for $195 per person. Inquire on direct bookings for discounts. *Lihu'e Airport; 800-972-4666; 808-246-4666; fax 808-246-3966; e-mail for reservations: heliop@aloha.net; e-mail for information: info@airkauai.com; www.airkauai.com.*

Bali Hai Helicopter Tours Owned and operated by James Lee and his staff. Family discounts. Four-passenger Bell 206B Jet Ranger helicopter. Two basic tours: Bali Hai Grandeur Tour 55 to 60 minutes, $139 per person; Bali Hai Splendor Tour 45 to 50 minutes, $110 per person. Highway 50, Hanapepe, next to Lappert's Ice Cream Shop on the way to Waimea. Departs from Port Allen Airport. *P.O. Box 626, Hanapepe, HI 96716; 800-325-TOUR; 808-335-3166; fax 808-335-5615; e-mail: blh@aloha.net; www.balihai-helitour.com.*

HeliUSA They fly A-Stars. Three basic air tours are offered and take in the major scenic highlights of Kaua'i. The 30-minute Bali Hai is $99 per person. The 45-minute Garden Isle Special is $135 per person. The 60-minute Garden Isle Deluxe is $179 per person. *Departs Princeville Resort Airport; 866-936-1234; 808-826-6591; www.heliusa.com.*

Inter-Island Helicopters Operates Hughes 500 with two sit-up-front and two sit-in-back seats, each have their own window. They like to fly with the doors off so photos will come out clear, and their two-way intercom allows communication between pilot and other passengers. They fly from Port Allen Airport in Hanapepe. The one-hour tour covers Olokele Canyon, three Waimea Canyon valleys, then over Koke'e to Napali Coast. They also have a one-hour-forty-five minute Waterfall Adventure tour that includes a stop at their private landing pad and a short walk on the boardwalk to a waterfall with time for a picnic lunch and a quick swim in the pond. Waterfall weddings are also available. *P.O. Box 156, Hanapepe, HI 96716; 808-335-5009; fax 808-335-5567.*

Island Helicopters Flies A-Star helicopters and also a six-passenger A-Star. Depart from Lihu'e. They specialize in just one tour, the "Kaua'i Grand," 55 to 60 minutes in length, which takes in all the major scenic attractions of Kaua'i. Per person rate, $200; from Lihu'e Airport. *P.O. Box 831, Lihu'e, HI 96766; 808-245-8588; 800-829-5999; fax 808-245-6258; e-mail: fly@islandhelicopters.com; www.islandhelicopters.com.*

★ ***Jack Harter Helicopters*** Flies Bell Jet Ranger, tours depart Lihu'e Airport. Jack originated helicopter tours on Kaua'i in the 1960s. They offer two standard air tours and cover all the major scenic attractions of Kaua'i. The 60-minute flight runs $165 per person; the 90-minute flight is $235 per person. *4231 Ahukini Road, Lihu'e; 888-245-2001; 808-245-3774; e-mail: jharter@aloha.net; www.helicopters-kauai.com.*

Ni'ihau Helicopters Flies an Augusta helicopter that departs from Hanapepe. The flight circles Ni'ihau and lands briefly on one of the beaches. They are a little difficult to reach, with short office hours, and tour offerings are limited to mostly hunting and fishing excursions. *P.O. Box 370, Makaweli, HI 96769; 808-335-3500; fax 808-338-1463.*

Ohana Helicopter Tours Flies A-Star, departures from Lihu'e Airport. Owner-pilot Bogard Kealoha is a local, born and raised on Kaua'i. There are two separate tours offered. The 50- to 55-minute Mokihana tour is $146 per person; the 60- to 75-minute Maile tour is $186. Both tours take in all the major attractions and features. *341 Rice Street, #204, Lihu'e; 808-245-3996; 800-222-6989; fax 808-245-5041; e-mail: info@ohana-helicopters.com; www.ohana-helicopters.com.*

Safari Helicopters Flies the A-Star and departs from Lihu'e Airport. Their three- and four-camera video/sound system, with two-way intercom, captures your trip with pilot's narration. They offer one basic Kaua'i air tour, the 55-minute Deluxe Waterfall Safari for $149 to $189 seasonal rate per person; check out the internet booking special for $139. *P.O. Box 1941, Lihu'e, HI 96766; 808-246-0136; 800-326-3356; e-mail: info@safarihelicopters.com; www.safariair.com.*

South Sea Helicopters Departs Lihu'e Airport, flies Bell Jet Ranger. Seasonal rates available, inquire when booking. Choose the 45- to 50-minute "Kaua'i Special Flight" air tour at $115 to $135 per person; the 60-minute "Golden Eagle Flight" air tour at $130 to $160 per person; or the 75-minute "Flight of the Canyon Bird" air tour at $173 to $198 per person. Tours take in the best of Kaua'i's scenic highlights. *Lihu'e Airport, 3901 Mokulele Loop, Box 32, Lihu'e, HI 96766; 808-245-2222; 800-367-2914; fax 808-246-9586; e-mail: 2ssh@gte.net; www.southseahelicopters.com.*

Will Squyres Helicopter Tours Tours depart Lihu'e Airport. Will Squyres began his company in 1984 with 22 years of flying experience. He uses six-passenger A-Stars. The "Ultimate Kaua'i Adventure" air tour is 60 minutes and visits the Waimea Canyon, Napali Coastline, Wai'ale'ale Crater and the famous *Jurassic Park* waterfall, as well as settings used in many other films made on Kaua'i. Per person cost is $159; private charters for 1 to 6 people available at $950. *P.O. Box 1770, Lihu'e, HI 96766; 808-245-8881; 888-245-4354; e-mail: squyres@aloha.net; www.helicopters-hawaii.com.*

HIKING

(Also see "Parks" section below for information on several hiking trails.)

Hiking on Kaua'i is a delightful experience, and guides are not generally needed. The state is trying to control commercial activities on public trails by limiting the trails that can be used by tour companies. For instance, no guided tours are allowed along the Kalalau trail. So please help support the state's rules, don't sign up for any such hikes. Also, if you are considering hiring a guide, ask if they comply with state trail rules. If they don't, don't hire them. This is just one way the state is trying to protect the trails from overuse and ensure quality experiences for those who use these public resources.

A few good rules to follow: be prepared—take rain gear (where needed), water and food; always let someone know where you are hiking and when you should be back; stay on trails since it's easy to get lost and many steep drop-offs are hidden under a blanket of ferns; never jump from waterfalls into pools; don't drink untreated water anywhere on the island. In Koke'e, be prepared for cool weather.

The Hawai'i State Department of Land and Natural Resources, Division of Forestry & Wildlife has free (if you go in person) trail maps of Kaua'i available. If you are contacting them in advance, you will need to send a self-addressed stamped envelope with your request, and probably a small fee for handling. Call or write for requirements to the Department of Land and Natural Resources, Division of Forestry and Wildlife, 3060 Eiwa Street, #306, Lihu'e, HI 96766; 808-274-3433.

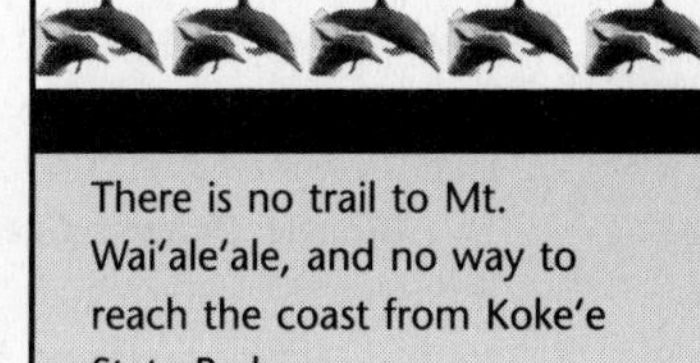

There is no trail to Mt. Wai'ale'ale, and no way to reach the coast from Koke'e State Park.

Also check the Na Ala Hele Trail and Access System website, www.hawaiitrails.org, for details on hiking trails throughout the Hawaiian islands, along with relevant hiking information.

Hiking Outfitters

★ ***Kaua'i Adventure Trek*** This outfitter combines half-day adventure treks with biking, hiking and optional swimming. (*See* "Bicycling/Motor Biking" above for details on this adventure.) Includes picnic lunch and drinks. Two treks daily at 8:15 a.m. and 10 a.m., leaving from Kilohana Plantation (home of Gaylord's). Rates: $85 per person. *3-2087 Kaumuali'i Highway, Lihu'e, HI 96766; 808-245-3440; cell 808-635-8735; e-mail: inquiries@kauaiadventuretrek.com; www.kauaiadventuretrek.com.*

Kaua'i Mountain Tours Mike and Terri Hopkins, under the name Aloha Kauai Tours, operate a number of hiking excursions into different areas of Kaua'i. They also offer water/kayak and land tours;

check the website for details. Hikes range from easy to moderate to difficult; some combine van or four-wheel-drive offroad vehicle rides to more remote trailheads. Hikes cover areas such as Koloa to Maha'ulepu Coast and Kilohana Crater, with a beautiful 360-degree island view. There is also a trek to Blue Hole near Mt. Wai'ale'ale in the island's interior, plus other hikes through Kaua'i's splendid Koke'e Park, Waimea Canyon trails, *koa* forests and much more. Rates: Kauai Backroads Half Day $50 (kids $44); Aloha Kauai Tour Full Day $90 (kids $63); Blue Hole Half Day $65 (kids $50). *Aloha Kauai Tours, 1702 Haleukaua Street, Lihu'e, HI 96766; 808-245-7224; 800-452-1113; e-mail: tours@gte.net; www.alohakauaitours.com.*

Kaua'i Nature Tours Kaua'i Nature Tours offers day trips with short hikes led by experienced local guides. These guides and tours are generally well done. However, we can't recommend their Napali hike because it is not legal, despite their rationalization that they should be allowed to offer it because they help maintain the trails. Instead, choose from a number of interpretative tours, including Waimea Canyon Explorer, Maha'ulepu Coast Hike, and Beaches of Kaua'i Excursion. Tour/hike rates: $82 (kids 12 and under $45). These unique day-long tours include transportation, a picnic lunch and refreshments. Hikers should be reasonably fit, have good walking shoes and sun protection. Most of the tours leave from Po'ipu Beach Park at 9 a.m. and return by 4 p.m. Also available are week-long adventure vacations. *P.O. Box 549, Koloa, HI 96756; 808-742-8305; 888-233-8365; e-mail: teok@aloha.net; www.teok.com.*

Olokele Canyon Overlook Tour This 3.5-hour excursion combines an offroad vehicle or van ride plus some limited hiking on a tour of sugar plantation fields, a working cattle ranch and the irrigation system at Makaweli on Kaua'i's south side. This tour takes in the Olokele Canyon Overlook and the water intake at Olokele Canyon. Learn about the Gay & Robinson Plantation, Makaweli Ranch, the 1904 Olokele ditch system, history, culture, flora and fauna of the area. It's quite scenic and interesting. Gay & Robinson Tours. *2 Kaumakani Avenue, Kaumakani, HI 96747; 808-335-2824; e-mail: toursgnr@aloha.net; www.gandrtours-kauai.com.*

★ ***Princeville Ranch Hiking Adventures*** This outfitter/guide offers three different adventures, and they are highly recommended. The "Hidden Hanalei" hike is three hours, easy to moderate, hiking trails around Hanalei Bay and Namolokama, $59 per person. The "Waterfall Excursion" is four hours, a moderate loop trail through lush ranch uplands, with panoramic overlook and plunging 100-foot Kalihiwai Falls, $74 per person. The "Jungle Waterfall Adventure" combines a kayaking excursion up a jungle stream and short hike through the jungle to a waterfall, $89 per person. Kids 12 and under and seniors get a 10 percent discount. They provide daypacks, water bottles, healthy snacks, walking sticks, *tabis* (special Japanese shoes for walking through water), even rain gear (just in case), plus informative and educational insight into the history, culture, flora and fauna of the area. *P.O. Box 224, Hanalei, HI 96714; 808-826-7669; 888-955-7669; fax 808-826-7210; e-mail: prha@aloha.net; www.kauai-hiking.com.*

The **Sierra Club** publishes a quarterly newsletter, *Malama*, available by subscription for $7 per year. A sample of the newsletter can be received by writing them, including a $1 fee and a self-addressed and stamped envelope. Also available is *Hiking Softly in Hawai'i*, a guide to the enjoyment of the Hawaiian wilderness with useful information on how to obtain hiking and camping permits, etc. Available for $4 from the Sierra Club. Sierra Club, Hawai'i Chapter, P.O. Box 2577, Honolulu, HI 96803. Visitors can write to the Kaua'i group a couple of months prior to their arrival and request a schedule by sending a self-addressed stamped envelope and a $1 fee. They can also check the calendar listing in *The Garden Island* newspaper for upcoming hikes. Advance registration is necessary for all outings in the event of last-minute changes due to inclement weather. They suggest a $3 donation for each person participating in the outings. Several excellent references are available for the interested hiker. (See ordering information at the back of this guide.) Craig Chisholm is the author of *Kaua'i Hiking Trails*, *Hawaiian Hiking Trails* and *Hawai'i: The Big Island Hiking Trails*. His guides provide excellent topographical maps, good directions and detailed information, including the number of calories you can expect to burn, time required to travel the trail roundtrip, and elevation.

The **Koke'e Natural History Museum** offers a series of guided hikes in the scenic uplands of West Kaua'i. Hikes are led by one of the trained volunteers of the Koke'e Natural History Museum. The hikes vary in length and in difficulty and since space is limited, call ahead to reserve your spot. A $2 donation is requested. Tours include a hike along cliff and canyon trails to Waipo'o Falls, hikes along the fairly strenuous Pihea trail or a family hike along Berry Flats Trail. Along the way your interpretative guide will explain about the flora and fauna discovered on your hike. *For dates and times of hikes call 808-335-9975.*

Hiking Trails

Awa'awapuhi The Awa'awapuhi Trail, one of 29 trails listed in *Kaua'i Hiking Trails*, is reprinted here with permission. Author Craig Chisholm comments that this trail takes a bit more effort than some, but "it is well-marked and the view at its end is, in my opinion, the most impressive in Hawai'i." The moderately difficult hike takes 2.25 hours up and 1.5 hours down. Roundtrip is 6.5 miles. The highest point is 4,100 feet and the lowest point is 2,560 feet. Awesome views of Napali Coast and its isolated, hanging valleys make the Awa'awapuhi Trail one of the best for photographing Hawai'i. The trail descends 1,500 feet through native dryland forests to twin viewpoints above the cliffs that drop into the remote Awa'awapuhi and Nualolo valleys. The floors of these rarely visited valleys are accessible only by water, and then only after difficult climbing from the sea. However, the trail provides good vantage points of the great fluted walls enclosing the valleys and forest wilderness. The various scenic viewpoints afford a good opportunity to watch the sunlight and shadows play on the cliffs and sea. Mornings and afternoons, helicopters flutter like dragonflies in and out of the valleys below, while cruise boats zip along the coast. There's a nice overlook and grassy rest point at trail's end. The trail is in very good condition, most of the way, and marked about every quarter to half-mile. The Division of Forestry and Wildlife has labeled many endemic plants along the route and has published an interpretive guide that is available at their office in Lihu'e or at the Koke'e Museum. At first the broad trail leads north and goes up a little. It then descends (with switchbacks), generally in a northwesterly direction. At approximately three miles from the start, the Nualolo Cliff Trail, which is a connector from the Nualolo Trail, leads in from the left (south). Soon after this junction, the Awa'awapuhi Trail ends at the metal-railed viewpoints. Do not go close to the rims of the canyons. The small stones covering the hard surfaces on the eroded areas, like ball bearings on concrete, provide treacherous footing. The drop to the valley floor on either side is between 1,500 and 3,000 feet, depending on the bounce. The plants in the native dryland forest are rare and the danger of fires extreme; thus, neither overnight camping nor fires are permitted. *To get there*: From Koke'e State Park Headquarters go 1.6 miles up Highway 550 toward the Kalalau Lookout. The trailhead is on the left, in the Napali-Kona Forest Reserve, across from a dirt road and just before the 17-mile mark on the Highway. Take your own food and plenty of water. (While this trail may be a bit rugged for family travel with young children, there are many other trails outlined in Chisholm's book that are less strenuous and of shorter duration.)

Kalalau Trail/Napali Coast This time-worn trail of 11 miles starts next to Ke'e Beach at the end of Highway 56. There you will find parking, bathrooms and showers. A sign at the beginning of the trail will provide you with all the pertinent information you will need for your hike. (Maps, permits, mileage, restrictions, etc.) The first two miles to Hanakapi'ai and additional 1.8 miles to Hanakapi'ai Falls is as far as most people go. The roundtrip hike to the beach will take at least half a day, and plan a full day for the waterfall hike. These hikes are strenuous, and not recommended for young children or people with knee problems. Bring your own drinking water and snacks. (See "Parks—State Parks" below for complete description of the Kalalau Trail.) Hikers venturing on from Hanakapi'ai will need overnight camping permits, which you get from the State Parks Office.

Koke'e State Park/Waimea Canyon Trails System There are numerous hiking trails in the Koke'e State Park and adjoining Waimea Canyon. Only a couple of the trails are highlighted here. It is suggested that hikers obtain maps, brochures and trail guides for details on the hiking trails in these areas. These are some great hikes; however, helicopters are frequent and low-flying in these areas, so don't expect silence. *Upper and Lower Waipo'o Falls* Access this trailhead 1.4 miles below (south) Koke'e Lodge on the Koke'e Road at Halemanu Road. Parking is on both sides of the road. Follow Halemanu Road .8 miles to the trailhead. A marked trail junction indicates the Canyon and Black Pipe Trails. Past this is a second junction, hang left on the Canyon Trail. *The Upper and Lower Waipo'o Falls and Canyon Trail* hike is one of the Waimea Canyon's more enjoyable. This is a moderately difficult 3.2 mile roundtrip of about 2 to 3 hours. The trail passes through the cool montane forest, alive with the sounds of birdlife, and meanders down deeper into the canyon, crossing a small stream and arriving at a bare knoll. There are great views of the surrounding colorful walls and cliffs of Po'omau Canyon. There are also some surprising wind-eroded rock arches high on the cliffsides. Below this bare knoll a short distance is Koke'e Stream, with the Upper Falls to the left. To the right, the main trail leads to the Lower Falls. The Upper Waipo'o Falls has a large pool and is surrounded by boulders, rocky outcroppings and heavy vegetation. It's a great place to relax and stick your feet in the water. The Lower Waipo'o Falls, a short distance down stream, has several smaller pools and spreads out into showering cascades as it tumbles down a sheer drop. Avoid going too close to the edge. Find a rock or grassy patch to sit on and enjoy your picnic lunch while basking in the magnificent canyon views. It's an incredible experience in solitude. Take food, water and sun protection.

HORSEBACK RIDING

Horseback trail riders are afforded the opportunity to enjoy some of Kaua'i's most breathtaking scenery. On the North Shore, you can take a four-hour ride to a mountain waterfall. Near Waimea, visitors can enjoy the island's only ocean rides while watching the sun sinking slowly over the island of Ni'ihau. At Po'ipu Beach, a three-hour breakfast trail ride encompasses scenic views of the ocean, beaches and mountains. These are among a few of the offerings from Kaua'i's horseback trailride outfitters listed below.

CJM Country Stables Located 1.5 miles past the Hyatt Regency Kaua'i Hotel, owner Jimmy Miranda and his crew will take you into hidden valley ranchland, past secluded beaches and bays to discover the picturesque beauty of the Po'ipu area on horseback. The "Secret Beach Breakfast Ride" is a three-hour ride that includes gourmet cowboy coffee and a continental breakfast, offered three days a week on Tuesday, Thursday and Saturday at $75 per person. The "Hidden Beach Ride" is a two-hour ride through the ancient Maha'ulepu area of the South Shore, twice daily except Sunday at $65 per person. The "Beach Swim/Picnic Ride" is a three-and-a-half-hour beach swim and riding excursion, with a picnic lunch included, offered three times a week on Monday, Wednesday and Friday at $90 per person. *1731 Kelaukia Street, Koloa, HI 96756; 808-742-6096; fax 808-742-6015; e-mail: cjm@aloha.net; www.cjmstables.com.*

Espirit De Corps Riding Academy The standard three-hour "Fast Half Ride" includes trotting and cantering, with panoramic ocean and mountain views at $99 per person. The five-hour "WOW!!! Ride" passes along ridges of an old lava flow, and exotic beauty of Kaua'i's mountains and meadow uplands, snack included at $250 for minimum of three guests (five maximum). An "All-Day Adventure Ride" is eight hours and includes a stop at a mountain swimming hole and lunch for $350 for a minimum of two guests or $300 for a minimum of four guests. Private "Honeymoon Rides" are also available. Private rides with longer arena lesson are available for the less-experienced rider. Private lessons are also available. *P.O. Box 269, Kapa'a, Kaua'i, HI 96746; 808-822-4688; e-mail: riding@kauaihorses.com; www.kauaihorses.com.*

Princeville Ranch Stables/Adventures on Horseback A family-owned business since 1978, Donn and Gale Carswell offer a variety of trail rides. Minimum age is 8 years. All riders must be in good physical condition. Weight-limit restrictions: 180 pounds for women, 220 pounds for men. Long pants recommended, closed shoes are a must. The three-and-a-half-hour "Waterfall Ride" involves riding across ranchland and a short, steep hike (without the horse) down to the base of the Kalihiwai Falls (about 10 minutes). It includes a picnic lunch and swim at $110 per person. The two-hour "Cattle Drive Ride" shows you what it's like to be a real Hawaiian *paniolo* (cowboy), rounding up cattle at sunrise and driving them across ranchlands to a corral at $125 per person. The "Anini Bluff & Beach Ride" is a three-hour adventure along a scenic bluff to spectacular 'Anini Beach, and includes a light snack and swimming at beach at $100 per person. The "Panoramic Paniolo Country Ride" is a fantastic one-and-a-half-hour ride across Princeville Ranch, taking in all the scenic vistas of the magnificent Hanalei Mountains, 'Anini Beach and distant Makana. $55 per person. Most rides offered daily, except Sunday. *P.O. Box 888, Hanalei, HI 96714; 808-826-6777; 808-826-7473; fax 808-826-7210; e-mail: pstable@aloha.net; www.kauai.net/kwc4.*

Silver Falls Ranch Trail Rides This outfitter has various trail rides through the Mount Namahana area near Kilauea in the North Shore region. The one-and-a-half-hour "Greenhorns Trail Ride" is for beginners and scaredy cats (gulp!), and focuses on basic riding skills at $69 per person. The two-hour "Hawaiian Discovery Ride" takes in beautiful and peaceful country forest settings and great views of the mountains at $78 per person. The three-hour "Silver Falls Ride" takes in a natural mountain pool and waterfall, combining a great trail ride, swim and a picnic lunch at $105 per person. Private rides also available. *P.O. Box 692, Kilauea, HI 96754; 808-828-6718; fax 808-828-0131; e-mail: sfr@hawaiian.net; www.hawaiian.net/~sfr.*

HUNTING/SHOOTING RANGES

There are no commercial hunting guides currently operating on Kaua'i. Those interested in hunting might inquire with the hunting shop listed below. Public hunting areas allow seasonal hunting for game birds such as ring-necked pheasant, chukar partridge, Japanese quail, doves and others. Seasonal hunting is also allowed for feral goats, wild pig and black-tailed deer. For hunting information contact the Department of Land & Natural Resources, Wildlife Division. They can help you with enforcement and licensing information as well as hunting guidelines. 808-274-3433.

The Hunting Shop of Kaua'i This is a full-service fire arms and hunting shop that also includes archery. It is the only authorized Matthews dealer. They also do repairs. **Shooter's Paradise** (808-246-4867), an indoor shooting range, is also located here. Firearm Safety training courses are offered. *3156 Oihana, Lihu'e; 808-245-3006.*

Ni'ihau Safaris, Ltd. Departs from Port Allen Airport. This outfitter offers exclusive full-day hunting safaris for wild boar and feral sheep (plus fishing) to the privately owned island of Ni'ihau. The island is owned and operated as a working ranch by the Robinson family. There is a small resident population of Hawaiians on the island. They also operate Ni'ihau Helicopters as a joint operation. Hunters must have a Hawai'i State hunting license, which Ni'ihau Safaris will assist in acquiring. There are some rigid rules to follow on Ni'ihau, such as no alcohol or smoking allowed. Hunting daily rate: $1650 per person, four hunters maximum. Observers allowed on trip at $400 per person. Free-chase hunts and stalking are the rule. Game is plentiful, but it is not an easy hunt. The daily rate includes use of fire arm, one ram and one boar, and one guide per hunter, plus dressing crew to handle animals taken, lunch, snacks and cold drinks. Advance reservations and deposits are required. Office hours are 8 a.m. to 2 p.m., Monday through Saturday. Kaumakani, 18-mile marker on Kaumuali'i Highway #50 between Hanapepe and Waimea towns. *P.O. Box 690370, Makaweli, HI 96769; 877-441-3500; 808-335-3500; fax 808-338-1463.*

KAYAKING

With its many navigable rivers and streams, Kaua'i is a jewel for the kayaker. You can choose an adventure on your own on the Wailua, Hulei'a and Hanalei rivers, take a guided tour or go on a group expedition. There are also various sea kayaking adventures to be enjoyed along the Napali Coast and South Shore areas, but they are recommended for the experienced kayaker or with a guided excursion group.

Although Kaua'i has many rivers and streams, only a few are deep and long enough to be used for kayaking. These include the Wailua, Hanalei, Hulei'a and Kalihiwai rivers. Each river has its own personality and unique picturesque scenery. The Hulei'a River follows the striking Ha'upu Ridge, passing by the Menehune Fish Pond and the Hulei'a National Wildlife Refuge. The Kalihiwai River, with its mouth at Kalihiwai Bay near Kilauea, travels through lowland areas of Kaua'i. The Hanalei River twists through the valley past fields of taro. The Wailua River is accessible from Wailua State Park. Depending on the seasons and surf, sea kayaking locations vary. In the summer months, the North Shore may often be calm and perfect for various skill levels. A Napali coast trip is a 16-mile kayak adventure and can be accomplished in one day or more, depending on weather conditions and camping permit availability. In the winter, the southern shore of the island offers many options. For more information, pick up a copy of *Paddling Hawai'i* by Audrey Sutherland at local bookstores.

Aloha Canoes & Kayaks This outfitter offers several kayaking excursions. The three- to three-and-a-half-hour "Kayak Adventure Tour" combines kayaking, hiking and swimming on the Hulei'a River for $82 with lunch, $70 without. The three-and-a-half-hour "Hawaiian Double Hull Canoe Adventure" is a hike, swim and canoe outing for $82 with lunch. The one-and-a-half-hour "Hawaiian Double Hull Canoe Paddle Tour" just cruises the Hulei'a River for $60 per person. They also offer an Ocean Kayak Tour, including snorkel and swim for $150 per person. *P.O. Box 3502, Lihu'e, HI 96766; 808-246-6804; 877-473-5446; fax 808-245-6912; e-mail: kayaks@hawaiian.net; www.hawaiikayaks.com.*

Island Adventures This outfit features a two-and-a-half-hour guided kayak excursion on the Hulei'a River, site of the legendary

Menehune Fishpond. The Hulei'a River is in the heart of the 241-acre Hulei'a National Wildlife Refuge, with four endangered bird species under protection here. The river is famous as a location for scenes from such movies as *Raiders of the Lost Ark* and *The Lost World*. Each person is taught kayak control during a safety briefing. The trip includes a picnic snack with juice. You paddle up, and then are brought back by boat. Departs Nawiliwili Small Boat Harbor twice daily, 8:30 a.m. and 12:30 p.m. Rate: $49 adults, $29 children 4 to 12. They also operate True Blue Charters (fishing) and Rainbow Running (sailing/snorkeling). *P.O. Box 1722, Lihu'e, HI 96766; 808-245-9662; 888-245-1707; fax 808-246-9661; e-mail: info@kauai-by-kayak.com; www.kauai-by-kayak.com.*

Kaua'i Water Ski & Surf Kayaks are among the variety of equipment available for rent here. Single- or two-person kayaks rentals, surfboards, bodyboards, snorkel gear, waterskis, mountain bikes, etc. Open Monday through Saturday 9 a.m. to 9 p.m. *Kinipopo Shopping Village, 4-356 Kuhio Highway, Kapa'a, HI 96746; 800-344-7915; 808-822-3574; e-mail: surfski@aloha.net.*

Kayak Adventures This outfitter offers a standard five-hour "Wailua River Kayak Tour Waterfall Adventure," four-mile roundtrip paddle, with a short hike to a waterfall for $85 per person; kids 12 and under are $65. They also have custom ocean kayak excursions and two-hour surf lessons for $65. *P.O. Box 4821, Princeville, HI 96722; 808-826-9340; e-mail: kayaking@aloha.net; www.extreme-hawaii.com/kayak.*

Kayak Ecotour "A True Kayak Experience." They take small groups (no more than 8) to hidden waterfalls, quiet rivers, lonely beaches and enchanted ponds. "Please bring your boy/girl scout's attitude, bathing suit, sports or beach footwear, hat, suntan oil, camera and an open mind." The price includes a gourmet sandwich and beverages for the family, kayaks, and all the equipment. All tours are $75 adults. Children under 10 years are $40. River tours range from two to five hours. They also have three special ocean kayak tours: "North Shore Beach Discovery," "East Side Beach Explorer" and "South Shore Beach Adventure." Ocean tours are weather dependent. They also rent kayaks. *P.O. Box 884, Kapa'a, HI 96746; 808-822-9078, 808-639-7718, 808-652-2665, 808-652-3833; e-mail: valentin@hawaiian.net; www.kauai-kayaking.com.*

Kayak Kaua'i Outbound Their one- or multi-day guided tours are available year round. They can be geared to the active adventurer or to the whole family. Full-day "Napali Sea Kayak Voyage" is $160; "Secret Falls Paddling & Hiking Adventure" to Ho'olalaea Falls is five hours for $80; "Blue Lagoon Hanalei River" tour is three hours for $60; "Sea Kayak Po'ipu is a full-day trip for $115; "River Rental Packages," where you rent your own kayak and create own tour, is single kayak $26, double kayak $50. They also rent surfboards, hiking and camping equipment rentals, and bicycles. *P.O. Box 508, Hanalei, HI 96714; 808-826-9844; 800-437-3507; fax 808-826-7378; Kapa'a shop 808-822-9179; e-mail: info@kayakkauai.com; www.kayakkauai.com.*

Kayak Wailua This outfitter has kayak rentals available to explore the Wailua River on your own: single for $25, double for $55. They also offer a guided "Wailua River Kayak Tour," including a hike to Secret Falls, the 125-foot Ho'olalaea Falls, on the upper reaches of the river for $85 per person. *4-350 Kuhio Highway, Kapaa; 808-822-3388; e-mail: info@kayakwailua.com; www.kayakwailua.com.*

Outfitters Kaua'i This outfitter has a full line of one- and two-person kayak rentals and tours available. Information and maps on kayaking locations are also provided. Tours include: "Napali Coast Kayak," a full-day 16-mile paddle for $145 per person; a five-hour "Jungle Paddle Stream & Waterfall Hike" to Ho'olalaea Falls for $84 per person, kids 12 and under $72; the four-hour "Hidden Valley Falls Kayak Adventure" on the Hulei'a River, with picnic lunch for $84, kids $72—same tour without lunch $72 adults and $60 kids. *2727A Po'ipu Road, P.O. Box 1149, Po'ipu Plaza, Po'ipu Beach, HI 96756; 808-742-9667; 888-742-9887; fax 808-742-8842; e-mail: info@outfitters kauai.com; www.outfitterskauai.com.*

Paradise Outdoor Adventures Rental bikes and kayaks. They also feature guided kayak trips, including a five-hour "Wailua Jungle Tour" for $85 per person, kids under 11 $60; "Sea Kayaking Whale Watch" (seasonal) along the South Shore to Po'ipu for $99 per person; "Napali Coast" is a full-day tour, 16 miles for $175. *4-1596 Kuhio Highway, Kapa'a, HI 96746; 808-822-1112; 877-42-BOATS; fax 808-822-4224.*

Pedal and Paddle They rent kayaks for self-guided river trips. Daily rentals of single- and two-person kayaks available. Call for prices. *Ching Young Village, Hanalei; 808-826-9069.*

Tropical Kayak Co. They have a full line of kayak rentals: single for $20, double for $40. Rent a kayak and do your own river paddling excursion. They are just five minutes south of the Wailua River. *3-4684 Kuhio Highway (51), two miles north of Lihu'e Airport, a quarter mile past the traffic light on right side (ocean) of the highway; 808-632-0011.*

Wailua Kayak Adventures Kayak rentals $15 to $30 to do your own river excursion. Guided tours include: four- to five-hour "Wailua Secret Falls Tour" to Ho'olalaea Falls for $75 per person; three-hour "Wailua Falls Hiking Tour" for $50 per person; three- to four-hour "Jungle River Safari" for $50 per person. Morning and afternoon departures. *P.O. Box 197, Kapa'a, HI 96746; 808-822-5795, 808-639-6332; fax 808-822-5795; e-mail: sacredriver@hawaiian.net; www.kauaiwailuakayak.com.*

Wailua Kayak & Canoe This outfitter has kayak rentals, single for $25, double for $50. They also do guided river tours. The three-hour "Wailua River Trip" takes in the Fern Grotto and Rope Swing, snack included, for $60 per person. The five-hour "Secret Falls Trip" includes hike to Secret Falls (Ho'olalaea Falls), Rope Swing and lunch for $80 per person. *169 Wailua Road, Kapa'a, HI 96746; 808-821-1188.*

LAND TOURS

There are several tour operators offering various general scenic attraction coach/bus or van tours for sightseeing, plus some more adventurous operators that offer backcountry, offroad specialized tours and excursions. Check with the following land tour operators for details.

Aloha Kaua'i Tours This outfitter/operator offers two basic land tour packages that explore various areas of Kaua'i in vans or 4x4 offroad vehicles. They also have hiking and water/kayaking adventures as well. Check their website for latest offerings, rates and applicable discounts. *1702 Haleukana Street, Lihu'e, HI 96766; 808-245-8890, 808-245-7224; 800-452-1113; e-mail: tours@gte.net; www.alohakauai tours.com.*

- **Kaua'i Backroads** is part of Aloha Kauai Tours. They depart for a half-day tour twice daily at 8 a.m. and 1 p.m. Travel former cane roads in the comfort of an air-conditioned four-wheel-drive van to remote areas. Learn about Kaua'i's history as you travel scenic backroads up to Kilohana Crater, past reservoirs and old Koloa town to the rugged coastline of Maha'ulepu, then take the tunnel through the Ha'upu Range back to the plantation home. A photographer's dream. Adults $50, children $44.
- **Kaua'i Mountain Tour**, another branch of Aloha Kauai Tours, offers 4x4 mountain-van tours that last six to eight hours and include picnic lunch for $90 adults, $63 children. Tours go beyond the normal land excursions in their 12-passenger air-conditioned vans. With their competent guides you'll discover the backroad beauty of "upcountry" Kaua'i as well as the Hawaiian history and culture and flora-fauna of the region. Explore Koke'e State Park and the Pali-Kona Forest. While you can hike in on many of these roads to the lookouts visited, the four-wheel-drive vehicle can get you much closer to the lookouts. This is an excellent option, especially for those who are unable to hike. Nothing on the trip was more that a light walk. The van was cool and comfortable, although there was some expected jostling that occurs over the rough back roads. The guide led an informative narration for almost the entire seven hours of the trip. Examining different types of plants and flowers,

learning about their uses, and viewing the majestic Waimea Canyon from several vantage points were some of the highlights. The excursion included a leisurely picnic lunch. While many choose to drive up to the Waimea Canyon and Koke'e Park independently, you'll miss out on learning much about some of the secret treasures that Kaua'i has to hold.

Kaua'i Backcountry Adventures This tour group takes guests on a tubing adventure down the Lihu'e Plantation's historic Hanama'ulu irrigation ditch system. Tube riders go through tunnels, flumes and open canals. Headlamps are provided on these guided three-hour tours, which include lunch. Call for rates and times. *P.O. Box 183, Hanama'ulu, HI 96715; 808-245-2506; 888-270-0555; e-mail: adventure@kauaibackcountry.com; www.kauaibackcountry.com.*

Kaua'i Paradise Tours Island sightseeing in a six-passenger van to Waimea and Kalalau or the North Shore. There are two basic six-hour tours offered. Tour 1: Waimea Canyon, Koke'e Park, Kalalau Valley and other west Kaua'i sights for $66 per person. Tour 2: Kilauea, Hanalei, Haena, Ke'e Beach and other East Coast/North Shore highlights for $66 per person. Or combine a land tour with helicopter trip for an additional $129, or the Fern Grotto Boat Cruise for an additional $15. Narration available in English or German, with owner/tour guide Max Dereyl. Basic tours with add-ons, extra two hours, $88. *P.O. Box 3927, Lihu'e, HI 96766; 808-246-3999; 800-404-3900; cell 808-639-9833; fax 808-245-2499.*

Polynesian Adventure Tours They offer four basic sightseeing tour packages that take in island highlights. Rates depend on pickup origin. Tour 1: Waimea Canyon/Wailua River—covers canyon views and Fern Grotto cruise for $60 to $73, children under 12 $43 to $56. Tour 2: Waimea Canyon Experience—covers canyon views and west Kaua'i sights for $40 to $60, children under 12 $30 to $50. Tour 3: North Shore Excursion—covers all the attractions of Hanalei area for $28 to $43, children under 12 $18 to $33. Tour 4: Waimea Canyon/North Shore Excursion—combines all the attractions of west Kaua'i, North Shore and Hanalei for $60 to $65, children $54 to $58. *3113 B Oihana, Lihu'e, HI 96766; 808-246-0122; 800-622-3011; e-mail: sales@polyad.com; www.polyad.com.*

Robert's Hawai'i They offer full- and half-day tours to major scenic attractions of the island. The "Waimea Canyon & Fern Grotto Tour" is 8 hours for $59 per person, children under 12 $44; the five-hour "Waimea Canyon Tour" includes west Kaua'i sights at $40 per person, children under 12 $30; "Fern Grotto" includes Wailua River cruise, 4 hours for $40 per person, children under 12 $30; the four-hour "Hanalei Valley and North Shore Tour" at $33 per person, children under 12 $23. All tours are by comfortable air-conditioned mini-coach. Book online and save. *808-245-9558, 808-539-9400; 800-831-5541; www.robertshawaii.com.*

Trans Hawaiian Three trips available: "Hanalei and Ha'ena Tour" visits the Wailua River and its ancient temples, Opaeka'a Falls, Kilauea Lighthouse and Refuge, Lumahai Beach, Hanalei Bay, the wet and dry caves at Ha'ena and Ke'e Beach. "Waimea Canyon Tour" tours Nawiliwili Harbor, the Menehune Fishpond, Russian Fort Elizabeth, Waimea Town, Waimea Canyon, Kalalau Valley Lookout, Koloa, Po'ipu and Spouting Horn. "Waimea Canyon/Wailua River Tour" is a full-day trip that circles the island from the eastern shore to the northern. Prices quoted vary depending on pick-up location. Ask about discounts for children. *1770 Haleukana, Lihu'e, HI 96766; 808-245-5108; www.transhawaiian.com.*

LUAUS (*See* Chapter 3)

MOVIES/MOVIE RENTALS (*See also* Theater)

Coconut MarketPlace A twin theater with bargain prices for matinees (before 6 p.m.) is located here. *4-484 Kuhio Highway, Wailua; 808-821-2324.*

Kukui Grove Cinemas This complex has four screens in its theater. *Kukui Grove Shopping Center, 4368 Kukui Grove, Lihu'e; 808-245-5055.*

The Princeville Hotel The hotel has complimentary movies for guests shown four times daily in their private cinema. Non-resort guests who dine at the hotel receive complimentary cinema passes for the evening. *5520 Ka Haku Road, Princeville; 808-826-9644.*

Waimea Community Theatre Offers a variety of films. *991 Kaumuali'i Highway, Waimea; 808-338-0282.*

If you have a VCR at your accommodation, there are plenty of options for renting movies. If you don't have a machine you can rent one. **Blockbuster** videos is the island's biggest chain. Their main outlet is at Waipouli Town Center, 4-771 Kuhio Highway, next to Foodland; 808-822-7744. They have drop-off boxes at other places around Kaua'i. It's about $5 for a three-day rental. Other video stores are scattered around the island. **Foodland** stores and **Longs** have good selections.

A few other video rental outlets: **Canyon Video** *9814 Kaumuali'i Highway, Waimea, 808-338-1441*; **Hanalei Video & Music** *5-5190 Kuhio Highway, Hanalei, 808-826-9633*; **Hot Flix Video Rentals** *5470 Koloa Road, Koloa, 808-742-1154*; **Kauai Video Rentals** *4480 Ahukini Road, Lihu'e, 808-245-7675, 9905 Waimea Road, Waimea, 808-338-0303, or 4469 Waialo Road, Hanapepe, 808-335-3942*; **Kilauea Video** *4244 Kilauea Road, 808-828-0128.*

MOVIE/FILM TOURS

Hawai'i Movie Tours If you're a movie buff, or even if you're not, you're sure to enjoy one of Kaua'i's most unusual island tours. Hawai'i Movie Tours travels around the north and eastern shores of the island with a guided narrated tour of some of Kaua'i's most famous movie locations. Ground tours, combined with air and sea tours, are also available. They have arranged special permission to visit private estates and other hidden places not open to the public. As you travel around the island, their on-van video equipment shows clips of a fraction of the movies and commercials filmed on Kaua'i. The film snippet provides an ideal introduction to the scenic location you're about to visit. (Trust us, it's impossible to visit many of the filming scenes on your own.) The five-hour "Standard Tour" includes lunch for $95 per person, children under 12 $76. The "Deluxe Tour" is 12 hours (offered three days a week) and includes a comprehensive tour of varied movie sites by helicopter, ground and river-boat cruise, ending with a fantastic luau for $265 per person. The "4x4 Offroad Tour" is a half-day in a 15-passenger offroad van that includes lunch and takes in numerous sites where famous movie scenes were filmed for $105 per person, children under 12 $95. Book early as tours fill up rapidly. Check the website for discounts or special offers. Maximum 10 people per tour. Hotel pickup available. Their office is located behind Beezers in Kapa'a. *4-1384 Kuhio Highway, Kapa'a, HI 96746; 800-628-8432; 808-822-1192; e-mail: tourguv@hawaiian.net; www.hawaiimovietour.com.*

Film Flicks Hawaii Historical Adventure Tours This tour operator is noted here even though they differ somewhat from the operator listed above. Film Flicks Hawaii offers comprehensive island tours, taking in the scenic highlights and popular attractions of Kaua'i. The 15-passenger van used is TV/VCR equipped and shows informational video clips of Kaua'i history, culture and subjects of interest to visitors. The tour includes visits to favorite places to shop, dine and experience. Hotel pickups available. Deluxe Tour is six hours and includes lunch for $89 per person, children under 12 $69. *3412 Rice Street, Lihu'e, HI 96766; 877-632-0066; 808-632-0066; e-mail: information@filmflickshawaii.com; www.filmflickshawaii.com.*

MUSEUMS/GARDEN TOURS/CULTURAL TOURS

Kaua'i offers some of the finest garden and cultural tours in the Hawaiian chain. Be sure to find time to take in at least one of the following varied options.

MOVIES MADE ON KAUA'I

Some of these will be familiar names and, as for others, well, there is good reason they never made it big on the big screen!

2002—*Dragonfly;* 2001—*Jurassic Park III, Manhunt, To End All Wars;* 2000—*Dinosaur;* 1998—*Six Days, Seven Nights; Mighty Joe Young;* 1997—*George of the Jungle;* 1996—*The Lost World—Jurassic Park II;* 1995—*Outbreak;* 1994—*North;* 1993—*Jurassic Park;* 1992—*Honeymoon in Vegas;* 1991—*Hook;* 1990—*Flight of the Intruder, Lord of the Flies;* 1987—*Throw Mama from the Train;* 1986—*Islands of the Alive;* 1983—*The Thorn Birds, Uncommon Valor;* 1981—*Behold Hawaii, Body Heat;* 1981—*Raiders of the Lost Ark;* 1979—*Seven, Last Flight of Noah's Ark;* 1978—*Deathmoon, Acapulco Gold;* 1977—*Fantasy Island, Islands in the Stream, King Kong, Waterworld* (television); 1974—*Man with the Golden Gun, Castaway Cowboy;* 1970—*The Hawaiians;* 1969—*Lost Flight;* 1968—*Yoake No Futare, Lovers at Dawn;* 1966—*Hawaii;* 1965—*Lt. Robinson Crusoe, U.S.N, Operation Attack, None but the Brave;* 1963—*Gilligan's Island* (pilot episode), *Donovan's Reef;* 1962—*Girls! Girls! Girls!* (original title *Paradise Hawaiian Style*), *Diamond Head;* 1961—*Blue Hawai'i, Seven Women From Hell;* 1960—*Wackiest Ship in the Army;* 1958—*South Pacific;* 1957—*Forbidden Island, Jungle Heat, Voodoo Island;* 1956—*Beach Head, Between Heaven and Hell, She Gods of Shark Reef, Thunder Over Hawaii;* 1953—*Miss Sadie Thompson;* 1951—*Bird of Paradise;* 1950—*Pagan Love Song;* 1933—*White Heat*

—Courtesy of Hawai'i Movie Tours

The National Tropical Botanical Garden The National Tropical Botanical Garden is a nationally chartered, privately funded, nonprofit organization, the nation's only tropical botanical garden chartered by the U.S. Congress. Headquartered on Kaua'i, its principal mission is research, conservation and education relating to the world's tropical plants. The NTBG consists of five distinct gardens in the Hawaiian islands and in Florida. The three Kaua'i gardens are: Lawa'i, Allerton and Limahuli, with another on Maui. *P.O. Box 340, Lawa'i, HI 96765; 808-742-2623; e-mail: tours@ntbg.org; www.ntbg.org.*

★ ***The Lawa'i Garden*** Located on Kaua'i's southern shore in the lush Lawa'i Valley, the Lawa'i Garden was the first site to be acquired by the National Tropical Botanical Garden and is where the National Tropical Botanical Garden Headquarters is. (*See* Chapter 2 for information on the gardens.) Reservations are required for the separate tours of the Lawa'i and Allerton Gardens. Only guided tours are available at the Lawa'i Garden and operate Tuesday through Saturday, 9 a.m., 10 a.m., 1 p.m. and 2.p.m., and are approximately two-and-a-half hours each, walking at an easy pace for about one mile. Tour fee is currently $30 for each tour. *For information on scheduled tours and reservations, contact: 808-742-2623; e-mail: tours@ntbg.org; www.ntbg.org.*

★ ***The Limahuli Garden*** This garden on Kaua'i's North Shore is an area of overwhelming natural beauty. Located .7 of a mile from Ha'ena Park and well marked with a sign and a Hawaii Visitors Bureau marker, this is another branch of the National Tropical Botanical Garden. This lush garden offers a walking tour that leads uphill through a 15-acre garden and forest to a beautiful viewpoint overlooking the ocean. This is a three-quarter-mile loop trail, steep in some areas. Comfortable walking shoes are necessary; umbrellas are provided for occasional showers. You'll see ancient taro terraces, many of the plants introduced to Hawai'i by the early Polynesians, as well as plantings of native Hawaiian species and the pristine Limahuli Stream. The guided tours are two to two-and-a-half hours long; self-guided tours are about one to one-and-a-half hours. Advanced reservations are required for guided tours; they request visitors meet promptly for their tours. If you must cancel your reservation, phone at least two hours in advance of your scheduled tour. All visitors are met by the National Tropical Botanical Garden staff at the garden's entrance. Parking area and restroom facilities are available. Picnic lunches are not allowed on the grounds. Guided tours are offered Tuesday to Friday, and Sunday at 9:30 a.m. to 4 p.m., $15 per person. Self-guided tours, including a descriptive booklet are $10 per person during the same times. *Ha'ena; 808-826-1053 for information; e-mail: tours@ntbg.org; www.ntbg.org.*

★ ***Grove Farm Homestead*** This Lihu'e example of old-style plantation living was the home of George N. Wilcox until 1978. A fascinating two-and-one-half-hour tour is given. This, in our opinion, is the best cultural tour on the island. Advance reservation only. Admission $5. Currently tours are offered Monday, Wednesday and Thursday 10 a.m. and 1:10 p.m. Call to verify schedule. (*See* Chapter 2 for additional information.) *P.O. Box 1631, Lihu'e, HI 96766; 808-245-3202.*

Guava Kai Plantation Guava Kai Plantation in Kilauea has some 480 acres of guava orchards under commercial cultivation. (*See* Chapter 2 for additional information.) Visit the plantation's visitors center and discover how guava is grown and processed into a variety of treats. There is a self-guided tour that includes a view of the orchard and the processing plants, as well as an informative eight-minute video. A manmade fish pond and an assortment of native Hawaiian plants are yours to enjoy as you stroll the grounds. The snack bar, open only in the summer months, sells ice cream, juice, breads and other bakery items made with guava. There are free samples of guava juice, jams, jellies and coffee. Since they are owned by Maunaloa, they also sell their products at slightly lower rates than retail outlets. *Hours:* 9 a.m. to 5 p.m. *Kuawa Road, just off Kuhio Highway (Route 56), watch for sign; 808-828-6121.*

★ ***Kamokila Hawaiian Village*** Kamokila Hawaiian Village has been around for several years. The quaintness and authenticity of this re-created village gives a glimpse of an early Hawaiian lifestyle. The $5 admission fee includes a guided tour. A guide explains the meanings of each of the various thatched structures and their uses. Experiences include opening a coconut for guests to sample (the young green ones have soft pudding-like coconut meat), picking flowers for your hair, and even picking a fresh guava off the tree to eat. Dashing between huts to avoid the off and on again rainshowers, our guide played the ukulele and sang as we explored the birthing place, the sleeping huts and other markers of early Hawaiian life. It does what the oversized Polynesian Cultural Center on O'ahu can never do: provide a truly personalized and interpretive cross-cultural experience. Guests can buy a lei for $2 or a freshly made pandanus hat for just a little bit more. *Located opposite Opaeka'a Falls, the Kaumo'o Road entrance is just past the Wailua Bridge on the Wailua River, Wailua; 808-823-0559.*

Kapa'a History Tour This 90-minute walking tour, led by interpretive guides familiar with the history and architecture of old Kapa'a Town, begins and ends at the Pono Kai Resort. Learn about Kapa'a's history as an agriculture service center for the once-bustling sugar cane and pineapple industries as well as the culture, heritage and colorful multiethnic population of the area. Adults $15, children under 12 $7. Call for schedule. *Kaua'i Historical Society, P.O. Box 1778, Lihu'e, HI 96766; 808-821-1778, 808-245-3373; www.kauaihistoricalsociety.org.*

Kaua'i Coffee Company Visitor Center & Museum Make a stop at this informative and interesting visitors center and museum to learn about the island's coffee industry. This is Hawai'i's largest coffee estate and you can sample a freshly brewed cup, view exhibits and displays tracing the coffee growing, harvesting and production process of estate-grown premium coffees. A retail gift shop features unique Kaua'i gifts, freshly ground and whole-bean coffees and lots more. Free admission. *870 Kalewili Road (located on Highway 540, which leads off from Highway 50 near 'Ele'ele and Port Allen), P.O. Box 8, 'Ele'ele, HI 96705; 800-545-8605; 808-335-0813; fax 808-335-3149; www.kauaicoffee.com.*

Kaua'i Historical Society Archive This is the official historical documents archive of Kaua'i and is housed in the historic County Building in Lihu'e. It holds varied historical collections, documents, records, books, papers, donated memorabilia, etc., on various Kaua'i subjects. It's free and open to the public by appointment. *4396 Rice Street, Lihu'e, HI 96766; 808-245-3373.*

The Kaua'i Museum Through murals, artifacts and artwork, discover how the islands have changed since Captain Cook's arrival at

Waimea in 1778. The Museum Shop specializes in Hawaiian memorabilia, Hawaiian books and local crafts. They also have rotating exhibits so there will be something new and different every time you visit. Admission $5, seniors $4, children under 17 free. *Hours*: Weekdays 9 a.m. to 4:30 p.m., Saturday 10 a.m. to 1 p.m. Closed Sunday. The first Saturday of the month is free and they feature special family events and activities. *4428 Rice Street, P.O. Box 248, Lihu'e, HI 96766; 808-245-6931; fax 808-245-6864; e-mail: museum@midpac.net; www.kauai.qpg.com.*

★ ***Kaua'i Sugar Plantation Tours*** Hawaii's cultural history can be intimately explored through the heart of the sugar plantation. The two-hour bus tour, conducted by Gay & Robinson Tours LLC, includes the history of the plantation, its operation, processing, the plantation's miles of irrigation systems, and views of the private plantation lands. Harvesting operations are seasonal, with the months of April through October the best times to visit. Tour routes depend on the day-to-day operations. If you don't have time for the full tour, stop by their office and view the historic displays. The office is located in the historic Field Office (circa 1900) on Kaumakani Avenue. From Lihu'e, take Highway 50 just past mile-marker 19, turn left on Kaumakani Avenue. All visitors on the tour are required to wear safety equipment to enter the factory. They must also wear pants (shorts are okay), low-heeled, closed shoes and they will be provided with safety glasses and hard hats. Cost of the tour is $40. *Hours*: Office open 8 a.m. to 4 p.m. Monday through Friday, with the exception of plantation holidays. Tours are at 9 a.m. and 1 p.m., Monday through Friday. *Gay & Robinson Tours LLC, Kaumakani Avenue, Kaumakani; 808-335-2824; fax 808-335-6852; e-mail: toursgnr@aloha.net; www.gandrtours-kauai.com.*

Kiahuna Plantation Kiahuna offers free self-guided tours of their Moir (or Pa'u a Laka Garden) and Hawaiian Gardens. Guided tours are available as well. *2253 Poipu Road, Koloa; 808-742-6411.*

Kilohana Kilohana is reminiscent of the grandeur and elegance of an earlier age, when sugar was king and prosperity reigned, and owners would build luxurious homes. One of the grandest plantation homes on Kaua'i was Gaylord Parke Wilcox's Kilohana. (*See* Chapter 2 for more information.) Today, in addition to the gift shops, galleries and Gaylord's Courtyard Restaurant, you can take a carriage ride tour of this 35-acre estate. The "Carriage Ride" (808-246-9529) is a romantic excursion around the grounds, complete with a short narration. The rides are available daily from 11 a.m. to 6:30 p.m. for $8 adults and $4 children. Admission to Kilohana and its grounds are free. The shops are open daily from 9:30 a.m. to 9 p.m. *See* Chapter 3 for dining options here. *Located just outside Lihu'e, 3-2087 Kaumuali'i Highway (Route 50); 808-245-5608; fax 808-245-7818.*

★ ***Koke'e Natural History Museum*** contains geographic maps of Kaua'i along with exhibits of native plant and bird species. Admission is free, but donations are accepted. They regularly offer free or inexpensive guided hikes and other interesting annual activities. Great book section, interesting local products for sale and their staff is friendly and helpful. Check their website for calendar of events, hiking information, canyon and state park information, birds, etc. *P.O. Box 100, Kekaha, HI 96752; 808-335-9975; www.aloha.net/~kokee.*

Koloa Heritage Trail This is essentially a self-guided excursion in the Po'ipu Beach Resort and Koloa area on the south side of Kaua'i. Look for a copy of the "Koloa Heritage Trail" guide/map where visitor information is available. The guide/map details 13 different historic sites and attractions in the Koloa and Po'ipu Beach areas. Included are Spouting Horn Park, Prince Kuhio Birthplace and Park, Koloa Landing, Po'ipu Beach Park, Hapa Road, Koloa Jodo Mission, Sugar Monument, Koloa Missionary Church, Yamamoto Store and Koloa Hotel and others. These sites give a sense of the history, culture and heritage of the region. A free copy of the guide/map can be obtained by contacting the Po'ipu Beach Resort Association. *P.O. Box 730, Koloa, HI 96756; 808-742-7444; fax 808-742-7887; e-mail: info@poipu-beach.org; poipu-beach.org.*

Na 'Aina Kai This is a combination botanical garden, sculpture park and hardwood plantation consisting of 12 acres of landscaped gardens surrounded by 45 acres of exotic fruit trees and 110 acres of tropical hardwoods. Tours are available Tuesday, Wednesday and Thursday and require advance reservations. Visitors must be 13 or older. The "Garden and Plantation Tour," by motorized car tram, is three hours and is given at 8:30 a.m. and 1:30 p.m. It takes in the various gardens including the Orchid House, Shower Tree Park, Ka'ula Lagoon Garden, Poinciana Maze, International Desert Garden, Carnivorous Plant House, Forest Garden, Hardwood Plantation and Ocean Overlook Gazebo at a cost of $35 per person. The "Walk on the Wild Side Walking Tour" is 4 to 5 hours and begins at 8 a.m. It includes most of the previous stops plus Kuliha'ili Canyon, Koli Ridge Bird Garden, and the Makai Meadow and Marsh at a cost of $70 per person. It's a three-mile guided walking trek requiring some ascents and descents on pathways and steps. Comfortable walking shoes, hats and sunscreen are recommended. *4101 Wailapa Road, P.O. Box 1134, Kilauea, HI 96754; 808-828-0525; fax 808-828-0815; e-mail: naainakai@msn.com.*

Ni'ihau Safaris, Ltd. This outfitter offers exclusive full-day hunting safaris for wild boar and feral sheep, plus fishing as well, on the privately owned island of Ni'ihau. Those interested in a cultural tour of the "Forbidden Island" can join a hunting party as an observer for the helicopter trip over to Ni'ihau. (See listing under "Hunting/ Shooting Ranges.") *P.O. Box 690370, Makaweli, HI 96769; 808-335-3500; 877-441-3500; fax 808-338-1463.*

★ ***Waimea Sugar Mill Camp Museum and Plantation Lifestyles Walking Tour*** Reservations are required for this historical and unique tour, which is limited to 12 people. Learn about life in the plantation camps. Volunteers lead a tour that begins at the administration building of the Waimea Plantation Cottages. The tour is currently offered Tuesday and Saturday at 9 a.m. and lasts about one hour. Cost is $6 adults, $5 seniors (65 and older), and children $4 12 and under. *Kaumuali'i Highway, P.O. Box 1178, Waimea, HI 96796; 808-335-2824, 808-337-1005.*

★ ***Wai'oli Mission House*** Guided tours of the 19th-century New England-style home of island missionaries Abner and Lucy Wilcox home are available at no charge. Open to the public Tuesday, Thursday and Saturday from 9 a.m. to 2:45 p.m. Donations appreciated. (*See* Chapter 2 for more information.) *P.O. Box 1631, Lihu'e, HI 96766; 808-245-3202.*

West Kaua'i Technology & Visitor Center This is a unique place to gain an understanding of the Waimea area. It's a one-of-a-kind educational technology center and museum. Pictorials, graphics and displays with touch-sensitive screens provide information on all of Kaua'i's activities, not just Waimea. (*See* Chapter 2 for additional information.) The museum blends the history of the area with information on the nearby Pacific Missile Range Facility. Not an easy task to undertake, but one that seems to work here. *Hours*: 9 a.m. to 5 p.m. *9565 Kaumuali'i Highway, Waimea; 808-338-1332.*

PARKS

County Parks

Anahola County Park Located on the northeast coast on Highway 56 north of Kapa'a town. This is a one-and-a-half-acre beach park with showers, toilets, swimming and camping pavilions.

'Anini Beach Park Located on the north coast, Highway 56, turn-off road is two miles past Kilauea town. Turn right after a big bridge, Kalihikai, and drive for .2 mile, then turn left onto Anini Road to a deadend sign. It's another .2 mile to the campsite. There are two acres here, camping pavilions, toilet, showers, picnic tables, barbecue and swimming. It's got a nice beach with a large reef-protected swimming area. Very popular with local families.

Ha'ena Beach Park Located on the North Shore, Highway 56, a few miles before the end of the road where the hiking trail to Napali

Coast begins. Camping is permitted under the trees, in designated areas. The 4.7-acre park has pavilions, toilets, showers, tables and barbecue grills. Swimming is unsafe in winter due to a strong riptide.

Hanalei Beach Park Located at Hanalei on the North Shore. In Hanalei town, turn right on Aku Road, then make another right and follow this beachfront road until it ends at Black Pot Park, which has a large parking lot and pier. This is a 1.5-acre park with pavilion, toilets, tables and barbecue grill. Camping is available at Black Pot Park. Restaurants, grocery stores, etc., located in town nearby.

Hanama'ulu Beach Park Located on the southeast coast .5-mile from Hanama'ulu Town. From Highway 56, turn right at Hanama'ulu Road across from Hanama'ulu Café until you come to a fork. Stay on Hanama'ulu Road going down a hill until you come to the beach area. Camping is permitted under the trees. The 6.5-acre park has tables, toilets, pavilion, barbecue and showers.

Lucy Wright Park Located at Waimea on the southwest coast. From Highway 50, turn left on Alawai Road just past the bridge as you enter town. Campsites can be seen from the main highway on your left. The 4.5-acre park has toilets, showers, swimming and surfing.

Salt Pond Beach Park Located on the southwest coast. From Highway 50, turn left at Lele Road on the west side of Hanapepe town and stay on the road passing a veterans cemetery. Turn right at Lolo Kai Road and continue for a quarter mile, passing the dry salt pond beds. Park on the left side of the road. This 6-acre park has pavilion, tables, toilets, showers, surfing, swimming and is a popular snorkeling area. Camping is available for about 50 people.

State Parks

Hanakapi'ai Beach Primitive tent camping is allowed near the beach, one night only. See preceding section to contact State Parks Department for required overnight camping permits. The road on the North Shore ends at Napali State Park, where you'll find the trailheads for some of Kaua'i's most incredible hikes. Be sure to wear good sturdy hiking boots or, if you wear tennis shoes, bring old ones since the dirt and mud will cause permanent staining to your footwear. The roundtrip to Hanakapi'ai Beach can be done in a day. It is a distance of two miles from Ke'e and may take 1.5 to 2 hours to get there. (*See* Chapter 5 for more information.) You may see remnants of a fishing village and a farming community that once resided here. As mentioned before, due to the remoteness of this coastline, beach lovers need to use extra caution. This is a remote wilderness area and help would be a long time in reaching you should anyone get hurt. As with other North Shore beaches, surf and currents are extremely hazardous. Even the Department of Land and Natural Resources recommends you avoid the ocean along Napali. A hike to this beach is better in summer when the ocean is calmer (albeit still very dangerous) and the trail has had time to dry out from spring rains.

Kalalau Primitive camping is available near Hanakoa Stream, near the mouth of the Kalalau Valley (near the waterfall) and just behind the beach at Kalalau. Maximum camping stay at Kalalau is five consecutive nights. Stream water only is available for cooking and drinking. Remember to purify the water as it breeds *leptospirosis*. From Ke'e, it is an 11-mile trek along the steep cliffs of the Kalalau Trail to Kalalau Beach and the campsites. Due to the rugged terrain

In the late 1950s, Dr. Kenneth Emory, working on behalf of the Bishop Museum, began a project to study the Nualolo Kai area. In Hawai'i's early days, the valley contained all the materials to sustain a substantial native Hawaiian population. The bark of the *hau* tree was used for making twine and the very soft wood was well suited for canoe outriggers and fires. Salt was gathered from the sea, the streams offered freshwater shrimp, and along the shore were *opihi* (limpets) and *pipipi* (tiny black limpets). The *kukui* tree filled a variety of needs of the early Hawaiian people. For example, canoe hulls were made from the wood of the tree while the nuts, rich in oil, were strung together to make an imperfect, but adequate, candle. The bark was used to dye fishing nets. The leaves of the *lauhala* (pandanus) trees were woven into mats. The *noni,* another tree in the valley, had medicinal properties that were valuable for the early Hawaiians. Robert Krauss, columnist for the *Honolulu Advertiser,* during a trip to visit Dr. Emory in the valley, wrote in his book *Here's Hawai'i,* " . . . the gnarled tree with the lumpy fruit is the *noni.* It has medicinal properties. The Hawaiians tied *noni* leaves over boils for drawing out infection. The green juice from the crushed pulp of a young *noni* apple, used as a gargle, is good for sore throat. Taken internally it will cure fish poisoning." It is unknown why the Hawaiians left this valley, but Emory speculated their leaving may have been influenced by the arrival of the early missionaries, who preferred to have their congregations more centralized. Many archaeological sites remain in this area and should never be disturbed by visitors.

and steep elevations, it may well take an entire day to reach the beach. As you leave Hanakapi'ai Valley, the hiking becomes more strenuous, climbing 800 feet in elevation. After passing through the Ho'olulu and Waiahuakua hanging valleys, you enter the Hanakoa Valley, home to many native lowland forest plants. Camping is available near the Hanakoa Stream. In the late 1800s there were terraces of coffee plants grown here (a few stragglers remain). These cleared areas are now campsites. There is an unmarked one-third-mile trail to Hanakoa Falls, but the unmaintained trail has eroded in some places, making hiking hazardous. The next five miles of trail travels through a section that offers little protection from the sun. Crossing the Kalalau Stream near the mouth of the valley rewards the weary hiker with a small waterfall. Camping is only allowed by this sand beach. During the summer, sea caves just beyond the waterfall can be used as shelter, but during winter and high surf, they are filled with water. An easy two-mile trail follows the Kalalau Valley and ends at a pool in the stream. The area was inhabited until 1919 and taro and other crops were grown here. Now the valley is filled with wild Java plum, guava and a mango tree or two. Remember to treat any *heiau* you find with respect. In the late 1960s and early 1970s the area was repopulated, this time by hippies. Faced with serious sanitation problems, the state implemented a program that limited access to the area by restricting the number of camping permits. Boat and helicopter landings also came under restrictions. With no fronting reef and strong currents, it is dangerous to swim here at any time of the year. Hiking and camping is best here during the summer months, but it is also more difficult to obtain a permit.

Koke'e State Park For information on cabin rentals contact Koke'e Lodge, Koke'e State Park, 3600 Koke'e Road, P.O. Box 819, Waimea, HI 96796; 808-335-6061. Cabins should be booked as far in advance as possible, at least three to four months, and are $35 and $45 per night per cabin, plus tax. Cabins sleep 3 to 6 people with five-day maximum stay. The cabins are *very rustic* and self-contained, with kitchen, refrigerator, cookware and eating utensils, hot shower, bedding, linens, towels provided. These are backpacker-hiker cabins and not first-class tourist lodgings. The cooler climate of upcountry Kaua'i will give you a very different camping experience compared to the beachfront facilities. Koke'e State Park encompasses some 4,345 acres with commanding views of the lush Kalalau Valley from the 4,000-foot-elevation lookout.

Many nearby trails throughout the park offer varied daytime excursions to points along the rim of Waimea Canyon. Information on the hiking trails in Koke'e Park can be obtained from the Division of Forestry and Wildlife, Department of Land and Natural Resources,

3060 Eiwa Street, Lihu'e, HI 96766; 808-274-3433. Hikes range from a .1-mile walk that leads to an overlook of Waimea Canyon to a 3.5-mile trail through forested terrain. Trails into the neighboring forest reserves include Nualolo, Awa'awapuhi, Honopu, Pihea and Alakai Swamp trails. The Koke'e Natural History Museum offers a series of guided hikes in the scenic uplands of West Kaua'i. Hikes are led by one of the trained volunteers of the Koke'e Natural History Museum. The hikes vary in length and in difficulty and since space is limited, they ask that you call ahead to reserve a spot. A small donation is requested. Tours include a hike along cliff and canyon trails to Waipo'o Falls, hikes along the fairly strenuous Pihea Trail or a family hike along Berry Flats Trail. Along the way your interpretative guide will explain about the flora and fauna you encounter along your hike.

Miloli'i State Park Camping restricted to maximum of three nights. Accessible by boat only, from May 15 through Labor Day, weather permitting. Located on the northwestern coast of Kaua'i in Napali Coast State Park. These 40 acres are equipped with a restroom and picnic area, and allow primitive tent camping only and small boat access. No drinking water available.

Nu'alolo Kai No camping allowed and day-use permit is required. It is accessible by small boat only, weather permitting. Many tour boat operators use this oceanfront spot for snorkeling trips as a part of their Napali boat tours.

Polihale State Park The park provides showers, restrooms, picnic tables, barbecues, camping pavilions and drinking water. Shore fishing and beach combing are good activities, but swimming is safe only when conditions are favorable (mostly in summer months) due to strong offshore and hazardous currents. Where Napali meets the west side of Kaua'i is where you'll find Polihale. Located at the end of a five-mile-long dirt road off Kaumuali'i Highway (Route 50) about 7 miles past Kekaha town and just past the Pacific Missile Range Facility at Barking Sands. There are 138 acres of wild coastline here with a wide sandy beach and large sand dunes. It's a scenic setting with great views of the high sea cliffs of Napali Coast extending northward. It's also a very warm and windy desert-like climate and there are pavilions that offer some shade from the hot rays of sun, although no shade trees to speak of.

POLO

You might not expect to find this recreational option on a Hawaiian island, but polo season begins in late April and runs through September. Matches are held each Sunday at the **'Anini Polo Field**, across the road from 'Anini Beach, at 3 p.m. *Access is via the western Kalihiwai Road.*

RIVER EXCURSIONS (*See also* Kayaking)

Smith's Tropical Paradise/Smith's Boats This organization cruises up the Wailua River to the famous Fern Grotto. Trips start at 9 a.m., with the last boat departing at 2:30 p.m. or 3:30 p.m., depending on the day of the week. They last 1 hour, 20 minutes. The current scheduled departures are every half hour from 9 a.m. to 11:30 a.m. and 12:30 p.m. until 3 p.m. An additional 3:30 p.m. departure on Monday, Wednesday and Friday. No reservations are needed, just arrive 15 minutes before departure time. Adults $15, children 2 to 12 $8. They are located near the mouth of the Wailua River on Wailua Road at the Wailua Marina State Park. *Smith's Tropical Paradise, 174 Wailua Road, Kapa'a, HI 96746. Cruise information 808-821-6892; 808-821-6893; fax 808-822-4520; e-mail: smiths@aloha.net.*

Wai'ale'ale Boat Tours Inc. Fern Grotto Cruises are offered by this group as well. Lasting 1.5 hours, they go up the Wailua River, offering music, hula, historical facts and legends along the way. Adults $15, children $8; senior discounts. Trips start at 9 a.m. and run on the half-hour until 3 p.m. or 3:30 p.m., depending on the season. *Wailua State Park Marina, Wailua at 6455 Makana Road, Kapa'a, HI 96746; 808-822-4908; fax 808-823-0822.*

Hanalei Water Sports They offer Outrigger Canoe Tours of 1.5 hours up the Hanalei Bay and River for $55 adults, $45 child. They also have a sunset canoe tour $65. *Ka Haku Road, Princeville Hotel, Princeville, HI 96722; 808-826-7509; fax 808-826-1166.*

RUNNING

Kaua'i has no official running organization. If you'd like to know more about marathons or running events see "Calendar of Annual Kaua'i Events" in Chapter 1 or call the Kaua'i Athletic Club, Foot Locker or Dan's Sports Shop, as they usually have entry forms and information for any current running events. Also check the events calendars for the Hawai'i Visitors & Convention Bureau at www.gohawaii.com and/or Alternative-Hawaii at www.alternative-hawaii.com.

SCUBA DIVING

Scuba divers can explore the General Store, a 65- to 80-foot-deep reef with a variety of marine life and a 19th-century steamship, or the Sheraton Caves, which have interesting lava formations and plenty of green sea turtles. At Koloa Landing divers might discover bottles or fittings from old whaling ships and parts of the train track that once ran between Koloa and the area's sugar mill. On the North Shore there are underwater lava tubes and archways. While on the eastern shore, divers can explore the wreck of the *Lukenbach*, a German freighter that sank 40 years ago. Off Ni'ihau there are 130-foot-deep reef walls with abundant marine life, considered by some to be the best diving in Hawai'i.

Popular shore-diving beaches include Makua Beach (Tunnels) on the North Shore and on the southern shore near Po'ipu Koloa Landing and Prince Kuhio Park. If you'd like to do an introductory scuba dive, a boat dive on Kaua'i will run you $75 to $100. Shore dives are available from several dive companies. Dive certification usually takes two or more days; some offer PADI, while others offer NAUI. The cost of certification on Kaua'i starts at $225. A few dive companies offer prescription masks. Most of them offer a three-tank dive to Ni'ihau ($235 to $270), a little steep, but quite an adventure to see the reef wall. Some dive shops suggest that visitors with limited time do PADI dive preparation on the mainland and then they can be certified on Kaua'i in just two days. Classes are generally no more than six persons. Private lessons, which run slightly more, are also available. Many of the following dive companies also rent gear.

★ ***Bubbles Below*** This outfit offers scuba charters that specialize in marine biology. Their 35-foot vessel *Kaimanu* takes eight divers out at a time. They have a variety of dives, including a multilevel drift dive. Morning 2 Tank Dive, 4.5 hours, 7:30 a.m. to noon, $100; Afternoon 2 Tank Dive, 4.5 hours, 12:30 to 5 p.m., $100. Snorkelers/riders are $50. They offer a Ni'ihau/Lehua Rock Dive Trip, but warn that rougher channel conditions make this a trip for the hearty, with the 20-mile open-ocean crossing usually taking an hour to go across and an hour and a half to come back. The all-day trip includes three tanks at three different locations. This trip runs twice a week. If you are interested in underwater photography, they have a professional camera system for rent. Ni'ihau/Lehua Rock Dive is $235 per person. Night and Twilight dives are two-tank dives for $100. Equipment is available for rent, including wetsuits, regulators and buoyancy compensators. Owners Linda and Ken Bail have years of experience. Linda began her scuba diving experience at age six and has instructed divers since 1977 as a NAUI course director and PADI master–scuba diver trainer. Ken has been a NAUI instructor and PADI master–scuba diver trainer since 1982. They share their love for the marine environment and include the marine ecosystem in their briefing. *P.O. Box 157, 'Ele'ele, HI 96705; 808-332-7333, 808-822-3483; e-mail: kaimanu@aloha.net; www.aloha.net/~kaimanu.*

Dive Kaua'i Scuba Center Dive tours, boat charters, equipment rentals, introductory dives and PADI certification are your take here.

Scuba introductory tours are $98 to $125, 2 tank shore dives for certified divers $78, 2 tank boat dive $95, night dive $78, scooter dive $98, PADI certification $225 and up. Equipment rental by day or week. *976 Kuhio Highway, Kapa'a, HI 96746; 800-828-3483; 808-822-0452; e-mail: email@divekauai.com; www.divekauai.com.*

★ ***Fathom Five Divers*** This is a full service dive store and PADI certification organization. Introductory dives from one of their two 26-foot dive boats. They visit more than 20 dive locations ranging from 30 to 90 feet. Some dive sites include Sheraton Caves, General Store, Ice Box, Brennecke's Ledge, Turtle Bluffs and Zack's Pocket (named after their Hawaiian boat captain who discovered this site). Their dive sites are only 10 to 15 minutes from the harbor, which makes a two-tank boat dive a half-day trip and provides adventures for both the experienced and beginning divers. Maximum of six divers. Introductory two-tank boat dive, no experience necessary $135 includes class, dives and gear. Introductory shore dive with one-tank $95. Their 4- or 5-day course for PADI certification includes lectures, diving each day, and two boat dives on the last day. $369 for all. Open-water check-out dives available for $230. *3450 Po'ipu Road, P.O. Box 907, Koloa, HI 96756; 800-972-3078; 808-742-6991; www.fathom-five.com.*

Hanalei Water Sports They offer PADI scuba certification and have daily guided snorkel and scuba tours, as well as rentals. Located on the beach at the Princeville Hotel, they conduct their dives from the shore or offer special dive tours to Tunnels Reef, Koloa Landing or Ahukini Landing. Guided snorkeling tour (1 hour) includes pool lesson, equipment and wet suit for $35. (Two-hour surf lessons, including equipment, are also available.) Scuba dives $105 to $140 for introductory dives, certified divers $75 to $125. *5570 Ka Haku Road, Princeville Hotel, Princeville, HI 96722; 808-826-7509; fax 808-826-1166.*

Mana Divers Scuba This operator is a PADI dive center. They choose from several dive sites depending on conditions and offer introductory dives, Eco-informed guided dives, PADI instruction and specialty dives, private tours and specialized dives, and night dives for certified divers. Their Discover scuba diving experience is for mature guests 8 years and older at $35 for 1.5 to 2 hours. It's a chance to get a little hands-on dive at a minimal cost. The experience can include a lagoon dive and the fee can later be applied to an ocean dive if desired. Refresher dives $85. Introductory dives $110/$75 based on weather permitting. Offered to mature guests 12 and older. Maximum depth 40 feet, average depth 20 feet. *4310 Waialo Road, Bay 3, Hanapepe, HI 96716; 808-335-088; e-mail: manadivers@hawaiian.net; www.manadivers.com.*

Nitrox Tropical Divers and Sunrise Scuba Adventures No swimming skills are required for this diving experience. They do shore dives and outfit you in shallow water where the scuba gear becomes weightless. They conduct all dives from a calm beach and keep the group size down to six divers. The minimum age for all scuba activities is 12 years, with parental consent. All beginners are required to participate in a *free* scuba orientation in calm shallow water prior to the ocean dive. Prices are $98 for intro dive tour for uncertified divers; $98 for shore or boat dive for certified divers. Underwater Scooter Tour $98. Kayak Dive Tour, $98. Snorkel Tour, $48. PADI certification available. They are a PADI 5-STAR enriched air facility. *976 Kuhio Highway, P.O. Box 1255, Kapa'a, HI 96746; 808-822-7333; e-mail: doctrox@aloha.net; www.sunrisescuba.com.*

North Shore Divers They offer a variety of adventure dives, boat dives, night dives, crack and wall diving, shark dives, turtle dives, lobster fest. Shore dives: 1 tank, $98; 2 tanks, $128; 2 tank boat dive, $175. Dives for certified divers: 1 tank shore dive, $78; 2 tank shore dive, $108; 2 tank boat dive, $135; 1 tank turtle, shark or lobster fest dives, $78; night dive, $78; scooter dive, $98; certification course, $350 per person. *P.O. Box 577, Hanalei, HI 96714; 877-688-3483; 808-826-1921, 808-828-1223; e-mail: sacredseas@hotmail.com; garden-isle.com/nsdivers.*

Ocean Odyssey This outfitter offers a variety of dive tours, boat dives, scuba certification courses, intro scuba dives and more. Check their website or call for latest rates and details. *P.O. Box 957, Lawai, HI 96765; 808-245-8681; www.oceanodyssey-kauai.co.*

Ocean Quest Watersports Owners Jeannette and George Thompson specialize in small groups, no more than 4 persons, and offer excursions for beginners or advanced divers. North Shore eco tours are their summer specialty; South Shore tours in the winter. Diving tours are also available for the "Differently Abled." They include dives at Tunnels, Ahukini and Koloa landing, other advanced sites can be arranged. For certified divers, 1 tank dive $60 to $75; 2 tank dive $80 to $95; night dive $60 to $75; certification course $450 per person; Intro Discover Scuba Dive $95; Boat Dive $100 to $125. *P.O. Box 514, Kapa'a, HI 96746; 808-821-1000; e-mail: info@trykauai.com; www.trykauai.com.*

★ ***Seasport Divers*** Excursions depart aboard their 32-foot, 12-passenger boat from the Kukui'ula Boat Harbor. With 26 different dive sites to choose from, they appease all levels of diving enthusiasts. They offer a morning (8 a.m. to noon) or afternoon (1 p.m. to 5 p.m.) two-location dive or an evening (6 p.m. to 9 p.m.) one-tank dive. Underwater videos will be filmed by the divemaster and are available for $39.95. They also offer 35 mm camera rentals. Certified divers 2 tank dives $95 to $115, 1 tank dives $80; 2 tank shore dives, $85 to $120, 1 tank $70 to $95; intro boat dive $135, snorkelers/riders $55; certification course starts at $225 per person. Ni'ihau All Day Dive $250 to $270. They also offer referral dives and advanced certification. They offer complimentary pool lessons daily. Call for the scheduled lesson nearest your location. Reservations are suggested. Also available are watersport equipment rentals including snorkel gear, boogie boards, beach chairs and scuba gear. *2827 Po'ipu Road, P.O. Box 639, Koloa, HI 96756; 808-742-9303, 808-245-2592; 800-685-5889; e-mail: seasport@pixi.com; www.kauaiscubadiving.com.*

Wet 'n Wonderful This diving company specializes in shore dives for both the novice and experienced diver. First-time divers can take an introductory course with a one-tank dive for $110, or enroll in a four- or five-day course to become a certified PADI diver. Certified divers are charged $80 for one tank. All equipment is provided; guests can have a video of their adventure for a separate fee. Dives are conducted at 8:30 a.m., 11 a.m. and 1:30 p.m. at Koloa Landing, Makua (Tunnels) on the North Shore, or Ahukini Landing (near the Lihu'e Airport), with the location determined by water conditions. Night dives are offered to certified divers. Free pool demonstrations at various hotels. Call for information. *808-822-0211.*

SEA EXCURSIONS, SAILING, CRUISES (*See also* Snorkeling)

Sea excursion options on Kaua'i are more limited than on some of the other islands, but what makes it special on the Garden Island is the intimacy of the trips. Most outfitters use small boats, with as few as 6 people and a maximum of 25, so that the experience is more personal.

Depending on the time of year, the roughness of the water varies greatly. If you are concerned about motion sickness there are several over-the-counter medications to take. Dramamine has been used by millions of people for years, however, many who have used this for motion difficulties have been so significantly affected by the sleepiness (which is a side effect for some individuals) that they virtually sleep away the entire trip. While this might be an option for avoiding discomfort, those who take it can't be having nearly as much fun as those who remain alert! Bonine is another medication that can be purchased over the counter and for some people has less of a drowsy effect. Ginger, which can be purchased in capsules at health food stores, is recommended as a preventative for motion sickness. Another non-medicinal alternative are wrist bands that use acupressure points to suppress motion sickness. Check with your physician to discuss options that might work for you (given other medications you may already be taking). Using simple techniques such as keeping your eye on the land or horizon and avoiding a heavy, greasy meal before a boat trip are the only precautions most people need to use. A final note that bears mentioning. Most of these small craft *do not* have bathroom facilities on board. In some cases, there might be a *lua* (Hawaiian word for toilet), but it may not be available for public use. The larger boats will have facilities. It is recommended that you ask when booking.

Court rulings and a mandate by former Governor Ben Cayetano have impacted commercial cruise boat operations in the Hanalei area. The State of Hawai'i banned commercial boating operations from Hanalei Bay where many Napali Coast tours used to originate. Many tour boat operators relocated to boat harbors on the south and west sides of the island. After considerable legal battling, a court decision upheld the ban and now most commercial boating operations are in the Kukuiula Small Boat Harbor at Lawai in Po'ipu, the Port Allen Harbor on the south side or Kikiaola Harbor at Kekaha on the west side.

Blue Dolphin Charters, Ltd. Snorkel, sun, fish, eat, try out their water slide, and scuba aboard their 56-foot sailing trimaran *Tropic Bird.* The 5-hour Deluxe Napali Coast Tour is $99 per person, and includes a continental breakfast and sandwiches for lunch. The 7-hour Deluxe Ni'ihau Island Tour is $139 per person. The 3-hour Napali Sunset Cruise is $65 per person. The 2-hour Romantic Po'ipu Sunset Sail is $45 per person. Departs from Port Allen and Kukuiula Harbor at Po'ipu. *4380 Maha Road, P.O. Box 869, 'Ele'ele, HI 96705; 808-335-5553; 877-511-1311; e-mail: dolphin@aloha.net; www.kauaiboats.com.*

Bluewater Sailing Their 42-foot all-aluminum, Navy reconnaissance hull power boat, the *Northwind* is certified for 32 passengers, but 20 are "invited" on the cushioned, shaded seating in the open-air cabin or outside deck seating. A swim-step and freshwater showers are added conveniences for snorkelers, and all gear is provided along with a deli box lunch and soft drinks. Bluewater Express tours on the *Northwind*: The 5-hour Napali Coast Experience is $110 for adults, kids under 12 $85; the 4-hour Sunset/Napali Coast Tour, adults $90, kids under 12 $65. Private charters for *Northwind*: 5-hour Experience is $2,200; the 4-hour tour is $1,700. You can also choose their snorkeling trips aboard their 42-foot Pearsen ketch, *Lady Leanne II*. Summer sail rates: the Half-Day Sail to Makua is adults $105, kids under 12 $85 (this includes light meal); 2-hour Sunset Sail is adults $60, kids $55; Half-Day Charter is $1,260; Charter Sunset Sail is $720. Winter sail rates: Half-Day Sail is adults $105, kids under 12 $85; Sunset Sail for adults $60, kids $55; Half-Day Charter is $1,260; Sunset Sail is $900. The "Express" departs from Port Allen. The sailing excursions depart from Hanalei in the summer, Port Allen in the winter. Exclusive charters available for either vessel. *P.O. Box 1318, Hanalei, HI 96714; 808-828-1142; fax 808-828-0508; e-mail: bluwat@aloha.net; www.sail-kauai.com or www.bluewater-sailing.com.*

★ ***Captain Andy's Sailing Adventures*** These are great cruises, offering good value and comfortable boats. Their motto says it all, "Nobody has more fun!" Sail aboard the 55-foot catamaran *Spirit of Kaua'i*. Seasonal whale watching. This vessel was designed and built for Capt. Andy in the Virgin Islands, then tested out on the 12,000-mile trek to Kaua'i. This operator offers several cruises. The 5.5-hour Napali Coast Snorkel/Barbecue Cruise is offered for adults at $109, kids under 12 $79. The 4-hour Napali Dinner Cruise is adults $99, kids under 12 $69. The 5.5-hour Napali Coast Snorkel/Picnic Sail is offered for adults at $109, kids under 12 $79. The 5-hour Napali Snorkel/Sunset Sail is adults $109, kids $79. The 2-hour Po'ipu Cocktail Sail is adults $59, kids under 12 $40. Departs Port Allen and Kukuiula Harbor in Po'ipu. *P.O. Box 876, 'Ele'ele, Kaua'i, HI 96705; 808-335-6833; fax 808-335-6838; e-mail: fun@sailing-hawaii.com; www.sailing-hawaii.com.*

★ ***Captain Sundown*** The *Ku'uipo* is a 15-passenger sailing catamaran. The operator has a 6-hour Snorkel Sail-Napali Coast daily 9 a.m. to 3 p.m. (April-November only) that shows you the whole Napali Coast—dolphins, flying fish—with snorkeling and lunch for $135. A 4-hour Whale Watch Sail (December-April only) departs twice daily, 9 a.m. and 2:30 p.m., for $75. The 3-hour Bali Hai Sunset Sail goes every evening, 4 to 7 p.m. for $68. The boat is also available for private charters, 2, 4, 6 hours or more, call for rates. Winter whales guaranteed. *P.O. Box 697, Hanalei, HI 96714; 808-826-5585; e-mail: sun_down@aloha.net; www.captainsundown.com.*

Catamaran Kahanu This outfit tours Napali coastline in their power 36-foot catamaran. Maximum 18 passengers. Covered area and private restroom. There are power engines on this catamaran so you can cruise near the coastline. Whale tours offered seasonally. The 5-hour Napali Coast Morning Tour runs adults $105, kids under 12 $75. The 4-hour Napali Coast Sightseeing Tour is adults $85, kids under 12 $65. Departs from Port Allen. *P.O. Box 51006, 'Ele'ele, HI 96705; 808-335-3577; fax 808-828-0935; e-mail: kahanu@hawaiian.net; www.catamarankahanu.com.*

Hanalei Sport Fishing & Tours One of three companies allowed to depart from Hanalei Bay, this outfitter offers a 3.5-hour tour of Napali Coast, complete with 45 minutes of snorkeling or swimming with dolphins. Lunch is included. They also have a 2-hour mini-Napali sightseeing-only cruise. The full tour is $125, mini-tour $110. *P.O. Box 9, Hanalei, HI 96714; 808-826-6114; www.napalitours.com.*

HoloHolo Charters The 61-foot *HoloHolo* is a motor vessel/catamaran custom built on Kaua'i. Large trampolines and a huge open-air cabin. The HoloHolo offers a 7-hour Napali-Ni'ihau Supertour, 7 a.m. to 2 p.m., adults $156, children under 12 $109, that includes a continental breakfast, lunch and snorkeling. The *HoloHolo* also offers a 3.5-hour Napali Sunset Tour, adults $85, kids under 12 $60, that includes champagne for adults and dinner *pupus*. Aboard their 48-foot sailing catamaran *Leila* you can enjoy their 5-hour Napali Sail, adults $109, kids under 12 $75, that runs twice daily, 7 a.m. to noon and 1 to 6:30 p.m. Seasonal whale watching. Children must be 6 years and older for excursions, 5 years and older on sunset trips, no expectant mothers. Departs from Port Allen Harbor. *Located at the 'Ele'ele Shopping Center, 'Ele'ele, HI 96705; 808-335-0815; 800-848-6130; fax 808-335-0916; e-mail: reservations@holoholocharters.com; www.holoholocharters.com.*

Kaua'i Sea Tours This cruise operator sails out of Port Allen Harbor. The ride to the Napali Coast from this direction is 1.5 hours. They offer various cruise packages with choice of power catamarans or ocean rafts. The 6-hour catamaran Deluxe Nualolo Kai Day Tour is adults $135, children under 12 $105. The 5-hour catamaran Half-Day Nualolo Kai Tour is adults $119, kids under 12 $89. The ocean raft 5-hour Sightseeing Tour is adults $132, kids under 12 $105. The ocean raft Half-Day Tour is adults $108, kids under 12 $78. The seasonal catamaran Napali Sightseeing/Sunset/Whale Watch Tour, 4 hours, is adults $89, kids under 12 $59. The seasonal ocean raft Napali Sightseeing/Sunset/Whale Watch Tour, 4 hours, is priced the same. The 5-hour raft tour includes a beach landing at Nualolo Kai, with a narrated hike of the area and time to snorkel. *P.O. Box 51004, 'Ele'ele, HI 96705; 800-733-7997; 808-826-7254; e-mail: seatour@aloha.net; www.seatours.net.*

Kaulana Pali Kai Tours Group or private charters. Sunset cruises, snorkeling, whale watching aboard this 25-foot *Bayliner Trophy*. Freshwater shower and enclosed toilet. Departs Kiki'aola Harbor in Kekaha. Their Napali run costs $96 per person for the 4.5- to 5-hour cruise that includes lunch and refreshments. *4573 Akialoa Road, Kekaha, HI 96752; 808-337-9309.*

★ ***Liko Kaua'i Cruises*** Board their 49-foot power catamaran with bathroom, freshwater shower and shaded area for a relaxing cruise experience. Their 5-hour Morning or Afternoon Napali Coast Snorkel Tour is $110 for adults, kids under 12 $75. The 2.5-hour Napali Sunset Cruise is $75 for adults, kids under 12 $45. Day cruises include lunch/snacks/beverages. There's a sunset sightseeing cruise three times a week, with snacks and soft drinks. Seasonal whale watching. Departing from Kiki'aola Harbor near Kekaha, check-in is at their office in Waimea. *9875 Waimea Road, P.O. Box 18, Waimea, HI 96796; 808-338-0333; 888-SEA-LIKO; fax 808-337-1544; e-mail: liko@aloha.net; www.liko-kauai.com.*

Na Pali (Eco) Adventures Led by a trained naturalist, this outfitter's boats use 100-percent recycled fuel made from cooking oil.

They use motor-powered, hard-body catamarans (passenger maximums of 26 and 35) on a trip along the Napali Coast that provide a smoother and drier ride than the inflatables or rafts. The morning Napali Coast Tour/Onboard Picnic trip is 5 hours, with snorkeling and sightseeing, and includes a full lunch for $115 adults, $86 kids. The 3.5-hour Napali Coast Sunset Tour is adults $80, kids $45. The 6-hour Ultimate Napali Coast Tour, Snorkel, Whale Watch and Onboard Picnic Tour is seasonal, adults $115, kids $75. The seasonal 3.5-hour Napali Coast Sunset/Whale Watch runs adults $85, kids $45. The 2-hour seasonal Whale Watch Cruise is adults $59, kids $35. An underwater microphone allows you to hear the whales' musical conversation. Departs from Port Allen Harbor. *4310 Waialo Road, Highway 541, 'Ele'ele, HI 96705, P.O. Box 1017, Hanalei, HI 96714; 808-826-6804; fax 808-826-7073; 800-659-6804; e-mail: reservations@napali.com; www.napali.com.*

★ ***Na Pali Explorer*** Enjoy a Napali excursion on the comfortable adventure raft *Na Pali Explorer*. This 48-foot rigid hull inflatable is mounted on Scarab ocean racing hulls and is powered by twin Volvo turbo supercharged diesels that each generate 230 horsepower. Needless to say, the *Na Pali Explorer* travels pretty quickly, cruising at 25 knots and the potential to reach 33 knots. This vessel offers a smoother, more comfortable ride than the zodiac-type raft experience. Capacity is 49 passengers, but we're advised they take only 35. There are two tours. The 5-hour Napali Snorkel Expedition coastal tour is $118 for adults, kids under 12 $70, and includes light meal/beverages. The 3.5-hour Napali Coast Expedition sightseeing/swim cruise is $79 for adults, kids under 12 $59. The seasonal Whale Watching Expedition is $79 for adults, kids under 12 $59. There's also a chance to swim and snorkel (gear provided) on a protected reef with a beach landing at Nualolo Kai, an ancient Hawaiian fishing village (weather permitting). Comfort features include a canopy for shade and padded seating. Their expert naturalists share little-known facts about marine life and Hawaiian places along the way. Departs Kikiaola Harbor in Kekaha. *9935 Kaumuali'i Highway, Waimea, HI 96796; 808-338-9999; 877-338-9999; fax 808-335-0188; e-mail: napali@hawaiian.net; www.napali-explorer.com.*

Rainbow Runner Sailing This outfitter offers the 42-foot Kantola-designed Trimaran with a maximum of 18 passengers. A one-hour Kalapaki Fun Sail is one featured cruise: $45 adult/$35 children. High-performance speed sailing. Includes soft drinks/juices. Their Nawiliwili Sunset is $59 adults, $39 children and includes champagne and snacks. Other short cruises are available. All trips include performance sailing and seasonal whale watching. Departs Nawiliwili Small Boat Harbor or Kalapaki Beach, weather permitting. *P.O. Box 1722, Lihu'e, HI 96766; 808-632-0202; fax 808-246-9661; e-mail: kamal@kauaifun.com; www.sailingkauai.com.*

SNORKELING (*See also* Scuba Diving; Sea Excursions)

Po'ipu Beach is generally good for beginner and intermediate snorkelers. If weather conditions are just right, Makua (Tunnels) on the North Shore is a wonderful spot for intermediate snorkelers, as is Ke'e and Hideaways during calm summer seas. Since weather and ocean conditions cause very dramatic day-to-day differences in the snorkeling conditions, a dive shop is a great place to find the tip for the best spot of the day. The staff usually is friendly and eager to ensure you have a great snorkeling experience.

A number of divers carry little packages of smelly fish food pellets. However, it's not a good idea to feed the fish as it can make them more aggressive and provides them with a false habitat, develops dependency and is not their natural food supply.

Kids take to snorkeling with little effort. The only difficulty might be in their excitement when they spot the fish for the first time. They may forget they have a snorkel in their mouth when they try to shout out their glee. For the child who lacks confidence, use water wings or a "noodle" for extra buoyancy. A life jacket, of course, provides even more security. An adult may find taking a paddle board out and positioning themselves over the top of it (face in the water on one side and feet in the water on the other) a way to get over their initial jitters. Rest assured that snorkeling is much easier than swimming. All you have to do is float and breathe. Lydgate is a fine beach for the novice child snorkeler. It has a very sheltered area that will inspire confidence. Perhaps the most difficult thing for a beginner (child or adult) snorkeler is just getting into the water. Waves make this a more difficult task. Once in the water and enjoying the sights, they'll wonder why they never tried it before.

Rental equipment is available at locations around the island. With snorkel gear you will get what you pay for. Prices range from $4 to $5 a day—and up. Silicon gear is preferred, but you generally won't find that at the economy prices. If you plan on adding snorkeling to your list of regular recreational activities, you may find it worthwhile to invest in your own set of gear. You can pick up an inexpensive set of fins, mask and snorkel for a child at Longs Drug Store, Big Kmart or Walmart. Better yet, bring your own gear from home.

Several cruise operators include snorkeling adventures in their various excursions. Several are listed here as well as the "Sea Excursions, Sailing, Cruises" and "Scuba Diving" sections above.

Blue Dolphin Charters, Ltd. See "Sea Excursions, Sailing, Cruises" for various Napali snorkeling adventures. *808-742-6731.*

Bluewater Sailing See "Sea Excursions, Sailing, Cruises" for a combination sightseeing-snorkeling excursion on Napali Coast. *808-828-1142.*

Capt. Andy's See "Sea Excursions, Sailing, Cruises" for snorkeling and sightseeing cruises along the Napali Coast. *808-335-6833.*

Capt. Sundown This outfitter offers a daily Napali snorkel-sail to North Shore's best spots. *808-826-5585.*

Catamaran Kahanu See "Sea Excursions, Sailing, Cruises" for snorkeling thrills along the famed Napali Coast. *808-335-3577.*

Fathom Five See "Scuba Diving" for trips to secluded south-side dive sites. *808-742-6991.*

Hanalei Sport Fishing & Tours See "Sea Excursions, Sailing, Cruises" for snorkeling along the Napali Coast. *P.O. Box 9, Hanalei, HI 96714; 808-826-6114; www.napalitours.com.*

Hanalei Surf Company This organization offers a range of rental equipment: mask, fins and snorkel at $20 per week; boogie board, $30 per week; wet suits, $4 per day. Optical masks are available. *5161 Kuhio Highway; 808-826-9000.*

Holoholo Charters See "Sea Excursions, Sailing, Cruises" for catamaran sailing cruises that include snorkeling adventures. *808-335-0815.*

Kaua'i Sea Tours See "Sea Excursions, Sailing, Cruises" for ocean power raft excursions on Napali Coast that include snorkeling. *808-826-7254.*

Liko Kaua'i Cruises See "Sea Excursions, Sailing, Cruises" for Napali Coast power catamaran cruises that offer snorkeling adventures. *808-338-0333.*

Mana Divers Scuba See "Scuba Diving" for snorkeling for non-divers. *808-335-0881.*

Napali Eco Adventures See "Sea Excursions, Sailing, Cruises" for their sightseeing and snorkeling cruise adventures. *808-826-6804.*

Pedal and Paddle Hanalei See "Sea Excursions, Sailing, Cruises" for information about their rentals. Regular or optic masks and snorkel set is $5 day/$20 week (but the good news is their rental week is eight days long!). *808-826-9069.*

Rainbow Runner See "Sea Excursions, Sailing, Cruises" for information about their adventure sails and snorkeling on Kaua'i's east and south shores. *808-632-0202.*

SeaFun Kaua'i SeaFun is a shore-based, half-day, guided snorkeling tour. Some of the island's best snorkeling is inside protective reefs where boats cannot go. Transportation (from most hotels), including wet suit, instruction and snacks and drinks, are included in their fee. An underwater video of your tour is available for an additional fee. Experienced snorkelers will appreciate learning more about the environment from marine biologist experts. They snorkel off Lawa'i Beach and Prince Kuhio Park. Rates: $69 adults (age 13 and up), $53 children (5 to 12 years). *1702 Haleukana Street, Lihu'e, HI 96766; 808-245-6400; 800-452-1113; fax 808-245-4888; e-mail: tours@gte.net; www.alohakauaitours.com.*

Snorkel Bob's This outfit has locations throughout the islands, and specializes in renting snorkeling gear. They offer snorkeling tours on various boats and provide maps to get you to the best spots. Weekly snorkel gear rentals are available, or you can buy equipment and sell it back before you leave. You can even return it to another Snorkel Bob on another island. (They also act as an activity center so you can book luaus and other outings through them.) *4-734 Kuhio Highway, Kapaa, 808-823-9433; and in Koloa at 3236 Po'ipu Road, 808-742-2206; www.snorkelbob.com.*

True Blue Charters & Ocean Sports See "Fishing" for information on their snorkel/dive cruises on the east and south shore coasts. *808-245-9662, 808-246-6333.*

SNUBA

Snuba Kaua'i Snuba, as it sounds, is a blend of snorkeling and scuba. The air source is contained within a floatation raft that follows you as you move beneath the ocean. The guided underwater tour includes personalized instruction, fish food and equipment. Rates are $55 per person. They take small groups, 1 to 6 divers at a time. Tour length is 1.5 hours with 35 to 40 minutes underwater. They dive from Lawa'i Beach in Po'ipu on the South Shore. *P.O. Box 4318, Kapaa, HI 96746; 808-823-8912; e-mail: snuba@aloha.net; www.hshawaii.com/kvp/snuba.*

SPAS & FITNESS CENTERS (*See also* Retreats *in Chapter 2*)

Ever considered taking a vacation from your vacation? Well, here's a tip for you! Let's face it, shopping, beaches, terrific dinners, hikes, fabulous lunches, swimming . . . well, you know, it all gets pretty tiring! Indulge yourself in some personal relaxation and rejuvenation by signing up for a massage from one of the many private therapists or a session at one of the island's spas.

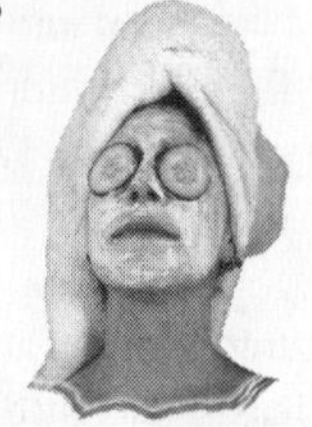

★ ANARA Spa The most sophisticated is the ANARA Spa at the Hyatt Regency. (ANARA is an acronym for "A New Age Restorative Approach.") When you consider the amenities, it is one great value. Select a facial, half-hour or 50-minute massage, or perhaps an herbal wrap. With any of their pampered treatments you'll get a full-day pass to enjoy their spa facilities. It's recommend getting there in advance of your appointment. There are ladies' and mens' facilities, which are private, as well as some coed facilities. The coed area offers a complete exercise room and a lap pool, or for the less aerobically inclined, sun or shade on lounge chairs around the pool, a light lunch or a jacuzzi. In both the women's and men's facilities you'll find a private jacuzzi, 12-jet jacuzzi shower, eucalyptus steam room, sauna, multi-person jacuzzi, lava rock outdoor shower garden and more lounge chairs. Get in that relaxation mode and then enjoy your therapy treatment. When you're finished, there is more time to choose from the aforementioned facilities before freshening up with their specially formulated mango-scented shampoos, conditioners and body soaps. Make it a whole day event! Prices for daily spa membership, inclusive with any spa/salon treatment: hotel guests $15/non-guests $20. Massage therapy or skin-care treatments run $55 to $130. Loofah scrubs, personal training sessions, herbal wraps and other services $35 to $90. Can't decide? Try a mini-day at ANARA for $215, or the ANARA Sampler for $115, or discover the new you with the six-hour Day at ANARA for $325. Open daily from 6 a.m. to 8 p.m. Salon service are also available. Any salon services over $40 includes a complimentary ANARA spa membership for that day. *Hyatt Regency Hotel, 1571 Po'ipu Road, Koloa; 808-742-1234 for reservations.*

Princeville Health Club and Spa On the North Shore in Princeville, this spa offers massages, facials, seaweed wrap and aromatherapy treatments, along with a complete health and fitness facility. Passes start at $15 per day (for hotel guests only), weekly rates run $45 and monthly passes are $95. The Spa Experience includes: use of whirlpool sauna, steam room, 25-meter lap pool, personal locker, robe, unlimited classes, one-hour *lomi lomi* massage for $130 for Princeville hotel guests, Spa guests $140. Spa admission is included in regular Prince and Makai Golf Course green fees. Unlimited daily exercise classes, including body conditioning, step aerobics, aquacize and yoga are offered. Spa hours are Monday to Saturday from 9 a.m. to 6:30 p.m., Sunday 9 a.m. to 4:30 p.m. *Prince Golf and Country Club, 5-3900 Kuhio Highway, Princeville, HI 96722; 808-826-5030; www.princeville.com.*

STATE FOREST RESERVE CAMPSITES

Na Pali-Kona Forest Reserve Campsites Located approximately four miles east of Koke'e State Park headquarters on the Camp-10 Road. A four-wheel-drive vehicle is required as the road is steep, rutted and often muddy. The two campsites available are: **Kawaikoi Campsite,** a three-acre open grass field surrounded by Koke'e plum trees and native *koa* and *ohia* forest. The Kawaikoi Stream flows next to the camping area. There are two picnic shelters and a composting toilet. No drinking water available—bring your own or treat stream water. Maximum stay allowed is three consecutive nights. Campsite accommodates up to 30 people. **Sugi Grove Campsite** is a shady campsite located across Kawaikoi Stream from the Kawaikoi Campsite. The

Kawaikoi Stream Trail, which is one of the most scenic streamside trails in Hawaii, runs 1.75 miles upstream from the Sugi Grove Campsite. There is a single picnic shelter, a pit toilet and space for several tents. No drinking water—bring your own or treat stream water. Maximum stay allowed is three consecutive nights. Campsite accommodates up to 10 people.

Pu'ukapele Forest Reserve Campsites Running cool mountain streams and sheer vertical valley walls are part of the Waimea Canyon camping experience. Access to this area is via the Kukui Trail that starts approximately .75 mile beyond miler-marker 8 on Highway 550, the Waimea Canyon Drive. The maximum stay at any of these Waimea Canyon campsites is four consecutive nights. The four campsites available are: **Wiliwili Campsite**, a small one-shelter campsite; **Kaluahaulu Campsite**, a small one-shelter campsite that should not be used in stormy weather due to dangers of flash floods in the canyon; **Hipalau Campsite**, a small one-shelter campsite; and **Lonomea Campsite**, a small one-shelter campsite. None of these sites have drinking water, but stream water at the sites can be treated or boiled for drinking.

SURFING

'Anini Beach This operator offers instruction in both surfing and windsurfing; intro and certification lessons; rental equipment, sails, boards, etc. *P.O. Box 1602, Hanalei, HI 96714; 808-826-9463.*

Hanalei Surf Company This company rents fiberglass surfboards for $15 per day, $65 per week. Soft surfboards $12 per day, $50 per week. Boogie boards rent for $5 per day, $20 per week. *5161 Kuhio Highway; 808-826-9000.*

Kayak Kaua'i Outbound Offers Hawaiian surfboarding lessons, $35 per hour lesson. *Kapa'a 808-822-9179; Hanalei 808-826-9844, 800-437-3507; e-mail: outbound@aloha.net.*

Learn to Surf School This instructional operator offers guaranteed surf lessons that will teach you how to do it. They offer surf lessons daily and daylong. Rates: 1 person/1 hour, $30; 1 person/1.5 hours, $35; 2 persons/1 hour, $50; 2 persons/1.5 hours, $60. Group rates available. *Hanalei 808-826-7612.*

Margo Oberg's Surfing School Located between the Kiahuna Plantation and the Sheraton in Po'ipu, Margo won world titles seven times between 1968 and 1981. Her school has been operating for well over 25 years. Daily lessons are offered three times at $45 per person with 6 to 7 in a class; 1-hour instruction, half-hour practice time. Private lessons $75. *Po'ipu Beach 808-742-8019, 808-639-0708.*

Progressive Expressions, Inc. In Koloa since 1974, this organization manufactures and sells surfboards, bodyboards and surfing accessories for all ages. *5420 Koloa Road; 808-742-6041.*

TENNIS

Kaua'i County has eight free municipal public tennis courts that are available on a first-come, first-served basis. Available courts are in Waimea, Kekaha, Koloa, Kalaheo, Lihu'e, Wailua Homesteads, Wailua Houselots and Kapa'a New Park.

Many hotels have courts available for both public and guest use. Tennis facilities are located at resorts around Kaua'i. Call them for open hours and rate details: **Hanalei Bay Resort**, *Princeville 808-826-6522*; **Kaua'i Lagoons Racquet Club**, *Lihu'e 808-241-6000*; **Kiahuna Tennis Resort**, *Po'ipu 808-742-9533*; **Po'ipu Kai Tennis Complex** *808-742-1144*; **Princeville Resort Tennis Complex**, *Princeville 808-826-3620*; **The Tennis Garden**, *Hyatt Regency Kaua'i 808-742-1234.*

THEATER

Kaua'i Community College opened its Performing Arts Center/Theater in 1995. The beautiful hall seats 550 persons and adds an exciting dimension to theater possibilities on Kaua'i. They currently offer an annual concert series and special performances throughout the year. It is proving to be an invaluable community cultural resource. *For information on upcoming events, call 808-245-8311 or 808-245-8270.*

The **Kaua'i Community Players** performs several productions annually for children and adults. Call 808-245-7700 for more information on plays and dinner theater productions.

The Kaua'i Village Theater has a 62-seat capacity and offers foreign and unusual films as well as an occasional live production. *4-831 Kuhio Highway, Kapa'a, HI 96746 in the Kaua'i Village Center; 808-821-1588.*

The **Radisson Kauai Beach Resort** stages "A Nite of Broadway" Dinner Theater and Musical Revue. Held at different times throughout the year, this is a series of favorite Broadway musical performances. Shows begin with a no-host cocktail party at 6 p.m., followed by a dinner buffet. One recent edition of the show included selections from *Les Miserables*, *The Phantom of the Opera* and *Guys and Dolls*. The show changes so audiences can come back and enjoy new songs for continuing family entertainment. The sets and buffet dinner are intertwined to create an entertaining evening of food, drama, music and fun. Cost is $65 per person inclusive of tax and tip. *Call Show-tunes 808-245-8046.*

Waimea Theatre, the 1938 art deco–era influenced theater has 500 seats. The small-town rural movie house has gone through a number of renderings—a warehouse, retail space—and Hurricane Iniki assisted with renovations, destroying the decorative marquee. Over the course of several years, preservation and patience have saved the landmark structure and restored its vitality. The theater now offers a variety of films and live productions. *Waimea 808-338-0282, 808-338-2027.*

WATERSKIING

Kaua'i Water Ski & Surf Co. See "Kayaking" above. Rates for waterskiing run $100 per hour, $55 per half-hour, accommodates up to two people. They ski up the Wailua River. Monday through Friday 9 a.m. to 5 p.m. *Kinipopo Shopping Village, 4-356 Kuhio Highway, Kapa'a, HI 96746; 800-344-7915; 808-822-3574.*

WHALE WATCHING

Whale watching is seasonal, officially December 15 through May 15, although a few stragglers may linger into May and some anxious for those warm waters of the Hawaiian islands may arrive a bit ahead of schedule. The best vantage points for whale watching are from areas along the north, east and south coasts, or from one of the boats that make excursions out in search of these magnificent mammals. See "Sea Excursions, Sailing and Cruises" above for more information. You can also view them from the Kilauea lighthouse. A good pair of binoculars is useful.

WILDLIFE REFUGES

As you pass the Princeville Shopping Center you are at mile-marker 28 on Kuhio Highway 56. Opposite the shopping center is an overlook area with a great view of the Hanalei Valley, the taro patches and distant mountains. The road winds on down the Princeville bluff a mile or so to the one-lane iron bridge spanning the Hanalei River. This section of the highway passes through the **Hanalei Wildlife Refuge**. (*See* Chapter 2 for more information about the refuge.)

Located along the Hulei'a River in southeast Kaua'i near Lihu'e is the **Hulei'a National Wildlife Refuge**, which is home to the endangered *koloa* duck and other rare water birds. (*See* Chapter 2 for more information about the refuge.) The lands, once taro and rice fields, are now breeding and feeding grounds for a variety of waterfowl. The refuge is located in a relatively flat valley along the Hulei'a River, which is bordered by a steep wooded hillside. Special permits are issued annually to a commercial kayaking business for access through an upland portion of the refuge.

The **Kilauea Point National Wildlife Refuge** was established in 1974 and is recognized as Hawai'i's largest seabird sanctuary, a place that is home to more than 5,000 seabirds. (*See* Chapter 2 for more information about the refuge.) The refuge is open to the public daily from 10 a.m. to 4 p.m., closed some federal holidays. Admission is $2 by donation. *Kilauea Point, P.O. Box 87, Kilauea, Kaua'i, HI 96754; 808-828-1413.*

WINDSURFING

Once again, weather conditions will determine where this activity is best suited. 'Anini is the best for beginners. Located near Princeville, it offers a lagoon with protected waters and steadily blowing winds that make it ideal for the beginning or intermediate windsurfer. Advanced windsurfers enjoy Tunnels on the North Shore and Maha'ulepu on the South Shore. There are two windsurfing schools that provide instructional lessons and equipment rentals.

'Anini Beach Windsurfing This group offers windsurfing equipment rentals at $50 per day. Intro and certification lessons available; three-hour windsurfing lessons for $65. *P.O. Box 1602, Hanalei, HI 96714; 808-826-9463.*

Windsurf Kaua'i This certified school features new boards, windsurf rentals and surf lessons for people of all abilities. The first lesson is guaranteed to get you up on the water. *P.O. Box 318, Kilauea, HI 96754; 808-828-6838.*

Recommended Reading

Bailey, Paul. *Those Kings and Queens of Old Hawaii*. Tucson, Arizona: Westernlore Press. 1975.

Ball, Stuart M. *The Backpackers Guide to Hawai'i*. Honolulu: University of Hawaii Press. 1996

Barrere, Dorothy. Pukui, Mary K., Kelly, Marion. *Hula, Historical Perspectives*. Honolulu: Bishop Museum. 1980.

Beekman, Allan. *The Ni'ihau incident: the true story of the Japanese fighter pilot*. Honolulu: Heritage Press of Pacific. 1982.

Berger, Andrew J. *Bird Life in Hawai'i*. Honolulu: Island Heritage. 1993.

Berger, Andrew J. *Hawaiian Birdlife*. Honolulu: University of Hawaii Press. 1994.

Bird, Isabella. *Six Months in the Sandwich Islands*. Tokyo: Tuttle. 1988.

Carter, Frances. *Hawai'i for Free*. Mustang Publishing. 1997.

Carter, Frances. *Hawaii on Foot*. Honolulu: The Bess Press. 1990.

Chisholm, Craig. *Hawaiian Hiking Trails*. Lake Oswego: Fernglen Press. 1994.

Chisholm, Craig. *Hawaiian Hiking Trails: The Guide for All Islands*. Oregon: Fernglen Press. 1999.

Chisholm, Craig. *Kaua'i Hiking Trails*. Lake Oswego: Fernglen Press. 1991.

Clark, John R. K. *Beaches of Kaua'i and Ni'ihau*. Honolulu: University of Hawai'i Press, 1990.

Clark, John R. K. *Hawai'i's Best Beaches*. Honolulu: University of Hawai'i Press. 1985.

Clay, Horace F. and Hubbard, James C. *The Hawaii Garden Tropical Exotics*. Honolulu: University of Hawaii Press. 1987.

Cook, Chris. *Kauai—The Movie Book*. Honolulu: Mutual Publishing Co. 1996.

Crites, Jennifer. and Crow, Gerald L. *Guide to Hawai'i's Sharks and Rays*. Honolulu: Mutual Publishing Co. 2001.

David, Reginald E. *Hawai'i's Birds*. Hawai'i Audubon Society. 1996.

Dawrs, Stu. *Discover Kauai—The Garden Island.* Honolulu: Island Heritage. 1999.

Daws, Gavan. *Hawai'i, the Islands of Life.* Honolulu: Signature Hawai'i. 1988.

Daws, Gavan. *Shoal of Time: A History of the Hawaiian Islands.* Honolulu: University of Hawaii Press. 1974.

Day, A. Grove and Stroven, Carl. *A Hawaiian Reader*, Vol. I. Honolulu: Mutual Publishing Co. 1985.

Day, A. Grove. *A Hawaiian Reader*, Vol. II. Honolulu; Mutual Publishing Co. 1998.

Day, A. Grove. *Hawai'i and Its People.* Honolulu: Mutual Publishing Co. 1993.

Day, A. Grove. *Mark Twain in Hawai'i: Roughing It in the Sandwich Islands.* Honolulu: Mutual Publishing Co. 1990.

Elbert, Samuel H. *Hawaiian Antiquities and Folk-Lore.* Honolulu: University of Hawai'i Press. 1959.

Fielding, Ann. *Hawaiian Reefs and Tidepools.* Hawai'i: Oriental Pub. Co.

Fielding, Ann and Robinson, Ed. *An Underwater Guide to Hawaii.* Honolulu: University of Hawaii Press. 1991.

Harrison, Craig. *Seabirds of Hawai'i: Natural History & Conservation.* NY: Comstock Pub. 1990.

Hawai'i Audubon Society. *Hawai'i's birds.* Honolulu: The Society. 1993.

Hobson, E. and Chave, E. H. *Hawaiian Reef Animals.* Honolulu: University of Hawaii Press. 1990.

Hoover, John. *Hawai'i's Sea Creatures: A Guide to Hawai'i's Marine Invertebrates.* Honolulu: Mutual Publishing Co. 1999.

Hoover, John. *Hawai'i's Underwater Paradise.* Honolulu: Mutual Publishing Co. 1998.

Hoover, John. *A Pocket Guide to Hawai'i's Underwater Paradise.* Honolulu: Mutual Publishing Co. 1997.

Juvik, Sonia P. and Juvik, James O. *Atlas of Hawai'i.* Honolulu: University of Hawaii Press. 1998.

Knudsen, Eric Alfred. *Kanuka of Kaua'i.* Tongg. 1944.

Knudsen, Eric. *Teller of Tales.* Honolulu: Mutual Publishing Co. 1946.

Koch, Tom. *Six Islands on Two Wheels: A Cycling Guide to Hawaii.* Bess Press, Honolulu, HI. 1990.

Laudan, Rachel. *The Food of Paradise—Exploring Hawaii's Culinary Heritage.* Honolulu: University of Hawaii Press. 1996.

London, Jack. *Stories of Hawai'i.* Honolulu: Mutual Publishing Co. 1965.

Ludwig, Myles. *Kaua'i in the Eye of Iniki.* Hanalei Bay, Kaua'i: Inter-Pacific Media. 1992.

McMahon, Richard. *Adventuring in Hawai'i: Hawai'i, Maui, Molokai, Lanai, Oahu, Kauai.* Sierra Club. 1996.

McMahon, Richard. *Camping Hawai'i—A Complete Guide.* Honolulu: University of Hawaii Press. 1997.

Merlin, Mark. *Hawaiian Coastal Plants.* Pacific Guide. 1995.

Merlin, Mark. *Hawaiian Forest Plants*. Honolulu: University of Hawaii Press. 1996.

Morey, Kathy. *Kaua'i Trails: Walks, Strolls, and Treks on the Garden Island.* Berkeley, CA: Wilderness Press, 1991.

Moriarty, Linda. *Ni'ihau Shell Leis*. Honolulu: University of Hawai'i Press. 1986.

Pratt, Douglas. *A Pocket Guide to Hawai'i's Beautiful Birds*. Honolulu: Mutual Publishing Co. 1996.

Pratt, Douglas. *Enjoying Birds in Hawai'i*. Honolulu: Mutual Publishing Co. 1993.

Pratt, Douglas. *Hawai'i's Beautiful Birds*. Honolulu: Mutual Publishing Co. 1998.

Pratt, Douglas. *Pocket Guide to Hawai'i's Trees and Shrubs*. Honolulu: Mutual Publishing Co. 1999.

Pratt, Douglas. Bruner, P.L. and Berrett, D.G. *A Field Guide to the Birds of Hawaii and the Tropical Pacific*. Princeton, N.J.: Princeton University Press. 1987.

Pratt, Helen. *Hawaiians: An Island People*. Vermont: C.E. Tuttle. 1991.

Pukui, Mary and Korn, Alfons. *The Echo of Our Song*. Honolulu: University of Hawai'i Press. 1973

Pukui, Mary Kawena et al. *The New Pocket Hawaiian Dictionary*. Honolulu: The University of Hawai'i Press. 1975.

Pukui, Mary Kawena. *Tales of the Menehune*. Honolulu: Kamehameha Schools Press. 1985.

Rayson, Ann. *Modern Hawaiian History*. Honolulu: The Bess Press. 1984.

Rayson, Ann. *The Hawaiian Monarchy*. Honolulu: The Bess Press. 1983.

Rayson, Ann and Bauek, Helen. *Hawai'i: The Pacific State*. Honolulu: The Bess Press. 1997.

Riznik, Barnes. *Waioli Mission House*. Kaua'i: Grove Farm Homestead. 1987.

Ronck, Ron. Kauai: *A Many Splendored Island*. Honolulu: Mutual Publishing Co. 1985.

Russo, Ron. *Hawaiian Reefs: A Natural History Guide*. Wavecrest Publishing. 1994.

Sanburn, Curt. *Kauai Travelogue*. Honolulu: Mutual Publishing Co. 1996.

Smith, Robert. *Hawai'i's Best Hiking Trails*. CA: Hawaiian Outdoor Adventures. 1994.

Smith, Robert. *Hiking Kaua'i—The Garden Isle*. Long Beach, CA: Hawaiian Outdoor Adventures. 1999.

Soehren, Rick. *The Birdwatcher's Guide to Hawai'i*. Honolulu: University of Hawai'i Press. 1996.

Sohmer, S.H. *Manual of the Flowering Plants of Hawai'i*. Honolulu: University of Hawaii Press. 1990.

Sohmer, S.H. and Gustafson, R. *Plants and Flowers of Hawaii*. Honolulu: University of Hawaii Press. 1987.

Stevenson, Robert Louis. *Travels in Hawai'i*. Honolulu: University of Hawai'i Press. 1973.

Stone, Robert. *Day Hikes on Kauai*. Red Lodge, Montana: Day Hike Books Inc. 1997.

Tabrah, Ruth. *Kaua'i, The Unconquerable Island*. Las Vegas. K.C. Publications. 1988.

Tabrah, Ruth. *Ni'ihau, the last Hawaiian Island*. Kailua, HI: Press Pacific. 1987.

Tava, Rerioterai and Keale, Moses K., Sr. *Ni'ihau: The Traditions of a Hawaiian Island*. Honolulu: Mutual Publishing Co. 1989.

Teilhet, Darwin. *Russian Flag Over Kaua'i*. Honolulu: Mutual Publishing Co. 1986.

Thrum, Thomas G. *Hawaiian Folk Tales*. Honolulu: Mutual Publishing Co. 1998.

Titcomb, M. *Native Use of Fish in Hawai'i*. Honolulu: University of Hawai'i Press. 1952.

Valier, Kathy. *On the Na Pali Coast*. Honolulu: University of Hawai'i Press. 1988.

Westervelt, William. *Hawaiian Historical Legends*. Honolulu: Mutual Publishing Co. 1999.

Westervelt, William. *Hawaiian Legends of Ghosts and Ghost Gods*. Honolulu: Mutual Publishing Co. 1999.

Westervelt, William. *Myths and Legends of Hawai'i*. Vermont: C.E. Tuttle. 1991.

Wichman, Frederick. *Kaua'i Tales*. Honolulu: Bamboo Ridge Press. 1985.

Wichman, Frederick. *Polihale and Other Kaua'i Legends*. Honolulu: Bamboo Ridge Press. 1991.

Wong, Helen and Rayson, Ann. *Hawai'i's Royal History*. Honolulu: The Bess Press. 1987.

Yau, John. *Hawaiian Cowboys*. Black Sparrow. 1995.

Zurick, David. *Hawaii, Naturally*. Berkeley, CA: Wilderness Press. 1990.

Index

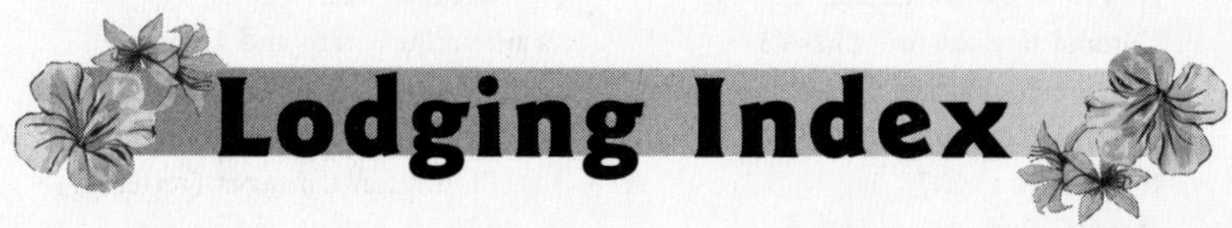

Lodging Index

Dining Index

Dining Index by Cuisine

Hawaiian Regional Cuisine

International

Italian/Pizza

Japanese

Korean

Luaus

Mediterranean

Mexican

Pacific Rim Cuisine

Pupus

Salads/Salad Bars

Sandwiches

Seafood

Paradise Family Guides

Ideal for families traveling with kids of any age—toddlers to teenagers—Paradise Family Guides offer a blend of travel information unlike any other guides to the Hawaiian islands. With vacation ideas and tropical adventures that are sure to satisfy both action-hungry youngsters and relaxation-seeking parents, these guides meet the specific needs of each and every family member.

Hidden Guides

Adventure travel or a relaxing vacation?—"Hidden" guidebooks are the only travel books in the business to provide detailed information on both. Aimed at environmentally aware travelers, our motto is "Where Vacations Meet Adventures." These books combine details on unique hotels, restaurants and sightseeing with information on camping, sports and hiking for the outdoor enthusiast.

The New Key Guides

Based on the concept of ecotourism, The New Key Guides are dedicated to the preservation of Central America's rare and endangered species, architecture and archaeology. Filled with helpful tips, they give travelers everything they need to know about these exotic destinations.

Ulysses Press books are available at bookstores everywhere. If any of the following titles are unavailable at your local bookstore, ask the bookseller to order them.

You can also order books directly from Ulysses Press
P.O. Box 3440, Berkeley, CA 94703
800-377-2542 or 510-601-8301
fax: 510-601-8307
www.ulyssespress.com
e-mail: ulysses@ulyssespress.com

PARADISE FAMILY GUIDES

____ Paradise Family Guides: Kaua'i, $16.95
____ Paradise Family Guides: Maui, $16.95
____ Paradise Family Guides: Big Island of Hawai'i, $16.95

HIDDEN GUIDEBOOKS

____ Hidden Arizona, $16.95
____ Hidden Bahamas, $14.95
____ Hidden Baja, $14.95
____ Hidden Belize, $15.95
____ Hidden Big Island of Hawaii, $13.95
____ Hidden Boston & Cape Cod, $14.95
____ Hidden British Columbia, $18.95
____ Hidden Cancún & the Yucatán, $16.95
____ Hidden Carolinas, $17.95
____ Hidden Coast of California, $18.95
____ Hidden Colorado, $15.95
____ Hidden Disneyland, $13.95
____ Hidden Florida, $18.95
____ Hidden Florida Keys & Everglades, $12.95
____ Hidden Georgia, $16.95
____ Hidden Guatemala, $16.95
____ Hidden Hawaii, $18.95
____ Hidden Idaho, $14.95
____ Hidden Kauai, $13.95
____ Hidden Maui, $13.95
____ Hidden Montana, $15.95
____ Hidden New England, $18.95
____ Hidden New Mexico, $15.95
____ Hidden Oahu, $13.95
____ Hidden Oregon, $15.95
____ Hidden Pacific Northwest, $18.95
____ Hidden Salt Lake City, $14.95
____ Hidden San Francisco & Northern California, $18.95
____ Hidden Southern California, $18.95
____ Hidden Southwest, $19.95
____ Hidden Tahiti, $17.95
____ Hidden Tennessee, $16.95
____ Hidden Utah, $16.95
____ Hidden Walt Disney World, $13.95
____ Hidden Washington, $15.95
____ Hidden Wine Country, $13.95
____ Hidden Wyoming, $15.95

NEW KEY GUIDES

____ The New Key to Costa Rica, $18.95
____ The New Key to Ecuador and the Galápagos, $18.95

Mark the book(s) you're ordering and enter the total cost here ⇨ [ ]

California residents add 8.25% sales tax here ⇨ [ ]

Shipping, check box for preferred method and enter cost here ⇨ [ ]

❑ Book Rate (free) ❑ Priority Mail/UPS Ground (call for rates)
❑ UPS Overnight or 2-Day Air (call for rates)

Billing, enter total amt. due here and check payment method ⇨ [ ]

❑ CHECK ❑ MONEY ORDER

❑ VISA/MASTERCARD____________________ EXP. DATE ________

NAME____________________ PHONE ____________

ADDRESS____________________________________

CITY ____________________ STATE________ ZIP __________

MONEY-BACK GUARANTEE ON DIRECT ORDERS PLACED THROUGH ULYSSES PRESS.

About the Authors

JOAN CONROW is a journalist who has been living on Kaua'i since 1987. She was previously on the staff of *The Honolulu Advertiser* and was Kaua'i bureau chief for the *Honolulu Star-Bulletin*. She is currently a contributing editor of *Hawaii Magazine*. Ms. Conrow writes extensively about Hawai'i and its natural world and culture, and her work has appeared in *Audubon*, *National Wildlife*, *Sierra* and many other national and regional publications.

CHRISTIE STILSON, a native Oregonian, is one of the original authors of *Paradise Family Guides: Kaua'i*. She first visited the Hawaiian islands in the late 1970s and loved Hawai'i so much, she began writing travel guides for the islands. Christie and her two children have been frequent visitors to the Aloha State ever since.